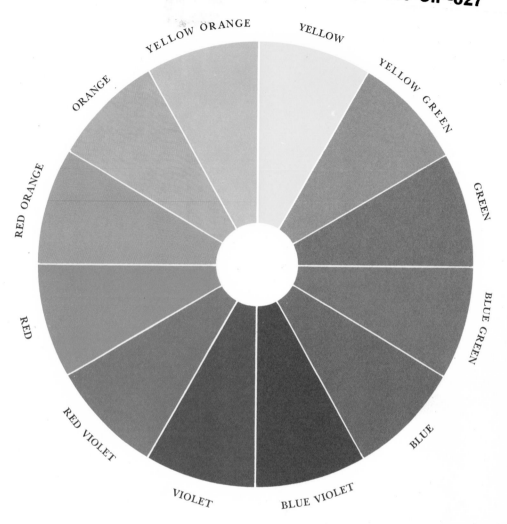

Primary colors: yellow, red, blue

Secondary colors: orange, violet, green

Tertiary colors: yellow orange, red orange, red violet,
blue violet, blue green, yellow green

The Key to Weaving

This wall hanging, **Pine in Winter,** won the British-American Oil Company prize at the London District Weavers Exhibition in 1956. It was woven by Violet M. Black, Wolfville, Nova Scotia, in the half-dukagång technique of natural black, gray, and white homespun yarn.

Second Revised Edition

The Key to Weaving

A Textbook of Hand Weaving for the Beginning Weaver

MARY E. BLACK, O.T.R.

Master Weaver, Guild of Canadian Weavers;
Formerly Director, Handcrafts Division,
Department of Trade and Industry,
Province of Nova Scotia, Canada

MACMILLAN PUBLISHING CO., INC. / NEW YORK
COLLIER MACMILLAN PUBLISHERS / LONDON

Macmillan Publishing Co., Inc.
866 Third Avenue, New York, N.Y. 10022
Collier Macmillan Canada, Ltd.

Library of Congress Cataloging in Publication Data

Black, Mary E
The key to weaving.

Edition for 1957 published under title: New key to weaving.
Bibliography: p.
Includes index.
1. Hand weaving.   I.   Title.
TT848.B5   1979   746.1′4   79–26177
ISBN 0–02–511170–1

10 9 8 7 6 5 4 3 2

This edition is an entirely new and re-set edition of the previous edition which was entitled *New Key to Weaving*.

Printed in the United States of America

Dedicated
to
E. B. and V. M. B.

Contents

1 THE LOOM 1

Frame or Primitive Types · Types With Combined Reed and
Heddle Construction · Foot- and Hand-Treadle Looms · Fly-
Shuttle Looms · Choosing a Loom · Parts of a Loom ·
Function of the Parts of the Loom · Measuring and Marking
the Reed · Marking the Harnesses · Colored String Heddles
Used to Facilitate Threading · Marking the Heddles ·
Wires or Ropes to Hold Lease Sticks · Frame for Holding
Drafts · Screw Hooks · Pincushion and Shoelaces.

2 DRESSING THE LOOM 13

1. The Warp · 2. Method of Determining Number of Warp
Threads Needed to Weave a Web or Piece of Material a Given
Width · 3. Method of Determining Length of Warp Needed
to Weave a Web a Given Length · 4. Method of Determining
Amount of Yardage Needed to Warp a Loom to Weave a Piece
of Material a Given Size · 5. The Guide String · 6. Handling
the Spools or Cones of Warp · 7. Methods of Winding a
Warp · 8. Tying the Lease · 9. Chaining the Warp ·

on 4-Thread Plain-Weave Huck · Huck Lace · M's and O's:
4-Harness, 2-Block; 6-Harness, 3-Block; 8-Harness, 4-Block ·
Waffle Weave: 4-Harness; 5-Harness; 8-Harness · Warp Face,
Ripsmatta · Texture Weaves.

Inside Selvedge Edges · To Correct Errors Caused by Uneven Tying and Faulty Tension · Uneven Spacing of Weft Threads in Web · Imperfect Diagonals in Pattern Weaving · Causes of Broken Threads · To Repair Broken Warp Threads · To Repair Warp Slipping on Beam · To Add New Weft Threads · Winding Two Threads Together on the Shuttle · To Prevent Threads on Shuttles From Tangling When Placed in a Cupboard · Tying New Warp Ends Onto Old Warp Ends · For New Warp to be Tied Onto Old Warp Ends in Front of the Reed · For New Warp to be Tied Onto Old Warp Ends on the Back of the Loom · To Thread a New Pattern With Warp That Is on the Beam · Salvaging Samples · To Keep Weaving Clean · To Determine Correct Sleying for Threads of Unknown Size · To Figure Amount of Material to Weave a Garment · Following Treadling Draft · To Mark Blocks · To Weave Two Identical Pattern Units · To Weave Narrow Webs on Wide Looms · To Unweave a Web · Knots · Fringes: Hemstitched; Simple Knotted; Double Knotted; Twisted; Braided; Half-Hitch; Uncut Loop Fringe; Swedish; Flossa; Auto Rug Fringe · Fringe Woven on Four Sides · Gimp, Two Webs Woven Simultaneously · Slits or Holes · Cords.

Foreword

When the first issue of *The Key to Weaving* appeared in 1945, the majority of weavers were content to follow such drafts and treadling directions as were available to them from the few experienced weavers who were generous enough to pass along their knowledge.

Today, however, the trend is entirely different. Even the beginning weaver is curious to know the structure of the weave; the correct ratio between threads, sleying, and fabric; the mechanics of the loom; and something about the history of weaving. He or she is interested in weaving pieces that are technically correct as well as those calling for creative expression.

Couched in simple terms, *The Key to Weaving* answers the many questions which puzzle the beginner; the weaver unable to obtain formal instruction; the weaver who lacks stimulating contacts through membership in a weaver's study group; the weaver who likes to experiment; and the weaving teacher.

This new edition of *The Key to Weaving* adds directions for techniques which previously have not been found in the weaving literature as well as directions for interesting new ways to use the better-known ones.

A long-needed, and frequently asked for, chapter on color in weaving will assist the weaver in producing more attractively colored articles by explaining the fundamental theory of why and how colored threads blend and change when combined on the loom.

A comprehensive chapter on fibers is also included, with specific directions for the processing of sheep's wool. And "Ready Reference Tables" will help weavers during the changeover to the metric system.

Mary E. Black, O.T.R.

Wolfville, Nova Scotia, Canada
January 1980

Acknowledgments

Weaving techniques and pattern drafts, like cooking recipes, are passed from person to person until their origins and frequently their names are lost. As a result, it is difficult, in a text such as this, to give credit where credit is due.

The author is cognizant of, and deeply grateful for, the help and inspiration gained from studying the publications of many outstanding weavers, from occupational therapists, craft instructors, and friends with whom she has been associated over the years, and from the many weavers from far and near whose letters and interesting samples have been a source of pleasure.

No weave or variation of same used in the book has been reproduced knowingly without permission first being obtained from the weaver originating it, where the originator has been known to the author.

How to Use This Book

This book is strictly a textbook and should be used as such.

To get the most from the book, the lessons should be studied in the order in which they appear.

A student of arithmetic would not jump about his textbook from simple addition to fractions then back again to subtraction, nor in the study of English grammar from the A B C's to essay writing.

If the directions are followed carefully, step by step, the interested student will soon become familiar with the basic weaving structures and prepare himself for the more advanced study of the many variations and extensions of these weaves.

No effort has been made to include threading drafts other than those needed to illustrate the various points under discussion, but ample references have been given for source material to which the weaver can refer.

The author makes no claim that the methods presented are the best or only ones to use, but they are methods that have been successfully used to present weaving techniques to many students in a simple, progressive manner.

The material in the text is based on notes gathered and used over a period of years as a student of weaving in Canada, the United States, and Sweden, in study groups, as a weaving instructor in psychiatric occupational therapy, and in the Handcrafts Program of the Province of Nova Scotia.

The Key to Weaving

chapter 1

The Loom

Webster defines a loom as "a frame or machine for interweaving yarn or threads into a fabric, the operation being performed by laying lengthwise a series called the warp and weaving in across this other threads called the weft, woof, or filling."

Modern weavers use the same principles of weaving as those employed by the primitives, but numerous inventions have changed a slow, laborious hand process into a highly mechanized, productive industry.

Primitive man first stretched twisted root fibers from tree to tree, interlaced other fibers across these by hand, and fashioned the first crude web or piece of cloth. Then came a type of loom still found in remote sections of the world where modern methods have not penetrated. To make this loom, one end of the warp was attached to a stick which was securely fastened to two pegs driven into the ground; the other end of the warp was tied around a stick which in turn was tied to the body of the weaver to keep the warp tight. Then, to form a shed, the weaver dug a hole in the ground for his legs, tied cords to some of the warp threads, and manipulated these cords with his feet. The shuttle bearing the weft thread was passed through this opening, whereas it had previously been woven over one thread, under one thread across the entire warp. Later man devised a method whereby a flat stick was woven under alternate threads and turned on its edge to give a shed; this, however, still left the remaining threads to be picked up by the fingers or shuttle. This difficulty was solved by tying bits of string to the alternate threads, then tying these to another stick, which, when lifted, brought these alternate strings up. This method is still used by the Indian weavers in the southwestern United States. In some countries these simple looms were hung horizontally and in others they were used in a vertical position.

The American pioneers constructed large cumbersome looms of hand-hewn timbers. On these looms they wove the cloth which they needed from the flax and wool grown in their new country. The sturdy, beautiful fabrics which have been handed down to us from this period attest to the cleverness and ability of the weavers of the colonies. These materials often were dyed with roots, barks, and leaves. Later, as the colonists could afford them, fine fabrics were sent from France and England.

Then came the Jacquard loom, on which intricate designs were woven through the employment of a series of many hundreds of perforated cards. The process was difficult, but we read that the "card boy," though frequently exhausted at the end of his day's work, still had strength to protest when his loom became power driven.

A study of the history of weaving is a fascinating hobby in itself, but can only be lightly touched upon here. Fortunately, we have been able to trace the evolution of the loom and weaving down through the centuries through pictures and other descriptive relics. Primitive peoples and those who have retained the old methods possess a heritage of talent which enables them to produce textiles rich in design, coloring, and texture. Sometimes these designs are symbolic; others record historical events; and still others tell stories of the daily lives and activities of the people of the countries in which they originated.

The revival and interest in hand-loom weaving during the past five decades has been responsible for the marketing of a variety of types of table and floor looms. These, in general, have been patterned after the Scandinavian and early colonial types rather than commercial looms.

Although there is some overlapping in construction, looms in general can be divided into four classes.

FRAME OR PRIMITIVE TYPES

Various types of frame looms, which lack both heddles and beaters, can be purchased. Weaving is accomplished on these looms by passing a shuttle over one then under one thread, back and forth across the warp as in darning. Some of these looms have a small triangular bar, with slots, which is turned in various directions to manipulate the threads and form a shed through which to pass the shuttle. In still other types a flat stick is woven in, under one and over one thread across the loom; then this stick is turned on edge to form a shed. The alternate threads are threaded through string eyes tied to another stick. This stick when raised lifts in alternating sequence the threads not controlled by the flat stick.

Material woven on a frame loom, by a beginner, often is poor in structure, with uneven beating and edges. However, when the work is done by an experienced weaver, who uses the techniques and artistic designs and colors of the primitive weavers or the very fine Scandinavian processes, the product can be beautiful and sturdy.

FIG. 1. Back-strap loom used by primitive peoples

TYPES WITH COMBINED REED AND HEDDLE CONSTRUCTION

The simplest method of obtaining a shed automatically is through the use of a special type of blocked reed. The reed is supported by and operates in slots fastened to the sides of the upright beams of the loom. Every other dent in the reed is blocked off so that every alternate thread can go only halfway up the reed, thus forming the shed. The reed also acts as a beater.

The old-fashioned Barbour loom was of this type. Small table looms, which can be obtained at the present time, embrace this principle. A fair grade of weaving can be done on these looms when properly threaded and operated by careful, experienced weavers. The beginner, however, finds them somewhat difficult to manipulate.

FOOT- AND HAND-TREADLE LOOMS

The treadle type of loom, which is the type most frequently used by modern weavers, consists of an upright frame from which 2 to 16 harnesses with heddles are hung from the overhead beam of the loom. Threads are threaded through the heddles in predetermined sequence to form plain or pattern weaving, and the harnesses are manipulated either by foot or hand treadles, levers, pedals, or ropes. Some types "trip" automatically, returning the harness back to the original position, but most of them are operated entirely by hand or foot.

Under this general heading of hand- and foot-treadle looms are the following:

2-, 4-, 6-, 8-, 12-, and 16-harness floor or foot looms
2-, 4-, 8-, and 10-harness table looms

There are two types of floor looms, the counterbalanced and the jack. Counterbalanced looms operate with a sinking shed, that is, the harnesses are drawn down when the treadles are pressed to the floor. Jack looms have a somewhat more complicated mechanism and operate with a rising shed, by which the harnesses are drawn up when the treadles are pressed to the floor.

Hand looms usually operate with a rising shed, although some can be obtained which operate with a sinking shed. Hand levers of various kinds control the harnesses. Before beginning to weave, check the operation of the levers or treadles to determine whether the harnesses sink or rise; then follow the treadling directions given for the particular type of loom. The finished weaving is the same in each case. Should the wrong treadling be used by the inexperienced weaver, the pattern may be upside down. There is little harm if this occurs, for the web can be reversed when it is removed from the loom. During the weaving, some difficulty may arise in "squaring" the pattern, but if the diagonals are carefully followed there should be little real trouble.

FLY-SHUTTLE LOOMS

Fly-shuttle looms are similar in construction to the floor loom with the exception that the shuttle runs in a "shuttle race" along the lower beam of the beater. The shuttle is propelled very rapidly back and forth through the shed by the automatic action of two rawhide picks tied to an overhead rope. This rope is manipulated from side to side by one hand, while the other hand works the beater back and forth.

This loom is generally found in 2-harness types although some semi-commercial weavers use a 4-harness loom. These looms cannot be recommended except for weavers who are interested only in rapid production of unlimited quantities of plain, coarse fabrics, such as dish toweling, drapes, cloth, etc. The operation of these looms is tiresome and noisy, but they serve a most useful purpose in institutions where the product can be utilized by the organization and the patient needs a simple, repetitive, monotonous activity. Products of fly-shuttle looms sold commercially should be so marked.

CHOOSING A LOOM

It is not possible to give definite advice to the beginning weaver as to what type or size of loom he should purchase, but several factors should be taken into consideration.

Is the weaving being done for commercial purposes or as a hobby? If it is to be used commercially, a sturdy, easily and quickly prepared and operated loom is essential; if for a hobby, time and effort need not be considered, as little but one's self-entertainment is at stake.

The size of articles to be woven should be considered. If small articles such as bags, scarves, etc., are to be woven, a small loom will be sufficient; but if large articles such as bedspreads, blankets, baby blankets, table linens, tweeds, dress materials, or upholstery materials are to be woven, a large, wide loom will be required. Strips of materials can be woven on a narrow loom and sewn together, but the results are never as pleasing as when the material has been woven on a wider loom.

Finances will, to a large degree, determine the size and quality of the loom, but the weaver is urged to be quite sure that the loom he is buying is sturdily built of hardwood, or its life will be short and the weaving of poor quality.

Space in which to place the loom and its equipment must also be considered; it is not comfortable working around a large loom in cramped quarters. It is better to restrict the size of the loom than to fill up a small room with a large loom, leaving little space for living. A sturdily built loom with a folding back will pass through doorways and, when not in use, will require only a small amount of space.

If the weaver is content with simple types of weaving, and lacks the time and inclination to delve deeply into the subject, a 2-harness loom is recommended. Many beautiful designs, patterns, color effects, and textures can be worked out on a 2-harness loom. Overshot patterns are not possible on less than four harnesses. Many Scandinavian and primitive techniques can be worked out most successfully on the 2-harness loom, and are limited only by the ability and interest of the weaver.

The 4-harness loom will do all that the 2-harness loom is capable of, plus overshot, simplified summer and winter weaves, twills, and many other techniques. On general principles, a 4-harness loom is recommended over a 2-harness loom because of its greater possibilities.

The interested weaver who wishes to progress from the simple types through to the more intricate patterns is advised to consider the 4-harness loom, constructed with space for the later addition of an extra set of four harnesses to make an 8-harness loom.

There are some very good 4- and 8-harness looms on the market, and the average weaver will find much satisfaction in owning and operating a sturdy 15- or 20-in. table loom. Such table looms, operated at the front with levers, are especially good for therapeutic purposes. A fairly good rhythm can be obtained on this loom.

There is considerable controversy among experienced weavers as to which is the better type, a rising-shed or counterbalanced loom. Some prefer the rising-shed type with direct-action tie-up, claiming they can concentrate on what the harnesses are doing and need not be concerned about the treadles. They feel also that treadling variations can be quickly executed since it is not necessary to change the tie-up. The rising-shed loom is particularly good when weaving patterns that call for treadling one harness against three as it is possible to get a perfect shed without difficulty. This cannot be said of a counterbalanced loom on which it is sometimes necessary to weave the web upside down to get the shed to open wide enough for the passage of the shuttle. Also, as he grows older, the weaver finds it increasingly difficult to crawl under the loom to tie up the treadles!

On the other hand, devotees of the counterbalanced loom and the newer type rising-shed loom, which use the regulation tie-up with two or more harnesses tied to one treadle, claim there is considerable conservation of both time and energy when one foot manages several harnesses.

Here again the preference is largely personal but the beginning weaver is urged to thoroughly test and investigate the different types of looms before deciding which to purchase.[1]

PARTS OF A LOOM

A loom consists of many parts, and the weaver will do well to familiarize himself with the names when he first begins to weave, as frequent reference is made to them throughout the text.

The loom, Fig. 2, is composed of a frame of four sturdy corner posts, Nos. 1, 2, 3, and 4, joined together at the top and bottom with four cross beams, Nos. 5, 6, 7, and 8, and two floor beams, Nos. 9 and 10, across the front and back. Two upright side beams, Nos. 11 and 12, are fastened to Nos. 5 and 6, between which is supported a roller No. 13, from which the harnesses No. 14 are hung.

Across the front of the loom, fastened to Nos. 2 and 3, is the breast beam No. 15, and across the back of the beam, fastened between Nos. 1 and 4, is the slab stock, back beam, or thread carrier No. 16.

Extending across the front of the loom, and fastened to side beams Nos. 5 and 6, well back from the front of the loom, are the cloth beam No. 17 and the cloth-beam rod No. 18 (not shown in the illustration). In a similar position at the back of the loom are the warp beam No. 19 and the warp-beam rod No. 20 (not shown in illustration).

The beater, No. 21, may be hung either in the Scandinavian manner from the top of the loom frame, or it may be bolted to the floor beams Nos. 7 and 8. Inserted between the top and bottom beams of the beater is the reed No. 22. The ends of the beater, Nos. 23 and 24, are called the swords. It is here, at the end of the reed, that one looks for the numbers designating the number of dents to the inch of the reed (page 14).

The harness frames, No. 14, hold the heddles, **No.** 25. The harness frames are tied to the heddle horses, No. 26, at the top, and at the bottom to the lams, No. 30, which are fastened to the inside of the upright beam, No. 11. These lams are tied to the treadles or foot pedals, No. 27.

Ratchet wheels, Nos. 28 and 29, are fastened to the end of the cloth beam, No. 17, and warp beam, No. 19. Dogs or pawls are screwed to the beams, Nos. 4 and 6, opposite the ends of the cloth beam, No. 17, and warp beam, No. 19.

FIG 2

FUNCTION OF THE PARTS OF THE LOOM

Parts 1 to 13 inclusive serve only to form a rigid structure or frame to hold the workable parts of the loom which, in turn, have a definite duty to perform.

The harnesses, No. 14, hold the heddles, No. 25.

The heddles, No. 25, may be of string, steel, or twisted wire (page 9). Through eyes in the heddles are passed the warp ends which, when stretched taut, provide the base on which the web or cloth is woven.

The heddle horses, No. 26, serve to keep the harnesses in alignment, and permit them to be operated either as single units or in sets, as desired.

The lams, No. 30, connect the harnesses to the treadles, No. 27, and control the pattern structure. Pressure on the treadles, No. 27, pulls the harnesses down, opening the shed through which the shuttle (page 9) carrying the weft thread is passed.

The beater, No. 21, serves a double purpose. It holds the reed, No. 22, which, in turn, keeps the warp ends equally spaced and in alignment as they pass from the warp beam, through the heddles, and are tied into position to the cloth-beam rod. Its second function is to pack or pound the weft threads back into place against the edge of the web as one shot after another is laid in place. The manner of hanging the beater is not important, but it must work smoothly and be fastened with accurate alignment or the weaving will not be correct (page 574). The overhead beater usually has a spring attachment to pull and hold the beater back against the upright beam, out of the way, when not in use. When the beater is fastened to the floor beam, it usually returns to its position through its own weight and leverage when lightly touched by the weaver after the beating stroke has been completed.

The warp beam, No. 19, holds the supply of warp (page 34). Modern looms are frequently equipped with sectional warp beams (page 24).

Some looms are built without a slab stock or back beam, No. 16. The completed web passes over the breast beam, No. 15, and continues down under and around the cloth beam, No. 17.

Considerable variation is found in the type of ratchet wheel, crank, and dog, but they all serve the purpose of holding the warp and cloth beams in position, thus maintaining a constant tension on the warp.

MEASURING AND MARKING THE REED

Marking the reed at the halfway and quarter points facilitates the centering of the web in the loom. To have the spacing permanently marked saves counting each time the loom is threaded with a new warp. When warps are centered in the loom, the balance is better and the whole loom is neater.

The reed is inserted in grooves in a movable frame called the beater (page 6).

Measure the width of the reed and find the center dent.

Place a piece of colored yarn in the dent.

To check for accuracy, count the dents beginning at the left edge of the reed and count toward the center; then begin at the right and count toward the center. Use a warp hook to count the dents. If measurement with tape has been incorrect, move the colored yarn to the correct dent.

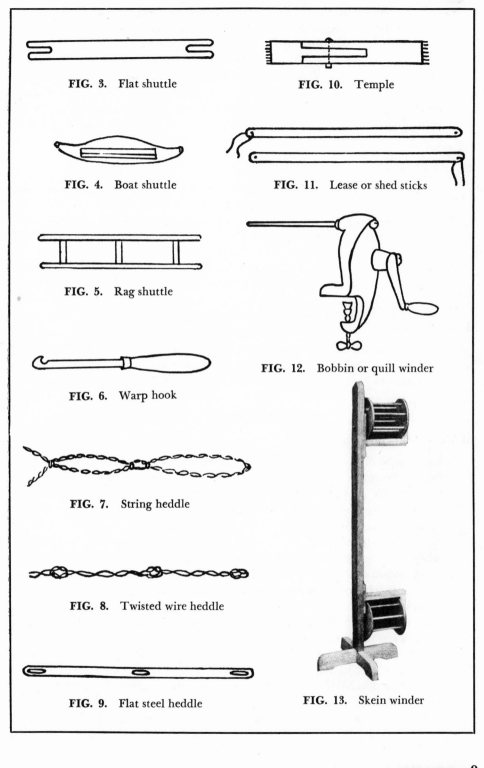

FIG. 3.   Flat shuttle

FIG. 4.   Boat shuttle

FIG. 5.   Rag shuttle

FIG. 6.   Warp hook

FIG. 7.   String heddle

FIG. 8.   Twisted wire heddle

FIG. 9.   Flat steel heddle

FIG. 10.   Temple

FIG. 11.   Lease or shed sticks

FIG. 12.   Bobbin or quill winder

FIG. 13.   Skein winder

Measure again and find halfway points between the ends of the reed and the center dent, both to the right and the left. Mark with colored yarn.

With a fine paintbrush and some bright enamel paint, mark the beater frame directly in front of and behind the dents marked with the colored yarn. If for any reason the reed should be removed from the beater, be sure to check for correct placement when it is put back. Scratches can be made on the paper that is wound around the reed between the dents.

MARKING THE HARNESSES

To speed up threading and to aid in eliminating mistakes, paint the lower heddle bars of harnesses 1 and 3 to distinguish them easily from harnesses 2 and 4. In threading, the weaver will immediately sense his mistake before he makes it if he should start to thread a No. 3 heddle when it should be a No. 2, etc.

COLORED STRING HEDDLES USED TO FACILITATE THREADING

Users of string heddles can greatly hasten and facilitate the threading process if all heddles on harnesses 1 and 3 are light colored, and all those on harnesses 2 and 4 are a dark color.

MARKING THE HEDDLES

For 2-harness, twill, and simple pattern weaving, each harness should have the same number of heddles. As patterns become more complicated, it may be necessary to move heddles from one harness to increase the number needed on another, but for the beginner it is advisable to have the same number on each harness.

By counting, find the middle heddle on each harness and either securely tie a colored thread through the eye, or paint the heddle. Count again and find the halfway heddle between the one in the center and the right and left ends. Either tie colored thread through these eyes also, or paint the heddle.

When threading begins on a 2-harness loom, the required number of heddles can be found easily.

For instance, if 90 heddles are required to thread a 2-harness loom for a 6-in. web, one half of these heddles will be on harness No. 1 and the other half on harness No. 2. The center heddle would be counted as heddle No. 1, and 22 heddles to the right and 22 to the left of the one in the center would make a total of 45 heddles. The same method would be used on harness No. 2, making a total of 90 threads, the number required. On a 4-harness loom, the total number would be divided first by four, and then would be subdivided. On an 8-harness loom the total number would first be divided by eight and then subdivided, to insure the correct number of heddles being counted off.

WIRES OR ROPES TO HOLD LEASE STICKS

Time is saved and the threading of the loom facilitated if permanent wires are fastened to the upright beams of the loom to hold the lease sticks (Fig. 14).

Pass a double strand of wire through the screw eyes on the beams. Even the ends and twist them to a point about halfway between the slab beam and the upright beam. Insert the end of a lease stick, and make three twists in the wire. Insert another lease stick, and twist the ends of the wire up to the screw eye in the upright beam. Pass the end of the wire through the screw eye and fasten them securely. Do the same on the other side of the loom.

These wires are not in the way, yet are always available to hold the lease sticks in place when the new warp is being entered.

If for any reason, wires are not available or cannot be used, cut four cords of equal length (two for each side of the loom), and tie knots in the center of them to make loops for eyes for the lease sticks. These knots remain permanently tied. One end of the double cord is tied to the upright beam of the loom and the other to the back beam. Weavers who prefer to let the lease sticks "float" need not be concerned with this, but it is an advantage for beginners.

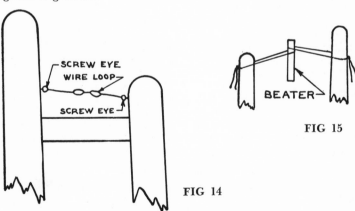

SCREW EYE
WIRE LOOP
SCREW EYE

BEATER

FIG 15

FIG 14

It is convenient, also, to have a piece of cord with knotted ends at hand to tie the beater midway between the breast beam and the upright beam to hold it in position during the entering of the warp. This releases both hands for threading and sleying, and does away with unexpected motions of the beater which might pull the threads out of the reed (Fig. 15).

FRAME FOR HOLDING DRAFTS

A small wooden frame with a wooden back, faced with soft cardboard or sheet cork, with a cleat to screw it to the loom frame, is excellent for holding the threading draft (Fig. 16).

SCREW HOOKS

Screw hooks screwed in along the outside upright supporting beam of the loom afford a convenient place to hang shuttles, shed sticks, scissors, etc.

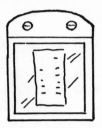 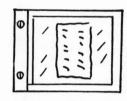

FIG 16

PINCUSHION AND SHOELACES

A small hard pincushion fastened to the side of the upright supporting beam on the loom provides a convenient spot to keep pins and needles.

Shoelaces with tinned ends are easily tied and untied and are useful for many purposes around the loom.

chapter 2

Dressing the Loom

"Dressing the loom" is the term used to describe the process of preparing the loom for weaving.

Many important processes must be completed before the actual weaving can begin. Many preparatory steps are necessary, beginning with the preparation of the warp and continuing through to the winding of the shuttles. The logical sequence of these steps is as follows:

1. Preparing the warp
2. Calculating the number of threads needed
3. Calculating the length of the threads
4. Calculating the yardage of material needed
5. Attaching the guide string
6. Handling the spools or cones of warp
7. Methods of winding a warp
8. Tying the lease or cross
9. Chaining the warp
10. Methods of dressing the loom
11. Transferring the lease sticks
12. Beaming the warp
13. Threading and sleying
14. Tying the warp ends
15. The tie-up
16. Testing the loom
17. Filling the shuttle and winding the bobbin
18. Weaving
19. Finishing

1. THE WARP

Warp threads run lengthwise in the loom. Back and forth, across these stretched threads, a shuttle is passed carrying the weft threads. The interlocking of these two sets of threads forms what is called the cloth or web.

2. METHOD OF DETERMINING NUMBER OF WARP THREADS NEEDED TO WEAVE A WEB OR PIECE OF MATERIAL A GIVEN WIDTH

Sample Illustrated   6 in. wide when completed. At the end of the reed will be found a flat metal rod (page 6). On this rod two numbers have been stamped. The first number indicates the width of the reed and the second the number of spaces, openings, or dents per inch in the reed. Thus a 20–15 combination would indicate that the reed is 20 in. wide and that 15 openings or dents appear to the inch.

To determine the number of warp threads needed to weave a web or piece of material 6 in. wide, multiply the number of inches (6) by 15, the number of dents to the inch in the reed. This equals 90 threads single sley, which indicates that one warp end or thread is drawn through each dent in the reed. When a fine thread is used, two warp ends are drawn through each dent, thereby doubling the number of threads required, or 180. This is called double sleying.

During the process of weaving, the edge threads draw in. To offset this, allow a few extra threads, usually enough to thread an extra inch in width. However, there is some variation in the amount drawn in by weavers, as well as in different materials and weaves. So after the first few webs have been woven, the weaver will know how many extra threads are indicated. If, as just described, the weaver draws in the web enough to narrow it an inch, plan to thread 7 in. instead of 6 in. This will equal 7 × 15, or 105 threads for a single sley or 210 threads for a double-sley web 6 in. wide when completed.

3. METHOD OF DETERMINING LENGTH OF WARP NEEDED TO WEAVE A WEB A GIVEN LENGTH

Sample Illustrated   6 in. wide, 12 in. long. Estimate or measure the length of the article to be woven, including hems or fringe. To this measurement must be added:

A. The loom waste which is the measured distance between the back beam and the breast beam (Fig. 2).

B. The amount of warp used in tying ends onto the warp and cloth beam rods, approximately 6 to 8 in.

C. The shrinkage that may occur when the tension of the web is released. Most experienced weavers allow 3 in. per yard to cover this and the initial finishing, particularly for wools and cottons.

It is an advantage to record the length of all warp chains and the overall length of the finished material or article both before and after washing. From these records the actual waste can definitely be established.

D. Allowance for samples to be woven for notebook.

E. Allowances for experimenting with various weaves and color arrangements before the actual weaving begins. Weavers seldom if ever wind only enough warp for one article.

Therefore, for an article 12 in. long with allowance to take care of the foregoing, the warp should be wound 12 plus 24 in. or a total of 36 in.

4. METHOD OF DETERMINING AMOUNT OF YARDAGE NEEDED TO WARP A LOOM TO WEAVE A PIECE OF MATERIAL A GIVEN SIZE

A. Multiply the number of ends per inch by the width in the reed by the length of warp, for instance: width 6 in., length 12 in., sleyed to the inch 15.

B. Add to the above:

Extra allowance to cover "draw-in" at edge, which changes width measurement to 7 in.;

Extra allowance for shrinkage and that part of the warp that cannot be used (page 14), which changes length measurement to 36 in.

C. Now that the measurements in length and width have been determined, figure the yardage and number of threads needed.

D. Multiply:

15 threads to the inch, the sleying, by

7 in., the width of the web
___

105 threads required

E. Multiply:

105 the number of threads required by

36 in. length of the threads required
___

3780 in. total amount of warp needed (or 105 yds.)

The yardage per pound of cotton is usually given on the inside of the cone, or in the literature describing the thread, so it is a comparatively simple matter to figure the amount needed from this information.

However, when the yardage per pound is not given, it can be worked out from the following formula:

"The count of cotton" yarn is based on the formula of the number of yards that are spun from a pound of raw cotton.

The basis of this formula is the spinning of a pound of cotton into 840 yd. of No. 1 yarn. Yardage per pound of all other sizes of cotton yarn is figured from this formula.

No. 2 cotton would be one half the size and contains 1680 yd. per pound.

No. 3 cotton would be one third the size and contains 2520 yd. per pound.

No. 10 cotton would be one tenth the size and contains 8400 yd. per pound.

No. 12 cotton would be one twelfth the size and contains 10,080 yd. per pound.

When 2, 3, or more threads of a single-ply yarn have been twisted together to make a single thread, they are called plied yarn and are designated thus:

20/2 thread which is composed of 2 threads of a No. 20 single-ply yarn twisted together.

10/3 thread which is composed of 3 threads of a No. 10 single-ply yarn twisted together.

In calculating for a 2- or 3-ply yarn, remember that the count must be reduced to a single equivalent; for example, multiply 840 yd. by 20 and divide by 3, which equals 5600 yd.

A plain 50/50 web requires slightly less thread for weft than for warp so no loom waste is involved.

For a balanced 50/50 weave (page 53), the warp and weft threads must be of the same size although they may be of a different material. Therefore, purchase approximately the same amount of thread for the weft and the warp.

Where a patterned web, such as the overshot (page 226) or the crackle (page 307), is to be woven, half of the thread purchased should be pattern thread and half tabby thread.

For a warp-face web (page 88), approximately twice as much warp thread as weft thread is required; while for a weft-face web (page 94), almost twice as much weft thread as warp thread is needed.

One of the most difficult webs for which to figure the material requirements is a textured upholstery web in which threads of several sizes and materials are used. In this case, experience is the greatest help.

The count of wool yarn is based on the formula of 560 yd. spun from 1 lb. raw wool.

The count of linen yarn is based on the formula of 300 yd. spun from 1 lb. raw flax.

The count of jute, hemp, ramie, grass linen, etc., are all calculated on the linen count. Silk, rayon, nylon, and the many other new synthetic threads are measured in meters and weighed in decigrams.

5. THE GUIDE STRING

The length of warp having been determined, cut a piece of heavy brightly colored twine this length, and place it in position on whatever device is chosen for winding the warp. When tied in position, this string acts as a guide along which the warp threads follow in succession. It sometimes will be found that the guide string is too short to reach even the minimum distance between the pegs. If this happens, lengthen the guide string.

6. HANDLING THE SPOOLS OR CONES OF WARP

The warp always should be fed slowly off the ball or spool and be wound onto the warping device with an even tension. The position of the spool or ball from which the warp is fed usually is determined by the individual weaver. What is convenient for one may not be for another, but, in general practice, the ball usually is placed to the right of the winder, and guided by the right hand around the pegs of the warping device.

Balls can be placed in deep pitchers to prevent them from rolling on the floor.

A 12-in.-long round stick can be placed in the center of a tube of warp. This allows the tube to ride freely on the right hand, the thread unwinding easily and regularly.

If large cones are used, they can rest on the floor, and if placed in proper position in relationship to the winder, the thread should feel easily and evenly. If, however, the cone upsets, change its position or place it in a box. The thread should feed directly from the top of the cone and not from an angle (Fig. 17).

Boards with dowels sunk in them, over which the cone or tube can be placed, can be made to rest on the floor.

On a table warping reel, the spool rides on a wooden rod which runs lengthwise under the reel proper. The spool travels along this rod from left to right and back again as the winding proceeds, releasing the thread with an even tension.

FIG 17   **RIGHT**   **WRONG**

7. METHODS OF WINDING A WARP

When warping a loom, every thread must be of even tension and length. Therefore, it can easily be seen that some device is needed to control the length and tension of the threads.

Several methods are available:

A. Table and chairs
B. Blocks of heavy wood with sturdy upright pegs clamped to a table
C. Warping board
D. Pegs in door frame
E. Table warping reel
F. Floor warping reel
G. Warping directly from spool rack onto sectional warp beam.

A. Table and Chairs Place a straight-back chair at each end of a kitchen or dining-room table, with the seat underneath the table and the back close to it, to prevent slipping (Fig. 18).

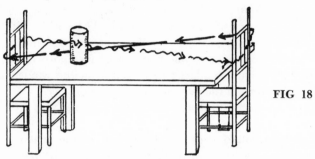

FIG 18

1. Place a tomato-juice can or other high, straight-sided can filled with stones or sand, 18 in. from the left end of the table.

2. Tie a colored guide string to the farthest edge of the chair at the left end of the table, and carry it along the top of the table in front of the can and around the back of the chair at the right end of the table. Continue back to the left end of the table, passing the string behind the can, and tie it to the edge of the chair nearest the winder. It will probably be necessary to either lengthen or shorten the guide string to have it reach exactly between the two chairs, as the length of the table controls the distance and length of the warp. Keep in mind that it is always better to have a warp that is a little too long rather than a little too short.

If the guide string has been correctly placed, it will, on its return journey, cross itself between the can and the chair at the left-hand end of the table. This crossing or alternation of threads forms a lease or cross known as the porrey-cross.

3. Tie the end of the warp thread to the chair at the same spot where the guide string started, and follow the line of the guide string around the can and chairs. Watch the chairs carefully so that the tension of the warp does not pull them over onto the table thus causing the last threads to be shorter than the first. Continue until the required number of threads have been wound. Methods of counting threads, tying in lease sticks, and chaining warp are given later in the text (pages 19 and 23).

In Fig. 18, the wavy line represents the guide string passing from left to right. The solid line represents the guide string passing back of the can and back to the chair at the left end of the table.

4. During the process of winding the warp, the threads should be counted frequently. This counting is done at the porrey-cross or lease, although some weavers find it easier to count elsewhere.

5. After a number of threads have been wound, start counting at the bottom thread which lies just above the colored guide string, anywhere along the warp.

6. Count off 25 or 50 threads. Pass the ends of a heavy cord or piece of carpet warp under the bottom threads, and bring one end up on each side of the warp. Tie a single knot around the 25 or 50 threads. Tie a double knot around each 100 threads. Let the ends of the cord fall down onto the board out of the way of the winding of the threads.

B. Blocks With Upright Pegs   Three of these blocks are necessary. They should be made of pieces of ¾-in. hardwood (maple or oak) approximately 4 in. square. The pegs should be 6 in. long, 1 in. in diameter, and should be sunk completely through the base of the block (Fig. 19).

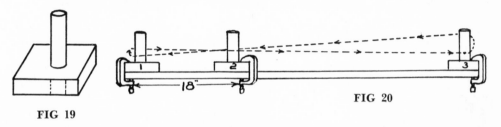

FIG 19

FIG 20

1. Clamp one peg at each end of a table, near the edge (Fig. 20). The exact distance apart is determined by the length of the guide string. Clamp the third peg 18 in. to the right of the first peg and in line with it and peg No. 3.

2. Tie a colored guide string around peg No. 1, carry it in front of peg No. 2, continue around peg No. 3, and back to peg No. 1, going between pegs Nos. 1 and 2 in a direction opposite to the first turn. The guide string follows around the pegs in the direction of the arrows.

3. Tie a warp thread to peg No. 1, and follow the colored guide string around and around until the required number of threads have been wound (page 19).

C. Warping Boards   When a longer, heavier warp is required than it is possible to wind by any of the previously described methods, a warping board is used.

Two types of warping boards are in common use. We shall call them board *A*, Fig. 21, and board *B*, Fig. 22. In order to stand up under the tension of many tightly wound warp threads, the boards are made of heavy oak or maple, with sturdy 1-in. pegs sunk entirely through the frames. When in use, the warping boards can be hung on the wall at a height convenient for the winder, or they can be laid flat on a table.

Board *A:* Warp capacity is 300 coarse or 600 fine threads, approximately 15 yd. long; measurements of board: length, 72 in.; width, 12 in.; thickness, 1¾ in.; pegs: diameter, 1 in.; length, 8½ in.; sunk completely through the base.

Board *B:* Warp capacity is 300 coarse or 600 fine threads, approximately 8 yd. long; measurements of board: length, 36 in.; width, 24 in.; thickness, 1¾ in.; pegs: diameter, 1 in.; length, 8½ in.; sunk completely through the base. The line in Fig. 21 shows the route of warp between pegs *A* and *M* and between pegs *D* and *A* on the return. On both types of boards there should be a series of holes across the bottom so that pegs *B* and *C* can be placed to bring the porrey-cross at the right distance from *A*. Looms vary, and different methods of threading call for different placing of the cross.

1. Tie a colored guide string to peg *A*, as shown on the warping boards (Figs. 21 and 22), pass it behind peg *B*, in front of peg *C*, around peg *D* to pegs *E, F, G, H, I, J, K*, and *L*, turning around peg *M*, as shown in Fig. 21, and around peg *L*, as shown in Fig. 22, and follow the guide string back to peg *A*.

2. Tie a warp thread to the peg at *A*, and follow the colored guide string around and around until the required number of threads have been wound. Be sure that the threads cross and alternate each time between pegs *B* and *C*. Continue until the required number of threads have been wound (page 19).

D. Pegs in Door Frame   The weaver who lacks room for either a large warping board or floor reel can easily solve the problem of warp winding by converting a convenient door frame into a warping board. Bore holes along each frame of the door, approximately 1½ in. deep, to hold pieces of doweling 1 to 1½ in. in diameter and 8 in. long. (Pieces of broomstick serve very well.) Space the holes so that they are 36 in. apart, thus providing an easy check on the length of warp being wound. Drill a series of holes, of the same size as above, in a thick board, the end holes so placed that the board will slip easily over any two pegs lying directly opposite each other on the door frame. Insert the pegs, around which the porrey-cross is made, in this board, bringing the cross where it is needed. These pegs correspond to pegs *B* and *C* as shown on the warping boards (Figs. 21 and 22).

The procedure of winding is similar to that used with other types of warping boards. Once the warp is wound and removed from the pegs, they are withdrawn from the door frame and stored away in a small box. Short pegs with wooden rosette tops, finished to match the door frame, are inserted in the holes. This decorative door frame attracts little attention.

E. Table Warping Reed (Fig. 23)   The table warping reel was designed especially for the home weaver and others with limited working and storage

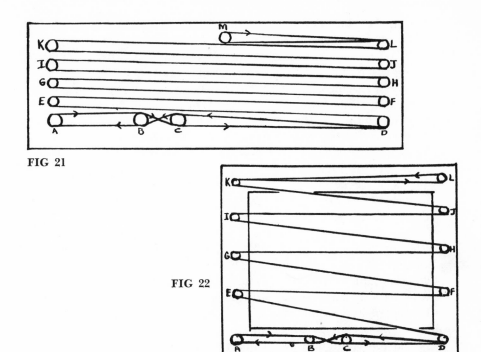

FIG 21

FIG 22

space. It comes apart and requires little storage space, but can be assembled quickly and set up on any convenient table. The operation is simple and easy, and the speed is controlled entirely by the wishes of the weaver. The table warper has a maximum capacity of 300 fine threads approximately 8 yd. long. Heavier warps, such as wools and carpet warp, can be wound in two or more sections, each section being removed as wound. The guide string is left in place as the sections are removed.

1. Tie colored guide string to peg *A*, Fig. 23, and guide it with the left hand while the right hand turns the reel. (If desired, the reel may be set up so that the left hand turns the reel and the right guides the thread.)

FIG 23

2. Pass the guide string to the left of peg *B*, right of peg *D*, left of peg *E*, making the necessary number of turns around the reel to peg *F*.

3. Reverse the turning of the reel and guide the string back to the left of peg *E*, left of peg *G*, right of peg *C*, and back to peg *A*.

The spacing of the guide string along the reel is governed entirely by the length of the string. Longer lengths of warp will be spaced more closely together on the reel, shorter lengths farther apart.

Warp can be wound very quickly on this type of winder, but care must be taken not to wind more quickly than the eye can follow to keep the strand of thread following along in its correct course.

4. Place a spool of warp on the rod under the reel, and pass its end through screw eye *X*. Continue winding until the required number of threads have been wound (page 19).

F. Floor Warping Reel (Fig. 24)   This method of winding the warp is recommended when long warps with many hundreds of threads, such as for drapes, blankets, bedspreads, etc., are needed. This reel is also used for winding warp for sectional warp beams when a spool rack is not available. Because of its size, this type of warping reel is used principally in schools, occupational-therapy shops, weaving studios, and by home weavers where special rooms are devoted to weaving. The reel is large and requires considerable space to operate and store. Unless it is especially constructed with movable pegs, it does not lend itself to the winding of short warps.

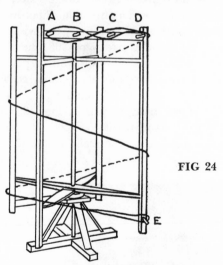

FIG 24

The capacity of this type of warping reel is approximately 1000 threads, 20 or more yards long. The usual size of the reel is 60 in. high including the base, with 27- to 36-in. wings.

Tie a colored guide string to peg *A*, pass it over peg *B*, under peg *C*, over *D*, and down and around the reel to peg *E*. Pass the string around peg *E*, and back along the same route to and on top of pegs *D* and *C*, and under pegs *B* and *A*. As with the table warping reel, the guide string must be spaced around the reel according to the length of the warp required. Continue until the required number of threads have been wound (page 19).

8. TYING THE LEASE

Regardless of the manner in which the warp has been wound, the next step is the same for all methods. After the required number of threads have been wound, tie a shoelace around the lease, or porrey-cross, made by the crossing of the threads between the two top pegs. Be sure the lace is inserted in the right place, passing around the two sets of warp threads.

To prevent the warp from tangling, and to keep the threads in the correct order, tie pieces of cord tightly around the warp at intervals of 24 or 36 in.

9. CHAINING THE WARP

If you know how to crochet, the process will be easy, as the hand and arm take the place of the crochet hook. However, if you do not know how to crochet follow the steps shown in Fig. 25. With the left hand, hold the warp firmly in front of peg *E* (Fig. 24), and remove the peg with the right hand. Chain the warp with the right hand, and insert the foot or a piece of stick into the reel to act as a brake, as the reel is likely to turn more quickly than the chaining can be done.

The warp, chained closely to the peg *C*, is held carefully to prevent its

FIG 25

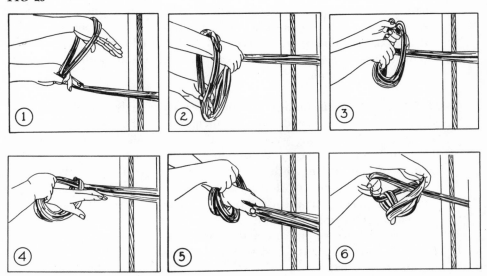

falling to the floor. If the chain is very long, it is thrown over the weaver's shoulder. This prevents the chain from unraveling and tangling.

Once the chaining has been completed the warping can be started.

If the chain is not to be placed immediately on the loom, the ends of the shoelace tying the porrey-cross are passed through the last hoop and tied tightly.

10. METHODS OF DRESSING THE LOOM

There are several methods of dressing a loom. The beginning weaver is advised to study and experiment with the various methods, then decide which one suits him best.

Some weavers will claim that a certain method is the only one, others will prefer an opposite method, while another group will choose a method which they themselves have compounded.

The method is irrelevant, what is important is that the process be easy for the individual and that it results in an evenly tensioned, well-wound warp.

Several warping methods are described here. They are:

A. Sectional warping
B. Warping the loom with a raddle
C. The Swedish method of warping
D. The Beriau method of warping
E. Threading from the front of the loom
F. Threading from the back of the loom

After the warp has been wound, the cross or lease tied, and the warp chained off the warping board or reel and taken to the loom, the process of dressing the loom begins. The weaver can choose any one of the six methods described and, if the directions are followed carefully, should have no difficulties. It is advisable for the new weaver to start with a short warp of rather coarse cotton.

A. Sectional Warp Beaming   Winding the warp directly from the spool rack onto the warp beam has distinct advantages over other methods, especially for the winding of long warps on large looms. This method can be used only on looms equipped with sectional warp beams. It is not a difficult matter to convert the ordinary warp beam into a sectional one if a carpenter is available, or if the weaver himself is handy with tools. This method of warping is a distinct time saver, and if properly done, is most satisfactory. One of its disadvantages, however, is that it requires a number of spools of warp of one size and color (sometimes as many as 40 or 60). Unless the weaver plans to weave a number of articles with the same warp, it can be seen that this method would require a considerable financial outlay as this complete spool yardage is seldom required for a single warping of a loom.

[An alternative to the purchase or winding of the many spools required for the foregoing method is to wind the number of threads required for each section on the warping board or reel (page 22). For instance, if 26 threads were needed for each section, these should be wound the desired length on the warping reel. The lease should be tied with a shoelace and chained, beginning at the end where the lease has been tied.]

A spool rack is also required. Some looms come equipped with a rack; however, if one is not furnished, it can be made quite easily and inexpensively.

FIG 26

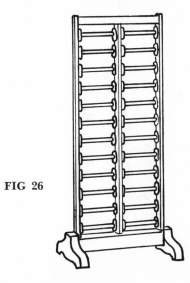

The sectional warp beam differs from the ordinary beam in that it is divided into some 10 to 20 sections. The demarcation of the sections is made with wooden pegs, usually 4, set equidistant around the beam. The warp lies in these sections instead of being spread evenly along the beam.

1. Decide upon the width of the article to be woven—illustrated, 7 in.

2. Determine the number of threads required to weave the article (width of article multiplied by number of dents per inch, page 14).

3. Find the center of the reed (page 8).

4. Measure from the center to the left along the reed a distance of half the width of the web (3½ in.). Measure the same distance to the right. This will center the web in the loom. Place pieces of colored yarn in the dents.

5. Cut two pieces of twine long enough to tie onto the breast beam, pass one end of each piece through the reed, and tie the ends onto the warp beam. Pass the other ends through the marked dents, and tie. These pieces of twine must run in a perfectly straight line from the breast beam to the warp beam; they must not angle. These threads mark the sections on the sectional warp beam within which the warp will be wound. They are removed before the winding starts.

6. Divide the total number of ends required (7 × 15 = 105) by the number of sections lying inside the pieces of twine. For instance, if 105 warp ends are needed to weave a piece 7 in. wide on a 15-to-the-inch dent loom, the 105 threads would be divided by the number of sections bounded by the twine, in this case 4. Therefore, 26 threads would be wound in each one of the four sections (27 would be wound in one to give the extra thread to make an even 105).

7. A guide string, or some method of measuring the amount of warp wound onto the roller, is very necessary, as each section must have the same length of warp wound around it. Looms which come equipped with a sectional warp beam are usually constructed with a roller which measures a yard around, made in the form of crossed bars. These looms also have a gauge to measure the yardage. However, with a converted warp beam, it will be necessary to cut a guide string the length of the warp to put on the loom, and wind it around one of the sections before winding the warp. Count the number of turns. The same number of turns should then be used to fill all the sections. It is wise for the weaver to train himself from the beginning to start and stop the turns at some specified place, as for instance when the handle is at the bottom of the turn. Now remove the guide string.

8. Place 26 spools on the spool rack, with all ends coming from the spools in the same direction, either from under or over the top of the spool. Care must be exercised to see that this is done, or trouble will ensue when the winding begins. Place the spool rack about 4 ft. away from the back of the loom.

9. Place the metal warp guide in the slot on the top of the back beam, or hold the guide if there is no slot. Start with the spool on the lower left-hand side of the spool rack, and thread the end through the lower left hole in the guide. Continue threading the threads through in rotation,

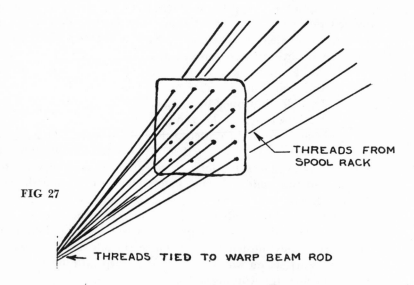

THREADS FROM SPOOL RACK

FIG 27

THREADS TIED TO WARP BEAM ROD

being careful to take them in order and avoid crossing. If crossed the threads will break during the winding (Fig. 27).

10. The tape or cord that is fastened to the center of each section should be wound around its respective section to prevent it flopping around during the winding. At this point, it is a good idea to check the direction in which the warp beam should be turned so that the dog will engage correctly in the ratchet wheel to hold the warp at a tension. Some beginners have been unfortunate enough to turn the warp beam in the wrong direction for the entire winding and others have wound some of the sections in one direction and some in the opposite. Check carefully, as incorrect winding will cause unpleasant trouble.

After all ends from the spool rack have been threaded through the guide, or through a tension box if one is used, tie them into the loop of tape or cord fastened to the center of the section they are to fill. While there is no rule governing which section should be filled first, it seems logical to start with the center one and then fill in the sections first on one side, then the other.

11. After the warp ends have been fastened securely and the number of turns have been determined, the actual winding of the warp onto the beam can begin. It will take a little practice to learn how to wind the warp so that it does not pile up into the center of the section and slide off at the edges next to the pegs, which would cause trouble when the weaving begins. To offset this, as the beam turns, guide the warp with the left hand (the right hand is holding the guide plate) close to and along one side of the pegs for two turns of the beam, then cross over and fill up close to the pegs on the opposite side, and finally fill in the middle. Repeat this routine, going close to the pegs at first, then filling in the center until the required number of turns have been made. At all times be sure that the warp is higher near the pegs than it is in the center of the section. Always keep in mind the smoothness with which a spool of thread is wound. While it is not possible to attain this by a hand method of winding, there is no excuse, except the carelessness of the weaver, for a poorly wound warp. If a tension box is used, follow carefully the directions that come with it. The person winding the warp beam should be responsible for keeping track of the number of turns, but it is advisable for both the winder and the weaver to keep the count. This is no time for conversation. While no definite harm will result if there are a few more turns on one section than on another, it is a waste of warp because the remaining warp usually is too short to be used either for a small loom or for weft.

12. After the required number of turns have been made and the first section has been filled, stop the winding with the crank handle down. If the warp beam seems inclined to turn of itself, place a small stick in the wheel to hold it steady, thus releasing the hands of the person who has been doing the winding for more important matters. The person who has been guiding the warp now holds it away from the beam and toward the spool rack, while the winder spreads the warp threads flat, and pastes a piece of

gummed paper or Scotch tape across the threads about 20 in. from the beam (Fig. 28). This keeps the threads in the position in which they came from the spool rack and were wound around the warp roller. The gummed paper substitutes for lease sticks to keep the threads in order. Still holding the warp tightly with the left hand in front of the guide plate, have the winder cut the warp directly behind the gummed paper (between it and the guide plate), but in front of the left hand. Care must be taken to prevent the cut ends from slipping through the guide plate. With a safety pin, fasten the cut ends to the warp that has been wound on the beam. This pin holds them securely while the winding of other sections progresses. Some looms come equipped with a small wooden peg with a slot (Fig. 29) to slip over the cut threads, in place of the gummed paper.

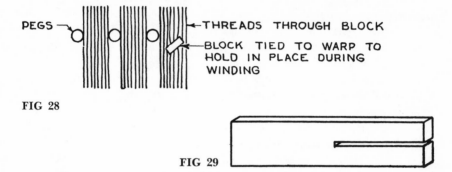

PEGS →

←THREADS THROUGH BLOCK

←BLOCK TIED TO WARP TO HOLD IN PLACE DURING WINDING

FIG 28

FIG 29

13. Untie the tape of the next section, tie the group of warp ends just cut to the loop, and wind the section. Proceed with each section in turn until all have been wound.

If the warp has been wound on the warping reel, tie the end loop of the chain to the loop of the tape on the warp beam. The ends need not be cut and passed through the metal warp guide (Fig. 27) as a lease has already been wound in. Keep the chain from twisting, taking care to wind it on as flat as possible. When the end of the warp is reached (the end where the cross is tied in), fasten the shoelace securely to the warp that lies around the beam with a safety pin.

When all the sections have been filled, turn the beam so that the tied ends are up, and carefully insert the lease sticks through the crosses on each section of the beam. Remove the pieces of shoelace. Unwind a sufficient quantity of the warp to allow the lease sticks to pass up over the back beam (page 6) and slip into place in the wire loops (page 11). The warp is now ready to be threaded through the heddles.

B. Warping With a Raddle The following directions are for warping a loom with a raddle and are recommended for long warps of many threads.

1. Wind the warp by any of the prescribed methods. The handling of long, wide warps may be facilitated by winding them in two or three sections, each one the same length and with the same number of threads.

Remove the warp from the warping device, chain, and insert the lease sticks. Rest the warp chain on a chair or stool placed in front of the loom to relieve the pull on the chain.

2. Remove the beater. Start at the center of the harnesses and push one half the heddles back as far as they will slide on the harnesses to the right and the others to the left. If there does not seem to be sufficient room for the warp to spread out to the required width on the back beam, it will be necessary to detach the harnesses and drop them to the floor. No definite directions can be given for this because of the great variation in types of looms, but the weaver will soon learn the most simple method. In some looms it is possible to lift out the overhead roller (Fig. 2, No. 13), but in other types the process may not be so simple. In any event, if it is possible to warp the beam without removing the harnesses do so as both time and labor will be saved.

3. Insert the ends of the lease sticks into the loops of wire or cords extending from the back of the loom frame to the warp beam (page 11). Tie the ends of the lease sticks together.

4. Tie the warp chain securely to the breast beam. Do not stretch the warp nor allow it to hang loosely between the lease sticks and the breast beam. It should be snug but not at a tension.

5. Remove the top from the raddle and clamp the bottom part securely to the back beam, being careful to center it.

6. Insert the warp-beam rod through the looped ends of the warp which lie between the lease sticks and the back beam.

7. Remove the ties holding the cross at the lease sticks and carefully spread the warp ends along the warp-beam rod to the right and the left, being careful that the threads lie in order as they come from the cross.

8. The width of the web having been determined, start at the center of the raddle, and measure one half the width of the web from the center to the left and the other half from the center to the right. Now divide the number of raddle spaces lying within this area into the total number of warp threads. For instance, if the material is to be 10 in. wide, and the warp is 100 threads, and there are 10 spaces within this area, then 10 threads would go in each raddle space.

9. Having determined the number of threads in each section of the raddle, hold the bar slightly in front of the raddle as you face it, just above the pegs of the open raddle, and place the groups of threads in their assigned spaces taking care to carry them, without crossing, directly from the lease sticks through the raddle and around the bar. It may be necessary to rearrange some of them on the bar but this is a simple matter. It is best to hold the bar back far enough so that the warp threads are taut, though not stretched. With wide warps it is easier if two people are available while the threads are being distributed, so one can hold the bar and the other distribute the threads.

10. As soon as the threads are all in order, place the top bar back on the raddle and tie it in place.

11. Securely tie the warp-beam rod to the second rod that is already in the warp-beam apron, with not less than 5 ties, being sure that they are tied securely.

12. If the material is to be striped, plaid, or tartan, check for mistakes in warping the threads as they can be seen easily and corrected.

C. Swedish Method 1. Remove the reed from the beater and set it up in the wooden holders (Fig. 30) on a table with the warp chain on the table in back of the reed. Place a heavy weight such as a tailor's iron on the warp chain. Put the lease sticks in, tie the ends together, and remove the ties holding the cross or lease.

FIG 30

Some weavers remove the reed and rest it on two sticks extending lengthwise through the loom from the back to the breast beam. Rest the ends of the lease sticks on the same sticks that hold the reed. Support the warp chain on a stool placed inside the loom. Place the ends of the warp close to the reed where they can be reached easily. No matter which method is chosen, the next step is the same.

2. Figure out the width of the finished material and mark the reed so that the warp will lie within this area.

3. Sit facing the reed and, with the left hand starting at the right, pick up a group of eight threads. Take them in the order in which they lie on the lease stick, and place them on the warp hook which has been inserted through the dent at the edge of the right-hand boundary of the cloth. The group of eight threads is pulled through (page 31).

Seven dents in the reed are skipped, the hook placed in the eighth dent, and eight more threads are picked up and pulled through. This step is repeated until all the ends are drawn through the reed.

4. Pass the warp-beam rod through the looped ends in front of the reed and remove the whole warp to the loom.

5. Standing in front of the loom, pass the warp-beam rod through the loom and securely tie it to the rod which lies within the hem of the warp-beam apron.

6. Place the reed in the beater. The lease sticks are now in the warp chain in front of the reed. Some weavers prefer to leave the lease sticks loose, floating on the warp. Others fasten them to the back beam.

7. Change the lease sticks and begin warping (page 32).

D. Beriau Method 1. In the Beriau method, the shed sticks are tied securely to the cloth beam with the looped ends of the warp chain toward the harnesses.

2. The person sitting in front of the loom picks up a group of eight warp ends and hooks them onto the warp hook which has been inserted from the back into the proper dent in the reed by the assistant who sits at the back of the loom. This is called rough sleying.

3. When all the warp ends have been pulled through (skipping seven dents in the reed between each group of eight threads) and have been slipped over the warp-beam rod, transfer the lease sticks (page 32). The warp now is ready for winding (page 36).

E. Threading From Front of Loom 1. Tie the lease sticks securely to the breast beam.

2. Cut the warp chain loop where it lies between the breast beam and the harnesses.

3. Measure the reed and place the warp so it will be centered (page 37).

4. Insert the warp hook through the reed from the back to the front in the dent marking the right-hand side of the web. Pull the first warp thread through. Proceeding from right to left, draw all the warp ends through the reed.

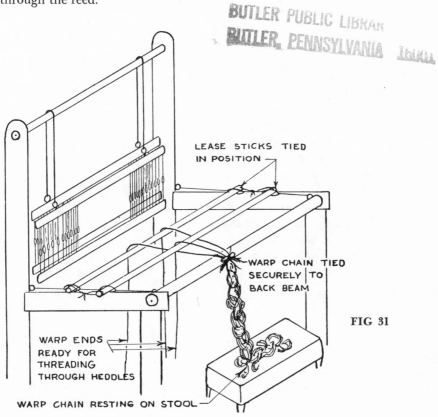

LEASE STICKS TIED IN POSITION

WARP CHAIN TIED SECURELY TO BACK BEAM

FIG 31

WARP ENDS READY FOR THREADING THROUGH HEDDLES

WARP CHAIN RESTING ON STOOL

5. Thread the warp ends through the correct heddles (page 38).

6. Tie the warp ends in small groups to the warp-beam rod (page 34).

7. Untie the lease sticks from the breast beam and tie the ends together. The lease sticks lie directly in front of the reed.

8. Wind the warp onto the warp beam (page 36).

9. When the end of the warp chain reaches the breast beam, cut and tie the ends onto the cloth-beam rod.

With this method it is not necessary to either rough sley the warp or transfer the lease sticks, as with the Swedish and Beriau methods, or wind the warp twice as with method *F* in which the loom is threaded from the back. While the method may at first seem a bit awkward, once the procedure is thoroughly understood and practiced, the sleying, threading, and beaming go very quickly.

F. Threading the Loom From the Back   1. Insert the ends of the lease sticks into the warp, one on each side of the cross tied in the warp. Then insert the ends of the sticks into the loops of wire or rope extending from the back of the loom frame to the back beam (page 11). Tie the ends of the lease sticks together.

2. Tie the warp chain securely to the back beam using the ends of the cord or shoelace to tie the last loop of the chain (page 31, Fig. 31).

3. Push the heddles back from the center of the harnesses toward each end of the harness frames. Pass the end of the warp chain through this space toward the front of the loom, to determine if the threads are long enough to go through the heddles and reed and not slip out. If necessary, undo another loop of the chain. Shake the end of the warp chain gently to straighten the threads and cut them.

4. Drop the end of the warp chain down into the space back of the harnesses and in front of the lease sticks.

5. Untie or carefully cut away the heavy twine used to mark the number of threads while winding, and gently spread the loosened threads in order in each direction along the top of the lease sticks. Shake gently and pull the loose threads toward the front of the loom if any of them seem uneven or difficult to find.

6. Tie the beater midway between the harnesses and the cloth beam to prevent its moving during the process of threading.

Everything is now in order to begin the threading of the warp ends, as they lie in position on the lease sticks, through the heddles and reed (page 36).

11. TRANSFERRING THE LEASE STICKS

There are several schools of thought on how to place the lease sticks while beaming the warp. In the Swedish method, they are left loose in the warp chain (being securely tied at the ends) and are pushed back toward the

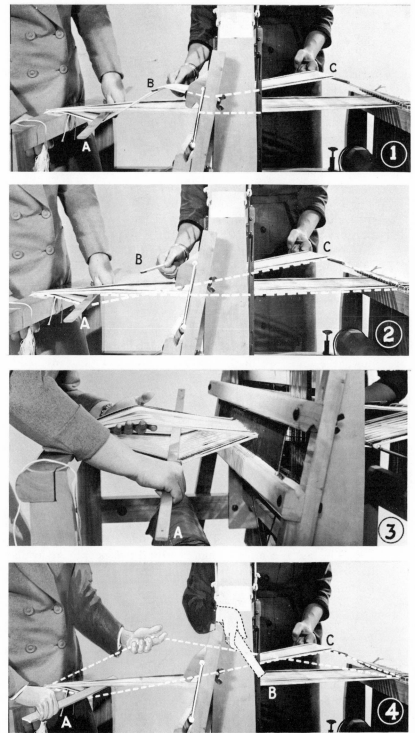

FIG 32

DRESSING THE LOOM 33

end of the warp chain as the beaming proceeds. In the Beriau method, the lease sticks are tied to the breast beam during the process of fastening the warp to the warp-beam rod, but are transferred to the back beam before the winding begins. This transferring of the lease sticks also takes place in the Swedish method *after* the warp is beamed and not before.

However, since it is used in both methods, the directions for making the change are given here, although the weaver must remember that the change can be made in the Swedish method before or after the warp is beamed. In methods *A, B, E,* and *F,* no transfer is necessary.

The lease stick designated as *A* is the one which lies next to the cloth beam; lease stick *B* lies next to the harnesses.

It requires two people to transfer the shed to the back of the loom. The person standing in front of the loom holds the warp chain tightly in his right hand and with his left hand pushes lease stick *A* down as far as possible onto the lower set of threads. The person at the back of the loom lifts lease stick *B* as high as possible with the right hand, while inserting a third lease stick *C* with the left hand into the shed between the two sets of threads at the back of the loom near the apron rod (Fig. 32). Note the position of the cross.

Lease stick *B* is now removed (Fig. 32).

The weaver at the front of the loom now pushes shed stick *A* toward the reed, lifting the upper set of threads with the left hand and pushing down the lower set of threads with lease stick *A*. This action forces the cross back through the reed where it is held in place by lease stick *B*. The two lease sticks are now tied together to the top of the back beam or left floating.

For the Beriau or Swedish method, the beaming of the warp can now start.

12. BEAMING THE WARP

To produce good weaving, it is necessary that the warp be properly beamed. This is not difficult to do if the directions are followed carefully in every step. The task is completed more easily if two people are available. Regardless of the method used in dressing the loom, follow these directions for beaming the warp:

1. Have at hand sheets of lightweight cardboard, heavy glazed paper, or thin wind-in sticks. Do not use newspapers, as they are too soft and the printer's ink soils the warp.

These papers or sticks keep the warp at an even tension and spacing as it is wound on the beam. It is important to fold a hem, about 1 in. wide, at each side of the paper or cardboard on every second or third sheet. A double fold is better for the paper, while a single fold is sufficient for the cardboard (Fig. 33). If the fold is not made, the tension of the warp will crush the ends of the paper and the warp will slide off. The result is such that even an experienced weaver will lose patience. If the warp extends across the entire beam, place the folds of the paper close to the edges of the wheel at the ends of the beam, or directly next to the upright frame if the beam has no wheels. When the warp does not extend across the entire beam, the folded, built-up edges of the paper hold the warp in position within its designated limits. The folds at the edges of the paper serve the same purpose as the sloping ends on a spool of thread (Fig. 33).

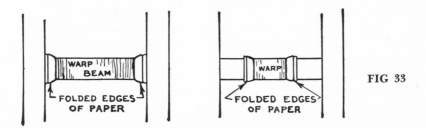

FIG 33

Thin wind-in sticks, the length of the width of the cloth and warp beams and approximately ¾ in. wide, can be used in place of the paper or cardboard. Some weavers use both paper and sticks for the same warping.

2. Remove all laces and cords from the warp chain. The assistant who holds the warp chain should stand back at least 6 or 8 ft. from the loom. The end of the warp chain can rest on the assistant's shoulder or on a chair or stool.

Tug briskly on the chain a few times to straighten the warp and get the threads in the right order. Avoid combing loose threads back with a comb or the fingers. Instead, lift each thread carefully and carry it back behind the hand that is holding the warp chain. At this point the warp chain is divided in the center, one half being held in each hand, as one holds the reins in driving a horse (Fig. 34).

FIG 34

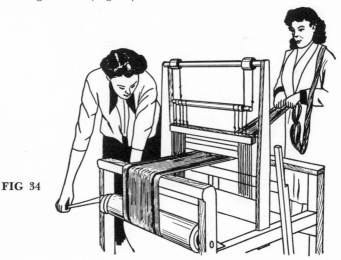

3. The winding can now begin. Turn slowly and watch the beam to be sure that the apron or ropes, if the loom is equipped with ropes, roll smoothly into place around the beam.

4. Special care must be taken at this point if the warp ends have been tied to the rod (page 42). As the knots wind around the beam and are about to be covered by another turn of the warp, insert the cardboard, a heavy, folded piece of paper, or a wind-in stick over the knots. It is important that this be done, or the threads will sink into the spaces, bunching over the knots, and the warp cannot be wound with an even tension.

5. After one or two turns have been completed, undo more of the warp chain, straighten the threads, and divide and hold them for another turn. Crossing and tangling of the threads may occur in the porrey-cross between the lease sticks or directly in back of them. It is important that all knots be detected and loosened before the winding is started or broken threads will result.

6. As soon as the warp has been straightened, the winding continues. Wind-in sticks or hemmed papers sometimes are inserted at every turn. Continue winding until all the warp has been wound on the beam. Much of the success of weaving depends on the care with which the warp has been put on the loom.

If the foregoing steps have been carefully executed, the warp should wind on easily and without snarls. After experience has been gained, it is possible to warp the beam with a 16-yd. warp of 800 or 900 threads in less than an hour.

If the warp gives any trouble at the lease sticks, beat sharply with the palm of the hand on top of the sticks. Avoid handling the warp more than is necessary. One weaver, experienced in the use of homespun wool, winds in a cross at each end of her warp, thus being assured that each thread lies in perfect order throughout the entire length of the warp.

Leave the warp ends in front of the back beam sufficiently long to thread through the heddles and reed. It facilitates operations if the beater is securely tied halfway between the harnesses and the breast beam. Some weavers take the reed out of the beater, lay it flat, and sley.

13. THREADING AND SLEYING

Let us return for a moment to the various methods of dressing the loom.

With method *A*, the sectional warp beam (page 24), the warp, if wound in sections on a warping device, will have the lease sticks in the shed and be ready for the threading.

If the sections have been wound directly from the spool rack, there will be no shed, but the threads will have been inserted into the slot in the wooden peg or stuck in order on a piece of gummed paper.

Each section is taken separately, as the threading proceeds, and unwound from the warp beam until it is long enough to reach up over the back beam, through the heddles and reed, and to the cloth-beam rod. This is done by passing the group of threads around the beam, *not* by turning the warp beam. Be sure that the group of threads lies flat on the back beam and that there are no twists in the threads between the two beams.

Thread the threads in order, from either the block or the gummed paper; do not crisscross them or there will be difficulty when the weaving starts.

With the Swedish method, *C* (page 30), the warp has been beamed and runs through the reed which is in the beater. The lease sticks may still be between the front of the reed and the end of the warp chain. If so, transfer them to the back of the loom (page 33), where they are either placed in the wire supports (Fig. 14) or tied to the back beam. The warp ends are cut and pulled through the reed toward the back beam where they are allowed to hang down.

In the Beriau method, *D* (page 31), the lease sticks, which had been transferred and tied to the back beam before the warp was rolled onto the beam, will remain in this position. The warp ends are cut in front of the reed, pulled through it, and allowed to fall down at the back of the loom as in the Swedish method.

In methods *C* and *D,* the reed has served as a guide in distributing the threads evenly on the warp beam. If the harnesses have been removed for these methods of warping, they must now be replaced.

Everything is now in order to begin the threading:

1. A warp of white carpet warp, 36 in. long, of 105 threads, has been wound.

2. The warp is in position on the loom. The heddles are strung on harness frames. On a 2-harness loom, the frame nearest the front of the loom is harness No. 1. The frame at the back of the loom is harness No. 2. There should be an equal number of heddles on each frame. On a 4-harness loom, the front harness is No. 1, the back No. 4.

3. Find the center heddle on each frame. These were marked with pieces of colored thread when the loom was first brought into use (page 10). Slide these heddles to the exact center of each harness. Count the remaining heddles, and slide them toward the center. There will be 26 heddles on each side of these center heddles, a total of 105, the number needed to thread the number of warp ends wound for the sample. If a 4-harness loom is being used, divide the thread evenly among the 4 harnesses.

4. Insert a piece of colored yarn in the dent in the exact center of the reed, which has been previously determined (page 8). Count off 52 dents to the left and 52 to the right of this center marker, and insert colored yarn in these dents. The object of this procedure is to locate the center of the loom so that the web will be placed in the center of this space. This facilitates the weaving and makes for a more "shipshape" appearance of the loom.

Some weavers prefer to start threading at the center, finding the

FIG 35

middle thread in the warp, the center thread on the pattern, and the middle heddle on the designated harness. Threading proceeds first to the right, then to the left. This method might confuse the beginner, as part of the pattern draft must be read from the left to the right and the rest from right to left. However, after the weaver once becomes familiar with the reading of drafts, this method is recommended as there is no necessity of resorting to mathematics and counting of heddles to center the web accurately in the reed, and all unused heddles are evenly distributed at each end of the harnesses.

For ease in threading the pattern, it is advisable to make a copy of it on squared paper, and paste or pin it to the smooth side of a piece of corrugated paper (page 12).

The person at the front of the loom reads the pattern and finds the correct heddle through which the person at the back of the loom threads the warp end (Fig. 35). It is advisable for the person at the back of the loom to have a copy of the pattern, at least until the threaders become accustomed to reading and threading. In this way mistakes will be caught before they are made. As pattern drafts become more complicated, it is advisable to place a pin in each square as the designated thread is placed in the heddle eye. This helps prevent mistakes and, should the threading be interrupted, there will be no question as to where to begin when threading is resumed. Each repeat of a pattern should be carefully checked, and the threads tied in a loose knot as soon as a section has been threaded. It is much more simple to correct a mistake at this point than later on when perhaps two or three hundred threads may have been threaded.

One person working alone sits at the front of the loom. If the breast beam is removable, remove the beam as well as the beater and the reed.

Place a stool inside the loom in front of the harnesses. Put the warp hook (page 9) through the heddle designed as the first on the pattern draft and, with the left hand, reach through to the back beam, pick up the first thread on the right-hand side of the lease sticks, and hook it over the end of the hook, drawing it carefully through the heddle eye. Remove the thread from the hook and drop it so that it hangs loosely in front of the heddles on the first harness. Repeat this operation until all the threads are threaded.

Of the total of 105 threads warped, half, or 52 of these, are threaded into the heddles on the front harness and the remainder into the heddles on the rear harness, or evenly distributed between the four harnesses if a 4-harness loom is used. As these threads follow a system and alternate, it is necessary that a pattern be drafted to show their position.

5. American pattern drafts are always read from right to left, beginning with the first darkened square in the lower right-hand corner and up from the bottom to the top.

The darkened squares in Fig. 36 represent eyes in the heddles.

In looking at the pattern in Fig. 36, it will be noted that a thread passes first through a heddle on No. 1 harness, then a heddle on No. 2 harness, then returns to harness No. 1, repeating the operation until all threads have been threaded. Only two changes are possible, so one complete unit of the pattern occurs between blocks *A* and *B*. This is a harness draft or pattern.

FIG 36

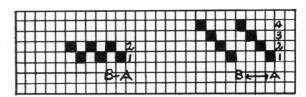

6. Begin threading by inserting a pin in the first square at the lower right-hand corner of the pattern draft.

7. The first thread lying on the lease stick at the left of the person at the back of the loom (and at the right of the person at the front of the loom) is threaded through the first heddle at the left of the group previously counted off on the first harness.

Theoretically, one thread should lie on top of the lease stick, and the next underneath it, repeating this procedure across the entire warp. No matter how important the shed is, the weaver should not be greatly perturbed should some variation occur, as no great harm is done if three or four threads are out of order.

8. The warp hook is now inserted, with the hook up, into the dent at the right of the reed which has been previously marked with colored wool,

52 spaces to the right of the center of the reed. The warp end is looped over the hook and is carefully drawn through the dent by the person sitting at the front of the loom. Care is taken not to split the warp end, as this weakens it and causes later breakage. After being carefully drawn through, it is tightened and allowed to drop down in front of the reed. It should hang down about 10 in.

If preferred, the reed can be taken from the beater and laid flat on sticks lying between the front and back beams. The threads can be drawn through from the heddles as before. Some weavers prefer this method to that of the upright reed in the beater.

If one person is working alone, he first threads all the heddles, and then, standing in front of the loom, draws the threads through the reed toward himself. It is necessary to exercise the utmost caution in doing this, to prevent the threads crossing between the heddles and the dents, or the shed will not open correctly when the weaving is begun (page 572).

9. Move the pin to square No. 2 on the pattern. Take the next thread as it lies either under or over the lease stick, and pass it through the eye of the heddle on frame No. 2.

10. Pass the hook through the dent in the reed to the left of the first thread that has been drawn through, and pull this second thread through.

11. Continue this process, repeating the pattern from *A* to *B* until all the threads, or warp ends, have been threaded.

12. For safety, tie groups of warp ends together so they can't slip back through the reed.

The pattern draft is followed in exactly the same manner for the 4-harness loom as for the 2-harness draft. Reading from right to left and starting at the bottom, the dark squares are followed in sequence until four threads have been threaded into heddles on harnesses 1, 2, 3, and 4. Then the same sequence is repeated until all the threads are threaded.

14. TYING WARP ENDS ONTO THE CLOTH-BEAM ROD

The threading of the heddles and the sleying of the reed having been completed, the next step is the tying of the warp ends to the cloth-beam rod for methods *A, B, C,* and *D.*

1. Unroll the apron or ropes (page 6) that lie around the cloth beam, and bring them up outside and on top of the breast beam, unrolling them to their full length.

2. Untie one of the groups of warp ends tied up close to the reed during the sleying, and pass it up through the slit in the apron and around the rod (or through the loop in the rope) to determine if the warp is pulled through the reed far enough to tie a double knot. If not, release the ratchet on the warp beam and pull the group of warp ends gently toward the front of the loom until they are long enough.

3. Take the center group of warp ends and gently work any slackness

toward the ends. Then pull the group of threads toward the reed. Tie a single knot. When all groups across the loom have been tied, roll the beam a notch or two with the handle, then take the ends of each group again and give them a final pull toward the reed and knot a second time. If any groups seem slacker than others, this second pull will adjust them all and assure an even tension. This is method *A*.

In method *B*, the "bout" or "bight" or ends are passed over the rod, one half the group being brought up at the left and the other half at the right. The ends are pulled tight as above, tied in a single knot across the rod and the beam, and rolled a notch. Then the bouts are given the second tightening and tied in a second knot.

Method *C* begins like either method *A* or *B*, but instead of tying a second knot, a bow knot is tied. Some weavers find this to be the easiest method to tie and untie.

For method *D*, divide the warp into small bouts, about an inch or so wide at the reed. Straighten the warp ends and tie a hard knot as close to the end of the bout as possible. Cut lengths of stout cord, double, and loop over the warp rod. Turn the bout knot up over the warp and divide the bout into two parts (Fig. 37). Draw the two ends of the cord inserted into the bout back to within 2 in. or so of the rod and tie to it, with the warp at a tension. The cords remain on the rod for future use.

No matter which of these methods is used, the point is to have a warp, in which each thread is at the same tension. At this point, draw the fingers across the warp at right angles. Uneven tension can be immediately detected and remedied by untying and retying the "slack" or "too tight" groups of threads. The loom is now ready for weaving.

Those who have used method *F*, threading from the back of the loom (page 32), still have work to do.

Turning back for a moment, we find that the warp chain was securely tied to the back beam while the threading was done (page 32). Following this, the warp ends, after they were pulled through the reed, were tied to the warp-beam rod (Fig. 38).

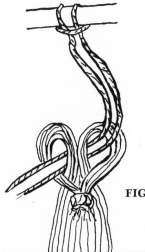

FIG 37

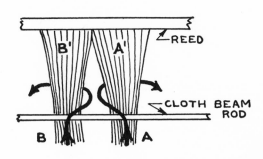

FIG 38

The procedure for beaming the warp for method *F*:

1. Untie the heavy cord or shoelace which ties the warp chain onto the back beam.

2. The person at the back of the loom should step back as far as possible and straighten the warp with a few brisk jerks on the chain. Then follow the directions for beaming the warp (page 34), winding in the flat sticks or cardboard until all the warp has been wound onto the cloth beam, leaving the ends long enough at the back to tie onto the warp-beam with the same knot that was used to tie the ends onto the cloth-beam rod (Fig. 38). The warp ends will be fairly even if the warp has been wound carefully.

It is important that each group of warp ends be tied with the same tension. To test the tension, run the fingers across the warp in front of the beater. If some sections feel loose and others tight, retie the slack sections. It is not possible to weave satisfactorily on a warp of uneven tension.

3. Release the dog that holds the cloth beam. Wind the warp toward the warp beam, holding the cloth-beam crank securely but not too tightly to keep steady tension on the warp. Wind in sticks or papers, as was done on the first winding of the warp onto the cloth beam. After inserting a stick or papers, hold the cloth-beam crank very tight, and turn the warp-beam handle against it. The result is a tightening of the warp on the beam that makes it compact and even.

4. Continue winding until the warp is wound back onto the warp beam.

5. If necessary, untie the warp ends from the cloth-beam rod, straighten, tighten, and retie.

The loom is now ready and weaving can begin.

15. THE TIE-UP

Because the weaver has only two feet, a method has been devised whereby one, two, or more harnesses can be operated together when necessary. This is called the tie-up. It plays an important part in weaving and varies from the simple tying of two harnesses to two treadles, as in 2-harness weaving, to the complicated tie-ups of 8-, 10-, and 12-harness looms.

Table looms do not require a tie-up as the harnesses are attached directly to the levers. One, two, or more levers can be depressed together as required. Most table looms have a rising shed, that is, the harnesses lift when the levers are depressed.

There are two types of floor looms in general use. One is the counterbalanced type on which one set of harnesses sinks while the other remains stationary when the treadles are depressed. This counterbalanced floor loom is also known as a sinking-shed loom.

A second type of floor loom is the rising-shed loom. When the treadles are depressed, the harnesses are raised. Such a loom is a rising-shed loom. Some rising-shed looms operate with a system of jacks while others are operated by direct push-up treadle action. There is also the Swedish counter-marche loom.

The bottoms of the harnesses of the counterbalanced loom (Fig. 2, No. 14) are connected to the lams (Fig. 2, No. 30) by chains or cords.

The beginning weaver is sometimes confused as to the purpose of the lams. They act only as a balance between the harnesses and the treadles and are always tied at a slight upward angle to the harnesses which lie directly above them. The pattern tie-up actually occurs between the lam and the treadle rather than between the harness and the lam. Once the harnesses and lams are fastened together they seldom are changed.

On most looms, there are a number of screw eyes or holes on the underside of the lams and on the upper surface of the treadles. When tied into the correct screw eyes, the harnesses draw down evenly, resulting in a perfect shed.

Connecting chains or cords are seen between the lams (Fig. 2, No. 30) and the treadles (No. 27). On most modern looms, the connecting link between the lams and the treadles is of cord or rope and is in two sections. The upper part is fastened to the lams, the lower to the treadles. The knot connecting the two is a snitch knot (Fig. 39).

FIG 39

This knot is used universally to tie up lams and treadles. It is made as follows: Loop *A*, coming up from the treadles, is doubled back across as shown at A'. The two ends of cord B, coming down the lams, are passed through loop *A'*. Loop *A'* is then tightened and drawn downward. The ends of loop *B*, drawn through *A'*, are tied with a square knot close to the bight.

On the counterbalanced floor loom, tie up the harnesses at a height that will permit the warp to lie in a straight line from the top of the back beam through the heddle eye, through the *center* of the reed, and over the top of the breast beam to the cloth beam, as shown in Fig. 40.

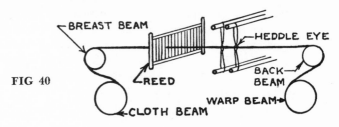

FIG 40

For a rising-shed loom, such as a jack loom, the warp should lie close to the *bottom* of the reed and across the shuttle race on a level with the heddle eye when the treadles are at rest (Fig. 41).

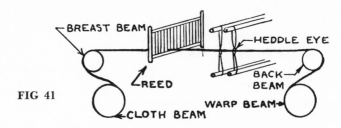

FIG 41

The harnesses on new looms usually are set at the correct height, but, if not, the height can be corrected by carefully retying the ropes. First, tie a piece of carpet warp to the back beam, thread it through the heddle and reed, and tie it to the breast beam. This thread will act as a guide.

The exact height at which the treadles are tied is left to the discretion of the weaver. The treadles must be high enough to open a shed wide enough to permit the easy passage of the shuttle, yet not so high that the weaver's knees bump against the finished web. Place pieces of wood or books under the treadles to hold them in position; tie the snitch knots.

Before attempting to tie the harnesses, rest the bottom edges on two boards that have been measured and cut to bring the harnesses to the height just described. The two boards must be exactly the same length or the harnesses will not hang true. As an alternate method, take shorter lengths of boards and place them on top of the harness frames between the frames and the rollers. Slip pieces of stout rope around the top bar of the harness frame and tie up the harnesses as tightly as the board will permit. This will hold the harnesses in place while the tie-up is being made.

Tie harness No. 1, the front harness, to the first lam, then to the treadle on the left, called treadle No. 1.

Tie harness No. 2, the back harness, to the second lam, then to the second treadle from the left, called treadle No. 2.

On a 4-harness loom in addition to the above:

Tie harness No. 3 to the third lam, then to the third treadle from the left, called treadle No. 3.

Tie harness No. 4 to the fourth lam, then to the fourth treadle from the left, called treadle No. 4.

This is called a direct tie-up and is adequate, at the moment, for the purposes of the weaver. When the tie-up is finished, remove the blocks of wood or books holding the harnesses and treadles in place. Be sure the harnesses are all level and the treadles all the same height from the floor.

The table loom, on which levers connect directly with the harnesses, and the floor loom with rising shed, on which the harnesses connect directly with the treadles, do not require a tie-up.

A full explanation of tie-ups appears later in the text (page 533).

16. TESTING THE LOOM

Foot loom—counterbalanced. Press the left treadle (No. 1) down to the floor. Note that the front harness (No. 1) sinks, or is pushed down to the floor.

Foot loom—rising-shed. Press the left treadle (No. 1) down to the floor. The front harness (No. 1) will then rise.

Hand loom. Pull down No. 1 hand lever, which is the one nearest the front of the loom. The mechanism varies with different types of looms.

Note that the front harness (No. 1) has been raised. It is quite important that the weaver remember that the action of the counterbalanced loom is directly opposite to that of the rising-shed loom. In 2-harness weaving this is not of any great consequence, but in some of the twills and in pattern weaving the pattern designs will be found to be upside down on the loom if a pattern written for a sinking-shed loom is woven on a rising-shed loom, and vice versa. As the weaver becomes familiar with treadling techniques he will learn how to overcome this.

The raising or lowering of the harnesses opens up a triangular space between the cloth-beam rod and the reed. This space is called the shed. The shuttle passes back and forth through the shed, interlacing the warp and weft threads to form a web.

Open the shed; glance into it to determine that all the threads are in alignment. Should the threads in the shed cross, it is a sign that they do not follow through in correct sequence from the heddles to the reed. Find the mistake and correct it (page 572).

17. FILLING THE SHUTTLE AND WINDING THE BOBBIN

Before the weaving can be started, the shuttle must be filled.

Wind a rug-loom shuttle (Fig. 5) with carpet rags.

Fill a flat or boat shuttle (Figs. 3 and 4) with white carpet warp, the same material with which the loom has been threaded.

The spool-like bobbin lies within the shuttle and is removed by grasping it in the middle and pulling up. In some shuttles the rod that passes through the bobbin is hinged to the shuttle at one end and will remain at right angles to the bobbin until snapped back into position. Other shuttles have a small spring at one end of the bobbin bar. When the bar is pushed back against the spring, the bar comes out of a slot at the other end and is easily removed.

Push the bobbin onto the winder shaft until it is tight. If the shaft is tapered, put on first the end of the bobbin having the larger hole.

Do not wind a bobbin by hand. A winder can be purchased at a reasonable price. Ingenious weavers have fastened a small spindle to a sewing machine, an electric beater, a milk separator, and a stationary

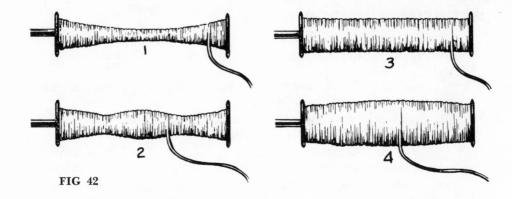

FIG 42

bicycle with the owner furnishing the power. Any method which turns a spindle is acceptable.

Make a few turns of the thread around the bobbin with the fingers, then:

1. Start turning the winder and fill up each end of the bobbin close to the inside of the wheel ends.

2. Run back and forth across the center and up on the two ends previously filled.

3. Now fill in the center of the bobbin until the thread lies in a straight line from end to end. Try to wind the bobbin as smooth as a spool of thread.

4. The last few turns will fill up the middle, making it higher than the ends. Take care not to make it higher than the sides of the shuttle or the bobbin will not pass smoothly through the shed nor turn easily in the shuttle.

5. When the bobbin is full, remove it from the winder shaft, and slip it onto the shuttle bar in such a way that when the bar is snapped back into place, the thread will come from underneath. Now pass the end of the thread through the hole in the side of the shuttle. Pull out a length of thread the width of the warp, and the shuttle is ready for use.

18. WEAVING

1. Weave in several rows of carpet rags to draw the threads together, and fill up the spaces left between the groups of warp threads as they were tied to the cloth-beam rod (Fig. 43). These rags also prevent the weaving from unraveling when it is cut from the loom. Remove the rags before you tie the fringe or hem the article.

2. On a 2-harness foot loom, push down treadle No. 1 (the one at the left), and on a hand loom, lever No. 1. For the 4-harness foot loom, push down treadles 1 and 3 together.

3. Insert the shuttle with the carpet rags into the shed from the left.

4. Slide the shuttle through to the opposite side (the shuttle rides on the tightly stretched warp threads) until the end of the rag hangs out about 1 in. at the left side.

5. Grasp the beater in the center, and pull or press it back toward yourself.

6. Release the lever or treadle, and pull or press down treadle No. 2. Use treadles 2 and 4 together for the 4-harness loom.

7. Grasp the beater in the center of the top bar again, and pull it with a quick motion against the piece of carpet rag, thumping the carpet rag back into place tightly against the knots. If the beater is grasped at one end instead of in the middle, there is danger of the web building up more at one end than at the other end (page 574).

The changing of the shed crosses the threads close to the edge of the web, holding the thread in place when beaten the second time. This is the fell.

The method of beating varies with, and is determined by, the temperament of the weaver and the type of material being woven. It can be done with one or two quick decisive strokes or "bangs," or the beater can be drawn back and the thread put in its proper place with a pressing motion.

8. Now that the shed has been changed, insert the shuttle from the right-hand side of the loom into the new shed, and slide it back to the left-hand side.

Do not pull the rag so tight as to pull the edge threads in at an angle to the beater which would cause the action of the beater to cut the threads. (To repair broken warp threads, see page 576.) Beat this second piece of rag back into position, change the shed, and proceed with this alternating sequence until the required number of rags have been woven in.

Some weavers prefer to introduce several rows of carpet warp at the beginning of the web instead of using rags to fill up the spaces between the groups of warp threads. This method saves both warp and time, although it is slightly more difficult for the beginner than the method just described. To use this method, open the shed, insert a shot of carpet warp, and beat it back as far into the groups of threads as possible. Hold the beater tight

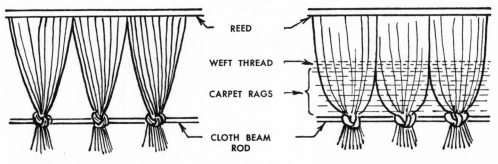

REED

WEFT THREAD

CARPET RAGS

CLOTH BEAM ROD

FIG 43

against this thread, change the shed, release the beater, and insert another shot of carpet warp. Continue changing the shed and inserting carpet warp until three shots have been entered. Do not beat until all three shots are in place; then beat back as tightly as possible. If done correctly, there will be much less space between the knots and the place where the threads are drawn evenly together and where the weaving can begin (the fell), than there is when carpet rags are used. It may be necessary to weave in two or three of the 3-thread groups to close the spaces. This will depend upon the number of threads in each bout tied to the cloth-beam rod.

The routine of weaving with a single shuttle embraces four steps:

1. Press treadles or levers down to open shed.
2. Beat weft back into position.
3. Pass shuttle through shed.
4. Beat weft back into position.

This procedure is called one "pick" or "shot" of weft.

In addition to these four operations, the weaver must watch the edges or selvedges. Weaving is judged by the evenness of the selvedges and the uniformity of the beating. Most weavers find that they can make a better selvedge on one side of the web than on the other; good selvedges are largely a matter of practice and care. If the weft thread is pulled through too far, the warp threads are pulled away from the straight line in which they should run from the warp beam, through the heddles and reed, to the cloth-beam rod. When this happens, the sharp edges of the steel reeds soon cut the thread. On the other hand, if the threads are not pulled tightly enough, there will be a series of loops along the selvedges. Experience and care alone will teach the weaver at just what tension the thread should be pulled to ensure a good selvedge and avoid broken edge threads. Some weavers use a temple to prevent the edges on bedspreads, rugs, suiting, and other wide materials from pulling in and breaking (Fig. 10).

After enough carpet rags or shots of carpet warp have been woven in to draw the spaces together, cut the end of the carpet rag or warp about 1 in. from the selvedge. Do not turn in.

Enter the shuttle bearing the weft thread from the left bringing it out at the right, as was done previously with the carpet rags. Leave about ½ in. of the weft thread extending beyond the web on the left-hand side. Turn this end back around the edge warp thread and into the shed (Fig. 44).

FIG 44

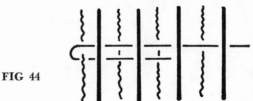

To add a new weft thread see page 578, Fig. 666. Now, weaving can begin following routine as previously outlined (page 46).

After the proportions have been planned and the measurements decided upon, weaving of the article may begin.

Sample Illustrated   6 in. wide, 12 in. long, white carpet warp.

Measuring String   Cut a fine piece of string the length of the article to be woven. Allow enough extra string to pass around the rag and tie the knot; fasten the end into the last row of carpet rag at the center of the web.

This string will wind in with the web as it is woven. When the end of the string has been reached, the article should be the correct length. As a precaution, unwind and measure the web before cutting it from the loom.

If the piece being woven is a long one, do not use the string, as it will pile up and make a ridge along the center of the web. Use a tape measure, pinning it to the selvedge, and tie a contrasting thread around the outer selvedge thread to mark each yard.

Winding Back the Finished Web   After a certain amount of material has been woven, the space between the reed and the edge of the web becomes so small that it is impossible to insert the shuttle. At this point the web must be rolled forward onto the cloth beam.

To do this, release the warp-beam brake (be careful that the beam does not roll forward quickly thus releasing a quantity of the warp), and slowly wind the completed web toward the cloth beam. Do not wind the cloth too far forward at once, or the edge of the web, the fell, will be too far back for the beater to reach properly, resulting in streaks in the weaving.

When enough web has been woven so that it begins to wind around the cloth beam, it is necessary to place wide flat sticks or folded glazed paper (page 34) over the warp-end knots, to prevent them from cutting into and stretching the web. The sticks or papers should be continued for the first few turns. This placing of the paper requires little effort, and the quality of the weaving is retained. If a light-colored web is being woven, it is well to pin a towel or piece of transparent plastic over it to protect it. The towel should extend from the edge of the web at the place where the weaving is being done, down over the breast beam, and to the edge of the cloth beam. The towel is moved as the weaving progresses.

19. FINISHING

A. To Hemstitch Ends of Web Before Removal From Loom

1. Start weaving in the usual manner, with rags or carpet warp.

2. Weave in two separate threads of carpet warp, with ends extending about 1½ in. beyond the sides of the web.

3. Weave 1 in. using the weft thread chosen for the web.

4. Lay the shuttle aside.

5. Thread a needle with a length of weft thread.

6. Remove the two threads of carpet warp.

7. Beginning at the left side of the web, pass the needle around the edge group of 5 to 8 threads, depending on the coarseness of thread used for the warp. The fringe looks better if groups of threads are not too large.

8. Run the needle and thread along the edge of the selvedge to fasten the end.

9. Take a stitch into the web.

10. Pass the needle under the next group of threads, slip it up through the loop formed by the thread, and tie a knot.

11. Take a stitch into the web.

12. There is less likelihood of web threads pulling down if a long-short method of stitching is used. Between the first two groups, sew into about three threads of the web; between the next group sew into only two threads; continue to alternate in this manner as hemstitching proceeds across the web.

13. Upon completion of the hemstitching, weave about 1 in., then run the needle, containing the thread used for hemstitching, along the selvedge, following, if possible, one of the warp threads. Clip the thread, which should be almost inconspicuous. Do the same with the 3-in. length left at the point where the hemstitching was started.

14. Weave the web the desired length. When finished, hemstitch across the web and finish the thread by darning carefully into the selvedge as was done at the beginning of the weaving.

15. Cut the web from the loom, allowing ½ or ¾ in. for the fringe.

If a second web is to be woven before removing the first, weave in fine rags until a wide enough space has been woven to allow for the length of fringes on both articles. For instance, if a fringe 1½ in. long is desired on each piece, fill in a space of 3 in. with rags or a piece of cardboard cut the correct width. After this has been done, weave in the two lengths of carpet warp and 1 in. of the web, and proceed with the hemstitching of the fringe on the second piece, following previous directions.

If a number of towels or pieces for a luncheon set are to be hemstitched after removal from the loom, much time in the drawing of threads can be saved if the following method is used.

Determine upon and weave the width of hem desired. For instance, if a 1-in. hem is desired, 2¼ in. must be woven because a little more than half the hem is turned back under.

After weaving the hem, weave in two separate threads of carpet warp of a contrasting color. Allow the ends of the carpet warp to extend 1 in. beyond the web on each side (Fig. 45).

Weave the center of the towel or the place mat.

Weave in two threads of carpet warp.

Weave the hem.

Proceed in this manner for each towel or mat.

After removal of the web from the loom, cut the pieces apart, turn the hems, and baste them down.

Draw out the two threads of carpet warp. Hemstitch the piece.

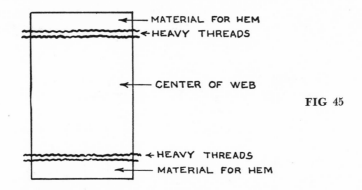

MATERIAL FOR HEM
HEAVY THREADS

CENTER OF WEB

FIG 45

HEAVY THREADS
MATERIAL FOR HEM

B. To Remove Web From Loom   Untie the warp threads from the warp-beam rod, and draw the remaining warp through to the front of the loom. Unroll the web from the cloth roller, and untie the warp threads from the cloth-beam rod.

If the ends have not been hemstitched and a knotted fringe is desired, remove the rows of carpet rags at the beginning and end of the weaving, and tie the fringe or sew the hem.

To Tie Fringe   The number of threads chosen for each group in the fringe depends upon the coarseness of the warp and the type of article made.

1. A group of threads is held in the right hand and twisted to the left until the entire length of the group of threads has been twisted up close to the weaving (Fig. 46).

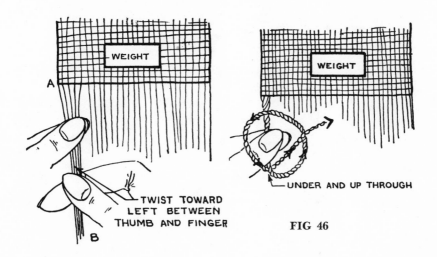

WEIGHT

WEIGHT

A

UNDER AND UP THROUGH

TWIST TOWARD
LEFT BETWEEN
THUMB AND FINGER

B

FIG 46

2. The fringe is held between the thumb and index finger of the left hand, about halfway up the twisted part of the fringe. The end of the fringe held in the right hand is passed on top of the fringe held in the left hand, brought down and up through the circle thus formed, knotted, and carefully tightened up close to the weaving. Twisting the groups of threads makes the knots much smoother and tighter, and easier to handle during the process.

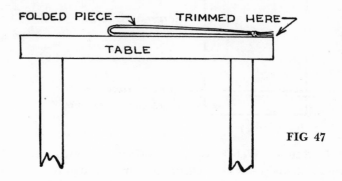

FIG 47

Fold the article in half, and place it on a table with the selvedge close to and parallel with the side of the table. The ends of the piece will then be at right angles to the end of the table, and can be trimmed evenly (Fig. 47).

Other types of fringe are shown later in the text (page 586).

chapter 3

Plain Weaves–
Loom Controlled

TYPE Balanced Weaves · PATTERN Plain Weave

The simplest fundamental weaving process is that of darning. Weft or woof threads are woven in across some previously sewn-in warp threads to fill up a hole.

This same result, that of weaving a web, can be executed on a loom. First, the warp threads are placed on the loom and threaded through the heddles and reed. They are then tightened, and through the manipulation of the harnesses, a space, called a shed, is opened. A shuttle carrying the weft thread is passed through this shed, the harnesses are changed, and the thread then is beaten back into position. Many repetitions of this procedure form cloth (page 46), known in weaving nomenclature as a web.

Any number of threads can be set to the inch in the reed for plain webs. The number may vary from a coarsely set 8/4 carpet warp for rag rugs to a closely set reed for very fine linen, rayon, nylon, or wool materials.

When the same size threads are used for warp and weft and the beating is correctly done, a 50/50 plain web is woven; that is, there are the same number of warp and weft threads to the square inch.

This type of web is commonly referred to as a "tabby" weave, but for the purposes of this text will be called a plain weave.

Plain 50/50 webs are difficult to weave since the beating must be done very carefully to avoid streaks. These streaks are easily seen if the material is held to the light. It is wise, when short lengths of plain material are being woven, to weave the whole piece at one sitting. Long lengths, of course, cannot be completed at one sitting. All that can be done when continuing again is to try to match the beat of the previous day. All plain weaves are not beaten in the same way. Wool threads are pressed, rather than beaten back into place; cotton and linen are given a sure, swift beat, repeating the beat, if necessary, after the shed has been changed. The article being made also influences the beat. Upholstery material should be beaten very hard, while a filmy scarf or stole should be beaten very, very lightly.

The plain weaves are divided into two groups: (1) those controlled by the action of the loom, and (2) those manipulated by the fingers.

Many variations are possible in each group. In the first group are the balanced weaves, those in which the warp and weft are of the same size or grist, though the material may differ, and the unbalanced weaves in which warp and weft differ in size.

In the second group, the finger-manipulated weaves, the emphasis is placed on decoration. The decoration may be incorporated into the web in addition to the threads which form the web; it may be superimposed on the surface in knotted or flat designs; or, as in tapestry weaves where colored weft threads are woven in following a predetermined design, it may form the web.

At this point it is advisable for the new weaver to concentrate on what is known as the structure of the weave and its connection with the harnesses, the threading draft, the treadling, the draw-down, and the finished web. For purposes of clarity, this has been worked out with black and white threads.

The loom has 2, 4, or 8 harnesses; but, for the first sample, work on the 2-harness loom. The dark threads are indicated on the charts by a black square and the white threads by a circle (Fig. 48):

■ DARK THREAD O LIGHT THREAD   FIG 48

Harness 1 is the one at the front of the loom next to the weaver; harness 2 is the one at the back of the loom. These harnesses are designated on the threading draft by two rows of symbols (Fig. 49).

HARNESS-2
HARNESS-1   FIG 49

Visualize the threads as they come from the lease sticks tied at the back of the loom (page 31). The first thread, a black one, will be threaded through a heddle on harness 1, followed by a white thread threaded through a heddle on harness 2. These two threads, shown in the bracketed section of the pattern draft (Fig. 49), form a unit of the pattern known as block *A*. All further threading from this pattern draft is simply a repetition of this unit or block. All weaves are composed of blocks, each with its own distinguishing arrangement of threads within the block. The threads vary greatly in number and arrangement.

Next, to discover what the web is going to look like, make a draw-down from the pattern draft.

Referring back to the threading draft, note that all the heddles on the uneven-numbered harness (1) are threaded with the dark thread and those on the even-numbered harness (2) with white thread (Fig. 49).

When actually weaving on the loom, depress treadle 1, which is tied to harness 1, and thus draw down all the dark threads. The result can be shown as well on the paper draw-down as on the loom (Fig. 50).

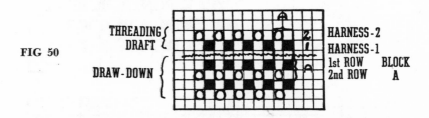

FIG 50

THREADING { DRAFT {

DRAW-DOWN {

HARNESS-2
HARNESS-1
1st ROW   BLOCK
2nd ROW   A

All the squares in row 1, which lie directly under the dark squares in the pattern draft, have been filled in with the dark symbol. This corresponds to the first row of weaving where all the dark threads have been covered by the black weft thread which the shuttle has carried through.

In row 2, the same thing happens with the white threads by depressing treadle 2 which is tied to harness 2. A shuttle carrying a white weft thread is passed through the shed covering all the white threads in the second row. These two shots of weft, the black and white, weave one complete unit, or block *A*, as outlined on both the pattern draft and the draw-down with the heavy black line. Weaving is simply a repetition of this two-thread block which produces a web or piece of material as the weaving proceeds.

Another factor to be considered here is the type of loom in use. On the sinking-shed loom (page 7), stepping on a treadle lowers the harness. On a rising-shed loom, stepping on the treadle raises the harness, which, in this case, would lift the wrong set of threads. Therefore, on a rising-shed loom the treadling is reversed, i.e., instead of treadling 1 then 2, the treadling would be 2 then 1 in alternating succession. Throughout this text, with a few exceptions, treadling is given for both types of looms.

Tie-ups are explained on pages 533 to 535.

Sometimes new weavers are puzzled as to the advantage of owning a loom with 4 or 8 harnesses rather than only 2. The major advantage, of course, lies in the greater development of special techniques and patterns that are possible with additional harnesses; yet one of the important factors, which is often overlooked, is that the threads can be distributed among a greater number of harnesses, lessening the weight on the treadles and eliminating the friction which occurs when many threads are crowded onto 2 harnesses.

With the plain weaves, the end result is the same whether the web is set and woven on 2, 4, or 8 harnesses.

On 4 harnesses the threading draft and draw-down are as shown in Fig. 51, while the 8-harness draft and draw-down are shown in Fig. 52. Fig. 53 shows the structure of the plain 50/50 weave.

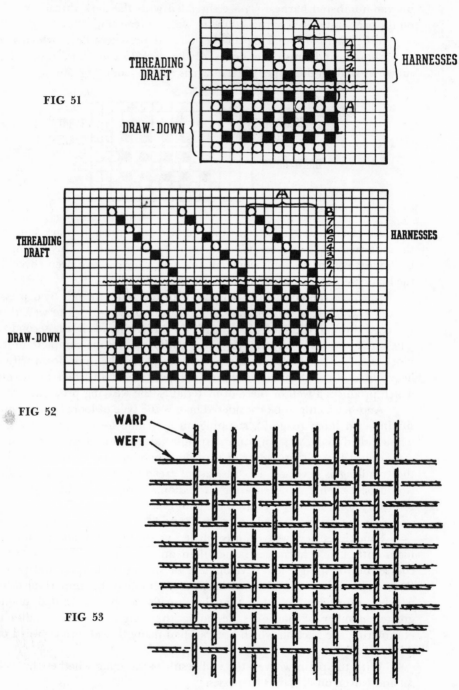

FIG 51

THREADING DRAFT

DRAW-DOWN

HARNESSES

THREADING DRAFT

DRAW-DOWN

HARNESSES

FIG 52

WARP

WEFT

FIG 53

TYPE Balanced Weaves · PATTERN Plain Weave

These samples (Figs. 54–63) show textures achieved through the use of various kinds and sizes of threads. All samples are threaded and treadled on a plain-weave draft (page 55) and illustrate the use of various materials.

FIG. 54
Warp: Carpet warp
Weft: Same

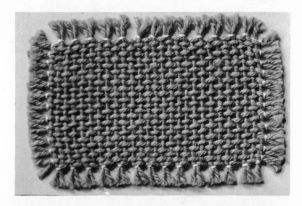

FIG. 55
Warp: Cotton, Egyptian,
     30/3
Weft: Same

FIG. 56
Warp: Linen, homespun,
     coarse, single-ply
Weft: Same

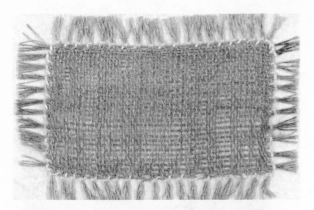

FIG. 57
Warp: Linen, homespun,
       fine, single-ply
Weft: Same

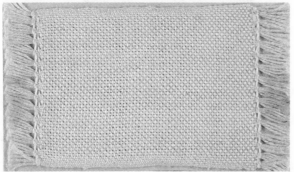

FIG. 58
Warp: Cotton, mercerized
       28/4
Weft: Same

FIG. 59
Warp: Perle cotton,
       No. 5
Weft: Same

FIG. 60
Warp: Yarn, homespun,
       single-ply, fine
Weft: Same

FIG. 61
Warp: Yarn, homespun,
   single-ply, coarse
Weft: Same

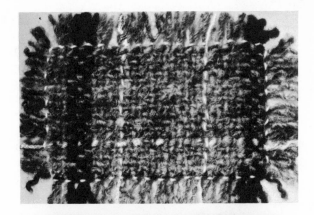

FIG. 62
Warp: Yarn, commercial,
   fine
Weft: Same, two strands
   together

FIG. 63
Warp: Yarn, commercial,
   knitting worsted
Weft: Same

TYPE Balanced Weaves · PATTERN 50/50 Plain Weave

Throughout weaving literature, the expression "50/50 weave" frequently appears. This is a weave in which the number of weft threads per inch is the same as the number of warp threads per inch. A 50/50 weave is found in the plain weaves, the twill and overshot weaves, and in other balanced weaves.

The beginning weaver should practice beating to obtain an even web. Actually, plain weaves are the most difficult to weave because there is no opportunity to cover up uneven beating in the web with overlying shots such as are woven into the overshot, summer-and-winter, and other patterns.

The processes that occur when the harnesses are raised and lowered in alternating sequence and the shuttle, which carries the weft thread, is passed back and forth through the shed have been explained (page 46).

Uses and Materials The uses for the plain weave and the materials from which it may be woven are unlimited. Not only is it a weave in its own right, but it is also the basis of many other weaves.

Sample Illustrated (Fig. 64)

WARP	WEFT	REED (dents per inch)	SLEY
Cotton, 8/4	Cotton, 8/4	18	Single

It has been found through years of use that the size of cottons does vary. The particular lot used to make this sample produced a 50/50 web set in an 18-dent reed, whereas a heavier 8/4 cotton would square up better in a 16-dent reed. The weaver should keep this in mind. No explanation can be given for this variation in the cottons. The skeined cotton thread seems to run a bit thicker than thread wound on tubes or cones.

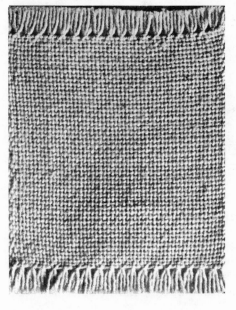

FIG 64

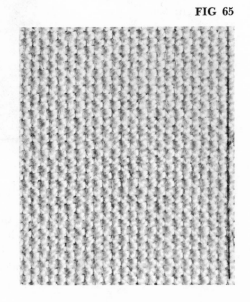

FIG 65

Threading and Treadling   Plain Weave

Tie-Up   Standard

Problem   Plan the warp, thread the loom, and weave a piece of material in plain 50/50 weave, at least 8 by 8 in., paying special attention to the edges and the beat.

TYPE Balanced Weaves · PATTERN 50/50 Plain Weave

Beginning weavers should strive for an even beat and good selvedges. This sample, woven of nylon wrapping twine, weaves up easily and quickly, is inexpensive, and lends itself well to interiors with a modern decor.

Uses   This material is suitable for place mats and runners. When loosely woven, it hangs beautifully and is excellent for drapes. The finished material washes easily, but shrinks considerably. It is stiff and boardlike when wet, but softens after drying and ironing. It lends itself well to the miscellaneous weaves (Chapter 11). The thread is slippery and may be difficult to handle for the beginning weaver. However, if care is taken to get a good tension and tie all knots securely, weaving with nylon will provide good experience in handling threads. The coarseness of the thread is in the beginner's favor.

Sample Illustrated (Fig. 65)

WARP	WEFT	REED (dents per inch)	SLEY
Nylon cord, No. 25	Nylon cord, No. 25	12	Single

Use a 10-dent reed if a softer material is desired.

Number of Threads Wound   60

Length of Warp   1 yd., set up on small loom for experimentation

Threading   Plain weave

Treadling   Plain weave

Problem   Choose any type of coarse thread, set up a sample, and experiment to obtain a sley which will give a 50/50 fabric.

TYPE Balanced Weaves ·
PATTERN Plain Web With Colored Weft Stripes

A simple fundamental method of decorating a plain 50/50 tabby web is to insert colored weft threads to make a border.

The new problem presented here is the method of turning in the ends of the colored threads so that they will be neat and secure. It is important that the beginning weaver learn how to do this correctly, because in all weaving there are ends to be turned in. The care and accuracy with which this is done constitutes the difference between good and bad weaving.

Instructions for starting the weft thread already have been given; the method for ending the weft thread before inserting the colored border threads is as follows (Fig. 66):

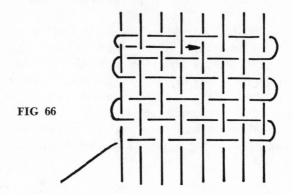

FIG 66

Cut the weft thread about 1 or 1¼ in. beyond the selvedge. With the same shed open through which the last shot was made, turn the cut end around the outside warp thread between the end thread and the warp thread which lies next to it. Carry the cut end into the shed close to the weft thread which is already there. Whether the edge warp thread lies on the top or bottom row of threads makes no difference; the weft thread must be turned around the edge thread. Now, change the shed and insert the colored weft thread, using the method just described to fasten the ends at the start and finish. In plain weaving, the colored thread may be started on the side of the web opposite from that where the last thread ended. This technique prevents the piling up of threads on one side which might result in that side being longer than the other. It is not possible to change the order of the threads when weaving twills, particularly tartans (page 416), as the change would throw the routine off and leave loose threads at the selvedges. It is not necessary to cut and turn in ends on checks, plaids, or tartans, as the selvedges either are hidden or cut off when garments are made. This is a considerable time-saver. Of course, on such articles as scarves or table linens, ends must be turned in. If the stripes are narrow, the different colors can be carried up the sides by passing the new weft thread around the old at the selvedge before the shuttle enters the shed. It takes practice to achieve a smooth selvedge while carrying threads, but it can be done.

The purpose of this text is to teach techniques, therefore, with a few exceptions, detailed directions will not be given for the weaving of specific articles. There are many fine publications[1] on the market which give full directions as to threads, sleying, draft, and size, and the beginning weaver is urged to subscribe to one or more publications until such time as he has gained sufficient knowledge and confidence to plan his own projects.

A list of articles to be woven, together with suitable threads and sleying, is given on pages 648 to 656; so the beginning weaver will know the different factors to be considered, the following directions are given for a sample of 8/4 carpet warp showing three border arrangements. The finished piece is 12 by 18-in. place-mat size. This is the minimum size accepted by many guilds for samples.

One of the unknown quantities of hand weaving is shrinkage. Many factors control this: thread composition, a combination of various threads, technique, beating, and sleying. If an article must meet certain specifications after washing, the only way to assure these dimensions is to make a sample which, upon completion, can be thoroughly washed. Accurate measurements must be recorded of the width set in the reed, the width when woven, and the shrinkage in length after tension release. It is always better for a sample piece to be slightly larger rather than smaller than the required size.

There are all kinds of border arrangements and color arrangements. Many weavers are at a loss when it comes to arranging borders, and it is a subject which requires a great deal of study. Borrow Swedish weaving books from the library;[2] the many colored illustrations will be helpful.

Sample Illustrated (Fig. 69)

WARP	WEFT	PATTERN	REED (dents per inch)	SLEY
Cotton, yellow, 8/4	Cotton, yellow, 8/4	Cotton, 8/4, assorted colors	16	Single

Length of Warp Chain   1 yd. plus loom waste (the measurement from breast beam to back beam). This allows for a fringe or wide hem as well as an extra sample.

Number of Threads in Warp   16 threads per inch × 14-in. width = 224 threads

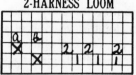

TIE-UP   THREADING DRAFT
2-HARNESS LOOM

FIG 67

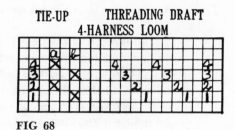

TIE-UP   THREADING DRAFT
4-HARNESS LOOM

FIG 68

Treadling–Sinking Shed

Treadling–Rising Shed

a ⎱	Repeat until required length	⎰ b
b ⎰	is woven	⎱ a

The sample illustrates three different stripe arrangements in colors that combine well with the yellow background (Fig. 69):

Weave   2½ in. with yellow thread for hem

STRIPE 1 ROWS	COLOR
3	medium blue
2	navy blue
3	orange
1	medium blue
1	navy blue
1	medium blue
1	navy blue
1	orange
2	navy blue
10	medium blue
*2	yellow
1	orange–center

From * reverse back to beginning of stripe.

Weave   3½ in. of yellow

FIG 69

STRIPE 2	
ROWS	COLOR
2	dark brown
2	yellow
2	dark brown
2	yellow
12	rust
*2	yellow
18	turquoise–center

From *, reverse back to beginning. The number of rust and turquoise threads can be varied, if desired.

Weave   3½ in. of yellow

STRIPE 3		
ROWS	COLOR	
2	dark green	
3	yellow	
5	gold	
3	brown	
*5	gold	
2	dark green	
3	yellow	center
2	dark green	
3	yellow	

From *, reverse back to beginning.

Weave   2½ in. of yellow for hem

FIG 70

Problem   Choose a background color, plan and weave a sample with three types of borders, each with a different color scheme, but all designed to harmonize with the background color.

Fig. 70 is a sample showing stripes of textured threads placed at random to contrast with the smooth background threads.

TYPE Balanced Weaves · PATTERN Warp Stripes, Equal Width

The next interesting variation of the plain web is the use of two colors in the warp, arranged in stripes.

The width of the stripes is determined by the number of warp threads of one color which are threaded at one time. Stripes can be of any width in keeping with the use of the article. Accurate counting of threads is necessary while winding the warp, or the stripes will be uneven and the result anything but pleasing.

One thing to be noted in weaving stripes is that, even though the warp is set at 16 threads per inch, and actually measures 1 in. at the reed, there is a draw-in during the weaving that results in the stripe being about one thread narrower at the edge of the web. This shrinkage must be taken into consideration and offset in sleying if it is absolutely necessary that the finished stripes, checks, plaids, or tartans measure a given number of inches in width. For general purposes, however, the stripe as set and woven is satisfactory.

Use For any article where stripes are desired: scarves, tablecloths, runners, pillow covers, luncheon sets, material for sportswear

Suitable Materials and Sleying Any thread can be used, but the ratio between warp and weft should be such as to produce a 50/50 fabric.

Sample Illustrated (Fig. 73)

WARP	WEFT	REED (dents per inch)	SLEY
Carpet warp, light and dark, 8/4	Carpet warp, light and dark, 8/4	15 or 16	Single

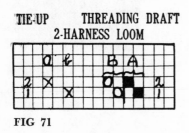

TIE-UP   THREADING DRAFT
2-HARNESS LOOM

FIG 71

TIE-UP   THREADING DRAFT
4-HARNESS LOOM

FIG 72

Thread A–2× } Repeat until the desired width has { Thread A–1×
Thread B–2× } been threaded.   { Thread B–1×

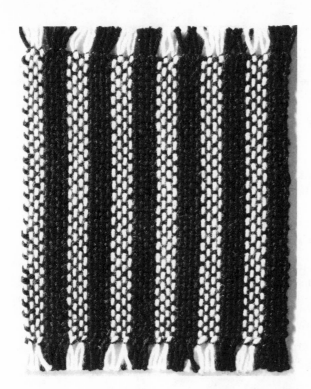

FIG 73

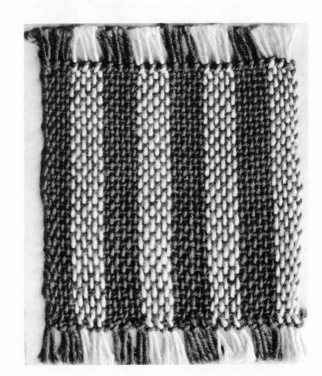

FIG 74

Treadling–Sinking Shed			Treadling–Rising Shed *(No Tie-Up)*

a $\}$	Repeat in alternating succession until	$\{$ *b*
b	desired length has been woven.	*a*

The weft thread can match either the light or dark warp thread.
Fig. 73 is a four-thread stripe; Fig. 74, a six-thread stripe.

TYPE Balanced Weaves · PATTERN Checks

Checks are made by alternating two colors of weft across a two-colored striped warp, such as is shown in Fig. 73, weaving in an equal number of weft threads and warp threads, and beating the web to obtain a perfect square.

Use Wherever checks are suitable: dress materials, scarves, breakfast sets and table linens, pillows, book covers, etc.

Suitable Materials and Sleying Any combination that will make a 50/50 fabric, for example:

WARP	WEFT	REED *(dents per inch)*	SLEY
Carpet warp, 8/4	Carpet warp, 8/4	18	Single
Cotton, 16/2	Cotton, 16/2	15	Double
Yarn, heavy homespun, 2 ply	Yarn, heavy homespun, 2 ply	12	Single
Yarn, fine, 16/2	Yarn, fine, 16/2	14	Double

Samples Illustrated (Figs. 79 and 80)

WARP	WEFT	REED *(dents per inch)*	SLEY
Carpet warp, light and dark, 8/4	Carpet warp, light and dark, 8/4	18	Single

Thread *A*–2× $\}$	Repeat until the desired width has	$\{$ Thread *A*–1×
Thread *B*–2×	been threaded.	Thread *B*–1×

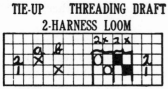

TIE-UP   **THREADING DRAFT**
2-HARNESS LOOM

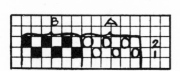

FIG 75

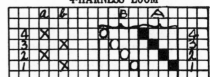

TIE-UP   **THREADING DRAFT**
4-HARNESS LOOM

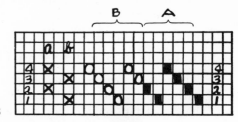

FIG 76

FIG 77

FIG 78

Treadling–Sinking Shed

Treadling–Rising Shed
(*No Tie-Up*)

	TREADLES OR LEVERS		
$\left.\begin{array}{c}a\\b\end{array}\right\}$ 2× dark thread		$\left.\begin{array}{c}b\\a\end{array}\right\}$ 2× dark thread	
$\left.\begin{array}{c}a\\b\end{array}\right\}$ 2× light thread		$\left.\begin{array}{c}b\\a\end{array}\right\}$ 2× light thread	

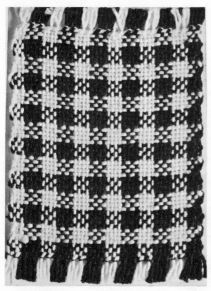

FIG 79

FIG 80

Carry the weft threads along the edge from one square to another; do *not* break off each time.

As scales are to the musician so checks are to the weaver. There is no better way to perfect or correct beating than by weaving checks. Weave checks and checks and checks, measuring each woven piece until the squares are perfect, with the same number of threads in the weft as in the warp.

Problem Plan, set up, and weave a dish towel of 16/2 cotton in 6- or 8-thread checks.

TYPE Balanced Weaves · PATTERN Tattersall Check

This check receives its name from the famous Tattersall Racing Club of early nineteenth-century London. Young men of that day dressed in the height of fashion for sporting occasions and this particular check was a favorite.

In pattern, it differs from a regular check or plaid in that it consists of a series of background checks of ¼-, ½-, 1-, or 2-in. squares, framed on all four sides by threads of two other colors. If the check is 2-in. square, there should be four warp threads on each side with four colored weft threads at the top and four at the bottom of the square. If the squares are small, ½- or 1-in. squares, two threads are used for the frame (Figs. 83, 84, and 85). This makes a daintier pattern. While the large square may be of any color, white or a light color usually is chosen with strong contrasting colors to frame the square. The weft colors are entered in the order in which they appear in the warp. When seen in a large piece, it is noticeable that the colored threads which frame the squares form an overcheck on the light background. This overcheck cannot be seen in the samples illustrated (Figs. 84 and 85), with the exception of the ¼-in. square (Fig. 84) where it does show up.

Uses For shirtings and sport blouses; shirtwaist dresses; children's skirts, blouses, shorts, and dresses; and dish towels

Suitable Materials and Sleying Materials chosen for this weave should be smooth and soft enough to beat into a firm but soft material. Perle cotton, rayon, and nylon, in sizes to correspond with the following, should be sleyed the same as the threads listed.

WARP	WEFT	PATTERN	REED (dents per inch)	SLEY
Cotton, 16/2	Cotton, 16/2	Cotton, 16/2	16	Double
Wool, 2/32	Wool, 2/32	Wool, 2/32	18	Double
Linen, round thread, 40/2	Linen, round thread, 40/2	Linen, round thread, 40/2	15	Triple

Samples Illustrated (Figs. 83, 84, and 85)

WARP	WEFT	PATTERN	REED	SLEY
			(dents per inch)	
Cotton, 20/2	Cotton, 20/2	Cotton, 20/2	18	Double

Order for Winding the Warp for the 1-in. Square Pattern (Fig. 85)

ROWS	COLOR
4	green to start, right selvedge
36	white
2	blue
36	white Repeat to thread desired width.
2	green
36	white
4	blue to end, left selvedge

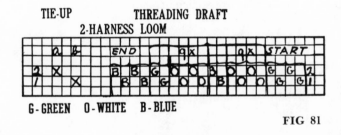

TIE-UP THREADING DRAFT
2-HARNESS LOOM

G-GREEN O-WHITE B-BLUE

FIG 81

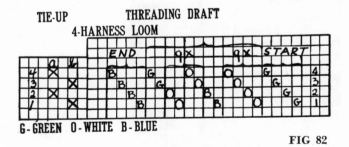

TIE-UP THREADING DRAFT
4-HARNESS LOOM

G-GREEN O-WHITE B-BLUE

FIG 82

Other colors frequently used on a light background are orange or yellow with black, red and black, brown and yellow, purple and mauve, brown and rust.

LEVERS OR TREADLES

$a = 1$ and 3; $b = 2$ and 4

a *b*	2× green, right selvedge start only	*b* *a*
a *b* *a* *b*	9× white, 36 shots	*b* *a* *b* *a*
a *b*	1× blue	*b* *a*
a *b* *a* *b*	9× white, 36 shots	*b* *a* *b* *a*
a *b*	1× green	*b* *a*
a *b*	36× white 2× blue } left selvedge to end	*b* *a*

Problem   Work out threading for the ½-in. squares (Fig. 83) and the ¼-in. squares (Fig. 84) and weave sufficient material of either pattern for a small boy's shirt.

FIG 83

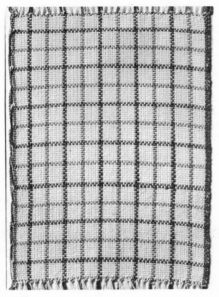

FIG 84

FIG 85

TYPE Balanced Weaves •
PATTERN Warp Stripes, Unequal Width

Unless the weaver has had some training in design and color, it is not advisable to attempt the arrangement of a variety of colors into stripes of unequal width, since the result may not be as artistic as desired. If puzzled about the correct placement of colors, the weaver can obtain help by referring to a piece of commercially woven material. Two or more shades of one color combined with a few threads of black and white is usually a safe combination.

Uses For scarves, drapes, pillows, upholstery, purses, sport shirts, blouses, skirts, etc.

Suitable Materials and Sleying Many. Refer to the stripes of equal width (page 66).

Sample Illustrated (Fig. 88)

WARP	WEFT	REED (*dents per inch*)	SLEY
Cotton, 8/4	Cotton, 8/4	15 or 16	Single

Arrangement of Warp Colors

ROWS	COLOR
8	light blue
2	black
8	light blue
12	dark blue
2	white
12	dark blue
44	threads for each repeat

Repeat as often as necessary to obtain the desired width, starting at the top each time.

For the sample shown (Fig. 88), the arrangement was used twice, ending with one repeat of 8 light blue, 2 black, 8 light blue to balance design.

For another pleasing but brighter arrangement, wind the warp as follows for a web of 100 threads:

ROWS	COLOR
22	dark green
7	light gray
4	black
*12	light green
10	orange–center

From *, repeat back to beginning.

If a wider web is required, do not repeat the 22 dark green at the start or there will be a double-width, dark-green stripe at intervals.

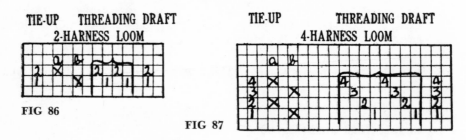

TIE-UP THREADING DRAFT
2-HARNESS LOOM

FIG 86

TIE-UP THREADING DRAFT
4-HARNESS LOOM

FIG 87

Threading Draft Correctly place the lease sticks in the warp (page 32). The threads must lie in the order in which they are wound since they are entered in this order in the heddles and reed.

Repeat the bracket portion of the threading draft until the desired width has been threaded.

Treadling For the weft, use any desired color. The lighter colors give the more pleasing result. The blue sample was woven with a light-blue thread resulting in a web with a pale, bluish cast. A light green was chosen for the second sample.

The beating must produce a 50/50 fabric.

Treadling–Sinking Shed		Treadling–Rising Shed (*No Tie-Up*)
TREADLES		**LEVERS**
		$a = 1$ or 1 and 3; $b = 2$ or 2 and 4
$a \,\}$ $b \,\}$	Repeat until desired length has been woven.	$\{$ b $\{$ a

FIG 88

Problem Plan the warp and weave a piece of striped material for a sunroom pillow or beach bag. Allow enough extra warp to weave a plaid sample (below).

TYPE Balanced Weaves · PATTERN Plaid

While checks are developed from striped warps that have the same number of threads in each stripe, plaids are developed from striped warps that have a different number of threads in each stripe.

Confusion often exists in the understanding and use of the words "plaid" and "tartan." A tartan, to be correct, must be woven on a 4-harness twill (page 408) and must be warped according to the "sett" of threads as approved and used by the various clans. The arrangement of the threads in a plaid, on the other hand, is governed only by the choice and desire of the weaver.

Uses In wool: skirts, jackets, scarves, bags, caps, shirts, couch throws, lounging robes, car robes. In cotton and linen: dresses, summer suits, bags, purses, luncheon sets, towels, runners, drapes

Suitable Materials and Sleying

ARTICLE	WARP	WEFT	REED (*dents per inch*)	SLEY
Lightweight webs, scarves	Fine yarn, 2/32	Fine yarn, 2/32	16–18	Double
Couch throws, coats, etc.	Medium yarn	Medium yarn	9–10–12	Double
Car rugs	Heavy knitting yarn, worsted or homespun, 3-ply	Heavy knitting yarn, worsted or homespun, 3-ply	10–12	Single
Linens	Linen thread, various sizes	Soft-twist linen, various sizes	15–20	Double, Triple

Sample Illustrated Threading and tie-up are the same as for the striped material. The only difference in the plaid is that the weft threads are entered to form a pattern, following in color the same order in which they lie in the warp. In planning wool warps, allow extra for shrinkage in both length and width.

To facilitate the designing and threading of plaids, break the striped warp up into blocks. A study of the warp reveals that there are two pattern areas which are repeated in alternating succession across the web. In Fig. 89, the first group of 8/4 cotton threads, block *A,* consists of 8 light blue, 2 black, and 8 light blue. The second group, block *B,* consists of 12 dark blue, 2 white, and 12 dark blue 8/4 cotton threads. These two blocks are threaded in alternating succession until the desired width has been threaded. If wide material is being woven, such as would be needed for a skirt, it is not necessary to end with the same block with which the threading began. If a scarf or stole is being woven, however, the pattern should be balanced; that is, if the threading begins with an *A* block on the right it should end with an *A* block on the left.

Treadling–Sinking Shed		Treadling–Rising Shed (*No Tie-Up*)
TREADLES		**LEVERS OR TREADLES**
		$a = 1$ or 1 and 3; $b = 2$ or 2 and 4
a ⎰ b ⎱	Repeat until desired length has been woven.	⎰ b ⎱ a

Order of Weft

		SHOTS	COLOR			SHOTS	COLOR
Block A	⎰	8	light blue	*Block B*	⎰	12	dark blue
	⎨	2	black		⎨	2	white
	⎱	8	light blue		⎱	12	dark blue

FIG 89

Repeat until the desired length has been woven. Beat the blocks to a square. If they do not square up, check for the trouble and correct it. If the warp threads are covered and it requires more than the given number of threads to square the block, use a finer reed. If, on the other hand, the weft threads do not beat back and the warp threads predominate, use a coarser reed.

A sample of plaid woven in fine, single-ply homespun wool, suitable for a jacket, is set and woven as follows (Fig. 90):

	SHOTS	COLOR		SHOTS	COLOR
Block A {	8	gray	Block B {	12	blue
	4	black		4	white
	8	gray		12	blue

This sample was threaded on the same threading as the 8/4 cotton sample (Fig. 89), with the same treadling. The sample was set double sley in a 10-dent reed, but after washing it seemed a little hard. A double sley in a 9-dent reed would be better.

To figure the number of yards of material required for a garment, lay out the pattern, arranging the pieces according to the width of the loom. If the loom is narrow, lay the pattern so it will take more length and less width. Tailors consider 28- to 30-in. widths satisfactory. Narrower widths also can be used if there is sufficient length. Allow for shrinkage.

In weaving yardages of either cotton or wool, it is permissible to carry the different weft colors from block to block. If scarves, stoles, or place mats are being woven, it is better to turn in the ends of each color as the required number of threads are woven.

After the material has been removed from the loom, wash, dry, and steam press it (page 626).

Problem Plan and set up a plaid warp of soft wool long enough to weave two scarves, one in plain-weave stripes and the other in a plain-weave plaid. Allow for a fringe at each end of the scarf.

FIG 90

TYPE Balanced Weaves · PATTERN Tie and Dye

This weave should appeal to weavers who enjoy dyeing material and to those patient weavers who like to experiment. It is by no means a new weave, as articles of clothing made from tie-and-dye material can be purchased in the market places of Mexico, Central and South America, many islands of the South Pacific, and elsewhere.

It is a weave that is seldom attempted by present-day weavers, although it is fun to play with, even if weaving a long web looks like quite an undertaking.

A folio picturing many samples of this weave, published in Japan,[3] shows how complicated the designs can become when there is sufficient "know-how" and experience behind the weaver.

Uses Aprons, sport shirts, and shirt material; kitchen and bathroom curtains.

Suitable Materials Cottons, wool, or other materials which will dye easily. Avoid linen; it is too difficult to dye.

Sample Illustrated (Fig. 92)

WARP	WEFT	REED (dents per inch)	SLEY
Cotton, 8/2	Cotton, 8/2	20 10	Single Double

Length of Warp 1 yd.

Number of Threads Wound 60

Threading and Treadling Plain weave

Tie-up Standard

Tie cord around lease, then remove the warp from the warping board or reel.

The warp length must be spread out its entire length and width and stretched. This is simple enough for a short length, such as for the sample, but a little difficult for a length of three or more yards, 36 in. wide.

For the short sample, slip round sticks through each end of the warp chain. Fasten the shed with a fine cord, left loose so that it will not prevent the warp from being spread out to its full width. It is very important that the shed not be lost.

Now, securely fasten the two sticks so that the two chains are stretched tight. Then spread the threads along each of the round sticks in the order in which they lie in the shed. When this is done, decide where the design units are to be placed (Fig. 91). With rags for the larger spots and cord for the smaller units, pick up the number of threads desired for the design and tie the rag or cord *tightly* around this area. If it is not tied tightly, the dye will seep in and there will not be sufficient contrast between the dyed background and the pattern unit. Those whose specialty is dyeing can get as ambitious as they like by dyeing and overdyeing to get subtle colorings, but the beginner would be wise to keep the first piece simple.

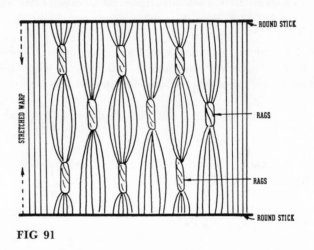

FIG 91

    The warp, after the design units have been tied, should look like Fig. 91.

    After all the ties have been made, loosen and remove the sticks, and chain the warp very loosely so the dye can penetrate the threads properly. Dye the chain, stirring constantly. Rinse the skein. Save the dye.

    Fasten the warp to the clothesline and hang a weight on the end of the chain. The weight will keep the threads in alignment. Once the warp has dried, cut away only enough rags to loosen the required length for threading. The more carefully the warp is put on, the better the results. The units of the design should be as perfectly aligned as possible.

    Tie on the warp ends, disturbing the tied and dyed warp groups as little as possible. Once the warp ends are tied, cut the rags away and roll on the warp.

    Before beginning to weave, however, wind a quantity of undyed weft on the warping board. The length should be the width of the warp as it lies in the reed. Now lay this weft across the warp and make rag ties where the weft lies over the undyed portions of the warp. Dye the weft threads in the same dye as was used for the warp.

    Now weave in the usual manner by filling in the spaces and weaving in a heading.

    It will require a little experimentation to determine exactly where the

FIG 92

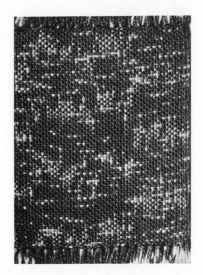

FIG 93

undyed portions of the weft should start and lie in the shed to give the desired pattern effect.

As was stated in the beginning, this weave is only for those with unlimited patience and a love for experimentation.

Sample 1 (Fig. 92): Set up and weave according to above directions.

Sample 2 (Fig. 93): Tie the warp and weft with cord at regular intervals, then dye. As no specific design is tied into the warp, the result is a hit-and-miss effect.

Finish   Steam press the material when it is removed from the loom. Unless the weaver is an experienced dyer, the material should be dry cleaned or washed very carefully.

Problem   Plan and dye the warp and weft for a small experimental sample.

TYPE Unbalanced Weaves · PATTERN Rag Mats

There probably are as many varieties of rag mats as there are people weaving them. They vary from the heavy, rough, hit-and-miss utilitarian types woven of material available in the farm home, to lovely, artistically designed mats of new material, carefully cut and woven.

Usually the interest lies in the weft, although, if the only material available is dark or lacks color, interest can be achieved by using a multi-color or striped warp.

Warp settings vary greatly, but in general and following the old order, most mats are woven on an 8/4 carpet warp set at 15 dents per inch.

Above all, rag mats should be firm, almost to the point of being stiff. There is no use or excuse for a sleazy mat.[4]

Among the French-Canadian weavers of Quebec, the rag mat has been brought to its highest standard of workmanship and design. The catalogne, as it is called there, is woven of carefully torn and sewn rags with the edges pressed and concealed in the center of the strip. Colors are arranged carefully and are combined so pleasingly, in spite of the great number used in each piece, that unless a catalogne of one definite color was desired, the mat harmonizes with practically any color scheme.

Uses Bedroom and bathroom mats, drapery, upholstery, and stair and hall carpeting

Materials Warp: cotton; weft: cotton, wool, flannelette, knit underwear, factory ends, stockings.

It is suggested that no effort be made to dye carpet rags, for it is difficult to obtain a permanent dye job. A closely set, gay warp will give the desired life to the mat.

Stockings should not be cut on the bias because they stretch too much during the weaving, have little body, and shrink up when the mat is removed from the loom. If nylon stockings are to be used, cut open the hem at the top and cut straight down. Remove the heels and toes. When weaving, alternate the ends of the stocking as they are entered; that is, enter one in the shed with the top of the stocking at the edge and the second one with the top slightly overlapping the foot of the first stocking. This keeps the weft more uniform. There are many methods of sewing carpet rags, but those sewn on the bias by hand are the nicest.

Sample Illustrated (Fig. 94) The accompanying sample is woven in two dark tones and one light. To accentuate the colors, a tabby thread is used between some of the rows of rags so that the dark warp threads will cover dark rags and the light warp will cover light rags.

WARP	WEFT	PATTERN	REED (*dents per inch*)	SLEY
Carpet warp, 8/4	Cotton, 10/2	Carpet rags	9	Double

Length of Warp 48 in. + loom waste; the finished mat is approximately 34 in.

Number of Threads in Warp 354

FIG 94

Warp Arrangement

24 threads white or light shade
  alternating with dark shade, No. 1
6 threads darks shade, No. 2
20 threads white or light shade
12 threads dark shade, No. 1
20 threads white or light shade

*6 threads dark shade, No. 2
178 threads white or light shade
  alternating with dark shade, No. 1–
  center
Repeat from * back to beginning.

Threading Plain weave 1, 2, 1, 2, (page 55) or 1, 2, 3, 4, etc. (page 55). **Care** must be taken when repeating the sections with alternating light and dark threads so that the light ones are threaded through No. 1, or, if four harnesses are used, through Nos. 1 and 3, and all the dark threads through No. 2 or Nos. 2 and 4.

Treadling 1¼-in. plain weave in carpet warp shade No. 1

ROWS OF COLORED RAGS		ROWS OF CARPET WARP, SHADE NO. 1	
4	dark	alternating with	4
3	light	alternating with	3
1	dark	followed by	1
3	light	alternating with	3
2	dark	alternating with	2

The body of the mat is woven throughout with two shades of light-colored carpet rags without the carpet warp between.

In weaving the border area, be sure the rags are all entered when treadle *b* (harnesses 1 and 3) is depressed, and the carpet warp when treadle *a* (harnesses 2 and 4) is depressed.

The central portion of the mat is treadled *a* and *b* with the rags, wound on two shuttles, entered in alternating succession until the desired length is woven. End with the border, in reverse, and the heading of 1¼ in. of plain weave.

Finish After removing the material from the loom, tie the warp ends in groups of eight or ten threads, each with a simple knot (Fig. 46).

Problem Prepare the rags, set up a warp, and weave a bath mat approximately 18 by 30 in.

TYPE Unbalanced Weaves · PATTERN Log Cabin

This old-time pattern is simple to thread and weave; the threading is changeable; and, if color combinations are well chosen, the material is most attractive. The log cabin goes well with either traditional or modern interiors where a simple geometric pattern is desired. The number of threads in each unit may be varied to suit the individual and the purpose for which the material is to be used. For upholstery, the blocks should be kept small. A hall runner or stair carpet would be more attractive with a plain center and a border along each edge.

Uses Upholstery, pillow covers, table scarves, rag and wool mats, place mats, bags, purses, and drapes

The log-cabin pattern can be set up and woven either on 2 or 4 harnesses. Threads of two colors alternate in the warp, the order of the colors changing at the edge of each block. For instance, block *A* consists of alternating light and dark threads repeated the required number of times (Figs. 97 and 101) while in block *B* the colors are reversed, running dark, light, dark, light. Two threads of the same color are adjacent where the blocks change, or in reverse.

Samples Illustrated (Figs. 97 to 101)

WARP	WEFT	PATTERN	REED (dents per inch)	SLEY
Carpet warp, 8/4	Carpet warp, 8/4	Carpet warp, 8/4	15	Single
Carpet warp, 8/4	Cotton, 16/2	Candlewick	15	Single

The log-cabin pattern can be woven with two threads of the same size, or with one heavy and one fine thread. Either is correct.

Length of Warp Wound 1 yd.

Number of Threads 60

To facilitate the winding of the warp for the log-cabin pattern, in which the dark threads alternate with the light, place a tube of the light thread on a stick and on top of this place a tube of the dark thread. This winds two threads together: first a light and then a dark. At every change of color, as designated on the threading draft, reverse the stick, bringing the bottom color to the top, thereby changing the sequence of the threads.

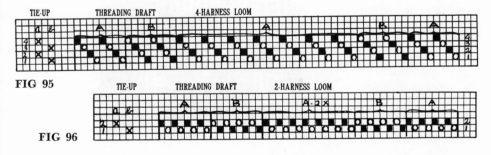

TIE-UP   THREADING DRAFT   4-HARNESS LOOM

FIG 95

TIE-UP   THREADING DRAFT   2-HARNESS LOOM

FIG 96

Treadling–Sinking Shed			Treadling–Rising Shed	
Block A			**Block B**	
TREADLE	COLOR		TREADLE	COLOR
a	light }	4× to square block A	{ b	dark
b	dark		a	light
b	dark }	4× to square block B	{ a	light
a	light		b	dark
a	light }	14× to square block A	{ b	dark
b	dark		a	light
b	dark }	4× to square block B	{ a	light
a	light		b	dark
a	light }	4× to square block A	{ b	dark
b	dark		a	light

To make a good edge on the log cabin, the thread which comes from behind must be carried, each time, over the one which has just been brought out of the shed, or it will pull into the shed leaving the edge warp thread unwoven.

Sample 1 (Fig. 97): Woven with both colors in 8/4 carpet warp.

Sample 2 (Fig. 98): Woven with one-strand 16/2 cotton. The change from one block to another is made on the fine thread shed.

Sample 3 (Fig. 99): Alternating with one-strand candlewick. The change between the blocks is made on the heavy shed.

Sample 4 (Fig. 100): Woven of 8/2 cotton.

Sample 5 (Fig. 101): Woven in log-cabin technique of silk stockings and 8/4 cotton warp in two shades of green.

Problem Plan and set up a place mat in a 12 by 18-in. log-cabin pattern using 8/4 carpet warp and candlewick for weft (Fig. 101).

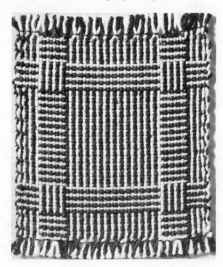

FIG 97

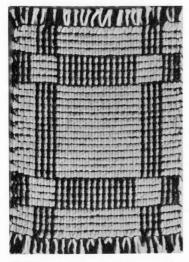

FIG 98

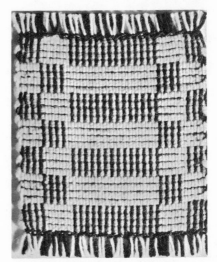

FIG 99

FIG 100

FIG 101

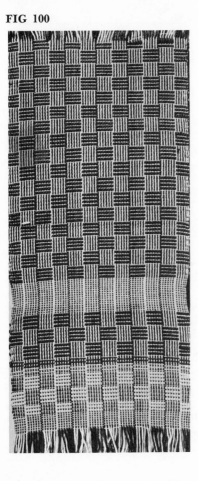

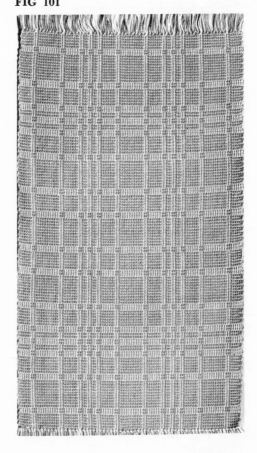

TYPE Unbalanced Weaves · PATTERN Warp Face, Plain

Warp-face weaving is a very firm, close weave, in which the warp threads almost entirely cover the weft threads.

This type of weaving is rather common among primitive tribes who achieve much of the beauty of their weaves through artistic arrangements of colored warp threads which they dye with bark, roots, grasses, etc.

Uses Commercially, this material is used where extra strength and wearing qualities are required as in canvases, ducks, floor coverings, etc. When woven on hand looms, the material is suitable for knitting bags, purses, pillow covers, etc.

Suitable Materials and Sleying Carpet warp, Egyptian cotton, or perle cotton are advised in preference to wool or linen warp. It is very difficult to obtain a clear shed with threads that are inclined to stick together when the treadles are operated.

WARP	WEFT	REED (dents per inch)	SLEY
Carpet warp	Carpet warp	15	Double
Cotton, Egyptian, 10/3	Cotton, Egyptian, 10/3	18	Double
Cotton perle, No. 3	Cotton perle, No. 3	15	Double

Sample Illustrated (Fig. 102)

WARP	WEFT	REED (dents per inch)	SLEY
Carpet warp, 8/4	Carpet warp, 8/4	18	Double

The secret of a successful warp-face weave is the close setting of the warp in the reed.

Length of Warp Wound 1 yd.

Number of Threads 60

Threading and Treadling Plain weave

Tie-Up Standard

The warp-face technique is simple, but sometimes it is difficult to get a good shed. The warp is sleyed so closely and the heddles are so close together that there is little opportunity for the threads and heddles to operate without friction. It is easier to weave this technique on a rising shed than on a counterbalanced loom.

Problem   Plan and set up the warp for a warp-face weave, then weave material for a beach bag.

FIG 102

TYPE Unbalanced Weaves ·
PATTERN Warp Face, Print or Chine

Chine webs are obtained by painting or stenciling a design on a closely set warp-face warp of a neutral color.

Commercially, this process is used to produce cretonnes and other prints.

Striking effects can be obtained through the use of good design and color. The dyes should be very bright and the pattern one of masses rather than of fine detail.

These imitation tapestries can be quickly and easily woven.

Uses   For wall hangings, pictures, pillow covers

Procedure   Wind the warp in the usual manner. Chain loosely, and tie the end with a piece of carpet warp to prevent unskeining. Soak the warp well in cold water for an hour or so; then boil in soap suds to remove all sizing; rinse and dry.

Thread the loom and wind the warp onto the warp beam in the usual manner. Tie a strong flat stick to the cloth-beam rod. Tie the warp ends onto this stick instead of onto the cloth-beam rod (Fig. 103).

Untie the flat stick from the cloth-beam rod.

Pull the warp forward, through the reed, and out in front of the loom until sufficient warp has been released for the entire design to be painted on.

Tie the stick to some stationary object, and brace the loom to prevent it from slipping.

On a drawing board place a piece of paper with the design inked on it and slip this under the taut warp. This provides a firm support on which to work.

With dye and a stiff brush, paint or stencil the design onto the warp. Work the dye well into and around all warp threads.

After the pattern has dried, rewind the warp toward the warp beam, and retie the stick to the cloth-beam rod.

Because of close sleying of the warp, it may be difficult to clear the shed. Working the beater back and forth, after the shed has been changed, may help. The fingers can be used to clear threads that are stuck together.

The warp threads almost completely hide the weft threads, yet there is some suggestion of background shading from these threads.

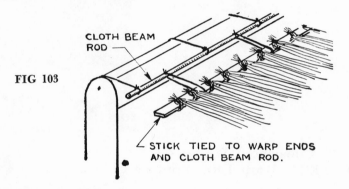

CLOTH BEAM ROD

FIG 103

STICK TIED TO WARP ENDS AND CLOTH BEAM ROD.

Suitable Materials and Sleying

WARP	WEFT	REED (*dents per inch*)	SLEY
Cotton, Egyptian, 10/3	Cotton, Egyptian, 10/3	20	Double
Carpet warp, 8/4	Cotton warp, 16/2	18	Double

Sample Illustrated (Fig. 104)

WARP	WEFT	REED (*dents per inch*)	SLEY
Carpet warp, 8/4 natural	Cotton, Egyptian, 10/3	18	Double

FIG 104

Threading   Plain weave

Tie-Up   Standard

Treadling   Plain weave

Problem   Design and weave a wall picture at least 12 by 18 in., preferably using an original design.

TYPE Unbalanced Weaves ·
PATTERN Stripes, Even and Roman

Interest can be added to a plain warp-face material by using a striped warp. Vertical stripes are brought out clearly in this type of sleying. Horizontal strips are indistinct and should not be attempted.

Uses and Suitable Materials   The same as for the plain warp face (page 88)

Sample Illustrated   Even stripes (Fig. 105)

Sample C is the firmest of the three pieces.

WARP	WEFT	REED (*dents per inch*)	SLEY
Sample A: Carpet warp, 8/4, turquoise and white	Carpet warp, 8/4, turquoise and white	18	Double
Sample B: Carpet warp, 8/4	Cotton, 8/2, white	18	Double
Sample C: Carpet warp, 8/4	Cotton, 16/2, white	18	Double

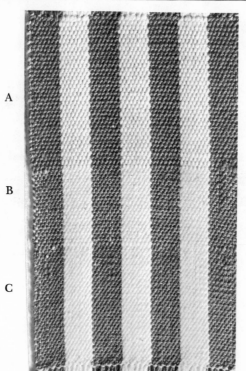

A

B

FIG. 105

C

To Wind Warp   Alternate 15 turquoise with 15 white, 3×. End with 15 turquoise.

Sample Illustrated   Roman stripe (Fig. 106).

WARP	WEFT	REED (*dents per inch*)	SLEY
Cotton perle, No. 5, blue, black, orange, yellow, and red	Cotton perle, No. 10, gold	15	Double

FIG 106

Number of Threads Required for Sample Illustrated   240

Warp 20 in. long, weaves piece 8 in. wide.
Wind the warp on a warping board in the following order:

THREADS	COLOR
10	black
10	orange
20	blue
*10	red
20	yellow—center

From *, reverse back to beginning. Thread the threads through in the order in which they were wound.

Threading   Plain weave

Tie-Up   Standard

Treadling   Plain weave
Beat warp face very hard.

Problem   Plan warp, set up, and weave material for an envelope purse.

TYPE Unbalanced Weaves · PATTERN Nova Scotia Drugget

Druggets found in the old homes of Nova Scotia are of two types. Both have warps of heavy homespun yarn, but in some, carefully cut and folded rags were used for filling while in others a single-ply, neutral-color homespun yarn was used. The warp, however, in both cases, was so closely set that the weft is practically invisible and can only be found by raveling back the weaving. Many very beautiful examples of these carpets can still be found in the "best rooms" of the more comfortable farm homes. The colors, vegetable dyed, seem to have improved with the passage of time and are the envy of the modern dyer.

Suitable Materials and Sleying

WARP	WEFT	REED (dents per inch)	SLEY
Double-ply homespun or heavy wool	Finely cut and folded carpet rags or single-ply homespun	10	Double

Threading   Plain weave

Tie-Up   Standard

Treadling   Plain weave

It is recommended that the drugget be woven only on a substantial floor loom that has a good shed, since the heavy homespun yarn, being set so close in the reed, causes a heavy strain on the loom. Sizing the yarn with a glue size (page 630) may help overcome some of the sticking.

Problem   Set up a small sample of a drugget for experience in treadling; plan colors carefully.

TYPE Unbalanced Weaves · PATTERN Weft Face

In the weft-face weave, as opposed to the warp-face weave, the weft completely covers the warp. The resultant weave, if closley beaten, is firm but not as durable a weave as the warp face. Stripes run horizontally instead of vertically. The success of a warp-face weave lies in the close set of the warp in the reed; in a weft-face weave the warp is widely spaced and the weft predominates. If coarse warp threads are used, they are sleyed every other dent. In Fig. 109, the threads are threaded single sley for 4 dents, 4 dents are skipped, and 4 dents are threaded single sley, and so on, until the required number of threads have been threaded. This varies the texture over the threading.

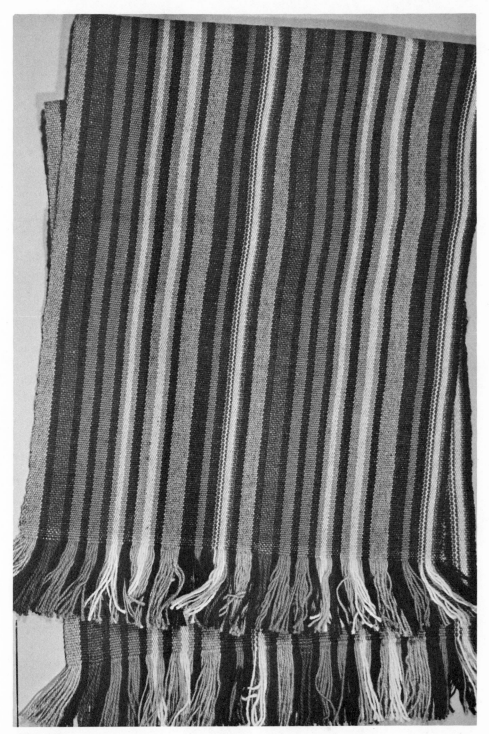

FIG 107

The beauty of a weft-face weave lies in the attractive arrangement of the weft in stripes or patterns.

Uses   Table covers, pillows, purses, wall hangings, knitting bags, etc.

Suitable Materials and Sleying

WARP	WEFT	REED (dents per inch)	SLEY
Carpet warp, 8/4	Carpet warp, 8/4	15	Every other dent
Cotton, Egyptian, 30/3	Cotton, Egyptian, 30/3	15	Single
Linen, tight twist	Wool, medium coarse	18	Every other dent

Samples Illustrated (Figs. 108, 109, and 110)

WARP	WEFT	REED (dents per inch)	SLEY
Figure 114: Carpet warp, 8/4	Carpet warp, 8/4	15	Every other dent
Figure 115: Carpet warp, 8/4	Carpet warp, 8/4	15	Single for 4 dents, skip 4. Repeat
Figure 116: Carpet warp, 8/4	Wool 2/16	15	Single

FIG 108

FIG 109   FIG 110

Length of Warp Wound   1 yd.

Number of Threads   50

Threading   Plain weave

Tie-Up   Standard

Treadling   Plain weave
Beat closely to cover all warp threads.

Problem   Set up the warp, plan the stripes, and weave the material for a purse.

TYPE Texture on Plain-Weave Threading · PATTERN Weft Texture

Plain webs can be varied by weaving in heavy weft threads at chosen intervals as the web progresses. When woven with self-colored thread, the variation is one of texture; when contrasting colors are used, the result is both texture and color variation. The variations which are possible are limited only by the imagination of the weaver (Fig. 113).

Use   To add interest to a plain web, household linens, dress and suiting materials, purses

Suitable Materials and Sleying Cotton, linen, or wool

Sample Illustrated (Fig. 113)

WARP	WEFT	PATTERN	REED (*dents per inch*)	SLEY
Cotton, mercerized, 16/2	Cotton, mercerized, 16/2	Carpet warp, 3 strands	15	Double

TIE-UP THREADING DRAFT
2-HARNESS LOOM
a b
2 X 2 2 2
1 X 1 1 1

FIG 111

TIE-UP THREADING DRAFT
4-HARNESS LOOM
a b
4 X 4 4 4
3 X 3 3 3
2 X 2 2 2
1 X 1 1 1

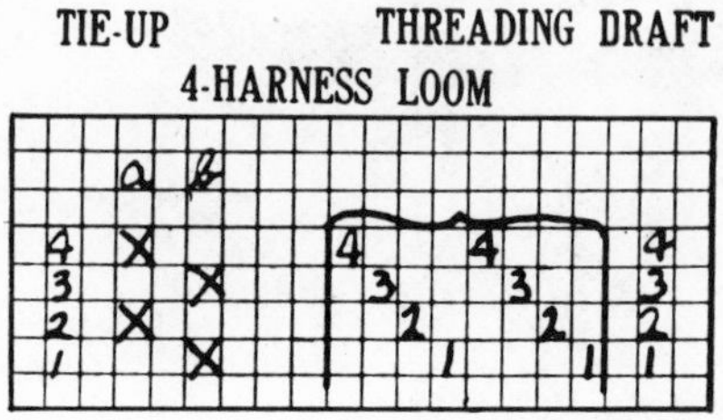

FIG 112

FIG 113

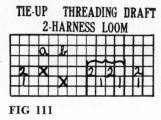

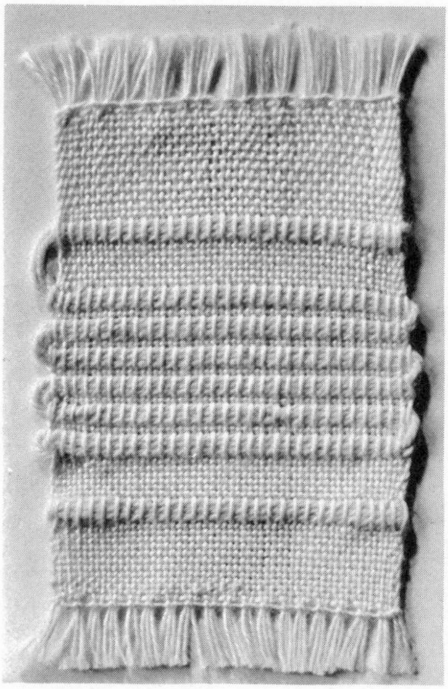

Treadling–Sinking Shed	Treadling–Rising Shed (*No Tie-Up*)
TREADLES	TREADLES OR LEVERS
	a = 1 or 1 and 3; *b* = 2 or 2 and 4
a, b } Cotton mercerized, 16/2	*b*, *a* } Cotton, mercerized, 16/2
a) Carpet warp (three strands together) in the same shed	*b*) Carpet warp (three strands together) in the same shed
b, *a* } Cotton, mercerized, 16/2	*a*, *b* } Cotton, mercerized, 16/2
b) Carpet warp (three strands together) in the same shed	*a*) Carpet warp (three strands together) in the same shed

Repeat as often as necessary to weave the required length, placing the heavy threads where desired.

Problem Try various threads for a textured effect on a plain weave.

TYPE Texture on Plain-Weave Threading · PATTERN Uneven Beating

This is the simplest, though certainly not the best method of achieving a textured effect on a plain weave threading. It consists of beating part of the web into a 50/50 plain weave and the rest into loosely woven borders. It weaves up quickly but it is not durable. It does not wash well as there is nothing to hold the weft threads in place, and whatever passes by catches easily into the long skips.

Use About the only use for this weave is to decorate a lightweight scarf or stole, or to weave stripes in sheer window curtains.

Materials Warp: cotton or wools; weft: materials which do not slip easily, such as nonmercerized cottons, fine wools, and cotton bouclés. Colored or textured threads can be introduced into either the 50/50 or the loosely beaten stripes.

Sample Illustrated (Fig. 114)

WARP	WEPT	REED (dents per inch)	SLEY
Cotton, 8/4	Cotton, 8/4	18	Single

Threading Plain weave

Tie-Up Standard weave

Treadling Plain weave

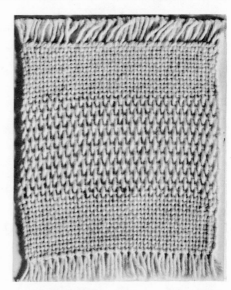

FIG 114

Beating Stripes of any width can be woven, though it is suggested that they be not wider than 2 or 3 in. with 1- or ½-in. bands of the 50/50 plain weave between. The plain-weave bands are beaten to give the 50/50 weave, while in the loosely beaten bands the weft threads are pressed, rather than beaten, back into place. Care must be taken to have the weft threads equally spaced in the open areas.

Problem Set up a short warp of wool and weave it in alternating 50/50 and loosely beaten rows of wool and bouclé of either the same or contrasting colors. Try out various widths for the stripes as well as different color combinations. The result should be a fluffy, colorful scarf.

TYPE Texture on Plain-Weave Threading · PATTERN Threads Spaced in Dents

Texture also can be achieved on a plain-weave threading.

The threading is the same as for all the plain weaves previously given, but here, for the first time, a variation in the sleying produces a different surface or texture.

Uses From the suggested threading, the weaver can work out many ideas which will be useful for rugs, drapes, pillow covers, and bags.

Suitable Materials and Sleying

WARP	WEFT	PATTERN	REED (*dents per inch*)	SLEY
Carpet warp, 8/4	Carpet warp, 8/4	Rug yarn Carpet rags Silk strips	15	Single for 3 dents Skip 3 dents Repeat as often as necessary

Sample Illustrated (Fig. 115)

WARP	WEFT	PATTERN	REED (*dents per inch*)	SLEY
Carpet warp, 8/4	Carpet warp, 8/4	Rug yarn	15	Single for 3 dents Skip 3 dents Repeat

Threading Plain weave

Tie-Up Plain weave

Treadling–Sinking Shed	Treadling–Rising Shed (*No Tie-Up*)
	TREADLES OR LEVERS
	$a = 1$ or 1 and 3; $b = 2$ or 2 and 4
A Carpet warp	*A* Carpet warp
a } Repeat as often as *b* } necessary.	*b* } Repeat as often as *a* } necessary.
B Rug yarn	*B* Rug yarn
a } Repeat as often as necessary in *b* } any desired color arrangement.	*b* } Repeat as often as necessary in *a* } any desired color arrangement.

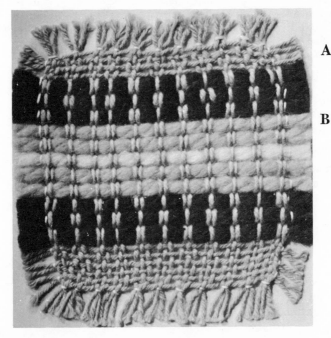

A

B

FIG 115

Problem   Set up a sample in accordance with above directions and experiment with various materials. Keep a record of the results for future reference.

TYPE Texture on Plain-Weave Threading · PATTERN Texture in Warp and in Weft

Further variations in plain weaves can be obtained by using different sizes of threads in the warp as well as in the weft. The size and placement of the threads is one of personal preference. The coarser threads can be used across the entire web, or only to form a border, as on towels or luncheon cloths.

Use To give added interest to plain-weave webs, such as household linens, woolen scarves, purses, and table covers.

Suitable Materials and Sleying

WARP	WEFT	REED (*dents per inch*)	SLEY
Cotton, Egyptian, 30/3	Cotton, Egyptian, 30/3	15 or 18	Double
Carpet warp, 8/4	Carpet warp, 8/4	15 or 16	Single
Linen, heavy	Linen, heavy	15 or 16	Single
Linen, 40/2	Linen, 40/2	20	Double
Wool, fine	Wool, fine	15	Double
Wool, coarse	Wool, coarse	12	Single

Samples Illustrated (Fig. 118)

WARP	WEFT	REED (*dents per inch*)	SLEY
Carpet warp, 8/4	Carpet warp, 8/4	15	Single
Cotton, mercerized, 16/2	Cotton, mercerized, 16/2	15	Double

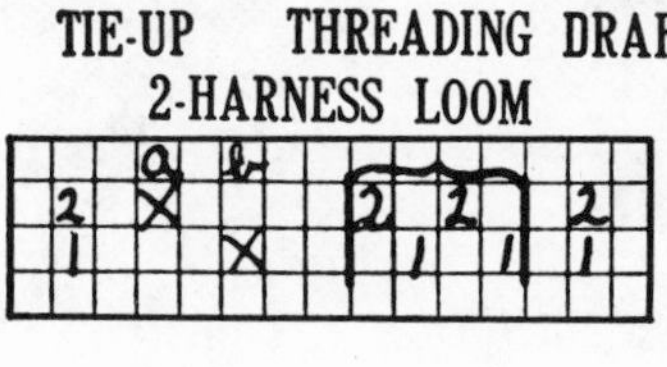
TIE-UP THREADING DRAFT
2-HARNESS LOOM
a b
2
1
X
X
2 2 2
1 1 1

FIG 116

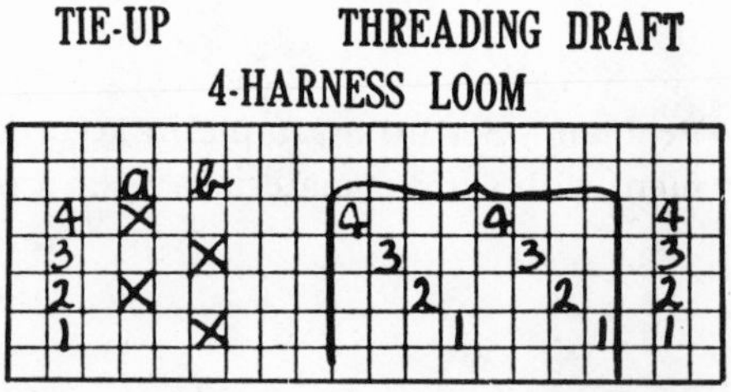
TIE-UP THREADING DRAFT
4-HARNESS LOOM
a b
4 3 2 1
4 3 2 1 4 3 2 1
4 3 2 1

FIG 117

Warp Wind the warp with 4 fine threads, then 4 coarse threads, and thread in this sequence.

Treadling–Sinking Shed	Treadling–Rising Shed (*No Tie-Up*)
TREADLES	**LEVERS OR TREADLES**
	$a = 1$ or 1 and 3; $b = 2$ or 2 and 4

Treadling–Sinking Shed (TREADLES)		Treadling–Rising Shed (LEVERS OR TREADLES)	
A		**A**	
a	Cotton, mercerized, 16/2	b	Cotton, mercerized, 16/2
b	Repeat as often as required	a	Repeat as often as required
B		**B**	
a	Carpet warp, 8/4	b	Carpet warp, 8/4
b	Repeat as often as required	a	Repeat as often as required
C		**C**	
a		b	
b	Carpet warp	a	Carpet warp, 8/4
a		b	
b		a	
a		b	
b	Cotton, mercerized, 16/2	a	Cotton, mercerized, 16/2
a	Cotton warp, 8/2	b	Cotton warp, 8/2
b		a	
	Repeat *C* as often as required		Repeat *C* as often as required

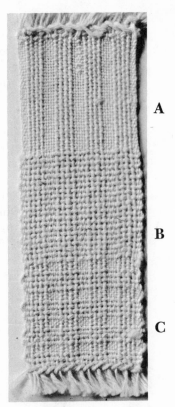

A

B

C

FIG 118

TYPE Texture on Plain-Weave Threading •
PATTERN Supplementary Threads Added to Warp

Colored threads can be added to any plain-colored warp to make stripes along the edges or to add interest in the center of the material.

Procedure   Decide on the colors of threads to be added. Cut them about 12 in. longer than the finished article. Plan the exact place for their insertion.

Beginning at the left side of the warp, draw these threads through the chosen heddles and dents. The original threads are left in place.

Attach ends of colored threads to the cloth-beam rod. If a woven web is on the loom, attach the ends of the threads with a pin as directed for a broken warp thread (page 576). Each new thread must run in a **straight line** from dent to point where it is fastened, otherwise it will cut.

After all new threads have been drawn in and fastened to the front of the loom, draw them snugly to the back of the loom. Tension may be secured in two ways. For instance, weights can be hung on the ends of each group. C clamps are excellent. If sufficiently heavy, they hold the threads at the same tension as the original threads. If the weights are too heavy, the threads are held too taut. If not heavy enough, the shed will not open properly. Another method is to fasten the ends of the groups of colored threads around the back beam. If the article to be woven is short (a short piece is recommended for the first attempt), this method is successful, but the threads must be untied and retied every time the warp is rolled forward.

If long threads are added, for a long piece of weaving, the entire warp should be wound forward onto the cloth beam, the new ends attached to the warp-beam rod, and the entire warp rerolled onto the warp beam.

Samples Illustrated   Figs. 119 and 120 show colored threads added to a plain web, and weft threads for additional design. Weft threads also can be used to make squared material. Luncheon sets can be made with a different colored stripe in each napkin.

Problem   Experiment by adding colored threads to plain warp.

FIG 119

FIG 120

chapter 4

Plain Weaves– Finger Manipulated

The finger-manipulated weaves do not work up as quickly as the loom-controlled weaves and are only for the careful, patient weaver to whom time is no object.

The many weaves of this group have the following in common:

1. They are all threaded on a plain-weave threading.
2. They are woven more easily with a flat than a boat shuttle.
3. A pickup stick can be employed with some of the weaves.
4. The pattern, in most instances, starts at the right selvedge and progresses to the left.
5. To begin the pattern, the outside thread at the right selvedge should be in the upper row of threads when the shed is opened.
6. A slightly slack warp aids in picking up the pattern threads with some of the techniques.
7. Care must be taken with all finger-manipulated weaves to prevent drawing in the selvedge in the pattern areas.
8. Turnings must be made accurately around the correct warp threads to insure the continuity of both pattern and background areas.

TYPE Pattern Threads Inserted Into Web · PATTERN Fleck

Interest can be added to plain-weave webs by inserting bits of contrasting-colored threads at random throughout the web (Fig. 121).

Uses   To decorate luncheon sets, towels, drapes, etc.

Suitable Materials and Sleying   Any material which is suitable for household linens and produces a 50/50 web.

105

Samples Illustrated (Figs. 121 to 123)

WARP	WEFT	REED (dents per inch)	SLEY
Cotton, mercerized, 28/3	Cotton, mercerized, 28/3	15	Double
Cotton, 8/4	Cotton, 8/4	18	Single

Threading   Plain weave

Tie-Up   Standard

Method of Introducing Flecks   The flecks or short pieces of thread are inserted at random in the shed, with the fingers, after the shed is changed. The ends of the threads are left loose on the wrong side, and are not carried from shot to shot (Fig. 121). They also can be left on the right side to form tufts (Fig. 122); this is attractive when a heavy yarn is used for decorating drapery material.

FIG 121

FIG 122

FIG 123

On a 4-harness loom, one harness can be raised where a direct tie-up is used and the decorative thread inserted in this shed, which is then closed. Then the shed for plain weaving is opened. The advantage of using one harness is that the warp threads do not cover as much of the pattern thread and more color shows.

If desired, the flecks can be set in at regular intervals to form a border or a design in the center of the web. In weaving a border or design, the ends of the threads can be carried from one part of the design to the other and not cut as described for the first method. Threads used for the flecks can vary in length and color as in hit-and-miss, or they can be of one color. The fleck weave offers a satisfactory method for using up old bits of colored thread (Fig. 121).

At the top of Fig. 122, another way of adding decoration is shown. The first row of threads for the bottom of the square are inserted in the shed with enough thread extending from each side to complete the figure. Five, or any desired number of rows of plain material are woven in. Then the ends of the thread from each side of the figure are carried along, parallel to the warp threads, and caught down by the next weft thread. The threads are then pulled back to the surface, another plain weft thread is woven in, and the operation is repeated with the decorative threads again brought back to the surface. Five plain weft threads now are woven in and the left-hand decorative thread is passed into the next shed and down through the warp at the upper right-hand corner. The right-hand thread is put down through the warp between the same threads to complete the square. The ends are cut on the wrong side and left hanging. Do not attempt to darn them in as darning would distort the shape of the figure. This material is not reversible.

Figures of any design may be woven in this manner.

Problem   On the end of a plain-weave warp, weave in various decorative threads with odds and ends of contrasting materials.

TYPE Pattern Threads Inserted Into Web · PATTERN Laid-In

When the laid-in technique is mentioned, we immediately associate it with the log-cabin, animal, and humorous mountainfolk designs of weavers

FIG 124

living in the highlands of the southern United States. These weavers are most adept in the laid-in type of weaving and their fingers fly as they weave towels, luncheon sets, aprons, and other articles with designs representing their environment.

The laid-in technique also is found in many other countries. During recent years, weavers of this technique have turned to conventional and abstract designs which will harmonize with modern interiors.

Uses To decorate household linens, aprons, drapes, curtains, table covers, pillows, wall hangings, and other fabrics

Materials Cotton, linen, wool, rayon, nylon, and metallics. To give the pattern character, the thread should be slightly heavier than the background threads.

Sample Illustrated (Fig. 126)

WARP	WEFT	PATTERN	REED (*dents per inch*)	SLEY
Cotton, 8/2	Cotton, 8/2	Cotton perle, No. 10	18	Single

Threading Plain weave

Tie-Up Standard

Treadling Plain weave

Design The design for the laid-in weave can be drawn on a sheet of plain paper and pinned securely under the warp. If the design is to start just above the heading, allow enough blank paper at the bottom of the design to tuck under the end of the warp or web to help hold it in place. Arrange it under the warp to bring the first line of the pattern at the chosen spot in the web. If the design is a geometrical or squared one, like the "Walls of Troy" for instance, it can be worked out on graph paper, each square representing two warp and two weft threads.

The design used for the sample (Fig. 125) was drawn on squared paper, but was fastened under the warp and followed in the same manner as a pattern on plain paper, since thread-by-thread accuracy was not desired.

As the weaving proceeds, the paper is pinned up closer to the fell, and the part that has been woven is either cut off or rolled in with the finished web. What must be guarded against is the shifting of the design paper.

Technique The weaving usually is done with the wrong side up next to the weaver. This facilitates both the turn-ins and the turning of the pattern threads. Some weavers prefer these turnings on the upper or right side. This is a matter of preference, governed somewhat by the design. As weavers disagree about which side shall be the upper side, so also they disagree as to the routine of the pattern and background threads. Some claim that the background thread should enter the shed first, others that the pattern thread should be first. From experience in weaving this technique, the results have been better when the pattern thread was thrown first, for it then can be placed in the exact position desired and beaten back without the interference of the background thread. Should the background thread be of a springy type, the pattern thread is quite likely to slip half under and half over the background thread in spite of the weaver's efforts to keep it in place. Many of the weavers in the southern United States follow the routine described here. This method also carries out the routine followed

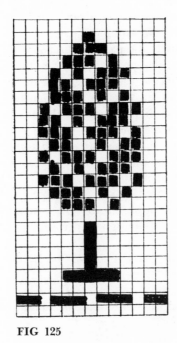

FIG 125

FIG 126

in much of our weaving in which the pattern thread is followed by the tabby thread. The weaver should experiment with both methods, then choose the one he prefers, following it consistently to the end of the pattern. What will happen when the routine is changed is shown in the second pattern row at the base of the tree in Fig. 126.

To Weave   Weave in the heading and the required amount of background, ending with the shuttle at the right selvedge and the outside selvedge thread in the upper row of threads. Pin the pattern in position under the warp.

1. Insert the pattern thread, which has been made into a butterfly (page 128), in the open shed from right to left. Turn the loose end around the warp thread that is at the right boundary of the pattern and back into the shed. Bring the butterfly to the surface at the left boundary of the pattern. If the pattern is in two or more distinct areas separated from each other by three or more threads, a butterfly will be required for each area because it is not good weaving to carry the pattern threads across the plain background from area to area. After the pattern thread or threads are in place, draw the beater gently back against the fell. This will hold the threads in place. Release the beater and without changing the shed, throw the background thread from right to left. Beat the thread back ever so lightly and open the opposite shed. Gauge the beating in laid-in weaving by the background areas rather than the pattern areas. If beaten tightly, the pattern areas build up into peaks and the background areas slope away from the patterns. The result is anything but pleasing. This fabric is loosely woven with a play of color between background and pattern threads.

2. With the new shed open, insert the pattern thread or threads from left to right, carefully following the design pinned under the warp. Press the thread back against the fell, release the beater, and throw the background thread through the shed from left to right. Beat lightly and change the shed. The pattern butterflies and the background threads must always travel in the *same direction* through the shed, that is all from right-to-left or all from left-to-right. The pattern thread is carried on top of the web, from pattern row to pattern row, unless the skips from area to area are over three threads, then the pattern thread must be cut, ended off in the shed, and started anew for the new area.

Continue with the right-to-left and left-to-right routine until the pattern has been completed. Watch the design paper. If it shifts, it will throw the pattern off completely.

3. Finish the article with a border to match the first border or in any manner desired.

Problem Make a simple design and weave a sample of a laid-in technique, paying special attention to the beating.

TYPE Pattern Threads Inserted Into Web · PATTERN Italian Laid-In

The Italian laid-in technique is recommended to the weaver who is looking for a speedy, effective method of decorating aprons, children's dresses, or articles for household use.

Any simple design can be used which need not be followed with the accuracy required for many techniques, and, if the weaver is clever with her fingers, the pattern can be woven in without a predrawn design. Simple initials can be woven with this technique.

A similar type of laid-in, the Calabrian, is woven on a pattern shed.

Uses As mentioned above and for place mats, towels, etc.

Materials For the warp and weft use those materials which are suitable for the article being woven. For the pattern, use bits of heavy perle cotton: any cottons that contrast in color, size, and texture with the background thread. If wools are used, as for instance on a pocket design for a child's dress, there should be no long skips to catch. Interesting effects are obtained with bouclés. When a heavy, natural-color linen is used against a pure white line background, the effect is rich and subtle.

FIG 127

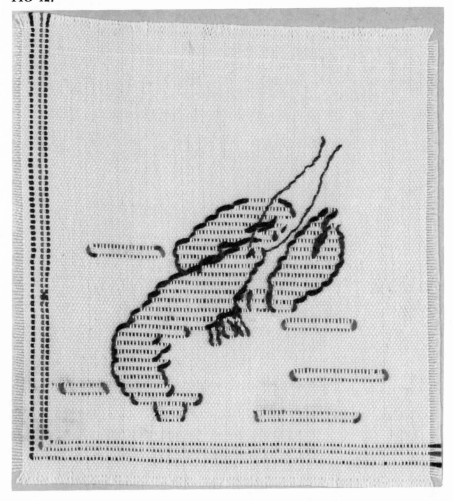

Sample Illustrated (Fig. 127)

WARP	WEFT	PATTERN	REED	SLEY
			(dents per inch)	
Cotton, 16/2	Cotton, 16/2	Cotton perle, No. 5	16	Double

Number of Threads in Warp   100

Threading   Plain weave

Tie-Up   Standard

Treadling   Plain weave

Weave with the right side up and finish off the ends on the back.

Weave the heading the desired length in a plain weave, choose the location of the pattern, and weave it in as follows:

1. Cut a piece of pattern thread about 18 in. long. Lay it in the open shed so that the middle of the thread is at the spot where the pattern is to start. Bring the ends of the thread out on the surface at the right and left boundaries of the pattern area (Fig. 128). Throw the tabby shuttle through the same shed from selvedge to selvedge, beat, open the opposite shed, and beat again. The background threads are not shown in Fig. 128.

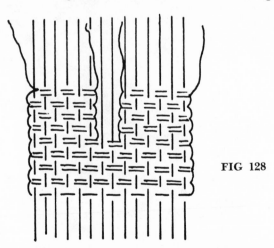

FIG 128

2. It is customary to weave an uneven number of rows of plain weaving, usually three, between each row of pattern threads, but this depends on the design. The pattern threads frame the pattern where they run at right angles to the weft, and sometimes the effect desired is gained best by a longer or shorter skip than the three threads would give, so weave in the background accordingly. Beat and open the new shed.

3. Insert the second pattern row according to the design, crossing the

two threads in the shed. The right thread passing to the left and the left to the right. Bring the ends to the surface. Follow this with a background thread, beat, close shed, beat again, and weave in the desired number of background threads. Continue with the routine until the entire pattern has been woven.

4. In some designs, where the pattern area divides into smaller units, the original thread continues up one unit, with a new thread laid-in for the new unit.

Problem   Set up a warp of linen or cotton and weave a guest towel with an original design at the end.

TYPE Pattern Threads Inserted Into Web · PATTERN Spanish Eyelet or Openwork

This weave, sometimes referred to as the Spanish-Lace weave, is one of the more attractive and lacy finger weaves, though it, too, is only for the patient weaver who will take time to make the weft turnings accurately and to beat the threads back carefully to form the correct pattern. Theoretically, the interest lies in the size and shape of the eyelets, yet very handsome effects are obtained by leaving the weft threads loose in the warp, instead of drawing them up into tight groups.

These instructions cover only the basic theory of the weave, but once it has been mastered the weaver can originate designs or follow the suggestions of leading weaving publications, in which the details covering the extension of the weave are given.

Uses   The weave is suitable for decorative borders on peasant skirts, drapes, and household linens. Interesting color effects can be achieved by introducing heavy threads in the border patterns of skirts, especially if the color choice is harmonious. Wool drapes with rows of heavy self-colored wool are quite striking where a formal effect is desired.

Suitable Materials   Avoid threads which slip easily for they will not stay in place too well.

Cotton, linens, and wool are suitable. The weft threads should be sturdy or they will break when the groups of warp threads are drawn up. Therefore, avoid single-ply linen or very fine single-ply wool. Heavy linen threads produce exceptionally nice pieces in this weave.

Sample Illustrated (Fig. 131)

WARP	WEFT	REED (dents per inch)	SLEY
Cotton, 8/2	Cotton, 8/2	18	Single

Threading   Plain weave

Tie-Up   Standard

Treadling   Background, plain weave

Pattern   After the heading of plain weave has been woven in the desired width, start the first row of the pattern. A slim poke or flat shuttle (page 9), carrying the weft thread, should be at the right-hand selvedge and the shed opened so that the outside thread is in the top row of threads.

1. There are to be 10 threads in each pattern area; therefore, pass the shuttle into the shed and bring it up to the surface between the fifth and sixth warp threads of the *upper* row of threads (the ninth and tenth threads in Fig. 129). With the tip of the shuttle, tap the weft back to the edge of the last row of plain weaving. The beater is not used for beating the pattern threads.

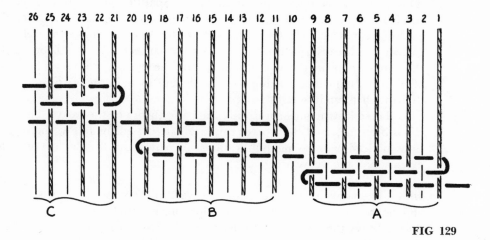

FIG 129

2. Change the shed.

3. Insert the shuttle back into the shed from left to right. Count the warp threads. There should be five threads lying on the *top* of the shuttle. Push the warp thread down against the first pattern shed and pull the weft thread tight enough to gather the warp threads into a bunch or "bouquet," as it is sometimes called.

4. Change the shed.

5. Again insert the shuttle from the right, but this time pass it under the first 10 *top* threads and bring it to the surface between the tenth and eleventh threads of the *top* row (the nineteenth and twentieth warp threads in Fig. 129).

6. Change the shed and beat back the thread with the shuttle point. Tighten the weft.

7. Again insert the shuttle in the shed from left to right, but this time bring it to the surface between the sixth and fifth *top* warp threads.

8. Change the shed and beat the weft into position with the shuttle point.

9. Insert the shuttle where it was taken out of the shed and return it, through the shed, to the left, bringing it out between the fifteenth and sixteenth *top* threads. Beat down the weft with the shuttle point, change the shed, and tighten the weft thread around the warp as for other rows.

10. Continue the above routine across the web to the left selvedge, dropping five warp threads but gaining five new ones every third row.

11. Once the left selvedge is reached, two courses are open to the weaver. The shed may be opened, the tabby thread returned to the right selvedge, and a second row of eyelets woven from right to left. If this is done to the weft pattern threads should turn around the same warp threads as in the first pattern row. Interesting effects also can be achieved by splitting the groups of warp threads (Fig. 130).

The alternate course is to weave in the pattern from left to right. In the center of the sample (Fig. 131), where the weft thread has not gathered up the warp threads into groups, the first two rows of lacelike designs slant in the same direction, while in the other two rows they slant in the opposite direction, forming a leaflike design. This is accomplished by weaving the

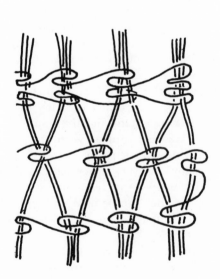

FIG 130

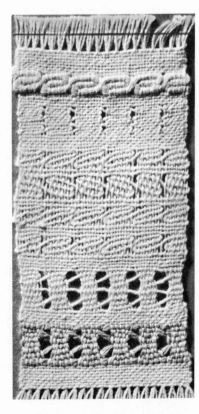

FIG 131

first pattern row as described in steps 1 to 11, ending with two rows of plain weave. The shuttle now will be on the left side. The second row of the pattern is then woven from left to right, reversing the procedure given above. That is, the shuttle passes under the first five warp threads in the upper row, returns to the left selvedge, then passes back from left to right and is brought out at the right of the tenth warp thread from the left selvedge in the upper row. This procedure is repeated across the web. It is necessary, when the weave is reversed, to turn the weft around the same warp threads as in the row directly beneath it. Before attempting to arrange the pattern threads, weave the pattern row completely across, then follow with a plain weave which is pressed into position by the beater. Arrange the pattern threads in the desired position in the warp. A large, blunt tapestry needle does this more efficiently than the shuttle point. Watch the selvedges in this weave. There is an inclination to draw them in.

Refer now to Fig. 131 which illustrates variations of the Spanish-Eyelet weave.

The first, or bottom, row above the plain weave is woven with a candlewick pattern thread which gives an entirely different effect than the second row, which is woven with 8/4 cotton on the slightly finer 8/2 cotton warp. In each of these rows, the pattern has been repeated twice.

The third section of the sample shows the lacelike design recently referred to in the text. It has been woven in the same manner as the two previous patterns except that the warp threads were not drawn up into groups. Perhaps this cannot be considered an orthodox way of weaving the Spanish-Eyelet technique, but it is one way of producing lacelike designs in sheer wool stoles or drapes.

In the fourth section of the sample, each row of the design has been beaten back tightly against the edge of the web, which is called the fell. The eyelets of this design are practically nonexistent and the result is not particularly interesting, but it does illustrate what happens when the pattern rows are beaten with the beater instead of the shuttle point.

In the top pattern area on the sample, a very heavy pattern thread has been beaten back tightly into the warp. Any resemblance to true Spanish Eyelet has been lost. However, the idea can be used and will work up rather quickly for borders on skirts or drapes where a color or material contrast is desired.

If the warp groups are to be split, it is necessary to have an even number of threads in each group, half of which are taken from each group to form the new group.

Further interest can be obtained by splitting the groups of warp threads after a few pattern rows have been woven. A very lacy, delicate effect can be achieved if fine threads are used.

Problem Practice various ways of weaving Spanish Eyelet, working out some original designs.

TYPE Pattern Threads Inserted Into Web With Fingers • PATTERN Danish Medallion

The Medallion, which is identified as "Danish," has been especially popular in the Scandinavian countries, although it also has been found in many other countries.

It is a weft weave in that the design is made by the weft threads. There are two methods of weaving in the weft threads, one of which gives a heavier design while the other is perhaps easier to weave. Instructions are given for both methods.

Use and Materials   The Danish Medallion effectively decorates the ends of scarves and stoles. If metallic and rayon or nylon threads of either finer or heavier grist than the background thread are used, the contrast against the dull wool is particularly pleasing. The medallions generally are outlined with a heavier thread, of either the same or a contrasting color. Place mats, or other household articles of cotton or linen, are practical and durable if two sizes and shades of natural linen are used. This weave lends itself well to decorative motifs on blouses and children's dresses. Designs worked out on graph paper can be followed easily, but the more simple the design the more effective the result.

Sample Illustrated (Fig. 135)

WARP	WEFT	PATTERN	REED (dents per inch)	SLEY
Cotton, 8/2	Cotton, 8/2	Perle cotton, 5/2	20	Single

Threading   Plain weave

Tie-Up   Standard

Treadling   Plain weave

To Weave

Method 1 (Fig. 135)   1. Thread a length of the pattern thread into a blunt tapestry needle or wind it onto a steel netting needle or shuttle.

2. Weave in a heading of the background thread, ¾ or 1 in. wide, or as wide as desired. Close the shed and beat when the heading has been completed.

3. Open the shed and throw the pattern-thread shuttle through it from left to right, turning in the thread end at the left selvedge. Beat and change the shed.

4. Weave in six rows of the plain weave with the background thread, beat, and change the shed.

5. Carry the pattern thread along the right selvedge and into the shed; the outside right selvedge should lie in the top row of threads.

6. Pass the netting shuttle or large needle into the shed, and bring it out with the point toward the weaver between the sixth and seventh threads. Place the left thumb on the pattern thread to hold it in position (Fig. 132).

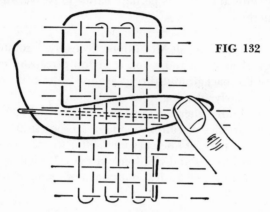

FIG 132

7. Pass the shuttle or needle down between the warp threads and bring it up between the first row of the pattern thread and the last row of threads of the background area.

8. Taking the thread which has been held down by the left thumb, twist it around under the point of the needle from right to left. It is important that the thread is turned in this manner each time, or there will be a twist in the weave.

9. Draw the needle up, out of the web, and toward you, then pull the thread taut, pull it toward the beater, and tighten it. The tying of this knot creates the hole between the medallion units; the tighter the knot, the larger the hole. Thought should be given here as to the effect desired. Which is to be emphasized, the holes or the design? When the knot is drawn up tight, the resulting design will be oval or round, depending upon the number of threads in the warp.

10. Continue with this routine across the web, following rows of plain weave with additional pattern rows, and ending with the plain weave heading.

Method 2 (Fig. 133) With the second method it is customary to use two shuttles, one to carry the background thread, the other for the pattern thread. However, if the material is not too wide, or if the design areas are small, use the steel netting shuttle or weave in a length of the pattern thread with the fingers. The pattern threads are double where they cross the web at right angles, resulting in a bolder design than that of the first method. After the heading, the first row of pattern thread, and the nine rows of plain weaving have been woven, proceed as follows:

1. Open the shed and insert the pattern thread from right to left, allowing it to lie loosely in the shed for the moment.

2. Push the crochet hook down through the web between the sixth and seventh threads, and between the last row of background weave and the first shot of pattern thread. Be sure the point of the hook is down.

3. Push the crochet hook up toward the edge of the weaving and hook it around the pattern thread where it lies loose in the shed, carefully drawing the loop to the surface toward you (Fig. 133).

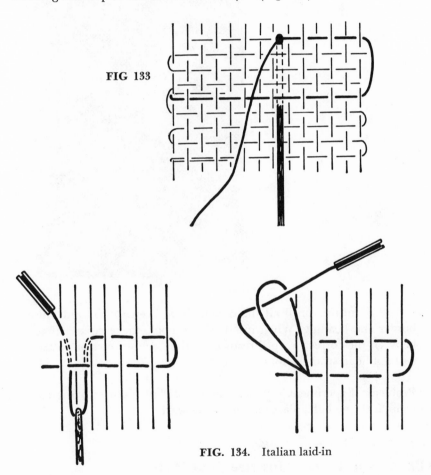

FIG 133

FIG. 134. Italian laid-in

4. When the loop is large enough, put the shuttle through from left to right. If the weaving is being done without a shuttle, pass the end of the pattern thread completely through the loop (Fig. 134).

5. Draw up the thread until the knot is at the edge of the web and pull it tight. Be sure the threads that form the loop are not twisted across each other.

6. Proceed as above toward the left, passing the shuttle under the desired number of threads, bringing the loop to the surface each time, and locking it.

7. If an over-all pattern is desired (Fig. 135), weave in a row of the pattern thread, from left to right, followed by the desired number of background threads, and weave in a second pattern row. In the sample, three background threads were used.

FIG 135

8. Continue until all the designs have been woven and finish with a border and heading. When inserting the hook, make certain that it passes between the correct warp threads each time or the rows of pattern threads will not lie in straight lines.

Problem Experiment with both methods. Plan and use an original arrangement at the end of a place mat or a wool scarf.

TYPE Design Threads Inserted Into Web · PATTERN Brooks Bouquet

This weave, named for Marguerite Brooks, an expert in bobbin lace, is simple and quick to weave once the process is learned. The weft thread is passed around a group of warp threads and pulled tight. The knot holds the groups in place. In the center of the spaces between the groups, a warp and weft thread cross at right angles.

Many variations are possible, both in the number of threads in each group and in the arrangement of the warp threads within the groups. A group of three to five strands of fine thread produces a very fine, sheer over-all pattern, while a grouping of eight or ten threads is more effective in the end border of a wool scarf or stole. The Brooks Bouquet does not offer the opportunities for color treatment or thread contrast found in the Danish Medallion, although a very pleasing effect can be obtained by graduating the colors of successive rows of the pattern from a light to a dark shade. The chief difficulty with this variation is concealing the ends; it can be done by a careful, painstaking weaver.

Use It is an effective weave for borders on wool scarves and stoles, household linens, curtains, blouses, and children's dresses.

Sample Illustrated (Fig. 136)

WARP	WEFT	REED (dents per inch)	SLEY
Cotton, 8/2	Cotton, 8/2	18	Single

For curtains: 16/2 cotton; for blouses: 40/2 linen; for stoles: 2/16 or 2/32 wool

Threading Plain weave

Tie-Up Standard

Treadling Plain weave

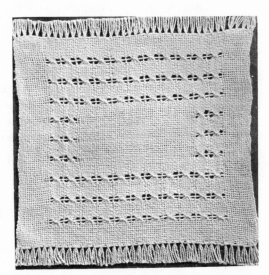

FIG 136

To Weave First weave in a heading of the desired width, alternating treadles *a* and *b* for the plain weave and ending at the right selvedge.

1. Open the shed. The right-hand outside thread should be in the upper row. If it is not, change the rotation of the plain weave so that it will be. Change the rotation by cutting and ending the weft and starting it from the opposite side.

2. The number of warp threads should be exactly divisible by the number of threads in each pattern area or group. In Figure 136, there are 120 threads in the warp, which provides considerable scope for the pattern arrangement.

3. Insert the shuttle from the right under 12 threads and bring it to the surface between the twelfth and thirteenth threads of the upper shed.

4. Carry the shuttle back to the right, across four threads of the upper row of threads, and insert it into the shed again, as before, bringing it out between the sixteenth and seventeenth threads.

5. With the right thumb and forefinger, hold the weft thread at the right selvedge where it enters the shed and, with the left hand, draw up the weft thread until it is taut and draws the first group of four threads tightly together.

6. Now pass the shuttle back to the right, across the upper row of threads, inserting it into the shed between the twentieth and twenty-first threads and bringing it out between the twenty-fourth and twenty-fifth threads. Draw up the knot to make the second group. Do not pull the knot so tight that it pulls one pattern area toward the next. The tension of the thread between the groups should be the same as that of a plain weave at the border. This is achieved by holding the thread in place while the knot around the group is being tightened. It will require practice to master this step.

7. Continue tying the groups until eleven have been tied. If the groups of thread have been counted off correctly, eight threads will remain for the left border. Beat, change the shed, and beat again.

8. Weave in the desired number of rows of plain weaving. In the sample, nine were woven in. In order to have the shuttle at the right selvedge to start the second pattern area, it is necessary to have an uneven number of threads between the weft threads which tie the knot. This will also bring up, in each pattern row, the same set of threads around which the first row of knots was made. There is no tying of threads in the lower row of the shed since the threads are held in place by the rows of plain weave in the pattern areas.

This weave proceeds quite rapidly once the first row is counted off since the shuttle enters and leaves successive rows at the same warp threads. Pattern arrangement is a matter of choice and imagination.

Problem Set up the warp and weave a child's scarf with at least three pattern rows separated with rows of plain weave.

TYPE Pattern Threads Inserted Into Web ·
PATTERN Leno Pickup

The leno weave is not only a familiar one, but it is also believed to be a very old, universally known weave.

Products of commercial leno looms, ranging from dishcloths to wool scarves, window curtains, and clothing, are found in practically every department store. The words "gauze" and "marquisette" are allied closely with leno but have a wider meaning than simply a weave-technique classification. Aside from the commercial method of weaving leno, there are two other ways in which it can be produced. One is by the addition of half heddles or doups to a standard foot loom and the other is with a pickup stick on any plain-weave threading. The directions given here are for the pickup method.

While this process does not move quickly, it is adequate for headings and decorative borders in household linens, wool scarves, and stoles. Its greatest virtue is that delicate, lacy materials can be woven with full assurance that the threads will not slip out of place. Leno is most effective if woven in a single color. A rough, single-ply linen weft on a two- or three-ply linen warp gives an interesting fabric.

Uses For household articles, such as dishcloths and curtains; for woolen scarves and stoles; and for the coarsely woven, cotton undershirt worn by those subjected to extreme cold.

Sample Illustrated (Fig. 137)

WARP	WEFT	REED (dents per inch)	SLEY
Cotton, 8/2	Cotton, 8/4	18	Single

Number of Threads in Warp 60

Threading Plain weave

Tie-Up Standard

Treadling Headings and background, plain weave

Treadling of Pattern Areas, Leno Pickup If obtainable, a fisherman's small, mesh, wooden netting shuttle is excellent. If unobtainable, a smooth, fairly wide pickup stick will be needed in addition to the flat shuttle.

Sample I (Fig. 137)

1. Weave in the heading in the usual manner, beat, and open the new shed. The shuttle should be on the right, and the right-hand outside warp

thread should be in the upper row of threads. With the left hand, draw back to the left the outside thread of the upper row, slip the point of the pickup stick under the first thread in the lower row and tip the point up over the top thread. This is more easily done if the warp is a bit slack. The lower thread now lies on top of the stick, and the first warp thread, which was originally at the right, is now underneath the stick.

2. With the left hand, draw the second thread in the upper row back to the right, slip the point of the pickup stick under the second thread in the lower row, and tip the point of the stick up over the top thread, which, when released from the left hand, slips under the stick. This may seem a bit awkward at first, but after a few threads have been picked up the process is quite rapid. Continue this pickup across the entire weft.

3. After all the threads from the under row are on the top of the stick, turn it up on its side, and check to be sure the crosses all lie in the same direction. Slip the flat shuttle through this shed from right to left.

4. Remove the pickup stick and beat. If the netting shuttle is used, draw it directly through the shed.

FIG 137

FIG 138

5. Change the shed and pass the shuttle through from left to right. Changing the shed automatically weaves the second row of leno.

6. Weave the third row, picking up the threads as you did for the first row.

7. Continue until the desired length has been woven.

Rows of plain weaving may separate the rows of the leno weave, or the pickup rows may follow along, one after another.

As with other weaves in this chapter, the weaver's imagination can be given free rein. Some variations are made by twisting two, three, or even four lower warp threads onto the pickup stick and over the same number of threads in the upper row. A 3-and-1 combination also is used, and the groups of threads split as in the Spanish Eyelet (page 113). As with other finger-manipulated weaves, pay special attention to the selvedges. They should not draw in.

Refer to Sample I (Fig. 137).

The tops rows show the single- or two-thread leno twist; the second row shows the double- or four-thread twist; and the third row the four-and-four-thread twist. These rows are followed by a wide row of single and double twist.

At the bottom is shown a simple pattern in pickup leno against a plain-weave background. This technique is particularly well suited for weaving ecclesiastical linens where simplicity is desired. Borders and symbols can be woven in wherever desired, which is somewhat difficult when the design is loom-controlled.

The design is drawn on graph paper, each square representing one twist. Due to variations in sleying, beating, and threads used, the weaving does not always work out exactly as planned on the paper, but once a sample is woven the weaver will know exactly how to proceed.

To keep the background areas the same texture as the headings, build them up by weaving to the edge of the leno design in the plain weave, change the shed, return the shuttle to the right selvedge, change the shed, and return to the edge of the pattern area. Weave the design over the designated number of threads in the leno pickup, continuing to the left selvedge in the plain weave. Change the shed and weave back to the pattern area; change the shed and return the shuttle to the left selvedge. This completes the build-up. A close study of the sample will show where the build-up is made. Change the shed.

Pass the shuttle through to the right selvedge and repeat the routine, starting with the build-up of the right area of the plain weave.

Sample II (Fig. 138)

This sample, woven in coarse thread, shows the manner in which the threads twist around each other. The light threads represent the upper row of threads and the dark ones the lower row.

Always remember, in making the twist, that no matter how many threads are involved, the thread or threads from the lower set of threads are lifted up and to the right over a corresponding number of threads in the upper row.

Problem Set up a sample and practice weaving various leno twists, ending with an original design.

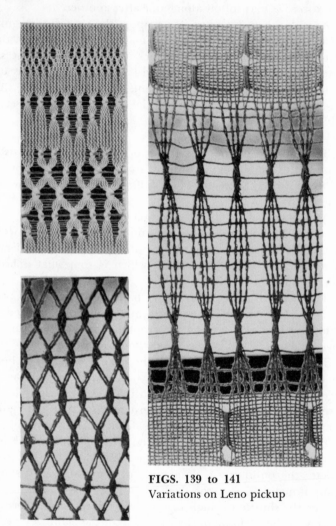

FIGS. 139 to 141
Variations on Leno pickup

TYPE Pattern Threads on Surface · PATTERN Brocade

Beautiful examples of brocade weaving are on display in museums throughout the world. Perhaps the most beautiful brocades originate in the Orient. These elaborately designed materials are woven of exquisitely fine silk threads and often embellished with gold and silver threads. Floral, bird, and dragon designs predominate.

"One of the finest specimens is the Danzig brocade . . . found in the Mariakirchen in Europe. It is a black silk brocaded with gold, the design being of polygon frames containing parrots, with dragons occupying the interspace."[1]

None of the brocades woven today are comparable to these priceless antiques, but the technique is one that can be adapted to our modern needs.

Weavers, however, disagree on the exact technique. One authority states that in a brocade technique the pattern weft naturally passes from selvedge to selvedge. Another feels that in the true brocades, the pattern weft is restricted to the limits of the design and does not pass from selvedge to selvedge. Others state that real brocading differs from other inlay weaves since the pattern weft is cut to the proper length before it is laid in the shed. Still others point out that there are only three kinds of brocade. In view of the variation of opinions expressed by serious students of brocade techniques, it seems that it can be woven to please the individual.

Space being too limited to illustrate the various methods, only one will be explained in this text, a simple brocade which can be elaborated on by the weaver.

Uses   To decorate aprons, skirts, place mats, or towels in geometric, stylized, or free-form designs. The gifted weaver can develop his own artistic designs for wall hangings, screens, and pictures.

Do not use the brocade weave where long skips on either the front or back of the material would be objectionable or where the web is sheer, since the pattern threads carried across the back of the material would show through.

Suitable Materials   Fine cotton, perle cotton, or linen for background; nylons, silks, and metallics for patterns. Use coarser material with shorter skips for aprons, bibs, blouses, and place mats.

Samples Illustrated (Figs. 144 and 145)

WARP	WEFT	PATTERN	REED (dents per inch)	SLEY
Sample 1: Cotton, 8/4	Cotton, 8/4	Cotton, 8/4	18	Single
	Cotton, 8/2	Rayon, medium	20	Single
Sample 2: Cotton, 8/2				

Threading   Plain weave

Tie-Up   Standard

Treadling   Plain weave

Design If a geometric design is desired, block it out on graph paper. If a stylized or free-form design (Fig. 145) is preferred, sketch it on paper.

To Weave Weave the heading in the desired width and decide on the placement of the pattern. It is easier to weave this technique with butterflies or bobbins than with a shuttle.

In a brocade, the pattern thread passes over the surface of the warp covering the desired pattern areas. Using a closed shed, bring up the pattern thread between the warp threads that lie at one end of the design, pass it over the pattern area, and then insert the pattern thread between the warp threads at the other edge of the design. Pass the shuttle or butterfly under the warp to the next area of the design, then bring it to the surface as described above. A tabby thread is thrown in between each pattern thread. There will be many loose threads and long pattern skips on the back of the material (Fig. 144).

This technique is woven with the right side facing the weaver.

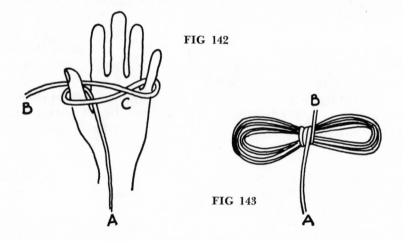

FIG 142

FIG 143

To Make the Butterfly Hold the left hand up with the palm toward the body, the thumb facing outward (Fig. 142). Hold the end of the thread *A* between the thumb and palm with the end hanging toward the wrist. Turn the thread across the thumb and in front of the palm between the ring and little fingers. Turn the thread around the little finger, across the palm, and between the thumb and palm, bringing it around the thumb and across the palm again, between the ring and little fingers. A figure 8 is formed by the crossing of the threads in the center of the palm at *C*. Continue to wind back and forth until a fair-sized butterfly has been wound. Cut the thread from the ball of weft, leaving an end about 6 or 8 in. Wrap this end, *B*, around the center of the butterfly at *C* several times, finishing with a couple of half hitches (simple knot). The butterfly (Fig. 143) unwinds easily when end *A*, which was held between thumb and palm during the winding, is pulled. Start weaving with end *A*.

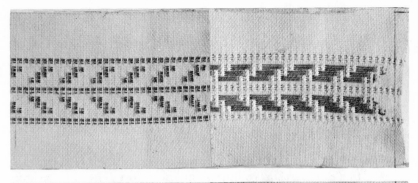

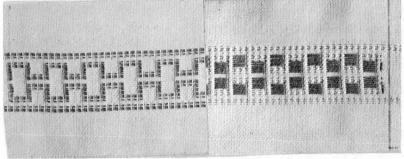

FIG 144

FIG 145

Problem Set up the warp and weave a small apron with a border in an original brocade design.

TYPE Pattern Threads on Surface ·
PATTERN Dukagång and Half Dukagång

People are inclined to think of dukagång as a distinctively Scandinavian weave, belonging specifically to Sweden, and, therefore, may be surprised to find it in general use in other countries. However, it is in Sweden that the weave has been highly developed and it is to the Swedish teachers that we turn for our information. A literal translation of the word *dukagång*, according to one Swedish teacher, is "straight little paths in the cloth." And this is what the weaver should strive for.

In Scandinavian countries, articles woven in this technique grace practically all homes and public buildings. Designs usually are stylized and similar to those used for rölakan and åklae. There are two types of dukagång, the whole and the half. The half dukagång is the more familiar. The threads which form the pattern areas lie on the surface of a plain-weave background being caught, or tied down, by every fourth warp thread (Fig. 150). In the whole dukagång, the background areas, as well as the pattern areas, are filled in (Fig. 149).

Uses For wall hangings and pictures, pillow tops, borders for draperies and skirts, purses, bags, tablecloths, household linens, simple designs on children's clothing, blouses, and aprons. This technique is not suitable for floor or car rugs.

Suitable Materials For the warp: either cotton or tow linen, the size depending on the article being woven.

For the weft: wool and cotton, both plain and perle, are suitable. Linen should not be used unless it is fine ply and closely sleyed. Single-ply linen is too springy. Threads that slip, such as rayon and nylon, are not satisfactory. Soft threads that pack in and stay in place are best. Fine, single-ply homespun yarns, vegetable-dyed, are excellent for wall hangings, pillows, and warm winter skirts.

Three strands of single-ply yarn in different shades, wound into the butterfly (Fig. 143) with one strand of the same single ply for the tabby

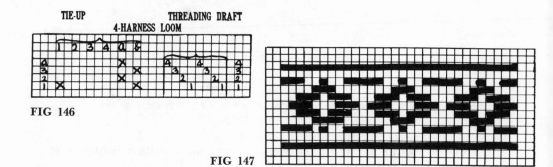

TIE-UP   THREADING DRAFT
4-HARNESS LOOM

FIG 146

FIG 147

thread, make a good combination for a wall hanging (see frontispiece). Cotton, linen, and perle cotton are good for household linens with designs in six-strand floss.

Samples Illustrated (Figs. 149 to 151)

WARP	WEFT	PATTERN	REED (*dents per inch*)	SLEY
Sample 1 (Fig. 149):				
Cotton, 8/4	Homespun yarn, 2-ply	Homespun yarn, 3-ply	16	Single
Sample 2 (Figs. 150 and 151):				
Cotton, 8/2	Cotton, 8/2	Homespun yarn, 2-ply	18	Single

Threading   Plain weave for both 2- and 4-harness looms

Tie-Up for 2-Harness Loom   Standard

Tie-Up for 4-Harness Loom   This is the first departure from the plain-weave tie-up and treadling that has appeared so far in the text. In the plain-weave tie-up, treadles *a* and *b* operate in alternating sequence and all pattern threads are picked up with the fingers. This weave is a combination of loom and finger manipulation.

In making the new tie-up, do not touch the tie-up for harnesses 2 and 4 (the *a* treadle) or 1 and 3 (the *b* treadle) which are used for the plain-weave background and the headings. Tie the lam which controls harness 1 to treadle 1; when this treadle is depressed it will pull down all the threads threaded on harness 1. These threads become the binder or tie-down threads which hold the pattern threads in place. The harnesses carrying the warp threads which lie under the pattern thread areas remain stationary.

The above instructions are for a counterbalanced loom. For a jack-type, rising-shed loom, or a table loom with levers where there is no tie-up, treadles 2, 3, and 4 are depressed together. This lifts all the threads except those threaded on harness 1, which are the tie-down threads.

To Weave   The following instructions apply to both the 2-harness pickup and the 4-harness techniques and to both the half and the whole dukagång.

Dukagång designs are drawn on graph paper. Each square represents three pattern threads; the vertical lines between the pattern squares represent the warp threads; the horizontal lines the tabby treads between the pattern rows.

Dukagång is woven with the wrong side facing the weaver. Check the under, or right, side for errors with a hand mirror. There is a type of dukagång woven right side up but there is doubt as to its correctness. It does not compare to the true dukagång in which each pattern thread is turned neatly around the designated warp thread and no little loops appear at the edges of the pattern areas.

There are two schools of thought regarding the tabby thread. Some authorities state definitely that there should be two tabby threads between each pattern row; others insist there should be only one. When a single tabby is thrown between the pattern shots, the pattern threads lie in pairs and it requires four pattern shots to square up the pattern. On the other hand, if two tabby shots are thrown between each pattern thread, three pattern threads usually will square the pattern.

The size of the pattern also affects the result. If the pattern thread is three times as heavy as the tabby thread, two tabby shots should be used. The background, too, must be considered. Does the finer thread produce a 50/50 plain-weave background? It is sometimes necessary, if the pattern thread is much coarser than the background thread, to build up the borders on each side of the pattern areas. It is not customary to bring the pattern threads to the very edge of the web. Again, if the tabby thread is too coarse, the pattern will lack compactness. Experiment to achieve a pleasing harmony between threads, sleying, and beating. Dukagång should be well beaten with a 50/50 background.

Dukagång can be woven on either a 2-harness loom, with the aid of a pickup stick, or on a 4-harness loom where the treadles bring up the threads which tie down the pattern threads. In either case the pattern threads are wound into butterflies or onto small shuttles and inserted with the fingers. During the weaving, all the butterflies enter the shed from the same direction, that is, all from the right or all from the left.

The first row of pattern should enter the shed on the right, after the a, "2–4," tabby shed has been closed and the tabby shuttle brought out at the right selvedge.

The ends of the pattern threads are caught down under the middle thread of each three-thread pattern square, being carried along in the pattern thread row under the center thread of three squares. When only one square is woven, the ends are left to be darned in with a needle after the weaving has been removed from the loom. It is not advisable to carry the pattern threads from one pattern area to another across the background. Each area should have its own butterfly.

If the border areas do not build up even with the pattern areas, enter an extra thread or two in the border area every few rows. This is done by taking the tabby shuttle to the edge of the pattern area, changing the shed, passing the shuttle out at the selvedge, changing the shed, and throwing the shuttle completely across. Build up the opposite edge in the same manner.

To Weave on a 4-Harness Loom   Weave the heading in the desired width in plain weave.

1. Open the pattern shed (treadle 1 on the counterbalanced loom; treadles 2, 3, and 4 on the rising-shed loom). From the right, insert the butterfly or bobbin carrying the pattern thread into the pattern shed of

one thread down, three threads up. Follow the design on graph paper where one square equals the three pattern threads. Bring the butterfly to the surface at the left edge of the last (left) pattern area. Turn the loose end around the nearest warp thread to its left and run the end under the middle thread of three pattern squares.

Make certain that the design is centered in the web, with the same number of threads in each side border. Then release the treadle, or treadles, and press the pattern thread firmly back against the fell.

2. Open the plain-weave shed, *b,* and throw the tabby shuttle from the right through to the left selvedge, beat hard, close the shed, and open the new pattern shed (treadle 1 or treadles 2, 3, and 4). If two tabby shots are required, open the opposite shed and return the shuttle to the right selvedge.

3. Repeat the pattern row from left to right. Be careful in making the turn. Do not pull the warp thread out of line, nor pull the pattern thread in under the weft thread. Beat and change the shed.

4. Weave the tabby row, beat, and close the shed. Open the pattern shed and weave the third pattern row, ending the pattern thread under the center thread of the last three pattern squares. At this point it requires four pattern threads to square the pattern weave in the fourth thread.

5. Continue weaving the pattern and tabby rows following the design on the graph paper.

The Pickup Half Dukagång on a 2-Harness Loom   After the heading has been woven in the desired width, proceed as follows:

1. Beginning at the right-hand selvedge, skip the first warp thread, pick up three threads on the pickup stick, skip the next thread, pick up three more warp threads, skip the next thread, and so on across the entire warp.

Find the center group of threads and count off the number of squares both to the right and left of the center square as called for in the design. The design will be exactly centered. Slip the unneeded groups off the ends of the pickup stick.

2. Turn the pickup stick on edge and insert the butterfly carrying the pattern thread into this shed. Working from right to left, bring the butterfly out to the left of the last pattern group of warp threads. Turn the loose end back around the first warp thread at its left, and under the center thread of the next three pattern groups. The end will beat in and not be conspicuous.

3. Remove the pickup stick; carefully beat the pattern thread into place.

4. Open the shed and throw the tabby shot through from right to left. Close the shed and beat. If two tabby threads have been used, insert the second one from left to right, close the shed, and beat.

5. With the pickup stick, start at the right and pick up the same group of warp threads as for the first pattern row. Turn the stick on edge and

return the butterfly, from the left, through to the edge of the right-hand side of the pattern area. Watch the warp thread around which the thread turns; do not pull it out of line. Do not pull the pattern thread under the other threads; it should lie flat and straight on the web. Avoid too loose a thread, for then a loop forms.

6. Remove the stick, beat, and open the tabby shed. Everything is ready for the third pattern shot, which is woven in the same way as the first row. Weave in a fourth pattern thread, or more if needed, to square the block.

7. Locate the position of the second pattern area, run in the pickup stick, turn the stick on edge, insert the pattern thread, and fasten in the end. Some weavers leave all ends loose until the piece is finished, then fasten them in with a needle, but the method of tucking them into the weave as described above is quicker and neater.

To Weave the Whole Dukagång   The directions for the whole dukagång closely follow those given for the half dukagång except that the background is filled in as well.

The background butterfly should be of the same kind and number of threads, but of a different color than the pattern butterfly. Insert the background butterfly from the right under the first group of pattern threads, bringing it out at the right of the first pattern area.

Start the pattern butterfly and bring it out at the left of the pattern area. Start the second background butterfly and bring it out at the left selvedge. There should be a butterfly for each pattern and background area.

Throw one or two tabby threads completely across the warp between each pattern and background row.

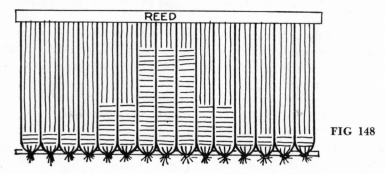

FIG 148

Fig. 148 shows how the pattern and warp threads lie in relation to each other in the half dukagång. In whole dukagång, the entire background area is filled with the horizontal pattern lines. The tabby threads are not indicated.

Problem   Set up the warp and weave an original design in a half dukagång on an apron, blouse pocket, or the end of a guest towel.

FIG. 149. Whole dukagång

FIGS. 150 and 151. Half dukagång

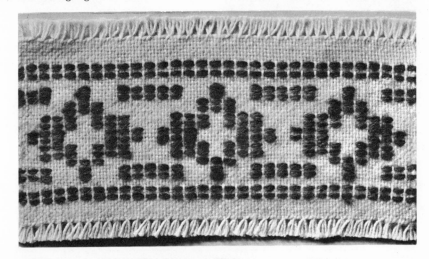

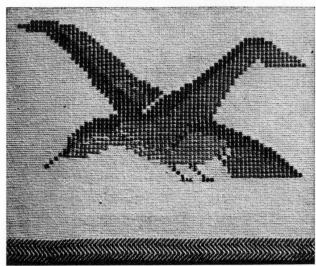

FIG. 152. Half dukagång

TYPE Pattern Threads on Surface · PATTERN Loops

Loops or tufted weaves are found quite universally. However, they have been brought to a higher state of development by the Italian, Spanish, Guatemalan, and French-Canadian weavers. The weave is simple and effective when the correct relationship between color and material is observed.

There are several variations of the weave. In the French-Canadian type, several rows of plain tabby weave are usually inserted between the tufted pattern rows. In an Italian piece, the pattern of several thicknesses of fine thread is inserted every row, while in a Spanish piece, the loops are twisted around the knitting needle to form a sort of knot. Patterns for this type of weave are usually simple, depicting either trees, stylized human figures, or stars. Colors usually are confined to one or two, as in the French-Canadian types, although in the others we find a variety (Fig. 155).

There is considerable flexibility in the weaving of looped or tufted patterns. After the technique has once been mastered, the patterns may be woven in freely without first sketching them on paper. Designs may be placed anywhere on the web, with as many plain rows of tabby weave between the designs as the weaver desires. This type of looping is effective but does not have the wearing qualities of those in which the pattern thread is tied around the warp threads (page 139). It does, however, weave up more quickly.

Use This weave is most commonly used for decorating bedspreads of homespun linen or yarn, luncheon sets, towels, and bureau covers.

Suitable Materials and Sleying

WARP	WEFT	PATTERN	REED (dents per inch)	SLEY
Cotton, 16/2	Cotton, 16/2	Cotton, 12/4	15	Double
Cotton, 16/2	Yarn, fine homespun	Yarn, medium weight homespun	15	Double
	Linen	Linen	15	Double

Sample Illustrated (Fig. 155)

Copy of unit from French-Canadian homespun bedspread.

WARP	WEFT	PATTERN	REED (dents per inch)	SLEY
Cotton, 8/2	Cotton, 8/4	Candlewick	18	Single

Number of Threads in Warp   60

Draw the design on graph paper. Each square represents one loop and contains three warp threads. Loops should not be placed closer together than every second square.

Threading   Plain weave

Tie-Up   Standard

Treadling   Background, plain weave

A double-pointed knitting needle and a crochet hook are required to pick up the loops. After the required heading has been woven in a plain weave, start the first looped row as follows:

Find the center of the web, and count threads to the left and right of this center thread, to correspond with the number of squares drawn across the pattern, Fig. 153.

FIG 153

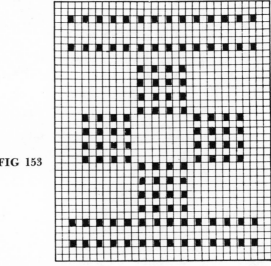

1. Open the shed and, with the tabby shuttle on the right and the right-hand outside thread in the upper row of threads, pass the pattern-thread butterfly through the shed from right to left, allowing it to lie loosely in the shed. Do not beat.

2. With the crochet hook, reach down between the second and third threads of the upper row, draw the pattern thread to the surface, and slip the knitting needle through the loop. Slide the knitting needle across the top of the next two warp threads lying in the top row and again reach down between the warp threads with the crochet hook. Draw the pattern thread to the surface and slip the knitting needle through the loop. Continue across the entire warp toward the left selvedge, keeping the knitting

needle on the surface and not in the shed. The pattern thread can be picked up with the fingers, but better tension is obtained when the hook is used.

The heavy lines in Fig. 154 represent the upper row of warp threads when the shed is open, the dotted lines the lower row. For purposes of clarity, the tabby threads are not indicated. Shown are the position of the knitting needle and the crochet hook when lifting the pattern thread preparatory to slipping it on the knitting needle.

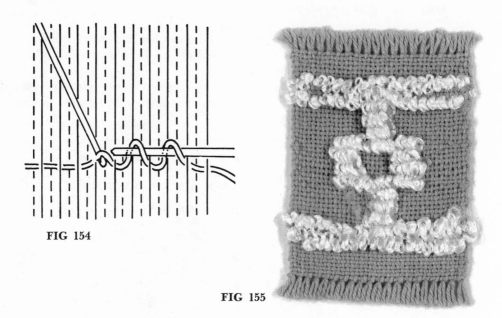

FIG 154

FIG 155

3. Enter the tabby shuttle in the shed with the pattern thread and out at the left selvedge. Beat, change the shed, beat hard, return the tabby shuttle to the right selvedge, beat, change the shed, and beat again. In this type of looping, where the loops all lie one above the other in a straight line and are not staggered, it is necessary to have an even number of tabby shots between each pattern row. This may vary with the design and materials used. In the sample (Fig. 155), there are six tabby shots between the first two pattern rows of the border and two shots between the other parts of the design. After the required number of tabby shots have been woven in, remove the knitting needle.

4. Repeat the first row (step 2), working from left to right. When the borders are woven, the pattern thread is carried along the selvedges or along the edge of the pattern area at right angles to the looped rows.

It may be awkward picking up the pattern thread from left to right but, with the crochet hook, pull the thread out of the shed and slip it over the knitting needle which lies on top of the warp. All the loops should twist in the same direction. Turn in the end of the pattern thread at the right selvedge and, at the same time, take the end which was left hanging out of the shed at the right, where the first pattern thread was entered, and carry it along the selvedge and into the pattern shed. This loop along the selvedge will match the pattern loop which lies along the left selvedge (Fig. 155).

5. Refer to the graph-paper design, count off the threads, and weave in the first row of the design area. This consists of four squares of three threads each. After the threads have been picked up and placed on the knitting needle and the loops have been beaten back against the fell, each end of the pattern thread, which is carried about ½ in. beyond the loops, must be turned into the shed to prevent it from pulling out.

If the pattern thread is larger than the background thread, build up the selvedges every second or third pattern row. This is done by taking the tabby thread in to the edge of the pattern thread, changing the shed, returning the tabby thread to the selvedge, changing the shed, and passing the tabby thread completely across the warp. The left border is built up in the same manner before returning the tabby shuttle to the right selvedge.

The warp can be sleyed to produce a loosely woven background, in which case it is not necessary to build up the borders. The sleying is entirely dependent on the article being woven.

6. Continue weaving, following the graph-paper design, and turning in the ends carefully. Watch the tension. All loops should lie with an even tension around the knitting needle. Watch particularly the end loops or any loops that cover only one or two squares isolated from the main part of the pattern.

Complete the sample by weaving in a border at the beginning.

Problem Set up the warp, design, and weave a baby bib with the loop technique.

TYPE Pattern Threads on Surface, Knotted · PATTERN Flossa

Although the Swedish flossa requires considerable skill and care in the weaving, it allows much freedom in the choice of color and design. Beautiful examples of the flossa can be seen in the museum at Scandia, in southern Sweden, and in many current and past weaving publications.

Thickly piled flossa rugs have been used throughout the Scandinavian countries for centuries and are as popular today as they were a hundred or more years ago. Flossa rugs require more wool than rölakan rugs but are softer and richer in appearance. Many modern rugs, commercially manufactured, are patterned from the designs of these Swedish rug weaves, but like the Oriental rugs, there is no comparison in feel and beauty between the machine-made and the hand-knotted weaves.

Uses For decorative wall hangings, pillow covers, draperies, upholstery, and, predominantly, floor rugs

Design Many subjects, including stylized trees, flowers, animals, and human figures and geometric designs, were and are used for flossa mat designs. Over-all designs composed of a repeated diamond are very popular. The diamonds sometimes are outlined with a dark color while the inside area is woven in a variety of designs; some diamonds are woven in a plain color, others with spots of contrasting color; other diamonds use two colors, one in the border and one in the large plain center. The elongated triangle appears in a variety of border designs, and is sometimes arranged with rectangles in an over-all design.

Draw the design on graph paper and color it. There are two warp threads to each square. The knot is tied around these two threads.

One of the things which puzzles weavers when they first study flossa and rölakan weaving is the subtle coloring. This is the result of years of understanding, appreciation, and use of color by Scandinavian weavers. All colors are bright, yet grayed, and harmonious. Many of them are based on colors found in nature. The gray, white, and yellow combination taken from the lichens on the rocks is a favorite one. Commercial dyers work closely with the various schools and guilds throughout Sweden and dye the yarns to their specifications. In this way, harsh and glaring colors are avoided. Many shades of one color are available and subtlety is gained by winding three or more single-ply colors together on the weft shuttle instead of using a two- or three-ply wool in a single color. Three shades of gray twisted together as they are entered in the shed produce a much more interesting effect than a two- or three-ply strand of plain Oxford gray.

Materials In general, no matter what rug technique is being used, materials should be strong, with plenty of body.

Linen, hemp, jute, or a tightly twisted glazed cotton, ranging in size from 8/3 to 10/5 are suitable. Do not attempt to weave flossa on a 4/8 cotton warp. It is much too soft and the results, even for a sample, will be disappointing.

Warp should be set at six, seven, or eight dents per inch. Two-ply or fine three-ply homespun yarn, or three single-ply strands of homespun twisted together, will beat down to cover the warp satisfactorily at these settings.

If obtainable, the Scandinavian nöthårsgarn, or cow yarn, is preferable to homespun. It has more body and a sheen not found in the homespun. Thrums from a carpet mill are a suitable substitute if they can be obtained in the desired shades.

Technique Flossa mats should be woven firm and tight, and beaten even to a boardlike stiffness, with special attention to the edges to prevent curling. The loom, which should be a 2- or 4-harness floor loom, should be very sturdy, for the beating is hard and vigorous.

The knot used to tie the pile is actually a Turkish or Ghiordes knot, but, through general use in the Scandinavian countries, it has come to be called the flossa or rya knot. Two rows of tabby weave after each row of knots hold them in place. The wider the flossa rod, the longer the pile. Where a longer pile is used, more tabby rows are required.

A flossa rod or bar is required for this technique, though there are weavers who cut their yarn and tie each knot individually. This tying method is perhaps best if there are frequent color changes and small pattern areas, but, in general, the rod hastens the weaving and assures the weaver of an even pile.

The flossa gauge bar or rod is a piece of metal varying in width from ⅜ to ¾ in. for flossa to 1 to 2 in. for rya.

There is a slit running lengthwise along the center of the bar and it is along this slit that the flossa knife or razor blade is drawn to cut the pile after the knots are tied and the two or more rows of tabby which follow the knots (pages 143 to 144) have been woven in and beaten.

There are several ways in which the gauge bar can be made if a Swedish one is not available. Cut two pieces of firm but thin metal: ⅜, ½, or ¾ in. wide, and 2 in. longer than the width of the warp. Solder the flat sides of these two pieces to a third piece which is about 1/16 in. narrower than the sides and which has been placed between the sides. Even up the three pieces at the bottom. This leaves a groove at the top edge 1/16 in. deep along which to draw the knife (Fig. 156).

FIG 156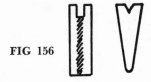

The flossa can be knotted around a flat, hardwood stick along one edge of which a groove has been made. A sharp knife or razor blade is drawn across the threads where they lie over the groove on the rod. The rod stands up at right angles to the warp.

Samples Illustrated (Figs. 162 and 163)

WARP	WEFT	REED (dents per inch)	SLEY
Hemp, 3-ply medium	Homespun, natural cream, gray, vegetable-dyed yellow, 2-ply	8	Single

Number of Warp Threads Wound   56

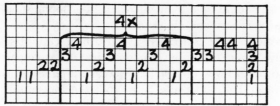

FIG 157

Threading

The first two and the last two threads on each selvedge are threaded through string heddles which have been tied in at each side of the metal heddles. The four edge threads on each side are double sleyed through the reed. The string heddles are cut away after the heading and the border have been woven in, and are tied in again after the body of the rug has been woven, to facilitate the weaving of the end border and heading.

Prepare the loom in the usual manner, then, at the start, weave in (alternating treadles *a* and *b*) about ¾ in. of hemp warp to regulate the threads and to make a firm heading against which to beat.

Wind a shuttle with the natural wool and weave in a border slightly over ½ in. wide.

To attain the necessary body and wearing qualities, the rug must be beaten very hard. It is advisable to weave in a few extra shots in the border as the beating of successive rows of weft will narrow it down a little. Be sure that the shuttle carrying the weft, of which the border has been woven, ends on the right side. Bring it to the surface between the two pairs of selvedge threads. Cut out the string heddles.

Make a small ball, or butterfly, of the same wool as that used for the border and insert the end into the open shed through which the shuttle carrying the border thread has just passed (Fig. 158).

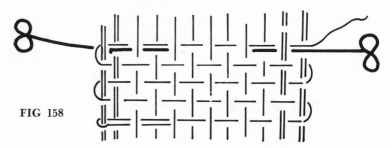

FIG 158

Prepare another ball or butterfly of the same material and insert the end far enough into the shed at the left selvedge so it cannot pull out.

To tie the first row of knots, close the shed and lay the flossa rod on the warp. Both ends of the rod should extend at least 1 or 2 in. beyond the selvedges. The rod must always be longer than the width of the pattern area because, once a foot or so of the knots has been tied, it is almost impossible to slide the bar, although some weavers claim to do so. If the bar slides, it is a sign that the knots have not been tied tightly enough.

The rod will not stand upright on the warp until a few of the knots have been tied tightly. The cutting groove of the rod should be on top. Eight or ten knots should be sufficient; as soon as they have been tied, straighten up the bar. If the rod is not straight and at right angles to the warp, the pile will be uneven when the knots are cut.

The first knot is tied around the first two warp threads on the left, which lie just inside the two pairs of selvedge threads.

To tie the knot (Fig. 159), pass the small ball or butterfly of yarn prepared for the knots under the first warp thread, working from left to right. Bring the butterfly up on the left side of the first thread, over the top of the first and the second threads from left to right, under the second

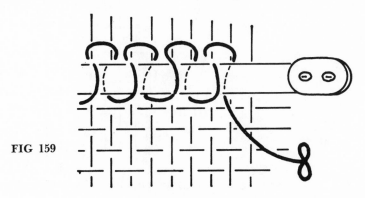

FIG 159

thread from right to left, and up between the two threads. Bring the yarn under the flossa rod and pull it tight. Continue in this manner, taking the wool from the back of the rod, across the front of the bar, under the third thread from right to left, across the third and fourth threads, under the fourth thread from right to left, and up between the third and fourth threads. Bring the wool under the flossa rod and pull the knot tight. Continue bringing the wool from the back and up across the front of the rod to the next pair of warp threads, etc., to the right edge of the pattern area. The last knot is tied around the forty-seventh and forty-eighth threads, which are just inside the two selvedge pairs on the right.

There are 24 knots across the width of the sample. A good pull on the thread tightens the knot where it passes around the flossa rod. This may seem awkward at first but with practice the process moves rapidly.

Tie all the knots on the sample but *do not* cut the pile. The edges must be built up, the tabby thrown, and measurements taken before the pile can be cut.

The knots are higher than the selvedge borders at each side and do not go directly to the edge of the weaving, thereby leaving a space on each side that must be filled in. It is here that the pairs of selvedge threads and the butterflies come into use.

Wind a butterfly of the same color and material as the bottom border and the right selvedge borders, and insert it with the last row of tabby threads between the two pairs of warp threads. Take the butterfly, which is hanging at the right selvedge, and bring it up from the outside between the two pairs of warp threads and the warp thread around which the last knot was tied (Fig. 160). Pull it taut, but not so taut that it pulls in the selvedge threads. Remember that a perfect selvedge is desired. Next, with the shed closed, pass the butterfly down between the two pairs and out at the very edge of the right selvedge. Repeat until the right selvedge has been built up to the depth of the knotted row.

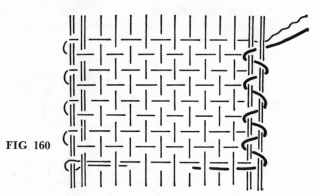

FIG 160

Pick up the butterfly hanging from the left selvedge and pass it between the pairs of selvedge threads, around the inner pair, back between the selvedge pairs, around the edge pair, and again between the selvedge pairs until the same number of threads have been inserted as for the right selvedge.

Pick up the shuttle, open the shed, and pass the shuttle through, bringing it out at the left selvedge between the two pairs of selvedge threads. Change the shed, return the shuttle to the right, and bring it down between the two pairs of selvedge threads.

Before proceeding with the next row of knots, beat the rug hard.

Draw the flossa knife across the top of the rod to cut the pile, then move the rod up to the edge of the weaving for the next row of knots. Unless a regulation flossa rod and knife are being used, exercise extreme care to prevent the knife or razor blade from slipping off the improvised rod and cutting the warp threads. The blade should be very sharp to cut the pile evenly. It does not take much imagination to picture what would happen to the warp if the knife slipped!

In flossa and half flossa, as in rölakan, a gauge is needed to measure the weft shots. Remember that on the graph paper, each square represents two warp threads. Each square represents the same space for the weft, although it may require more than two weft threads to fill this space.

To make a gauge, place light cardboard on the warp, next to and in front of the reed. Mark the cardboard for every other dent (Fig. 161). Since there is only one thread per dent, the width of two dents will represent the width and the height of the square on paper.

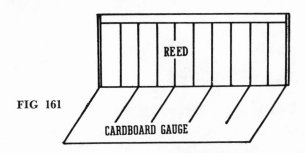

FIG 161

REED

CARDBOARD GAUGE

After the row of knots has been cut, measure with the guage from the bottom of the row of knots to the top of the tabby. This measurement should equal one unit of the gauge, that is, two warp threads or one square. If the woven area is too wide, either the warp has been sleyed too closely or the beating has not been hard enough. If the area is too narrow, add more tabby shots and build up the borders as previously described. Throw one or two shots more than seem necessary, since successive rows tend to beat these pattern rows back further than at first seems indicated.

When making the gauge, mark 10 or more units on it so several rows of knots can be measured at one time. One or two rows might be off slightly but not enough to show when measured individually, but the measurement of a number of rows will show any discrepancy.

The knots for the pattern areas of the sample illustrated are tied in the following order, with the tabby rows between:

Begin with 4 rows of white knots extending from selvedge to selvedge;

Area 1: 2 white, 4 yellow; 4 white; 4 gray; 4 white; 4 yellow; 2 white—repeat for 4 rows;

Area 2: 6 white; 4 gray; 4 yellow; 4 gray; 6 white—repeat for 4 rows;

Area 3: the same as Area 1;

Area 4: 2 yellow; 4 gray; 4 yellow; 4 white; 4 yellow; 4 gray; 2 yellow;

Area 5: the same as Areas 1 and 3;

Area 6: the same as Area 2;

Area 7: the same as Areas 1, 3, and 5;

End with 4 rows of white knots.

Before weaving the ½ in. of plain weave, cut off the butterflies, leaving ends ¾ in. long. Tuck and conceal these ends in the shed. Tie the string heddles around the outside pair of selvedge threads on the harnesses from which they were cut. Weave the border of wool followed by a ¾-in. heading of the hemp warp threads.

Before cutting the sample from the loom, examine it to be sure that

FIG 162   FIG 163

the pile is even. If any uneven spots are found, clip them with slightly rounded, surgical scissors. It is difficult, in fact almost impossible, to trim a mat with flat scissors. Flossa and half flossa should be as even as possible, without having a commercial look. After checking and clipping, cut the sample from the loom, leaving the warp sufficiently long to tie the desired fringe (page 586).

Problem   Work out a design on graph paper and weave a small sample.

The bath mat (Fig. 164) is woven on a tightly twisted six-strand cotton warp with cream-colored candlewick for the knots and tabby. The frogs are a medium shade of green with the connecting lines in a deeper shade of the green. The tadpoles are purple. The border was woven by the method described for the sample, using butterfles for the borders and a shuttle for the tabby thread.

TYPE Pattern Thread on Surface, Knotted · PATTERN Half Flossa

The half-flossa technique, which is used for rugs, is the forerunner of the modern sculptured or cut-pile rugs and carpets. Although these rugs

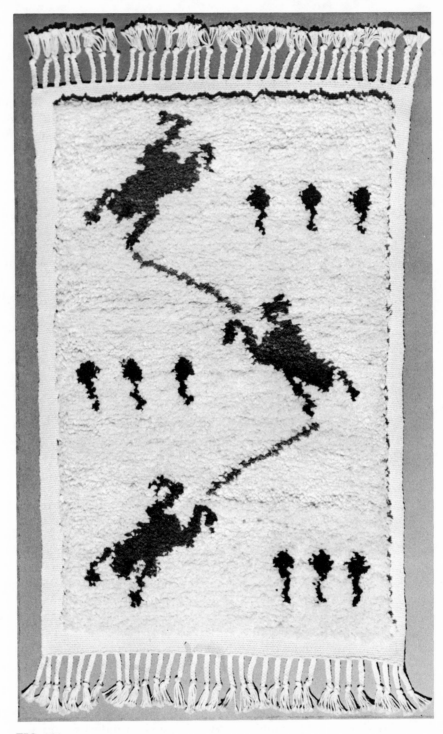

FIG 164

have won some popularity, they are hazardous to wearers of high heels and are difficult to keep clean.

"Halv-flossa" as it is called in Sweden, is suitable for wall hangings in which it is desirable to have part of the design, either trees, leaves, flowers, or an abstract design, stand out from the background (Fig. 166).

At first glance, it woud appear that the half flossa, in which only the design is knotted, would be less difficult and time consuming to weave than the whole flossa. This is not the case, at least for rugs, since the building up between the pattern areas necessitates the use of several balls, bobbins, or butterflies.

Sample Illustrated   The loom is threaded the same as for the whole flossa (Fig. 157) except that the two pairs of selvedge threads are threaded through the regular heddles since they are not cut away. With the half-flossa technique, the background is built up at the edges of the pattern area rather than just at the selvedges. The gauge is used (Fig. 161) and the beating must be very hard.

Weave the heading of the warp material, ¾ or 1 in. wide, beating it hard.

This is followed by a ½-in. border of the natural cream-colored home-spun, alternating treadles *a* and *b* for the plain weave.

Two rows of cream homespun flossa knots, with two rows of tabby between, are now woven in, building up the selvedges on both sides with butterflies. End the butterflies after the second row of knots and tuck the ends into the open shed.

Continue with another ½ in. of plain weave, alternating treadles *a* and *b* with the cream wool. Beat very well and measure with the gauge (page 145). End with the shuttles on the right side. This brings the weaving up to the design area. This time, the flossa rod is not to be used for the knots. Since the pattern areas are smaller than the background areas, the rod would only be in the way. Instead, the wool for the pattern areas is cut into 3¼-in. lengths which are used individually to tie each knot.

Prepare two cream-colored butterflies. The weft thread, which has been brought out to the right side, is considered the third butterfly. When a large rug is to be woven, and there are large background areas, it will save time to have the wool on a flat shuttle rather than made up into butterflies.

With the shed closed, tie a knot of the cut gray yarn around the ninth and tenth and one around the eleventh and twelfth threads from the left. Then tie one around the ninth and tenth and another around the eleventh and twelfth threads from the right. Do not count the selvedge-thread pairs on either side.

To Make the Knot   Lay the cut piece of wool on top of the two designated warp threads, for example the first and second, turn the two ends up between the two warp threads (Fig. 165), and pull them tightly toward you.

Try to keep the ends as even as possible, although they can be trimmed with curved scissors before the sample is taken off the loom. Open the shed to the last one used, tuck in the loose ends of the butterflies, close the shed, and beat hard.

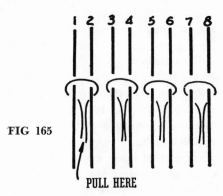

FIG 165

PULL HERE

Starting at the right selvedge, open the shed opposite the shed last used, carry the butterfly over the first eight threads, and bring it to the surface. Close the shed, beat, open the new shed, and return the butterfly back to the right selvedge. Close the shed and beat. This constitutes one complete cycle. Repeat as often as necessary to make the background area level with the top of the knotted area.

Now, starting on the left side of the two knots which were tied in, start the second butterfly and carry it through the open shed to the right side of the second pattern area, bring it to the surface, close the shed, beat, open the opposite shed, and return the butterfly to the right where it started. Repeat the operation until the same number of weft threads have been inserted between these two pattern areas as were woven in at the right side.

Weave in the background area to the left of the second pattern with the same number of threads as were used for the other background areas. End with the butterfly at the left side of the second pattern area. Change the shed, beat hard, pick up the right-hand butterfly and pass it completely across the web, change the shed, beat, and carry the butterfly across, through the shed, and out to the right edge.

Measure with the gauge. If the measurement is correct, proceed with another row of knots; if there are not enough threads, weave in another two rows of tabby completely across the web and back. When these threads have been woven in, comb them loosely back with the fingers, leaving the threads in scallops, and then beat.

As the weaving proceeds, it is necessary to carry the butterfly threads from one knotted area to another at right angles across the main body of the weaving. This is done on the wrong side and is hardly noticeable. The only alternative is to cut the threads and tuck the ends into the shed, though this would soon build up lumps around the edges of the pattern areas. If the color of the background and the pattern threads do not contrast too sharply the butterfly thread can be brought to the surface and clipped to the same height as the pattern threads.

The weaving proceeds in this manner. When a new pattern area extends to the right or left beyond the area just finished, the threads from the butterflies are cut and the ends concealed in the web. The loose end is started at the edge of the new area in the same manner in which it was started for the first area.

The weaver can easily follow the pattern design from the photograph showing the wrong side of the sample (Fig. 167). It is similar to the design used for the whole flossa (Fig. 162). The center parts of the areas are woven in yellow, the outside areas in gray.

The sample ends as it began, with ½ in. of plain weave in the cream homespun; two rows of flossa knots, also in the cream homespun; ending with ½ in. of cream homespun and the ¾-in. heading of warp thread.

Cut the knots and remove the sample from the loom, leaving an end long enough to tie the desired type of fringe.

FIG 166

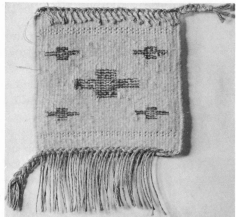

FIG 167

Two methods for ending this fringe are shown. At the top, the fringe ends have been caught down with thread and the ends clipped (Fig. 167). Later, a piece of stout cotton material will be sewn over these ends both to conceal them and to make a firm durable finish. The ends of the warp at the bottom of the sample have been carried back through the heading and left as a fringe.

Other methods of tying fringes are shown on pages 588 to 591.

Problem Prepare an original design and weave a small rug sample paying particular attention to the turning of the background threads, the gauge measurements, and the beating.

TYPE Pattern Threads on Surface, Knotted ·
PATTERN Finnish Ryijy or Rya

Rya rugs, according to some researchers, were first woven in Finland. They were used, however, in all the Scandinavian countries as floor rugs, bed and sleigh robes, and as blankets for animals to protect them from the intense cold.

One of the very old rya rugs examined in a Finnish exhibition showed the pile to be at least 2 in. long. Moreover, the rug was woven in a double-weave technique with pile on both sides, while the rows of binder weave between the knots were in rose-path instead of plain weave. This rug was well over one hundred years old, as attested to by the date and weaver's initials woven into one corner. It showed ingenious workmanship. This and other old rugs in the exhibition probably had been woven for bed coverings or sleigh robes, because they seemed softer and more pliable than the more modern, stiffer rugs which obviously were floor coverings.

The colors of the older rugs, though somewhat faded, suggested the use of vegetable-dyed yarns. The colors of the modern rugs were gay, but harmonious, and the weaving well done.

The rya floor rug is more popular among Scandinavian weavers than flossa because it can be woven much more quickly.

Design   The pile of the rya rugs is much longer than that used for even the deepest flossa rug, sometimes being as much as 1½ to 2 in. long. The flossa pile usually stands up, while the rya pile is designed to lie close to the background, covering it completely.

Because of this long pile, the design easily loses its identity. Therefore, concentration is on color and large, bold, geometric designs rather than on small compact ones. When viewed from a distance, the figures of the bride and groom surrounded by large hearts and flowers could be distinguished on some of the old wedding rugs seen at the Finnish exhibition. Other old rugs showed trees and houses; modern weaves revealed the trend to abstract designs.

Materials   The best of the rya rugs seem to have been woven on a strong, natural-colored linen warp. The choice of weft depended largely on the financial circumstances of the family and the purpose for which the rug was to be used. It varied from yarn made from animal hair, twisted with tow or hemp, to single-spun wool and linen of good quality in natural colors.

Technique   The loom is set up as for the flossa with two pairs of threads at each selvedge, double-sleying, and the outside pair on each side threaded through string heddles.

Rya rugs are started with the ¾-in. warp heading used to begin the flossa, the rölakan, and others. This is followed by the wool border. Be sure to weave enough so that the desired amount of border will show below the pile, which lies toward the weaver. Cut out the string heddles.

The gauge for rya is made in the same way as for flossa and rölakan. Lay the cardboard against the reed and mark every third dent (instead of every second dent as in flossa). The width of each space on the gauge equals one row of knots plus the plain weave between each row of knots.

If a longer pile is desired, make the gauge so that it is 1¼ to 1⅝ times the width of three warp threads and weave in more plain weave. In this case, the woven design will be elongated compared to the design on the squared paper. The ideal answer to this problem would be to have rectangular graph paper, as is used in Scandinavian weaving schools. The design also can be drawn full size on heavy paper with the design areas outlined heavily in black ink. This design then is pinned to the underside of the warp and followed without the necessity of graph paper. The gauge must be used at all times.

Whatever length of pile is decided upon, the edge of the pile should cover just the preceding row of knots. The technique of tying the knot is the same as for the flossa knot with the following exceptions:

1. The knot must be tied over a much wider flossa rod to make the longer pile which should be at least 1⅛ in. long. Many experienced Scandinavian weavers tie around their fingers rather than a gauge. Another method is to wind a single row of the yarn around a long stick, then cut the yarn along the length of the stick with a sharp knife, scissors, or razor blade. When cut, the pieces will be equal in length. With this method the flossa rod is not used, as the knots are tied separately around the designated warp threads. The stick should be of a size to make the pile, when tied, the correct length. There is no economy in cutting the pieces too long and then having to trim them off. Many weavers feel that the unevenness of pile on a rya rug adds to its beauty.

2. For the rya technique, the Ghiordes (yor-deez) knot is tied over two warp threads, the same as with the flossa technique, but one warp thread is skipped between each knot (Fig. 168). Number the warp threads from left to right. The knots are always tied from left to right in the following order:

    a) Tie the first knot around warp threads 1 and 2. (These are the threads which lie just inside the two pairs of selvedge threads.)

    b) Skip warp thread 3.

    c) Tie the second knot around warp threads 4 and 5.

    d) Skip warp thread 6.

    e) Tie the third knot around warp threads 7 and 8, and so on.

FIG 168

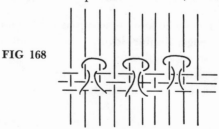

Plan the correct number of threads so that a single warp thread will not be left between the last knot and the two pairs of warp threads which form the right selvedge.

The background areas are built up around the knots at the selvedges in the same manner as for the flossa.

The width of plain weaving between the knotted areas has been described above. The majority of the old rugs studied had been woven in plain weave, a few in twill, and an occasional one in rose-path.

The rugs end in the same border arrangement with which they began, but the width of the wool border should be the same as that part of the first border which shows below the cut pile.

Rya rugs can have either a cut or uncut pile. When it is to be cut, and this is genarally done, do not cut the pile until at least two rows of plain weave have been woven in and the rod, if used, is ready to be released for the next row of knots.

FIG 169

Sample Illustrated (Fig. 169)

WARP	WEFT	PATTERN	REED (dents per inch)	SLEY
Hemp, 10/3 or 10/5	Wool, homespun, cream, 2-ply	Wool, homespun, three shades of green, 1- or 2-ply	8	Single

No design was used, but the colors were shaded from the darkest green for the bottom row to the lightest for the top row. The background is creamy-white homespun, woven in plain weave. Five strands of the single ply were used for each knot. For a heavy floor rug, three strands of the double ply would be advisable.

Problem   Design and weave a rya sample, stressing the color arrangement.

TYPE Pattern Threads on Surface · PATTERN Soumak

Oriental rugs were originally grouped under six general classifications: Persian, Turkish, Caucasian, Turkoman, Indian, and Chinese. Through the years, there have been many deviations from these original techniques and products, which, appearing under new names, have lost their identity.

Historians believe that the smooth-surface, kilim type of rug was probably the earliest form of rug weaving. Next came the soumak, from the Caucasian group, with its design superimposed on the surface rather than incorporated into the weaving as in the kilim or the rölakan. These were followed by the many pile-surface rugs which originated within various countries and bear the names of these countries: the Swedish flossa, the Turkish Ghiordes, the Persian or Sehna knotted rugs, and others.

A study of a piece of antique soumak carpet (Fig. 170), which dates back to the late seventeenth or eighteenth century, reveals many interesting things about color, design, material, and technique. The workmanship, though crude and primitive, does follow a logical pattern.

Design   Soumak designs are probably symbolic. They are composed of many small design areas which, in turn, form themselves into large over-all designs. The piece analyzed (Fig. 170) is a portion of the border of a large rug. The main design is flanked, both top and bottom, by a border of stylized birds.

The colors, undoubtedly vegetable dyes, are somewhat subdued and mellowed, yet clear, after years of use. The background blue is the beautiful Oriental indigo blue; the red is a shade that could have been dyed with madder or cochineal; and the golden yellow with saffron, a dye plant popular in ancient times. Soft green, medium blue, black, and a light creamy shade are used for emphasis and to outline various pattern areas.

Materials   It is difficult to come to any definite conclusion concerning the materials used in the antique soumak. A burning test indicated that the fibers used were wool, cotton, and hair. In some instances, as for the warp, these fibers have been twisted individually into single- and 2-ply strands of a soft but tightly twisted, tough cotton. It is possible that the weft might

FIG 170

have been goat or camel hair spun with wool to hold the shorter strands together. The very fine, 2-ply, tightly twisted, wiry pattern thread resembles the Scandinavian cowhair yarn in feel and luster.

Sample Illustrated   The sample (Fig. 171) was woven with coarse materials to illustrate the technique and to show the different surface textures achieved with pattern threads laid-in in both the twill and herringbone methods.

Because of the long skips, this combination of threads is impractical for a rug, as the threads would be caught and broken by whatever passed

FIG 171

FIG 172

over them. This sleying is, however, suitable for a pillow top or chair seat. The weft-face background is correct for these projects. Fig. 172 shows the reverse side.

WARP	WEFT	PATTERN	REED (dents per inch)	SLEY
Jute or linen, 10/3	Jute or linen, 10/3	Carpet thrums, 1-strand	15	Single

This sample will be similar in weight to the antique sample (Fig. 170). Carpet thrums are ideal for the pattern if they can be obtained in the desired colors.

Design motifs woven in the soumak technique in colorful wools, cottons, or synthetic threads can be used to decorate plain webs. These designs can be scattered at random over the web or planned to form borders.

As with all rug weaving, have two pairs of double threads at each selvedge. Do not count these double pairs of selvedge threads when planning or weaving the design as none of the pattern threads pass over them.

Technique The soumak technique is comparatively simple. It consists of rows and rows of stemstitching, one of the most simple of embroidery stitches, worked over a tightly woven tabby background. This stemstitching can be done on either the closed or open shed, but it is easier to do it across the closed shed. There are two methods of slanting the stitches. In one, each successive row lies in the same direction, and, in the other, the successive rows lie at an angle to each other. With the first, a twill-like effect results, with the second a herringbone.

There is no rule to determine the correct number of warp threads over which and under which the pattern thread shall pass. However, as the antique sample (Fig. 170) shows the pattern thread passing over four on the right or upper side of the rug and under two, perhaps this can be considered authoritative. It is customary to weave with the right side up, though it can be done with the wrong, or under, side up if the pattern area turns give trouble.

A row of tabby alternates with each row of pattern. Thread a sturdy 2- or 4-harness loom for a plain weave, add two pairs of selvedge threads on each side, double sley through the reed, but do not thread through the heddles.

Prepare the design on graph paper, paint a cartoon to be fastened under the warp, or ink the design directly on the warp (page 483).

Wind the tabby thread on a shuttle and the pattern thread on bobbins or butterflies (Fig. 143).

Start the weaving with a ¾-in. heading of heavy thread against which to beat. If a hem is desired, weave it with the tabby thread, ending with the shuttle at the right selvedge. Close the shed and beat hard.

With the bobbin or butterfly of pattern thread at the right selvedge, pass it under the two edge threads and bring it to the surface (Fig. 173). Working toward the left selvedge, cross the butterfly over these two threads and pass it under the first four warp threads; then bring it to the surface between warp threads 4 and 5.

Pass the thread back toward the right selvedge over two warp threads, then again under four warp threads, to the surface, and over two. Continue in this way across the width of the weaving (Fig. 173).

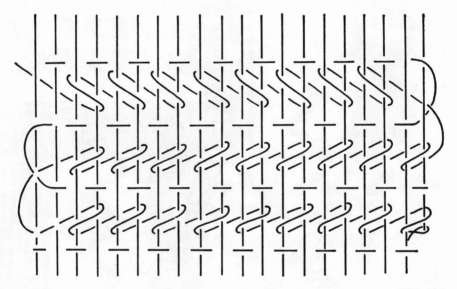

FIG 173

After the pattern thread has been carried completely across the web, beat it sharply back into position, open the shed, and insert the tabby. Once again, beat back tightly and close the shed. When correctly sleyed and beaten, the warp is completely covered.

The pattern thread, which now lies at the left, is carried under four threads, out to the surface, back toward the left selvedge, over two threads, down between the warp threads, under four again, and so on, across the web to the right selvedge. This order or repetition will produce a twill-like surface. Where the order is reversed, as shown in the top row of the diagram (Fig. 173), a herringbone effect is obtained. The antique sample shows the pattern threads lying in the same direction, giving a twill effect.

Carry the pattern thread completely across the web for several rows to weave the edge of the border design. The pattern threads will now travel back and forth over their own pattern area, filling it in with the desired color.

FIG. 174. Gamp showing various finger-manipulated weaves

Where there is a pattern area of only two or three threads, the color is laid across these threads, carried down between them and the next warp thread to the underside, passed under the same threads as have just been covered on the top surface, and brought back to the surface ready for the next pattern row. Do not pull this pattern thread too tightly or the warp threads will be pulled out of alignment.

The beating must be very hard throughout or the rug will be sleazy. End with a border and hem as at the start.

Problem Design, set up, and weave a small soumak sample using the threads listed above. Follow this by weaving a single design motif in the center of a plain web.

chapter 5

Twills

How appropriate is the saying "the twills begin but they never end!"

The late Marguerite Porter Davison[1] stated, "The number of variations to be gained in (twill) fabrics made by changing the sequence of the treadlings, by using different combinations of the tie-ups of the harnesses, by adding color variations in the warp and weft, or both, can not be figured mathematically."

Many a weaver, in doubt as to what threading to use, usually will settle the matter by saying, "I'll use a twill."

In view of the foregoing, it can be seen why no attempt can be made in a single chapter to discuss all the possibilities of twill threadings. Therefore, only some of the better known and fundamental ones, and a few of the more unusual ones are given.

There are plain right and left twills, zigzag twills, herringbone twills, bird's-eye and diaper twills, single-, double-, and triple-point twills, and many more. The slightest variation in threading or treadling produces a different result. In fact, there are so many twill threadings and treadling variations that an entire book could be written about them, and it would be a sizable volume.

A twill web is essentially a 50/50 fabric; that is, a fabric in which an equal number of weft threads and warp threads appear to the square inch. In many twill weaves, both sides of the web are the same; in others, the warp thread forms the pattern or design; and in still others, the pattern is formed by the weft threads.

Contrasting colors of warp and weft produce the most interesting fabrics in wool; in linens, pleasing results are obtained by the use of a single color or two shades of the same color.

All the weaving that has been described so far in the text has been listed as plain weave. Variations and/or decorations have been achieved by the introduction of heavy threads in either warp or weft or in both, through the insertion of colored threads with the fingers to form designs as in the tapestry weaves, by knotted threads forming patterns on the surface, or by other finger-manipulated methods.

In none of these weaves has a patterned web been produced mechanically through the operation of the harnesses controlled by the treadles, or, as in the case of a table loom, by the levers.

Here, then, we have the first of many departures from the plain weave; and since the twills form the background of many weaves including the overshot, a thorough understanding of the mechanics of the weave is of the utmost importance.

Particular attention should be given to this weave because it will recur in one form or another as long as the weaver continues to throw a shuttle.

TYPE Twill, Plain, 3-Harness · PATTERN Jeans

History does not identify the Jean in whose honor the 3-harness twill was named. Many teenagers would be surprised to learn that their favorite costume derived its name from the originator of this twill, who very likely was a mother searching for a cloth that children couldn't wear out.

The fewest number of harnesses on which a twill can be woven is three. Few weavers, if any, have 3-harness looms, but any 4-harness loom can easily be reduced to 3. The 3-harness twill weaves given in the following pages have little value except that they illustrate the technique of a twill weave on a minimum number of harnesses. Three-harness weaves are frequently found among the Scandinavian drafts. Much of the beauty of twill lies in the attractive color arrangements rather than in the structure.

Uses   In wool: for dress and coat materials, blankets, drapes, belts, or afghan strips and squares. In linen: for towels, luncheon sets, and other household linens. In carpet warp: for porch and chair pillows, drapes, and upholstery. In fine cottons: for sports wear.

Suitable Materials and Sleying

WARP	WEFT	REED (dents per inch)	SLEY
Wool, heavy	Wool, heavy	12	Single
Carpet warp, 8/4	Carpet warp, 8/4	18	Single
Cotton, 20/2	Cotton, 20/2	15	Double
Linen, 40/2 or 30/2	Linen, 40/2 or 30/2	18	Double

Sample Illustrated (Fig. 176)

WARP	WEFT	REED	SLEY
		(dents per inch)	
Cotton, 8/2	Cotton, 8/2	12	Double

The draw-down (Fig. 175) illustrates how weaving is done on paper. The policy of making draw-downs is followed for all the weaves in the text with the exception of those weaves for which they would be of little value. A full description of the draw-down is given later (page 535). The draw-down helps the weaver to better understand the structure of the weave.

Many things about weaving have become traditional and are accepted without question. One of these is the method used in making the draw-down. Weaving is actually done above the draft, while the draw-down is made below the draft. Usually this makes little difference. However, with the twill weave it weaves a right-hand twill on paper whereas in actual weaving on the loom the twill emerges as a left-hand twill. Generally speaking this is unimportant, since the material itself is correct. The left-hand twill is accepted generally as being the distinguishing mark of a hand-woven twill.

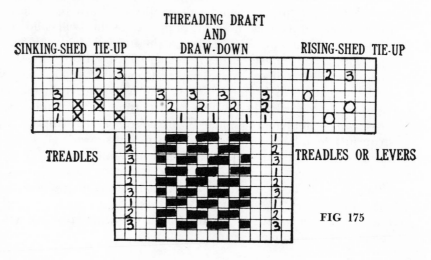

A further study of the draw-down shows that the twills are woven with an overlapping of one or more binder threads from the first shot into the second, from the second into the third, and from the third into the fourth, repeating this routine entirely across the web.

On the tie-up for the sinking-shed loom (Fig. 175) two harnesses are tied together to the first treadle, two to the second, and two to the third. When the treadle is depressed the two warp threads that are to be covered with the weft thread are pulled down. When the next treadle is depressed, the single thread that was up is drawn down, while the release of treadle 1 causes just one of the threads used to rise, the other being held down by treadle 2. This change of threads holds the first row of weaving in place. This happens with each row, a new thread being treadled, or drawn down, in combination with the last one from the previous group.

Quite the opposite happens on a rising-shed loom (Fig. 175). One thread only at a time is drawn up, leaving the two threads down that are to be covered by the weft thread. Notice that the spaces which were left empty on the sinking-shed tie-up have been filled in with circles to make the tie-up for the rising-shed loom. A detailed description of the tie-up is given later (page 533).

The numbers that appear at the left of the chart under the tie-up designate the order in which the treadles are to be used. The numbers across the chart on the right-hand side of the draw-down designate the order of treadling on a rising-shed foot loom, or the levers on a table loom.

The right side of the jeans twill (A, Fig. 176) is weft face, the reverse

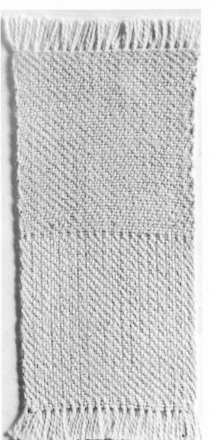

A

FIG 176

B

side (B), warp face, because the weft passes over two warp threads and under one.

In addition to the plain 3-harness jeans twill, further interest can be added by deviations in the treadling routine.

Treadling

A: Left twill

1
2 } Repeat as often as desired.
3

B: Right twill

3
2 } Repeat as often as desired.
1

C: Zigzag twill (not shown in Fig. 176)

1
2
3 } Repeat as often as desired.
2

Problem Thread a sample of a 3-harness twill and study the action of the harnesses, treadles (or levers), and rotation of threads. It is best to try this out on a rising-shed or table loom. Counterbalanced looms are not too suitable for off-balanced weaves.

TYPE Twill, 4-Harness · PATTERN Plain

The general theory just given for the twill weaves also applies to twills threaded on four or more harnesses.

As with other weaves, each additional harness adds one more change and allows for the extension of the weave. An odd or even number of harnesses can be added but weaving is simplified, particularly on a counterbalanced loom, if the harnesses are kept to even, rather than uneven, numbers.

Beginning weavers frequently are frustrated because the edge thread of the selvedge does not weave in. This should not cause too much worry.

If a plain twill is being woven on a sinking-shed loom with the threading starting on harness 1 on the right and ending on harness 4 on the left, start the shuttle for the first shot of the weft on the left on the 1–2 shed. If this is done, there should be no trouble. Where reverse twills are being woven, this rule does not hold as the reversing throws the routine off. The shuttle must be passed either between the two selvedge threads to pick up the loose thread before throwing it through the shed, or the whole matter ignored, cutting off the loose thread when the material is finished.

Suitable Materials and Sleying

WARP	WEFT	REED (dents per inch)	SLEY
Wool, fine	Wool, fine	18 or 20	Double
Wool, medium	Wool, medium	15	Single
Wool, coarse	Wool, coarse	12	Single
Wool, very coarse	Wool, very coarse	10	Single
Cotton, 20/2 or 30/2	Cotton, 20/2 or 30/2	15 or 16	Double
Carpet warp	Carpet warp	15 or 16	Single
Linen, 40/2 or 40/3	Linen, 40/2 or 40/3	18	Double

Notice that the warp and weft are always the same for twill weaves.

Sample Illustrated (Fig. 180)

WARP	WEFT	REED (dents per inch)	SLEY
Cotton, 8/2	Cotton, 8/2	12	Double

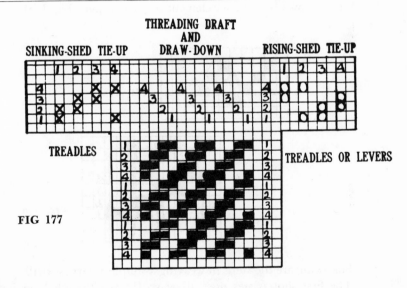

THREADING DRAFT
AND
DRAW-DOWN

SINKING-SHED TIE-UP

RISING-SHED TIE-UP

TREADLES

TREADLES OR LEVERS

FIG 177

Treadling If the rising-shed loom has no tie-up, or a table loom with levers is being used, depress two treadles or levers together:

3 and 4
4 and 1
1 and 2
2 and 3
} Repeat as often as desired.

Starting the thread from the left, this sequence eliminates the loose thread in the selvedge.

Recall, for a moment, the plain weaves (page 53) which were threaded in the same routine as the twill. The manner in which they were treadled to produce a plain weave was:

HARNESSES

$\left.\begin{array}{c} 1 \\ 2 \end{array}\right\}$ Woven in alternating succession on the 2-harness loom

$\left.\begin{array}{c} 1 \text{ and } 3 \\ 2 \text{ and } 4 \end{array}\right\}$ Woven in alternating succession on the 4-harness loom

$\left.\begin{array}{c} 1, 3, 5 \\ 2, 4, 6 \end{array}\right\}$ Woven in alternating succession on the 6-harness loom

$\left.\begin{array}{c} 1, 3, 5, 7 \\ 2, 4, 6, 8 \end{array}\right\}$ Woven in alternating succession on the 8-harness loom

These were all woven with opposite harnesses treadled together whereas there is an overlapping of harnesses in treadling the twill succession.

There are, on a 4-harness twill threading (aside from the 1–3, 2–4 plain weave), four possible treadling combinations. These are 1–2, 2–3, 3–4, 4–1, as shown by the encirclement in the diagram (Fig. 178).

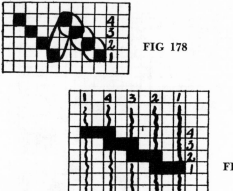

FIG 178

FIG 179

Following are the steps in weaving a simple 4-harness twill:

The first shot passes *over* all warp threads threaded on harnesses 1 and 2 and *under* all on 3 and 4.

The second shot passes *over* all warp threads threaded on harnesses 2 and 3 and *under* all on 1 and 4.

The third shot passes *over* all warp threads threaded on harnesses 3 and 4 and *under* all on 1 and 2.

The fourth shot passes *over* all warp threads threaded on harnesses 4 and 1 and *under* all on 2 and 3.

The weave resembles the side view of a stairs with extending treads (Fig. 179).

A continued repetition of the 1 and 2, 2 and 3, 3 and 4, 4 and 1 sequence, produces a left-hand twill.

A reversal of the sequence 4 and 1, 3 and 4, 2 and 3, 1 and 2, produces a right-hand twill.

A repeated sequence of the 1 and 2, 2 and 3, 3 and 4, 4 and 1, 3 and 4, 2 and 3, produces a zigzag twill.

FIG 180

Sampler   One of the "musts" for every weaver is the designing and weaving of a sampler of the various twill treadlings similar to Fig. 182.

The choice of color and arrangement should be the weaver's own. While the different treadlings and draw-downs are given in Fig. 181 for a sampler similar to the one shown, it should not be copied thread by thread. There is much more satisfaction to the weaver when the choice of threads, color, and design arrangement are his own.

In weaving a sampler, especially if it is for study purposes, it is wise to separate the different twill pattern bands. Do not attempt to do this with alternating bands of plain weave as it is very difficult to keep straight selvedges when changing from twill to plain weave and back again, as shown. This is due to the difference in weave structure. Bands of plain twill or color can be used effectively to separate the pattern bands. This is something with which to experiment.

On the draw-down (Fig. 181), the arrow designates a group of weaves

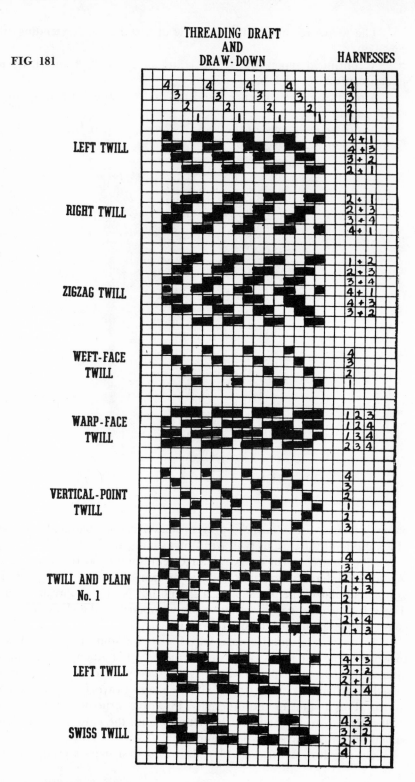

FIG 181

THREADING DRAFT
AND
DRAW-DOWN

HARNESSES

LEFT TWILL

RIGHT TWILL

ZIGZAG TWILL

WEFT-FACE
TWILL

WARP-FACE
TWILL

VERTICAL-POINT
TWILL

TWILL AND PLAIN
No. 1

LEFT TWILL

SWISS TWILL

THREADING DRAFT
AND
DRAW-DOWN

HARNESSES

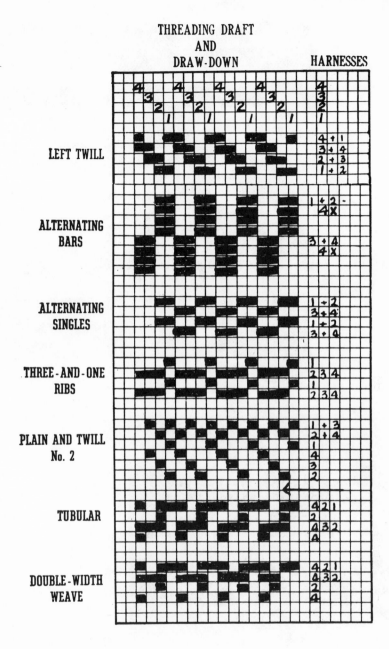

LEFT TWILL

ALTERNATING
BARS

ALTERNATING
SINGLES

THREE-AND-ONE
RIBS

PLAIN AND TWILL
No. 2

TUBULAR

DOUBLE-WIDTH
WEAVE

shown on the sampler (Fig. 182) which do not appear here. They were treadled directly on the loom and were not recorded.

Problem Plan and weave a small sampler using an original color combination and as many original treadlings as possible.

FIG 182

FIG. 183
More 4-harness twill
variations

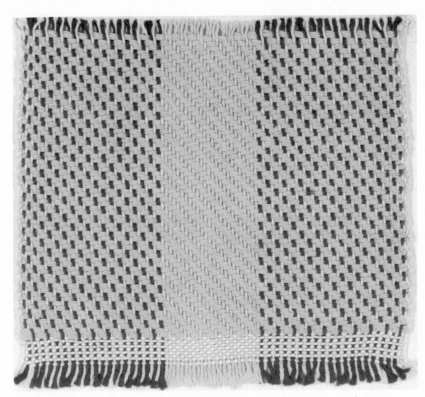

FIG. 184. Plain twill weave on mixed color warp

TYPE Twill, 4-Harness •
PATTERN Combined Plain and Twill

The astute weaver will have discovered long before this that the plain weave and the twill weave are set on the same threading. The difference is achieved through the treadling routine.

Plain and twill are the two weaves on which most other weaves are based. One of the most natural methods of decorating a plain web is to use bands of twill. One difficulty with this type of decoration, however, is the selvedge. With most materials, the twill weave draws in much more than the plain and is a challenge to the weaver. In the sample shown (Fig. 186), the material was suitable for this combination of weaves and the result was fairly satisfactory.

Uses For borders at the bottom and through the body of drapes; for borders at the ends of place mats, scarves, and the bottom of skirts; for formal drapes; and for ecclesiastical articles.

Suitable Materials and Sleying To be appropriate for the article being woven

Sample Illustrated (Fig. 186)

WARP	WEFT	REED	SLEY
		(dents per inch)	
White nylon package twine, No. 25	White nylon package twine, No. 25	12	Single

There is considerable shrinkage to nylon package twine, therefore allowance should be made to offset this. The sample illustrated was tried out for place mats and found satisfactory.

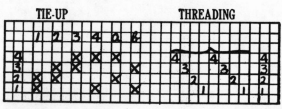

FIG 185

Repeat the bracketed section the required number of times to obtain the desired width.

Treadling–Sinking Shed		**Treadling–Rising Shed** *(No Tie-Up)*
		LEVERS
TREADLES		**OR TREADLES**
a b	Repeat for 18 shots to weave plain web.	1 and 3 2 and 4
1 2 3 4	Repeat for 21 shots to weave left-hand twill web.	3 and 4 1 and 4 1 and 2 2 and 3
3 2 1 4	Repeat for 21 shots to weave right-hand twill web.	1 and 2 1 and 4 3 and 4 2 and 3
a b	Repeat for 18 shots to weave plain web.	1 and 3 2 and 4

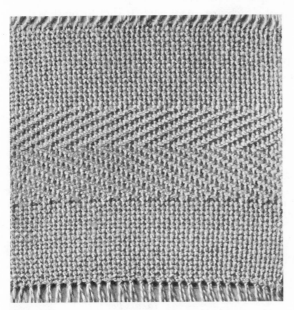

FIG 186

While weaving, watch the selvedge carefully so both the plain and the twill sections will be even.

Problem Plan and weave a set of two place mats with twill borders at each end. Allow sufficient warp for the hems or fringes between the mats.

FIG. 187
Another combined plain and twill weave

TYPE Twill, 4-Harness • PATTERN Return or Point Bird's-Eye

The bird's-eye, one of the finest of the patterned twills, is included in the group called diaper weaves and, until recent years, was the weave most generally used for this purpose. The weave is simple and there are various ways of treadling it, two of which are given here. It should be sleyed to give a firm but soft fabric, regardless of the materials being used.

Uses For fine linen toweling; fine, soft wool, baby blankets; or, if closely sleyed and beaten hard, for upholstery

Suitable Materials and Sleying

WARP	WEFT	REED *(dents per inch)*	SLEY
Wool, 2/32	Wool, 2/32	15	Double
Linen, 3-ply	Linen, 3-ply	15	Double
Cotton, 16/2	Wool, 2/32 or 2/16	15	Double

Sample Illustrated (Fig. 189)

WARP	WEFT	REED *(dents per inch)*	SLEY
Cotton, 8/2	Cotton, 8/2	15	Double

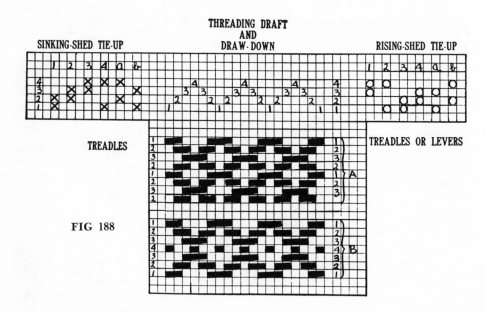

THREADING DRAFT
AND
DRAW-DOWN

SINKING-SHED TIE-UP   RISING-SHED TIE-UP

TREADLES   TREADLES OR LEVERS

FIG 188

A: Treadled as-drawn-in, the web lacks character and is uninteresting. The 1 and 4 harness combination is not included, as it does not appear on the draw-down.

B: Woven in twill succession 1 and 2, 2 and 3, 3 and 4, 4 and 1. A tiny, pointed figure emerges.

C: Woven in return twill 1 and 2, 2 and 3, 3 and 4, 4 and 1, 3 and 4, 3 and 2. Results in tiny, starlike figures.

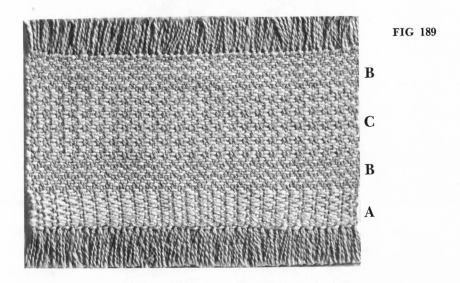

FIG 189

B

C

B

A

Problem   Thread three samples of the bird's-eye; one with fine linen, one with fine wool, and one with cotton. Weave and wash to test the sleying and beating. Keep accurate notes of the results for future use.

TYPE Twill, 4-Harness ·
PATTERN Return or Point Herringbone, Chevron, and Goose-Eye

The return group of twills includes such well-known favorites as the herringbone, the goose-eye, bird's-eye, and the Swedish rosengang or rose path.

A reverse and return twill are not necessarily the same. Harriet Tidball defines them in part as follows, "Return: the part of the pattern or draft which is the mirror image of the preceding part; that is, the second part, which repeats the first part in reverse," and "Reverse: the reverse in the direction of a draft or a pattern. This may or may not be the same as a return, as a reverse does not necessarily produce a symmetrical arrangement but may simply be part of a design elaboration."

The most familiar return twill is the herringbone, also called the

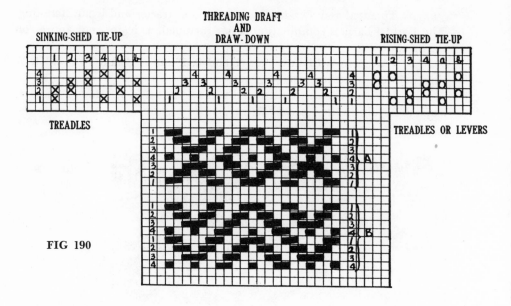

FIG 190

chevron. The goose-eye is the design formed when the draft is treadled as-drawn-in. The herringbone is used extensively for suitings and coatings, being rivaled in popularity only by the dornik twill (page 209) which, while threaded in practically the same way, is a more durable weave as the three skips at the turning points are eliminated. Other methods of threading this herringbone give only slightly different results.[2]

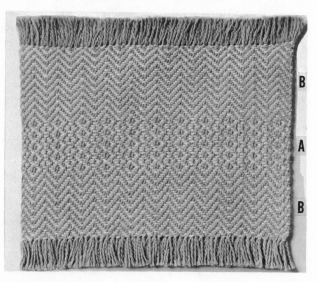

FIG 191

Materials and Sleying The same as those given for the plain twill. Linens and wools are considered the best threads for twill weaves, though some weavers achieve splendid results with other materials. The threads used should, of course, be suitable to the purpose of the finished material.

Problem With a homespun wool warp, set up a sample and treadle it in either method. Experiment with sleying, then test a swatch by washing and steam pressing. Allow enough warp for several samples and keep accurate notes of the experiment for future reference.

TYPE Twill, 4-Harness · PATTERN Return or Point Rose Path

Weavers do not progress too far into the return twills before they discover the Swedish rosengang or rose path, as it is known in this country. Authorities on rose-path samplers are Berta Frey and Marguerite P. Davison. Experienced weavers claim also that there are still many unrecorded treadlings.

There are many treadlings and several threadings for rose path, although only one threading and a few treadling variations are given here.

The rose-path threading is popular among modern weavers interested in texture weaving. It is as suitable in very fine upholstery as it is in coarse, loosely woven draperies. This is one weave that can be woven according to the weaver's choice.

Samples Illustrated

1 (Fig. 193)

WARP	WEFT	REED (*dents per inch*)	SLEY
Cotton, 8/2	Cotton, 8/2	12	Double

2 (Fig. 194)

WARP	WEFT	REED (*dents per inch*)	SLEY
Cotton, 8/2	Homespun, 2-ply	16	Single

Threading Rose Path (Fig. 192)

Tie-Up Standard

Treadling Sample woven on rising-shed loom

Sample 1

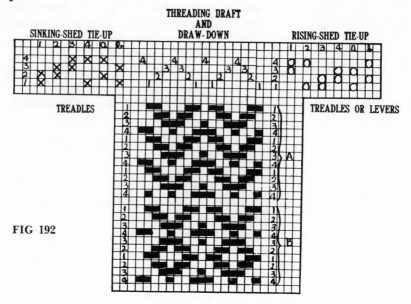

THREADING DRAFT
AND
DRAW-DOWN

SINKING-SHED TIE-UP   RISING-SHED TIE-UP

TREADLES   TREADLES OR LEVERS

FIG 192

Sample 2

Sinking Shed		Rising Shed
TREADLES, NO TIE-UP		**TREADLES OR LEVERS**
3 and 4 — 1× 4 — 12× 1, 2, 3 — 4× 2 and 3 — 4× 3 and 4 — 4× 4 — 3×	A. Trees, woven with tabby (page 179)	1 and 2 — 1× 1, 2, 3 — 12× 4 — 4× 1 and 4 — 4× 1 and 2 — 4× 1, 2, 3 — 3×

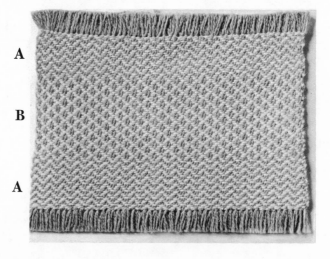

A

B

A

FIG 193

2, 3, 4		1
1, 3, 4		2
1, 2, 4		3
1, 2, 3	B. Woven without tabby;	4
1, 2, 4	repeat from top.	3
1, 3, 4		2
2, 3, 4		1
1, 2, 3		4

TREADLE, STANDARD TIE-UP   **LEVERS**

3		1 and 2
4		2 and 3
1		3 and 4
2	C. Woven as-drawn-in	4 and 1
1	without tabby	3 and 4
4		2 and 3
3		1 and 2
2		1 and 4

Repeat from top

3 — 1×		1 and 2 — 1×
4 — 1×		2 and 3 — 1×
1 — 1×		3 and 4 — 1×
4 — 1×		2 and 3 — 1×
3 — 8×		1 and 2 — 8×
2 — 1×		1 and 4 — 1×
1 — 1×		4 and 3 — 1×
4 — 1×		3 and 2 — 1×
3 — 1×	D. Border woven	2 and 1 — 1×
4 — 1×	with tabby	2 and 3 — 1×
1 — 1×		3 and 4 — 1×
2 — 1×		4 and 1 — 1×
3 — 8×		1 and 2 — 8×
4 — 1×		2 and 3 — 1×
1 — 1×		3 and 4 — 1×
4 — 1×		2 and 3 — 1×
3 — 1×		1 and 2 — 1×

Repeat from top, omitting first treadle 3.

Repeat from top, omitting first treadles 1 and 2.

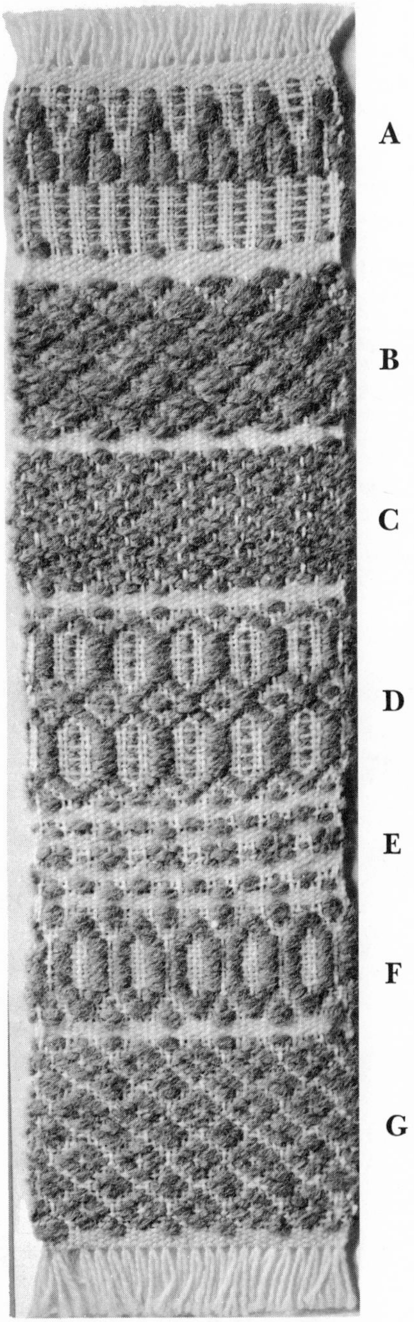

FIG 194

A
B
C
D
E
F
G

3 — 1× 4 — 1× 6 rows plain weave 2 — 1× 3 — 1× 2 — 1× 6 rows plain weave 4 — 1× 3 — 1×	E. Flowers, woven with tabby	1 and 2 — 1× 2 and 3 — 1× 6 rows plain weave 1 and 4 — 1× 1 and 2 — 1× 1 and 4 — 1× 6 rows plain weave 2 and 3 — 1× 1 and 2 — 1×

Repeat from top omitting first treadle 3.

Repeat from top omitting first treadles 1 and 2.

3 — 2× 4 — 2× 1 — 2× 2 — 10× 1 — 2× 4 — 2× 3 — 2×	F. Border, woven with tabby	1 and 2 — 2× 2 and 3 — 2× 3 and 4 — 2× 1 and 4 — 10× 3 and 4 — 2× 2 and 3 — 2× 1 and 2 — 2×

Repeat from top omitting first treadle 3.

Repeat from top omitting first treadles 1 and 2.

3 — 1× 4 — 1× 1 — 1× 2 — 1× 1 — 1× 4 — 1× 3 — 1× 2 — 1×	G. Treadled without tabby	1 and 2 — 1× 2 and 3 — 1× 3 and 4 — 1× 1 and 4 — 1× 4 and 3 — 1× 3 and 2 — 1× 2 and 1 — 1× 1 and 4 — 1×

Repeat from top.

Repeat from top.

Problem Set up a 2-yd. cotton warp and weave a sampler using as many different original treadlings and varieties of weft materials as possible. Try combinations of shiny and dull threads, dull and metallic threads, or rough and smooth threads. Use four different weights of thread:

Shuttle 1: Heavy thread

Shuttle 2: Medium-size thread

Shuttle 3: Fine thread

Shuttle 4: Very fine thread

Repeat in the same order. Dramatize the rose path with one contrasting, colored thread, the others in the same color.

TYPE Twill, 4-Harness •
PATTERN Double-Weave Interlocking

The setting and treadling given here produce a closely integrated material without skips or floats. The two webs are interlocked with a weft-face twill appearance on both the upper and under sides.

If two contrasting colors are used, there is a play of color between the threads of the surfaces.

Uses This weave, which deserves greater popularity than it is given, is suitable for soft baby blankets, car rugs, sports jackets, snowsuits, draperies, pillow tops, and bags.

Materials Any that are suitable for the article being woven.

Sample Illustrated (Fig. 196)

WARP	WEFT	REED (*dents per inch*)	SLEY
Cotton, 8/2	Cotton, 8/4	20	Double

The complete tie-up for this weave requires 8 treadles; therefore, as the average 4-harness loom only has 6, it is necessary to use a direct tie-up. Depressing a single treadle opens the upper shed while depressing 3 together opens the lower shed. As with the other double weaves, it is simpler and easier to get a good shed on a rising-shed loom than on a counterbalanced loom.

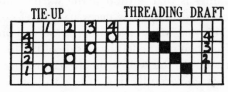

FIG 195

Treadling (*No Tie-Up*)

TREADLES OR LEVERS
1
1, 2, 3
2
1, 2, 4
3
1, 3, 4
4
2, 3, 4

FIG 196

Repeat the required number of times to weave the desired length. The beating should be light for woolen articles; hard for beach bags, lawn-chair covers, and porch pillows of heavy cotton.

Problem Set up the loom with 3-ply, fairly coarse yarn, and weave a baby blanket.

TYPE Twill, 4-Harness · PATTERN Double-Width Web

The width of blankets and luncheon sets frequently is restricted because of the width of the reed and, to obtain wide material, it is necessary to weave and join together two identical pieces. This difficulty can be overcome by weaving a piece of double-width cloth. The result is satisfactory if care is taken not to pull in the edges when weaving, thereby narrowing the fabric.

What actually happens in this double weave is that two pieces of cloth are woven simultaneously, one on an upper shed, and one on a lower shed. The shuttle passes from the upper to the lower, and vice versa, in such a way that the two webs are joined together down the center. One of the webs is woven on harnesses 1 and 2, the other on harnesses 3 and 4. An important point to remember is that, although the warp is double sley through the reed, the web is single sley. It is necessary, therefore, to choose threads for the warp and weft that will weave into a 50/50 web on a single sley.

The web is open on the left-hand side of the loom where two selvedges appear. The center of the web is on the right-hand side of the fold. This edge must be woven carefully or a streak will show up the middle of the web when it is removed from the loom and opened.

Use For any material required in a width wider than the available reed, such as blankets, car rugs, and luncheon sets. Add color interest by incorporating colored threads in either the warp or weft or both.

Suitable Materials and Sleying The choice of material depends upon the article to be made. Try out all materials to determine whether the threads used will produce a firm, satisfactory web.

Sample Illustrated (Fig. 198)

WARP	WEFT	REED (dents per inch)	SLEY
Carpet warp, 8/2	Carpet warp, 8/2	20	Double

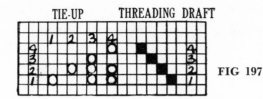

FIG 197

Do not thread the first 1 at the right selvedge when starting the threading or two warp threads will come together at the right (the center of the web).

To Weave   The treadling directions and tie-up are for a rising-shed loom. To weave on a counterbalanced loom, tie the blank spaces to the treadles. It may be difficult to get a good shed on the counterbalanced loom because of the close sleying and the treadling of one harness against three.

Harnesses 1 and 2, treadled in alternating succession, weave the upper web, while harnesses 3 and 4 weave the lower web. However, to weave the lower web, the upper row of threads on harnesses 1 and 2 must be lifted out of the way. For this reason, harnesses 1 and 2 are treadled in alternating succession with harnesses 3 and 4.

Order of Treadling

TREADLE	PASS THE SHUTTLE FROM
1	right to left
2	left to right
3	right to left
4	left to right

Repeat the required number of times starting with treadle 1 each time.

FIG 198

With Levers or a Direct Tie-Up

LEVER OR TREADLE	PASS THE SHUTTLE FROM
1	right to left
2	left to right
1, 2, 3	right to left
1, 2, 4	left to right

Extreme care in weaving this technique will bring good results.

Problem   Thread the loom and weave a baby blanket of wool with contrasting weft stripes.

TYPE Twill, 4-Harness ·
PATTERN Double Plain Weave, Tubular

Regardless of the width threaded in the loom, this technique produces a tube. Because of harness limitations, it can be joined only at the sides. There are only a few uses for this weave, but it is rather fun to do.

Uses   For purses, bags, pillow covers, and baby buntings

Suitable Materials and Sleying

ARTICLE	WARP	WEFT	REED *(dents per inch)*	SLEY
Pillow tubing	Linen, 30/2 or Linen and cotton, 30/3	Linen, 20/3	20	Double
Purses, bags, and pillow covers	Cotton, 20/2 or Cotton, 8/4	Wool, coarse	20	Double

Samples Illustrated (Figs. 200 and 201)

WARP	WEFT	REED *(dents per inch)*	SLEY
Cotton, 8/2	Cotton, 8/4	20	Double

These directions are for a rising-shed loom. Reverse the tie-up for a counterbalanced sinking-shed loom.

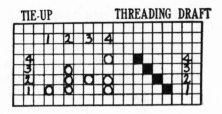

FIG 199

Order of Treadling

TREADLE	PASS THE SHUTTLE FROM
1	right to left
2	left to right
3	right to left
4	left to right

With Levers or Direct Tie-Up

LEVER OR TREADLE	PASS THE SHUTTLE FROM
1	right to left
1, 2, 3	left to right
2	right to left
1, 2, 4	left to right

FIG 200

FIG 201

Repeat the required number of times, starting with treadle or lever 1 each time.

The bottom of the tube or bag can be joined together by alternating treadles 1 and 3, 2 and 4 for a few rows. Turn this heading up, inside the bag or purse, and whip across the bottom to strengthen it.

It is not possible, by loom manipulation, to fasten two plain-weave surfaces together vertically. This is done with a pickup stick. The two surfaces are joined together horizontally by treadling one row of 1 and 3 or 2 and 4.

Add interest to a bag or purse by setting it for a weft-face fabric and weaving it in bright, gay, colored stripes. Or, set the warp in stripes and weave it either as a striped material or, by using two colors, as a checked material.

Problem Set up the warp and weave a wool or heavy linen bag or purse in gay colors.

TYPE Twill, 5-Harness · PATTERN Satin Weave Damask

True damask is a derivative of the satin weave which, according to commercial weaving books, is one of the three fundamental weaves. The other two are the plain weave and the twill.

Damask has long been the homemakers' choice for fine table linens. It is seen in small French restaurants in a red and white, two-block pattern, its simplest form; and in exclusive hotels in elaborately developed floral, bird, animal, or conventionalized patterns. Damasks in heavy, rich silks for upholstery and draperies reached their peak of popularity and workmanship just before the French Revolution when churches and homes were lavishly decorated with damasks and brocades, and the clergy and nobility were resplendent in garments of damask and brocade woven to their special orders. Paintings of the twelfth to the eighteenth centuries reveal many beautiful examples of these materials.

Damask has wonderful wearing qualities which explains why we find so many examples of it in museums.

The hand weaver will find it impractical to attempt patterns beyond the 10- or 15-harness, 3-block damask, as the loom becomes large and cumbersome and the treadle system unmanageable. For figured damask, a regulation damask or draw loom is required. While the technique seems very confusing to the neophyte, it holds a decided interest and challenge for the advanced weaver. Several hand weavers on this continent have damask looms and several places offer instruction. A helpful little publication on damask weaving is available in several Swedish centers[3] and can be obtained for a modest sum.

Uses Linen damask, by tradition, is used principally for tablecloths and upholstery. When woven of silk, damask is used for drapes, upholstery, clothing, and ecclesiastical purposes. Though usually associated with formal interiors and occasions, damask, if woven in block designs in the darker colors, rather than white or pastels, lends itself well to place mats for informal use.

Materials Fine, soft linens are a must for damask weaving. When procurable, a good Scottish, Irish, or Belgian linen is suggested. The mercerized linens are a better quality than the plain and, when laundered, are very handsome. In fact, the more mercerized linens are laundered, the more beautiful they become.

Threads can vary in size from very fine 60/2 sleyed at 60 threads per inch, to size 10/2 sleyed at 20 to 24 threads per inch. The size generally used is 40/2, set triple sley in a 15- or 18-dent reed. Beat hard, for there is nothing less desirable than a sleazy piece of damask.

Theory On the 8-harness loom it is possible to weave only one block, herein referred to as block *A*, of a 5-shaft damask.

Ten harnesses are required to weave a 2-block damask. One block shows the weft skips on the upper side, the other shows the weft skips on the underside, since the blocks are woven in alternating succession.

In the 5-shaft damask the weft thread floats over four warp threads and is caught down under every fifth warp thread. However, unlike the double plain weave, where the treadling forms a plain web, and the double twill weave, where the treadling is arranged to form a twill succession, the treadling for the damask is arranged to prevent any repetition that will form a pattern.

Sample Illustrated (Fig. 204)

WARP	WEFT	REED (dents per inch)	SLEY
Linen, 45/2	Linen, 45/2	18	Triple

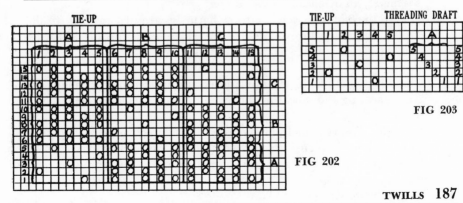

FIG 203

FIG 202

Repeat the threading for block *A* as often as necessary to obtain the desired width. A warp, 1 yd. long, was wound for the sample.

Treadling The treadles are depressed in the order in which they appear on the diagram, treadling from 1 through 5 and repeating the routine as often as required to weave the desired length.

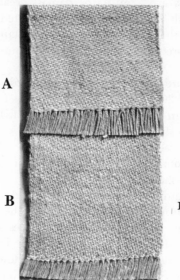

A

B   FIG 204

Problem Set up and weave a sample of 5-shaft damask. If a 10- or 12-harness loom is available, set up a 2-block pattern.

TYPE Twill, 6-Harness · PATTERN Plain

The theory which controls the 4-harness twills also controls the 6-harness; it is merely an extension of the former.

In the 6-harness version, three harnesses are tied to each treadle. This results in the weft thread passing over three warp threads with each shot, thus producing a somewhat softer and more pliable web.

Treadling Follow the treadling order as it appears on the tie-up chart (Fig. 206), repeating and repeating the sequence until the desired length is woven.

Problem Weave a small sample using any desired choice of yarns and colors and treadling sequence. Experiment. Keep notes of threads, colors, and treadling used, in the event it is desired to repeat the sample or parts of it.

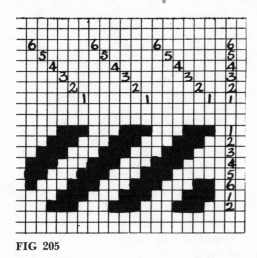

FIG 205

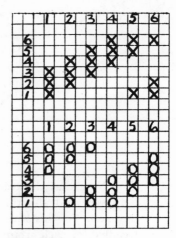

FIG 206

TYPE Twill, 6-Harness · PATTERN 2-Block, Reverse

This 2-block arrangement of a 6-harness reverse twill is equally appropriate for fine linen place mats, or, in heavy wool, for car rugs or coating. Sleying for the linen should be very close, and for the heavy wool a size 9 reed is suggested to give suppleness to the web.

While experimenting with this threading and variations of it, it was found that a much more subtle and interesting color effect was obtained by using two shades of one color of the linen or wool rather than two contrasting colors. However, to show up the weave structure the sample for the photograph (Fig. 179D) was woven with white and dark gray.

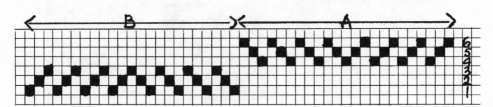

FIG. 207. Threading draft

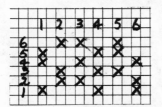

FIG. 208. Tie-up: sinking shed

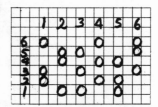

FIG. 209. Tie-up: rising shed

Treadling

TREADLES	HARNESSES
1	2, 3, 6, white
2	1, 4, 5, gray
3	1, 3, 5, white
4	2, 4, 6, gray
5	1, 2, 4, white
6	3, 5, 6, gray

Note that the treadling falls into groups of four pairs, on opposite harnesses, and also that where the pairs join, each has two harnesses in common. For instance, between the first and second pairs, threads are treadled for each group on harnesses 1 and 5. This results in a semi-double web as the weft threads form one group pack, or beat, down under two of the same warp threads as in the previous group. Where the pattern reverses, this does not occur, and there is a streak plainly visible in the woven web. For a second experiment, treadle 1, 4, 5, white, with alternating shots of gray on harness 1, 3, 5, and 2, 4, 6. After a square is woven, the gray and white threads are reversed, the gray becoming the pattern thread and the white the background thread. This treadling results in a softer web, is a more unusual weave than the return twill treadling as above, and is more interesting in the tonal nuances. This would probably weave a very good coating material if one-ply tweed yarn in two harmonious shades were used, with the darker shade for the background and the lighter for the top layer. It would also produce beautiful couch throws or shawls using the lightweight fluffy mohair yarns available from most weaving supply houses.

Problem Experiment!

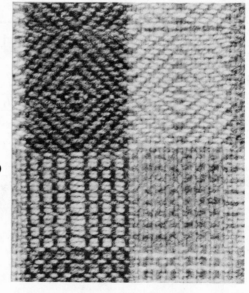

FIG 210

TYPE Twill, 6-Harness and Plain Weave ·
PATTERN Swedish Kypert och tuskaft

As the weaver delves more deeply into pattern structure, he appreciates the value of having extra harnesses with which to work. For example, the 6-harness pattern, *Kypert och tuskaft,* is a combination of a twill and plain weave which cannot be woven on four harnesses. The plain web in the center is threaded and woven on harnesses 5 and 6; the twill on harnesses 1, 2, 3, and 4. Further variations are possible by increasing or decreasing the width of the stripe and by changing the twill into a goose-eye threading.

Uses Household linens, dress materials, wool scarves, and blankets.

Suitable Materials and Sleying As for other twills.

Samples Illustrated (Figs. 212, 213, and 215)

WARP	WEFT	REED (*dents per inch*)	SLEY
Carpet warp, 8/2	Carpet warp, 8/2	8	Triple

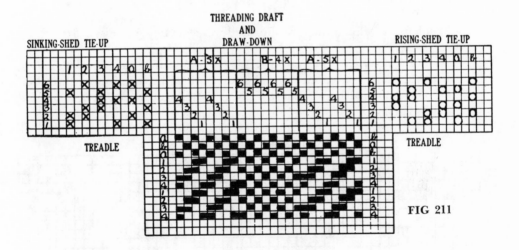

FIG 211

This combination weave presents the same problem with warp tension as the basket and plain weaves, the plain weave having a greater take-up than the twill. Long lengths of warp, such as for a tweed coat or suit, should be wound on two beams, one for the twill portions and the other for the plain weave.

In threading this draft, the *A* and *B* blocks can be repeated as often as necessary for the required width and any number of threads can be used

FIG 212

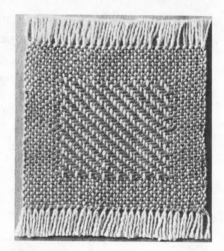

FIG 213

in each block. However, in threading, end with the *A* block to balance the design.

Regardless of the order in which the pattern is written, a three-thread skip appears every fourth weft row where the twill and plain weave join. This can be seen clearly in Figs. 212 and 213.

Problem Work out the threading and weave a sample of Fig. 213.

The reverse twill threading (Fig. 214) also can be used in combination with the plain weave, but remember that, where the two join, a thread on an odd-numbered harness must lie next to a thread on an even-numbered harness and vice versa.

THREADING DRAFT

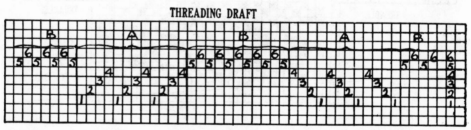

FIG 214

Repeat the threading the required number of times to set the warp to the desired width, ending on the left with the first four threads only of the *B* block to balance the design.

The tie-ups for both the sinking and the rising sheds are the same as for the twill and plain weave (Fig. 211). Material used for Fig. 215 was 8/4 cotton sleyed at 16 ends per inch.

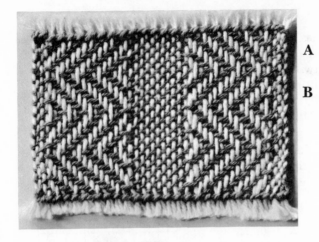

A

B

FIG 215

Treadling–Sinking Shed		Treadling–Rising Shed
1 ⎫		1
2 ⎪	Repeat twice.	2
3 ⎬		3
4 ⎭		4
3 ⎫		3
2 ⎪	Treadle once.	2
1 ⎬		1
4 ⎭		4

Repeat the required number of times to weave the desired length. Start at the top each time.

Problem Mixed threading. Student analyze same and weave sample (Fig. 216).

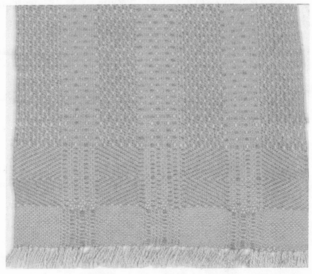

FIG 216

TYPE Twill, 8-Harness · PATTERN Plain

The theory of twills has already been explained. As more harnesses are added, more changes in pattern design are possible.

On an 8-harness twill threading (aside from the 1, 3, 5, 7; 2, 4, 6, 8 tabby weave) eight treadling combinations are possible:

1, 2;	2, 3;	3, 4;	4, 5;
5, 6;	6, 7;	7, 8;	8, 1.

As shown by the encirclement in the diagram (Fig. 217), however, unless the warp is very closely set, long overshots occur. To remedy this, the number of changes is reduced to four by treadling as follows (read across):

1, 2, 5, 6;	2, 3, 6, 7;
3, 4, 7, 8;	4, 1, 8, 5.

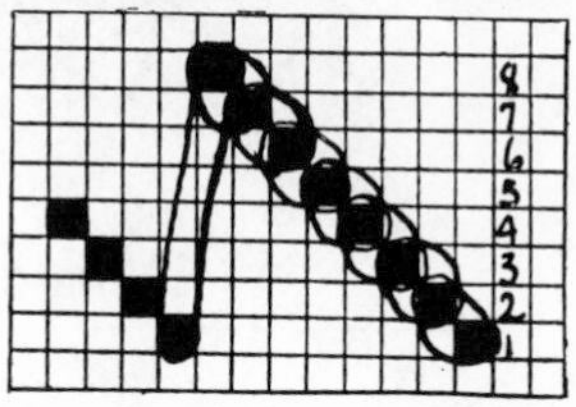

FIG 217

The theory of this is quite simple if the weaver thinks of the 8-harness loom as having two sets of four harnesses each, the front set numbered 1, 2, 3, 4; and the back set 5, 6, 7, 8. In order to balance the weave, harnesses 1 and 2 of the first set are used in combination with the first two harnesses of the second set which are numbers 5 and 6. For the second set, harnesses 2 and 3 of the first set and the second and third harnesses of the second set, or numbers 6 and 7, are combined, and so on until all possible combinations in sequence are used. From this fundamental theory many variations in weaves are developed.

The 8-harness twill threading offers much more opportunity for variation than the twill threadings on fewer harnesses. The web has more character, is firmer in texture, and has a definite right and wrong side. The warp shows very plainly in some webs, the weft in others.

Uses For dress and coat fabrics, household linens, bags, pillow covers, upholstery, and for any use for which twills are appropriate.

TYPE Twill, 8-Harness · PATTERN Treadling Variations

Sample Illustrated (Fig. 219)

WARP	WEFT	REED (dents per inch)	SLEY
Cotton, 20/3	Wool, fine	15	Double

The samples of the 8-harness twill weaves have been woven with the above selection of threads to emphasize the structure of the weave in the photographs.

It is customary to use the same thread or, at least, a thread of the same size for both the warp and weft in twill weaving.

Draw-downs and tie-ups usually are made for a sinking-shed loom, even though the draft calls for more than four harnesses. However, in this case (Figs. 218 and 220), the procedure has been reversed and O's appear in place of X's.

A study of tie-up *A* will reveal that treadles 1–5, 2–6, 3–7, and 4–8 are tied to the same harnesses. Actually it is only necessary to use four treadles, repeating the routine 1, 2, 3, 4 a second time to complete the 5, 6, 7, and 8 section. While this is true, in actual practice the full tie-up is usually given, and all treadles are used in the routine.

The most simple tie-up for the 8-harness twill is shown at *A*. This

THREADING DRAFT
AND
DRAW-DOWN

RISING-SHED TIE-UP

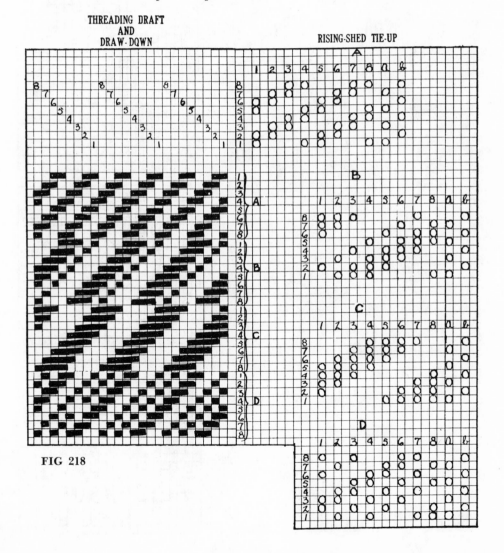

FIG 218

produces a balanced 2–2 twill, the weft thread passing over two threads and under two threads across the entire warp.

The first variation is shown at B (Fig. 218) where one warp thread is bound down, one thread up, then three down, then three up. This is the cheviot weave, a 3–1 weave.

At C there is still another variation, a 4–4 weave, four threads up, four down.

Treadling the D tie-up produces a much finer weave than any of the others with a one down, two up, two down, one up routine.

All of these treadlings are especially good for coatings, although they are a bit heavy for suitings. Place mats of either very fine or heavy linen are attractive in any of the 8-harness twill weaves.

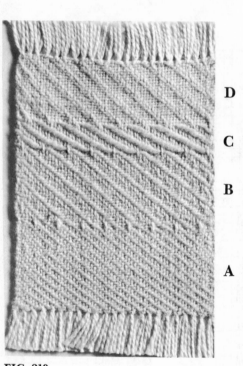

FIG 219

D

C

B

A

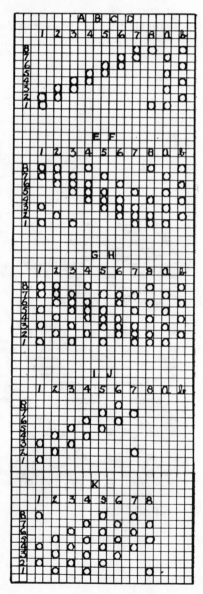

FIG 220

Additional Tie-Ups and Treadlings on the 8-Harness Plain Twill
Order of Treadling

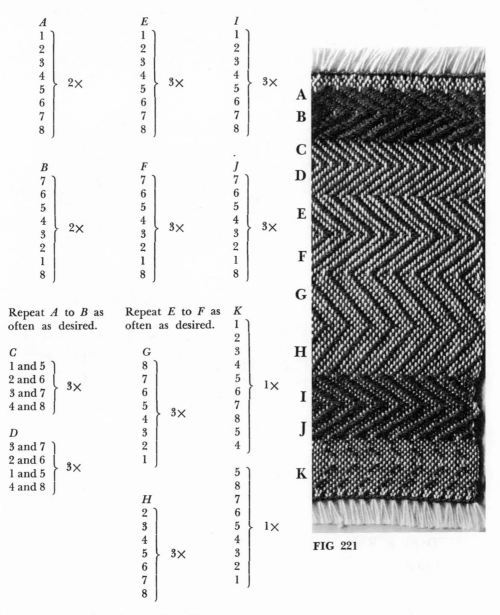

A
1
2
3
4
5 } 2×
6
7
8

E
1
2
3
4
5 } 3×
6
7
8

I
1
2
3
4
5 } 3×
6
7
8

          A
          B
          C
          D

B
7
6
5
4 } 2×
3
2
1
8

F
7
6
5
4 } 3×
3
2
1
8

J
7
6
5
4 } 3×
3
2
1
8

          E
          F
          G

Repeat A to B as often as desired.

Repeat E to F as often as desired.

K
1
2
3
4
5 } 1×
6
7
8
5
4

C
1 and 5
2 and 6 } 3×
3 and 7
4 and 8

D
3 and 7
2 and 6 } 3×
1 and 5
4 and 8

G
8
7
6
5
4 } 3×
3
2
1

          H

          I

          J

5
8
7
6
5 } 1×
4
3
2
1

          K

H
2
3
4
5 } 3×
6
7
8

FIG 221

Repeat G to H as often as desired.

Problem Thread the loom with 8/2 or similar size cotton and try out the twill treadlings as given above, striving for even beating.

TYPE Twill, 8-Harness •
PATTERN Swedish Kypert—Reverse Twill

The traditional return and bird's-eye twill weaves can be treadled on this threading. Many variations are also possible.

When closely sleyed of fine, firm threads such as the 3-ply linens, cottons, and synthetic threads, a very firm fabric, suitable for upholstery, results. It is also suitable for household linens when sleyed more loosely.

THREADING DRAFT AND TIE-UP FOR A,B,C,D,E,H,I,J,K

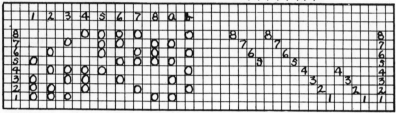

FIG 222

TIE-UP FOR F AND G

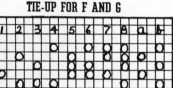

FIG 223

TIE-UP FOR L

FIG 224

Sample Illustrated (Fig. 225)

The sample illustrated (Fig. 225) was woven on an 8-harness table loom. It is suggested that it be woven in the following order on a floor loom to save changing the tie-up more than twice: *A B C D E H I J K F G L.*

Treadling/Rising Shed

Unit *A*
1 ⎫
2 ⎬ Repeat the desired
3 ⎪ number of times.
4 ⎭

Unit *B*
1 ⎫
2 ⎪
3 ⎬ 2×
4 ⎭

Unit *C*
5 ⎫
6 ⎬ 2×
7 ⎪
8 ⎭

Repeat the desired number of times.

FIG 225

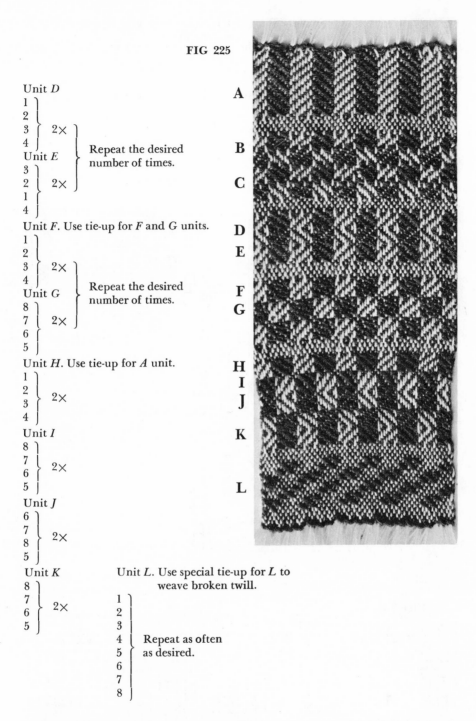

Unit *D*
1 ⎫
2 ⎪
3 ⎬ 2× ⎫
4 ⎭   ⎪ Repeat the desired
Unit *E* ⎬ number of times.
3 ⎫   ⎪
2 ⎬ 2× ⎭
1 ⎫
4 ⎭

Unit *F*. Use tie-up for *F* and *G* units.
1 ⎫
2 ⎪
3 ⎬ 2× ⎫
4 ⎭   ⎪ Repeat the desired
Unit *G* ⎬ number of times.
8 ⎫   ⎪
7 ⎬ 2× ⎭
6 ⎫
5 ⎭

Unit *H*. Use tie-up for *A* unit.
1 ⎫
2 ⎬ 2×
3 ⎪
4 ⎭

Unit *I*
8 ⎫
7 ⎬ 2×
6 ⎪
5 ⎭

Unit *J*
6 ⎫
7 ⎬ 2×
8 ⎪
5 ⎭

Unit *K*   Unit *L*. Use special tie-up for *L* to
8 ⎫   weave broken twill.
7 ⎬ 2×   1 ⎫
6 ⎪   2 ⎪
5 ⎭   3 ⎪
              4 ⎬ Repeat as often
              5 ⎭ as desired.
              6 ⎪
              7 ⎪
              8 ⎭

Problem Thread the sample as indicated and work out original treadlings
suitable for a linen towel or fine upholstery.

TYPE Twill, 8-Harness · PATTERN Point, Herringbone

It is on this threading that the herringbone, diamond, and other return twills are woven.

Uses For household linens and, in wools, for wearing apparel, blankets, and car robes.

Tie-Ups *A, B, C, D* are woven on the tie-up given in Fig. 226.

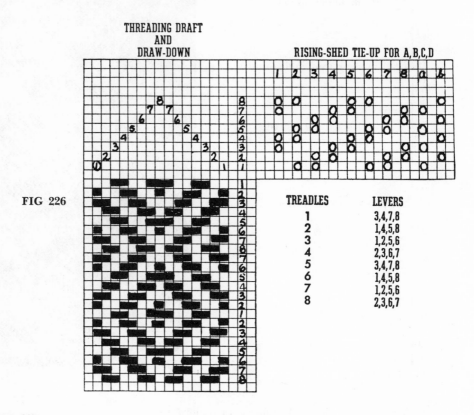

THREADING DRAFT
AND
DRAW-DOWN

RISING-SHED TIE-UP FOR A,B,C,D

FIG 226

TREADLES	LEVERS
1	3,4,7,8
2	1,4,5,8
3	1,2,5,6
4	2,3,6,7
5	3,4,7,8
6	1,4,5,8
7	1,2,5,6
8	2,3,6,7

FIG 227

TIE-UP FOR E AND F   TIE-UP FOR G AND H

Treadling–Rising Shed

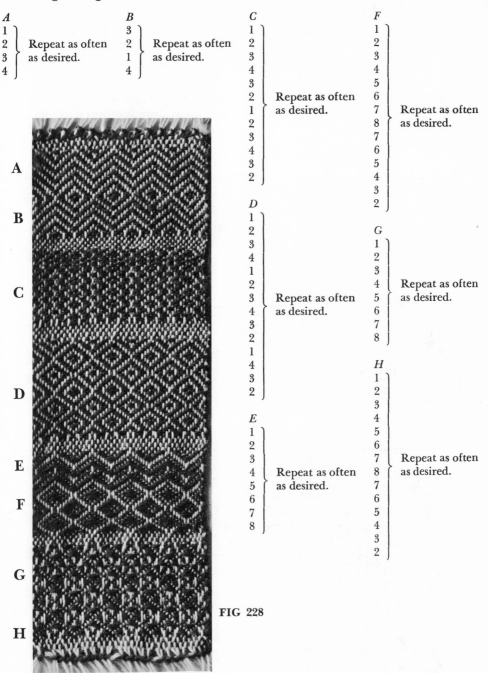

A		*B*		*C*		*F*	
1	}	3	}	1	}	1	}
2	Repeat as often	2	Repeat as often	2		2	
3	as desired.	1	as desired.	3		3	
4		4		4		4	

A
1 } Repeat as often
2 } as desired.
3
4

B
3 } Repeat as often
2 } as desired.
1
4

C
1 }
2
3
4
3
2 } Repeat as often
1 } as desired.
2
3
4
3
2

D
1 }
2
3
4
1
2
3 } Repeat as often
4 } as desired.
3
2
1
4
3
2

E
1 }
2
3
4 } Repeat as often
5 } as desired.
6
7
8

F
1 }
2
3
4
5
6
7 } Repeat as often
8 } as desired.
7
6
5
4
3
2

G
1 }
2
3
4 } Repeat as often
5 } as desired.
6
7
8

H
1 }
2
3
4
5
6
7 } Repeat as often
8 } as desired.
7
6
5
4
3
2

FIG 228

Problem   Thread the sample and try out the various treadlings.

TYPE Twill, 8-Harness •
PATTERN Double Point, Extended

The addition of a second point makes it possible to weave more interesting designs.

Four different tie-ups were required to weave the sample. It is suggested that, if only a sample is required, it be woven on a table loom where no tie-up is necessary. On the other hand, the floor loom can be warped with sufficient material to weave a pillow cover or a bag instead of just a sample. The beginner cannot have too much practice in tying up the treadles, and the extra warp will provide an opportunity to work out original treadlings.

Uses and Materials The same as those listed for the single-point twill. For coatings, have warp and weft of similar or blending colors, otherwise the weave will be "loud." Treadlings *C* and *D* are suggested for upholstery and *E* for pillow covers. Careful choice and gradation of colors is effective in the *E* treadling. Linen pieces woven with unbleached or white singles are particularly nice. They should be carefully sleyed and beaten to a 50/50 web.

THREADING DRAFT

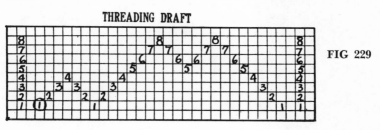

FIG 229

TIE-UPS

FIG 230

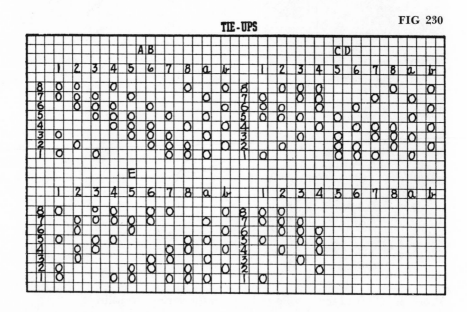

Treadling

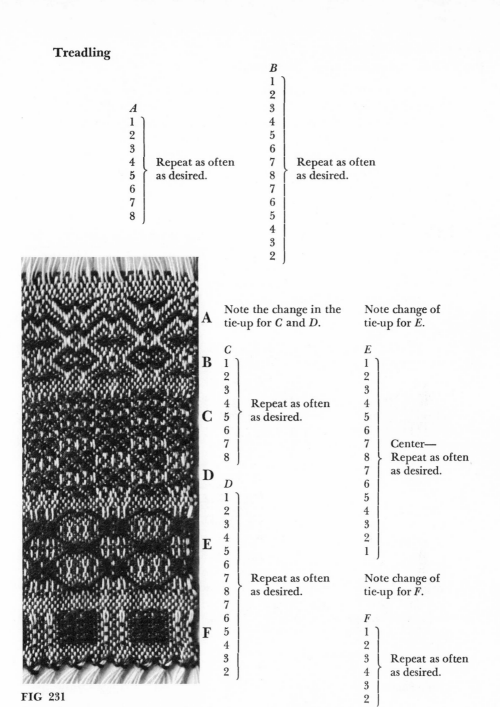

FIG 231

A
1 ⎫
2 ⎪
3 ⎪
4 ⎬ Repeat as often
5 ⎪ as desired.
6 ⎪
7 ⎪
8 ⎭

B
1 ⎫
2 ⎪
3 ⎪
4 ⎪
5 ⎪
6 ⎪
7 ⎪
8 ⎬ Repeat as often
7 ⎪ as desired.
6 ⎪
5 ⎪
4 ⎪
3 ⎪
2 ⎭

A

B

C

D

E

F

Note the change in the tie-up for *C* and *D*.

C
1 ⎫
2 ⎪
3 ⎪
4 ⎬ Repeat as often
5 ⎪ as desired.
6 ⎪
7 ⎪
8 ⎭

D
1 ⎫
2 ⎪
3 ⎪
4 ⎪
5 ⎪
6 ⎪
7 ⎪
8 ⎬ Repeat as often
7 ⎪ as desired.
6 ⎪
5 ⎪
4 ⎪
3 ⎪
2 ⎭

Note change of tie-up for *E*.

E
1 ⎫
2 ⎪
3 ⎪
4 ⎪
5 ⎪
6 ⎪
7 ⎪
8 ⎬ Center—
7 ⎪ Repeat as often
6 ⎪ as desired.
5 ⎪
4 ⎪
3 ⎪
2 ⎪
1 ⎭

Note change of tie-up for *F*.

F
1 ⎫
2 ⎪
3 ⎬ Repeat as often
4 ⎪ as desired.
3 ⎪
2 ⎭

Problem   Thread the loom with a sufficient amount of coarse cotton to weave a pillow cover using heavy yarn for the weft. Use original or given treadlings.

TYPE Twill, 8-Harness •
PATTERN Triple Point, Extended

Many variations can be treadled on this threading; some are given here, others appear on the linen sampler (page 208). It is an interesting weave, embracing a number of tiny figures which can be woven in any sequence to form the desired design.

Uses For linen and wool upholstery, pure linen toweling, bureau scarves, and place mats

Sample Illustrated (Fig. 234)

WARP	WEFT	REED (dents per inch)	SLEY
Cotton, 16/2	Wool, 2/16, or Fabri	15	Double

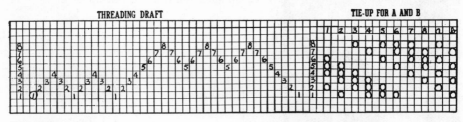

FIG 232

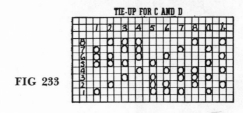

FIG 233

Treadling In weaving, note that the *A* and *B* treadlings are on one tie-up with the *C* and *D* on another. The plain-twill threading, 1, 2, 3, 4, 5, 6, 7, 8, can be repeated any number of times on each side for a border if desired.

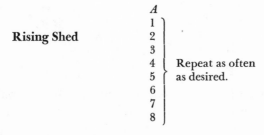

Rising Shed

A
1
2
3
4 } Repeat as often
5 } as desired.
6
7
8

B
1
2
3
4
5
6
7
8 Repeat as often
7 as desired.
6
5
4
3
2
1
2

D
1
2
1
2
3
4
5
6
7 Repeat as often
8 as desired.
7
8
7
6
5
4
3
2

C
1
2
3
4
5
6
7 Repeat as often
8 as desired.
7
6
5
4
3
2

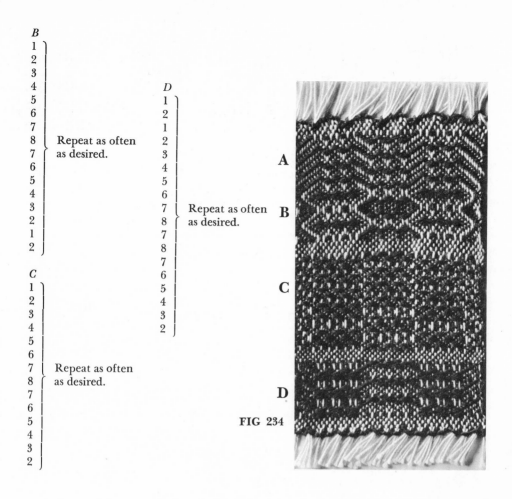

FIG 234

Problem   Set up the warp for a sample and work out the original treadlings.

TYPE Twill, 8-Harness •
PATTERN Extended Point, Swedish Rosenkransen M's and W's

This bordered arrangement is suitable for place mats, bureau covers, towels, and other household linens woven of fine threads, closely sleyed. For towels the side borders should be only about one third the width of the end border.

Materials and Sleying   Linen threads of various sizes and types, perle cottons, or rayons are good. Either use two closely related shades of a color or weave a piece entirely of one color. A strong contrast is not pleasing.

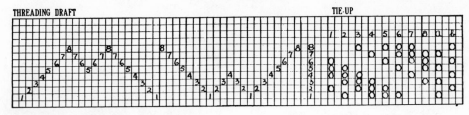

FIG 235

The borders are not shown on the draft. Allow for them when calculating the number of warp threads required.

Right border: thread 8, 7, 6, 5, 4, 3, 2, 1 ten times.

Thread the center M's and W's the required number of times ending with a W as at start.

Left border: thread 1, 2, 3, 4, 5, 6, 7, 8 ten times.

Treadling–Rising Shed

	TREADLES	LEVERS	
	6	1, 5, 7, 8	
	7	4, 6, 7, 8	
	8	3, 5, 6, 7	
	1	2, 4, 5, 6	
	2	1, 3, 4, 5	
	3	2, 3, 4, 8	
	4	1, 2, 3, 7	
	5	1, 2, 6, 8	

Repeat until a square twill corner appears

W-6	M-5	W-1, 5, 7, 8	M-1, 2, 6, 8
7	4	4, 6, 7, 8	1, 2, 3, 7
8	3	3, 5, 6, 7	2, 3, 4, 8
1	2	2, 4, 5, 6	1, 3, 4, 5
2	1	1, 3, 4, 5	2, 4, 5, 6
3	8	2, 3, 4, 8	3, 5, 6, 7
4	7	1, 2, 3, 7	4, 6, 7, 8
5	6	1, 2, 6, 8	1, 5, 7, 8
4	7	1, 2, 3, 7	4, 6, 7, 8
3	8	2, 3, 4, 8	3, 5, 6, 7
2 — Center	1 — Center	1, 3, 4, 5 — Center	2, 4, 5, 6 — Center
3 of W	8 of M	2, 3, 4, 8 of W	3, 5, 6, 7 of M
4	7	1, 2, 3, 7	4, 6, 7, 8
5	6	1, 2, 6, 8	1, 5, 7, 8
4	7	1, 2, 3, 7	4, 6, 7, 8
3	8	2, 3, 4, 8	3, 5, 6, 7
2	1	1, 3, 4, 5	2, 4, 5, 6
1	2	2, 4, 5, 6	1, 3, 4, 5
8	3	3, 5, 6, 7	2, 3, 4, 8
7	4	4, 6, 7, 8	1, 2, 3, 7
6	5	1, 5, 7, 8	1, 2, 6, 8

Repeat the M's and W's the number of times required to weave the article the desired size. Repeat the twill border on the second end, beginning with the bottom levers 1, 2, 6, 8 or treadle 5 and treadling to the top on each repeat.

Problem Weave a guest towel in fine linen using M's and W's threading with original border arrangement.

FIG 236

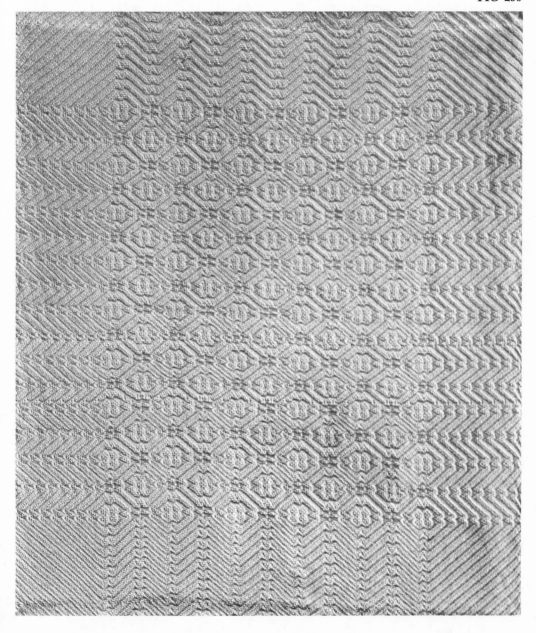

TYPE Twill, 8-Harness · PATTERN Extended Point, Sampler

A combined single-, double-, and triple-point twill was used to thread this sampler (Fig. 238). It was woven on a multiple-harness Swedish loom at the Vävskola in Saterglantan, Sweden. The thread used was Swedish linen, single twist, half bleach, No. 12 for the warp and unbleached No. 8 single

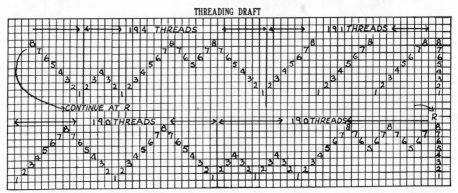

THREADING DRAFT

FIG 237

FIG 238

linen for the weft. The warp was double sleyed in a reed approximating an American 12-dent.

No tie-up or treadling directions are given for the sample, but tie-ups and treadlings for the 8-harness twills may be used as a guide.

Problem Set up a small sampler, experimenting with combined twill threadings and treadlings.

TYPE Twill, 4-, 6-, and 8-Harness · PATTERN Dornik or Broken

This is only one of the many broken twills. The dornik threading produces a sturdier material than the reverse twill (page 175). In the dornik threading, a harness is skipped at regular intervals, thus doing away with the three-thread skip which occurs where the threading of the other type reverses (Fig. 239). Like practically all of the twills, it can be threaded on either four, six, or eight harnesses.

Uses, Materials, and Sleying As for other twills; sleying and beating must be such as to produce a 50/50 material.

Sample Illustrated (Fig. 240)

WARP	WEFT	REED (dents per inch)	SLEY
Wool, 2/32, or Fabri	Same	14	Double

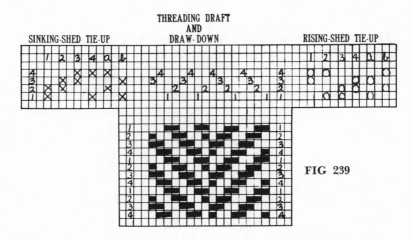

THREADING DRAFT
AND
DRAW-DOWN

SINKING-SHED TIE-UP

RISING-SHED TIE-UP

FIG 239

It is impossible to weave a plain weave on any of the dornik threadings, but the alternate treadling of *a* and *b* will weave a fairly satisfactory heading.

4-Harness Dornik

FIG 240

6-Harness Dornik

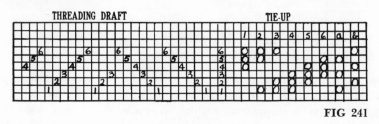

THREADING DRAFT   TIE-UP

FIG 241

Treadling Depress treadles or levers in the following order: 1, 2, 3, 4, 5, 6, and repeat in same order.

8-Harness Dornik

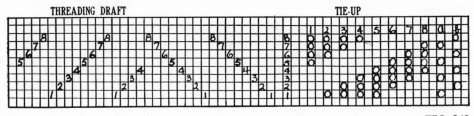

THREADING DRAFT   TIE-UP

FIG 242

Treadling Depress treadles in the following order: 1, 2, 3, 4, 5, 6, 7, 8, and repeat in the same order throughout the length of the warp.

Problem If an 8-harness loom is available weave a sample of the dornik in wool, suitable for a coat. If a multiple-harness loom is not available, weave a sample on a 4-harness loom and compare it with the herringbone sample (page 176).

TYPE Twill, 8-Harness •
PATTERN Double Weave 2-Block

The 4-harness double weave can be extended to 8 harnesses, greatly increasing the possibilities of the weave. This technique is an initial step leading to the many intricate processes of the multiple-harness double weave used to weave the beautiful old coverlets found in some museums.

The elaborate designs of pine trees, stars, and snowballs are beyond the possibilities of the 8-harness loom and the beginning weaver, but do offer a rewarding challenge to the weaver who has mastered the complicated tie-ups of 12- and 16-harness looms.

If tradition is to be followed, the warp for the double plain weave should be a combination of wool and cotton. Unless the cotton is a soft twist and the wool a hard twist, two warp beams will be needed, since wool and cotton stretch differently making it very difficult to maintain a satisfactory tension.

Uses   For bedspreads, heavy drapes, upholstery, pillow covers, and runners

Design   Two-block short drafts (page 545), either one of the many shown in various weaving publications or an original design. As the design is geometric, it is easy to arrange the blocks into a pleasing, well-balanced design.

Materials   Smooth materials retain the characteristics of the old pieces, but experiments with some of the bouclés and rough-textured materials might produce an interesting modern weave.

Use cotton, wools, and linens of similar grist: 8/4 cotton with a homespun or commercial wool of the same size for a heavy spread; fine wool and heavy linen for pillow tops and upholstery, and fine linen or cotton for bureau scarves or place mats.

Samples Illustrated (Figs. 244 and 245)

WARP	WEFT	REED (*dents per inch*)	SLEY
Lily cotton, mercerized, 20/2	Lily cotton, mercerized, 20/2	18	Triple

If a two-color block is desired, wind the two threads together in the warp. For a long, wide, cotton and wool warp, when two warp beams are available, wind the warps separately and beam each separately in the usual manner.

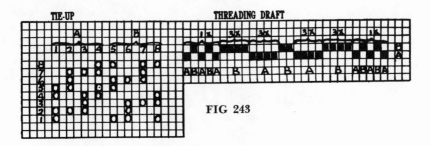

FIG 243

For the sample illustrated, 240 one-yard threads, alternating yellow and light green, were wound.

In the short draft, each block represents four threads; this sample has been threaded as follows:

A Block			B Block	
THREAD	HARNESS		THREAD	HARNESS
dark	1		dark	5
light	2		light	6
dark	3		dark	7
light	4		light	8

An important point to remember when weaving a double-web pattern is that two webs are being woven simultaneously, one on harnesses 1, 2, 3, and 4, the other on harnesses 5, 6, 7, and 8. Each pattern block requires four harnesses. If this fact is kept constantly in mind during the weaving, it will be easy to understand why half the dark and all the light threads must be drawn up when the dark block is being woven, and why half the light and all the dark must be drawn down when the light square is being woven. Remember that the warp threads in the squares alternate so that two changes are necessary for each square.

Take care to insert the shuttles so that the dark shuttle weaves the dark square and the light shuttle the light square.

Treadling The treadles are depressed in the order in which they are given on the tie-up chart:

Treadles 1, 2, 3, and 4 weave block *A* (repeat to square block).

Treadles 5, 6, 7, and 8 weave block *B* (repeat to square block).

One repeat of a block weaves a horizontal bar or line.

If a hand loom with levers is being used, depress the four levers together as shown on the tie-up for each treadle: 1 2 4 5; 2 5 6 7; etc.

FIG 244

FIG 245

Problem Set up a 2-yd. warp, designing your own pattern arrangement. Weave samples of the double weave, double twill weave (page 215), and false damask (page 218).

TYPE Twill, 8-Harness, 2-Block •
PATTERN Double Warp- and Weft-Face

In this weave, the warp-face and weft-face blocks alternate. In the warp-face blocks, the twill slants to the left, while in the weft-face blocks it slants to the right.

Uses This weave is more satisfactory than the fine damask weaves for everyday table linens, especially if woven of coarse linen. Towels of coarse linen, closely woven, will stand up to years of rugged use. Linen and wool double twill is suitable for upholstery if the design is made up of small squares, and fine cotton can be used for bureau covers and towels where the expense of linen is not justified. In soft wools, this is a good weave for couch throws and baby blankets as there are no long skips.

Materials Linen threads, varying in ply and size from very fine to coarse, are the first choice. Fine cottons, rayons, and soft wools are good.

Samples Illustrated (Figs. 247 and 248)

Sample 1

Use the same material, design, reed, and sley as for plain double and false damask.

Sample 2

WARP	WEFT	REED *(dents per inch)*	SLEY
Linen, natural, 20 singles	Linen, natural, 20 singles	20	Double

Treadling This is a three-one treadling in which the weft passes over three warp threads and under one.

    The treadles are depressed in the order in which they appear on the tie-up chart, with the treadling for each block repeated as often as necessary to square the block. One repeat of the treadling for either block weaves a bar. This treadling is for a rising-shed loom:

BLOCK A — TREADLES	BLOCK A — LEVERS
1	1, 5, 6, 7
2	2, 5, 6, 8
3	3, 5, 7, 8
4	4, 6, 7, 8

BLOCK B — TREADLES	BLOCK B — LEVERS
5	1, 2, 3, 5
6	1, 2, 4, 6
7	1, 3, 4, 7
8	2, 3, 4, 8

Order of Treadling for Sample 1

BLOCK	BLOCK (CONT.)
A — 1×	A — 1×
B — 1×	B — to square block
A — 1×	*A — to square block
B — 1×	B — 2× — center

From *, repeat *back* to beginning to complete pattern.

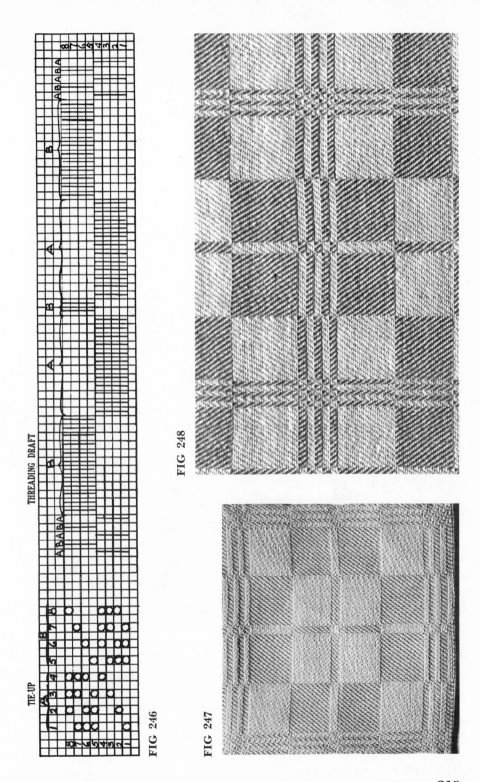

THREADING DRAFT

TIE-UP

FIG 246

FIG 247

FIG 248

TYPE Twill, 8-Harness · PATTERN Interlocking Double Weave

As with many other weaves, an 8-harness extension of a 4-harness weave allows a great deal more latitude in the weave, resulting in a much more useful and interesting material. This is true particularly of the interlocking-twill weave when extended from 4 to 8 harnesses.

Uses With this threading it is possible to weave material with a plain and a patterned side or even with two patterned surfaces, such as a tartan car rug with a different tartan on each side. This is not difficult if the weaver concentrates to keep the correct treadle routine and the correct order in the setts.

This weave is suitable for woolen sports jackets, snow suits, between-season coats, blankets, and car rugs.

Samples Illustrated (Figs. 250 and 251)

WARP	WEFT	REED _(dents per inch)_	SLEY
Homespun yarn, single ply	Homespun yarn, single ply	8	4 per dent

If two warp beams are available, wind the plaid warp and the plain warp separately in the customary manner on the respective beams. If all the warp is to be wound on one beam, wind the plain and plaid threads together, changing the colors of the plain warp as indicated on the chart.

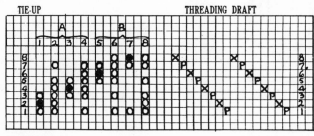

FIG 249

The threads for the upper side, indicated by _P_ on the threading chart, weave a plaid. They are threaded on the odd-numbered harnesses 1, 3, 5, and 7. The threads for the underside, which is a plain color, are indicated by an X and are threaded on the even-numbered harnesses 2, 4, 6, and 8.

The dark dots on the tie-up chart indicate the "stitching threads" which catch or stitch the two surfaces together. The stitching threads lie in

FIG 250   FIG 251

the lower, or plain, warp and are caught up in regular succession into the upper surface as the weaving proceeds. This results in considerable take-up, so a greater loom waste allowance than usual must be made to cover this take-up when winding the warp.

The order of treadling is as it appears on the tie-up chart. Start with treadle 1, depress the other treadles in order across the warp through treadle 8, then start with treadle 1 again, repeating the routine as often as necessary to weave the desired length.

Remember that treadles 1, 3, 5, and 7 weave the upper or plaid side and that the shuttles carrying these plaid threads must be entered in the order in which the colors have been wound in the warp (page 437). Treadles 2, 4, 6, and 8 weave the plain, or under, side of the material. The shuttles carrying the weft for the plaid side of the web and the shuttle carrying the weft for the plain web are thrown through the shed *in alternating succession.*

Problem   Set up a warp and weave a small sample, plaid or tartan (page 437) on top and plain underneath, preferably on an 8-harness table loom.

TYPE Twill, 8-Harness · PATTERN False Damask

A true damask requires a minimum of 10 harnesses and 10 treadles for a 2-block pattern. As this text does not carry the student beyond the techniques possible on 8 harnesses, directions are given for a 2-block type of damask generally referred to as "false-damask."

Damasks are distinguishable by the alternation of the warp surface and the weft surface blocks. Although it is possible to produce damask on an 8-harness setting, the surface lacks the beauty of a true damask.

Uses   Place mats, informal table covers, and upholstery

Materials   Linens, fine cottons

Sample Illustrated   Same material, threading, and sleying as for the double-face twill and 2-block double plain weave. (Cotton was used in preference to linen for the sample since it photographs more clearly.)

Treadling   The treadles are depressed in the order in which they appear on the tie-up chart. Repeat the treadling for each block as often as necessary to square it before passing on to the next block.

One repeat of the block weaves a bar.

If a hand loom with levers is being used, depress the four levers together as shown on the tie-up for each treadle: 1, 3, 4, and 7; 1, 2, 3, and 5; etc.

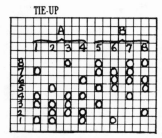

TIE-UP

FIG 252

FIG 253

Problem On the same threading as used for the plain weave, 2-block, 8-harness, weave a sample of false damask.

TYPE Twill, 4-Harness •
PATTERN Double Weave, Finnväv and Mexican

Finnväv, one of the most popular weaves in Finland, has been traced back to the sixteenth century. It is known in Finland as Täkänä, though technically, it is called *lastakudos* or stickweave.

Double weaving probably reaches its highest point of development in the Finnväv, in which it is possible to weave any design that can be drawn on graph paper.

Uses This weave was first used in Finland for linen towels, chest covers, and wool blankets. Later, interesting designs were developed and the technique was used for drapes, pillows, upholstery, and wall hangings. Many excellent wall hangings may be seen in public buildings and churches throughout the Scandinavian countries.

Materials Wool, linen, or cotton, or a combination of any two, depending upon the use of the article. Towels should be of very fine linen, closely set, and pillow tops and wall hangings of heavy cotton and wool, or linen and wool.

Technique There are two types of Finnväv: the reversible (Figs. 254 and 255) and the nonreversible (Figs. 256 and 257), and two methods of

FIG 254

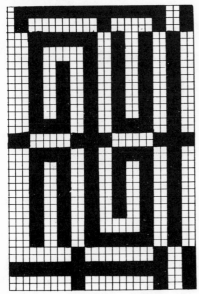

FIG 255

weaving: the true Finnväv and the Mexican weave. Both weaves and both methods are described here.

It is difficult to do this weave on small floor looms and table looms because there is little room to manipulate the sticks between the breast beam and the heddles. A rising-shed loom is recommended since a better shed can be obtained than on a counterbalanced loom.

In addition to the regular loom equipment, it is necessary to have a flat shed stick or sword, all smoothly finished.

It is easy to make mistakes in picking up the pattern. The mistakes are not always discovered at once and are called "raindrops." One or two are permissible as long as they are not too conspicuous and do not throw an important part of the pattern out of line. Raindrops should, of course, be avoided entirely.

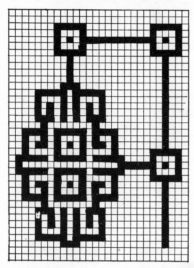

FIG 256

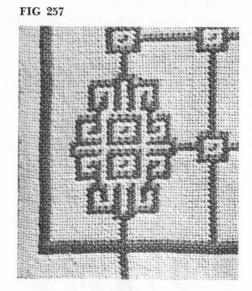

FIG 257

Design   Designs for Finnväv are drawn on graph paper and may be as simple or complicated as desired. The beginning weaver is urged to start with a simple one.

These directions are for a rising-shed loom with a direct tie-up (page 533).

Warp   In making the warp, alternate two dark and two light threads. Set up the loom threading 1, 2, 3, 4—1 and 2 threaded in dark threads, 3 and 4 in light threads. This is a double cloth, therefore the reed must be sleyed double. With 8/2 cotton use reed 18, double sley, 36 ends per inch. In weaving, beat 50/50, 18 threads on the top web, 18 threads on the lower web. Four threads, two dark and two light, correspond to one unit or one square on graph paper. These methods, Finnväv and Mexican, produce a reversible material. The pattern has a jagged edge on the bottom of the horizontal blocks and on the left side of the vertical blocks.

Weaving   To weave two fabrics, the light fabric above and the dark below, depress:

TREADLE	
3 4	light weft
1, 3, 4 2, 3, 4	dark weft

To weave dark fabric above and light below, depress:

TREADLE	
1 2	dark weft
1, 2, 3 1, 2, 4	light weft

Treadling—Reversible Finnväv   To weave a pattern with a dark figure and a light background, depress:

Treadles 1 and 2, raising all the dark threads of the warp. Using a pickup stick, pick up the dark threads which correspond to the first horizontal line of the pattern. Turn the pickup stick on edge.

Treadles 3 and 4, producing a cross behind the reed and between the parts of the warp. Insert a round stick under this cross. Remove the pickup stick.

Treadles 1, 2, and 3. Insert a sword (a smooth stick approximately 2 in. high) through the shed that develops above the round stick. Turn the sword on edge to make the shed and weave a shot of light weft. Remove the sword.

Treadles 1, 2, and 4. Insert the sword as before. Weave the second shot of light weft. Remove all the sticks.

Treadles 3 and 4, picking up the background threads, splitting the pair on each side of the pattern.

Treadles 1 and 2, making a cross. Insert the round stick as before.

Treadles 1, 3, and 4. Insert the sword and weave a shot of dark weft. Remove the sword.

Treadles 2, 3, and 4. Insert the sword, weave the second shot of dark weft, and remove all the sticks.

These four shots complete one unit of the pattern.

Treadling—Nonreversible Finnväv The nonreversible Finnväv gives a straight line on all four sides of the pattern. To achieve this either the Finnish or Mexican weaving method can be used, although the Finnish method gives a better shed and nicer edges. In the warp, break off the two light threads on the left-hand selvedge.

Refer to the Finnväv directions for warp and weaving. Depress:

Treadles 3, 4, raising all light threads of the warp. Using a pickup stick, pick up the background threads. NOTE: The pickup stick must *not* go over the background threads on either side of the pattern blocks. Turn the pickup stick on edge.

Treadles 1 and 2, producing cross behind the reed and between the parts of the warp. Insert the round stick under this cross. Remove the pickup stick.

Treadles 1, 3, and 4. Insert the sword through the shed that develops above the round stick. Turn the sword on edge to open the shed, and weave a shot of dark weft. Beat. Remove the sword.

Treadles 2, 3, and 4. Insert the sword as before. Weave the second shot of dark weft. Remove all the sticks.

Treadles 1 and 2. Pick up the dark threads corresponding to the first horizontal line of the pattern.

Treadles 3 and 4, making a cross. Insert the round stick as before.

Treadles 1, 2, and 3. Insert the sword and weave a shot of light weft. Remove the sword.

Treadles 1, 2, and 4. Insert the sword. Weave the second shot of light weft. Remove all the sticks.

NOTE: In weaving a pattern, the last tabby must end off on treadle 4 before beginning the pattern. The background is picked up first, then the pattern. When a block is only one unit wide, the horizontal *pattern* threads should *not* be picked up; the result is a horizontal straight line.

Treadling—Mexican Method The Mexican method is a simpler and more rapid way of doing the Finnväv. Refer to the Finnish method for the warp, weaving, and treadling. Depress:

Treadles 1 and 2. Using the pickup stick, pick up the dark threads corresponding to the first line of the pattern. The pickup stick should be laid flat in the warp and pushed back close to the reed.

Treadle 3. Weave a shot of light thread. Do not beat.

Treadle 4, leaving the pickup stick in the shed. Beat against the shed and push the stick against the reed. Insert the shuttle, remove the pickup stick, and beat.

Treadles 3 and 4. Pick up the background in pairs, but split first and last pairs outlining each side of pattern area, and push the stick against the reed.

Treadle 1. Weave a shot of dark thread. Do not beat.

Treadle 2, leaving the pickup stick in the shed. Beat against the shed and push the stick against the reed. Insert the shuttle, remove the pickup stick, and beat.

These four shots complete one unit of the pattern.

Problem Set up the warp and weave a small sample using both the Finnväv and Mexican methods.

FIG. 259
Designed and woven by
Evelyn Longard,
Nova Scotia

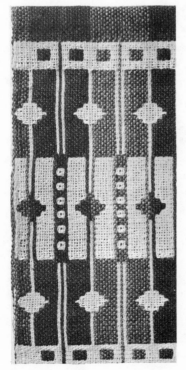

FIG. 258
Designed and woven by Joyce Chown,
Nova Scotia

FIG. 260.   Designed and woven by Elizabeth Wittenberg, California

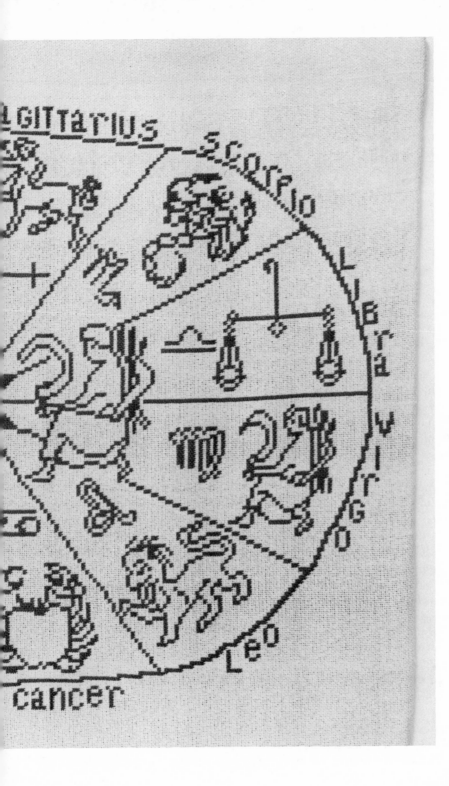

chapter 6

Overshot

In early Colonial days the overshot was a favorite of both the housewife and the itinerant weaver. Before cottons came into general use, homespun linen was used for the warp and tabby and homespun yarn dyed with indigo, madder, or other natural dyes for the pattern thread.

Of all the weaves, this one seems to have the greatest appeal to new weavers and, as a consequence, has probably been more abused than any other. Through the years it has been used for everything from bedspreads to clothing. Fortunately, present-day weavers have a keener appreciation of design and use their weaving knowledge with greater discrimination and effectiveness.

The origin of the technique remains obscure although Hans E. Wulff, author of *The Traditional Crafts of Persia*, believes it originated in Persia and then spread to other parts of the world. The name may first have been used to describe the long pattern overshot appearing at regular intervals across the surface of the plain-weave web. One weaver, at a loss for a definition, thought that it probably got its name because "the last thread of one pattern block overshoots the first thread of the next pattern block." A true definition, as a study of the weave will reveal.

Structure The overshot weave is a twill derivative. An examination of an overshot draft shows it to be made up of a repetitive sequence of the 1 and 2, 2 and 3, 3 and 4, and 4 and 1 twill blocks.

In the twill, each block contains only two threads; in the overshot, each block has been extended to at least four or six threads. Some blocks contain as many as ten or twelve threads. Such large blocks, however, are not practical since the long skips of the pattern thread are snagged too easily unless a very fine setting is used.

In the plain twill, when treadles 1 and 2 are depressed the weft thread passes over two warp threads only; in the overshot, because the draft is threaded 1 and 2 twice in succession (Fig. 261), four warp threads are covered. These wider spaces, which are opened up, are called blocks. For the purposes of study, the first block to the right will be called the *A* block.

The next set of threads lying to the left is the 2 and 3 set. This set is threaded twice forming the second or *B* block. The next set of threads to the left, 3 and 4 repeated twice, form the *C* block and the fourth and last set of threads, 4 and 1 repeated twice, form the *D* block.

When set down on graph paper, the threading draft looks like Fig. 261.

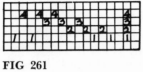

FIG 261

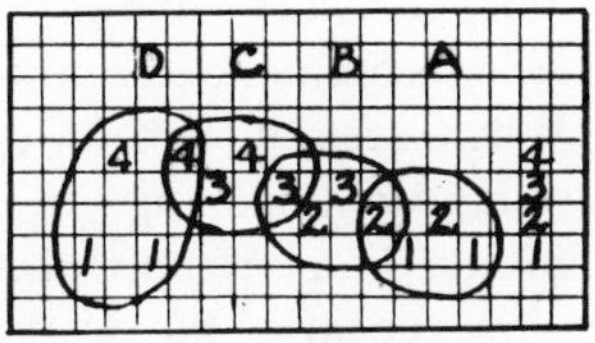

FIG 262

To aid in separating and naming the blocks, each one is encircled as in Fig. 262. One threading of these four blocks comprises one design unit of this pattern. In examining the blocks, note that the thread enclosed in the small circle is common to two blocks.

It is important to know how the woven pattern will look before going to the trouble and expense of winding a warp and threading the loom. A simple solution is to make a picture or draw-down of the web. To do this, write down the threading draft again. At least two repeats of the draft are needed to test the point where the first repeat ends and the second begins, as it is here that mistakes are likely to be made. With some drafts an unexpected design occurs here, and it is well to know whether or not it is pleasing.

This is how the draw-down will look:

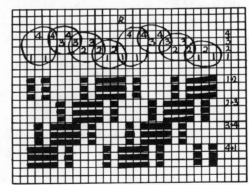

FIG 263

Note how the blocks overlap in the weaving. The last thread of one block becomes the first thread of the next block.

Remember this when threading. If the last thread of one block is threaded on the same harness as the first thread of the next block, one of these threads must be omitted or a mistake will occur. In the above draft the 1, at *R* on the draft, ends the first unit and a 1 also begins the next unit, so one of these should be skipped. Remember to thread the 1 at the end of the very last unit on the left to balance the pattern design. In many drafts throughout the text, the thread common to both units is encircled to warn the weaver to be careful.

While overshot weaves can be threaded on 6 and 8 harnesses it is not customary to do so. The process of compiling the draft is somewhat complicated and there are so many beautiful and satisfying 4-harness overshot weaves that it is not necessary to extend the weave.

Mary Atwater[1] shows a few 8-harness overshot weaves in her text which are recommended to interested weavers for study.

When seen in a draw-down, the foregoing draft weaves a very uninteresting web, lacking in design. The twill-like rows would continue indefinitely. To give more character the pattern can be reversed at the end of the first repeat of the draft and threaded so. This point where it reverses is called the turning point and lies at the center of the draft at *R*.

In reversing a pattern draft in overshot, it is necessary to make the turn on an uneven number of threads. This is done by adding an extra thread as in the case above, or by omitting a thread. Usually a thread is added, otherwise the center turning block may look too small, resulting in a poorly balanced design.

Here we have a more interesting figure which is known as the cross motif in overshot weaving. A return repeat weaves the diamond (Fig. 264).

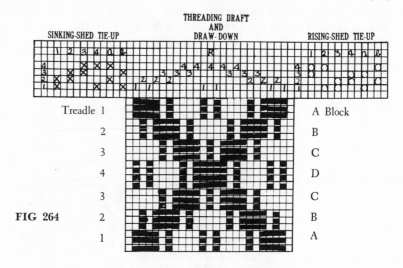

FIG 264

Treadling In weaving a pattern as-drawn-in, each block must be squared. As the successive blocks are treadled, a 45-deg. angle line will extend from the first block at the lower right-hand corner of the web to the upper left-hand corner. As previously noted (page 535), draw-downs or weaving on paper are written below the draft; actual weaving on the loom takes place above the draft. To see how the actual weaving will look, turn the draw-down upside down, hold it against a strong light, and look through it from the back.

It is necessary to choose the correct threads and sleying and to beat correctly or a 50/50 web with the pattern units correctly squared will not be achieved.

A 50/50 plain weave.

B Weft thread too coarse. Causes web to wrinkle.

C Weft thread too fine.

D Correct ratio between threads. 50/50 plain weave background; 45 diagonal. Requires hard beating.

E Pattern thread too coarse for fine warp thread, sley, and design. Distorts design.

F Pattern and tabby thread too similar in size. Pattern loses character.

G Tabby thread too coarse for pattern threads.

H Tabby thread too fine. Background not 50/50 weave. Harder beating might produce 45 diagonal 50/50 background.

I 50/50 plain weave. Warp and weft same thread.

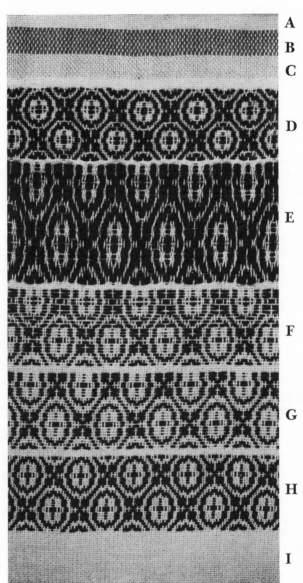

A
B
C
D
E
F
G
H
I

FIG 265

The tabby or binder thread should be slightly finer than the warp thread, and the pattern thread coarser than either but soft, so it will pack back closely into place.

Fig. 282 shows the correct ratio between threads. It requires experimentation to achieve this because threads vary and the desired ones are not always available.

Pattern blocks, with the exception of the turning blocks which will be discussed later (below), are always composed of an even number of threads. Theoretically, in weaving to square the block, it would seem that the same number of shots should be thrown as there are warp threads in the draft.

However, the thread which is common to the two blocks, the one which shows in the small circle between the larger circles, must be compensated for in some way, so one less pattern thread is woven in than the number of warp threads. This shows why only three, instead of four, pattern threads are shown on the draw-down.

On the draw-down a series of dots are seen between the pattern thread strokes. These are single threads which are common to the blocks being woven, but as they are part of other blocks they come up singly rather than in pairs or groups. These dots are called half tones.

In looking at an overshot web there are three things to notice: (1) the plain-weave background; (2) the long pattern-thread skips, shots, or floats; and (3) the half tones. Because of the structure of the overshot weave, the pattern threads could be cut away and a plain-weave background would remain.

When a pattern is reversed, a process common to all overshot weaves except the 2-block pattern on opposites (page 255), there is a turning point. Where this occurs, an even number of pattern shots are thrown. The procedure for the reverse pattern is the same with one less weft shot than warp threads in the block to keep the tabby threads running in correct relationship to the groups of pattern threads. According to the tabby sequence, pattern shots are either paired or unpaired. Consequently, to keep the pattern the same in reverse, the same tabby shot must be used between the same pattern shots to form the same pairs.

Weaving The treadling routine for plain weave, which makes the background for overshot weaving is:

SINKING SHED		RISING SHED	
TREADLE — HARNESSES		TREADLE — HARNESSES	
a	2 and 4	a	1 and 3
alternating with		alternating with	
b	1 and 3	b	2 and 4

To this treadling routine are added alternating shots of pattern threads woven in according to a particular treadling sequence.

Practically all overshot patterns are drafted in such a way that harnesses 1 and 3 and harnesses 2 and 4 are used in combination for the plain background weave, leaving the four combinations 1 and 2, 2 and 3, 3 and 4, 4 and 1, the twill sequence, for the pattern shots.

To fix the sequence of overshot pattern weaving clearly in mind, it is advisable to weave a sample threaded on the sample draft given in Fig. 264. Use the following treadling, reading down the columns.

HARNESSES	THREAD	HARNESSES	THREAD
1 and 3 —	tabby	1 and 3 —	tabby
1 and 2 —	pattern	3 and 4 —	pattern
2 and 4 —	tabby	2 and 4 —	tabby
1 and 2 —	pattern	3 and 4 —	pattern
1 and 3 —	tabby	1 and 3 —	tabby
1 and 2 —	pattern	3 and 4 —	pattern
2 and 4 —	tabby	2 and 4 —	tabby
2 and 3 —	pattern	1 and 4 —	pattern
1 and 3 —	tabby	1 and 3 —	tabby
2 and 3 —	pattern	1 and 4 —	pattern
2 and 4 —	tabby	2 and 4 —	tabby
2 and 3 —	pattern	1 and 4 —	pattern

Complete the star using draw-down (Fig. 264) and above treadling as guides.

It is obvious from the foregoing that it would be quite impossible and unnecessary to write such detailed directions for patterns, particularly those which embrace many and frequent changes.

In its abbreviated form, the foregoing treadling would be written as follows:

Tabby: 2 and 4—*a* for sinking shed; *b* for rising shed
1 and 3—*b* for sinking shed; *a* for rising shed
Pattern: 1 and 2—3× block *A*—sinking shed; 3 and 4—rising shed
2 and 3—3× block *B*—sinking shed; 1 and 4—rising shed
3 and 4—3× block *C*—sinking shed; 1 and 2—rising shed
4 and 1—3× block *D*—sinking shed; 2 and 3—rising shed

or, as they would be shown on the tie-up:

BLOCK	TREADLE
A —	1
B —	2
C —	3
D —	4

Remember that the tabby shots alternate with the pattern-thread shots.

If, by chance, the tabby treadling has not been given with the pattern draft, it is simple to discover what it is. Depress the different treadles in trial combinations until two are discovered which bring the alternate threads up in the reed. The pattern will be written on the remaining combinations.

To determine which treadles open the sheds for the different blocks, depress the treadles in various combinations. The combination which opens the first space of more than two threads at the right selvedge can be called block *A*. Successive openings to the left during the experimental treadling become blocks *B*, *C*, and *D*.

Experienced weavers seldom use a written treadling draft. They simply follow the diagonals, weaving blocks from right to left. Weavers who wish to become experts should learn this method early in their training period. It means complete freedom from written directions. It cannot be emphasized too strongly that weavers should train themselves to think of all weaving in terms of blocks rather than as numbers on a chart.

As patterns become more complicated, more changes occur, but they are simply woven in as they appear on the threading draft, squaring up the blocks and following the 45-deg. angle which forms naturally when weaving as-drawn-in.

The secret of obtaining attractive overshot webs depends largely on: correct ratio between the threads (page 229), uniform and firm beating, and the sequence of the shuttles.

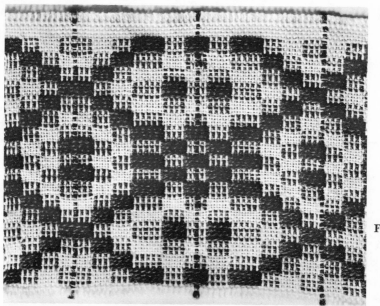

FIG 266

While no definite rule governs the routine sequence of the tabby or weft thread shuttle, it is a general rule that the tabby shuttle should follow the pattern-thread shuttle from the same side.

If the web looks sketchy and the pattern threads do not pack back tightly against one another, unweave back to the beginning and start with the opposite tabby. If this does not remedy the difficulty, check the tabby thread against the pattern thread (page 229), check the sleying (page 229) and the beating (page 229).

A few things to keep in mind about the overshot weave are:

1. It is a two-shuttle weave. One shuttle carries the tabby thread, which binds the pattern shots in place and also weaves the plain-weave background. The pattern shuttle carries a heavier, softer thread, generally twice as large as the tabby thread. It lies on the surface, being tied down into the web at regular intervals.

2. Blocks progress on the diagonal and the last warp thread of a block is always the first thread of the next block.

3. All blocks, except the turning blocks, contain an even number of threads.

4. When weaving as-drawn-in, pattern blocks are always woven with an uneven number of shots except for the turning block which is woven with an even number of shots.

5. All blocks in the same horizontal row in overshot are the same height, and all blocks in the same vertical row are the same width.

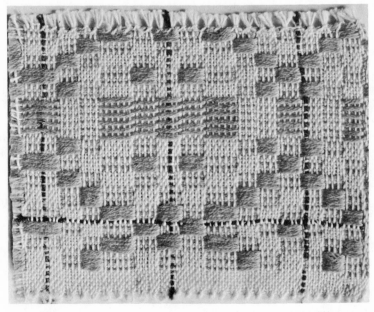

FIG 267

Problem   Using the foregoing information as a guide write a draft, thread a loom, and weave samples as shown in Figs. 266 and 267.

TYPE Overshot · PATTERN Motifs

Overshot patterns are divided into groups, each of which has its own distinguishing motif or design. The structure of overshot patterns is based on combinations of these motifs, interest and design being created through various arrangements. Further changes are possible through variation in the treadling.

These fundamental motifs, or design units, are known as cross, rose, star, table, diamond, and wheel. Few patterns are drafted on any one motif. The patterns are made up of combinations of two or more motifs, and are somewhat intricate and elaborate.

The cross is the most familiar motif and the first one which the weaver will encounter when weaving as-drawn-in. The rose threading is the same as the cross threading but the treadling is different (page 251). The different effects of the two treadling methods show up plainly in the Lover's Knot and Whig Rose patterns (pages 246 and 248). Tables are composed of small squares, one set of squares alternating with a second set. Patterns are set up with tables separating other units such as roses, diamonds, or wheels.

Diamonds appear between other units. They can be seen in nearly all overshot drafts, especially those treadled as-drawn-in. They seem to bind the other units together into a complete design.

The wheel appears frequently, particularly in the larger overshot patterns. It is the wheel which brings curves, or rather the suggestion of curves, into weaving. Actually the curves are an optical illusion brought about through carefully planned twill-succession treadling.

The new weaver should be warned that wheels are not easy to weave. There must be a perfect relationship between the warp, weft, and pattern threads, and the sleying and beating. Even experienced weavers find it difficult to weave perfectly round wheels without first spending considerable time trying out different thread combinations and sleying. Different looms will give different results with identical threads and sleying. Atmospheric conditions and the weaver's temperament can throw the wheel off balance.

Many old Colonial overshot drafts have been collected, studied, classified according to their predominating motifs, and recorded for our use. Books containing these drafts may be obtained from libraries, bookstores, or the publishers.[2]

Not long after beginning the study of weaving, the student will recognize the motifs in the threading drafts as readily as in the woven piece. The serious student will soon arrange his own drafts and treadling arrangements.

TYPE Overshot ·
PATTERN Diamond and Cross, Honeysuckle or Pine Bloom

The Pine Bloom or honeysuckle pattern (Fig. 269) is one of the most popular among amateur weavers. Its popularity may be due to the fact that the units are small and the many variations possible in treadling produce attractive allover designs as well as interesting narrow borders (Fig. 269).

This design is not suitable for bedspreads or drapes since the units are small and become uninteresting when spread over a large surface.

Materials and Sleying Any that are suitable for overshot and the purpose for which the piece is being woven.

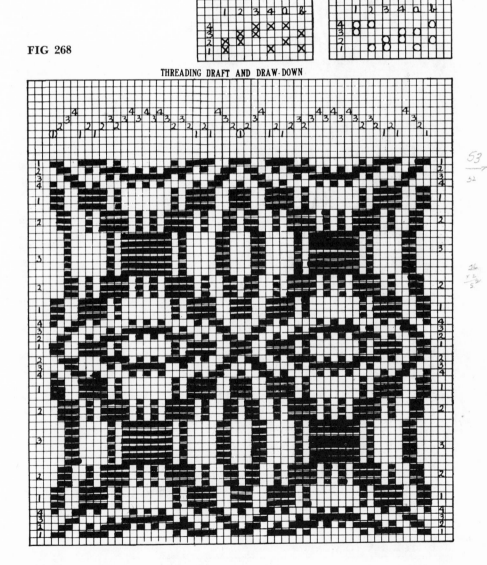

FIG 268

Treadling—Sinking and Rising Shed

A. Light	4 — 2×	2 — 2×	2 — 5×	4 — 2×
Green	3 — 2×	1 — 2×	3 — 2×	1 — 2×
TREADLE	2 — 4×	4 — 2×	4 — 2×	4 — 2×
3 — 2×	*B.* Dark	3 — 2×	1 — 2×	3 — 2×
2 — 3×	Green	2 — 4×	2 — 4×	*E.* Apricot
1 — 2×	3 — 2×	1 — 2×	3 — 2×	2 — 4×

4 — 2×
1 — 2×
2 — 2×
C. Light
Green
3 — 2×
2 — 2×
1 — 2×
4 — 2×
3 — 2×
2 — 4×
1 — 2×
4 — 2×
3 — 2×
D. Rust
3 — 2×
4 — 2×
1 — 2×
2 — 4×
3 — 2×
4 — 2×
3 — 2×
2 — 4×
1 — 2×
4 — 2×
3 — 2×
2 — 5×
3 — 2×
4 — 2×
1 — 2×
4 — 2×
3 — 2×
2 — 4×
1 — 3×
4 — 3×
3 — 10×
4 — 3×
1 — 3×
2 — 4×
3 — 2×

3 — 1×
4 — 1×
1 — 1×
2 — 1×
3 — 1×
4 — 1×
3 — 1×
4 — 1×
3 — 1×
2 — 1×
1 — 1×
4 — 1×
3 — 1×
2 — 4×
1 — 1×
F. Gold
1 — 1×
2 — 4×
3 — 1×
4 — 1×
1 — 1×
2 — 1×
1 — 1×
4 — 1×
3 — 1×
G. Light Tan
3 — 18×
4 — 1×
1 — 1×
4 — 1×
3 — 9×
H. Dark Tan
3 — 9×
4 — 1×
1 — 1×
4 — 1×
3 — 1×

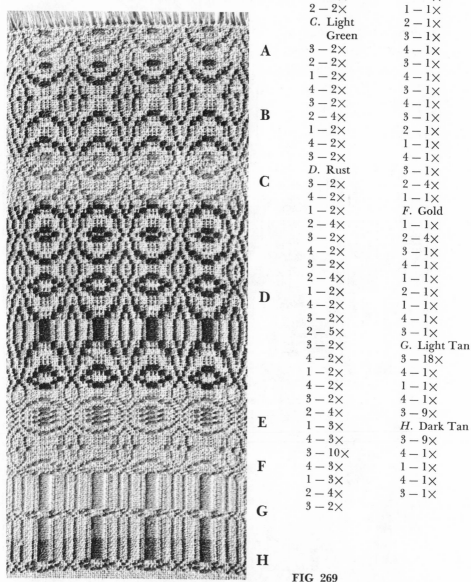

A
B
C
D
E
F
G
H

FIG 269

WARP	WEFT	PATTERN	REED *(dents per inch)*	SLEY
Linen, 40/3, tan	Linen, 40/3, tan	Cotton, perle, 6-strand, colored	15	Double

There are several ways of threading honeysuckle; the one used in Fig. 268 is one of the standard methods.

Problem Set up four repeats of the honeysuckle draft and weave a sampler using original treadlings and colors.

TYPE Overshot •
PATTERN Diamond and Cross, Orange Peel

This was a favorite for coverlets, both in the single and double versions, among Colonial weavers. Some weavers feel that both sides of the web are equally attractive and that either could be used for the upper or right side.

In the sample (Fig. 271) only part of the peel unit appears. A second repeat of this part of the draft is necessary to complete the unit.

Uses Especially good for coverlets, drapes, pillows, etc., where a large, yet compact design is desired

Suitable Materials and Sleying As for any overshot pattern in keeping with use of finished web.

Number of Threads to One Complete Pattern Unit 88 for single orange peel; 122 for double orange peel.

Thread *A* to *B* the number of times required to obtain the desired width, continuing through to *C* if the double version is being threaded. This begins and ends the pattern in the center of the peel.

Sample Illustrated (Fig. 271)

WARP	WEFT	PATTERN	REED *(dents per inch)*	SLEY
Cotton, mercerized, 28/4	Cotton, mercerized, 28/4	Yarn, fine	15	Double

THREADING DRAFT

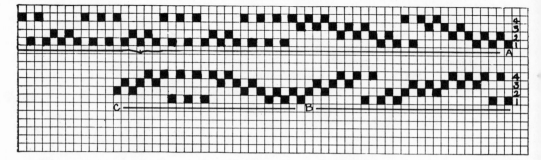

SINKING-SHED TIE-UP

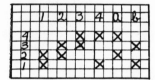

RISING-SHED TIE-UP

FIG 270

FIG 271

TREADLES			TREADLES OR LEVERS	
1 — 3×			1	3 and 4 — 3×
2 — 3×			2	1 and 4 — 3×
3 — 3×			3	1 and 2 — 3×
4 — 3×	Weaves one half of the Orange Peel.		4	2 and 3 — 3×
1 — 3×			1	3 and 4 — 3×
2 — 3×			2	1 and 4 — 3×
3 — 3×			3	1 and 2 — 3×
4 — 4×	3× — Weaves the table.		4	2 and 3 — 4×
1 — 4×			1	3 and 4 — 4×
4 — 4×	To balance the table.		4	2 and 3 — 4×
3 — 3×			3	1 and 2 — 3×
2 — 3×			2	1 and 4 — 3×
1 — 3×	Weaves the second half of the Orange Peel.		1	3 and 4 — 3×
4 — 3×			4	2 and 3 — 3×
3 — 3×			3	1 and 2 — 3×
2 — 3×			2	1 and 4 — 3×

Begin at the top and repeat until the desired length has been woven.

1 — 3×	End with on the last repeat only to balance the design.		1	3 and 4 — 3×

Problem Thread three repeats of the draft, balancing the design at the end. Use fine threads, closely sleyed, with an appropriate pattern thread.

TYPE Overshot •
PATTERN Radiating with Table, Maple Leaf

This pattern is similar to the old Blooming Flower pattern but is more interesting because of the addition of a table motif. The result is more pleasing and, when used for large objects such as bedspreads and drapes, the threading produces a better design, lacking the monotony of the Blooming Flower pattern.

The table threading given in the sample (Fig. 273) is somewhat reduced because of the width restriction of the loom on which the sample was woven. The complete table unit is about the size of one fourth of the flower unit.

Use As for any overshot pattern where a fairly large design can be utilized

Suitable Materials and Sleying As for any overshot pattern in keeping with the article being woven

Number of Threads to One Complete Pattern Unit   Table, 67; leaf, 173

Threading Draft   See Fig. 272

        Thread *A* to *B* twice for the table motif.

        Thread *B* to *C* once for the leaf motif.

        Repeat until the desired width has been threaded. Thread *A* to *B* twice on the last repeat to balance the pattern. If the leaf motif is to be repeated, do not thread the No. 1 at *B* on the repeat.

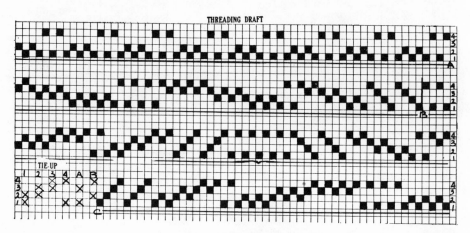

FIG 272

Treadling–Sinking Shed

TABLE

4 — 4× } Repeat the required number of times to square
1 — 4× } the table.

LEAF

1 — 1× ⎫		1 — 7×	1×	3 — 1× ⎫		4 — 7×	
2 — 1×		2 — 5×	(cont.)	2 — 1×		3 — 7×	
3 — 1× ⎬ 2×		3 — 5×		1 — 1× ⎬ 2×		2 — 5×	
4 — 1× ⎭		4 — 3×		4 — 1× ⎭		1 — 5×	1×
1 — 3× ⎫		1 — 3×		3 — 3× ⎫		4 — 3×	(cont.)
2 — 3×		2 — 3×		2 — 3×		3 — 3×	
3 — 3×		3 — 3×		1 — 3×		2 — 3×	
4 — 3× ⎬ 1×		4 — 1× ⎫		4 — 3× ⎬ 1×		1 — 3×	
1 — 5×		1 — 1×		3 — 5×		4 — 1× ⎫	
2 — 5×		2 — 1× ⎬ 2×		2 — 5×		3 — 1×	
3 — 7×		3 — 1× ⎭		1 — 7×		2 — 1× ⎬ 2×	
4 — 7× ⎭		4 — 10× — Center				1 — 1× ⎭	

TABLE

1 — 4× } Repeat the required number of times to square
4 — 4× } the table.

        If weaving an overall pattern, do not repeat the table treadling each time as given at the beginning.

TABLE

2 and 3 — 4× }
3 and 4 — 4× } Repeat the required number of times to square the table.

LEAF

3 and 4 — 1× ⎫		3 and 4 — 7×		1 and 2 — 1× ⎫		2 and 3 — 7×	
1 and 4 — 1× ⎬ 2×		1 and 4 — 5×		1 and 4 — 1× ⎬ 2×		1 and 2 — 7×	
1 and 2 — 1× ⎭		1 and 2 — 5×		3 and 4 — 1× ⎭		1 and 4 — 5×	
2 and 3 — 1×		2 and 3 — 5×	1×	2 and 3 — 1×		3 and 4 — 5×	1×
3 and 4 — 3×		3 and 4 — 3×	(cont.)	1 and 2 — 3× ⎫		2 and 3 — 3×	(cont.)
1 and 4 — 3×		1 and 4 — 3×		1 and 4 — 3×		1 and 2 — 3×	
1 and 2 — 3×		1 and 2 — 3×		3 and 4 — 3×		1 and 4 — 3×	
2 and 3 — 3×		2 and 3 — 1× ⎫		2 and 3 — 5×		3 and 4 — 3×	
3 and 4 — 5× ⎫ 1×		3 and 4 — 1× ⎬ 2×		1 and 2 — 5× ⎬ 1×		2 and 3 — 1× ⎫	
1 and 4 — 5×		1 and 4 — 1×		1 and 4 — 5×		1 and 2 — 1× ⎬ 2×	
1 and 2 — 7×		1 and 2 — 1× ⎭		3 and 4 — 7×		1 and 4 — 1×	
2 and 3 — 7×		2 and 3 — 10× — Center				3 and 4 — 1× ⎭	

TABLE

3 and 4 — 4× }
2 and 3 — 4× } Repeat the required number of times to square the table.

FIG 273

TYPE Overshot ·
PATTERN Wheel and Rose, Young Lover's Knot

This is one of the oldest and most popular of the Colonial overshot patterns and justly so. The correct choice of threads and sleying, colors and balance make it an ideal design for use in Colonial and Cape Cod cottage-type interiors. It should be used with restraint, however, as too much of it is confusing.

Uses and Suggested Materials   The same as for other overshots

Sample Illustrated (Draft, Fig. 274)

WARP	WEFT	PATTERN	REED (dents per inch)	SLEY
Cotton, 30/3	Cotton, 30/3	Wool, 2/18	15	Double

Number of Threads to One Complete Pattern Unit   125

Treadling   The Young Lover's Knot is treadled as-drawn-in (Fig. 275):

TREADLE		LEVERS	
1 — 3×	2 — 2× — Center	3 and 4 — 3×	1 and 4 — 2× — Center
2 — 3×	1 — 2× of rose	1 and 4 — 3×	3 and 4 — 2× of rose
3 — 3×	2 — 8×	1 and 2 — 3×	1 and 4 — 8×
4 — 4×	1 — 9×	2 and 3 — 4×	3 and 4 — 9×
3 — 3×	4 — 5×	1 and 2 — 3×	2 and 3 — 5×
2 — 3×	3 — 4×	1 and 4 — 3×	1 and 2 — 4×
1 — 3×	4 — 2×	3 and 4 — 3×	2 and 3 — 2×
4 — 5×	3 — 4×	2 and 3 — 5×	1 and 2 — 4×
3 — 4×	4 — 5×	1 and 2 — 4×	2 and 3 — 5×
4 — 2×	1 — 3×	2 and 3 — 2×	3 and 4 — 3×
3 — 4×	2 — 3×	1 and 2 — 4×	1 and 4 — 3×
4 — 5×	3 — 3×	2 and 3 — 5×	1 and 2 — 3×
1 — 9×	4 — 4×	3 and 4 — 9×	2 and 3 — 4×
2 — 8×	3 — 3×	1 and 4 — 8×	1 and 2 — 3×
1 — 2×	2 — 3×	3 and 4 — 2×	1 and 4 — 3×

Repeat as necessary ending with treadle 1 three times to balance.

Problem   Thread two repeats of the pattern draft (250 threads) and weave a balanced sample with an original choice of threads and sleying.

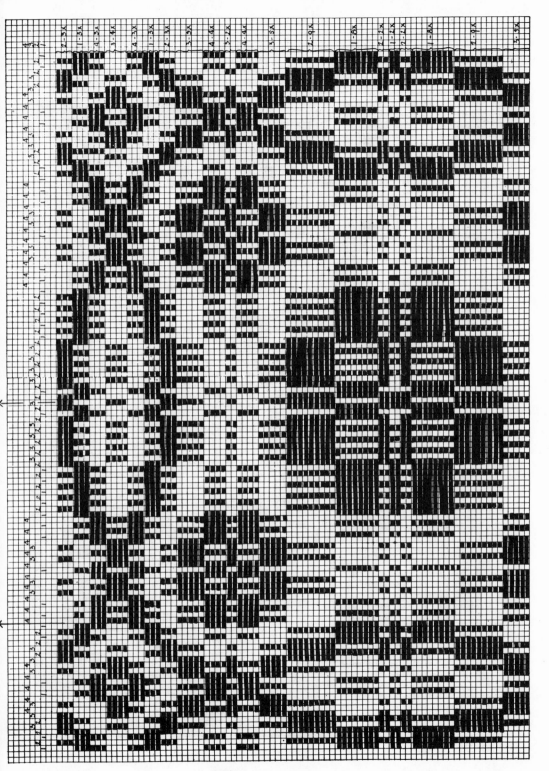

THREADING DRAFT AND DRAW DOWN

FIG 274

FIG 275

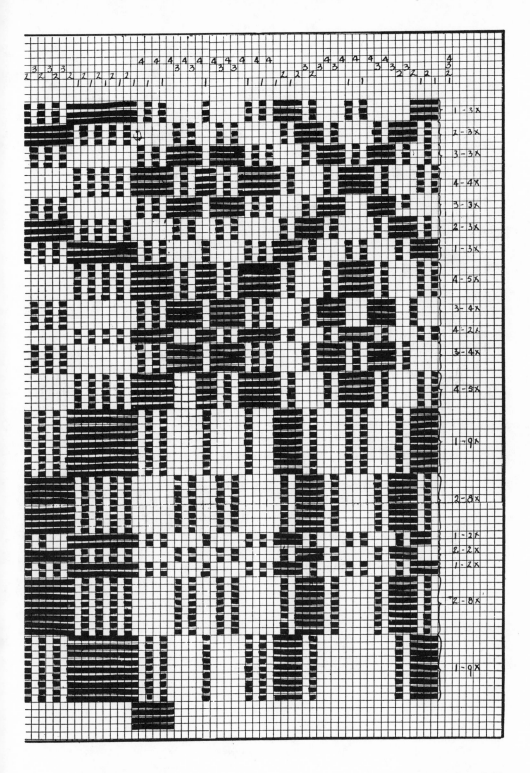

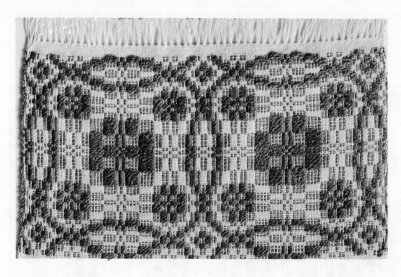

FIG 276

TYPE Overshot ·
PATTERN Wheel, Young Lover's Knot—Miniature

The sample (Fig. 278) demonstrates how a rather large, bold pattern (Fig. 276) can be reduced to one which is fine, dainty, and compact, without destroying the original design characteristics. This is accomplished by threading fewer threads in each section of the draft.

Not all patterns lend themselves to this treatment, for sometimes a reduction of the number of threads in any one section throws the whole pattern out of alignment. It is interesting, however, to experiment with the reduction of large patterns to finer, miniature versions. Compare the miniature draft with the draft for Young Lover's Knot (Fig. 275).

Fine threads and sleying are used for this type of pattern as large threads and coarse sleying would destroy the design.

Uses   Can be used for any article where a fine over-all design is appropriate, such as night-table covers, small pillows, book covers, upholstery materials, household linens, etc.

Suitable Materials and Sleying

WARP	WEFT	PATTERN	REED (dents per inch)	SLEY
Cotton, Egyptian, 40/3	Cotton, Egyptian, 40/3	Yarn, fine	18	Double
Linen, 40/3	Linen, 40/2	Linen, 30/2, 6-strand floss	18	Double

FIG 277

Sample Illustrated (Fig. 278)

WARP	WEFT	PATTERN	REED (dents per inch)	SLEY
Cotton, Egyptian, 40/3	Cotton, Egyptian, 40/3	Yarn, very fine	18	Double

Number of Threads to One Complete Pattern Unit   49

On the draw-down the first arrow at the right marks the center thread of the pattern, the second arrow the completion of the center block from which the pattern reverses, and the third arrow the end of the complete pattern. The arrows down the right side mark the same points for the treadling (Fig. 277).

FIG 278

Treadling

TREADLE

1 — 1×	4 — 2× — center
2 — 1×	3 — 2×
3 — 1×	4 — 4×
4 — 2×	3 — 3×
3 — 1×	2 — 1×
2 — 1×	1 — 2×
1 — 2×	2 — 2×
2 — 2×	1 — 2×
1 — 2×	2 — 1×
2 — 1×	3 — 1×
3 — 3×	4 — 2×
4 — 4×	3 — 1×
3 — 2×	2 — 1×

Start at the top and repeat the desired number of times. On the last repeat end with treadle 1 once to balance the design.

The twill border added at each side of the sample is not shown on the draft (Fig. 273). This was threaded 1, 2, 3, 4 three times on the right. For the left border thread 4, 3, 2, 1 three times.

Problem Choose any simple overshot draft and reduce it to a miniature pattern. Weave a sample, first on paper then on the loom.

TYPE Overshot · PATTERN Wheel and Rose, Whig Rose

The frequent appearance of wheel patterns in the overshot, summer and winter, and double weaves during the early Colonial days is indicative of the motif's popularity. It is combined with crosses, diamonds, stars, tables, and roses. The Whig Rose (Fig. 282) shows the wheel combined with one large and four small roses with diamonds in the corners between the wheels.

Other popular wheel patterns include chariot wheels, the Young Lover's Knot, and four wheels.

Uses For bags, purses, pillows, table covers, etc., and particularly coverlets and drapes

Suitable Materials and Sleying As for other overshot patterns and in keeping with the use for which it is planned

Sample Illustrated (Fig. 277; Draft, Fig. 274)

WARP	WEFT	PATTERN	REED (dents per inch)	SLEY
Cotton, Egyptian, 30/3	Cotton, Egyptian, 30/3	Wool, medium, 2/16	15	Double

The same threading draft is used for the Lover's Knot and Whig Rose (Fig. 274). The difference in the design is created by the treadling. The former is woven as-drawn-in while the Whig Rose is woven rose fashion (page 251).

A little-known threading, "Gertrude's Fancy,"[3] shows alternating blocks threaded and woven one as-drawn-in, the next Rose fashion, and so on across the quilt. It is an unusual and attractive weave.

Number of Threads to One Complete Pattern 125

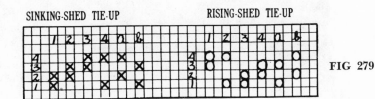

SINKING-SHED TIE-UP   RISING-SHED TIE-UP

FIG 279

Treadling

Sinking Shed			Rising Shed		
TREADLE			**LEVERS**		
1 — 2×	2 — 3× — Center		1 and 4 — 3×	3 and 4 — 2× — Center	
2 — 2×	1 — 3× of rose		3 and 4 — 3×	1 and 4 — 2× of rose	
1 — 8×	4 — 3×		2 and 3 — 3×	3 and 4 — 8×	
2 — 9×	3 — 4×		1 and 2 — 4×	1 and 4 — 9×	
3 — 5×	4 — 3×		2 and 3 — 3×	1 and 2 — 5×	
4 — 4×	1 — 3×		3 and 4 — 3×	2 and 3 — 4×	
3 — 2×	2 — 3×		1 and 4 — 3×	1 and 2 — 2×	
4 — 4×	3 — 5×		1 and 2 — 5×	2 and 3 — 4×	
3 — 5×	4 — 4×		2 and 3 — 4×	1 and 2 — 5×	
2 — 3×	3 — 2×		1 and 2 — 2×	1 and 4 — 3×	
1 — 3×	4 — 4×		2 and 3 — 4×	3 and 4 — 3×	
4 — 3×	3 — 5×		1 and 2 — 5×	2 and 3 — 3×	
3 — 4×	2 — 9×		1 and 4 — 9×	1 and 2 — 4×	
4 — 3×	1 — 8×		3 and 4 — 8×	2 and 3 — 3×	
1 — 3×	2 — 2×		1 and 4 — 2×		

Start at the top and repeat the desired number of items ending with 2 — 3× to balance the design.

Start at the top and repeat the desired number of times ending with 3 and 4 — 3× to balance the design.

If the pattern thread is too heavy the wheels appear oval (Fig. 281); if too light, they will be flat or squat. To produce perfect circles, warp, weft, and tabby must be carefully chosen, and beating must be even (Fig. 280).

FIG 280

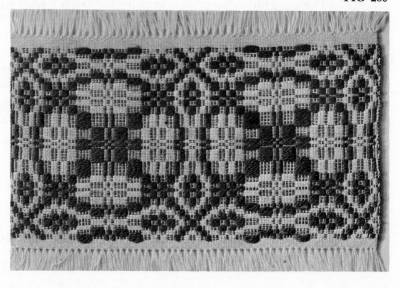

FIG 281

Problem   On the Lover's-Knot threading draft, weave a balanced sample of the Whig Rose. Use an original choice of thread and watch sleying.

CONVERSION OF TREADLING FROM AS-DRAWN-IN OR STAR TO ROSE FASHION

Many weavers mistakenly think that rose-fashion treadling is simply a reversal of the treadling, for example, the use of rising-shed treadling on a sinking-shed loom. What actually takes place is the reversal of the order of the blocks. Only those drafts which have star figures can be woven rose fashion. The pattern design must be studied and a decision made as to which star in the design will be used to make the transposition.

Using as an example the chart shown, start with the turning block at the center of the draft which is a *C* (3 and 4) block, and change its position with the *D* (1 and 4) block which lies next to it. It will follow across the entire draft that all *D* and *C* blocks will change position. Likewise all the *A* (1 and 2) and *B* (2 and 3) blocks will change position.

In chart form, the blocks before and after the transition would appear as follows:

Star Blocks	A	B	C	D	C	D	C	B	A
Harnesses	1 & 2	2 & 3	3 & 4	1 & 4	3 & 4	1 & 4	3 & 4	2 & 3	1 & 2
to									
Rose Blocks	B	A	D	C	D	C	D	A	B
Harnesses	2 & 3	1 & 2	1 & 4	3 & 4	1 & 4	3 & 4	1 & 4	1 & 2	2 & 3

In transposing or reversing the treadling from star to rose fashion, it is important to remember that the change must start from the turning block in the middle of the star. Each block is treadled the same number of times in the rose treadling as in the star so that the figure remains the same size as the original. The diagonal is not the same in rose weaving as it is in the woven as-drawn-in treadling. The difference in the appearance of the two methods shows up plainly in the draw-down (Figs. 274 and 275) and in the overshot sampler (Fig. 282).

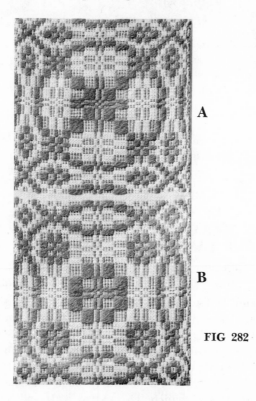

A

B

FIG 282

The plain weave between the two wheels indicates where the treadling changes from star (or woven as-drawn-in) (Fig. 282, A) to rose fashion (Fig. 282, B). The Lover's Knot woven rose fashion is known as Whig Rose.

GROUP Overshot ·
PATTERN Rose and Star, Snail's Trail, and Cat's Paw

This is one of the few patterns that is descriptive of its name. It is easy to visualize a cat stepping gingerly back and forth over a snail, fascinated to the point where it has no desire to hinder its progress. There may be little or no relationship between the pattern design and the name, for frequently patterns are named to honor individuals or to commemorate an historical event.

Although the design looks intricate, the structure of this pattern is simple, the snail's trail being composed of three repeats of twill blocks and the cat's paw being woven in rose fashion.

Use As for any overshot pattern weave, particularly coverlets

Suitable Materials and Sleying As for any overshot pattern, in keeping with the article being woven

Sample Illustrated (Fig. 285)

WARP	WEFT	PATTERN	REED (dents per inch)	SLEY
Cotton, Egyptian, 30/3	Cotton, mercerized, 20/2	Wool, fine, 2/32	18	Double

Number of Threads to One Complete Pattern Unit 126. The first 51 thread the snail's trail, the remainder the cat's paw (Fig. 283).

Treadling–Sinking Shed		Treadling–Rising Shed	
TREADLES		**TREADLES**	**LEVERS**
2 — 3×		2 — 3×	1 and 4 — 3×
3 — 5×	3× weaves snail's trail	3 — 5×	1 and 2 — 5×
4 — 3×		4 — 3×	2 and 3 — 3×
1 — 5×		1 — 5×	3 and 4 — 5×
2 — 9×		2 — 9×	1 and 4 — 9×
3 — 8×		3 — 8×	1 and 2 — 8×
2 — 4×	Weaves first paw	2 — 4×	1 and 4 — 4×
3 — 8×		3 — 8×	1 and 2 — 8×
2 — 9×		2 — 9×	1 and 4 — 9×
1 — 9×		1 — 9×	3 and 4 — 9×
4 — 8×		4 — 8×	2 and 3 — 8×
1 — 4×	Weaves second paw	1 — 4×	3 and 4 — 4×
4 — 8×		4 — 8×	2 and 3 — 8×
1 — 9×		1 — 9×	3 and 4 — 9×

Repeat, starting at the top each time, until the desired length has been woven. End with the snail's trail to balance.

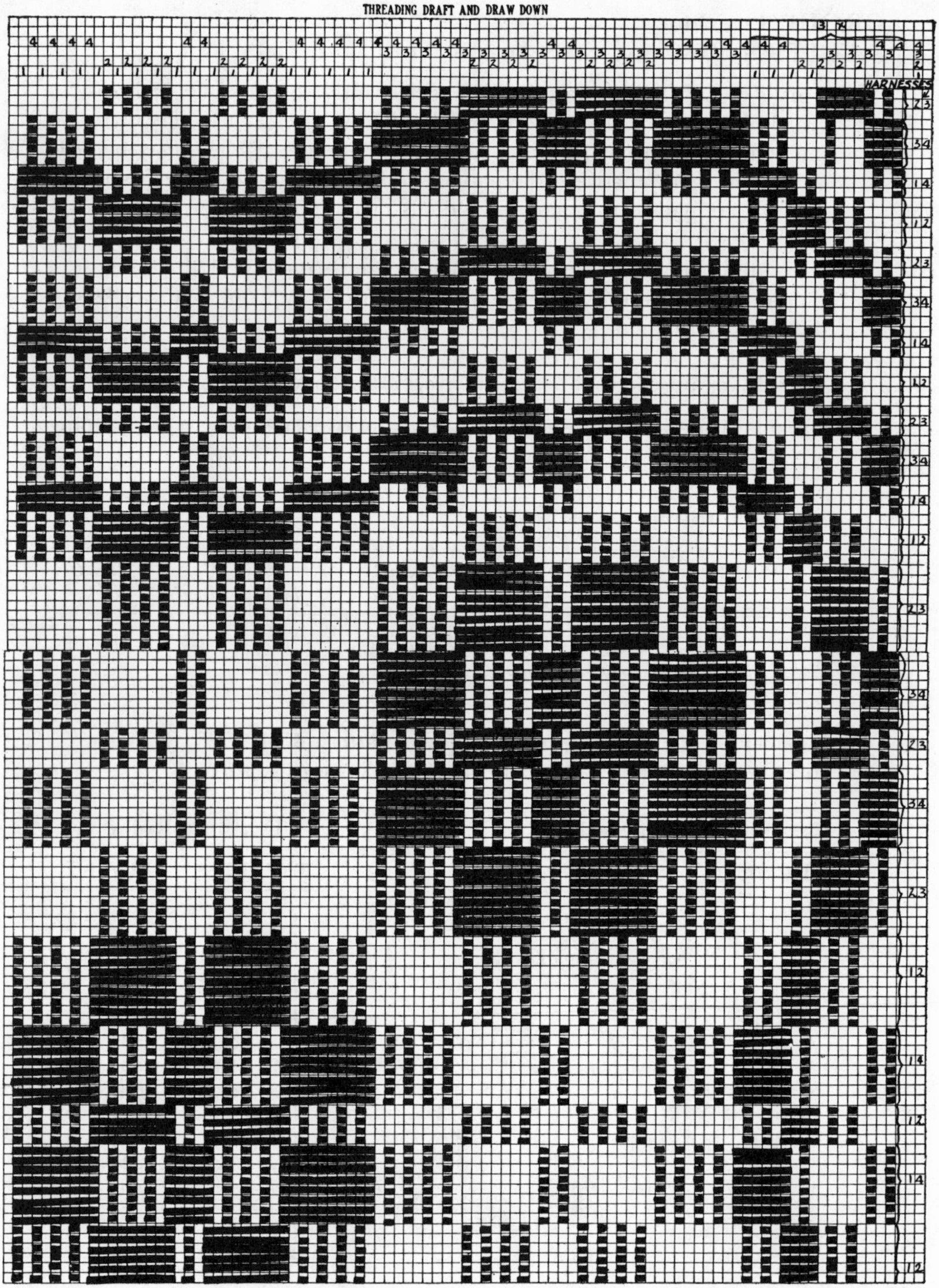

FIG 283

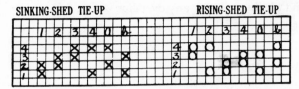

FIG 284

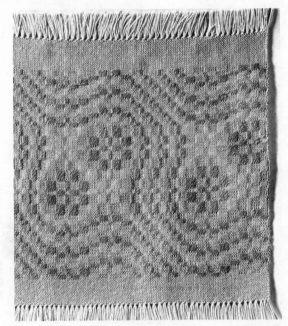

FIG 285

Problem Thread the loom with three repeats of the draft using 8/2 or 8/4 cotton for warp. Weave a porch pillow cover with a plain-weave back. Select threads and sleying carefully.

TYPE Overshot · PATTERN Patch, 2-Block on Opposites

One of the simplest and most fundamental of the overshot patterns is the square, 2-block pattern "threaded on opposites." In this threading, the same number of threads are used in each block, and the required number of tabby and pattern shots are woven in to produce a perfectly square block.

The term "to thread on opposites" means that block *A* is threaded on harnesses 1 and 2, while block *B* is threaded on harnesses 3 and 4. No thread is common to both blocks and there are no half tones in the background. Harness combinations 2 and 3 and 1 and 4 are not needed in the treadling to weave the simple 2-block pattern.

Use As for any overshot weave

Suitable Materials and Sleying As for any overshot weave, in keeping with the article being woven

Sample Illustrated (Fig. 287)

WARP	WEFT	PATTERN	REED *(dents per inch)*	SLEY
Cotton, Egyptian, 30/3	Cotton, Egyptian, 30/3	Yarn, fine	15	Double

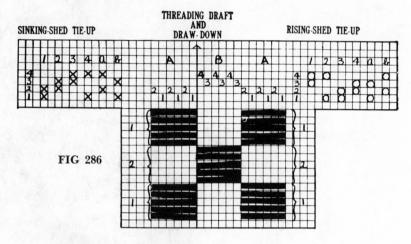

SINKING-SHED TIE-UP   THREADING DRAFT AND DRAW-DOWN   RISING-SHED TIE-UP

FIG 286

FIG 287

Treadling–Sinking Shed	Treadling–Rising Shed
	LEVERS
Block A — Treadle 1	Block A — Treadle 1 — 3 and 4
Block B — Treadle 3	Block B — Treadle 3 — 1 and 2

Problem Thread a 2-block pattern on opposites and weave a shopping bag of heavy cotton.

TYPE Overshot •
PATTERN 2-Block, on Opposites, Monk's Belt

Additional interest and variation are given the simple 2-block pattern (page 255) by breaking up the blocks into uneven units and treadling elongated figures instead of squares.

The pattern so produced is called monk's belt, and is one of the most popular among beginning weavers. It is Scandinavian in origin and in those countries forms the basis of much of the weaving used for wall hangings, table covers, and drapes, and, in some sections, for colorful peasant aprons.

It is an interesting and versatile weave, with numerous treadling variations. While different monk's belt threadings will be found, they vary but little and the end results in design are practically the same.

Materials and Sleying As for other overshot weaving, keeping in mind the use of the finished web.

Sample Illustrated (Fig. 290)

WARP	WEFT	PATTERN	REED _(dents per inch)_	SLEY
Cotton, 40/2	Cotton, 40/2	Perle, 6-strand	15	Double

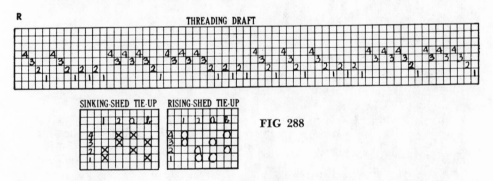

FIG 288

For the sample (Fig. 290), the pattern draft was threaded to _R_ from right to left, then threaded back to the beginning; _R_ marks the center of the sample. Do not thread the "4" twice on the return.

Treadling The blocks may be treadled any desired number of times.
 Treadle 1 weaves the _A_ block threaded on harnesses 1 and 2
 Treadle 2 weaves the _B_ block threaded on harnesses 3 and 4

The other blocks, 2 and 3 and 4 and 1, are accidentals and are not woven. The tabby treadles *a* and *b* are woven in alternating succession between the pattern shots.

Directions are given for weaving a fringe on four sides for plain weaving (page 593). The same technique is applicable to 4-harness pattern webs, except that the pattern thread is carried entirely across the extra

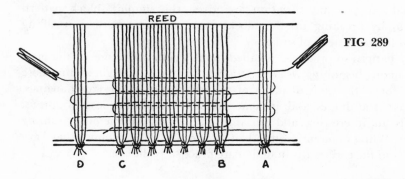

FIG 289

FIG 290

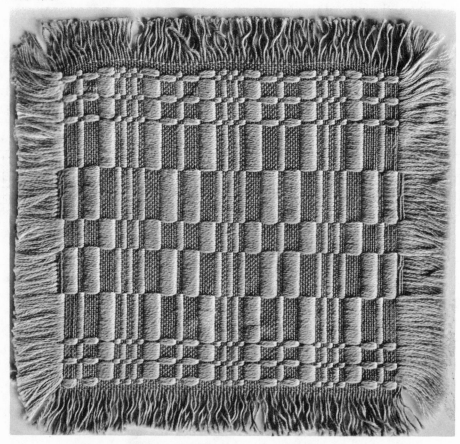

threads set up on the sides of the main web, *A* to *D,* and the tabby thread is carried only across the main body of the warp, *B* to *C* (Fig. 289). This results in a heavier fringe on the sides than on the ends. If the fringe should be the same weight and color on all sides, carry the tabby thread all the way across and the pattern thread only across the main web, *B* to *C* (Fig. 289).

Problem   On the monk's belt threading, weave a small square, fringed on four sides. Use original treadling.

TYPE Overshot •
PATTERN Monk's Belt Variation Pattern Set in Warp

Many weavers are puzzled by the method used to set patterns in the warp and question the advantages of this technique over the crackle, summer and winter, or overshot weaves.

The greatest advantage is that patterns can be woven lengthwise in the material, as, for example, along the edge of draperies. This weave is also a time-saver for those who weave peasant skirts. Many color nuances can be introduced into borders without the necessity of changing shuttles every few rows. The weave requires only one shuttle.

However, there are also several disadvantages.

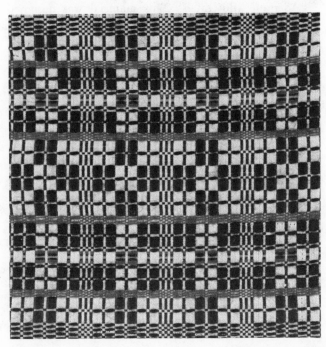

FIG. 291.   Use imagination in draft arrangement and color choice to give interest to a simple pattern

A rising-shed loom facilitates the weaving and, if the warp is to be longer than that required for a neck scarf or a few place mats, a second warp beam must be used or the tension between the fine background threads and the heavy pattern threads will be lost.

There are long skips on the back of the material. For many uses, such long skips would not be important. If necessary, they could be caught down to the back of the material with an occasional weft tie-down thread treadled between the patterns. This thread would appear as a fine dot across the plain-weave areas.

A very tight tension is necessary for the best results and a firm, tight beat is required.

The pattern threads should be at least twice the size of the background threads, which should be set to weave a 50/50 plain-weave web.

On a 4-harness loom, there can be only two pattern blocks since harnesses 1 and 2 are required for the plain weave. This leaves harnesses 3 and 4 for the pattern, allowing only two changes. For weavers who own 6- or 8-harness looms there are unlimited possibilities for extending this technique into the field of multiple-harness weaving.

Uses   For borders in place mats, aprons, skirts, drapes, and neck scarves, and on the fronts of blouses and dresses.

Materials   Any that are suitable for the kind of article or material being woven

Sample Illustrated   This material was designed for a child's skirt.[4] The black band at the bottom represents a row of black velvet ribbon. Above this band are rows of flowers in various shades of one color on a white background.

WARP	WEFT	PATTERN	REED _(dents per inch)_	SLEY
Rayon, 2/16	Rayon, 2/16	Rayon, 2/8	15	Double

Order for Winding the Warp for Fig. 294

NUMBER OF THREADS		COLOR
Wind 200	White rayon — Place on lease sticks	
24	light pink	
24	medium pink	Wind in order and place on second set
24	dark pink	of lease sticks.
4	black	

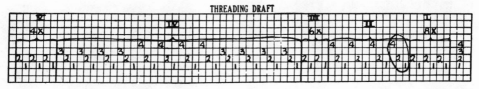

FIG 292

Order of Threading All threads on harnesses 3 and 4 are heavy, colored pattern threads.

1. Thread the right border with white 2/16 rayon for the bottom of the skirt.
2. Thread the first pattern band with black 2/8 rayon on harness 4 only.
3. Thread the plain-weave area with white 2/16 rayon, varying the width if desired.
4. Thread the first flower border with dark pink 2/8 rayon on harnesses 3 and 4 only.
5. Thread the plain-weave area between the flower borders with white 2/16 rayon.
4. Repeat for the second flower border with medium pink 2/8 rayon threaded on harnesses 3 and 4 only.
5. Repeat for the plain area between the flower borders by threading white 2/16 rayon.
4. Repeat for the third flower border with light pink 2/8 rayon threaded on harnesses 3 and 4 only.
5. To end, repeat as often as required, using the white 2/16 rayon, to weave the top of the skirt as wide as necessary.

Vary the pattern by threading a wider or narrower hem, by threading wider or narrower rows of plain weaving between the pattern bands, or by adding rows of flowers.

Sleying In sleying, the colored threads on harnesses 3 and 4 are sleyed through the same dent as the threads on harnesses 1 and 2, which they adjoin. The threads encircled at the beginning of section II on the threading draft illustrate the order in which the threads are sleyed together.

Treadling The entire piece is woven with one shuttle carrying 2/16 white rayon.

SINKING-SHED TIE-UP

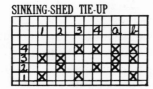

FIG 293

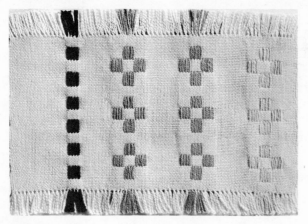

FIG 294

FIG 295

Sinking Shed		Rising Shed (*No Tie-Up*)
TREADLES		**TREADLES OR LEVERS**
a b	Plain weave, 4×, 8 shots	1 2
2 1	4× — first unit of flower	1 and 4 2 and 4
4 3	4× — second unit of flower	1 and 3 2 and 3
2 1	4× — first unit of flower	1 and 4 2 and 4

Begin at the top and repeat as many times as necessary to weave the required length.

The plain weave always must be treadled *a* when following pattern treadle 1, and pattern treadle 2 always must follow treadle *b* for the plain weave, otherwise two threads will appear together in the same shed.

Problem   Proceeding from the theory given above, work out the threading for a scarf (Fig. 295) and weave it. A 2/16 wool is suggested for the plain weave, with the same material doubled for the pattern.

TYPE Overshot ·
PATTERN 4-Block Patch, Poor Man's Damask

A 4-block overshot weave in which accidentals appear has been developed from the 2-block patch pattern (page 255).

Harriet Tidball defines accidentals as "a weft skip of two threads which occurs in the half-tone areas of four-block overshot patterns written on opposites, at the point where one half-tone area shifts to another."[5]

These two-block skips are apparent in both the draw-down (Fig. 296) and the sample (Fig. 297). I is woven on opposites; II is woven star fashion.

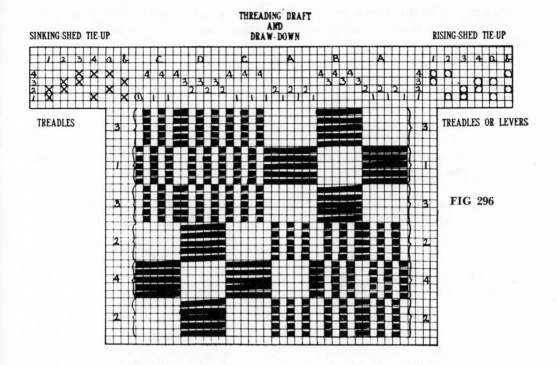

THREADING DRAFT
AND
DRAW-DOWN

SINKING-SHED TIE-UP

RISING-SHED TIE-UP

TREADLES

TREADLES OR LEVERS

FIG 296

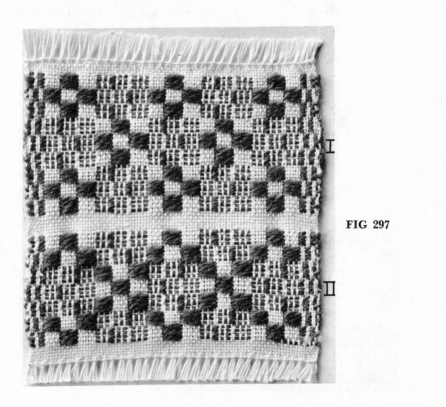

FIG 297

In this weave, set with six threads in each block, blocks with seven threads occur at regular intervals. These seven-thread blocks are unavoidable in this method of threading because, regardless of how the threads within the blocks are arranged, sooner or later a combination occurs which brings in the extra thread. A study of the draft shows how and why it happens. In the threading used here, the extra threads occur wherever the *A* and *C* blocks adjoin.

This peculiarity appears in such Swedish weaves as small flowers, which is very similar to poor man's damask. However, in the small-flowers' draft, the second figure is broken up into smaller units making a more pleasing design.

Problem Thread blocks *A* and *B* as on the draft but experiment with blocks *C* and *D,* breaking each one up into small units. Weave a sample.

TYPE Overshot ·
PATTERN Units From Wind-Flower

The sample (Fig. 299) illustrates the method by which single units from the same or various patterns can be combined to give new and different effects.

Any one of the units can be repeated many times, if desired, and the order changed, or they can be combined with units from other patterns to form new designs.

Suitable Materials and Sleying As for any overshot weave.

Thread *A* to *B* twice for the right selvedge. If a border is desired at the edges, repeat *A* to *B* six times.

Thread *B* to *C* twice for Block I.

Thread *C* to *D* once for Block II.

Thread *D* to *E* once for Block III.

For a continuous repeat of the flower unit, *C* to *D,* add a thread in the No. 4 heddle to prevent two No. 3 heddles from being threaded to-

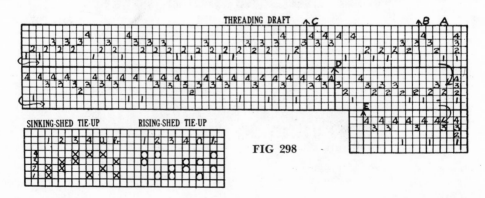

THREADING DRAFT

SINKING-SHED TIE-UP   RISING-SHED TIE-UP

FIG 298

gether. In repeating the table unit, *D* to *E,* omit the No. 4 heddle at *D* to avoid having two No. 4's together.

No attempt has been made to balance the units into a perfect square in the sample illustrated. The three units are given simply to show how they can be threaded and treadled in any combination by the weaver.

Sample Illustrated (Fig. 299)

WARP	WEFT	PATTERN	REED *(dents per inch)*	SLEY
Cotton, Egyptian, 20/3	Cotton, mercerized, 28/4	Yarn, fine	15	Double

Treadling–Sinking Shed		Treadling–Rising Shed
TREADLES		**LEVERS**

Treadling–Sinking Shed		Treadling–Rising Shed
A: Selvedge		*A:* Selvedge
a b } 4×		{ 1 and 3 { 2 and 4
B: Border		*B:* Border
1		⌈ 3 and 4 — 1×
4		⎪ 2 and 3 — 1×
3	Repeat until a square has been woven.	⎨ 1 and 2 — 1×
2		⎪ 1 and 4 — 1×
1 — 2×		⎪ 3 and 4 — 2×
2 — 2×		⌊ 1 and 4 — 2×
E: Bars		*E:* Bars
3 — 4×		⌈ 1 and 2 — 4×
1 — 14×	Repeat until a square has been woven.	⎨ 1 and 4 — 14×
3 — 4×		⌊ 1 and 2 — 4×
2 — 2×		1 and 4 — 2×
1 — 2×		3 and 4 — 2×
D: Table		*D:* Table
4 — 2×		⌈ 2 and 3 — 2×
3 — 2×		⎪ 1 and 2 — 2×
4 — 2×		⎪ 2 and 3 — 2×
3 — 2×		⎪ 1 and 2 — 2×
4 — 2×		⎪ 2 and 3 — 2×
3 — 4×		⎪ 1 and 2 — 4×
4 — 2×	Repeat until a square has been woven.	⎨ 2 and 3 — 2×
3 — 4×		⎪ 1 and 2 — 4×
4 — 2×		⎪ 2 and 3 — 2×
3 — 2×		⎪ 1 and 2 — 2×
4 — 2×		⎪ 2 and 3 — 2×
3 — 2×		⎪ 1 and 2 — 2×
4 — 2×		⌊ 2 and 3 — 2×

Treadling–Sinking Shed		Treadling–Rising Shed
TREADLES		**LEVERS**
C: Flowers		*C:* Flowers
1 — 2×		3 and 4 — 2×
2 — 2×		1 and 4 — 2×
3 — 2×		1 and 2 — 2×
4 — 2×		2 and 3 — 2×
1 — 2×		3 and 4 — 2×
2 — 2×	2×	1 and 4 — 2×
1 — 2×		3 and 4 — 2×
2 — 2×		1 and 4 — 2×
1 — 2×		3 and 4 — 2×
4 — 2×		2 and 3 — 2×
3 — 2×		1 and 2 — 2×
2 — 2×		1 and 4 — 2×

D — TABLE C — FLOWERS B — BORDER

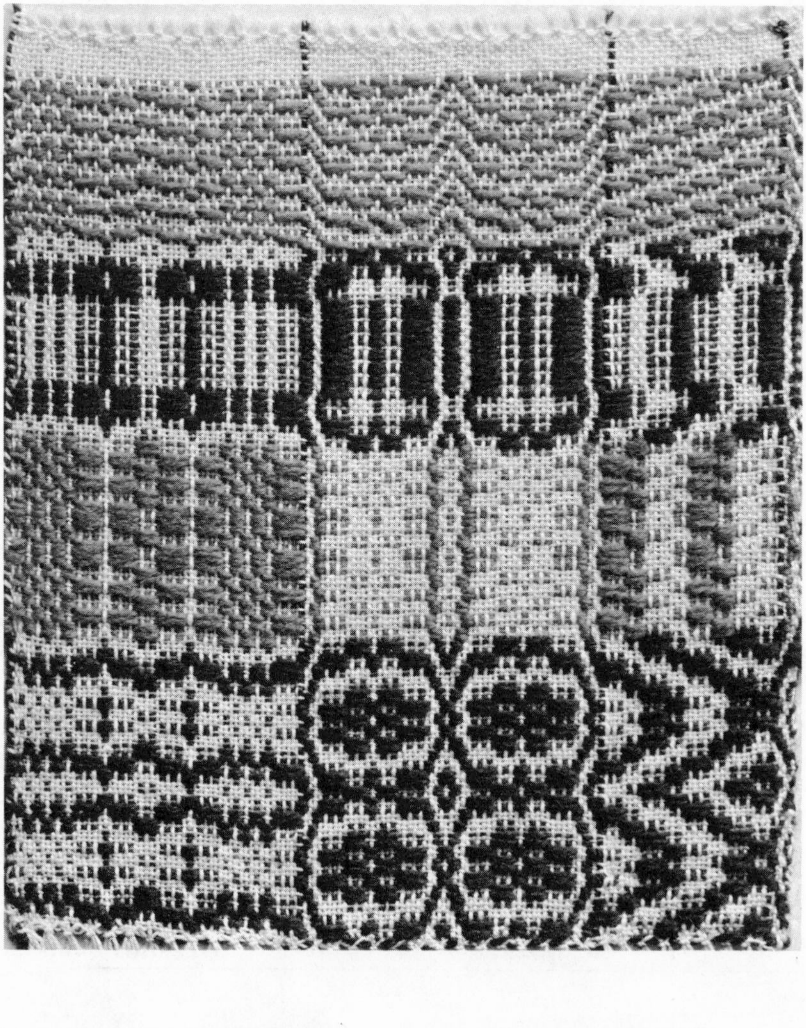

A — HEADING

B — BORDER

E — BARS

D — TABLE

C — FLOWERS

FIG. 299

Figure 299 will suggest ways in which units can be taken from pattern drafts and used to originate new drafts.

Problem Choose any two familiar overshot threading drafts, take a unit from each, and combine into an original draft. Work out on paper and, if pleasing, weave a sample.

TYPE Overshot · PATTERN Picked-Up Design

Small units from overshot patterns can be used separately as borders or small, scattered designs on a plain web. Although this requires more time and patience than the usual method of weaving, the result more than repays the weaver in added attractiveness and originality. The units of the design may be placed in rows, hit-and-miss over the web, staggered, or as a border on four sides, with a plain-web center. To achieve such results, cover only those warp threads which place the pattern in the correct position.

The weaver can experiment with any unit from any overshot threading to obtain unusual and pleasing results.

Use As for any overshot pattern

Suitable Materials and Sleying As for any overshot pattern and in keeping with article being woven

Samples Illustrated (Figs. 301 and 302)

WARP	WEFT	PATTERN	REED (dents per inch)	SLEY
(Fig. 293):				
Linen, 30/3	Linen, 30/3	6-strand floss	15	Double
(Fig. 294):				
Cotton, mercerized, 40/2	Cotton, mercerized, 40/2	Wool, fine	18	Double

Thread the draft the desired number of times, ending with the *A* unit to balance the design on the left.

FIG 300

SINKING-SHED TIE-UP   THREADING DRAFT   RISING-SHED TIE-UP

Treadling Treadling directions are not given for this sample as the illustration (Fig. 302) shows quite clearly what has been done. The treadlings at *A* are as-drawn-in; those at *B* are picked up using only the desired part of the design.

Problem On any overshot threading, pick up design areas making an arrangement which would be suitable for a place-mat decoration.

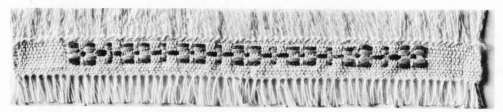

FIG 301

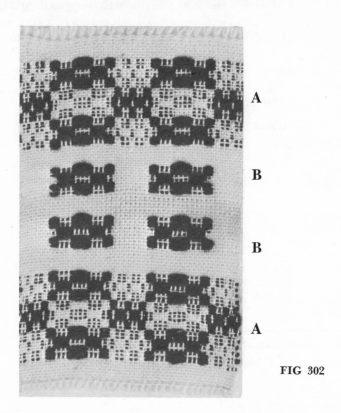

A

B

B

A

FIG 302

TYPE Overshot · PATTERN Alternate Treadling Methods

It is not necessary to limit overshot treadlings to the conventional as-drawn-in or rose-fashion methods with one shuttle carrying the tabby thread and the other the pattern thread.

Many textured materials are treadled on overshot threadings (Fig. 304). While the design characteristics of the finished web bear little resemblance to the original, the overshot threading serves as a satisfactory basis on which to weave materials in the modern mood.

Shown in the sampler (Fig. 304) are treadlings from other weaves which are adaptable to the overshot threading. Only a few of the many textured effects which can be woven on this threading will be shown here.

In weaving a sampler choose and arrange the colors carefully so that they will harmonize in the finished piece, even though the small units have each been designed to illustrate a specific point.

The original threading draft chosen for the sampler is comprised of a rose or wheel unit and small, connecting diamonds. This draft provides ample opportunity for the weaver to place the emphasis wherever he chooses.

Sample Illustrated (Fig. 304)

WARP	WEFT	PATTERN	REED (dents per inch)	SLEY
Crochet cotton, 30/3	Cotton, 16/2	Wool, 1/16	14	Double

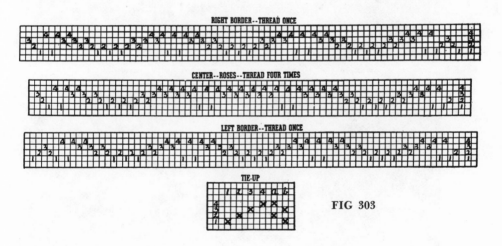

FIG 303

Treadling Beginning at the bottom of the sampler and reading up, the treadlings are:

1. As-drawn-in
2. Flame point
3. On opposites
4. Honeycomb
5. On opposites
6. Italian
7. Rose fashion

Plain bands between the patterns are woven standard twill treadling.

1. Woven As-Drawn-In Directions for this method of treadling are given on page 228.

Three strands of 2/32 wool were wound together on the shuttle for the pattern thread and a single strand of cotton 16/2 was used for tabby. The bands of weaving which separate the pattern bands are treadled 12, 23, 34, 41 using three strands of 2/32 wool wound together on the shuttle.

FIG 304

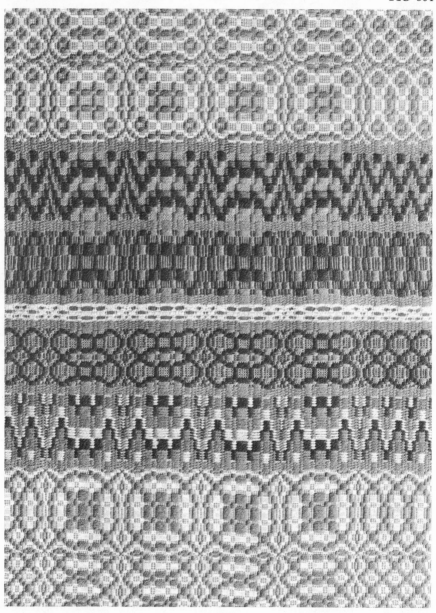

2. Flame Point Four shuttles, each carrying a different color, are required for this weave. Three strands of 2/32 wool are wound together on each shuttle. Directions for weaving are given on page 288.

These colors, designated as *A, B, C, D,* advance in a regular sequence, the second color (*B*) Group 1 becoming the first color in Group 2; the first color (*A*) in Group 1 becoming the last color in Group 2; and so on.

This is accomplished by passing the *A* color, after weaving, to the bottom of the group of shuttles which should be kept, in the order in which they are to be woven, on a chair or table beside the loom.

3. Woven on Opposites Two colors, one light and one dark, are required for this treadling.

The shuttles are thrown in on opposite sheds. One shuttle follows the twill succession of 12, 23, 34, 41, while the other is thrown in on the shed opposite to that last treadled. For instance, 1 and 2 pattern; 3 and 4 background; 2 and 3 pattern; 1 and 4 background, etc. This becomes clear as the weaving proceeds. This is a form of boundweaving but, in this particular sample, the sleying is close and the weft threads cannot pass around and completely cover the warp threads as they do in true bound-weaving.

Treadling

1 and 2 — dark		3 and 4 — dark	
3 and 4 — light	Group I	1 and 2 — light	Group III
1 and 2 — dark		3 and 4 — dark	
3 and 4 — light		1 and 2 — light	
2 and 3 — dark		2 and 3 — dark	
1 and 4 — light	Group II	1 and 4 — light	Group II
2 and 3 — dark		2 and 3 — dark	
1 and 4 — light		1 and 4 — light	
3 and 4 — dark		1 and 2 — dark	
1 and 2 — light	Group III	3 and 4 — light	Group I
3 and 4 — dark		1 and 2 — dark	
1 and 2 — light		3 and 4 — light	
1 and 4 — dark			
2 and 3 — light			
1 and 4 — dark			
2 and 3 — light			
1 and 4 — dark			
2 and 3 — light	Group IV		
1 and 4 — dark			
2 and 3 — light			
1 and 4 — dark			
2 and 3 — light			
1 and 4 — dark			
2 and 3 — light			

In repeating, end each block with the same shot as at the beginning to bring two pattern-thread colors together.

4. Honeycomb Treadling The honeycomb, as pointed out in the section covering the weave, is one that can be treadled on many overshot drafts.[6] A larger sample than shown here would demonstrate better the adaptabilities of this draft for honeycomb.

Traditionally, the tabby thread of the honeycomb is the same color value as the warp. In this sampler, which is dark, a large light area of honeycomb would disturb the harmony of the whole sampler so the band of honeycomb was kept to a minimum.

Treadling

1 and 3 2 and 4	1×, heavy thread, 6 strands, 2/32 Wool
3 4	10×, 1 strand, 2/32 Wool
2 and 4 1 and 3	1×, 6 strands, 2/32 Wool
2 1	10×, 1 strand, 2/32 Wool
1 and 3 2 and 4	1×, 6 strands, 2/32 Wool

5. Woven on Opposites Practically the same treadling was used for this sampler as for No. 3.

The former was woven with three strands of 2/32 wool wound together on the shuttle while single strands only were used for this sample.

Treadling
1 strand 2/16 wool, dark
1 strand 2/32 wool, light

COLOR		TREADLES	
A	—	1 and 2 3 and 4	4× — Group I
B	—		
A	—	2 and 3 1 and 4	4× — Group II
B	—		
A	—	3 and 4 1 and 2	4× — Group III
B	—		
A	—	1 and 4 2 and 3	4× — Group IV
B	—		

Balance with Group I if desired. Units can be squared or elongated to suit the design desired.

6. Italian Fashion Most weavers find it difficult to distinguish, at a glance, between the flame point and the Italian method, or fashion, of weaving.

There are several technical differences between the two patterns, but an easy way to identify them is to remember that the flame point has four blocks, each of a different color, while the Italian method has only three colors.

In the Italian method, the treadling progresses while the order of the colors remains constant. This is in direct contrast to the flame point which is explained in the section on boundweaving (page 287).

Treadling Throughout the weaving the heavy pattern thread is *A*. There are three colors.

COLOR	TREADLES	
A	—	1 and 2
B	—	2 and 3 } Repeat 3× — Group I
C	—	4 and 1
A	—	1 and 2 — once to end block
A	—	2 and 3
B	—	3 and 4 } Repeat 3× — Group II
C	—	1 and 2
A	—	2 and 3 — once to end block
A	—	3 and 4
B	—	4 and 1 } Repeat 3× — Group III
C	—	2 and 3
A	—	3 and 4 — once to end block
A	—	4 and 1
B	—	1 and 2 } Repeat 3× — Group IV
C	—	3 and 4
A	—	4 and 1 — once to end block

Treadling advances one to right (clockwise) at beginning of each group. Color remains constant.

7. Rose Fashion A comparison of the two ends of the sampler will show the difference in appearance between treadling as-drawn-in and treadling rose fashion. Directions for converting the treadling as-drawn-in to the rose fashion already have been given (page 251).

Three strands of 2/32 wool were used for the pattern threads, 16/2 cotton for the tabby.

Treadling

Border TREADLES		*Roses* TREADLES	
2 and 3 — 1×	Weave only once at	2 and 3 — 1×	Weave between border
1 and 2 — 2× }	beginning and end	1 and 2 — 2× }	and main pattern at be-
2 and 3 — 1×	of border.	2 and 3 — 1×	ginning and end only.

Border TREADLES		Roses TREADLES	
3 and 4 — 3×		3 and 4 — 3×	Small rose
1 and 4 — 3×		1 and 4 — 3×	
1 and 2 — 3×		1 and 2 — 3×	
2 and 3 — 6×		2 and 3 — 6×	
1 and 2 — 3×		1 and 2 — 3×	
1 and 4 — 3×		1 and 4 — 7×	Large rose
3 and 4 — 4×		3 and 4 — 4×	
1 and 4 — 3×		1 and 4 — 10×	
1 and 2 — 3×	Weaves border.	3 and 4 — 4×	
2 and 3 — 6×	Squared at	1 and 4 — 7×	
1 and 2 — 3×	corners	1 and 2 — 3×	Small rose
1 and 4 — 3×		2 and 3 — 6×	
3 and 4 — 4×		1 and 2 — 3×	
1 and 4 — 3×		1 and 4 — 3×	
1 and 2 — 3×		3 and 4 — 3×	
2 and 3 — 6×		1 and 2 — 3×	
1 and 2 — 3×		2 and 3 — 1×	To end border
1 and 4 — 3×		1 and 2 — 2×	
3 and 4 — 3×		2 and 3 — 1×	

8. Shadow Fashion Overshot treadled in shadow fashion (Fig. 305) produces a rather blurred, indistinct pattern that can be very handsome where a subtle color blend is desired. Do not confuse the shadow method of treadling with Shadow Weave Technique (page 297).

Exercise care in choosing the draft for this method of treadling for, if the skips are too long, the effect will be spidery. On the other hand, if the skips are too short, the heavy thread cannot be beaten back properly and a poor background results. To treadle shadow fashion, use the shuttle which carried the tabby thread for the pattern shots and the heavier pattern thread for the *a* and *b* tabby shots.

The threading draft used was the Maltese Cross.

Problem Try out the various methods of treadling given above on any overshot threading. Originate others using a variety of threads and weave a piece of upholstery suitable for a chair of modern design.

TYPE Overshot · PATTERN Border Treadlings

Weaving is of little value unless the weaver trains himself, from the start, to be independent of written directions, to think of the various techniques in terms of blocks, and to develop new uses for the techniques learned.

Among the simpler projects are place mats, towels, aprons, baby bibs, and, later, a peasant skirt, all of which require borders.

Design and color go hand in hand in weaving borders. They must be

FIG 305

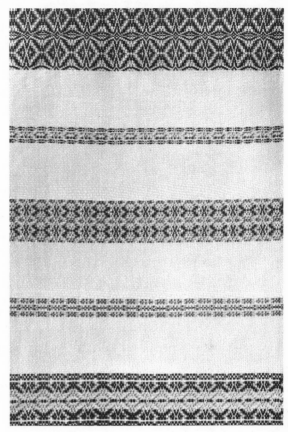

FIG 306

placed in the correct relationship to each other and to the article being woven. Colors must be harmonious, gaily contrasting, subtle, or in pastel arrangements (page 634).

It is wise, at first, to use not more than three or four colors. If four are used, two of them might be different shades of one color. Use less of the heavy, dark colors than of the light, gay colors. Dark threads are better if placed at the top or bottom of the borders. Work toward the center with the lighter colors, then outward again. Do not use the colors in equal proportion. They are more interesting when unequal.

Most overshot drafts can be used for borders, except those with large units especially designed for bedspreads or draperies.

The borders shown in Fig. 306 were treadled on a Maltese-Cross threading. The one at the bottom is woven with two shades of rust and a dark brown. It is a somewhat heavy color combination against white but might be used for a towel or place mat. It would be pleasing against a dark tan background.

The darker lines which outline the second border are dark brown with a yellow line between. Two shades of pale green form the center lines. In combination with narrower borders of the same colors both above and below, such a border would be suitable for the end of a guest towel. The center border is suitable for the ends of place mats. The colors are shades of blue and pale yellow with white.

The colors of place mats should harmonize with the china. Plain china is attractive on a place mat with a design, flowered china on a plain mat. An interesting project for a study group is to plan mats to complement their china.

The fourth border is in delicate lavender and pink shades suitable for a guest towel. Pastel blues and pinks or shades of green or yellow could be used. For modern bathrooms use the strongly contrasting colors of the fixtures and walls, or those in the shower curtain.

The color distribution in the top border is too even. The top and bottom of the border are dark red and the circles turquoise. The effect would have been more pleasing if a row or two of the turquoise had been introduced close to the edges at the top and bottom of the border.

Hostess aprons with gay borders always make welcome gifts. Peasant skirts of wool, cotton, or linen are the envy of nonweaving friends. However, be careful when placing the border; it should be within the lower third of the skirt.

No treadling directions are given for the borders, as similar ones can be treadled on practically any overshot threading.

Problem On an overshot threading, weave a sampler with five borders using different colors and threads for each one.

TYPE Overshot and Plain Weave ·
PATTERN Miniature Young Lover's Knot
With Plain-Weave Border

To further extend border techniques, the accompanying sample shows the Young Lover's Knot (page 248) woven with a plain weave border around it. This is achieved by threading the pattern according to the draft given on page 247 and utilizing two extra harnesses, 5 and 6, to thread the plain border on each side of the pattern. This method is extremely useful where it is desirable to weave an article with motifs of an overshot pattern (page 267) instead of an over-all design. This can be done on four harnesses, but it is time consuming as the shuttles must be passed up and down through the warp threads at the boundaries of the different units, and the effect is not as smooth. Care must be taken, in this weave, to use a small pattern thread which must be well beaten back. Otherwise, the center part will build up much more quickly than the border, due to the fact that the pattern thread does not pass across the border.

Use For household linens where it is desirable to have a plain web decorated with contrastingly colored motifs.

Suitable Materials and Sleying As for overshot weaves using fine linen or mercerized cotton for the pattern thread.

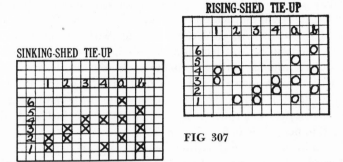

SINKING-SHED TIE-UP

RISING-SHED TIE-UP

FIG 307

Treadling Follow the treadling directions for the Young Lover's Knot (pages 244 to 245). For the plain weave, treadle *a* and *b* in alternating succession. Note that these treadles are tied to harnesses 5 and 6 which carry the border threads.

Problem Add a plain-weave border to any overshot pattern, work out the treadling, and weave a sample.

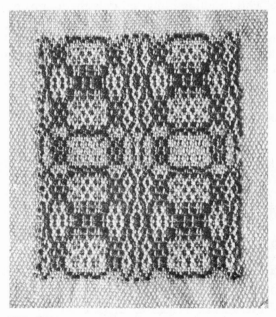

FIG 308

TYPE Overshot and Twill Weave ·
PATTERN Young Lover's Knot With Twill Border

Here the Young Lover's Knot is combined with a twill border made possible by the addition of a seventh and eighth harness (Fig. 309).

The original overshot draft, Young Lover's Knot (pages 244 to 245), is threaded and treadled exactly as written for four harnesses plus the addition of a 4-harness twill on each end and side.

As harnesses 1, 2, 3, 4 are taken up with the overshot part of the pattern, the twill is threaded on harnesses 5, 6, 7, 8, repeating the threading the required number of times to make the border the desired width.

Recall for a moment the routine treadling of the 4-harness twill. It runs 1, 2; 2, 3; 3, 4; 4, 1. Now, when the same thing happens on the second set of harnesses, the routine is exactly the same but with the numbers changed to become 5, 6; 6, 7; 7, 8; 8, 5.

In addition to the treadling for the overshot part of the pattern, and the twill border as just explained above, there must be a tabby treadling to bind the overshot portion of the pattern together. In this case it runs 1 and 3, and 2 and 4. At this point there are three sets of numbers to deal with. Some of these numbers are common to each shot so they can be sorted out as follows for a rising-shed loom. For the border at each end of the piece use: 1, 2, 5, 6; 2, 3, 6, 7; 3, 4, 7, 8; 1, 4, 5, 8.

A study of these sets of numbers will reveal that the first two in each set read across, following the routine of a 4-harness twill, while the last two in each set follow the same twill routine but on harnesses 5 to 8 inclusive.

The pattern thread follows the exact treadling given for Young Lover's Knot. This treadling brings up only the four-pattern sheds through which the shuttle passes, confining itself only to this section.

In addition to the tabby treadling, consideration must be given to the weaving of the twill border along the sides. It is necessary to add to a tabby running 1, 3 and 2, 4, threaded on the first four harnesses, the treadling for the twill threaded on harnesses 5 to 8. The tabby would run: 1, 3, 5, 6; 2, 4, 6, 7; 1, 3, 7, 8; 2, 4, 5, 8 for a sinking-shed loom, the opposite for a rising-shed loom.

RISING-SHED TIE-UP

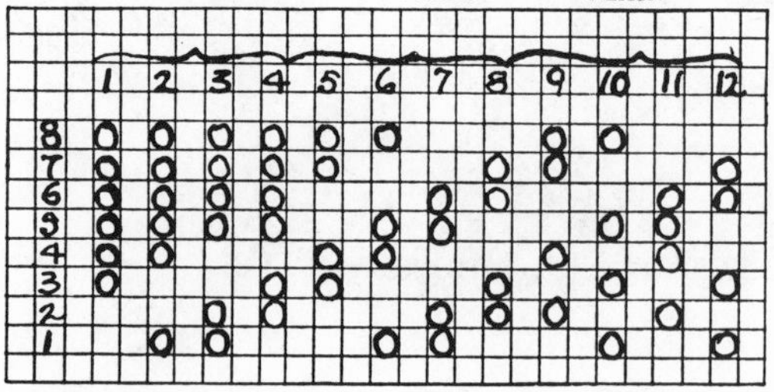

FIG 309

This may seem confusing at first, but if worked out carefully, step by step, it will clarify itself as the weaver proceeds.

Border Treadles 5, 6, 7, 8 repeated the desired number of times

Overshot Center Follow the treadling routine for the Young Lover's Knot, alternating with plain-weave treadles 9, 10, 11, 12 for the desired length and ending with a border as at the start.

Problem Add a twill border to any 4-harness overshot threading, work out the treadling, and weave a sample.

FIG 310

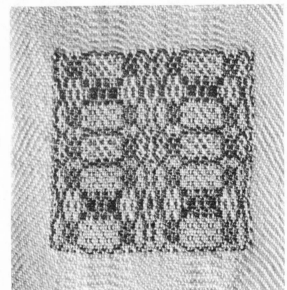

TYPE Vertical Borders

Horizontal or crosswise borders or stripes, as previously described (Fig. 306) are not difficult to weave, as they are simply color or treadling variations of the draft. These can be any width, and placed at the top or bottom, or spaced at intervals in the web.

A vertical border placed at the selvedge to add color or design to the center part of the web is a different matter. It must be part of the threading draft, but differ in design. To weave a plain border around a patterned 4-harness web (Fig. 308) or a patterned border around a plain web requires two extra harnesses. The huck weave (page 372), the Bronson weave (page 337), and a few other 4-harness techniques are exceptions, as the draft structure is such that plain and pattern units are combined in the draft itself.

FIG 311

The simplest vertical border which can be added, and one which will in most cases give a satisfactory finish to a patterned web, is a plain twill threading (Fig. 278). However, when woven it will not materialize as the conventional 1, 2, 3, 4 twill design, but will take on the general characteristics of the draft which it borders, in the center of the web (Fig. 311).

When adding a twill or other border, decide on the width, and be sure the proportions are in keeping with the main part of the web; plan the number of threads required, half on the right side, half on the left; and thread in the usual manner. For the right border, the twill sequence will run 1, 2, 3, 4 and the left 4, 3, 2, 1 so that the twill will run in the same direction on both sides of the web. Start the weaving with the conventional twill treadling, 12, 23, 34, 14, and weave the end border so it will be the same width as the side borders. In threading, if the border draft ends with a thread, on harness 1, for example, and the main part of the draft begins with a thread on harness 1, it will be necessary to add a transition thread between the two on either harness 2 or 4. Many of the old overshot coverlet drafts included border treadlings, some of which were completely different from the center part of the coverlet, while others were composed of one, or possibly more, units taken from the coverlet design and repeated a sufficient number of times to weave the border the desired width. It is not difficult to add a border design to an overshot draft. The most simple method of doing this is to choose from the overshot coverlet, or other draft drawdown, a unit which appeals, and make a draw-down of it. Place this draw-down at the edge of the coverlet draw-down, placing the squares so they match perfectly, and study the effect. If the point where the two join is not pleasing, try adding or deleting small units such as diamonds, tables, stars, or roses, any of which could well unify the two parts of the design.

The width of a border in proportion to the center, the main part of the web, and the size and type of the design must be given careful study. In the overshot sample shown (Fig. 312), the border is both too wide and heavy in the pattern design to be acceptable. One threading of the rose design, with the center design repeated a sufficient number of times to obtain the required width, would have made a more pleasing and appropriate design. Or the two parts of the draft could have been reversed using four repeats of the rose for the center area with the required number of

FIG 312

repeats of the center draft threaded on each selvedge to form a border. Borders can of course be added to other techniques such as summer-and-winter, crackle, etc.

Problem Choose an overshot draft design border for same and weave sample.

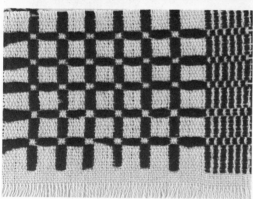

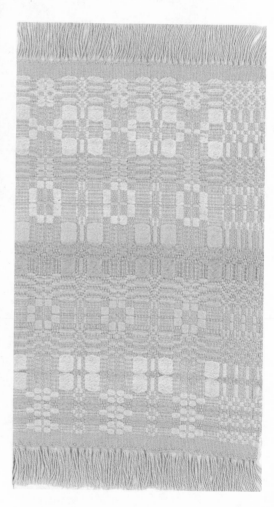

FIG. 313. Simple vertical border obtained by reducing, at the edge of the web, the number of threads in the pattern units

FIG. 314. Border obtained by repeating number of threads in one small unit of draft

TYPE Overshot Borders · PATTERN Popcorn

This weave is a method of treadling rather than a technique.[7] The draft resembles any of a number of overshot drafts, any one of which could produce the popcorn effect which well illustrates the name. To obtain the desired "puffed" effect, the warp must be widely spaced, and it is necessary to make an extra allowance beyond the calculated warp measurements to offset the take-up. Hard beating on a slack warp is required.

Sample Illustrated (Fig. 316)

WARP	WEFT	REED (dents per inch)	SLEY
Cotton, 8/2	Mop cotton, 12-strand *or* Cotton roving, 3- or 4-ply	16	Single

SINKING-SHED TIE-UP　　TO END　　　THREADING DRAFT　　　SELVEDGE　RISING-SHED TIE-UP

FIG 315

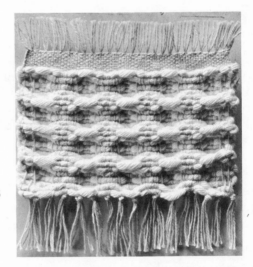

FIG 316

Thread the selvedge at the right. Thread the bracketed section the required number of times. (For Fig. 316, the bracketed section was repeated five times.) Balance the pattern with the end threads at the left.

Treadling   Treadles 3 and 6 weave the plain weave for the hem. If so desired, the mats may be fringed; but, with a fine, widely spaced warp the result is not too satisfactory. The hemmed mats are more attractive.

TREADLES	TREADLES
1	1
2	2
3	3
4	4
5	5
6	6
5	5
4	4
3	3
2	2

Start at the top each time and repeat the required number of times, ending with a 1 to balance the design.

Problem   Thread and weave four mats in the popcorn treadling, or pillow top with popcorn borders at each end.

TYPE Overshot Borders · PATTERN Imitation Pile

The tufted or pile technique provides a satisfactory substitute for those who do not wish to spend the time required to weave a true flossa rug. This rug does not possess the wearing qualities of a true flossa rug, for in the flossa, each pattern thread (which becomes the pile) is knotted around a warp thread. In the tufted technique, the pile thread simply lies in the web and is removed easily by vigorous shaking or thorough vacuum cleaning. However, if the web is tightly beaten and the pattern or pile thread fairly coarse, the rug will wear for a reasonable length of time.

Uses   For borders on draperies, bath mats, toilet-seat covers, pillow covers, baby bibs, aprons, skirts, and cotton jackets; and for small rugs.

Sample Illustrated (Fig. 318)

WARP	WEFT	PATTERN	REED (dents per inch)	SLEY
Carpet warp	Carpet warp	Candle wicking, heavy yarn	12	Double

Thread *A* to *B* 4× for the right selvedge.

Thread *B* to *C*, the center of the rug, the number of times required to obtain the desired width.

Thread *C* to *D* once only, on the last repeat, to balance the pattern.

Thread *D* to *E* 4× for the left selvedge.

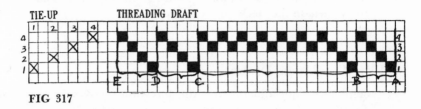

TIE-UP   THREADING DRAFT

FIG 317

The depth of the pile is controlled by the number of 3–4's threaded in sequence in the *B–C* unit of the threading. In the sample, Fig. 318, threaded in this manner, the pile is ¼ in. deep.

Treadling–Sinking Shed

HEADING FOR HEM

1 and 3 ⎱
2 and 4 ⎰ Carpet warp 3 in.

PATTERN WOVEN WITH A TABBY

1 and 3	Carpet warp	⎫
3 and 4	Candle wicking	Repeat as
2 and 4	Carpet warp	often as
3 and 4	Candle wicking	necessary.

Treadling–Rising Shed

HEADING FOR HEM

2 and 4 ⎱
1 and 3 ⎰ Carpet warp 3 in.

PATTERN WOVEN WITH A TABBY

2 and 4	Carpet warp	⎫
1 and 2	Candle wicking	Repeat as
1 and 3	Carpet warp	often as
1 and 2	Candle wicking	necessary.

FIG 318

End with a plain-weave heading.

The pile may be cut either before or after removal from the loom. With sharp-pointed scissors, a sharp knife, or, preferably, surgical scissors, cut through the center of the overshot bars and fluff up the cut ends with the fingers or a brush. The pile will cover the background web after a little use.

Problem Weave a baby bib using this method of decoration.

The two preceding weaves illustrate the very different results which may be obtained when the orthodox treadling from one technique, in this case the overshot, is replaced by the treadling of a different technique, or even by a weaver's original treadling. Examples of some of these results are shown on the "techniques gamp."

TYPE Combined Drafts

This technique differs from the foregoing weaves in that two drafts are integrated, forming a threading that can be treadled to produce either of the original draft patterns or an entirely new one which shows some features of the two originals. The chief advantage of these combined drafts is that they provide an opportunity to weave a great many different patterns on a long warp without rethreading.

They are interesting to the weaver who enjoys experimenting with draft writing but, as they are a bit involved for the beginner, they are not dealt with in this text. Those who wish to try them will find examples in Gertrude Greer's text,[8] and in some of the Scandinavian texts.

Weavers who have 6- or 8-harness looms will be interested in weaving linen and wool webs using a combination of the plain and one of the many twill weave techniques. A study of the accompanying draft reveals that the twill sections of the web are threaded on harnesses 5 and 6.

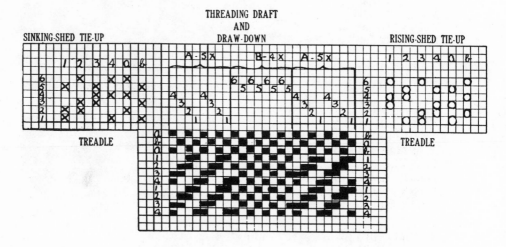

THREADING DRAFT
AND
DRAW-DOWN

SINKING-SHED TIE-UP

RISING-SHED TIE-UP

TREADLE

TREADLE

Problem Design, thread, and weave a linen place mat or woolen scarf using the above as a guide.

chapter 7

Variations and Extensions on Twill Threadings

**TYPE Variations and Extensions on Twill Threadings •
PATTERN Boundweave**

There are a number of weaves, some well known and frequently used and others not quite so well known, which do not completely conform to any one standard technique. They show deviations, such as the overshot, which is actually an extension of the twill technique.

Boundweaving, the shadow weave, and others show certain characteristics which tie them to a "mother" technique but permit them to stand on their own. In some texts we find various weaves grouped under a classified heading, such as, for instance, the spot family weaves, with each bearing its own individual name.

The weavers who enjoy experimenting can study the various techniques which follow in this chapter, compare their similarities and differences, and perhaps carry the study to the point of composing a weave structure distinctly their own.

TYPE Weft-Face • PATTERN Boundweave

The weft-face weave offers unlimited possibilities for weaving colorful pieces without the time-consuming task of inserting the colored threads with the fingers, as in the tapestry weaves. The treadles open the required sheds and the weaving is done entirely with flat or boat shuttles.

Boundweaving is not, in itself, a technique. It is a method of treadling.

The warp may be set on rose path, a point twill (page 177) with which it is usually associated; on summer and winter (page 311); or on overshot, particularly the well-known honeysuckle threading (page 235). Drafts should be chosen with care, however, since drafts with long overskips or many small, closely integrated units are not practical.

Aside from different methods of threading, there are various ways in which boundweaving can be treadled. Directions for three treadling methods are given here. The first, considered by many weavers to be the correct method, is the flame point. In this treadling, four shades of one color are used. The order of treadling never changes from the standard 1–2, 2–3, 3–4, 4–1 of the twill succession. It is the progression of the colors which forms the color harmony; the top color of each unit moves to the bottom of the following unit (page 289). A second method, popular in Sweden, is the boundweave woven on opposites. The rose path threading is used and the treadling is more variable than that used for other types of boundweaving.

Stylized figures, animals, flowers, trees, and abstract designs form a third group. Some very amusing designs have been published, but the adventuresome weaver can design his own on graph paper. It is surprising that these figures can be produced wholly through color changes while the treadling routine remains constant.

Uses   Because of the rather stiff web, this weave is limited to wall hangings, floor rugs, purses, bags, and cushion covers.

Materials   The warp must be firm linen or cotton. In Sweden linen is preferred to cotton. However, a hard-twisted cotton serves very well. Wool is best for the weft as it packs in well; linen or the springy synthetic threads should not be used. The size of the weft can vary from 2/16 wool to the coarse homespuns, depending upon the purpose of the fabric.

Sleying   Sleying is very important in boundweaving. The warp must be set so that the wool weft can be taken back to cover it, yet the result must be a firm piece of weaving. The pattern is destroyed if the warp is not entirely covered.

Samples Illustrated

1. Flame point on Honeysuckle Threading[1] *(Fig. 320)*

WARP	WEFT	REED	SLEY
		(dents per inch)	
Cotton, 8/4	Wool, soft 2-ply, four shades of blue	12	Single

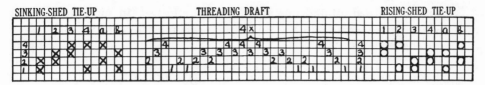

FIG 319

Treadling

TREADLE	COLOR		TREADLE	COLOR	

Unit 1:
1	dark blue	
2	medium blue
3	blue	} 3×
4	light blue

Unit 3:
1	blue
2	light blue
3	dark blue	} 3×
4	medium blue

Unit 2:
1	medium blue
2	blue
3	light blue	} 3×
4	dark blue

Unit 4:
1	light blue
2	dark blue
3	medium blue	} 3×
4	blue

FIG 320

Start at Unit 1 and repeat as many times as desired.

For the sample, each unit was treadled three times to give a more pointed effect to the design which, with the type of wool used, would otherwise have been rather flat. If desired, units 1, 2, 3, and 4 can be repeated in the order given above or in the reverse order, as 1, 2, 3, 4, 3, 2, then 1, either to balance the design or to begin a new sequence.

It is less confusing if the shuttles are kept in the order in which the colors are thrown through the shed. Place the shuttles on the end of the bench, on a chair, or on a small table at the side of the loom.

Good edges are difficult to obtain with this weave. The weft threads must be turned around one another or interlocked. In some instances, it will be necessary to slip the shuttle between the selvedge threads to keep the edge smooth.

2. *Variation of Twill Threading (Fig. 322)*

WARP	WEFT	REED (*dents per inch*)	SLEY
Cotton, 8/4	Wool, homespun, 2-ply: paddy green, yellow, dark green, turquoise	10	Single

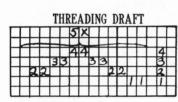

THREADING DRAFT

FIG 321

FIG 322

Two threads are threaded together on each harness (Fig. 321). The result is a larger, bolder figure than would be possible with the regulation threading. This combination threading, wide sleying, coarse wool, and hard beating produces a heavy material suitable for rugs. The tie-up is the same as that for the honeysuckle boundweave (Fig. 320).

Treadling

Unit 1: TREADLE	COLOR		*Unit 2:* TREADLE	COLOR	
1	paddy green		1	yellow green	
2	yellow green	5×	2	dark green	5×
3	dark green		3	turquoise	
4	turquoise		4	paddy green	

Unit 3:			Unit 4:		
TREADLE	**COLOR**		**TREADLE**	**COLOR**	
1	dark green		1	turquoise	
2	turquoise	} 5×	2	paddy green	} 5×
3	paddy green		3	yellow green	
4	yellow green		4	dark green	

3. Boundweaving Woven on Opposites (Fig. 324)

Because of the many variations possible in treadling this pattern and to encourage the weaver to use originality in his weaving, no treadling directions are given for sample 3, which was woven in Sweden.

To select four or more colors which harmonize, start with black and white and add two bright colors. Choose brown and tan and add rust and green or yellow, or begin with two grays and add two bright colors.

Bands of twill treadlings have been used at each end of the wall hanging and between the pattern rows. These twill rows accentuate the pattern rows and make the transition from one pattern and color to another much easier.

WARP	WEFT	REED (dents per inch)	SLEY
Carpet warp, 8/4 or Linen, heavy 2-ply	Homespun, 2-ply	10	Single

THREADING DRAFT

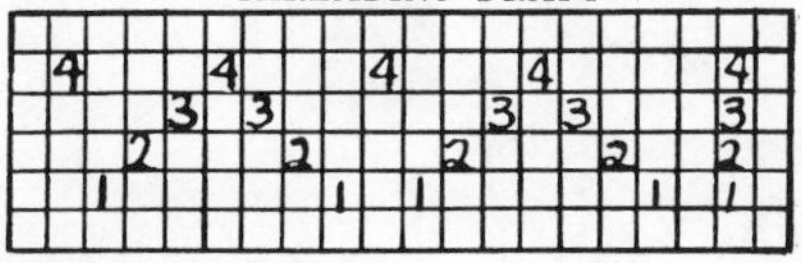

FIG 323

Rose-Path Treadling Draft Repeat the draft the required number of times to thread the desired width.

Tie-Up Standard

Treadling For boundweaving woven on opposites use any of the many rose-path treadlings. The difference between those woven with a tabby and boundweaving is that, instead of inserting a tabby thread on the usual 2 and 4 and 1 and 3 routine, a weft thread, of the same size and weight, but of a different color from the pattern thread, is thrown in between the pattern threads on the shed opposite that used for the pattern thread which directly preceded this weft thread.

The routine would be:

TREADLES	THREAD	TREADLES	THREAD
1 and 2	pattern	3 and 4	pattern
3 and 4	background	1 and 2	background
2 and 3	pattern	1 and 4	pattern
1 and 4	background	2 and 3	background

Problem These wall hangings or samplers appear in several of the Scandinavian weaving books and leaflets on sale in bookstores, but the weaver is urged to work out his own treadling and color arrangement rather than copy them. A study of Fig. 324, followed by some experimenting with treadling and color arrangements, will be helpful.

FIG. 324. Designed and woven in Sweden by Mary E. Black, Nova Scotia

4. Trees Woven in Boundweaving (Fig. 325)

As has been mentioned, the designs for figures can, with a little imagination, be amusing or stylized.

First work out the design on the graph paper, then sketch in the threading above the design. Some surprising results can be accomplished on four harnesses.

In weaving figures, choose one color for the background. Throw it on the same shed each time. For sample 4, for example, white was chosen and was woven each time on treadle 2 for the sinking shed and on treadles 4 and 1 for the rising shed.

WARP	WEFT	REED *(dents per inch)*	SLEY
Cotton, 8/2	Homespun, 2-ply	10	Single

Threading and Tie-Up   Rose path, Sample 4 (Fig. 325).

Treadling–Sinking Shed

TREADLES	COLOR	
3	white	
4	white	
1	white	3× for bottom border
2	white	
3	green	
4	green	
1	green	4× for base of tree
2	white	
3	green	
4	white	
1	white	12× for trunk of tree
2	white	
3	green	
4	green	
1	green	12× for branches of tree
2	white	
3	green	
4	white	
1	white	4× for tip of tree
2	white	
3	white	
4	white	
1	white	4× for top border
2	white	

Treadling–Rising Shed

TREADLES	COLOR
1 and 2	white
2 and 3	white
3 and 4	white
4 and 1	white
1 and 2	green
2 and 3	green
3 and 4	green
4 and 1	white
1 and 2	green
2 and 3	white
3 and 4	white
4 and 1	white
1 and 2	green
2 and 3	green
3 and 4	green
4 and 1	white
1 and 2	green
2 and 3	white
3 and 4	white
4 and 1	white
1 and 2	white
2 and 3	white
3 and 4	white
4 and 1	white

5. Boundweaving on Rose Path (Fig. 326)

WARP	WEFT
Cotton, 8/2	Homespun wool, fine, single-ply

REED (dents per inch)	SLEY
16	Single

Threading and Tie-Up The same as for sample 4 (Fig. 325)

Problem Using sample 4 (Fig. 325) as a guide, work out the treadling for sample 5. Experiment with original treadlings.

6. Humanesque Figures (Fig. 329)

WARP	WEFT	REED (dents per inch)	SLEY
Cotton, 8/4	Wool, homespun, 2-ply	14	Single

These figures were threaded on a return twill and were woven in gay colors with a bit of metallic for highlights in shoes and buckles.

The order for threading the blocks shown at the top of the chart

FIG 325

FIG 326

FIG 327

THREADING DRAFT   FIG 328   FIG 329

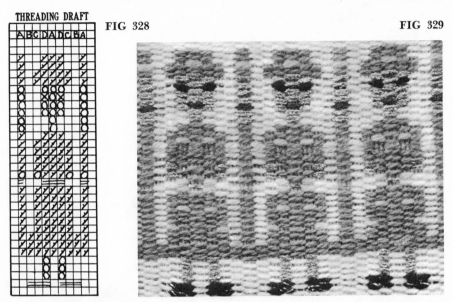

(Fig. 328) to weave one figure is as follows: *A, B, C, D, A, D, C, B, A*. If the threading is repeated, do not thread the *A* block at the left until the last repeat to balance the design. If it is threaded at both the start and finish, a double bar will occur between the figures when the pattern is repeated.

Treadling Use the treadling notes for the Pine Tree (page 293) as a guide in treadling the "girl with sunglasses"[2] (Fig. 329), recalling that a background thread must be entered between each pattern thread. Where a solid-color border is desired, treadle the blocks in the twill succession: *A, B, C, D*. Repeat as often as necessary. The bottom of the girl's skirt was woven in the *A, B, C, D* order without the white background thread being entered between the pattern threads.

Figures set on five or six harnesses[3] stand alone rather than having a part in common with the figure on either side, as a study of the figures (Fig. 330–331) will show. However, unless particular care is taken, a "post" between the figures will show, as can be seen between the row of dogs (Fig. 332).

In each case repeat the threading from *A* to *B* as many times as necessary to obtain the required width ending with 1, 5, 1 or 1, 6, 1 to balance the design.

VARIATIONS AND EXTENSIONS ON TWILL THREADINGS   295

There are two methods of treadling: (1) the regular twill succession which is easy to remember. It does however allow some of the threads to slide out of place. Method 2 holds all the threads in alignment resulting in better results designwise.

Treadling Sequence
5-harness: Method A 12, 23, 34, 45, 51   Method B 12, 34, 51, 23, 45
6-harness: Method A 12, 23, 34, 45, 56, 61   Method B 12, 34, 56, 23, 45, 61

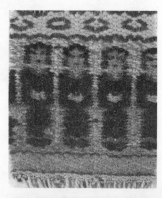

FIGS. 330 to 332
Boundweave figures set on 4, 5, and 6 harnesses. Designed and woven by Minnie Simpson, York, England.

Boundweave is particularly interesting to those weavers who like to experiment. It can be full of surprises. Children love it and are quite capable of producing interesting results once they understand the theory.

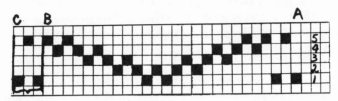

FIG. 333. 5-harness threading

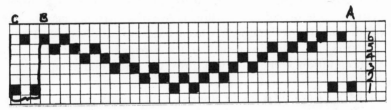

FIG. 334. 6-harness threading

TYPE Twill Variations and Extensions ·
PATTERN Shadow Weave

Shortly after the First World War, Mrs. Mary Meigs Atwater presented to the charter members of her Shuttle Craft Guild, and to other interested weaver friends, directions for an unusual weave which previously had not been in circulation. She did not state its source, whether it was an original technique, or one she had discovered during her studies of woven samples in the many museums she visited in this country and during her trips to Central and South America. She named it Shadow Weave, which well describes its appearance.

Though Shadow Weave is usually set on a twill sequence threading, it is not a true twill, but rather a plain weave with two thread skips, which because of the use of two colors, one dark, one light, alternating in both warp and weft, make shadows between the changes of the hatching. Its two-color threading resembles somewhat the log cabin (page 84) weave, also the Swedish Mattor, yet a close study of the finished web reveals that the Shadow Weave threads run at a 45-deg. angle with a distinct dark row alternating with a distinct light row with the edge threads interwoven with each other in a definite feather stitch pattern. One set of threads, either the dark or the light, weaves on a twill succession of 1, 2, 3, 4, while the other set follows a 4, 1, 2, 3 succession. Shadow Weave is usually set on a twill, point twill, or extended point twill draft, though advanced weavers have experimented with other types of drafts with excellent results.

The web when woven of sturdy threads is very firm and durable and suitable for upholstery, pillow covers, bags, and other purposes where a long-wearing material is required. When woven loosely on a fine silk or mercerized warp with soft wool weft, it produces beautifully soft and pliant shawls, afghans, baby blankets, and scarves. Place mats woven of round thread linen are also most attractive. Although there is a decided diagonal pull to the finished web, it springs back into place when released and holds its shape well.

Threads The beginner would be well advised to start with a coarse thread for both warp and weft, both threads of the same grist, one a light color, the other dark. 4/8 cotton was used for the two samples shown (Figs. 337 and 339). The dark squares on the draft represent dark threads, and the circles white or light-color thread. Additional colors may be experimented with once the technique has been tried and understood. The drafts are a bit tricky to write down on the graph paper and threading requires close concentration as one error will throw the whole design out of line.

Tie-Up Regardless of the number of harnesses required for the threading draft, the standard twill tie-up is used.

Sample 1

Several repeats of the draft given below should provide a sufficiently large sample to start with.

WARP	WEFT	REED	SLEY
		(dents per inch)	
Cotton, 4/8	Cotton, 4/8	15	Single

FIG. 335. 4-harness Shadow Weave draft and tie-up

FIG. 336. 4-harness tie-up rising shed

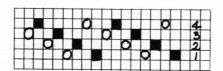

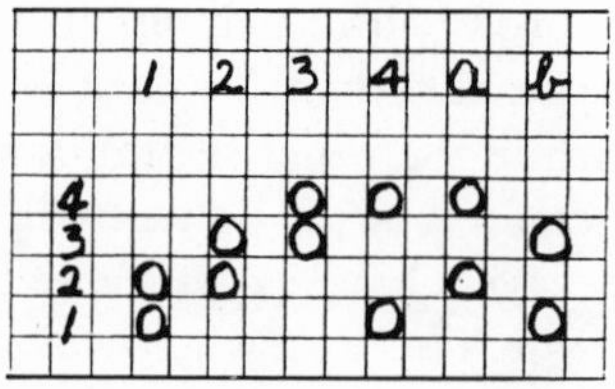

Treadling a

1 dark
2 light
3 dark
4 light
} repeat and repeat

Treadling b

1 dark
3 light } 4 times
2 dark
4 light } 4 times
} repeat as desired

Treadling c

1 dark   3 dark
4 light 2 light
2 dark   4 dark
1 light 3 light
} repeat as desired

Sample 2

4-harness Reverse Twill   Threads, reed, sley, tie-up same as for sample 1

TREADLE		TREADLE		TREADLE		TREADLE	
3 light		2 light		3 light		2 light	
1 dark		3 dark		1 dark		3 dark	
4 light		1 light		4 light		1 light	
2 dark	twice	2 dark	twice	2 dark	once	2 dark	once
1 light		4 light		1 light		4 light	
3 dark		1 dark		3 dark		1 dark	
2 light		3 light		2 light		3 light	
4 dark		4 dark		4 dark		4 dark	

FIG. 337. 4-harness reverse Shadow Weave

FIG. 338. 4-harness Shadow Weave reverse draft

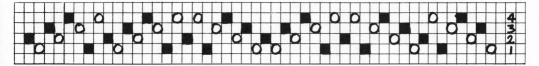

Repeat for allover design

The "featherstitch" crossing of the threads mentioned above is plainly visible along the diagonal lines of this design.

Sample 3

Shadow Weave set on 4-harness overshot draft Threads, reed, sley, tie-up same as for previous samples.

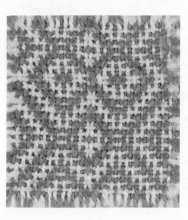

FIGS. 339 and 340
4-harness Shadow Weave
set on overshot draft

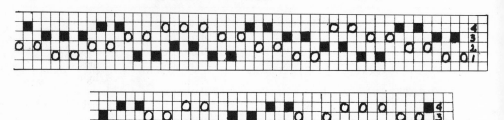

Treadling

	A Block TREADLE			B Block TREADLE		
1 light	3 dark			4 light	2 dark	
1 "	3 "			4 "	2 "	
2 "	4 "			3 "	1 "	
2 "	4 "	} 2 times		3 "	1 "	} 1 time
3 "	1 "			2 "	4 "	
3 "	1 "			2 "	4 "	
4 "	2 "			1 "	3 "	
4 "	2 "			1 "	3 "	

Sample 4

6-Harness Twill   Threads, reed, sley, tie-up same as for previous samples.

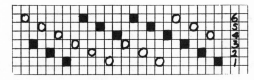
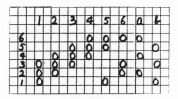

FIGS. 341 and 342.   6-harness Shadow
Weave draft and tie-up

Treadling

1 dark	4 dark
4 light	1 light
2 dark	5 dark
5 light	2 light
3 dark	6 dark
6 light	3 light

Sample 5

8-harness Reverse Twill   Threads, reed, sley, tie-up same as for previous samples.

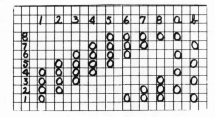
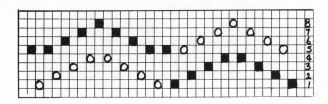

FIGS. 343 and 344
8-harness Shadow Weave
draft and tie-up

Treadling (*Fig. 1*)		Treadling (*Fig. 2*)	
TREADLE		**TREADLE**	
(*Figure 1*)		(*Figure 2*)	
1 dark	5 light	2 light	5 dark
2 dark	6 light	3 light	6 dark
3 dark	7 light	4 light	7 dark
4 dark	8 light	5 light	8 dark
5 dark	center	8 dark	center
8 dark	4 dark	7 dark	4 light
7 light	3 dark	6 dark	3 light
6 light	2 dark	5 dark	2 light
5 light	1 dark		

The foregoing is a short, concise description of the Shadow Weave. To record in detail its many ramifications and possibilities and the experiments which have been done with it by weavers[4] over the years would require much more space than is available in this text. It is unfortunate that most of the early notes and samples have been lost or destroyed, as the technique, which was never extensively circulated, produces some of the most unusual and beautiful designs possible on a handloom.

FIG. 345. Shadow Weave on multiple harness threading

TYPE Twill Variations and Extensions ·
PATTERN Letter Weave

Directions have been given throughout this chapter for various techniques suitable for weaving letters or designs, but the one given here is especially to be recommended.[5] Once the technique is understood, the weaving proceeds rapidly and has the advantage of a neat reverse side without mirrorwise letters and no long floats. At first glance the weave might be mistaken for dukagång (page 130), however, on close scrutiny it will be noted that the background is different than that of the half-dukagång (page 130). It is actually a surface inlay on alternate rows of plain weave. In order to obtain a proper relationship between the letters (Fig. 346) when used to form a word, it is advisable to work out the design on squared paper. In drawing the design, make strokes across the lines rather than in the squares. It is important to consider the spaces between the letters. Some, for instance, *A, F, J, L, P, T, V, Y,* will need to be placed more closely than letters *H, N, B, D, O,* which are more solid in outline. Spaces between words need watching. Avoid word-spaces which overlap those above or below; the effect of "rivers" in the script detracts from the appearance of the finished piece. After the design is completed, pin it on the wall and study it from across the room. Poor spacing can be detected immediately. To determine the number of threads needed to weave the design, count the "points" in the longest line of the script, add extra threads for margins or decorative borders, double this number, and add one thread to make an uneven number of threads in the warp.

Threading Draft   Any draft on which a plain 50/50 web can be woven.
    For the sample shown (Fig. 347) the threads chosen were:

Warp   White or natural cotton size 2/8 or 2/12
    This technique requires three shuttles carrying wefts as follows:
    Shuttle No. 1 weaves the *A* tabby. The thread for the *A* tabby should be similar in size and color to the warp thread. Use a stranded thread, such as a six-strand embroidery floss, as it gives more pleasing results than a hard-twisted thread such as the warp.
    Shuttle No. 2 weaves the *B* (or binder) tabby. For this use a *very fine* thread the same color as the pattern thread.
    Shuttle No. 3 weaves the pattern. Here again use stranded rather than twisted thread, which should be somewhat larger and of a deeper and stronger color than the warp thread.
    Shuttles Nos. 1 and 2 can be weaver's choice, that is either boat or flat shuttle (page 9), but shuttle No. 3, carrying the pattern thread, must be a wide flat shuttle unless the weaver prefers to use a boat shuttle plus a fairly wide pickup stick, which after the pattern has been picked up can be turned on edge to hold the shed open for the insertion of the pattern thread.

To Weave   This order of treadling must be carefully followed throughout the entire piece. For clarity the tabby weave sheds are called A (harnesses 1 or 1–3) and B (harnesses 2 or 2–4).
    Open shed A and throw shuttle No. 1 with the tabby weft; beat.
    Open shed B and throw shuttle No. 2 with the fine thread, the binder

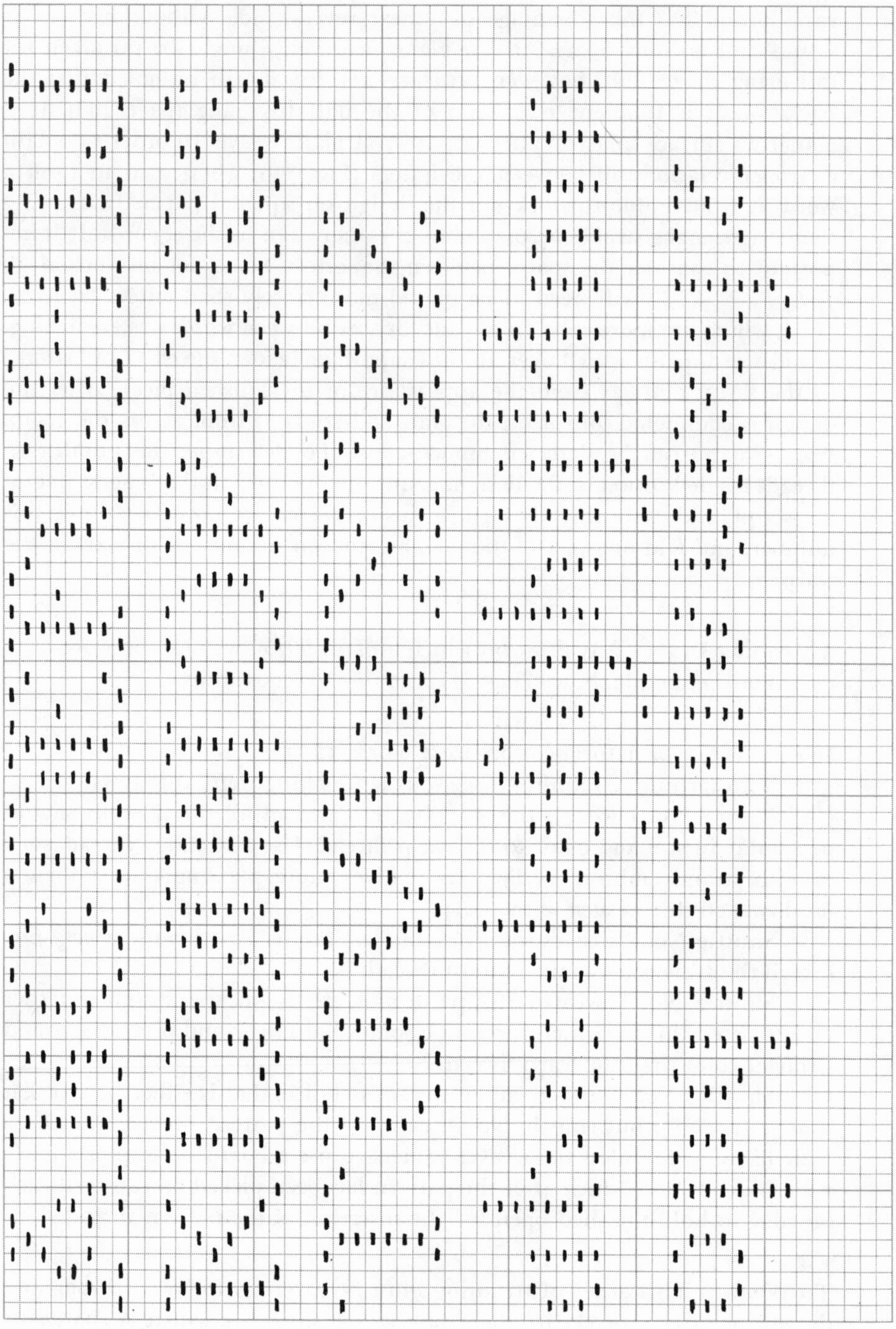

FIG 346

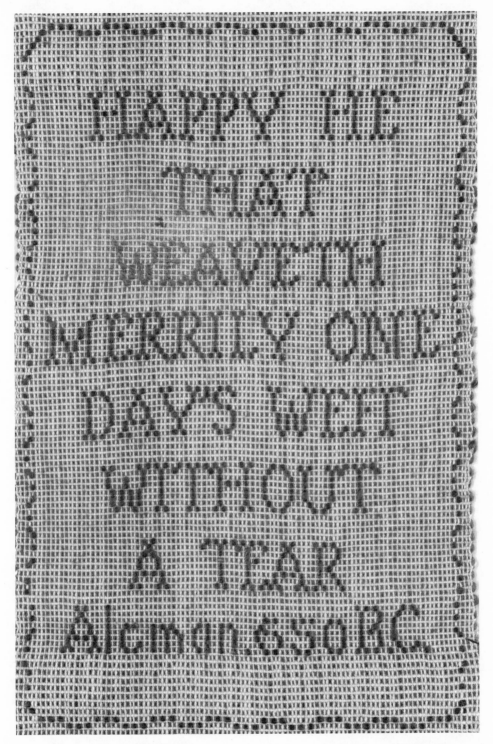

FIG. 347. Letter weaving, designed and woven by Minnie Simpson, York, England

tabby, but do not beat or change the shed. Throw shuttle No. 3 with the pattern thread into this open shed but from the opposite side. Beat and close shed. Beat hard a second time. Continue with this routine until a border of the desired width has been woven.

To begin the words, throw shuttle No. 2 through shed B. Keep the shed open. Find the center design point of the bottom row of the design and with a pickup stick, double-ended knitting needle, or a ruler, pick up the design from the center, working in both directions toward the selvedges, passing over an end in the upper warp layer for each "point" in the design. If this basic pickup is correctly centered, the other rows follow easily. The pickup stick can be discarded and the flat shuttle No. 3, with the pattern thread, used to pick up the rest of the design as shown on the graph paper. The weaving progresses more evenly and quickly on a tight warp. Use a firm beat.

chapter 8

Crackle Weave or Jämtlandsväv

The Jämtlandsväv,[1] or crackle weave, is a useful weave having characteristics of both the overshot and the summer-and-winter weaves. However, the
long skips of the overshot weaves are missing and there is more opportunity
for variation in design than in the 4-harness summer-and-winter weaves.

In the Jämtlandsväv, or crackle weave, the weft passes over three warp
threads and is bound down by every fourth warp thread. The pattern is
drafted on four blocks of three harnesses each. Patterns requiring six or
more harnesses also can be drafted on the crackle weave. Drafting
Jämtlandsväv, or crackle weave patterns, is interesting, but the transition
from one block to another can be confusing. The structure of the crackle-
weave blocks is as follows:

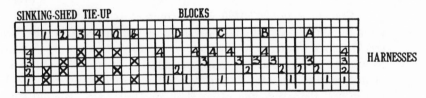

FIG. 348. Crackle

The threads shown between the narrow lines are the "incidental"
threads described below. Each block is composed of four threads in the
form of a point twill (page 177).

Threading
Repeat each block as many times as desired, one after the other, always
inserting the incidental (Fig. 348) between the blocks. The incidental thread

307

for each block is a repeat of the first thread of the block; that is, the incidental for block *A* is 1; for *B*, 2; for *C*, 3; and for *D*, 4 (Fig. 349).

These are shown in the draft (Fig. 348) between the narrow lines. Sometimes the incidentals are encircled (Fig. 643). If, in the crackle pattern, it is desirable to skip blocks, for example, skipping from an *A* to a *C* block without threading the *B* block, it is necessary to use the *B*-block incidental as well as the *A*-block incidental to preserve the continuity (Fig. 350).

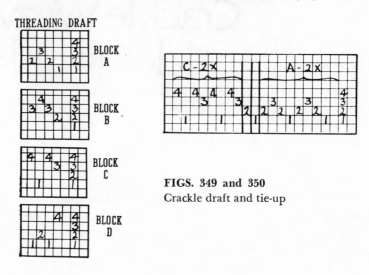

FIGS. 349 and 350
Crackle draft and tie-up

In the crackle, blocks cannot be woven individually as in many other techniques. It will be found that:

Block *A* weaves with block *D*	Block *C* weaves with block *B*
Block *B* weaves with block *A*	Block *D* weaves with block *C*

Crackle is not a 50/50 weave; that is, it does not square when the same number of threads are woven in as are threaded in the block. Each crackle block is squared with whatever number of pattern threads is required to weave the block as-drawn-in. Crackle blocks are difficult to keep track of during the weaving. A large-headed pin thrust through the last block woven will help keep the place. This pin follows a diagonal course across the weaving.

Jämtlandsväv can be treadled three ways. Sample 1 (Fig. 352) has been treadled as listed, squaring the blocks as in overshot weaving and using both tabby and pattern threads. Sample 2 (Fig. 352) has been treadled like the summer-and-winter weave, alternating blocks 1 and 2, 2 and 3, etc., and using the same threads as for Sample 1. Sample 3 has been treadled like the boundweave, using two pattern threads, contrasting in color and equal in size.

Uses   Bags, purses, table covers, upholstery, drapery, rugs, etc.

Suitable Materials and Sleying Use those materials suitable for overshot or summer-and-winter weaves and in keeping with the article to be woven. The warp and the tabby thread should be about the same size, with the pattern thread slightly larger. Because of the lack of long overlaps, a coarse pattern thread is not suitable since all threads should pack well back into the web.

Sample Illustrated (Fig. 352)

WARP	WEFT	PATTERN	REED (dents per inch)	SLEY
2/16	2/16	Fine yarn	16–18	Double

FIG. 351. Crackle draft

THREADING DRAFT

Treadling–Sinking Shed	Treadling–Rising Shed (*No Tie-Up*)
Sample 1 — Tabby a *and* b	*Sample 1 — Tabby* 1–3 *and* 2–4
1 — 4×	3 and 4 — 4×
2 — 4×	1 and 4 — 4×
3 — 4×	1 and 2 — 4×
4 — 4×	2 and 3 — 4×
1 — 4×	3 and 4 — 4×
2 — 4×	1 and 4 — 4×
3 — 4×	1 and 2 — 4×
4 — 4×	2 and 3 — 4×
3 — 4×	1 and 2 — 4×
2 — 4×	1 and 4 — 4×
3 — 4×	1 and 2 — 4×
Sample 2 — Tabby a *and* b	*Sample 2 — Tabby* 1–3 *and* 2–4
1 ⎫ 2 ⎬ 3×	3 and 4 ⎫ 1 and 4 ⎬ 3×
3 ⎫ 2 ⎬ 3×	1 and 2 ⎫ 1 and 4 ⎬ 3×
1 ⎫ 2 ⎬ 3×	3 and 4 ⎫ 1 and 4 ⎬ 3×
4 ⎫ 1 ⎬ 3×	2 and 3 ⎫ 3 and 4 ⎬ 3×
4 ⎫ 3 ⎬ 3×	2 and 3 ⎫ 1 and 2 ⎬ 3×
4 ⎫ 1 ⎬ 3×	2 and 3 ⎬ 3×

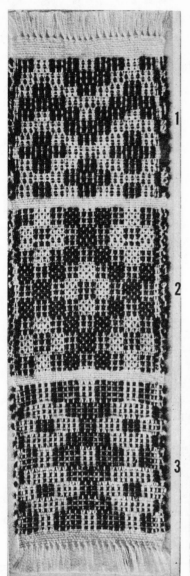

Sample 3 — No tabby, both threads same size	Sample 3 — No tabby, both threads same size
1 ⎱ 4× 3 ⎰	3 and 4 dk. ⎱ 4× 1 and 2 lt. ⎰
2 ⎱ 3× 4 ⎰	1 and 4 dk. ⎱ 3× 2 and 3 lt. ⎰
3 ⎱ 3× 1 ⎰	1 and 2 dk. ⎱ 3× 3 and 4 lt. ⎰
2 ⎱ 3× 4 ⎰	1 and 4 dk. ⎱ 3× 2 and 3 lt. ⎰
Repeat required number of times, starting at top.	Repeat required number of times, starting at top.
1 ⎱ 4× 3 ⎰	3 and 4 dk. ⎱ 4× 1 and 2 lt. ⎰
On last, repeat only to balance.	On last, repeat only to balance.

FIG 352. Crackle treadlings

FIG 353

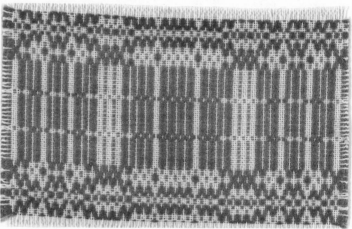

Problem Weave a small sample of crackle using an original block arrangement and fine wool and metallic materials.

chapter 9

Summer-and-Winter Weaves

TYPE Summer-and-Winter, 4-Harness · PATTERN 2-Block

The weaver interested in a logical, clear-cut, disciplined weave, yet one which offers many opportunities for original designs and treadling, should turn to the summer-and-winter technique. Its origin is unknown, but many samples showing its beauty and versatility have been found in Pennsylvania and adjacent states.[1] The old pinetree coverlets woven in this technique are especially interesting and attractive.

Some weavers feel that the summer-and-winter weaves lack the grace and beauty of the overshot weaves because the units are geometric in form, yet it is this geometric characteristic which makes it possible to write down summer-and-winter threadings in the block, or short-draft, form.

The weave is firm and even and, in contrast to overshot weaves, there are no long weft skips, for the weft is tied down by every fourth warp thread. In designing a summer-and-winter piece, the four-thread units, called blocks, can be placed in any order and repeated as often as necessary, although the arrangement should be pleasing and well balanced.

Uses Table linens, pillow covers, drapes, upholstery, coverlets, wall hangings, skirts, aprons

Suitable Materials Cotton, fine wool, rayon, nylon, perle cotton, metallics, and linen. Linen should be used only by the experienced weaver. Metallic threads, subtly combined with fine rayon, nylon, cotton, or wool, produce beautiful modern materials. The structure of the weave lends itself to fine materials, yet large, effective wall hangings can be woven of coarse wool and cotton. The weft and pattern threads should be soft enough to pack well into place between the warp, producing a firm, yet pliant material. The correct choice of threads and sleying plus accurate beating should produce a 50/50 fabric with a 45-deg. angle when woven "as-drawn-in."

Structure and Theory In the summer-and-winter weave, regardless of the number of harnesses involved, harnesses 1 and 2, the first two at the front of the loom, almost always carry the tie-down threads while the remaining harnesses carry the pattern threads. The reason for using the two front harnesses to carry these threads is that every other thread is threaded on these two, while the pattern threads may be divided among as many as six harnesses. Mechanically, it is easier to operate the loom with the tie-down threads in this position. Some weavers prefer to thread the tie-down threads on the back harnesses and this can be done; but, for the beginner, the use of the two front harnesses will simplify matters.

Because the first two harnesses are needed for the tie-down threads, it is possible to weave only 2-block patterns on a 4-harness loom. Four-block patterns (page 323) require six harnesses; 6-block patterns (page 329), eight harnesses; and so on.

The weaver should remember that, regardless of the number of harnesses being used, harnesses 1 and 2 always are reserved for the tie-down threads and must alternate in the threading between the pattern threads. In weaving, one or the other must be treadled with the pattern thread.

Harnesses 1 and 2, treadled together, make the *a* tabby which, for the summer-and-winter weave, is called the tie-down tabby. The remainder of the harnesses, 3 and 4 on a 4-harness loom; 3, 4, 5, and 6 on a 6-harness loom; or 3, 4, 5, 6, 7, and 8 on an 8-harness loom, when treadled together make the *b* tabby, called the pattern tabby. For multiple-harness summer-and-winter weaving, the first and second harnesses, when used separately in combination with a pattern harness, are called the X and Y tie-down threads. A detailed description of their function is given later in the text (page 325).

The Threading Draft The short-draft form of draft writing generally is used to thread summer-and-winter, as it is much simpler and quicker than the longer, thread-by-thread method.

Remember that each square of the short draft contains four threads, two of which always appear on harnesses 1 and 2, and the other two on pattern harnesses 3 and 4, 5 and 6, or 7 and 8 (for the more advanced

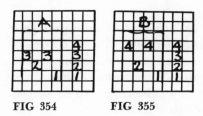

FIG 354   FIG 355

weaves). Thus, in a 2-block pattern, the first block, block *A*, is threaded as in Fig. 354, and block *B* as in Fig. 355.

The same sequence would be carried on if more harnesses were involved, as for instance, 1, 5—2, 5; 1, 6—2, 6; etc.

The draft may call for several repeats of block *A*, in which case it would be written as in Fig. 356. This repetition consumes both time and paper, so the short-draft form is used (Fig. 357). The first three squares on the short draft represent all the threads shown in the thread-by-thread draft (Fig. 356).

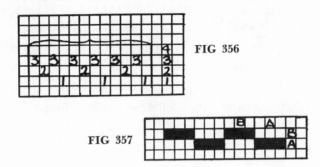

FIG 356

FIG 357

The weaver soon appreciates the short draft, once its possibilities for extension and use with certain weaves are understood. Some of these possibilities are discussed on page 545.

To help the student understand the relationship between the thread-by-thread draft and the short draft, both drafts are given for the first sample. It is suggested that the weaver thread from the short draft, then check the threading against the thread-by-thread draft if there is any doubt about the process.

Treadling   There are many ways of treadling the summer-and-winter weave.

The design may appear in the weft or in the warp, though it generally is conceded that the side with the weft predominating is the right or upper side. Treadling may be in pairs (page 315) giving the pleasing bird's-eye background which is a distinguishing feature of the weave.

Other methods are in singles or nonpairs (page 316) and a treadling which produces an effect resembling dukagång or overshot.

The samples illustrated (Figs. 360, 361, and 362) are threaded on the draft given (Fig. 359) and treadled in the various methods mentioned above.

It is important in all summer-and-winter weaving to insert the tabby shuttle correctly or the pattern sheds will not lie in the proper relationship to each other and the desired pattern effect will not be obtained. For example—and not all weavers may agree—it is preferable to enter the pattern tabby between the pairs of weft threads to produce the bird's-eye background.

Samples Illustrated

	WARP	WEFT	PATTERN	REED	SLEY
				(dents per inch)	
	Egyptian cotton, 30/3	Egyptian cotton, 30/3	Wool, 2/16	15	Double

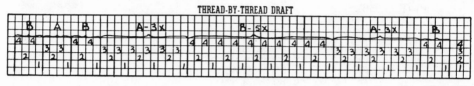

FIG 358

Starting at the right, thread the pattern as follows:

BLOCK

$B - 1\times$
$A - 3\times$
$B - 5\times$
$A - 3\times$
$*B - 1\times$
$A - 1\times$ — center

FIG 359

After threading to the center, repeat the order from * back to the first *B* block.

The sequence of threading the blocks as written in the short draft is as follows:

BLOCK	THREADS	
$B - 1\times$	4 (to begin design)	
$A - 3\times$	12	
$B - 5\times$	20	
$A - 3\times$	12	Repeat the required number of times to thread the desired width.
$*B - 1\times$	4	
$A - 1\times$	4 (center)	
Repeat from *	back to $A - 3\times - 12$	
$B - 1\times$	4 (to balance the design at the end)	

To prevent the edges from drawing in and spoiling the squareness of the first *A* block, a single *B* block, 1, 4, 2, 4, was threaded at each edge for this sample. These *B* blocks are ignored in treadling as they are not a part of the design. A selvedge threaded on harnesses 1, 3, 2, 4 would be just as effective.

All samples illustrated were woven "as-drawn-in" to square following the sequence of the blocks as given above.

Tie-Up There are several ways of tying and treadling the summer-and-winter weaves, some simple, some more complicated, as in the multiple-harness weaves.

The purpose of a tie-up is to connect the harnesses to the treadles so their manipulation will lift up the threads that are not wanted, leaving down the threads that are to be covered. To have the patterns in the various blocks show on the surface of the material and to have them appear in the weft, these threads must be raised. To do this, tie up the treadles as follows:

Sinking Shed			Rising Shed		
BLOCK	**TREADLE**	**TIED TO HARNESSES**	**BLOCK**	**TREADLE**	**TIED TO HARNESSES**
A	1	1 and 3	*A*	1	2 and 4
A	2	2 and 3	*A*	2	1 and 4
B	3	1 and 4	*B*	3	2 and 3
B	4	2 and 4	*B*	4	1 and 3
TABBY			**TABBY**		
a	*a*	1 and 2 (tie-down tabby)	*a*	*a*	3 and 4 (tie-down tabby)
b	*b*	3 and 4 (pattern tabby)	*b*	*b*	1 and 2 (pattern tabby)

For a table loom with hand levers or a rising-shed floor loom with direct treadling, there would be no tie-up. The levers or treadles follow the line of figures given at the extreme right of the above chart.

Sample 1 (Fig. 360) Treadled in the conventional method on pairs

Sinking Shed			Rising Shed	
TREADLE	**HARNESSES**		**TREADLE**	**HARNESSES**
b	3 and 4		*b*	1 and 2
1	1 and 3		1	2 and 4
a	1 and 2		*a*	3 and 4
2	2 and 3	Block *A*, repeat three	2	1 and 4
b	3 and 4	times to square.	*b*	1 and 2
2	2 and 3		2	1 and 4
a	1 and 2		*a*	3 and 4
1	1 and 3		1	2 and 4

TREADLE	HARNESSES		TREADLE	HARNESSES
b	3 and 4		b	1 and 2
3	1 and 4		3	2 and 3
a	1 and 2		a	3 and 4
4	2 and 4	Block B, repeat five	4	1 and 3
b	3 and 4	times to square.	b	1 and 2
4	2 and 4		4	1 and 3
a	1 and 2		a	3 and 4
3	1 and 4		3	2 and 3

Complete the sample by repeating the block as follows:

BLOCK	BLOCK (CONT.)
A — 3×	A — 3×
B — 1×	B — 5×
A — 1×	A — 3× — Weave after the last repeat only to balance.
B — 1×	

When weaving in pairs, there must be exactly eight threads to the block, four tabby and four pattern, and the block must be square. The choice of threads, sleying, and beating must be such as to achieve this. In Fig. 360, extra *A* and *B* blocks have been woven in the center to square the large square.

Sample 2 (Fig. 361)   Treadled in singles or nonpairs

Sinking Shed   **Rising Shed**

TREADLE	HARNESSES		TREADLE	HARNESSES
b	3 and 4		b	1 and 2
1	1 and 3		1	2 and 4
a	1 and 2		a	3 and 4
2	2 and 3	Block *A*, repeat three	2	1 and 4
b	3 and 4	times to square.	b	1 and 2
1	1 and 3		1	2 and 4
a	1 and 2		a	3 and 4
2	2 and 3		2	1 and 4

TREADLE	HARNESSES		TREADLE	HARNESSES
b	3 and 4		b	1 and 2
3	1 and 4		3	2 and 3
a	1 and 2		a	3 and 4
4	2 and 4	Block *B*, repeat five	4	1 and 3
b	3 and 4	times to square.	b	1 and 2
3	1 and 4		3	2 and 3
a	1 and 2		a	3 and 4
4	2 and 4		4	1 and 3

FIG 360

FIG 361

Complete the sample by repeating the blocks as follows:

BLOCK	BLOCK (CONT.)
$A - 3\times$	$A - 3\times$
$B - 1\times$	$B - 5\times$
$A - 1\times$	$A - 3\times$ — Weave after the last repeat only to balance.
$B - 1\times$	

With this treadling, do not be concerned over the size of threads or sleying as the units do not have to be squared unless the weaver prefers. This treadling gives more freedom in designing than when the treadling is done in pairs.

Sample 3 (Fig. 362)   Treadled in overshot or dukagång fashion

Treadling–Sinking Shed			**Treadling–Rising Shed (*No Tie-Up*)**
			USE TREADLES OR LEVERS
TREADLE	**HARNESSES**		**HARNESSES**
a	1 and 2		3 and 4, pattern tabby, left to right
1	1 and 3		2 and 4, pattern thread, right to left
b	3 and 4		1 and 2, tie-down tabby, right to left
1	1 and 3	Block *A*,	2 and 4, pattern thread, left to right
a	1 and 2	three times	3 and 4, pattern tabby, left to right
1	1 and 3		2 and 4, pattern thread, right to left
b	3 and 4		1 and 2, tie-down tabby, right to left
1	1 and 3		2 and 4, pattern thread, left to right

FIG 362

TREADLE	HARNESSES		HARNESSES
a	1 and 2 ⎫		3 and 4, pattern tabby, left to right
4	2 and 4 ⎪		1 and 3, pattern thread, right to left
b	3 and 4 ⎪		1 and 2, tie-down tabby, right to left
4	2 and 4 ⎬ Block *B*,		1 and 3, pattern thread, left to right
a	1 and 2 ⎪ five times		3 and 4, pattern tabby, left to right
4	2 and 4 ⎪		1 and 3, pattern thread, right to left
b	3 and 4 ⎪		1 and 2, tie-down tabby, right to left
4	2 and 4 ⎭		1 and 3, pattern thread, left to right

Complete the sample by weaving the remaining blocks as follows:

BLOCK	BLOCK (CONT.)
$A - 3\times$	$A - 3\times$
$B - 1\times$	$B - 5\times$
$A - 1\times$	$A - 3\times$ — Weave after
$B - 1\times$	the last
	repeat only
	to balance.

The weaver is free here to treadle any number of times to achieve a personal design. There are no rules restricting his choice of material or the order of the treadling.

Problem Design a simple, short draft for summer-and-winter, and weave a sampler using the three methods of treadling.

TYPE Summer-and-Winter, 5-Harness · PATTERN 3-Block

The first departure to be made from the 4-harness, 2-block type of summer-and-winter is the addition of a fifth harness which permits the weaving of side borders.

THREAD-BY-THREAD DRAFTS
FOR BLOCKS A, B, AND C

FIG 363

FIG 364

SHORT DRAFT
FOR BLOCKS A, B, AND C

Order of Threading

BLOCK	THREADS	
C — 5×	20 — at the start only for the right border	
A — 3×	12	
B — 5×	20	
A — 3×	12	
B — 1×	4	Repeat the required number of times to thread the desired width.
A — 1×	4	
B — 1×	4	
A — 3×	12	
B — 5×	20	
A — 3×	12 — once at the left to balance the design	
C — 5×	20 — at the end for the left border	

Tie-Up This tie-up is made for the rising-shed loom since it is rare to find a counterbalanced loom with a fifth harness. The tie-up for all the samples which follow are given for the rising-shed loom since the samples are multiple-harness weaves and are woven more easily on a rising-shed loom.

FIG 365

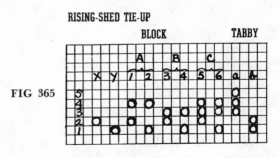

Sample 4 (Fig. 366)   Treadled in pairs

Order of Treadling

BORDER — Weave desired width.	BLOCKS
Treadle *y* — pattern thread	B and C — 5×
Treadle *b* — tabby thread	A and C — 3×
Treadle *x* — pattern tread	B and C — 1×
Treadle *a* — tabby thread	A and C — 1×
	B and C — 1×
	A and C — 3×
	B and C — 5×

Method of Treadling Pairs

Heading: 16/2 cotton

Treadle *a* and *b* in alternating succession. Repeat until the necessary width has been woven, ending with treadle *a*.

Border: Wool, treadled as above

TREADLE	
b	
5	
a	
6	Repeat for the required width.
b	
6	
a	
5	

FIG 366

Block *A* TREADLE	Block *B* TREADLE
b	*b*
1	3
a	*a*
2	4
b	*b*
2	4
a	*a*
1	3

In changing from block to block, be sure the tabby thread is correct.

Problem Compare the picture of Sample 4 (Fig. 366) with Sample 1 (Fig. 360), find the error in the treadling, and weave a correct sample. Also, treadle the sample in singles and overshot (page 317) using the directions for the 4-harness treadlings as a guide.

TYPE Summer-and-Winter, 5-Harness ·
PATTERN 3-Block, Snowball and Pine Tree

This design was developed on the second figure of a Snowball-and-Pine-Tree short draft written on blocks *D, E,* and *F* on harnesses 6, 7, and 8. As this is only a part of a draft which makes use of five harnesses, it could have been written, too, on blocks *A, B,* and *C* on a 5-harness loom. It illustrates the adaptability of the short draft and the ease with which a part of a draft can be developed.

Materials

WARP	WEFT	PATTERN	REED (*dents per inch*)	SLEY
Cotton, 8/4	Cotton, 8/2	Wool, knitting, 4-ply	9	Double

THREADING DRAFT

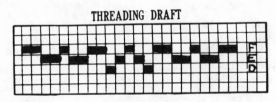

FIG 367

RISING-SHED TIE-UP

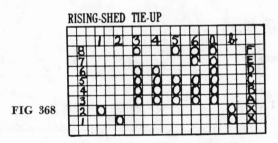

FIG 368

This tie-up allows the pattern blocks to be drawn down as desired and woven over in color.

Pine Tree (Fig. 369)

TREADLE COLOR		TREADLE COLOR	
8 — tabby	⎫	8 — tabby	⎫
1 — pattern		1 and 5 — pattern	
7 — tabby		7 — tabby	
2 — pattern	To weave base	2 and 5 — pattern	Blocks *D* and *E*, to
8 — tabby		8 — tabby	weave top of tree
2 — pattern		2 and 5 — pattern	(first row)
7 — tabby		7 — tabby	
1 — pattern	⎭	1 and 5 — pattern	⎭
8 — tabby	⎫		
1 and 3 — pattern		Repeat treadling for	
7 — tabby		block *E*, the trunk	
2 and 3 — pattern	Block *E* — 5×, to	of tree, second row.	
8 — tabby	weave trunk	8 — tabby	⎫
2 and 3 — pattern		1 and 6 — pattern	Block *D* — 2×, to
7 — tabby		7 — tabby	weave the cross be-
1 and 3 — pattern	⎭	2 and 6 — pattern	tween the top of
8 — tabby	⎫	8 — tabby	the trees and to
1 and 5 — pattern		2 and 6 — pattern	start the border
7 — tabby		7 — tabby	
2 and 5 — pattern	Blocks *D* and *E*, to	1 and 6 — pattern	⎭
8 — tabby	weave top row of		
2 and 5 — pattern	trunk		
7 — tabby			
1 and 5 — pattern	⎭		
8 — tabby	⎫		
1 and 4 — pattern			
7 — tabby			
2 and 4 — pattern	Blocks *E* and *F*, to		
8 — tabby	weave first branch.		
2 and 4 — pattern	Repeat block *E* for		
7 — tabby	trunk		
1 and 4 — pattern	⎭		

Alternate the
treadling for blocks
E, and *E* and *F*,
for five branches.

Treadle the tabby and pattern colors in the same order as before.

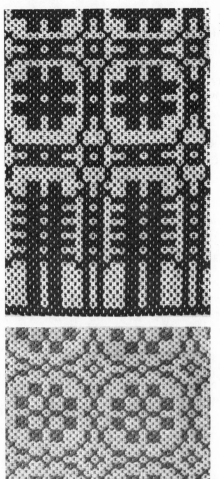

FIG 369

TREADLE	NUMBER OF TIMES	
4	1	
3	1	To weave the
4	1	border
6	2	

Snowball

Treadle as for the branches of the tree

TREADLE	BLOCK	
3	E — 2×	
4	E, F — 2×	
3	E — 2×	To weave the
4	E, F — 2×	snowball
3	E — 2×	

TREADLE	BLOCK	
6	D — 1×	
4	E, F — 1×	To weave the
3	E — 1×	border
4	E, F — 1×	between the
6	D — 1×	snowballs

Repeat the snowball and the center as many times as desired.

Problem Work out the treadling for the sample shown at the bottom of Fig. 369.

TYPE Summer-and-Winter, 6-Harness • PATTERN 4-Block, Pine Tree

As additional harnesses are added, designs can be extended to become more interesting and intricate. This is particularly true of the lovely old Pine Tree designs which were favorites in early Colonial days. Mary M. Atwater[2] has studied the old quilts and from them has developed drafts which are a joy to weavers. A simplified version of the Pine Tree is given here with additional samples showing weaves which illustrate how versatile the weave really is.

Uses The Pine Tree in the summer-and-winter weave is particularly good for wall hangings, drapes, and bedspreads; and for borders in place mats, towels, bureau scarves, and sport skirts.

Materials As listed for the 4-harness summer-and-winter weaves. The material should be suitable for the article being woven.

Sample 5 (Fig. 375)

Order of Threading

BLOCK

D — 2× — at start only	
A — 1× ⎤	A — 1× ⎤
B — 1×	B — 1×
C — 1×	C — 1×
D — 1×	D — 1×
C — 1×	C — 1×
D — 1×	D — 1×
C — 1×	C — 1×
B — 1×	B — 1×
A — 1×	A — 1×
D — 6×	D — 2× ⎦
A — 3×	
B — 3×	Thread once at the end to
C — 3×	balance the design.
B — 2×, center	
C — 3×	
B — 3×	
A — 3×	
D — 6× ⎦	

Repeat the required number of times, starting at the top each time to obtain the desired width.

FIG 371

FIG 370

THREAD-BY-THREAD DRAFT FOR BLOCKS

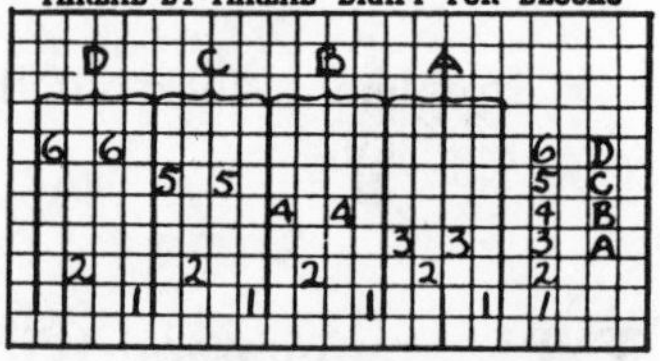

SHORT DRAFT

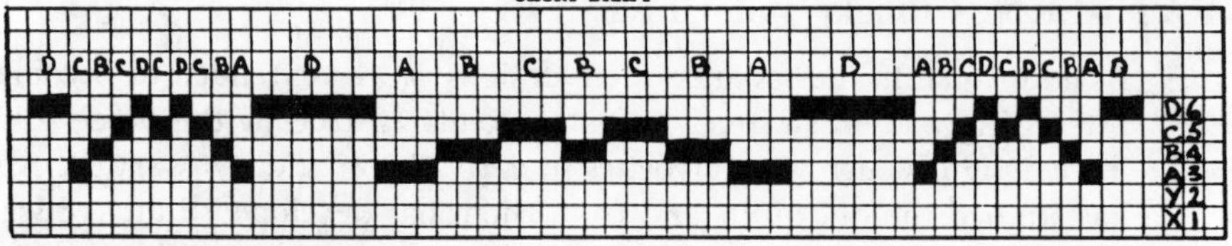

Tie-Up In studying the tie-up (Fig. 372), note that ten treadles are required.

Since few 6- or 8-harness looms are equipped with the required number of treadles, it is necessary to find some method of cutting down the number.

There is an abbreviated tie-up requiring only eight treadles which can be used (Fig. 373). Some weavers do not like the abbreviated tie-up since it is necessary to depress two treadles at once, instead of only one at a time as with the full tie-up. This, however, should not prove a deterrent to new weavers who have not formed weaving habits as yet.

A comparative study of the two tie-ups reveals the differences.

Starting with the *A* block, note that on the full tie-up (Fig. 372) it is tied to two treadles: treadle 1 with the pattern harnesses tied with the tie-down harness *X* (2); and treadle 2 with the pattern harnesses tied with the tie-down harness *Y* (1). On an abbreviated tie-up chart, the three block-*A* pattern harnesses are tied alone to treadle 1; the three block-*B* pattern harnesses are tied alone to treadle 2, and so on across the chart. The *X* and *Y* tie-down treadles are not tied with any of the pattern harnesses. These tie-down harnesses are treadled with the various pattern treadles.

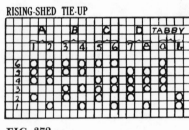

FIG 372

FIG 373

Treadling for the Blocks

BLOCK	PATTERN TREADLE	PLUS	TIE-DOWN TREADLE
A	1		*X*
A	1		*Y*
B	2		*X*
B	2		*Y*
C	3		*X*
C	3		*Y*
D	4		*X*
D	4		*Y*

Regardless of the treadling method used—pairs, singles, or overshot method—or the arrangement of the blocks, when using an abbreviated tie-up either the *X* or *Y* tie-down harnesses must be used with the pattern harnesses.

Order of Treadling Blocks The branches of the Pine Tree can be woven in any order and by any method. The sample (Fig. 375), can be woven in singles, alternates, or nonpairs, with the blocks treadled in the following order:

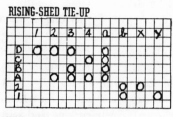

RISING-SHED TIE-UP

FIG 374

TREADLE

$$X \atop Y \Big\}$$ Alternate with tabby *a* and tabby *b* for 12 shots.

BLOCK

$$1 - 2\times \atop 2 - 2\times \Big\}$$ weaves A B C ⎱ base
weaves B C ⎰ trunk
3 — 2½ in.   C

$$\left.\begin{array}{l}2 - 2\times \\ 1 - 2\times \\ 3 - 2\times \\ 2 - 2\times \\ 1 - 2\times \\ 3 - 3\times\end{array}\right\}$$ large branches

$$\left.\begin{array}{l}2 - 1\times \\ 1 - 1\times \\ 3 - 3\times \\ 1 - 1\times \\ 2 - 1\times \\ 3 - 2\times \\ 2 - 1\times \\ 3 - 1\times \\ 2 - 1\times \\ 3 - 3\times\end{array}\right\}$$ top branches

4 — 2×   top border

FIG 375

TYPE Summer-and-Winter, 6-Harness • PATTERN 4-Block, Pine Tree Treadled As-Drawn-In

The advantage of weaving a sample as-drawn-in is that the relationship of the blocks to each other and the design that they form are shown. The same result is obtained with a draw-down. However, the actual weaving with the threads proves the accuracy of the sleying and the choice of threads and shows whether the blocks square up and a 45-deg. angle can be woven.

The design in sample illustrated 6 (Fig. 376), woven on the Pine Tree threading, does not resemble a pine tree but does produce an attractive over-all design that could be extended for drapes or upholstery. The lower part of the design is woven in singles, the upper half in pairs. The background effect is quite different; after studying each half, the weaver should decide which background he wishes to use for his own particular purpose.

FIG 376

Sample 6 (Fig. 376)

Order of Treadling

BLOCK

$D - 2\times$ — at start only	
$A - 1\times$	
$B - 1\times$	
$C - 1\times$	
$D - 1\times$	
$C - 1\times$	
$D - 1\times$	
$C - 1\times$	
$B - 1\times$	Repeat the
$A - 1\times$	required number
$D - 6\times$	of times to weave
$A - 3\times$	the required
$B - 3\times$	length.
$C - 3\times$	
$B - 2\times$ — center	
$C - 3\times$	
$B - 3\times$	
$A - 3\times$	
$D - 6\times$	

End border treadling:

$A - 1\times$
$B - 1\times$
$C - 1\times$
$D - 1\times$
$C - 1\times$
$D - 1\times$
$C - 1\times$
$B - 1\times$
$A - 1\times$
$D - 2\times$

Weave once at the end to balance the design.

Tie-Up   Fig. 373
    End border treadling as shown on page 320.

Problem   Plan and weave a pillow top with cotton and wool on the Pine Tree threading, treadled as-drawn-in. Weave in singles, pairs, or overshot effect, as desired.

TYPE Summer-and-Winter, 6-Harness •
PATTERN 4-Block, Borders Treadled on Pine Tree Draft

Sample illustrated 7 (Fig. 377), treadled on Pine Tree threading (Fig. 370), is suggested for borders on skirts, drapes, bags, and aprons.

The possibilities of the weave do not show up to advantage in a black-and-white photograph, but when woven in wide or graduated-width borders in subtle coloring or metallics on fine wools, this weave can be very beautiful. There are unlimited possibilities here for the weaver who is interested in costume designing as an adjunct to weaving.

Sample 7 (Fig. 377)

The blocks are treadled in the same sequence for all four samples:

BLOCK
$A - 3\times$
$B - 1\times$
$D - 2\times$
$C - 1\times$
$D - 2\times$
$B - 1\times$
$A - 3\times$

The bottom border, sample 7 (Fig. 377), is treadled in singles and shows the design in the weft. The second border is treadled in singles but the treadles used were the opposite of those used for the first border, bringing the design up in the warp instead of the weft. The third border is woven with the overshot or dukagång method; and the top, or fourth, is woven in pairs. All samples have a narrow border at both the top and the bottom and are treadled:

X (harness 1)
Tabby *a* (tie-down tabby)
Y (harness 2)
Tabby *b* (pattern tabby)
Y (harness 2)
Tabby *a* (tie-down tabby)
X (harness 1)

Order of Treadling the Blocks

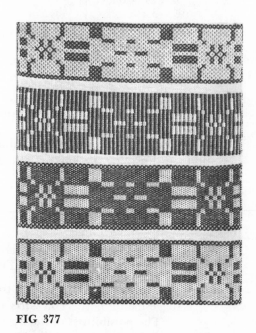

FIG 377

BLOCK	TREADLE	OR LEVERS
A	1	2, 4, 5, 6
	2	1, 4, 5, 6
B	3	2, 3, 5, 6
	4	1, 3, 5, 6
C	5	2, 3, 4, 6
	6	1, 3, 4, 6
D	7	2, 3, 4, 5
	8	1, 3, 4, 5

A tabby thread is entered between each row of pattern threads. Always be certain that the pattern tabby, levers 1 and 2 or harnesses 3, 4, 5, 6, are between the pairs of threads when the blocks are woven in pairs.

Problem On the 6-harness Pine Tree threading, work out treadlings for borders suitable for a child's skirt.

TYPE Summer-and-Winter, 8-Harness ·
PATTERN 6-Block, Spider Web

The fortunate owner of an 8-harness loom can derive much pleasure from working out variations on the summer-and-winter weave. Once the technique is thoroughly understood, it is easy to design, thread, and weave original patterns.

The almost unlimited number of variations adds interest to a seemingly simple threading and repetition is not necessary.

For experimental purposes, an 8-harness table loom rather than a floor loom is recommended; but the weaver who wishes to produce yardage definitely should have a multiple-harness rising-shed foot loom. After the tie-up has been made, the weaver treadles the blocks in whatever order he desires. The tie-up need not be changed. The lack of a sufficient number of treadles usually can be solved through the use of an abbreviated tie-up.

The short draft for the Spider Web lends itself well to further development and experimentation; sample 8 (Fig. 383) is woven as-drawn-in.

Sample 8 (Fig. 383)

WARP	WEFT	PATTERN	REED *(dents per inch)*	SLEY
Egyptian cotton, 30/3	Egyptian cotton, 30/3	Wool, 2/16	15	Double

SHORT DRAFT

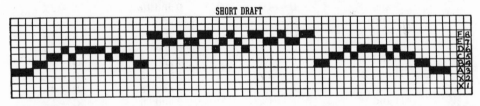

FIG 378

REGULATION RISING-SHED TIE-UP

SKELETON RISING-SHED TIE-UP

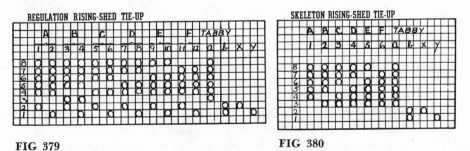

FIG 379

FIG 380

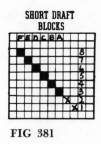

FIG 381

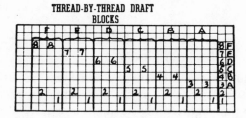

FIG 382

Number of Threads Required to Weave 244

An experiment in designing on the loom was tried with this sample. Note the difference between the upper and lower corners of Fig. 383. In the upper corners, the design seems to have grown out of the border; in the lower, the space seems awkward. It could be remedied by introducing a space of similar width between the side border and the first figure, necessitating a change in the threading.

Treadling The blocks of sample 8 (Fig. 383) are woven in pairs with the treadling sequence of the blocks exactly the same as the threading sequence:

TREADLE	BLOCK	TREADLE	BLOCK
End border (page 320)		9 and 10	$E - 1\times$
3 and 4	$B - 2\times$	7 and 8	$D - 1\times$
5 and 6	$C - 2\times$	11 and 12	$F - 2\times$
7 and 8	$D - 1\times$	9 and 10	$E - 2\times$
5 and 6	$C - 1\times$	11 and 12	$F - 1\times$
7 and 8	$D - 4\times$	9 and 10	$E - 2\times$
5 and 6	$C - 1\times$	11 and 12	$F - 2\times$
7 and 8	$D - 1\times$	3 and 4	$B - 2\times$
5 and 6	$C - 2\times$	5 and 6	$C - 2\times$
3 and 4	$B - 2\times$	7 and 8	$D - 1\times$
11 and 12	$F - 2\times$	5 and 6	$C - 1\times$
9 and 10	$E - 2\times$	7 and 8	$D - 4\times$
11 and 12	$F - 1\times$	5 and 6	$C - 1\times$
9 and 10	$E - 2\times$	7 and 8	$D - 1\times$
11 and 12	$F - 2\times$	5 and 6	$C - 2\times$
7 and 8	$D - 1\times$	3 and 4	$B - 2\times$
9 and 10	$E - 1\times$	End border (page 320)	
11 and 12	$F - 1\times$		

The A block (1–3 and 2–3) weaves the borders at the sides and must be treadled in combination with all the other blocks. Therefore, harness 3 is tied to each pattern treadle if a sinking-shed loom is used. Harness 3 is not tied to each pattern treadle for a rising-shed loom since it must lie in the lower shed so the warp will be covered with the pattern thread. Harness 3 is tied in Fig. 380. Note that block *D* is common to both the corner figures and the center figure.

Problem   Design an 8-harness summer-and-winter draft and weave a sample.

TYPE Summer-and-Winter, 8-Harness ·
PATTERN 6-Block, Treadling Variation on Spider Web

One of the surest ways for the weaver to determine whether or not he really understands a weaving technique is to experiment with it, trying out various treadlings and materials. The results are not always just what the weaver may have had in mind but they at least give some play to his latent creative ability.

Sample 9 (Fig. 384)   Threaded on the same short draft as sample 8 (Fig. 383) and given here for the weaving student to test his ability to reproduce the piece without benefit of direction

In addition to working out the treadling for the sample, it is suggested that the weaver try original treadlings of his own, keeping in mind the uses to which they could be put.

Further developments of the summer-and-winter weave are discussed under the section on the short draft (page 545).

Borders   The borders in Fig. 384 suggest designs from which to weave borders for aprons, skirts, bags, drapes, towels, place mats, etc.

A 6-harness summer-and-winter threading was chosen and all were woven with a tabby between the pattern threads.

The bottom row of the sampler was treadled in overshot fashion, the

FIG 383

FIG 384

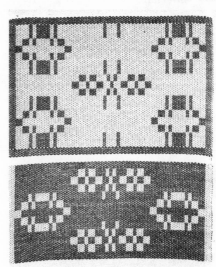

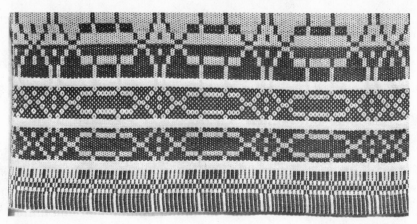

FIG 385

block arrangement woven at random. A quite different effect might have been achieved by a different block sequence. The tie-up was the standard 6-harness summer-and-winter tie-up (page 325). The treadling for a rising-shed hand loom:

LEVERS	SHOTS
2, 6	16
2, 3, 4, 5	4
1, 6	4
2, 3, 4, 5	4
1, 3, 4, 6	8

The second border from the bottom of the sampler was woven on alternates or singles (page 316).

LEVERS
6
5
4
3
4
5
6

The pattern shows up in the warp as it does also in the next border, treadled in pairs (page 320) with the blocks treadled in the same order as the second border.

The first part of the top border is woven with the pattern showing in the warp; the second part of the border at the top of the sampler shows the pattern in the weft.

TREADLING: PART I LEVERS		TREADLING: PART II LEVERS	
2, 6	6×	1, 3, 4, 5	2×
1, 6		2, 3, 4, 5	
2, 5	4×	1, 3, 4, 6	3×
1, 5		2, 3, 4, 6	
2, 4	3×	1, 3, 5, 6	4×
1, 4		2, 3, 5, 6	
2, 3	2×	1, 4, 5, 6	6×
1, 3		2, 4, 5, 6	

Problem   Weave an apron on summer-and-winter threading with original borders.

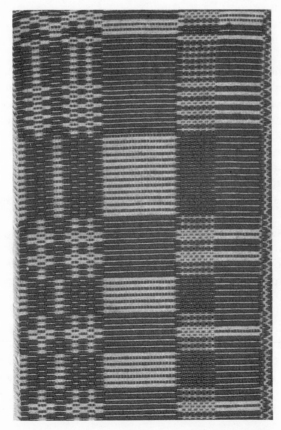

FIG. 386.   Summer-and-Winter, showing corner treatment

TYPE Summer-and-Winter •
PATTERN Single Unit Design on Plain Background

After a thorough study of the summer-and-winter technique as presented on preceding pages, it is suggested that the weaver test his versatility by designing and weaving a set of ecclesiastical book markers (Figs. 387 and 388) using this technique which lends itself particularly well to weaving a single unit design on a plain background. The book markers are not difficult to weave, though care must be taken to ensure that selvedges are perfect, that the marker and its backing are a constant and equal width throughout, the beating even, and that there is no visible piecing of warp, weft, or pattern thread.

The first step, after the finished length and width of the marker has been determined, is to draw the desired design on graph paper. By doing this, good proportions and pleasing placement of the design in relationship to the marker's length, length of bottom fringe, and finish at the top can be established. To give stability to the marker, a backing, woven in plain weave of the warp and tabby threads, is woven in a continuous length with the marker, so allowance must be made for this when planning the warp.

It is suggested that fine mercerized or preferably fine silk thread in white, red, green, or purple, to comply with the various church seasons, sleyed closely in a fine reed, be used. A good quality of gold thread interwoven with the finer silk, or mercerized threads, produces a strikingly rich effect.

Once the width and length of the marker, plus the length of the backing and loom waste, have been calculated, the warp wound and the loom dressed, the weaving can be started in the usual manner with an inch or so in plain weave using the tabby thread. When this is completed, check the smoothness of the web, the selvedges and beating, and uniformity of width. If these are all correct, the backing can be started and continued until a piece half the length of the marker is to be when finished, has been woven. The knotted gold fringe (pages 588 to 589) is now woven. The thickness of the fringe will be determined by the number of gold threads used together for each knot. If the gold thread is fine, it may require from eight to ten strands; if heavier, four to six. The fringe should not appear skimpy nor should it be too heavy and thus overpower the size and design of the marker. The knot itself makes an attractive heading. The weaver should use his own discretion whether or not to add any further decoration.

When the fringe and other decoration, if added, is completed, the design of the unit as drawn on the graph paper is woven in. The three treadlings used for the sample shown are the three standard summer-and-winter treadlings (page 313), each giving a quite different effect.

When the design is completed, sufficient background to fill in the space above the design to the top of the marker is woven, and the top finished according to the design plan. This could be a few rows of gold thread, using perhaps four to six strands together to give body, or it could

FIG 387

FIG 388

be a matching or narrower gold fringe similar to the bottom fringe. Tying the flossa knots in this direction is a bit tricky as they are being tied upside down; however, if a little patience and ingenuity are exercised it can be done, and the fringe will hang properly.

Beyond the top finish, weave a half inch or so of the backing, similar to that woven at the beginning of the marker, and hemstitch across the fell to prevent raveling when the piece is cut from the loom. Cut the marker from the loom and with the fingers carefully fold and crease the backing up and under at the top of the gold fringe and along the length of the marker. Be sure the selvedges of both marker and backing are in alignment (if woven carefully they should be of uniform width), and baste the two together. With a fine needle and fine thread, starting at the top of the bottom fringe, overhand the two selvedges together with inconspicuous stitches. Do not fold the marker over the fringes to hold it steady while sewing, but hold the two selvedges together between thumb and forefinger, thus preventing any "humping" of the two. Start the sewing of the second selvedges at the top of the bottom fringe, as was done with the first side, and again sew toward the top of the marker.

Finish the backing at the top as neatly as possible, cutting off surplus material and concealing the ends under the gold fringe or whatever decorative finish is used at the top.

The marker should not need pressing, but if it does, lay it face down on the ironing board, cover with a slightly damp cloth, and press with a warm iron, carefully avoiding the gold fringe.

It is a matter of preference whether or not to cut the loops of the gold fringe.

chapter 10

Bronson

While this weave has been found in old English books under the name of "Spot" weave and in modern German and Swedish texts under the name of *gerstenkörnern* and *droppdäll,* it was during the study of the old Bronson notebooks[1] that Mary Atwater discovered and developed the weave and presented it to American weavers as the Bronson weave.

Marguerite Davison refers to the weave as "Barley Corn," while Edward Worst uses the name of some individual of historic note.

There are more opportunities for design development in this weave, especially on multiple-harness looms, than with any other weave except possibly the summer-and-winter.

Uses The weave usually is thought of as a linen weave, but it is just as suitable for articles of cotton or wool. It is popular for linen and cotton tea cloths, place mats, and bureau scarves, especially when woven with bands of plain weave between the pattern areas and with plain-weave borders (Fig. 392).

With firm but soft wools it is good for baby and bed blankets and couch throws. In very fine wools, closely set, it makes attractive dress material; in fine wool, loosely set, lovely scarves and stoles. Fine cotton warp, closely sleyed, woven in overshot fashion with rough linen or fine wool makes excellent upholstery. Wall hangings and cushion tops of cotton and wool, or cotton and perle cotton, can be handsome when set on multiple-harness threading.

Suggested Materials and Sleying As this is a 50/50 weave, it is advisable to use the same material for both warp and weft, though the weft can be different as long as it is the same size. Attractive color arrangements are possible with this weave, although the smartest pieces are those woven of fine, round, white or unbleached linen thread.

WARP	WEFT	REED (*dents per inch*)	SLEY
Cotton, 16/2	Cotton, 16/2	16	Double
Cotton, 8/2	Cotton, 8/2	12	Double
Cotton, 8/4	Cotton, 8/4	18	Single
Linen, 8 cord	Linen, 8 cord	10	Single
Linen, fine, 40/3	Linen, fine, 40/3	18	Double
Linen, coarse	Linen, coarse	10	Double
Wool, 2/32	Wool, 2/32	18	Double
Wool, 2/16	Wool, 2/16	14	Double
Cotton or linen, medium	Perle cotton, 6-strand	15	Single

Singles linen produces exquisite pieces with long-wearing qualities. Highly glazed or slippery threads are not recommended. The spot Bronson should be sleyed a little closer than is usual for the plain weave.

Structure The Bronson weave is a 50/50 one-shuttle weave with every other thread threaded on the same harness, in this text on harness 1. These alternate threads could be threaded on the back harness but the mechanical action of the loom is better if the heavier harnesses are on the front. Before threading, make certain that there are sufficient heddles on harness 1 to thread the required width. Harness 1, which carries every other thread, is the *b* tabby, while the remaining harnesses, which carry pattern threads, make up the *a* tabby. To weave plain borders and plain areas between the pattern figures, tabbies *a* and *b* are treadled in alternating succession.

The short draft (page 545) rather than the thread-by-thread draft can be used for the Bronson weaves, particularly those set on the multiple-harness loom.

There are two distinct types of Bronson weave, the spot and the lace. Either can be designed to weave the point Bronson, which is a method of arranging the blocks. There is also the rep Bronson, which is a method of treadling.

TYPE Bronson, 4-Harness · PATTERN 2-Block

In treadling, the weft thread passes over the surface of all blocks threaded on one set of harnesses and weaves a plain weave over all blocks threaded on the other harnesses. Tabby treadle *b* weaves the plain weave between the pattern shots. This can be clearly seen on the draw-down (Fig. 389).

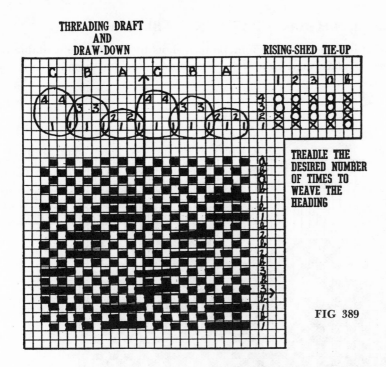

THREADING DRAFT AND DRAW-DOWN

RISING-SHED TIE-UP

TREADLE THE DESIRED NUMBER OF TIMES TO WEAVE THE HEADING

FIG 389

FIG 390

Like the overshot, there is in this four-thread block weave a thread common to the adjoining blocks which weaves in with each block as it is treadled, resulting in the weft passing over five threads. To weave this, four shots are needed to complete one unit: two pattern shots and two tabby shots.

TYPE Bronson, 4-Harness · PATTERN 2-Block Variations

A variation in treadling with four pattern shots instead of two, suitable for the edges of place mats or towels. The border can be threaded twice or three times.

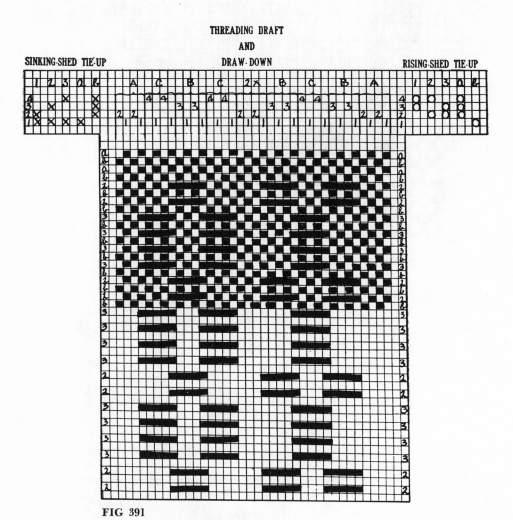

THREADING DRAFT AND DRAW-DOWN

SINKING-SHED TIE-UP   RISING-SHED TIE-UP

FIG 391

WARP	WEFT	REED (dents per inch)	SLEY
Linen, No. 30 singles	Linen, No. 30 singles	15	Double

Treadling In this sample (Fig. 392) the *A* block is not treadled as a block; treadles *a* and *b* are treadled in alternating succession to weave the plain-weave headings at the beginning and end of the piece.

> *Heading:* treadles *a* and *b* in alternating succession
> *Block B:* harnesses 1 and 3, treadle 2—2×
> *Block C:* harnesses 1 and 4, treadles 3—4×

Repeat the required number of times to weave the desired length, remembering to throw tabby *b* between each pattern shot.

FIG 392

TYPE Bronson, 5-Harness · PATTERN Point, Spot Setting

While the weaver with imagination can arrange interesting designs with the 4-harness Bronson-spot draft, the addition of a fifth harness increases the scope of the design considerably.

A curious thing about the old draft which is used here is that some of the blocks are two-thread blocks and others four-thread. This variation in the number makes a much more interesting design and points out the versatility of the weave.

There is a distinct right and wrong side to the weave, the weft predominating on the upper or right side and the warp on the under or wrong side. In glancing at a piece of Bronson-spot weaving in color, the student may at first think it a piece of overshot. A close examination of the background will show that the colored pattern threads alternate with the tabby thread and, as mentioned above, the pattern shows in the warp threads on the back. Also, the pattern skips are more uniform and much shorter than in most overshots.

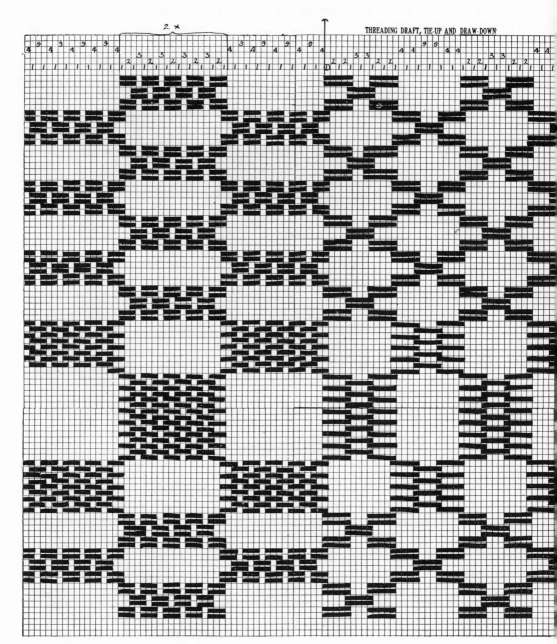

THREADING DRAFT, TIE-UP AND DRAW-DOWN

FIG 393

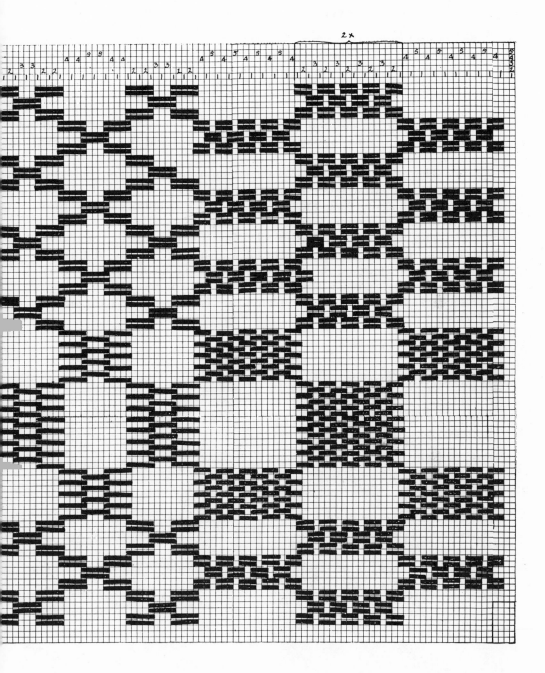

Samples Illustrated (Figs. 394 and 395)

WARP	WEFT	PATTERN	REED (*dents per inch*)	SLEY
Linen, 30/3	Linen, 30/3	Linen, 30/3	15	Double
Linen, 30/3	Linen, 30/3	Perle cotton, 6-strand	15	Double

Tabby *b* has not been shown on the draw-down (Fig. 393), which accounts for its squat appearance when compared with the sample (Fig. 394).

The 1–3 block which weaves the center of the rose is shown only once on the draw-down in order to keep it as small as possible. Only 19 threads are shown as against 34 in the sample. This block should be threaded twice to have the proper proportions in the woven piece.

This type of Bronson is treadled in a routine somewhat similar to overshot in that the blocks are treadled a sufficient number of times to square them. However, there is this difference, the tabby thread is always thrown on the *b* treadle. The *a* tabby is used only to weave, in alternating sequence with the *b* tabby, the plain-weave headings at the start and the finish.

FIG 394

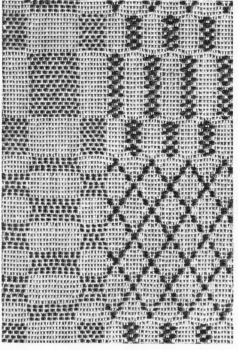

FIG 395

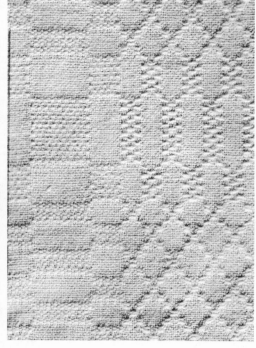

The contrast of the two samples (Figs. 394 and 395), one woven in linen and one in colored perle cotton, is quite marked. For those who enjoy working with color this weave offers an opportunity for color blending rather than color contrasts. The colored thread is bound down into the background producing a subtle shaded effect.

TYPE Bronson, 8-Harness · PATTERN Point, Spot Setting

The diamond threading (Fig. 396) can be arranged in a number of ways.

It can be threaded in single units across the warp with plain areas between; two diamonds can be threaded together with a plain area between each pair; or the diamond can be threaded in continuous succession. The last is not recommended as it bears too close a resemblance to a point-twill weave. The virtue of the spot Bronson is that single pattern motifs can be woven.

There is considerable difference in the appearance of the two samples (Figs. 398 and 399). The linen piece is of a medium fine, closely woven texture, which, after repeated washing and ironing, has a beautiful sheen. The other sample, woven for a bureau cover, is in stripes of medium and pale blue, pale green, apricot, and yellow. The difference in the materials used and the end results obtained points out the value of putting on long warps. In this technique, where the pattern thread is interwoven as part of the background, even a white warp takes on color.

Samples Illustrated (Figs. 398 and 399)

WARP	WEFT	PATTERN	REED (dents per inch)	SLEY
Linen, 30/3	Linen, 30/3	Linen, 30/3	18	Double
Linen, 30/3	Linen, 30/3	Perle, 6-strand	18	Double

Order of Threading

Thread the plain-weave border at the right, thread 1 and 2 for 10 threads.

For a single diamond, thread once from K to L.

For a double diamond, thread twice from K to L, omitting the 1-and-2 block at the start of the repeat.

Thread a plain weave between L and M, 1 and 2 for 16 threads.

Thread a motif between M and N.

Thread a plain weave on 1 and 2 for 16 threads.

Repeat the pattern the desired number of times, ending with either a single or a double diamond and a plain-weave border of 10 threads to balance the design.

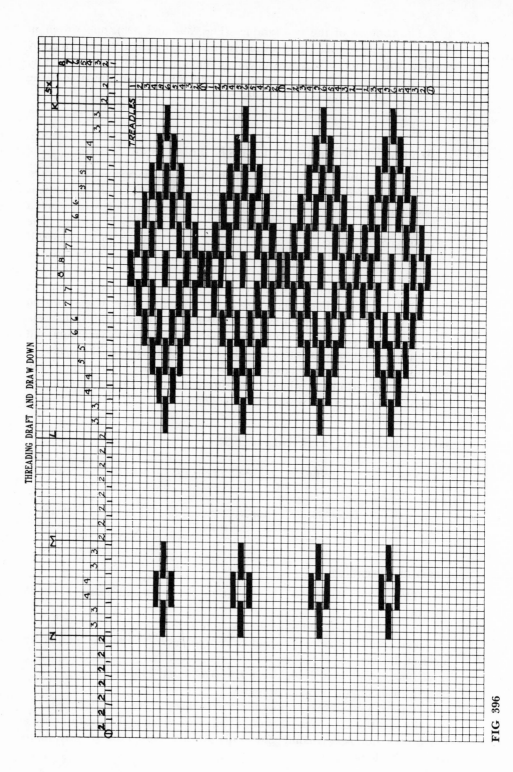

FIG 396

Treadling–Rising Shed

TREADLES	LEVERS
1	2, 3, 4, 5, 6, 7
2	2, 3, 4, 5, 6, 8
3	2, 3, 4, 5, 7
4	2, 3, 4, 6, 8
5	2, 3, 5, 7, 8
6	2, 4, 6, 7
5	2, 3, 5, 7, 8
4	2, 3, 4, 6, 8
3	2, 3, 4, 5, 7
2	2, 3, 4, 5, 6, 8
1	2, 3, 4, 5, 6, 7

RISING-SHED TIE-UP

FIG 397

Do not weave the last "1" when repeating the diamond unless two colors are being used. Weaving treadle 1 twice will keep the color bands a uniform width. For the plain-weave headings use treadles *a* and *b* in alternating succession until the desired width has been woven.

Problem Design an original Bronson draft, thread, and weave. Use original treadlings and a variety of threads.

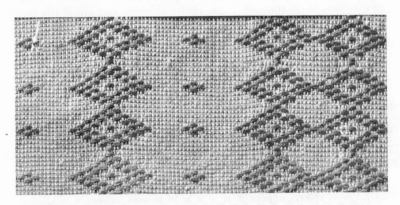

FIG 398

FIG 399

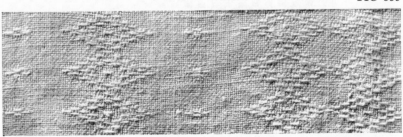

TYPE Bronson II, 5-Harness •
PATTERN With Tie-Down Thread

All of the samples so far have been woven on a draft that is limited in that none of the blocks can be repeated in succession. This cuts down the design possibilities.

There is a second type of Bronson threading, called Bronson II by Mary Atwater, which utilizes a tie-down thread between the blocks. The addition of this thread makes it possible to repeat any block any number of times in succession.

Each block is threaded as in the other method (Fig. 400), except that in Bronson II, a 2 is added between each block and each block consists of 6 threads (Fig. 401). The 2 has been encircled for purposes of clarity only.

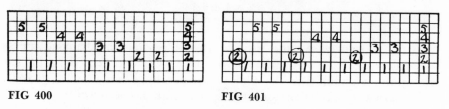

FIG 400   FIG 401

With this threading, the 1–2 block does not exist as a separate block, but is used to weave the plain borders or plain-weave areas between pattern areas. The threads on harness 1 are tabby threads and those on harness 2 now are used to tie down the long warp skips which occur if the block is repeated more than once.

Compare this draw-down of Bronson II (Fig. 402) with the draw-down

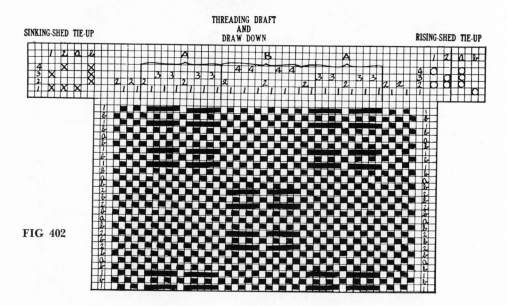

SINKING-SHED TIE-UP

THREADING DRAFT
AND
DRAW DOWN

RISING-SHED TIE-UP

FIG 402

for Bronson I (Fig. 389) and note the difference in the structure of the weave.

This second type of Bronson threading can be treadled in two ways: as for spot and point (Figs. 389 and 398) or as a lace weave so similar to the Swedish lace weave that it is often mistaken for it. An explanation of the difference is given under the Swedish lace weave (page 358). When woven Bronson lace fashion, the warp should be sleyed more loosely than for the spot Bronson and a unit must be repeated at least twice for each block before the window will appear. The *a* tabby, thrown every sixth shot, weaves the bar across the window.

The sample (Fig. 404) shows a 2-block pattern arrangement suitable for a soft wool scarf or, in linen or cotton double sley, for a towel or place mat. While the Bronson weave is at its best when woven in a single color, a scarf could be accented by threading some of the blocks in color and crossing them with the same color weft.

The arrangement of the blocks for Fig. 404 is as follows:

Repeat harnesses 1 and 2 the desired number of times for the plain-weave border.

BLOCK	THREAD
A	2×
B	3×
A	2×
B	2×
A	3×
*B	4×
A	4× — center

Repeat from * back to beginning.
The threading for the blocks is:
Plain weave at edge: 1, 2; 1, 2; 1, 2 the required number of times.
Block *A:* 1, 3; 1, 3; 1, 2.
Block *B:* 1, 4; 1, 4; 1, 2.

Tie-Up for Lace Weave

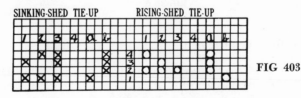

FIG 403

Treadling Treadle the blocks in the order in which they are drawn in or in any preferred order, as in Fig. 404, which starts with the *B* block. Repeat the desired number of times.

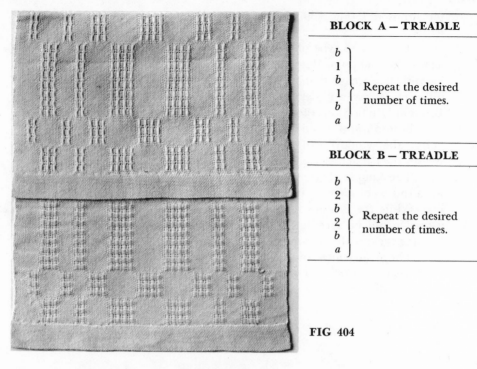

$$\left.\begin{array}{l} b \\ 1 \\ b \\ 1 \\ b \\ a \end{array}\right\} \text{Repeat the desired number of times.}$$

BLOCK B — TREADLE

$$\left.\begin{array}{l} b \\ 2 \\ b \\ 2 \\ b \\ a \end{array}\right\} \text{Repeat the desired number of times.}$$

FIG 404

Weave the plain-weave headings by alternating treadles *a* and *b*. Treadle 3, as shown on the tie-up, is used only when it is desirable to weave the two blocks together as for a border across the end.

TYPE Bronson, 4-Harness, Short Draft · PATTERN Place Mat

Sample Illustrated (Fig. 406)

WARP	WEFT	REED (*dents per inch*)	SLEY
Linen, 8 cord	Linen, 8 cord	10	Double

Treadling Arrangement

Plain-weave border: 16 threads
Pattern border: 4×
Center: as long as desired

Pattern border: 4×
Plain-weave border: 16 threads

The further one delves into the intricacies of the Bronson weave, the more fascinating it becomes, with its many possibilities for original designing.

As with the summer-and-winter weave, the Bronson can be threaded from the short draft (page 545) which, when analyzed, permits the weaver to get a good idea of the appearance of the woven design before undertaking any threading or weaving.

The ideal situation is, of course, for the weaver to design his own short draft and then work out variations on the original draft design as-drawn-in.

Problem Thread a sample of the Bronson II draft (Fig. 405) and treadle in lace fashion.

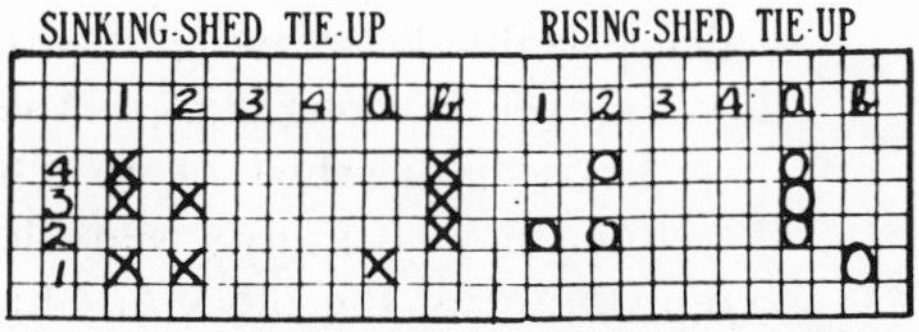

FIG 405

SINKING-SHED TIE-UP   RISING-SHED TIE-UP

THREADING DRAFT AND DRAW-DOWN

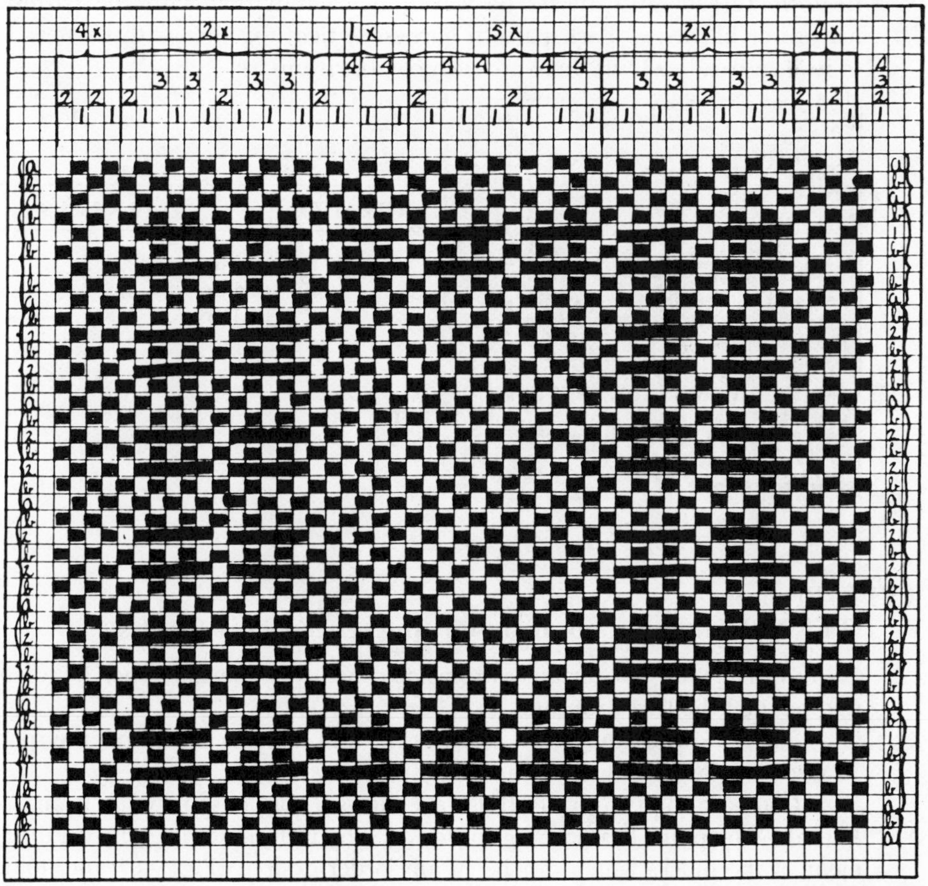

This is not difficult if these rules are followed:

1. Each block of the draft contains six threads, threaded:

Plain weave, on harnesses 1 and 2

Block *A*, on 1–3, 1–3, 1–2, repeated as many times as desired

Block *B*, on 1–4, 1–4, 1–2, repeated as many times as desired

Block *C*, on 1–5, 1–5, 1–2, repeated as many times as desired

and so on to the limit of the number of harnesses on the loom. Remember that there are always two blocks less than the number of harnesses, for harnesses 1 and 2 are required for the plain weave.

2. In making the draw-down and in treadling, pay no attention to the small 1–2–1 block which appears between each pattern block. Actually it is not a block. The two "1's" are the tabby threads which are treadled in combination with all pattern threads, and the 2 acts as a tie-down thread which permits the weaving of intricate patterns. It ties the pattern threads down, preventing long skips on the back of the web.

3. Use rising-shed tie-up. On a rising shed all harnesses are down; therefore, to weave any given block or blocks, raise all pattern harnesses except those for the block or blocks being woven. Harness 2 carrying the tie-down thread must always be woven in combination with the pattern harness or harnesses. Each pattern harness is tied, together with harness 1, to its own treadle. Thus there are such combinations as:

TREADLE		HARNESSES
1	tied to	2, 4, 5,
2	tied to	2, 3, 5,
3	tied to	2, 3, 4.

FIG 406

TYPE Bronson •
PATTERN Variations on Bronson and Lace Short Drafts

Many weavers are not certain as to what constitutes the difference between the spot and the lace Bronson.

The following multiple-harness drafts and samples show how the spot Bronson is converted into the lace Bronson.

Compare the two drafts. The first shows a simple spot point Bronson II draft. The point has nothing to do with the technique; it is the arrangement of the blocks which can be in any order desired (Figs. 407 and 408).

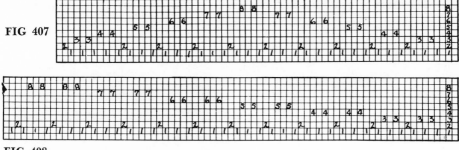

FIG 407

FIG 408

Repeat back to start, beginning with harness 7 when threading.

In the lace Bronson, each block is repeated twice; otherwise the order of threading is the same as for the spot Bronson (Fig. 389).

The tie-up for Figs. 410 and 411, to be woven as-drawn-in, is the same (Fig. 409).

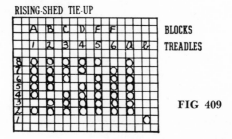

FIG 409

The spot Bronson (Fig. 410) is treadled as-drawn-in, using the treadles in order from 1 to 6 then reversing back to the start.

Because the blocks are threaded twice for the lace Bronson weave, the sample shows only one complete diamond rather than one complete diamond with half the second diamond appearing on each side. Keep this in mind when converting a spot Bronson to a lace Bronson.

The order of treadling the blocks for the multiple-harness spot Bronson (Fig. 410) is:

TREADLE	
Tabby *b*	
Pattern harness 1	Weaves block *A*.
Tabby *b*	
Pattern harness 1	

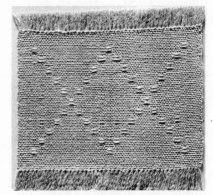

FIG 410

The order of treadling the blocks for the multiple-harness lace Bronson (Fig. 411) is:

TREADLE	
Tabby *b*	
Pattern harness *i*	
Tabby *b*	
Pattern harness 1	
Tabby *b*	
Tabby *a*	Weaves block *A*.
Tabby *b*	
Pattern harness 1	
Tabby *b*	
Pattern harness 1	
Tabby *b*	
Tabby *a*	

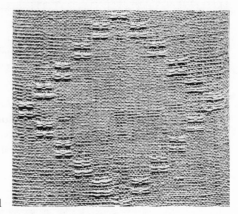

FIG 411

All succeeding blocks are treadled in the same way by depressing the correct treadle for the block being woven.

When using a table loom with levers to weave a block, depress lever 2 and all the other pattern levers except the one for the particular block being woven. For instance, if block 8 is to be woven, depress levers 2 through 7. Harness 1 is not included as it is tabby *b*.

FIG 412

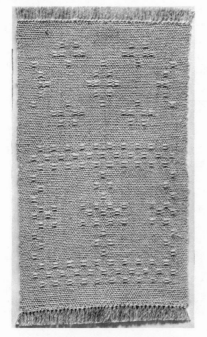

FIG 413

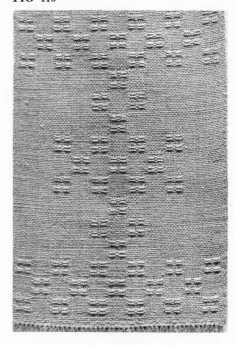

When treadling the sample as-drawn-in, the blocks follow in the order *A, B, C, D, E, F* and repeat back to the start if desired. As with all other types of weaving, the *F* block, which is the turning block, is not repeated. On the second repeat the *A*-block lever is not depressed. The *A* block is, however, woven at the end of the last repeat to balance the design on the left side of the web.

The most interesting method of weaving the multiple-harness spot or lace Bronson is on a table loom where the harnesses can be operated in any desired order or combination without a tie-up. This usually limits the width of the material to 20 in. or less. However, this width is quite sufficient for place mats and towels or for experimenting with various design arrangements for wider articles.

The blocks of the two additional samples (Figs. 412 and 413) are treadled in the same order. The design at the top of the spot-Bronson sample does not appear on the lace-Bronson sample.

A close study of the two samples will reveal the similarity of design.

The order of treadling the blocks for both samples is:

Rising Shed

LEVERS

2, 4, 6, 8 ⎫	
2, 3, 5, 7 ⎬	
2, 4, 6, 8 ⎭	
2, 3, 4, 5, 6, 7 ⎫	
2, 3, 4, 5, 6, 8 ⎬	
2, 3, 4, 5, 6, 7 ⎭	
2, 3, 4, 6, 8 ⎫	
2, 3, 4, 5, 7 ⎬ Center	
2, 3, 4, 6, 8 ⎭	
2, 3, 4, 5, 6, 7 ⎫	
2, 3, 4, 5, 6, 8 ⎬	
2, 3, 4, 5, 6, 7 ⎭	
2, 4, 6, 8 ⎫	
2, 3, 5, 7 ⎬	
2, 4, 6, 8 ⎭	

For the lace weave, repeat each bracketed section twice. The order of treadling the individual blocks was given on page 354.

For a rising-shed foot loom with tie-up, tie the treadles to the harnesses in the order given above, i.e.:

TREADLE	HARNESSES
1	2, 4, 6, 8
2	2, 3, 5, 7
3	2, 3, 4, 5, 6, 7.

The tree (Fig. 414) woven in Bronson lace was set on the same threading as the previous samples (Figs. 412 and 413). It was treadled directly on the loom without first making a design. This simple Bronson-point threading lends itself to many original treadlings. The short draft is by far the quickest and easiest method of threading for the multiple-harness Bronson. The short draft in the short-draft study can be woven in this technique (page 338).

Problem Work out the treadling for weaving a tree on paper or directly on the loom.

TYPE Bronson Short Draft

Setting the Bronson on the short draft (page 545) created a number of problems. As there are several single units in the Bronson draft, it would

FIG 414

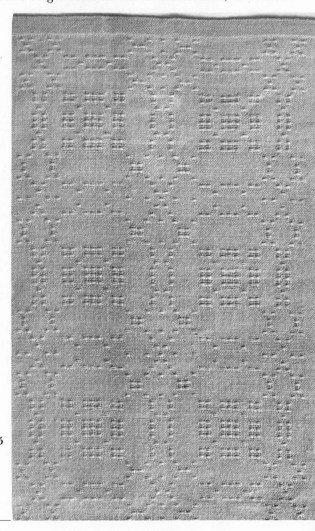

FIG 415

cut down the width and the number of threads if the spot unit was used in this figure of single units.

Care had to be taken so that the beginning and end blocks contained a balanced number of threads by adding or omitting the 2, 1 on each side of the design where it starts or ends against a *C* block, which is threaded lace fashion.

In weaving, only four shots should be used for the spots, since six pack down too much to square the block. This arrangement produces a beautiful Bronson variation (Fig. 415).

Several different threading arrangements were tried but the following brought the best results. The weaver who enjoys problems is urged to experiment with this particular one, for interesting and original results can be obtained.

Materials and Sleying

WARP	WEFT	REED (dents per inch)	SLEY
Linen, 40/2	Linen, 40/2	15	Triple

Treadling Treadle blocks in the Bronson routine (page 545), arranging blocks in the same order as for other short-draft study weaves.

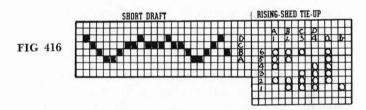

FIG 416

FIG 417

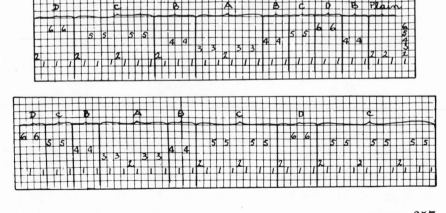

Problem Design an original Bronson draft, thread and weave. Use original treadlings and a variety of threads.

TYPE Swedish Lace

This lace weave is similar in general appearance to the Bronson lace weave. It is thought to have originated in Sweden, though samples of the lace have been found in other countries. There are many threading variations but, regardless of the one used, the end result appears to be the same. The draft used here is a Scandinavian version from the Vävskola at Saterglantan, Sweden.

The structure of the Swedish lace weave suggests that it is a derivative of the huck weave. It is a 2-block weave, each block consisting of five threads tied down by a sixth thread. It is this sixth thread which, when crossed by a weft thread, forms the little window between the units of the blocks which is a distinguishing feature of the weave. The web is reversible; the right side shows the pattern in the weft, the wrong side in the warp. Washing seems to group the threads more closely together, showing the pattern to better advantage.

Normally, the blocks contain three repeats of the basic unit as shown on the draft, blocks *A* and *B* (Fig. 419); but, if desired, the number can be varied according to the directions given for the Bronson lace draft (Fig. 411).

Actually, there is so little difference between the finished appearance of Swedish lace and Bronson lace that weavers are at a loss to differentiate between them.

In the Swedish lace weave, there is one thread in common between the two blocks; while in the Bronson lace, each block is a separate unit with a single thread lying between the blocks. Also, there are three rows of plain weave between the pattern blocks in the Bronson lace and only two in the Swedish lace. The Swedish lace weave is essentially a 4-harness, 2-block weave, while the Bronson lace can be extended to a multiple-harness weave.

An abbreviated draw-down of the structure of the two weaves, showing the difference between them, is given in Fig. 418. There are other technical structural differences but those just indicated will enable the beginner to distinguish between the two.

Uses, Materials, and Sleying As for the Bronson weave.

Sample Illustrated (Fig. 420)

WARP	WEFT	REED (*dents per inch*)	SLEY
Cotton, 8/2	Cotton, 8/2	12	Double

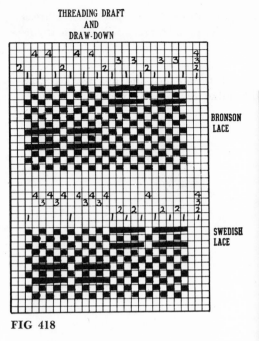

THREADING DRAFT
AND
DRAW-DOWN

BRONSON
LACE

SWEDISH
LACE

FIG 418

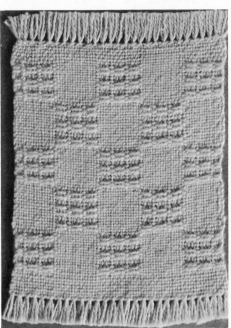

FIG 420

FIG 419

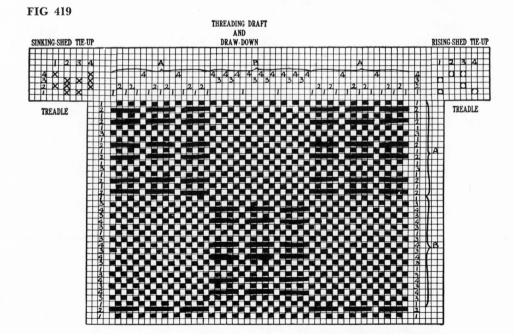

SINKING-SHED TIE-UP

THREADING DRAFT
AND
DRAW-DOWN

RISING-SHED TIE-UP

TREADLE

TREADLE

In treadling, the weaver should concentrate on the plain-weave areas to obtain a 50/50 fabric. If this is done the pattern areas will adjust themselves. It is difficult to get a good selvedge with this weave.

Problem Set up small samples of the Bronson lace and the Swedish lace weaves. Compare them carefully and familiarize yourself with the differences.

chapter 11

Miscellaneous Weaves

**TYPE Miscellaneous, 2-Harness,
Grouped Warp and Weft Threads ·
PATTERN Basket Weave**

While the uses for this weave are somewhat limited, it is used universally and directions are found in the weaving literature of many countries. The basket weave can be threaded on two, four, six, or eight harnesses, with each showing its own distinguishing characteristics.

There are several ways of threading the 4- and 6-harness versions, yet the end result is practically the same. The drafts given here are from the Vävskola at Saterglantan, Sweden.

Some weavers claim that a true basket weave must be threaded on six harnesses. While this may be a matter of controversy, the actual weaving of the 6-harness type is undoubtedly the easiest. The 6-harness pattern is also more attractive than that of the 2- or 4-harness types. Variations can be woven on the 6-harness threading which are not possible on the others, and the basket weave threaded on four or more harnesses can be combined with plain or twill weaves.

While not as sturdy or easy to weave as a true basket weave on six harnesses (page 365), the basket weave on two harnesses offers the owner of a 2-harness loom an opportunity to achieve a seemingly advanced technique on a simple threading.

Uses In wool: for couch throws, lightweight blankets, baby blankets, pillow covers, and drapes; in fine linen, cotton, or synthetic-fibers: for upholstery,

361

if closely sleyed. The well-known drapery material, monk's cloth, is a basket weave.

Suggested Materials and Sleying   Use the same material for both the warp and the weft.

WARP AND WEFT	REED (dents per inch)	SLEY
Wool, knitting, heavy 4-strand	8	Double
Wool, Germantown	10	Single
Wool, fine	12–15	Double
Cotton, 8/4	18	Single
Cotton, 8/2	12	Double
Linen, fine	15	Triple

Wool should be sleyed to produce a firm, yet soft, material, while linens and cottons for table mats should be closely sleyed to prevent sleaziness. Material for upholstery should be very hard and firm.

Samples Illustrated (Figs. 422 and 423)

WARP	WEFT	REED (dents per inch)	SLEY
1. Cotton, mop, 12-strand rug	Cotton, mop, 12-strand rug	8	Single
2. Wool, knitting, 4-strand	Wool, knitting, 4-strand	8	Double

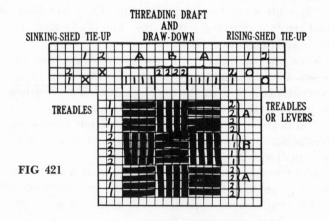

THREADING DRAFT
AND
SINKING-SHED TIE-UP   DRAW-DOWN   RISING-SHED TIE-UP

TREADLES   TREADLES OR LEVERS

FIG 421

The foregoing draft indicates that the blocks consist of four warp threads crossed by four weft threads. This number can be varied if the weaver so desires.

FIG 422

FIG 423

Different arrangements can be used in weaving this pattern, all of which are attractive. Alternate light threads with dark, making a check; weave the entire piece in one color, either on a plain or striped warp; or produce stripes by alternating four rows of dark weft with four rows of light weft threads (Fig. 422). Four strands of weft are woven through each shed before changing the levers; therefore, it is necessary to pass the shuttle between the selvedge threads to prevent the weft thread from pulling out as the shuttle is returned to the opposite side. The weft threads must lie side by side in the shed, flat and smooth. If the threads twist over each other, the completed fabric will not be correct.

It is difficult to get a good selvedge on the 2- or 4-harness basket weave. There is an inclination to pull the weft thread too tight when turning it around the edge warp thread. A good way to offset this is to leave the weft loose in the open shed and press it back against the fell before returning the shuttle through the shed for the second shot. This routine should be followed for each of the four shots in turn. If this is not done, a poor selvedge will be noticed immediately. In basket weaves, do not beat the weft but pull it back snugly into place, regardless of the number of harnesses used. A flat shuttle is advised for narrow widths and small looms.

Problem Set up a sample of the basket weave on two harnesses, experimenting with threads suitable for upholstery.

TYPE Miscellaneous, 4-Harness
Grouped Warp and Weft Threads •
PATTERN Basket Weave

Threading the basket weave on four harnesses makes it possible to weave headings for hems and end borders. It is also possible to separate the blocks of the basket weave with bands of either plain or reverse twill. The bands of twill add to the attractiveness of the pattern, but present a problem in warp tension. If any material of length is to be woven, two warp beams will be required. As few looms of the type used by beginners are equipped with two beams, the weave will not be presented here.

Uses and Materials   The same as for the 2-harness basket weave

Thread the *A* and *B* blocks in alternating succession until the desired width has been threaded, ending with an *A* block to balance. Notice that the treadling for the plain weave deviates from the general rule of 1 and 3, 2 and 4 found in most weaves; here it is 2 and 3, 1 and 4.

The rearrangement of the thread sequence within the blocks presents an appealing problem to the weaver who enjoys experimenting. The general rules governing the 2-harness basket weave apply as well to the 4-harness version.

Problem   Plan and weave a cotton place mat on the threading given above, paying particular attention to the edges.

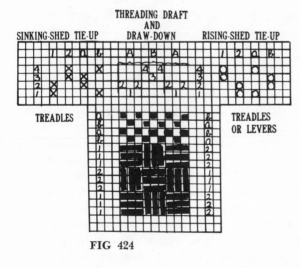

FIG 424

FIG 425

TYPE Miscellaneous, 6-Harness
Grouped Warp and Weft Threads ·
PATTERN Basket Weave

The 6-harness version of the basket weave generally is accepted as the true basket weave. At first glance, the web resembles the 2- and 4-harness weaves, but, upon closer examination, it is found to be quite different in structure. There are two seven-thread blocks. Three threads of each block form the pattern, while four act as binder or tabby threads.

The pattern (Fig. 427) is more interesting than that of the 2- and 4-harness weaves, and proceeds more rapidly, for the binder or tabby thread eliminates the necessity of always turning the weft threads around the edge threads to hold them in place.

Uses, Materials, and Sleying   As this is a multiple-harness weave, it is suggested that a rising-shed loom be used. The sinking-shed tie-up is given as it is from this that the draw-down is made.

Problem   Plan and weave a baby blanket using the 6-harness basket-weave threading.

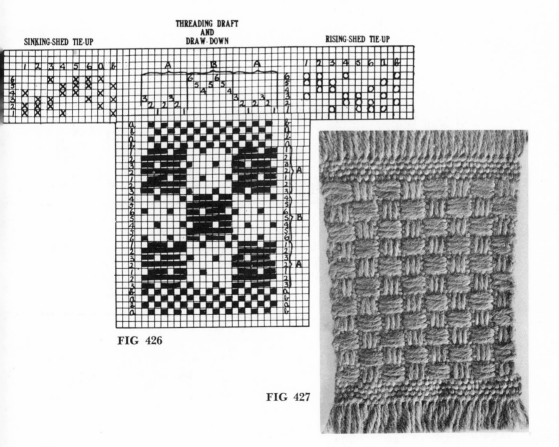

THREADING DRAFT
AND
DRAW-DOWN

SINKING-SHED TIE-UP

RISING-SHED TIE-UP

FIG 426

FIG 427

TYPE Miscellaneous, 8-Harness
Grouped Warp and Weft Threads ·
PATTERN Basket Weave

The advantage of threading the basket weave on eight instead of six harnesses is that borders can be added and bands of plain weaving can be threaded between the basket areas.

A problem with this method, however, is that of warp tension. The warp in the plain-weave areas tightens up much more quickly than that in the basket areas.

The effect of the basket weave set off with bands of plain weave is quite striking on baby blankets and fine linens; but, for the best results, a rising-shed loom with two warp beams should be used.

Uses, Materials and Sleying   As for the 2-harness basket weave

Sample Illustrated (Fig. 429)

Order of Threading (Fig. 428)

Thread plain-weave border (7 and 8) at right, twice.
Thread *A* and *B* blocks, three times.
Thread *A* block once to balance.
Thread plain-weave border (7 and 8) at left, twice.

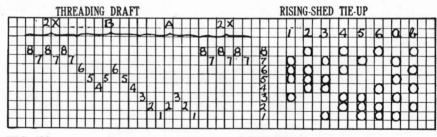

FIG 428

Thread the blocks in the desired order, but remember that, where the plain-weave borders threaded on harnesses 7 and 8 join together with the basket-weave areas threaded on harnesses 1 to 6 inclusive, the threads on the even-numbered harnesses must be next to the threads on the uneven-numbered harnesses, and vice versa. The necessary adjustments are made by reversing the threading order of harnesses 7 and 8.

Treadling

Treadle *a* and *b* in alternating succession for the desired number of shots for the heading or border.

Block *A:* Treadles 1, 2, 3, 2, 1, 2, 3

Block *B:* Treadles 4, 5, 6, 5, 4, 5, 6

Blocks *A* and *B* are treadled in alternating succession for the desired length, ending with block *A* to balance the design.

Weave a plain-weave border to balance the border at the beginning.

FIG 429

Problem Set up a loom with a combination basket and plain weave, experimenting with various arrangements.

TYPE Miscellaneous •
PATTERN Honeycomb Scandinavian Spetsväv

The honeycomb is another old and well-known weave and, like the waffle weave, the name is descriptive of the texture of the web.

This weave, with its many variations of threading, treadling, and color arrangements, produces an attractive, rather heavy web which, at a distance, resembles lace. When the web is examined, however, it reveals a closely woven background which fills in what appeared at first glance to be holes. Names given to these pseudo holes by various weavers are dents, dimples, eyes, pockets, and depressions.

A heavy thread outlines the dents; the effect is more pleasing if this thread is the same color as the warp. Dents of the same color, woven in fine thread, produce a single color web. Dents also can be a contrasting, darker color.

Generally, the Scandinavian spetsväv is woven with finer, more closely sleyed threads than the honeycomb, and quite frequently, the same thread is used for the dent and the outline thread. It would almost appear from some of the illustrations of the spetsväv that it is an embossed rather than an indented web. To judge from the picture, the spetsväv seems firmer and sturdier than the honeycomb weave with which we are familiar.

Curved lines, seldom seen in hand weaving, are possible with the honeycomb weave, especially if the warp is left a bit slack and the heavy tabby thread is left loose in the shed before beating. This combination of loose warp and tabby threads gives the tabby an opportunity to curve around the fine, plain-weave, background areas.

There are two methods of weaving these background areas or dents. The warp may be closely sleyed resulting in a 50/50 plain weave or it may be more coarsely sleyed to produce a weft-face material. The weft-face material is suitable for rugs or upholstery where a very firm fabric is desirable.

Uses The spetsväv originally was used for bedcovers, pillow covers, bureau covers, and table covers and still is in general use in many Scandinavian homes. The honeycomb is suitable for household linens, upholstery, pillow covers, small mats, purses, and bags. It produces attractive evening bags of fancy threads and metallics, and smart afternoon bags in contrasting fine and heavy linens or cottons. Because of the long skips on the back, its use is somewhat limited.

Suitable Materials and Sleying

WARP	WEFT	PATTERN	REED (dents per inch)	SLEY
Cotton, 10/3	Yarn, heavy 3-ply	Cotton, 10/3	15	Double
Yarn, fine	Yarn, heavy 3-ply	Yarn, fine	15	Double
Carpet warp	Yarn, heavy 3-ply	Carpet warp	15	Single
Cotton, 16/2	Cotton, 16/2	Fine perle, rayon or wool	15	Double
Rayon, fine	Rayon, fine	Metallics, silk, rayon	15	Double

Threading There are true honeycomb drafts, but many of these produce a pattern which seems a bit formal due to the introduction of frequent tie-down threads to control the long skips on the back of the web. The true honeycomb, such as the monk's belt, is usually a 2-block draft, threaded and woven on opposites.

Many beautiful overshot drafts, set on a great variety of threadings and treadled honeycomb, are presented in Marguerite P. Davison's book.[1]

If consideration must be given to the back of the web, choose the pattern draft carefully. If the long skips are not objectionable, some excellent results can be obtained with the use of a larger overshot threading.

Sample Illustrated

1. *Threaded on a Regulation Honeycomb Threading (Fig. 431)*

WARP	WEFT	PATTERN	REED (*dents per inch*)	SLEY
Carpet warp	Yarn, heavy 3-ply	Carpet warp	15	Single

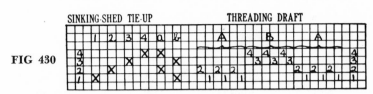

FIG 430

SINKING-SHED TIE-UP   THREADING DRAFT

Repeat the *A* and *B* blocks as often as required to thread the desired width, ending with the *A* block to balance.

Treadling–Sinking Shed	Treadling–Rising Shed
A: Fine thread	*A:* Fine thread
1 and 3 ⎱ 6×	2 and 4 ⎱ 6×
2 and 4 ⎰	1 and 3 ⎰
B: Coarse thread	*B:* Coarse thread
1 and 3 1×	2 and 4 1×
C: Fine thread	*C:* Fine thread
2 ⎱ 3×	1, 3, 4 ⎱ 3×
1 ⎰	2, 3, 4 ⎰
D: Coarse thread	*D:* Coarse thread
2 and 4 1×	1 and 3 1×
E: Fine thread	*E:* Fine thread
3 ⎱ 3×	1, 2, 4 ⎱ 3×
4 ⎰	1, 2, 3 ⎰

There are two methods of treadling the heavy threads between the dents. The first method is the regular system for treadling a plain weave,

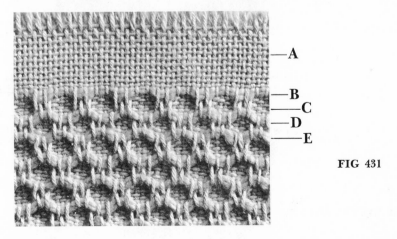

—A

—B
—C
—D
—E

FIG 431

that is, *a* (treadles 2 and 4) and *b* (treadles 1 and 3) are treadled in alternating succession throughout, the tabby threads crossing over the area between the blocks where they come together. In the second method, the tabby threads are treadled in the following sequence: tabby *a* (2 and 4) and tabby *b* (1 and 3) followed by tabby *b* (1 and 3) and tabby *a* (2 and 4). In the second method, the heavy tabby threads pack down more closely around the dents or background areas. Both methods are correct.

This weave requires hard beating.

2. *Variation on Threading Sample 1 (Fig. 432)*

A variation of sample 1 can be obtained by threading block *A* (treadles 1 and 2) eight times, equalling 16 threads, and block *B* (treadles 3 and 4), eight times, equalling 16 threads. Repeat the threading as many times as desired; then thread block *A* (treadles 1 and 2) three times, equalling six threads, and block *B* (treadles 3 and 4) three times, equalling six threads. Repeat as often as necessary.

The large blocks can be alternated with the small blocks across the web to make various arrangements.

Treadle the blocks in the order as-drawn-in with an equal number of weft threads and warp threads in each block.

FIG 432

3. *Honeycomb Set on 1000 Flower Threading (Fig. 434)*

WARP	WEFT	PATTERN	REED (*dents per inch*)	SLEY
Cotton, 8/2	Cotton, 8/2 double	Cotton, 8/2 Cotton, mercerized, 30/3, *or* Nylon, No. 10	12	Double

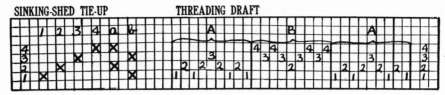

FIG 433

Thread blocks *A* and *B* in alternating succession as often as required to thread the desired width. End with an *A* block to balance the design (Fig. 434).

Treadling–Sinking Shed			Treadling–Rising Shed (*No Tie-Up*)
TREADLES			**TREADLES OR LEVERS**
$\left.\begin{matrix} a \\ b \end{matrix}\right\}$	As often as desired for a plain weave heading		$\left\{\begin{matrix} \text{1 and 3} \\ \text{2 and 4} \end{matrix}\right.$
$\left.\begin{matrix} 1 \\ 2 \end{matrix}\right\}$ 4×	Fine thread, block *A*	4×	$\left\{\begin{matrix} \text{2, 3, 4} \\ \text{1, 3, 4} \end{matrix}\right.$
$\left.\begin{matrix} a \\ b \end{matrix}\right\}$ 1×	Heavy nylon thread	1×	$\left\{\begin{matrix} \text{1 and 3} \\ \text{2 and 4} \end{matrix}\right.$
$\left.\begin{matrix} 3 \\ 4 \end{matrix}\right\}$ 4×	Fine thread, block *B*	4×	$\left\{\begin{matrix} \text{1, 2, 4} \\ \text{1, 2, 3} \end{matrix}\right.$

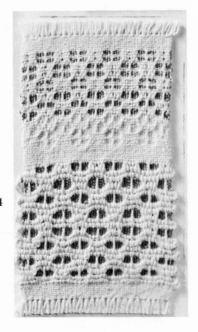

FIG 434

Order of Treadling Blocks *A, B, A, B*—twice; *A, B,* ending with an *A* block to balance

	ALL WHITE SAMPLE	
TREADLES		TREADLES OR LEVERS
$a \atop b$ } 1×	Heavy thread	1× { 1 and 3 2 and 4
$1 \atop 2$ } 3×	Fine thread, block *A*	3× { 2, 3, 4 1, 3, 4
$a \atop b$ } 1×	Heavy thread	1× { 1 and 3 2 and 4
$3 \atop 4$ } 3×	Fine thread, block *B*	3× { 1, 2, 4 1, 2, 3

Order of Treadling Blocks *A*—twice; *B*—once; *A*—once

	WHITE WITH DARK DENTS	
$a \atop b$ } 1×	Heavy thread	1× { 1 and 3 2 and 4
$1 \atop 2$ } 4×	Fine thread, block *A*	4× { 2, 3, 4 1, 3, 4
$a \atop b$ } 1×	Heavy thread	1× { 1 and 3 2 and 4
$3 \atop 4$ } 4×	Fine thread, block *B*	4× { 1, 2, 4 1, 2, 3

Order of Treadling blocks *A, B, A, B*—twice; *A*—twice; *B*—twice; repeat the required number of times to weave the desired length.

To weave a 4-block pattern, treadle *A*—1 then 2; *B*—2 then 3; *C*— then 4; *D*—4 then 1; repeat each the required number of times.

Problem Thread and weave a sample of the honeycomb.

TYPE Miscellaneous, 4-Harness •
PATTERN 5-Thread Block, Huck or Huckabuck

Most people are familiar with this weave since it is popular for hand towels. The weave is used universally, is very versatile, is adaptable for many purposes, and there are many variations of it.[2] In fact, there are so many of these variations, most of which bear so little resemblance to the original distinguishing neat little oval huck design that it could be asked why the huckaback isn't simply listed as one of that much larger group frequently referred to as the spot weaves. However, as much of the literature classifies

FIGS. 435, 436, and 437. Variations on the honeycomb weave

it and its many derivatives as huck, it seems pertinent to continue it under that classification.

Uses Huck is most pleasing when woven of fine linen thread, closely sleyed. Its many threading and treadling variations make it an acceptable weave for contemporary use. Specifically, it is used for toweling and table linens; wool scarves and stoles; fine cotton, wool, and synthetic-fibered upholstery; rayon and cotton draperies set with irregular spacing in the reed; and fine wool or cotton dress materials set in three-thread blocks.

Suitable Materials and Sleying

WARP	WEFT	REED (dents per inch)	SLEY
Linen, 40/2	Linen, 40/2	18	Double
Cotton, 30/3	Cotton, 30/3	15	Double
Wool, 2/16	Wool, 2/16	10	Double
Wool, 2/32	Wool, 2/32	12	Double

Samples Illustrated

1. (Fig. 439)

Cotton, Egyptian, 30/3	Cotton, Egyptian, 30/3	15	Double

2. (Fig. 440)

Linen, 40/2	Linen, 40/2	18	Double

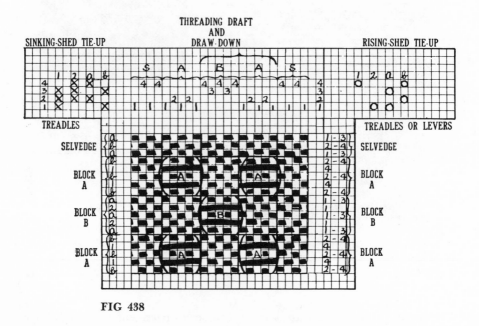

FIG 438

Threading, Sample 1 Thread selvedge, right side, once, 4 threads.
  Thread bracketed sections, blocks *A* and *B,* repeated five times.
  Thread block *A* to balance.
  Thread selvedge, left side, once, 4 threads.

Treadling Sample 1 Follow treadling given above (Fig. 438), repeating as often as necessary to weave the required length, ending with an *A* block to balance the weave.

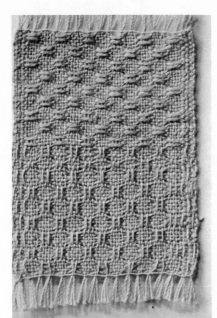

FIG 439

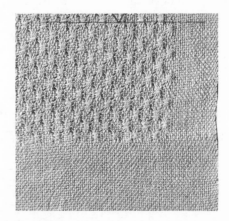

FIG 440

The upper, or right, side shows the design in the weft. The lower, or under, side shows the design in the warp.

Threading, Sample 2 Thread right selvedge six times, 24 threads, for border.

Thread bracketed section, blocks *A* and *B,* as often as required for the desired width, using the draft (Fig. 438).

Thread block *A* to balance.

Thread left selvedge six times for border.

Treadling, Sample 2 Follow the draw-down (Fig. 438).

Weave the end border the same width as the side border, adding an extra piece to be turned under for the hem.

Weave the center part the desired length, treadling blocks *A* and *B* in alternating succession and ending with an *A* block.

End with a border to equal the border at the beginning.

Problem Weave a guest towel in huck, using fine cotton or linen, closely sleyed, with plain-weave borders on all four sides.

TYPE Miscellaneous, 4-Harness •
PATTERN Floating Thread Unit, Huck or Huckabuck

A slight change in the draft arrangement (Fig. 441) brings up vertical and horizontal floats as shown on the draft (Fig. 441) and the traditional huck oval disappears. Compare the two drafts. It is well to remember at this point that huck and other spot weaves all require two harnesses for the plain 50/50 weave background. The remaining two, four, or six harnesses are available for the floats.

The materials and sleying used for the following are the same as used for the preceding. The tie-up and treadling are for a rising shed; for a sinking shed simply transpose the numbers.

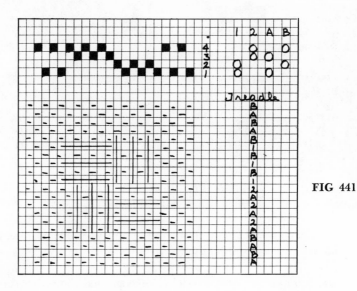

FIG 441

TYPE Miscellaneous, 6-Harness •
PATTERN Floating Thread Unit, Huck or Huckabuck

The addition of two extra harnesses produces a more involved, firmer web with more character (Fig. 442).

A comparative study of the drafts shown (Figs. 438, 441, and 442) will show the development from the simple huck to more intricate spot weaves.

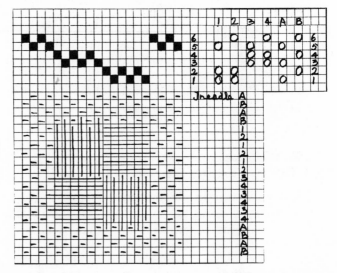

FIG 442

TYPE Miscellaneous •
PATTERN Spot on 4-Thread Plain Weave Huck Unit

Still another arrangement of the original huck draft (Fig. 438) gives an entirely different effect. In this draft (Fig. 443), the plain-weave background area is reduced to only four threads, which produces a web especially suited to wool. In fine wool this makes attractive wool scarves or dress material; in medium weight wool, baby blankets or afghans; and in coarse wools, pillow covers, bags, couch throws, or coatings. Although it is traditional that huck and other spot weaves be woven in a single color, it is suggested that, in addition to the color chosen for the four background threads, a second color be used for the horizontal and a third for the vertical floats. A much more subtle color effect is obtained if the chosen colors are from the same color family. Avoid contrasting colors.

As the weaving progresses it will be noted that there is no interweaving of the thread floats in the spots except as they cross each other in passing from the upper to the under side of the web.

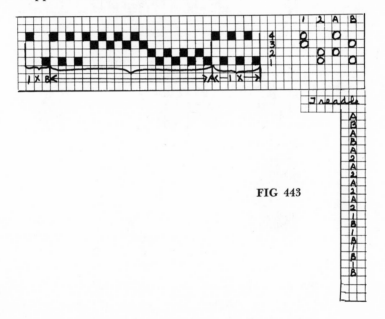

FIG 443

Problem Using the foregoing draft for a guide, extend draft to six harnesses. Weave sample.

TYPE Miscellaneous • PATTERN Huck Lace

In distinct contrast to the foregoing variations on the huck weaves, there is another group called the huckaback lace weaves. On these threadings, which require eight or more harnesses, can be woven some of the most beautiful webs which can be produced by the handweaver. The small oval unit which is the distinguishing mark of the huck technique is the central focal point of the huck lace weave. It can appear, according to the draft arrangement, in large diamond-shaped units against a plain weave background; in small units against a lace background; as small table units (Fig. 445) and so on. Its possibilities for design arrangement are unlimited.

The draft, tie-up, and treadling directions for a huck lace web follow. Although these are arranged to weave an alternating diamond design, there are many other designs which can be woven on the same draft by changing the order of the tie-up and treadling. It provides a challenge to the weaver desirous of producing original webs.

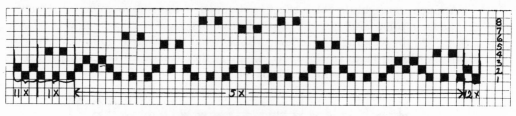

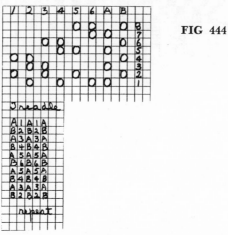

FIG 444

Fig. 445 shows section of linen cloth brought to Nova Scotia early in 1800 by Danish settlers. In some of the units the traditional huck threading can be seen, but of greater interest is the arrangement of the units which suggest the wheel, table, and star typical of many of the early overshot coverlet drafts.

TYPE Miscellaneous, 4-Harness •
PATTERN 2-Block, M's and O's or Swedish Sälldräll

The M's and O's, or as it is called in Sweden, the sällväv or sälldräll, is an attractive one-shuttle, 50/50, textured weave especially suitable for fine

FIG 445

linen threads. Many heirloom towels and tablecloths have been woven in this technique.[3]

Uses   While this weave has been popular commercially for wool scarves, cotton tablecloths, and luncheon sets, it is still of interest and a favorite among hand weavers for household linens, particularly fine linen table mats and tablecloths, scarves, and woolen baby blankets and afghans. Interesting drapery materials are possible when woven of heavy rayon or nylon threads combined with wool or linen. Sheer window curtains also can be woven.

Structure   M's and O's, a 2-block draft of eight threads each, can be extended to either a 3-block, 6-harness weave or a 4-block, 8-harness weave.

One of the M's and O's pattern blocks is written on the 1–2, 3–4 harness combination, referred to here as block *A*, while the other is on harnesses 1–3 and 2–4, referred to as block *B*. The pattern block shows 2 four-thread skips. The structure of the weave is such that the opposite block, the one not being treadled, weaves in a plain weave. Therefore, the pattern blocks alternate with the plain-weave blocks. Because of the block structure, a true 50/50 plain weave is not possible through an acceptable one, showing double threads at regular intervals, can be woven. The weave is completely reversible.

Different designs are possible by varying the number of repeats of blocks *A* and *B*. For example, block *A* might be repeated four times and block *B* eight times, resulting in a large block alternating with a small block. One threading of block *A* and one of block *B* would create stripes between the squares. Some old linens show the addition of a twill or bird's-eye section inserted between each block or used for borders.

The selvedge of M's and O's is greatly improved through the addition of four threads on each side, threaded 1, 2, 3, 4. These are not shown on the drafts nor are they treadled, but they eliminate the drawing in of the threads at the edge of the pattern blocks.

Watch the beating in the plain-weave areas for a 50/50 web must be woven. When this is done, the areas covered by the skips or floats adjust themselves.

Some of the blocks can be threaded in different colors. The colors of the weft and warp can be threaded in the same order, in the manner of a plaid. Plaid color arrangements are especially good for draperies. Refrain from using a color in the weft which contrasts with the warp; the result is unsatisfactory.

The blocks can be arranged in any order in which both sides of the design balance. If the design starts with an *A* block on the right, there must be an *A* block to balance it on the left, added after the last repeat of the pattern (Fig. 446).

FIG 446

THREADING DRAFT
AND
DRAW-DOWN

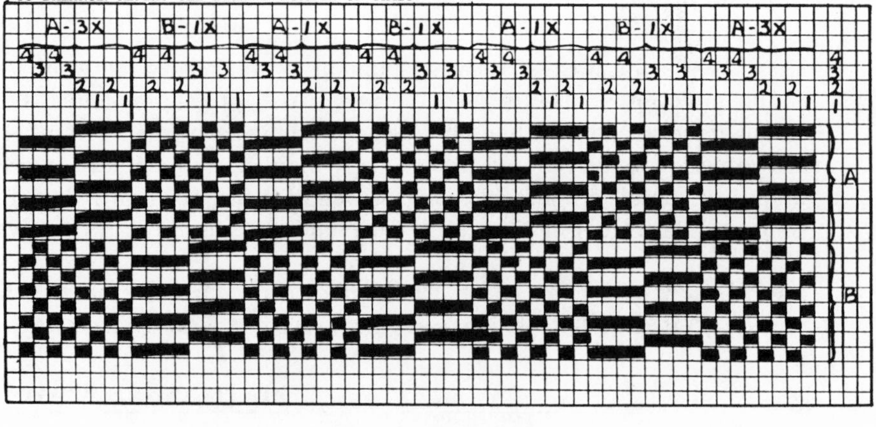

Sample Illustrated

1. (Fig. 448)

WARP	WEFT	REED *(dents per inch)*	SLEY
Cotton, 8/2	Dutch cotton, No. 8	20	Single

Number of Threads Wound 96 (an allowance has been made for four selvedge threads on each side, threaded 1, 2, 3, 4)

The first and last *A* blocks are threaded and treadled three times, as shown in sample 1 (Fig. 448), but are shown only once on the threading draft and draw-down (Fig. 446).

Tie-Up For rising shed tie blank spaces, or use direct treadling as given (Figure 447).

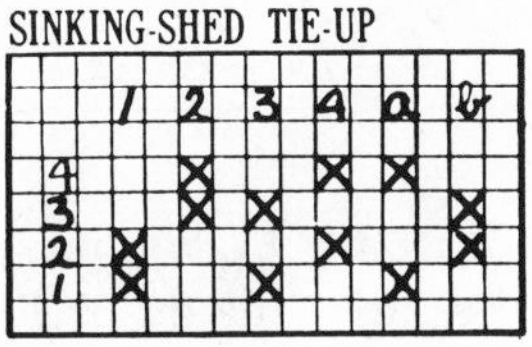

SINKING-SHED TIE-UP

FIG 447

Order of Treadling Follow the threading order.

FIG 448

		Sinking Shed		Rising Shed *(No Tie-Up)*
BLOCK	TREADLES		SHOTS	TREADLES OR LEVERS
A	1 2 }		24	{ 3 and 4 } 1 and 2
B	3 4 }		8	{ 2 and 4 } 1 and 3
A	1 2 }		8	{ 3 and 4 } 1 and 2
B	3 4 }		8	{ 2 and 4 } 1 and 3
A	1 2 }		8	{ 3 and 4 } 1 and 2
B	3 4 }		8	{ 2 and 4 } 1 and 3
A	1 2 }		24	{ 3 and 4 } 1 and 2

If headings are desired, treadle *a* and *b* in alternating succession until the required width has been woven.

2. *(Fig. 449)*

WARP	WEFT
Cotton, 8/2	Cotton perle, 10/3

REED *(dents per inch)*	SLEY
12	Double

Threading Arrangement of Blocks

BLOCK
A − 2×
B − 1×
*A − 1×
B − 7× − center

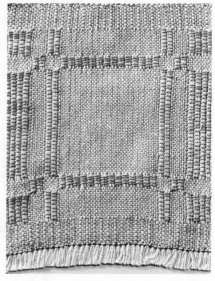

FIG 449

Repeat from * back to the beginning.

Use the threading draft (Fig. 446) for the blocks and treadle in order as-drawn-in.

3. *(Fig. 450)*

WARP	WEFT	REED *(dents per inch)*	SLEY
Natural linen, 65/2	Linen singles, 20	16	3 per dent

Threading   Arranged for a place mat or a guest towel.[4]

BLOCK

B ⎱
A ⎰ Alternate for 15 blocks, ending with block B for the right border.
A − 5×
B − 1× ⎱
*A − 1× ⎱ Repeat these five blocks, as a whole, the
B − 5× − center ⎰ required number of times to thread the
Repeat from * back to B − 1× ⎰ desired width.
A − 5×
B ⎱
A ⎰ Alternate for 15 blocks, ending with block B for the left border.

FIG 450

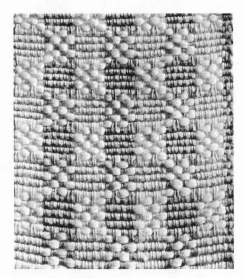

FIG 451

Treadling   Blocks are treadled in the order as-drawn-in, squaring each block.

Figure 451 shows M's and O's treadled on opposites and woven with candlewick cotton on a 16/2 double-sley two-color warp.

Problem   Experiment with treadling variations on any setting of M's and O's using various types of threads.

TYPE Miscellaneous, 6-Harness ·
PATTERN 3-Block, M's and O's

Using the same block structure found in the 4-harness M's and O's it is possible to extend the weave to a 3-block pattern set on 6 harnesses. This technique has not been covered by American weaving books, but one example does appear in a Finnish text.[5] In this publication, the blocks have been arranged to form a pattern but only the fundamental structure of the block has been explained. The weaver must originate his own design.

The sample illustrated (Fig. 453) required a great deal of experimentation to determine a satisfactory arrangement for the blocks and the threads composing the blocks.

The fundamental principle of the M's-and-O's structure is adhered to, for each block contains eight threads and, when woven, the pattern blocks show alternating four-thread skips surrounded by areas of plain weave. As with the 4-harness technique, a true 50/50 plain weave is not possible.

Through experimentation it has been learned that to prevent two blocks from weaving together, it is necessary to thread the *B* block 2–4; 2–4; 3–5; 3–5.

It has been found also that, because threads appearing on harnesses 2 and 3 in block *C* also are common to block *A* and *B*, it is not possible to weave the *A* block alone; the *C* block automatically weaves at the same time. The *B* and *C* blocks weave separately.

Another factor to consider is that the threads in one block must alternate between odd- and even-numbered harnesses (*B* block, Fig. 452), and in the other must follow the twill succession (*A* block, Fig. 452). All these facts must be considered when arranging the blocks in a pattern.

Uses and Materials   Same as for the 4-harness M's and O's

Sample Illustrated (Fig. 453)

WARP	WEFT	REED	SLEY
		(dents per inch)	
Linen, 30/2	Shoemaker's linen	15	Double

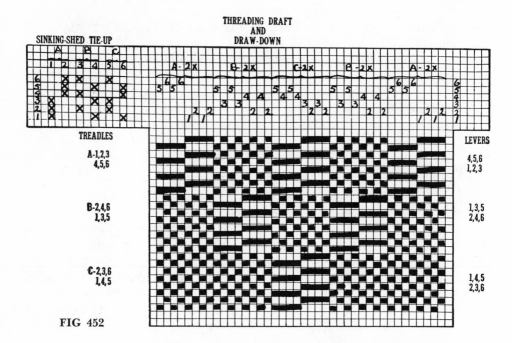

FIG 452

NOTE: In Fig. 453, 8 shots of the heavy linen have been used to show the weave structure; ordinarily, the piece would be woven with linen the same size as the warp, using 16 shots to a square.

In the sample, the blocks are each repeated twice, while on the draw-down, to save space, they are shown only once.

Treadling As this weave is set on six harnesses, it is advisable to use a rising-shed loom for the actual weaving will be easier. Therefore, the spaces shown on the tie-up (Fig. 452) would be tied up instead of the crosses.

The rising-shed treadling would be:

BLOCK	TREADLE	LEVERS	SHOTS
A	1	4:5:6 ⎫	16
	2	1:2:3 ⎬	
B	3	1:3:5 ⎫	16
	4	2:4:6 ⎬	
C	5	1:4:5 ⎫	16
	6	2:3:6 ⎬	

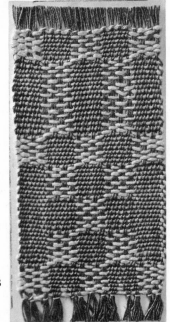

FIG 453

Repeat as often as required, beginning at the top each time, to weave the desired length.

Problem Work out a simple design arrangement of the 3-block, 6-harness M's and O's and weave a wool scarf.

TYPE Miscellaneous, 8-Harness •
PATTERN 4-Block, M's and O's

Two- and 3-block M's and O's on four and six harnesses have been discussed. Although practically nothing has been found in weaving literature covering the extension of the 2-block M's and O's to a 4-block weave, a study group has worked on this recently with the following results.

Block Structure One important point to remember when extending a 4-harness draft to an 8-harness draft is that, in addition to harnesses 1, 2, 3, and 4 on the original 4-harness draft, there is a second set of 4-harnesses, 5, 6, 7, and 8, which allows for a duplication of the pattern set in the same order.

All pattern blocks, when woven, should show the regulation M's and O's four-thread skips, with certain exceptions, with the plain-weave areas between the blocks.

A curious shading is noted in the web of the 4-block M's and O's. At first glance it appears to come from uneven beating, but a more careful inspection shows it to be caused by the fact that some background blocks are in plain weave while others have two-thread skips in the weave. The textured portions of the web are unusual and effective. As with the 4- and 6-harness M's and O's, there can be no true plain weave extending across the web. The closest weave to a plain weave to be achieved is woven by alternating treadles a—1, 4, 5, 8—and b—2, 3, 6, 7. Throughout the textured areas, groups of two threads together alternate with groups of two or more threads in the plain weave.

In arranging the blocks, a block on the twill sequence, *A* or *C*, must be followed by a block on the other sequence, *B* or *D*, so that both pattern and plain areas will be woven simultaneously.

Uses   As for M's-and-O's 2-block, 4-harness weave

Samples Illustrated

1. (Fig. 456)

WARP	WEFT	REED *(dents per inch)*	SLEY
Cotton, 8/4	Cotton, 8/4	16	Single

Coarse materials have been used to show the structure of the weave. The use of the materials and sleying given for the 4-harness M's and O's, the special design arrangements found in modern weaving books,[6] and copies from heirloom pieces will produce interesting effects.

To cut down the size of the draw-down, the blocks are shown only once, but they are threaded the number of times indicated over the bracket.

In making the tie-up, some harnesses from both groups (1, 2, 3, 4, and 5, 6, 7, 8) must be tied up together to prevent long skips on the back of the web.

Treadling

1. (Fig. 456)

This multiple-harness weave is set on a rising-shed loom using the tie-up shown in Figure 455.

THREADING DRAFT AND DRAW-DOWN

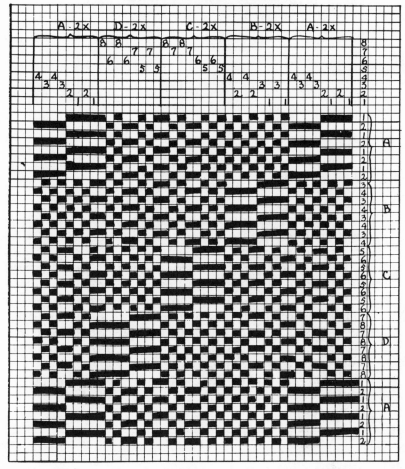

FIG 454

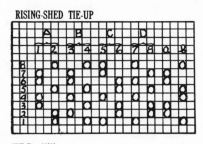

RISING-SHED TIE-UP

FIG 455

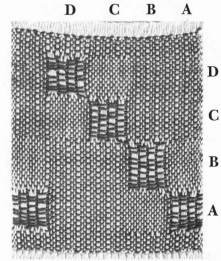

FIG 456

BLOCK	TREADLE OR LEVERS		
A	1	3 4 6 7	
	2	1 2 5 8	} Repeat to square block.
B	3	2 4 6 7	
	4	1 3 5 8	} Repeat to square block.
C	5	1 4 7 8	
	6	2 3 5 6	} Repeat to square block.
D	7	1 4 6 8	
	8	2 3 5 7	} Repeat to square block.

Repeat as often as required, beginning at the top each time.

2. (Fig. 459)

To achieve further interest and a sense of design, arrange the blocks in regular succession, then reverse the order at the D block back to the A starting block (Fig. 459).

Remember that the pattern is reversed on an uneven number of threads. In sample 2 the reversal occurs in the D block which normally is threaded 5–7, 5–7, 6–8, 6–8, but to obtain a correct repetition of the design, a mirror image, the threads must be reversed and will read 5–7, 5–7, 6–8, 6, 7–5, 7–5. Note that one 8 is omitted. If preferred, another 6 can be added and the draft will read 5–7, 5–7, 6–8, 6, 7–5, 7–5. The subsequent C, B, and A blocks will be threaded backward.

A close study of the draft will clarify the arrangement.

2. (Fig. 459)

WARP	WEFT	REED	SLEY
		(dents per inch)	
Cotton, 8/4	Cotton, 8/4	18	Single

Threading

BLOCK

A — 2×
B — 2×
*C — 2×
D — 11 threads only (this is the turning block)
Repeat from * back to beginning.

On the draw-down the blocks are shown only once. In designing a large piece, it possibly would be more attractive with the D block larger than the other blocks, rather than smaller; however, this is a matter of preference.

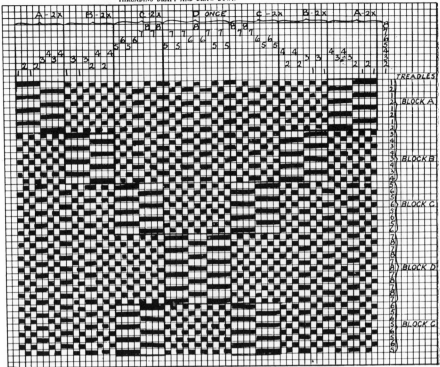

FIG 457

Treadling The blocks are treadled as-drawn-in according to the draw-down (Fig. 457). Treadles *a* and *b* are used in alternating sequence for the headings. Where the design reverses, it is necessary to change the treadling sequence. To be sure that the correct treadles are used, note the background threads; as in all plain weaves, they must alternate in correct sequence.

FIG 458

RISING-SHED TIE-UP

Rising Shed	**BLOCK**	**TREADLE OR LEVERS**	
	A	1	3 4 6 7
		2	1 2 5 8
	B	3	2 4 6 7
		4	1 3 5 8
	C	5	1 4 7 8
		6	2 3 5 6
	D	7	1 4 6 8
		8	2 3 5 7
	C	6	2 3 5 6
		5	1 4 7 8
	B	4	1 3 5 8
		3	2 4 6 7
	A	2	1 2 5 8
		1	3 4 6 7

The above treadling weaves one complete, balanced design. Start at *B* for the second repeat.

The two samples illustrated (Figs. 456 and 459) show the structure and explain the difficulties of the M's-and-O's technique when extended to a 4-block, 8-harness weave. A pattern is evident in one of the samples.

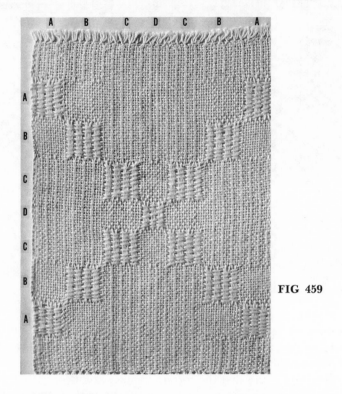

FIG 459

A further design development is shown later (Fig. 637) where the theory is applied to the short draft, resulting in an over-all patterned web, closely resembling the other short draft samples.

Problem Experiment with the arrangements of the blocks.

TYPE Miscellaneous, 4-Harness · PATTERN Waffle Weave

This is an old, universally used, one-shuttle weave whose name is descriptive of its texture. It is a 50/50 weave in that there are the same number of warp and weft threads in the finished square. The weave is characterized by long skips on the four sides of the square which has an indented center. Warp skips appear on the right and left of the square and weft skips at the top and bottom. The length of these skips diminishes with each weft shot. The center of the indentations shows a plain-weave structure. The figure is balanced by the first thread of the second repeat of the threading draft and by the first weft shot of the second repeat.

This single-block weave can be threaded on four, five, or eight harnesses. In the Scandinavian countries, the 5-harness threading is generally used.

The 4-harness type is the least satisfactory as the depressions, or indentations, are not as deep as those in the 5- or 8-harness types. However, if the warp is closely sleyed and the beating is firm but not hard, particularly for wool, the results are satisfactory. The 4-harness threading is given here for the many weavers who use the 4-harness looms.

Because of the structure of the weave, it is difficult to get a smooth edge with some materials. The wider the web and the softer the thread, the more difficult it is. There also is considerable drawing in of the web, even after removal from the loom, so a generous allowance, even to the adding of two or more extra blocks when threading and weaving, must be made if weaving to calculated measurements.

Uses Towels, washcloths, place mats, coatings and dress materials, baby blankets, and draperies. The weave is *not* recommended for upholstery because of the long skips and softness of the material. Some weavers, however, using a firm thread closely sleyed, have found that the under or wrong side has an interesting texture quite suitable for upholstery.

Suitable Materials and Sleying Soft threads are recommended for the waffle weave. Springy threads such as linens, synthetic threads, and the metallics should be avoided because of the long skips and because they do not beat back closely and stay in place. The type and size of thread should be chosen carefully and sleyed correctly for the material being woven. The size and kinds of thread chosen and the sleying largely determine its use. The warp should be set closer than for a 50/50 plain weave or the blocks will not weave square. The waffle weave can be woven in a single or in two or more colors arranged to give a variety of effects. This is a weave in which off-balance treadling occurs; that is, one harness is treadled against three. Without special equipment, it is difficult to get a good shed for such a weave on a counterbalanced sinking-shed loom. If a long yardage is planned, it is suggested that the weaving be done on a rising-shed loom.

WARP	WEFT	REED (*dents per inch*)	SLEY
Cotton, 8/4	Cotton, 8/4	18	Single
Cotton, soft and fine	Cotton, soft and fine	15–18	Double and triple
Wool, 2/16	Wool, 2/16	15	Double
Wool, 2/32	Wool, 2/32	18	Double
Wool, knitting, heavy	Wool, knitting, heavy	12	Single

Samples Illustrated

1. (Fig. 461)

WARP	WEFT
Cotton, 8/2	Cotton, 8/2

REED (dents per inch)	SLEY
12	Double

2. (Fig. 462)

WARP	WEFT
Cotton, 50/3	Cotton, 50/3

REED (dents per inch)	SLEY
15	Triple

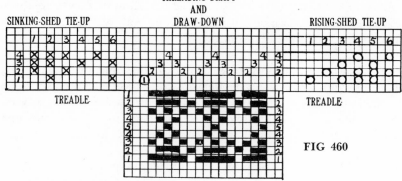

THREADING DRAFT AND DRAW-DOWN

SINKING-SHED TIE-UP

RISING-SHED TIE-UP

TREADLE

TREADLE

FIG 460

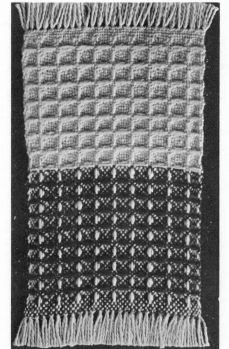

FIG 461

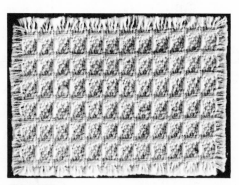

FIG 462

Treadles 3 and 6 (Fig. 460) weave the plain weave. In threading, repeat the draft as many times as required, omitting the encircled 1 until the last repeat.

At the end of the treadling draft, the treadle-1 shot has been added to balance the design. The treadling starts at the top each time after the last two, and is repeated in this sequence: 1, 2, 3, 4, 5, 4, 3, 2, (1).

Problem Plan the warp and weave a baby blanket in the waffle weave using a soft, coarse yarn.

TYPE Miscellaneous, 5-Harness · PATTERN Waffle Weave

Both the sample and the draw-down of the 5-harness waffle weave show a more complicated weave structure than the 4-harness version. The general outline of the weave remains the same, but there are more threads to the block resulting in a larger square. In threading the draft, repeat it the required number of times, omitting the encircled thread. When treadling, do not use the last thread shown on the draw-down. This thread and shot are used on the draw-down only to balance the design of the weave.

Uses and Materials The same as for the 4-harness waffle weave.

Sample Illustrated (Fig. 464)

WARP	WEFT	REED (dents per inch)	SLEY
Cotton, 8/2	Cotton, 8/2	12	Double

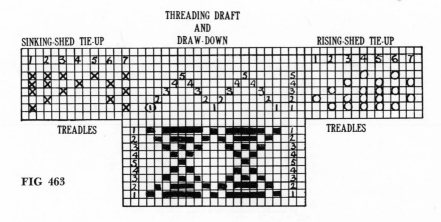

THREADING DRAFT
AND
DRAW-DOWN

SINKING-SHED TIE-UP

RISING-SHED TIE-UP

TREADLES

TREADLES

FIG 463

Problem Plan and weave a set of four pot holders of heavy cotton with the 5-harness waffle weave.

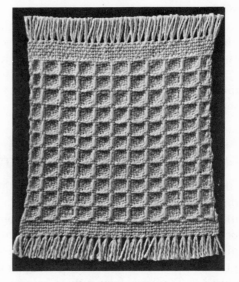

FIG 464

TYPE Miscellaneous, 8-Harness · PATTERN Waffle Weave

The 8-harness version of the waffle weave allows more opportunity for experimentation with materials and colors than is possible with the 4-harness waffle weave. The threading lends itself to the use of heavier threads and weaves very nice drapery.

Note that the threading is an 8-harness point twill. The skips are longer, with 14 warp and 14 weft threads in each block. The choice of materials and sleying should be such that the block will square when threaded and woven according to directions.

The general information covering the choice of material and sleying, as given for the 4-harness waffle weave, applies also to the 8-harness type.

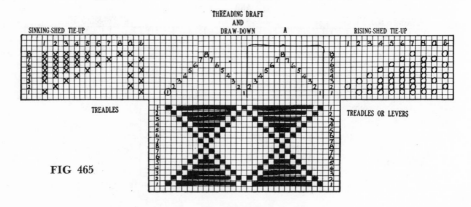

FIG 465

Uses, Suggested Materials, and Sleying As for the 4-harness waffle weave

The bracketed section, *A*, shows one repeat of the draft. In threading, repeat the draft as often as required, omitting the encircled 1 except for the last repeat when it is required to balance the design. Treadle *A* and *B* in alternating succession to weave the plain-weave headings. Repeat the treadling the required number of times to weave the desired length, omitting the treadle-1 row at the bottom except on the last repeat to balance the pattern.

FIG 466

Problem Set up an 8-harness waffle-weave sample using two or more colors and experiment with the crossing of these colors in the weft. Rayons and silks can be combined with fine wools to make suitable material for an evening bag or clutch purse, or use coarser materials for drapes.

TYPE Miscellaneous · PATTERN Warp Face Ripsmatta

Very little has been written in this country about the ripsmatta weave. Those who have worked with it probably know it as "matta" or as a glorified log-cabin weave. *Rip* is the Swedish word for "rep," a weave in which the closely sleyed warp is threaded in such a way that it completely covers the weft, producing a ridged material. *Matta* is the Swedish word for "mat," while *mattor* is the plural form.

The weaving of ripsmatta requires a strong loom and body, for the closely sleyed threads make it difficult to raise or lower the harnesses. The mat must be beaten very hard if it is to be firm. A rising-shed loom is easier to manage for this weave than a counterbalanced loom.

Uses If woven of heavy material, it is suitable for floor rugs; of lightweight materials, for heavy place mats, shopping bags, porch pillows, and runners.

Suitable Materials

WARP	WEFT	PATTERN	REED (*dents per inch*)	SLEY
Cotton, 8/4	Cotton, 8/4	Carpet rags	15	Double
Cotton, 8/4	Cotton, 8/4	Candle wicking	15	Double

Some authorities suggest alternating fine warp with heavy warp, but this does not seem too practical for a mat. Unless separate warp beams are used for the fine and the coarse threads, tension trouble could develop easily both on the loom and in the mat after removal from the loom.

For a pattern or filler on a heavy mat, use coarse, firm carpet rags or three or more strands of candlewick wound together on the shuttle.

Technique   Ripsmatta is a 4-block weave set on four harnesses. It can also be set on eight harnesses.[7] Arrange the pattern blocks on graph paper in an attractive design, keeping in mind that the

A block can be followed by either the *B* or *D* block,
B block can be followed by either the *A* or *C* block,
C block can be followed by either the *B* or *D* block,
D block can be followed by either the *C* or *A* block.

It is characteristic of this weave that two blocks always weave together, but the weaver has the choice of selecting, for the second block, the block either to the right or left of the main block. Some weavers do not bother with a design but thread the loom with blocks of varying width and treadle their pattern on the loom.

In addition to the changes that come from different arrangements of the four blocks, the design can be varied also by reversing the order of the treadling to bring up the opposite color. Experiment with this weave for there are many possibilities for its development. In some respects the weave resembles the log cabin; in others, the crackle; yet, it has definite characteristics of its own.

The threading of the four-pattern blocks is as follows:

BLOCK	HARNESSES		BLOCK	HARNESSES	
A	4 dark	3 light	*C*	3 dark	4 light
B	2 dark	1 light	*D*	1 dark	2 light

Samples Illustrated

1. (Fig. 468)

The sample is threaded as above with 20 threads in each block alternating dark and light throughout. One hundred and twenty threads were wound; 20 for each block.

The arrangement of the blocks is *A, B, C, D, A, B*.

WARP	WEFT	PATTERN
Cotton, 8/4	Cotton, 8/4	Candle wicking

REED *(dents per inch)*	SLEY
15	Double

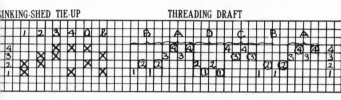

SINKING-SHED TIE-UP   THREADING DRAFT

FIG 467

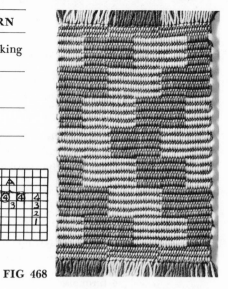

FIG 468

Tie-Up Standard

Length of Warp Twelve place mats will require a 9-yd. warp. Set up 1 yd. for a sample.

Number of Threads Wound 386

Treadling The following treadling brings up the dark blocks. If the light blocks are desired, reverse the treadling.

Sinking Shed		Rising Shed (*No Tie-Up*)
TREADLES		**TREADLES OR LEVERS**
	Block A	
	Block *D* weaves with block *A*.	
2	Candle wicking	1 and 4
4	8/4 cotton warp	2 and 3
	Repeat the desired number of times.	
	Block B	
	Block *A* weaves with Block *B*.	
b	Candle wicking	2 and 4
a	8/4 cotton warp	1 and 3
	Repeat the desired number of times.	
	Block C	
	Block *B* weaves with block *C*.	
4	Candle wicking	2 and 3
2	8/4 cotton warp	1 and 4
	Repeat the desired number of times.	
	Block D	
	Block *C* weaves with block *D*.	
a	Candle wicking	1 and 3
b	8/4 cotton warp	2 and 4
	Repeat the desired number of times.	

2. (Fig. 470)

WARP	WEFT	PATTERN	REED (dents per inch)	SLEY
Cotton, 8/4	Cotton, 8/4	Candle wicking	15	Double

Order of Winding and Threading Warp[8]   The warp for the plain borders is wound in a single color; for the design area it is wound: one thread dark, one thread light for the required number of threads.

COLOR		HARNESSES
BORDER (1½ IN. WIDE) FOR RIGHT SIDE		
46	20 rust (threaded in alternating succession on)	4 and 3
	2 yellow	2 and 1
	4 turquoise	4 and 3
	2 yellow	2 and 1
	10 rust	4 and 3
	2 yellow	2 and 1
	4 turquoise	4 and 3
	2 rust	2 and 1
CENTER — FIRST PART		
102	18 rust and turquoise (threaded in alternating succession on)	4 and 3
	18 rust and turquoise	2 and 1
	18 rust and turquoise	3 and 4
	18 rust and turquoise	1 and 2
	30 rust and turquoise	4 and 3

SINKING-SHED TIE-UP

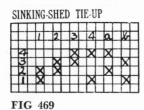

FIG 469

FIG 470

SECOND PART

90	18 rust and turquoise (threaded in alternating succession on)	2 and 1
	18 rust and turquoise	3 and 4
	18 rust and turquoise	1 and 2
	18 rust and turquoise	3 and 4
	18 rust and turquoise	2 and 1

THIRD PART

102	30 rust and turquoise (threaded in alternating succession on)	4 and 3
	18 rust and turquoise	1 and 2
	18 rust and turquoise	3 and 4
	18 rust and turquoise	2 and 1
	18 rust and turquoise	4 and 3

BORDER FOR LEFT SIDE

46	2 rust (threaded in alternating succession on)	2 and 1
	4 turquoise	4 and 3
	2 yellow	2 and 1
	10 rust	4 and 3
	2 yellow	2 and 1
	4 turquoise	4 and 3
	2 yellow	2 and 1
	20 rust	4 and 3

Treadlings

DIRECT TIE-UP		STANDARD TIE-UP	
1 and 4 candle wicking	4×	4	4×
2 and 3 cotton		2	
1 and 3 candle wicking	4×	a	4×
2 and 4 cotton		b	
2 and 3 candle wicking	4×	2	4×
1 and 4 cotton		4	
1 and 3 candle wicking	2×	a	2×
2 and 4 cotton		b	
2 and 3 candle wicking	4×	2	4×
1 and 4 cotton		4	
1 and 3 candle wicking	4×	a	4×
2 and 4 cotton		b	
1 and 4 candle wicking	4×	4	4×
2 and 3 cotton		2	
2 and 4 candle wicking	4×	b	4×
1 and 3 cotton		a	
2 and 3 candle wicking	4×	2	4×
1 and 4 cotton		4	
2 and 4 candle wicking	2×	b	2× — center
1 and 3 cotton		a	
2 and 3 candle wicking	4×	2	4×
1 and 4 cotton		4	
2 and 4 candle wicking	4×	b	4×
1 and 3 cotton		a	

TYPE Miscellaneous · PATTERN Texture

Texture weaves have an uneven or broken surface, and do not follow any specific pattern. A texture is felt as well as seen; it has a third dimension.

There are three ways to weave a textured material: through the use of threadings which are classified as true texture weaves; through the use of two, three, or more threads of different size, twist, and material; and through treadling. The first is the only true texture weave; the second and third are simply a means for obtaining a textured effect.

Textured materials are suitable especially for upholstery fabrics and draperies. Many of the samples for commercially produced, textured materials are designed and woven by hand weavers.

No effort has been made to cover the entire subject of texture weaving in this text. Several books and magazine articles are available to the weaver interested in texture weaving. It is much more interesting for the weaver to choose his own threads for weaving samples than to follow another's directions.

TYPE Miscellaneous · PATTERN Texture, Original Interpretation of an Old Threading

It has been said that a textured material is one without a pattern; however, since it is necessary to repeat certain units to weave the whole, a pattern does appear through the repetition of these units. As stated in the introduction, there are three ways of achieving a texture, or texture effect, in weaving.

The following pattern belongs in the first, or true, group. The threading does not follow any given technique; it is quite irregular as is the treadling.

Uses Textured material, while it has many uses, is used more for upholstery and drapes than for other purposes. Household linens woven in textured effects are attractive. Textured wool scarves frequently are softer and warmer than those woven in other techniques.

Materials The choice of threads for texture weaving is unlimited. Threads that contrast in size, twist, color, and sheen are acceptable. Linens, wools, and synthetic threads blend well together. Textured materials should be firm to withstand hard wear; textured drapery fabrics should be soft.

FIG 471

THREADING DRAFT

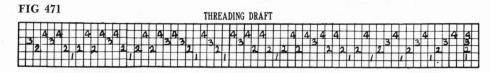

Sample Illustrated (Fig. 472)

WARP	WEFT	REED (*dents per inch*)	SLEY
Cotton, 8/2	Cotton, 8/4	18	Single

Tie-Up Standard

Treadling–Sinking Shed

Treadling–Rising Shed
(*No Tie-Up*)

TREADLE		LEVERS OR TREADLES
4 2	Repeat in alternating succession to weave the desired length.	2 and 3 1 and 4

First Block:

4		2 and 3
1		3 and 4
4		2 and 3
2		1 and 4
4	Repeat the required number of times to weave the desired length.	2 and 3
2		1 and 4
3		1 and 2
2		1 and 4
4		2 and 3
2		1 and 4

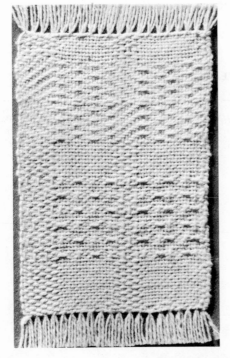

FIG 472

TREADLE		LEVERS OR TREADLES
1 ⎤		⎧ 3 and 4
2 ⎥ Repeat the required number of times to weave the desired		⎨ 1 and 4
3 ⎥ length.		⎩ 1 and 2
4 ⎦		2 and 3

Problem Work out the original threading and weave a place mat, or adapt the above threading for a fine wool scarf.

TYPE Miscellaneous •
PATTERN Texture, Assorted Sizes
Threads in Warp

The combination of fine and coarse threads in the warp produces an attractive textured fabric. It also provides an acceptable way to use up odds and ends of thread. These threads may be of different colors if well blended. A much more subtle effect is obtained if the threads are the same color but of a different texture, or if some are dull and others shiny. There is no limit to which the weaver's imagination can go to create textured fabrics with the aid of some of the recently published books.

Uses The textured weaves are fine for towels and place mats when woven in linen, and for upholstery when woven in wools.

Sample Illustrated

WARP	WEFT	REED (*dents per inch*)	SLEY
Linen, 6 cord	Linen, 40/2	16	Single
Linen, 25/2	Linen, 40/2	16	Double
Linen, 40/2	Linen, 40/2	16	Triple

FIG 473

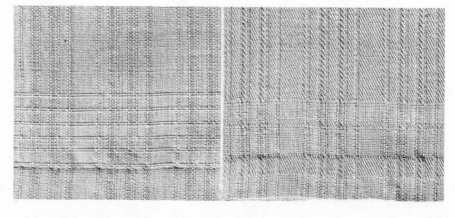

To Wind the Warp

THREADS	SIZE
12	40/2 — for right border
2	6 cord
12	40/2
2	6 cord
4	25/2
2	6 cord
12	40/2
2	6 cord	Repeat the required number of times for the desired width.
4	25/2
2	6 cord
12	40/2
2	6 cord
4	25/2
36	40/2
12	40/2 — for left border

Threading   Thread either on a 2-harness or a 4-harness loom for the plain weave, using a standard tie-up.

Sley carefully. The heavy six-cord thread is single sley, the medium size 25/2 is a double sley, and the fine 40/2 is triple sley in a 15- or 16-dent reed.

Treadling   The treadling for the sample at the left, Figure 473, is a plain weave in the fine linen 40/2, except for the few shots of heavy six-cord linen woven in for the border. The sample (Fig. 473) is woven with the fine linen 40/2, except for the few shots of heavy six-cord linen woven in for the border, in a combination of plain weave and twill weave which produces still another textured result.

Problem   Thread a linen, cotton, or wool sample with three sizes of thread and weave a sample in a plain weave. Experiment with various sizes of threads for the weft.

TYPE Miscellaneous, Grouped Warp and Weft Threads · PATTERN Texture

This arrangement of threads is a simple way of achieving a textured weave. A designated number of threads are threaded in a group of heddles on the same harness instead of being threaded according to a pattern or an alternating succession on two or more harnesses.

Uses   For luncheon sets, towels, upholstery materials when closely sleyed, purses, table covers, and scarves. The sleying and material determine the suitability of the finished fabric for various uses.

Design Use grouped threads in the same or contrasting colors as a border, leaving the center plain, or use grouped threads across the entire web.

Suitable Materials and Sleying

WARP	WEFT	REED (dents per inch)	SLEY
Carpet warp, 8/4	Carpet warp, 8/4	15, 16, or 18	Single
Cotton, Egyptian, 30/3	Cotton, Egyptian, 30/3	18	Double
Yarn, fine	Yarn, fine	15	Double
Yarn, heavy	Yarn, heavy	12	Single
Linen, 40/2	Linen, 40/2	20	Double

Samples Illustrated (Figs. 476, 477, and 478)

WARP	WEFT	REED (dents per inch)	SLEY
Cotton, 8/4	Cotton, 8/4	18	Single

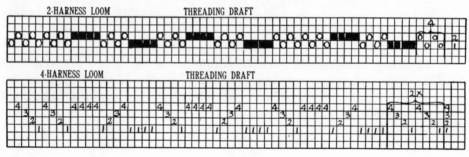

FIG 474

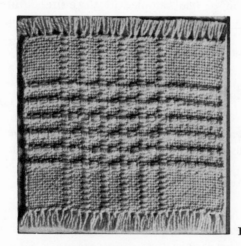

FIG 476

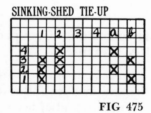

SINKING-SHED TIE-UP

FIG 475

FIG 477

FIG 478

Treadling–Four Harnesses

Sinking Shed		Rising Shed (*No Tie-Up*)
TREADLES		**TREADLES OR LEVERS**
a b	8×, plain-weave background thread	{ 1 and 3 2 and 4
1	pattern thread	4
a b	2×, background thread	{ 1 and 3 2 and 4
2	pattern thread	1
a b	2×, background thread	{ 1 and 3 2 and 4
1	pattern thread	4
a b	2×, background thread	{ 1 and 3 2 and 4
2	pattern thread	1
a b	2×, background thread	{ 1 and 3 2 and 4
1	pattern thread	4
a b	2×, background thread	{ 1 and 3 2 and 4
2	pattern thread	1
a b	8×, background thread	{ 1 and 3 2 and 4

The pattern thread is passed through the open shed four times. The shuttle is passed around the selvedge threads and care must be taken not to draw these too tight or the selvedge will pull in. The four threads should lie flat in the shed.

Problem Plan and weave a place mat of linen or cotton, 12 by 18 in., using grouped threads for accent.

TYPE Miscellaneous · PATTERN Texture on Twill

The upholstery fabric illustrated below was designed for a piece of maple furniture. The color choice was inspired by a trip to the ocean. Blues and greens for the sea, light green and white for the edge of the breaking surf, the gold metallic for flecks of sunshine, and the cinnamon chenille for the kelp and seaweed thrown on the sand by the tide (Fig. 479).

This sample was designed and woven by an interested, imaginative weaver. It is given as a suggestion rather than as a piece to be copied.

There are many articles that can be woven for the home or personal use. The weaver should be on the alert for new designs and unusual materials.

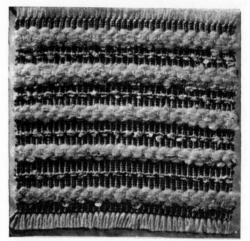

FIG 479

Sample Illustrated (Fig. 479)

WARP	PATTERN WEFT	REED *(dents per inch)*	SLEY
No. 114 Lily Mills, 5/2; turquoise, 476 and 1455	No. 114 Lily Mills, 5/2; turquoise, 476	16	Single
Cotton, 8/4, light birch and green	Lurex, gold Cotton, 8/4, birch green Bouclé, gold and white Chenille, cinnamon		

Threading Twill, threading perle and cotton at random. Do not thread in stripes.

Tie-Up Direct

It is simpler to weave this particular piece on a rising-shed loom with a direct tie-up than on a counterbalanced loom. This piece actually was woven upside down on a counterbalanced loom.

Treadling

1. Treadle plain weave, 8/4 cotton, starting with 2 and 4, then a tabby in turquoise, gold Lurex, turquoise, gold Lurex, and turquoise. Repeat.

2. Four rows chenille: treadles 1, 2, 3, and 4.

3. Repeat 1.

4. Three rows: treadle 3, gold and white; treadle 1, green cotton; treadle 4, gold and white.

5. Repeat 1.

6.

ROWS	MATERIAL	COLOR	TREADLES
3	chenille		1, 3, 1
1	bouclé	gold and white	4
1	cotton	green	2
3	chenille		1, 3, 1
1	bouclé	gold and white	4
1	Lurex	gold	2
3	chenille		1, 3, 1
1	cotton	green	2
3	chenille		1, 3, 1

Beating Very hard, to obtain a firm fabric

Problem Set up a sample on a mixed warp and work out an original upholstery idea using odds and ends of thread for the weft.

TYPE Miscellaneous · PATTERN Texture on Overshot

Treadling Try linen on treadles 1, 2, 3, 4; rayon on treadles *a* and *b;* and wool on treadles 1 and 2; all woven at random.

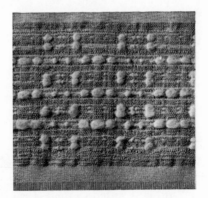

FIG 480

Problem Experiment with odds and ends of threads on the end of an overshot, summer-and-winter, or crackle warp, for drapery or upholstery material.

chapter 12

Tartan Weaves

GENTLEMEN—THE TARTAN!

"Here's to it;
   The fighting sheen of it;
   The yellow, the green of it;
   The white, the blue of it;
   The dark, the red of it:
   Every thread of it;
   The fair have sighed for it;
   The brave have died for it;
   Foemen sought for it;
   Honour the name of it;
   Drink to the fame of it —
The Tartan!"

The history of the tartans is long and involved. Throughout the centuries there has been much controversy over correct sett and coloring, but during the past decade an effort has been made to collect, standardize, and register all available information.

Among those whose work has been outstanding is Donald Calder Stewart, whose book[1] is accepted among hand weavers as being the most authentic and best suited to their purpose. There are other valuable books[2] which base their information on the *Vestiarium Scoticum,* published in 1842 by the Sobieski-Stuart brothers who claimed to be the grandsons of Prince Charlie and to have obtained their information from early sixteenth-century manuscripts. These manuscripts were never produced, yet, lacking better evidence, the Sobieski-Stuart work generally is looked upon as an authority.

The word "tartan," which is not Gaelic, slowly is being replaced by the word "breacan." The histories of the Scottish clans disclose that the bright cloth originally may have come into Scotland with the Roman conquerors. Records that have been found and accepted as authentic prove that tartans were in general use as early as the eleventh century.

In 1747, following the unsuccessful attempt of Bonnie Prince Charlie to regain the Scottish throne, tartans were barred and the clan system, as it originally functioned, was dissolved. It was not until 1782 that the antitartan law was repealed and tartans were again permitted, although there was no return to the clan system as it originally existed. It was during the period between 1747 and 1782 that many thousand Scotsmen left Scotland and emigrated to North America and Australia. It is to these early settlers that many Scottish Canadians and Scottish Americans trace their ancestry.

History records that district tartans were the forerunners of the clan tartan. In the early days, it was possible to recognize the district from which travelers came by their tartans.

District tartans are still worn, particularly by those who cannot lay claim to a clan tartan. Among the newest tartans to be acknowledged and registered by Sir Thomas Innes of Learney, Lord Lyon, King of Arms of Scotland, is the Nova Scotia tartan designed and put into general use in that province in 1954, and the new green and saffron tartan of Eire.

It is generally agreed by historians that most of the clans originally had four tartans: the chief's tartan, which was worn only by the chief and his immediate family, the clan tartan for use of all members of the clan and its sept men, the dress tartan of lighter colors for formal wear, and the subdued hunting tartan which blended into the heather and other vegetation of the moors and fens. Some clans have retained the four tartans while others have only one which is used for all occasions.

The royal family have their own tartans which under no circumstances should be worn by anyone outside the immediate family group. The newest royal tartan is one designed for Princess Margaret Rose. Queen Victoria's consort, Prince Albert, designed a tartan called the "Balmoral" which Queen Victoria used extensively in the royal household at Balmoral and as gifts for her friends.

Regimental tartans, as the name indicates, were designed for the exclusive use of various regiments. Over the years, however, the 42nd Black Watch tartan has been adapted for general use. The very beautiful azure and maroon tartan of the Royal Canadian Air Force, designed during World War II, is listed as a regimental tartan.

The two tartans used to denote occupation are the shepherd's check and the Clergy. There are many versions of the shepherd's check, which was probably chosen because it is not necessary to dye the wool, since the tartan or check is usually sett six threads of white, six threads of black homespun wool to the square. Some tartan books show the Clergy tartan in black, navy, and azure, others with navy, green, and black, but Donald C. Stewart states that, "The colors are often ill-reproduced, but should be black, gray and white."[3]

The tartan originally was wrapped about the body and belted in at the waist; the upper part was then thrown over the left shoulder, and fastened in place with a broach set with native stone called the Cairngorm. The portion thrown over the shoulder served as added protection against the cold mountain winds. The old Scottish song, "Come under my plaidie and sit down beside me," implies that there was room under the plaidie for more than the wearer! At first the tartan hung in loose folds, but later was pressed into pleats or kilts, and the excess piece cut off. This was fringed, thrown over the left shoulder and fastened with the Cairngorm.

The Cairngorm, or Scotch pebble, is an agatelike stone found in the Cairngorm mountains of Scotland. It is used in much of the silver jewelry worn with the Scottish national dress, vying in popularity with the amethyst and the topaz.

The word "plaid" has been used loosely when speaking of tartans. Actually it applies to the length of material thrown over the shoulder rather than to the sett.

The design of a plaid material can be any arrangement of threads and colors that pleases the weaver, woven across to form squares with the same arrangement of the threads as sett in the warp.

We usually think of tartans in relationship to kilts. According to correct tartan usage, kilts are worn only by men. However, the pleated skirt is properly worn by women, although the pleats should be laid in each square in its proper order, with the pattern of the tartan showing on the surface. This type of pleating also is correct for men's civilian dress. The pleating of the military kilt is notably distinctive. To attain the proper swing, the kilt pleats must be deep. It requires real craftsmanship to "shake a kilt." From 7 to 15 yd. of material may be required and the pleats must be planned very accurately so that the single, solid stripe of the tartan, no matter what its color, lies exactly at the edge or just inside the edge of each pleat. In addition to correct pleating, the kilt must fit the wearer with precision.

The edge of the pleat is basted according to the chosen design, whether it be the dark and light flat pleating of the Clergy kilt (Fig. 488), the pattern pleating of the MacPherson hunting skirt (Fig. 487), or the military pleating of the MacPherson military kilt (Fig. 490). Two other types of pleating are the knife and box.

The edge of the pleat must run straight with the warp, following the design of the sett. The pleats are laid in according to the hip measurement. The basted edge of the pleat is then slanted to fit from the hip line to the waist. This requires skill since, theoretically, the outside edge of the pleat should not deviate from a straight line. However, it is sometimes necessary to turn in the pleat slightly to fit the kilt to the body. Kilts for men are not much of a problem in this regard, but it is sometimes difficult to achieve the correct pleating when the waist measurement of a skirt is considerably smaller than that of the hip.

All pleats in a military kilt run straight from top to bottom with the exception of the two front ones, which flare a bit at the bottom and are fitted in at the top to conform to the figure. The edge of each pleat is hand-sewn for a distance of 6 or 8 in. down from the waist, depending on the height of the wearer. Kilts open on the right side. A plain piece of the tartan lies across the front of the figure. The pleats start just to the front of the right hipbone and continue around the body ending in front of the left hipbone, where the pleat is flared. An unpleated piece of the material, with the principal block of the tartan exactly centered, continues across the front and ends at the right where it is finished with three rows of narrow fringe. The kilt is fastened with two straps and buckles, one at the waistline, the other about 6 in. below. A jeweled pin, miniature dirk, or sterling-silver safety pin fastens the lower right edge of the kilt about 8 in. above the kilt bottom.

The inside tops of all the pleats, with the exception of the first and last, are cut away to lighten the kilt and remove the bulk from around the waist. Canvas is sewn in to hold the pleats in place, and the kilt, which is heavy, close to the hips. The top of the kilt is bound with a piece of the tartan cut on the straight of the material so it will not stretch.

Unless it is correctly made, a kilt will not swing properly. The bottom of the kilt should just touch the floor when the wearer kneels. Like all other full dress or service uniforms, the Highland costume must be correct in every detail. There is no costume today that carries more heraldry than the Scottish.

Two types of headdress are worn with the Highland costume. They are the tam or Balmoral, frequently referred to as the "bonnet"—"The bonnets of bonny Dundee," for example—and the small wedge-shaped cap called the Glengarry. The bonnet should display the personal crest, in silver, if the wearer possesses one. The crest of the chief of the clan, within a strap and buckle, may be worn by members of the clan. Under no circumstances should an ordinary clansman wear the crest without the strap and buckle which indicates that the wearer is merely displaying his chief's crest. The evergreen plant, or badge, should be worn on the bonnet behind the crest. Different accoutrements, such as the dirk, broadsword, sgian-dubh, sporan, special buttons, Cairngorms, and buckles each have their designated place on the various costumes. As Scottish women do not wear the kilt, neither is it correct for them to wear the sporan or purse.

For evening wear, Scottish women wear a silk tartan sash over the left shoulder, one end brought across the chest, the other across the back with the two ends fastened at the waist just above the right hip. Another less popular method is to drape the sash over the left shoulder. One end is left hanging at the front, the other is taken around the body, under the right arm, across the chest and fastened with a Cairngorm on the left shoulder. New directions have been received from Sir Thomas Innes of Learney, Lord Lyon, King of Arms of Scotland, regarding the wearing of the sash. These directions read as follows: "This stole (Arisaid) or wider form of Tartan sash, to be worn down the back only—as approved by the Lord Lyon King of Arms." This stole is an authentic version of the tartan sash fastened on either side of the waist at the back, about 4 in. from the fringed end, then looped up onto the right shoulder and fastened by the usual brooch to hang loose down the back to about hip level. Worn over light-colored evening dresses, these sashes add a decidedly gay note to Highland parties.

Although many Lowland Scottish families have adopted a recognized tartan, they do not use the kilt as freely as it is used in the Highlands. They more often use the tartan trews which are standard wear for Lowland regiments.

TARTAN COLORS

The colors most generally used in tartans are red, azure and dark blue, light and dark green, yellow, black, and white. Crimson is found in a few tartans such as the Menzies; the Lindsays use wine. Light or medium gray is displayed in the Anderson, Douglas, MacPherson Hunting, and Clergy tartans. A bit of mauve or purple is included in the MacFarlane, the Hay, the MacRae, the MacDougal, and several others.

The combination of the colors in some tartans is such that at a distance they blend into lovely greens, grays, or blues. This is particularly true of the R.C.A.F., the Anderson, and the Nova Scotia tartans.

It was during the revival and great popularity of tartans in the early Victorian era that the vivid colorings came into use. This probably was due to an attempt on the part of members of one clan to outdo the members of another at gay social and military events.

Until the advent of commercial dyes, all tartans were dyed with vegetable dyes which were indigenous to the locality. This accounts for the great variation in coloring. Even today with commercial dyeworks accessible to dye any quantity of yarn a given color, there is still considerable color variation in the commercial product. Many prefer their tartans in the ancient or vegetable-dyed colors which are perhaps more pleasing than many of the sometimes garish, modern commercial colorings. It is difficult to obtain vegetable-dyed wools for tartans. The closest substitute is the commercially reproduced vegetable-dyed wools available in Scotland.

Literature about tartans reveals many long lists of dye plants. For example, the gorse bark provides the shade of green which we associate with tartans and call the tartan green. Red dye is obtained from the red-tipped rock lichens, the yellow from heather, the blue from the blaeberries which are similar to our blueberries. Those who have used blueberries for dyeing will recall that the dye is a purplish, rather than a clear, blue. Alder bark can be relied upon to give a good black, while crotols and other plants produce good browns.

It seems strange that, in Scotland, with so many accessible dye plants that supply beautiful browns and tans, brown is seldom if ever found in the tartans. Students of tartan lore state that old tartans, which appear to have been woven with brown, show, upon examination, that they actually have been woven with black that has since faded.

There are so few really authentic, ancient tartans available for study that it is not possible to state with authority which shades are correct. Since the original tartans were dyed with vegetable dyes, there naturally would be considerable variation in the colors. Anyone who has struggled with vegetable dyes well knows the difficulties encountered with seasonal changes in the dye properties and the almost utter impossibility of matching a natural dye.

As there is no authentic chart to follow, tartan weavers often are at a loss to know which shades of the various colors should be used. The best advice that can be given is for weavers to obtain swatches from one of the better Scottish houses or manufacturers and follow these. As these swatches are expensive, it is wise to confine the request to one or two setts. Many Scottish export houses are endeavouring to interest customers in the ancient colorings rather than in those known as the standard tartan green and red.

Stewart[4] states: "How few colors are actually employed in a tartan is not always realized. Each color appears not only in its pure or solid form, but also in an equal blend with each other color. Thus, where only three are used, six tints result; where four are used, ten." He then gives the formula by which the resultant number is expressed.

THE TARTAN SETT

Outside of Scotland very few commercial firms are careful about the sett of tartans which explains the great variety on sale in our stores.

To be correct, tartans must be woven on a twill threading, the sett—which is the number and order of the colors—must follow closely that considered correct by the clan, and there must be the same number of threads per inch in both the warp and the weft. It is a 50/50 twill fabric. The sett should be adjusted to fit the object being woven. Obviously, more threads in a fine sleying are required for tie material than would be necessary for a car rug of heavy yarn set in a coarse reed. All units must contain an even, never an uneven, number of threads.

In Logan's *Description of Clan Tartans*[5] he states: "a web of tartan is 2 ft. 2 in. wide, at least within half an inch, more or less, so that the size of the patterns makes no difference in the scale. Commencing at the edge of the cloth, the depth of the colors is stated throughout a square, on which the scale must be reversed or gone through again to the commencement." He adds that "all clan tartans ought to have the colors so proportioned that they can be made up in the form of a kilt or belted plaid; that is, the stripes should be so arranged that in box plaiting, the distinguishing bars should appear without any overlaying, which prevents the free play of the feile-beg, and destroys the pleasing effect of loose drapery."

Logan's formulas are involved; they have been somewhat simplified by Adam and Innes. But it is the setts devised by Donald C. Stewart that are being used here because they are logical and have been tried and corrected. Stewart claims that the Logan formulas have many mistakes.

Stewart's setts have been adopted, according to his ruling, to various materials and for various purposes as noted in the following pages.

The large blocks of twelve or more threads are either enlarged or reduced for various thread settings. How this is done will be illustrated in the woven samples, each of which is accompanied by notes.

The motif of a tartan sett is the arrangement of groups of threads in a certain, prescribed order. Colors vary with different tartans but the original, basic number and order of threads remains unchanged.

For teaching purposes, it has been found advisable to break the setts into blocks. It is much less confusing and also follows the block system used with other techniques. For some reason this method has not been commonly practiced among tartan weavers but perhaps it will be used more generally in the future.

Practically all setts can be broken into two blocks, one showing a large area of a single color banded on both sides by a second color; the second showing more colors, fine lines, and squares.

Stewart's threading method is to follow the colors to the center bar, then reverse the order threading back to the start. The use of the *A* and *B* block system aids in designing the tartan article.

Thought must be given to the arrangement of the blocks. In studying tartans, it will be found that almost invariably the first and last blocks on the sides of the material are half-size blocks of the key color. This is done so that two pieces can be sewn together without any interruption of the design. If the weaver wishes to weave and join two pieces together, each piece must be woven with a perfect selvedge and the design units must be exactly the same size.

Apparently the early setts were not recorded, but were left to the memory of the capable men and women who dyed, spun, wove the material, and tailored the kilts. If any records were kept they undoubtedly were destroyed when, after the uprising, the clan and tartan systems were outlawed. In one sett, used in those Highland cottages where tartans are still hand woven, the different colors are wound around a flat stick in the order in which they appear both in the warp and the weft. During the weaving the stick is laid on the web and measurements are taken frequently to make sure the squares and lines are all in their correct order.

MATERIALS

As practically all hand-woven tartans are of wool, the rules which govern wool weaving should be observed. Materials should be soft enough to drape well yet should not be sleazy. Though tartans generally are associated with wearing apparel and are woven of wool, this does not rule out the use of other materials such as linen, cotton, silk, and some of the newer synthetic fabrics. Regardless of the material used, remember that the same threads are used for both the warp and the weft and are set to produce a 50/50 twill fabric.

WINDING TARTAN WARPS

Tartan warps, especially if there are many color changes, are tedious to wind.

If a warping reel is used, it is necessary to break the thread and tie on the new color at each color change. With some setts this will occur every other thread or every fourth thread while with others there are larger areas with less frequent color changes.

While warping on a peg warping board (Fig. 21) is somewhat slower than on a reel, it is sometimes quicker for tartan warps because the thread need not be broken at the color changes but can be left hanging down from the board ready to be picked up when needed. However, it is suggested that the cross, or shed, be placed at the opposite end of the warping board from which the threads are started and that the warp be chained from the end opposite the cross. This will facilitate warping the beam (page 34) as some of the threads may be carried quite a distance from block to block and so would not lie in correct order along the warp-beam rod.

Threading   The threading for tartans is the 1, 2, 3, 4 twill and the treadling can be either the standard or direct tie-up using the standard twill treadling:

Treadle 1 or 1 and 2 ⎫
Treadle 2 or 2 and 3 ⎪
Treadle 3 or 3 and 4 ⎬ Repeat as often as necessary.
Treadle 4 or 4 and 1 ⎭

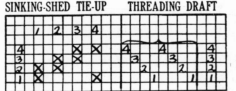

SINKING-SHED TIE-UP   THREADING DRAFT

FIG 481

Sleying It cannot be stated that a particular sleying is correct for tartans because there is such a great variation in wools as well as in the uses for which the materials are intended.

As with all woolen materials, it is better to double sley in a coarse reed than single sley in a fine reed. There is much less wear on the threads. For some materials sleying at three per dent is used. This is not always advisable since sometimes the line caused by the reed will not wash out. While this is not objectionable in some types of weaving, it cannot be accepted in tartan weaving.

One variant in tartan weaving is in the width of the stripes of color at the reed and in the web. Variation was found in all samples woven from the width of one or two threads in the finer materials to one eighth of an inch in the blanket sample. If the square must be a definite size when woven, allow for this variation in the sleying.

Tension It is important to keep the same tension on the warp at all times. Do not roll the warp forward in the center of a large square; wait until the square is finished or roll the warp forward before starting.

SELVEDGES

Each color should have its own shuttle. Learn to place them, in the order in which they are to be used, on the web within easy reach. If the correct number of threads have been woven into each square, the change of shuttles should occur on the same side each time. If not, check for a mistake either in treadling or counting.

When weaving material in which the selvedges will be hidden, it is permissible to carry the weft thread along the selvedge to the next block. This leaves skips of yarn along one selvedge. Do not do this over large blocks since the loose threads catch in pressing and handling.

Weave the selvedges as perfectly as possible, even though they are to be covered up in seams.

In making up skirts and kilts, use the material so that one selvedge is at the bottom and the other at the top. As the bottom of a kilt is never hemmed, one of the selvedges must be perfect. Plan the best selvedge for the bottom. Women's pleated skirts are hemmed, however, for the material is lighter in weight than kilt material and the pleats more widely spaced.

The selvedges on scarves, stoles, and other articles must be perfect. The weft thread must either be cut and turned in when the block is finished and another color picked up, or carried along the edge with the new color. If the latter method is used, the shuttle carrying the thread for the new block must turn around the old thread each time before it enters the shed. This demands care and slows up the weaving, but once the weaver becomes accustomed to doing it little time is lost. If the squares are large, it is better to cut the thread and insert the end in the shed in the customary manner (Fig. 44).

BEATING

The same number of threads in the warp and the weft plus a 45-deg. angle in the weaving should produce perfect squares in tartan webs. If not, the beating and sleying should be carefully checked and adjustments made.

Unless the beating is kept uniform throughout, the 45-deg. diagonal will be wavy instead of clear-cut and straight. Do not beat loosely and then crowd in a number of weft threads to square the pattern by beating the threads back tightly. In Fig. 482, *A* shows correct beating: 45-deg. angle; *B*, uneven beating; *C* beating too hard: angle less than 45 deg.

FIG 482

To acquire agility in weaving tartans, develop rhythm as quickly as possible. This assures ease in weaving, accuracy, and quantity. Once a good rhythm has been established, weave for as long a time as possible without stopping, for it is difficult to re-establish the rhythm once it has been broken. Tartan weavers are born, not made.

Not every weaver can make a success of tartan weaving, but those who have a natural flair for it can weave as many as 5 yds. in an eight-hour day. These weavers are steady, have good eyesight, and the ability to judge size, shape, and diagonal without the necessity of constant measuring. They are not bothered by what goes on around them, they can keep accurate count of the weft shots, do not know the meaning of nervous tension, and are perfectly happy day after day with the repetitive weaving of tartan webs. Rarely do they make a mistake.

MEASURING

Theoretically, all weaving should be measured with the tension released, but with tartan weaving this is not practical since it disturbs the tension too much and interferes with the rhythm of the weaver.

It sometimes happens that, upon removal of the material from the loom, steam pressing, and/or washing, the squares are not quite square and the angle not quite 45 deg. The answer to this is experimentation. Samples should be woven, accurate measurements kept, and results carefully noted and recorded, before starting a long web.

With some materials it may be necessary to weave the square a bit higher than wide with a resultant angle of 46 to 47 deg. to offset the shrinkage.

An example of this is found in the blanket sample (Fig. 484). The squares are not quite square, due to shrinkage, but the samples and data will serve to guide students or production weavers when setting up a heavy wool blanket, car rug, or knee rug.

FINISHING

Linen tartans should be washed well and ironed. The more they are laundered the nicer they become.

Woolen materials, such as suitings, knee rugs, and kilt material, should not be washed as washing removes much of the "body" from the material. Steam pressing and, later, professional cleaning should be used.

Blankets, throws, stoles, scarves, and baby blankets should be washed carefully with a mild detergent, allowed to dry, and then steam pressed to render them soft and fluffy. Do not wash wool in a washing machine; it mats the wool.

Articles woven of synthetic threads must be finished according to the directions furnished by the manufacturer.

COST AND SELLING

Materials for tartan weaving are comparable in cost to materials used for other types of weaving.

It is frequently necessary, however, to purchase a whole pound of wool or tube of linen to get only a few threads of a color called for in the sett. This increases the cost considerably and, unless the weaver plans to weave on a production basis, tartan weaving is not too practical. It is sometimes possible to exchange threads with another weaver. Remember that all the threads must be the same size if a true tartan is to result.

CLAN MACPHERSON

The tartans of the Clan MacPherson have been chosen to illustrate tartan weaving as the author is a sept man of this clan. It would be difficult to compile a complete list of all the clans and their various tartans so the weaves given here will serve as examples on which to base other clan tartan weaves.

Clan Chattan, the clan of the cats whose motto is "Touch not the cat bot (without) a glove," is one of the oldest and, at one time, was one of the strongest clans. It also has one of the stormiest histories of all the clans. In the middle of the twelfth century the clan members came to a tacit agreement and accepted MacPherson "son of the parson" as their chief. For years constant warfare waged between the MacPhersons, whose stronghold was at Badenoch, and the Murrays, the Grants, the Camerons, the MacIntoshes, and several other lesser clans and septs living along the surrounding border.

Like many other Highland clans, the MacPherson history is full of

FIG. 483. Cluny MacPherson

romance as well as strife, and a reference to the clan is made in Sir Walter Scott's novels and poems.

Cluny MacPherson was one of the most famous of the clan and it is from him that we have the well-known Cluny, or black and white dress, tartan.

The MacPhersons took an active part in the uprising of 1745. It was Ewen Cluny MacPherson who guided Prince Charlie to a safe hiding place and sheltered him until his escape to France. Cluny was known to be an ardent Jacobite and because of this affiliation his estates were confiscated and burned, his family scattered, leaving him destitute. Although he was entrusted with the care and distribution of the funds for the furtherance of the Jacobite cause, he lived in poverty, as his strict Scottish sense of honesty prevented him from using these funds for personal use.

In the novel *Kidnapped,* Robert Louis Stevenson devotes a whole chapter to Cluny, describing him as follows: "When we came to the door [of Cluny's Cage] he was seated by his rock chimney, watching a gillie about some cookery. He was mighty plainly habited, with a knitted nightcap drawn over his ears, and smoked a foul cutty pipe. For all that, he had the manners of a king and it was quite a sight to see him rise out of his place to welcome us."

In his description of the "Cluny's Cage," in which he was confined by illness for a time, David Balfour, the hero of *Kidnapped,* states: ". . . and the plaids upon the wall dwindled down and swelled out again, like fire-light shadows on the roof."

For many years Cluny lived a hunted fugitive from justice, moving about from place to place. Stevenson speaks of this when describing the "Cage." "This was but one of Cluny's hiding places; he had caves besides, and underground chambers in several parts of his country; and, following the reports of his scouts, he moved from one to another as the soldiers drew near or moved away. By this manner of living, and thanks to the affection of his Clan, he had not only stayed all this time in safety while so many others had fled or been taken and slain, but stayed four or five years longer and only went to France at last by the express command of his master. There he soon died and it is strange to reflect that he may have regretted his cage upon Ben Alder."

In 1784 the estates were restored to his son Duncan, whose descendants distinguished themselves with the Black Watch Regiment at Tel-el-Kebir.

Many years later, after the death of the twenty-third chief, Albert Cameron, Laird of Cluny MacPherson, the estates passed to a judicial factor and the arms and chieftainship were granted, by the Lord Lyon of the Court of the Lord Lyon, to Albert's nephew, Ewen George MacPherson of Cluny MacPherson.

While there does not exist a country stronghold or chief's residence in Scotland, relics of the clan, particularly the famous Green Banner, the Great Standard of the Chiefs under which the clansmen never knew defeat, are housed in the Clan Museum at Newtonmore in Inverness.

TYPE Tartan · SETT MacPherson, Cluny, Blanket Sample

There are few types of blankets, car rugs, or couch throws that are warmer or give better wear than a handwoven one of homespun yarn. The very nature of homespun wool, which is full of life and still contains some of the natural oil, offers greater warmth and protection from the elements than the most expensive of commercial blankets.

There is no economy, however, in purchasing a handwoven blanket, as the time element is such that it makes the selling price extravagant. But, as yarn is relatively inexpensive, it is both economical and enjoyable to weave a blanket for personal use. If a fluffy blanket is preferred, send it to a commercial woolen mill for "teasing."

Handwoven blankets are ideal for boys' rooms, hunting trips, camping, and other rough wear. Car robes and couch throws, too, are warm and serviceable.

Sample Illustrated (Fig. 484)

Materials

WARP	WEFT	REED (dents per inch)	SLEY
Homespun wool, 2-ply	Homespun wool, 2-ply	10	Single

Some weavers prefer to weave with homespun yarn which still retains the oil and then thoroughly wash the finished article. This procedure has advantages as well as disadvantages. Much of the homespun yarn available

FIG 484

today is very dirty and poorly dyed. There is a danger of excess dye running into the light-colored blocks, thereby completely ruining the finished article. Generally, it is advisable to wash the skeins first in a mild detergent and lukewarm water. If possible, hang the skeins in the shade outdoors to dry. Do not subject wet wool to freezing temperatures.

The wool used for the sample was washed first. A great deal of dirt and dye came out of both the red and black wool, requiring two washings in mild detergent and several rinsings. The wool, when dry, was light and fluffy and pleasant to work with. The yellow was home-dyed with onion skins. Homespun wool is strong, so even though the oil had been washed out there were no broken threads or difficulties with the shed. There was little or no shrinkage in length. If the yarn is washed first, the article is ready for use when taken from the loom. Dry cleaning does not remove the oil.

Number of Threads Wound for Sample   175

Length of Warp Chain   1 yd. plus loom waste (page 14)

Sett

BLOCK A	BLOCK B
30 white	20 black
*2 red	6 white
6 white — center	*8 black
Repeat from * back to beginning.	2 yellow —center
	Repeat from * back to beginning.

Because of the coarseness of the yarn and the sleying, the Cluny sett was reduced to half. As an uneven number of threads is never used in a tartan block, the units of 18 black threads were reduced to 8 threads each. This rearrangement of the sett produces units in keeping with the overall size of knee robes, car rugs, and blankets.

For the sample, the *A* block was threaded at the left, followed by the *B* block, and ending with one half the *A* block on the right. The weaver is at liberty to arrange the blocks in the order which seems most pleasing, beginning and ending with either one, but there *never* should be a change in the color arrangement of the threads within the blocks.

Threading Draft   Twill 1, 2, 3, 4 (page 160)

Tie-Up   12, 23, 34, 41 (page 42)

Treadling   Treadles 1, 2, 3, 4 repeated as often as necessary. If a tie-up is not used, treadles 12, 23, 34, 41 are repeated as often as necessary.

Beating   The beating should not be too hard and should produce a 50/50 fabric with a 45-deg. angle.

The arrangement of the blocks for a knee rug approximately 40 by 60 in. would be ½ block *A*, blocks *B, A, B, A, B*, and ½ block *A* to balance. This weaves a throw approximately 42 in. wide. The warp to be wound should be 2 yd. long plus loom waste. The warp ends are knotted into a fringe.

If a full-size blanket is desired, use the same arrangement as for the knee rug but wind a warp twice the length of the finished blanket, plus loom waste and allowance for shrinkage. The blanket will have to be joined down the center, requiring great care in weaving the blocks so they will match properly. Never join two pieces of tartan together on a single- or even a double-colored thread. To avoid this, when setting up the loom, thread the left selvedge to end with the 30 white, 2 red, 6 white. The first half of the blanket, plus the fringe or hem, should be woven as-drawn-in. Make sure the measurements of this half of the blanket are correct. If in any doubt, unroll the finished piece from the cloth beam and measure it. (However, never unroll the cloth unless absolutely necessary.) If perfectly satisfied that the length is correct, roll the cloth back on the cloth beam. Before starting to weave the second half of the blanket, cut away the outside six white threads at the left selvedge. When the two halves of the blanket are sewn together along this selvedge, six white threads appear together down the center white line of the *A* block with two red threads on either side. Careful weaving is necessary or the selvedge will draw in and this stripe will be narrower than the other *A*-block 6-thread stripe. If carefully woven and sewn, this seam will be inconspicuous. If a heavier blanket is preferred, sley 12 threads per inch instead of 10. Steam pressing will soften the blanket.

Problem Set up a short warp in tartan, arranged for weaving two lengths to be sewn together to make a single piece, such as a small blanket.

TYPE Tartan ·
SETT MacPherson, Hunting, Homespun Wool Sample

The MacPherson Hunting Tartan (Fig. 485) was designed to resemble, as closely as possible, the rough homespun vegetable-dyed material woven centuries ago by the men and women of the Scottish Highlands from wool from their own sheep.

The colors were obtained from natural dyes. Black from alder bark; red from mosses and lichens; blue from indigo; yellows and greens from many roots, barks, and plants. Grays were a mixture of the wool from black and white sheep. Equal quantities of black and white produced an Oxford gray; lighter and darker grays were the results from varying the proportions. White birch, chokecherry, and other native dyes also produce grays. In this country we do not have the mosses from which the Scottish people extracted their bright red, so we must depend on madder or cochineal. The cochineal is preferable as the madder red has a slightly bluish tint.

Uses Material of this weight is suitable for men's and women's sports jackets and coats, and children's coats and snowsuits. It is warm, sheds snow, rain, and mist, and withstands rough wear.

Material

WARP	WEFT	REED (*dents per inch*)	SLEY
Homespun, single-ply	Homespun, single-ply	9	Double

Number of Threads and Length of Warp Chain Depending upon the use of the material, homespun webs usually are set 36 in. wide. When woven, washed, and steam pressed, the webs usually narrow to about 30 in. wide which is a suitable width for garments.

Sample Illustrated (Fig. 485)

BLOCK A	BLOCK B
16 gray *2 red 2 blue — center Repeat from * back to beginning.	2 red 2 blue 2 red 16 black *2 red 2 blue — center Repeat from * back to beginning.

The order of the blocks in Figure 485 is *B, A, B*.

Threading Twill 1, 2, 3, 4 (page 160)

Tie-Up 12, 23, 34, 41 (page 42)

Treadling Treadles 1, 2, 3, and 4 are repeated as often as necessary. If a tie-up is not used, treadle 12, 23, 34, 41 together, repeating throughout. The blocks are treadled as-drawn-in and, as with all tartan weaving, each block is squared up with the same number of threads in the weft as in the warp, with a 45-deg. angle.

As this is a homespun weave, refer to the section covering this type of weave if the technique is not familiar (Sheep's Wool page 615).

Problem Arrange the threading for a purse or bag, and weave the article. These purses are attractive with a tweed suit or coat.

FIG 485

FIG 486

TYPE Tartan · SETT MacPherson, Cluny, Scarf

The dress tartan of the MacPherson clan is one of the most attractive and popular of the tartans, especially where a light-colored tartan is desired for dressy wear (Fig. 486). Although not suitable for general or rough wear, it is appropriate for women's skirts, vests, scarves, men's ties, and formal dress kilts.

Sample Illustrated (Fig. 486)

Materials Suggested

WARP	WEFT
1. *For light scarf* — Wool, 2/32	1. Wool, 2/32
2. *For heavy scarf* — Wool, 2/16	2. Wool, 2/16
3. *Tie material* — Wool, 2/32	3. Wool, 2/32

REED	SLEY
(*dents per inch*)	
1. 16	Double
2. 12	Double
3. 15	Double

Length of Warp   The actual length necessary to balance the pattern and add a fringe at each end of the scarf is 48 in. Allow additional wool for loom waste and take-up. If this is the first tartan piece to be woven and the weaver is a beginner, obtain enough yarn to first weave a generous sample and practice the beat. A size 12 by 54 in. is popular for men's scarves.

Number of Threads in Warp   330 wound as follows:

A Block		B Block		A Block	
30 white ⎫ 2 red ⎪ 6 white ⎬ Right side 2 red ⎪ of scarf 60 white ⎭		40 black ⎫ 6 white ⎪ 18 black ⎪ 2 yellow ⎬ Center 18 black ⎪ 6 white ⎪ 40 black ⎭		60 white ⎫ 2 red ⎪ 6 white ⎬ Left side 2 red ⎪ of scarf 30 white ⎭	

If preferred, the dark block *B* can be used on each side and the large white block *A* in the center. The arrangement given, however, is in accord with that generally used in Scotland. If the blocks are reversed, the black block *B* should start on the right with 20 black threads and end on the left side of the scarf with 20 black. The light block *A* in the center should begin and end with 60 white threads. The tartan should be woven as-drawn-in.

Threading   Twill 1, 2, 3, 4 (page 160)

Tie-Up   12, 23, 34, 41 (page 42)

Treadling   Treadles 1, 2, 3, 4 are repeated as often as required. If a tie-up is not used, treadles 12, 23, 34, 41 are repeated as often as necessary.

The blocks are treadled as-drawn-in, starting and ending with 30 white threads to balance the sides. Through the center of the scarf, the *A* block is woven with 60 weft shots at both the start and finish of the black block.

Where a soft, pliable article is desired, the beating must be well controlled. This is much more difficult to do than hard beating. Actually, the scarf is not beaten; rather, the threads are gently pulled back into place with the beater.

In finishing tartans of commercial wool, it is not customary to wash the material, as washing seems to remove some of the body from the web; but, in the case of a scarf or baby blanket, where softness is desired, it is best to hand wash the material carefully in lukewarm water and mild soap flakes. Do not wash wool in the washing machine as it fuzzes the wool. Handle the wet material as little and as carefully as possible, churning it under the water with a swimming motion to keep it agitated and permit the soap flakes to permeate all parts. When thoroughly washed, lift out the fabric with both hands and place it in lukewarm rinse water. Carefully squeeze the water out, do not wring. Roll the material in a heavy bath towel to soak up the excess moisture. Stand the rolled towel on end in the bathtub overnight. Remove the material in the morning and press it under a cloth. Avoid stretching the material, pat it with an iron, but do not rub it. If the fabric is dry when removed from the towel, steam press it under a damp cloth. The scarf should be soft and fluffy. There will be shrinkage of about 1 in. in width and from 2 to 3 in. in length.

Problem   Set up a scarf and weave it according to the directions given above.

TYPE Tartan · SETT MacPherson, Hunting, Sample Yardage

Before undertaking a length of wool yardage, it is advisable for the beginning weaver to practice on a sample length to become familiar with the winding of the warp, the arrangement of the sett for the width of the material, the handling of the shuttles, and the beating.

The small piece of woven material in Fig. 487 has been made up into a miniature pleated skirt to illustrate pattern pleating. In pattern pleating the pleats are so arranged that the design of the tartan shows up on the skirt or kilt just as it does on the web. To pleat a skirt in this design, measure the buttock and waist. Start with the desired block, in this case the dark *B* block, and follow with the second block, here block *A*. The pleats are laid in and basted across the length of the material according to the buttock measurement. As pointed out previously, skirts and kilts are made with the warp running around the skirt, rather than from top to bottom. The top of the pleat is now laid over the pleat directly next to it, at an angle to fit it into the waist measurement. The straight line at the edge of the pleat should not be changed any more than absolutely necessary. Sometimes pleats will lie one half or three quarters of a square further across the surface of the next pleat at the waist than at the buttock to offset the difference between the two measurements.

Sample Illustrated (Fig. 487)

Materials

WARP	WEFT	REED *(dents per inch)*	SLEY
Wool, 2/32	Wool, 2/32	18	Double

Length of Warp for the Sample   1¾ yd. The length of the warp required for a skirt is about 5 yd. including the allowance for loom waste and shrinkage. The height of the person, the sett used, and the method of pleating also will have to be considered when determining the length and width of the material required.

FIG 487

Number of Threads Wound for the Sample 176

Sett

A Block	B Block
32 gray	4 red
*4 red	4 azure
4 azure — center	4 red
Repeat from * back to beginning.	32 black
	*4 red
	4 azure — center
	Repeat from * back to beginning.

For this fine material the number of threads in the original sett has been doubled. The arrangement for the sample is as follows: ½ A block, B block, ½ A block.

For a full-size skirt, start with 32 black, 4 red, 4 azure, 4 red, 32 black, 4 red, 4 azure, 4 red. Repeat blocks A and B twelve times; end with 32 gray for the top of the skirt. (This arrangement will vary with the height of the wearer.)

Threading Twill 1, 2, 3, 4 (page 160)

Tie-Up 12, 23, 34, 41 (page 42)

Treadling Treadles 1, 2, 3, 4 are repeated as often as necessary. If a tie-up is not used, treadles 12, 23, 34, 41 are repeated as often as necessary. The blocks are treadled as-drawn-in, following the colors given in the sett.

Beating Throw the shuttle through the shed, press the thread back into place with a light beat, change the shed, release enough thread from the shuttle to reach three quarters of the way across the shed, throw the shuttle to the other side, press the thread back into place with a light beat, and change the shed. Continue in this manner.

This weight material requires very light, but even beating, the weft thread being pressed rather than beaten into place. Practice will be required before the 50/50 web with the 45-deg. angle will be achieved, so it is wise to allow sufficient warp for the first skirt length. The practice pieces can be used for a hat or as lapel lining for a plain jacket.

Finish Remove the web from the loom and send it to the laundry or cleaners for steam pressing. After the pleating, the skirt should be steam pressed to give it a professional look.

Problem Set up a 2-block sample using fine wool. Practice the beating. Plan a skirt length using the sample to figure measurements, and to check sley and beating.

TYPE Tartan · SETT Clergy, Yardage

Logan, on whose writings much of our knowledge of tartans is based, states, "The tartan which the Clergy wore is popularly believed to have been used by the Druids and Culders. The Highland ministers, it has been shown, went armed and generally dressed in the national costume."[6]

The clergy played an important part in the early history of the Clan MacPherson who claimed they were descendants of Muireach, the Parson of Kinguissie, Chief of Clan Chattan (1173). A literal translation of MacPherson is "son of the parson."

There are several recorded setts of the Clergy tartan. The one given here is the Breacan Nan Cleireach. The sett as given by Stewart has been re-arranged to fit a woman's skirt. Stewart states that leeway is permitted the weaver in arranging the sett to fit the width of the kilt or skirt. The tartans discussed previously have been 2-block tartans; this is a 3-block.

The weaving of fine wool tartan yardage is quite an undertaking and should not be attempted unless the weaver has had experience with wide wool yardages. However, if the weaver is willing to proceed slowly, to familiarize himself with the principles of tartan weaving and follow directions carefully, the results should be successful.

There are only a few of the darker tartans, the Black Watch and the Lindsay, for instance, which lends themselves well to a whole suit. Most tartans are much more effective if the tartan is used only for a skirt or a jacket, combined with a plain jacket or skirt in one of the colors from the larger blocks of the tartan, or with a harmonizing tweed jacket. Tartan skirts are more attractive if they are pleated in pattern, knife, box, or dark and light pleats rather than cut on the bias or finished as a tight skirt. A pleated skirt is more chic if not too long. The Clergy tartan is attractive in the dark and light pleating pattern.

Sample Illustrated, Tartan Yardage (Fig. 488)

Materials

WARP	WOOL
Wool, 2/32	Wool, 2/32

REED *(dents per inch)*	SLEY
18	Double

Number of Threads in Warp 1176
Length of Warp Wound 5 yd.

Sett

A Block	B Block	C Block
36 gray	36 black	4 white
*4 white	4 white	8 gray
4 gray — center	36 black	4 white
Repeat from * back to beginning.	——	*12 gray
——	76	4 white — center
84		Repeat from * back to beginning.
		——
		60

The following order of blocks gives a 32½-in. setting in the reed which is suitable for a woman's skirt. A tall person would require a wider setting.
36 gray threads on the right to start.
Blocks *B, C, B, A, B, C, B, A* (center), *B, C, B, A, B, C, B.*
36 gray threads on the left to end.
It is customary to weave a half block minus the turning threads, at each selvedge, though some tartan authorities prefer to end with a whole block.

Threading Draft Twill 1, 2, 3, 4 (page 160)

Tie-Up 12, 23, 34, 41 (page 42)

Treadling Treadles 1, 2, 3, 4, repeated as often as necessary. If a tie-up is not used, treadles 12, 23, 34, 41 are repeated as often as necessary.

Beating The beating follows the standard technique for all fine woolens. Open the shed, throw the shuttle, pull back the beater, change the shed, and follow with a gentle beat. Open the shed, with the beater held back against the edge of the web, release sufficient thread from the bobbin to go almost across the web (this is done by carrying the shuttle out at arm's length), release the beater, enter the shuttle in the shed, and proceed with the routine.

It will require quite a bit of practice to establish a rhythm, but with it will come confidence. After a few repeats of the blocks have been woven, it will become much easier. Make certain that there are the correct number of threads in each block and that the angle is the required 45 deg. Do not draw in the selvedges. Therefore it is not important that the selvedges be perfect, although having them perfect means greater satisfaction to the weaver.

The material should be steam pressed after removal from the loom. Do not wash it.

Problem Set up and weave an apron length of 16/2 cotton or a wool tartan stole for practice before attempting the wool yardage.

TYPE Tartan •
SETT MacPherson Clan Tartan, Sample Kilt Material

This tartan, sometimes referred to as the ancient MacPherson, is, when woven with vegetable-dyed yarns and pattern pleated, one of the most colorful and beautiful of the full-dress kilts. Another version of the clan tartan, Stewart No. 173, is very much the same, but has much smaller red blocks. The smaller blocks make more attractive skirts than the large ones.

Contrary to public belief, the "waggle" in the kilt is not executed by

FIG 489

FIG 488

the wearer. It is built in, and starts with a perfectly woven piece of material. As kilts are not hemmed, it is important to have a perfectly woven selvedge for the bottom. Do not draw in the edge warp threads too tightly thereby breaking them and distorting the shape of the edge block of the sett. Most weavers can weave a better selvedge on one side than on the other, therefore it is wise to plan the order of the shuttles so that the best selvedge will appear at the bottom of the kilt. It is not necessary to cut and turn in the weft threads where the color changes occur. Carry the threads from block to block on the selvedge for the top of the kilt, which is bound (Fig. 489).

Sample Illustrated (Fig. 490)
Materials

WARP	WEFT	REED (dents per inch)	SLEY
Wool, 2/16	Wool, 2/16	18	Double
For a lighter-weight boy's kilt:			
Wool, 2/16	Wool, 2/16	16	Double

Fine wool weaves beautiful kilt material but is somewhat expensive. Similar wools can be purchased in quantity at a lower price but the quantities are so large that their purchase is not practical for hand weavers who wish to weave only one or two kilts.

Length of Warp Wound 36 in. plus loom waste and 3-in. allowance for shrinkage and take-up

Number of Threads 596

A Block	B Block	A Block — to end
32 green	4 yellow	32 green
48 red	24 black	48 red
*8 azure	16 azure	8 azure
48 red — center	4 black	24 red
	4 azure	
Repeat from * back to beginning.	4 black	The bottom of a tartan skirt or kilt should break in the center, not at the edge, of a block.
	16 azure	
	48 red	
	4 white	
	*4 black	
	4 red — center	
	Repeat from * back to beginning.	

The number of threads used in the above MacPherson clan sett is double that given by Stewart. The reason for the increase is that fine yarn and close sleying were used. The pattern design would have been too fine for a kilt if the original number of threads had been used.

The width of the sample when set in the reed was slightly over 16½ in., when woven and steam pressed the width was approximately 15½ in.

In planning material for a man's kilt, repeat the A and B blocks the required number of times to weave the desired width, ending with the half A block.

FIG 490

Threading   Twill 1, 2, 3, 4 (page 160)

Tie-Up   12, 23, 34, 41 (page 42)

Treadling   Repeat treadles 1, 2, 3, 4 for the required length.

If a tie-up is not used, repeat treadles 12, 23, 34, 41 for the required length.

The blocks are woven as-drawn-in and, as with all tartan weaving, each block is squared up with the same number of threads in the weft as in the warp, with a 45-deg. angle.

Beating   The material for men's kilts should be beaten very hard, evenly, and firmly. The best routine is to open the shed, throw the shuttle, beat the weft back into position, change the shed, beat again with two sharp, hard beats, loosen enough thread from the bobbin to extend partway across the web, and then repeat the routine. Watch the selvedges carefully, particularly the one to be used for the bottom of the kilt. To avoid loss of rhythm, place the shuttles on the web in the order in which they are to be used.

Problem   On paper, plan material for a full-size kilt, using your own clan tartan. Then plan and weave sufficient material to make a kilt for a small boy.

TYPE Tartan · SETT MacPherson Clan Tartan, Cotton Sample

This sample was designed[7] to highlight a hand-thrown, azure-glazed, pottery breakfast set. The potter wished to display her own tartan place mats, yet did not want the focus on the mats but rather on the pottery. The use of the *B* block plus a few threads of the *A* block of the clan tartan, combined with an oatmeal cotton, seemed to be the answer.

This idea can be applied to side and bottom borders on drapes and borders on aprons and skirts.

Sample Illustrated (Fig. 491)

Materials

WARP	WEFT	REED	SLEY
		(dents per inch)	
Cotton, 8/2	Cotton, 8/2	14	Double

There is considerable variation in size in many of the 8/2 cottons, although all may be marked the same.

Number of Threads in Warp   382

Length of Warp   36 in. plus loom waste

FIG 491

The Sett

10 oatmeal for right border
*4 dark green
2 yellow
12 black
8 azure
2 black
2 azure
2 black
8 azure
24 red
2 white
**2 black
2 red — center
Repeat from ** back to and
including *.
234 oatmeal

The four green threads from the *A* block are placed next to the yellow threads at the beginning and end of the *B* block to prevent the yellow threads from losing their identity next to the oatmeal threads.

Threading   Twill 1, 2, 3, 4 (page 160)

Tie-Up   12, 23, 34, 41 (page 42)

Treadling   Repeat treadles 1, 2, 3, 4 for the required number of times.

Beating   This material requires fairly hard beating to obtain the 45-deg. angle with double sleying. Weave in the colors as set in the warp.

There is considerable shrinkage when 8/2 cotton is woven on the twill, therefore it is necessary to weave an extra inch or so. The tartan corner is woven in at the beginning so that, if the plain part is too long, it can be unraveled and fringed. It is suggested that, if a set of mats are being woven, the first one be cut off and washed to determine the amount of shrinkage. Do not have the iron too hot as the oatmeal thread burns very easily.

Problem   Plan, set up, and weave a tray cloth in an original tartan arrangement.

TYPE Tartan · SETT MacPherson Clan Tartan, Linen Sample

Fine, round linen thread weaves into lovely gay tartans for summer blouses and dresses, place mats, towels, and some household uses. It can be adapted to upholstery on bleached wood, and for drapes where it is desirable to carry out a tartan motif. Pine-panelled walls or walls with plain oatmeal paper make the best background for such drapes. To create a Highland atmosphere, pictures should preferably be of Scottish scenes or of persons dressed in the colorful Highland costumes. It is not wise to combine tartan drapes or upholstery with figured wallpaper or upholstery.

Sample Illustrated (Fig. 492)

Materials   As all linens are not guaranteed to be colorfast, it is wise to wash samples of them before undertaking any large pieces. Some threads tested for colorfastness in plain water did not run, although there was a slight bleeding of the blues and reds when tested in a mild detergent. The finished sample, washed in soap, left a slight purplish tinge in the water but there was no running of colors in the sample itself. Linen can be dry cleaned but it is through repeated washing and careful ironing that its beauty is brought out.

WARP	WEFT	REED	SLEY
		(*dents per inch*)	
Linen, 40/2	Linen, 40/2	20	Double

Number of Threads Wound   708

Length of Warp   18 in. plus loom waste, plus 6 in. for shrinkage and hems.

The sample piece was approximately 17⅞ in. in the reed and when taken from the loom was 16¾ in. wide. There was some additional shrinkage after washing and ironing.

The Sett

A Block	B Block
32 green	4 yellow
48 red	24 black
*8 azure	16 azure
48 red — center	4 black
Repeat from * back to beginning.	4 azure
	4 black
	16 azure
	48 red
	4 white
	*4 black
	4 red — center
	Repeat from * back to beginning.

For the square sample (Fig. 492) thread blocks *A, B, A* (Stewart's sett No. 172 has been doubled).

FIG 492

Threading Draft   Twill 1, 2, 3, 4 (page 160)

Tie-Up   12, 23, 34, 41 (page 42)

Treadling Repeat treadles 1, 2, 3, 4 for the required length. If a tie-up is not used, repeat treadles 12, 23, 34, 41 for the required length.

Beating The instructions covering linen weaving (page 606) apply to the weaving of linen tartans as well. Throw the shuttle across the shed, draw the beater back, change the shed, beat once or twice with sharp, quick beats, release a length of weft sufficient to cross the width of the web, and repeat the routine. Watch the selvedges for pulled-in threads, and measure the angle frequently. Be sure that, in each square, there are the same number of threads in the weft as in the warp and that the blocks are square.

Problem Plan and weave a square or place mat of linen, using the sett given, or plan an original plaid.

TYPE Tartan · SETT MacPherson, Cluny, Double Weave

For those with an 8-harness loom, an interesting project is the weaving of double-face materials (page 216).

An added challenge is the weaving of a double-face material with one side tartan and the other side plain. This is not particularly difficult, though strict attention must be paid to the winding of the warp, the threading, and the order of entering the shuttles during the weaving.

The tartan is woven on the upper side, as it is easier to follow the sett, and the plain material underneath. The really experienced weaver can plan a rug with a different tartan on each side.

This weave is suitable for car rugs and reversible material for sports jackets.

Sample Illustrated: Jacket Material (Fig. 494)

Materials

WARP	WEFT	REED (dents per inch)	SLEY
Wool, 2/16	Wool, 2/16	10 or 12	4 ends per dent (2 tartan ends and 2 plain ends)

Material sleyed in the 10-dent reed will be softer and lighter in weight and more suitable for women's and children's wear than that sleyed in the 12-dent reed, which produces a heavy material better suited to men's wear.

For a car robe use heavier wool. A coarse, single-ply homespun, set four threads per dent in a Number 10 reed, is a good choice.

Number of Threads Wound for Sample   180

Ninety of these threads are red and weave the plain back. The other 90, wound as follows, are for the tartan or upper side:

10 black	
30 white ⎤	
2 red ⎟	This is the *A Block* from the Cluny MacPherson sett, reduced to half
6 white ⎬	size, with a 10-thread black border on all sides.
2 red ⎟	
30 white ⎦	
10 black	

In weaving a larger sample or a piece of material, block *B* would alternate with block *A* the required number of times, ending on the left with an *A* block.

Block B

20 black
6 white
*10 black
2 yellow — center
Repeat from * back to beginning.

It will be an advantage if the loom is equipped with two warp beams since there is considerable take-up in the plain color due to the "stitching" together of the two sides, by the plain warp threads. If there are two warp beams, wind the plain color by itself, making a second warp chain of the tartan colors. Each chain is wound separately onto its own warp beam (page 216) and the two sets of shed sticks are tied together. The threads are threaded according to the draft and the color of the tartan given above, first taking a thread from the tartan warp, then one from the plain warp, and continuing in this sequence completely across the loom.

If the loom does not have two beams, when winding the warp carry the thread for the plain side of the material along with the threads for the tartan side throughout the winding. This will alternate the threads in accordance with the threading draft.

Threading Draft   The tartan, which is woven on the upper side, is threaded on odd-numbered harnesses 1, 3, 5, and 7, and is designated on the draft by an *O*.

The plain color, which is woven on the underside, is threaded on even-numbered harnesses 2, 4, 6, and 8 and is designated on the draft by an *X*.

To bind the two sides together it is necessary to tie up the harnesses so that, in each shot, a warp thread from the plain side is treadled in with the upper or tartan shed. In the tie-up draft these shots are shown by the black dots. These shots come up and under the center of the weft skip each time. The tie-up can be reversed to tie a thread from the upper tartan side down to the under, or plain, side. This, however, may weaken the color of the upper side. This thread actually sews the two pieces of material together and it is from this that it receives its name "stitching thread."[8] If this "stitching thread" is not tied in, the two surfaces will weave separately.

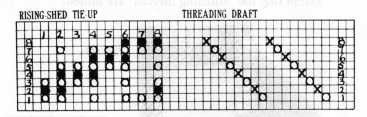

FIG 493

To Weave

TREADLE	THROW SHUTTLE CARRYING
1	tartan weft
2	plain weft
3	tartan weft
4	plain weft
5	tartan weft
6	plain weft
7	tartan weft
8	plain weft

Start again with treadle 1 and repeat until the desired length has been woven.

There are several things to consider while weaving this material. The order of the sett for the tartan must be followed correctly. The edge threads, which cross during the change from weaving the upper and lower sheds, should cross systematically to give a good selvedge. A 45-deg. angle must be maintained and all tartan blocks squared with the same number of weft and warp threads in each block. It simplifies the weaving a bit if the weaver remembers that the tartan is being woven on one set of harnesses and the plain web on a second set, the two webs being bound together with the "stitching threads."

This double weave should be woven more loosely, with slightly more than a 45-deg. angle to offset the take-up of the "stitching thread." Do not plan a long web unless the loom has two warp beams, or unless the material is to be cut off and the warp retied approximately every 2 yd. With a long web it is necessary to allow considerably more warp to offset take-up than is customary. Even in the small sample shown (Fig. 494), there was a loss of ¾ in. in length.

Note that the twill on the upper, or tartan, side is a left-hand twill, while that on the under, or plain, side is a right-hand twill. The action of these two webs, pulling against each other, makes a firm fabric.

The ends of a car robe can either be fringed or the two surfaces can be woven separately for ¾ or 1 in. at both the start and finish of the piece. After cutting it from the loom, fell the two open ends of the robe.

The tie-up for the open ends is the same as the tie-up given above except that the "stitching threads" are untied:

FIG 494

Untie **HARNESS** from **TREADLE**	
2	1
2 and 4	2
4	3
4 and 6	4
6	5
6 and 8	6
8	7
2 and 8	8

Retie the harnesses and treadles before starting to weave the robe proper.

Problem Plan and wind a narrow warp of 8/4 cotton for a sample double weave with a tartan top and plain bottom. Experiment with the sleying.

TYPE Tartan, 4-Harness •
SETT Cameron of Lochiel, MacLeod Dress

These two popular tartans are suitable for scarves, skirts, jackets, shirts, slacks, etc. The samples (Figs. 495 and 496) are woven of size 2/16 wool double sleyed in an 18-dent reed. This sleying produces a firm web; for a softer web, suitable for a woman's skirt or jacket, double sley in a 16-dent reed. Beating should produce a 50/50 web with a 45-deg. diagonal. Press the finished web under a damp cloth with a moderately hot iron.

TYPE Tartan, 4-Harness •
SETT MacLeod Dress

The district checks are as important to the Lowland families of Scotland as the tartans are to the Highlanders.

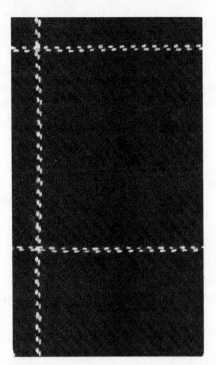

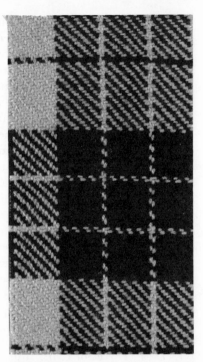

FIG. 495

Cameron of Lochiel
Sett

2 navy	2 white
4 red	2 navy
16 navy	12 red
8 red	6 green
16 navy	12 red
4 red	6 green
2 navy	12 red
	2 navy
	2 white

FIG. 496

MacLeod Dress
Sett

24 yellow	16 black
2 red	2 yellow
24 yellow	16 black
	2 yellow
	16 black

Although the district checks were developed at a much later period than the tartans, their history is equally as interesting. Originated by the Lowland families, the district checks were taken to the north of Scotland and adopted for use in the royal household at Balmoral by Queen Victoria. The district checks, also called border checks, do not have the gay coloring of the tartan but they do blend well with the heather and grouse indigenous to moor and fen. Because the yarns could be colored with dyes from local leaves, roots, and flowers, they were economically produced on the estates where the sheep were raised. The designing and weaving of the checks was originally a family matter, with such well-known families as the Chisholms, the Farquharsons, and the Strathspeys having their own distinguishing checks. Gun clubs and various regiments, such as the Seaforth Highlanders, also have their own checks.

The black and white shepherd's check (Fig. 498) is the simplest pattern of all the border or district checks and is incorporated in the setts of most of the richer patterns. It originated among the lowland shepherds who used it for their plaidies. Although it is not an established fact, it is possible that the shepherd's wives, unable to get enough wool of one color and tired of a pepper-and-salt mixture, worked out the alternate blocks or checks of black and white wool. Originally, and to a certain extent today, the black homespun wool used for the district checks was the wool taken from the black sheep; it was not dyed white wool. Because black sheep are seldom really black, the color variation was soft and a far more pleasing contrast to the creamy white wool than jet black commercially dyed wool.

True district checks, like the tartans, must be threaded and woven on a 2–2 twill with a 45-deg. angle, and an equal number of threads in the weft and the warp. They must be sleyed to produce a firm, but not hard or stiff, material and should preferably be woven of homespun wool.

After years of controversy, and probably based on the old expression "six-quarter wide," it has been established and accepted that the original shepherd's check sett was six white, six black, the colors alternating across the width of the warp in squares ¼ in. wide. Commercially it is produced in cottons, rayons, nylons, and other synthetic fibers.

Uses For wool coats, suits, men's jackets and scarves, women's skirts and dresses, and children's wear.

Suitable Materials and Sleying

WARP	WEFT	REED (dents per inch)	SLEY
Wool, 2/32	Wool, 2/32	14–16–18	Double for suiting and dresses
Wool, 2/16	Wool, 2/16	12–15	Double for suitings and coatings
Wool, homespun	Wool, homespun	8–10	Double for men's jackets and women's coats

Sample Illustrated (Fig. 498)

WARP	WEFT	REED (dents per inch)	SLEY
Wool, 2/32	Wool, 2/32	18	Double

For the warp, wind the required number of threads alternating six white, six black throughout.

Repeat the white and black six-thread blocks until the entire width has been threaded.

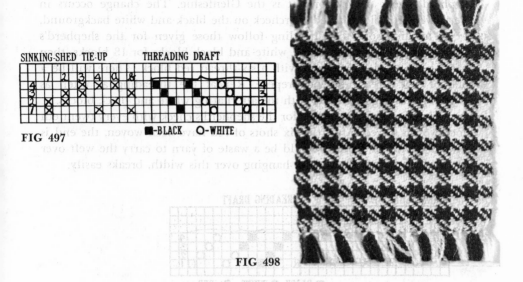

SINKING-SHED TIE-UP   THREADING DRAFT

FIG 497

■-BLACK   O-WHITE

FIG 498

Treadling–Sinking Shed		Treadling–Rising Shed (*No Tie-Up*)
TREADLES		**LEVERS OR TREADLES**
1		3–4
2		1–4
3	White — six shots	1–2
4		2–3
1		3–4
2		1–4
3		1–2
4		2–3
1		3–4
2	Black — six shots	1–4
3		1–2
4		2–3

Repeat the alternating black and white squares until the desired length has been woven.

Do not cut and turn in the weft at the end of the square. The weft thread will lie neatly and inconspicuously along the selvedge as it is carried from block to block and the shuttles are alternated. The shuttles change each time on the same side of the loom (page 416); if they do not, look for a mistake in treadling.

Problem   Plan, set up the warp, and weave a scarf using the shepherd's check pattern.

TYPE District Checks · PATTERN Glenfeshie

In studying the district checks, the first deviation we find from the basic shepherd's-check pattern or sett is the Glenfeshie. The change occurs in every twentieth block: a red overcheck on the black and white background.

The directions for threading follow those given for the shepherd's check (page 443). Alternate the white and black blocks for 18 blocks, then thread a white block and end with a six-thread red block. There will be a total of 120 threads for one repeat. Repeat the threading as often as necessary, starting each time with the alternating white and black blocks.

The treadling is the same for the shepherd's check with every twentieth block woven in red. After the six shots of red have been woven, the end is cut and turned in, since it would be a waste of yarn to carry the weft over the 20 blocks, while the thread, hanging over this width, breaks easily.

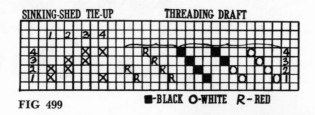

SINKING-SHED TIE-UP   THREADING DRAFT

FIG 499   ■-BLACK O-WHITE *R*-RED

FIG 500

Other district and gun club checks that are based on the six-thread shepherd's check are the popular Seaforth Highlanders' "Mufti" tweed with blocks of white, tan, and chocolate brown; the Ing of brick red and white;

the Dupplin of white, red, and chocolate brown; and many others. With the exception of the highly priced Scottish woolens, most district checks are woven with a four-thread shepherd's-check block.

Problem Weave a sample and plan material needed for a child's jacket.

TYPE District Check · PATTERN Glen Urquhart (Small)

Although the district-check weaves are accepted as standard for sportswear, it is seldom that hand weavers have troubled to examine the sett of the material with the intention of reproducing this popular weave.

Sample Illustrated

WARP	WEFT	REED	SLEY
		(dents per inch)	
Wool, 2/16	Wool, 2/16	16	Double

This sleying is suitable for jacket or suit lengths. For other yarns refer to the homespun (Sheep's Wool page 615) and tartan weaves (page 425).

Warp 102 threads wound as follows:

4 white 4 black 4 white	alternating for 12 blocks or for 48 threads
2 black 2 white 2 black	alternating for 24 blocks or for 48 threads

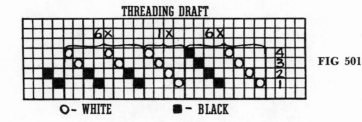

THREADING DRAFT

FIG 501

O - WHITE   ■ - BLACK

The above threading setts and weaves one complete unit. Two blocks of the repeat have been added on the left (Fig. 502). Repeat the required number of times to thread the desired width in the loom. When designed for yardage, the district checks, like the tartans, should begin and end in the center of the block.

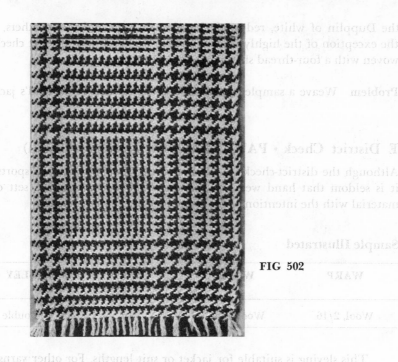

FIG 502

Tie-Up   Standard 2/2 twill

Treadling   Follow the order in which the warp is wound for color; the two-thread block is known as the basket block.

chapter 13

Tapestry Weaves

PLAIN—FINGER-MANIPULATED—WEFT-FACE

From the Book of Exodus (26:1–7, 31, 33) (King James Version) we read (and believe it applies to tapestry): "Moreover, thou shalt make the tabernacle with ten curtains of fine twined linen, and blue, and purple, and scarlet: with Cherubims of cunning work shalt thou make them. The length of one curtain shall be eight and twenty cubits, and the breadth of one curtain four cubits; and every one of the curtains shall have one measure. The five curtains shall be coupled together one to another; and other five curtains shall be coupled one to another. And thou shalt make loops of blue upon the edge of the one curtain, from the selvedge in the coupling; and likewise shalt thou make in the uttermost edge of another curtain, in the coupling of the second. Fifty loops shalt thou make in the one curtain, and fifty loops shalt thou make in the edge of the curtain that is in the coupling of the second, that the loops may take hold one of another. And thou shalt make fifty taches of gold, and couple the curtains together with the taches; and it shall be one tabernacle . . . and thou shalt make curtains of goats' hair . . . and thou shalt make a veil of blue, and purple, and, scarlet, and fine twined linen of cunning work: with cherubims shall it be made . . . and thou shalt make an hanging for the door of the tent."

Through the ages, and particularly today, the word "tapestry" has been used loosely to describe a large hanging or piece of upholstery worked in any of a number of techniques. According to Webster's *Dictionary*, the word "tapestry" is derived from the French word *tapis,* "a carpet," and is defined as "a heavy, hand-woven, reversible textile, commonly figured and used as a wall hanging, carpet, or furniture covering; also a machine-made imitation of it."

In her book,[1] Helen Candee points out that the word "tapestry" has been used indiscriminately to describe all sorts of wall hangings and names, in particular the famous "Bayeux Tapestry" which, according to Webster's definition, is not a tapestry at all. This so-called tapestry is over 200 ft. long and is embroidered with scenes depicting the conquest of England in 1066 by William the Conqueror.

A modern hanging, embroidered over the period from 1936 to 1954 by the Anderson family in the Cotswold district of England, has been called the "Notgrove Tapestry." However, the Embroiders' Guild of England states, "Though called a tapestry it is really a needlework hanging worked in grospoint and petitpoint."

The modern tapestry designer, Jean Lurçat, whose tapestries are woven in a section of the old tapestry works in Aubusson, France, is quite emphatic in stating that a true tapestry must be handwoven, it must be designed by an artist familiar with tapestry techniques, and the design must be understood by both artist and weaver.

In this text, a tapestry is considered to be a weft-face fabric, woven by hand, in which the various pattern areas join together with the background areas to form the web. Depending on the technique used, a tapestry may vary from the completely reversible Norwegian åklae, without slits or loose weft ends showing, to the French Gobelin, woven with slits which are later sewn together with the ends of the weft threads left hanging on the wrong side.

Many modern weavers, eager to weave a tapestry, use the first design that comes to hand, multicolored coarse wool, and bits of leather and metallics. With little regard to technique, they produce a hodgepodge which they glibly call a "modern."

The serious weaver, a purist at heart, will use the correct design and technique to produce a tapestry conforming to the standards laid down by the developers of the tapestry technique which he has chosen.

There are beautiful tapestries on display in museums all over the world, many of them as fresh in coloring as the day they were woven. This present state of preservation attests to the care with which the wools were dyed and the tapestries woven and handled through the years.

It is not known whether tapestry techniques were developed within each country or interchanged between countries through trade and commerce; but, because of the early dates to which tapestry fragments have been traced, students of textiles believe that the techniques were developed within the individual countries. Almost identical techniques are in common use among the Scandinavian weavers, the North and South American Indians, the Mexicans, the Slavic races, the French tapestry weavers, and among primitive, little-known tribes living in remote regions.

It is not unusual to find some deviation in technique in the weaves originating within the same country. The proximity of countries often influences the design or the technique. Polish kilims found near the Ukraine border show definite Russian characteristics, while those from

Podolia show a definite Turkish and Armenian influence. The weaving of the Navaho Indian remained crude until the tribe had contact with the Pueblos from whom they learned improved design and technique. Navaho weavings are considered superior to the Pueblo.

A student of tapestry weaves has little difficulty in naming the country in which a particular tapestry originated if it has been woven correctly.

The Loom   The terms "high-warp" and "low-warp" always are associated with tapestry weaving.

The high-warp, or haute-lisse, derives its name from the high, upright-, or vertical-type loom (Fig. 503) on which it is stretched. The low-warp, or basse-lisse, is stretched in the usual manner on a regulation floor or table loom. Both looms are so constructed that the warp can be held at a tension.

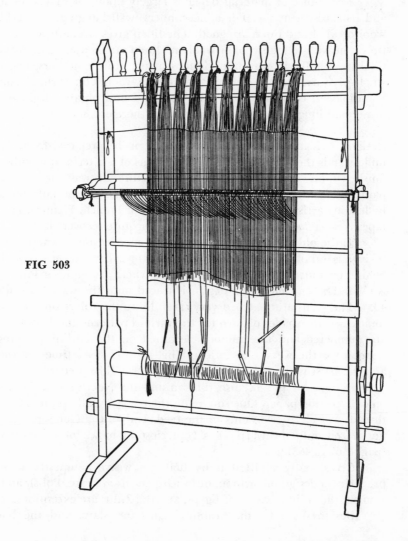

FIG 503

There are both warp and cloth beams and a method of changing the shed. One exception is the Navaho loom with a quite different method of warping (page 506).

Materials Before the introduction of cotton, wool and linen were the threads most commonly used for warp. Even though cotton warps are cheaper, tapestry weavers generally prefer a linen warp as it seems to give better body to the web. The best Navaho blankets are woven on wool warps. However, a tightly twisted cotton warp is acceptable. A coarse-ply linen or hemp-seizing twine are good and the price is reasonable.

For the weft, a variety of materials can be used: wool thrums from the carpet mills; regulation tapestry wools; two-ply commercial wools; one-, two-, or three-ply homespun; and the Scandinavian nöthårsgarn.

The choice of material depends largely upon the article being woven and its subsequent use. For table runners, wall hangings, or cushion tops, wool or wool and linen are good. The linen gives strength to the wool. For rugs, a heavier-weight wool or wool and linen can be used. The Scandinavian rölakan usually is woven of long-wearing, sturdy nöthårsgarn, a heavy, single-ply yarn spun of cow hair and coarse wool. This yarn, cheaper in the Scandinavian countries than pure wool and now obtainable in America, is firmer and longer-wearing than wool and, therefore, more practical for rugs.

Design It is important that tapestry designs be prepared by an artist who understands the possibilities and limitations of the technique, otherwise the finished piece may resemble a woven picture. It was the use of famous paintings for designs, rather than cartoons prepared especially for tapestries by leading artists, which led to the decline of French, Flemish, and English tapestries—a decline from which they never quite recovered.

In the old tapestry works and in the modern ones, where the tapestry revival is taking place, the colored design, called the cartoon, is placed behind or under the warp, depending on whether a high- or low-warp loom is used. The outline of the design is traced onto the warp with dots (page 483). The yarns are matched very carefully to the colors on the cartoon. In some cases, the shades of yarn for the various patterns and background areas are numbered and the numbers recorded on the outline drawing of the cartoon for the weaver to follow. This method saves time for the weaver and the artist is assured that the correct color will be used.

Designs for the Swedish rölakan and the Norwegian åklae are drawn on cross-section paper. One square on the paper usually represents two warp threads as well as two dents in the reed. Unlike the Gobelin, the design is not traced onto the warp. It is kept close at hand for constant reference (pages 467 to 468).

Occasionally a gifted individual can weave a tapestry without first preparing a design or cartoon, but such persons are rare. Polish and Navaho women, the child weavers of Egypt, and the Zulus are exceptions.

Designs used by the Scandinavians, the Slavs, and the North and

South American Indians usually are simple with traditional, stylized designs which frequently are repeated in the same or varied colors.

Practically all tapestry weaving is done with the wrong side facing the weaver, therefore, to be correct on the right side, designs with numbers or letters must be drawn in reverse.

Seemingly the old tapestries, full of detail in the design, required many colors. Actually the best of them have a very limited number of colors and shades, but these are blended cleverly. The many ways of shading tapestry designs will be discussed and shown later.

Threading Any threading which will produce a plain weave (page 97) is suitable for tapestry weaving on a standard low-warp loom. The high-warp, the Navaho loom, and other types of tapestry looms are threaded according to the directions for that particular loom.

Sleying As tapestry weaves are essentially a weft-face weave, the warp must be widely spaced at 8, 10, or 12 threads to the inch. Sleying will depend on the weights of both the warp and the weft and the article being woven. When correctly sleyed, the weft completely covers the warp. The warp should not be spaced too widely, however, or the weft will pack down too tightly, resulting in a spongy effect. If sleyed too closely, the weft will not cover the warp.

The Shuttle The weft thread may be left in short lengths, especially if the areas are small and the color changes frequent; wound into small bobbins (Fig. 555); made into butterflies (Fig. 143); or wound onto one of several types of tapestry bobbins or pins (Figs. 504 and 505).

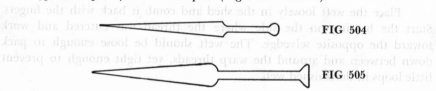

FIG 504

FIG 505

Weaving While each type of tapestry has its own technique, there are a few rules which apply to all.

With the exception of the Navaho, it is wise to start and end all tapestry weaving with a ¾- or 1-in. plain-weave heading woven with warp thread. These bands of plain weaving make a firm foundation against which to begin the weaving and to beat. The heading also helps to regulate the width of the weaving and holds the weft threads in place when the web is cut from the loom. For some weaves, the cartoon is pinned firmly to this heading. The headings are removed before the warp ends are knotted or tied into a fringe.

To prevent the selvedges from pulling in, the weft is laid loosely in the shed. With the fingers, it is pulled back in scallops to the edge of the fell so that it can completely cover the warp threads when beaten. It will take practice and experimentation to weave the selvedges properly, but if great care is taken at this point, there will be less trouble with selvedges later.

If the piece is to have a plain wool border use a shuttle, preferably a flat one for the high-warp loom, and weave in the border according to the width shown on the design sketch. Measure the width accurately.

The technique used will determine whether or not weft ends should be turned in or left hanging loose on the back of the tapestry. There are various methods for turning in the weft ends. One is to turn the weft thread around the warp thread and back into the shed. A second method is to leave the ends loose and, after a few rows have been woven, to run them up or down beside the warp threads with a needle, and cut the yarn off. Both methods are effective if carefully done. The threads should not show on either side of the web if the tapestry is to be reversible, nor should the thread be cut so short that it will work out, leaving a hole.

Beating The batten (Fig. 595), the reed (page 8), the bobbin (Fig. 504), or the tapestry fork (Fig. 506) is used to beat the weft threads back into position against the fell. The method used depends largely upon the type of tapestry being woven and is described in detail under each weave.

FIG 506

Place the weft loosely in the shed and comb it back with the fingers. Start the beating on the side where the thread was entered and work toward the opposite selvedge. The weft should be loose enough to pack down between and around the warp threads, yet tight enough to prevent little loops in the finished web.

Finishing the Ends Traditionally, each tapestry technique has its own method of finishing off the warp ends.

Blocking After removal from the loom all tapestries should be blocked and the warp ends finished. Small, sample tapestries can be steam pressed but this method is not advocated since it tends to flatten the threads, distorting the design. Blocking is the better method.

If soiled yarn has been used, the tapestry should first be washed thoroughly in a mild detergent dissolved in warm water. Whisk the tapestry up and down in the water. Avoid rubbing, rumpling, or wringing it as it is almost impossible to remove wrinkles. Be sure the colors are all runproof before washing the finished tapestry. Rinse the piece well and hang it on a line to drip-dry.

Proceed to block as follows:

1. Lay the finished tapestry on a flat, wooden surface such as the underside of a soft wood table or a piece of 5- or 7-ply veneer into which brads may be driven.

2. With a soft pencil, mark the wooden surface at each corner of the tapestry. With draftsman's square, join the four marks with lines that are exactly parallel. The corners will be right angles.

3. With brass or other small nonrusting brads, tack one selvedge with the edge parallel to one of the pencil lines. Start at the center of the selvedge and nail first in one direction, then the other, from the center toward the ends. Place the brads about ¾ in. apart.

4. Starting at the center of the side of the tapestry opposite that first tacked down, stretch it to the opposite line drawn on the board and tack. Make certain the tapestry is straight. Tack the four corners in place and tack back and forth from corner to center and vice versa.

5. After two sides have been tacked down, start at the center of one of the remaining two sides and tack toward one of the corners. Work carefully and be sure the end is not too full to fit into the space. If it is, start working from the corner toward the center and vice versa, easing the web into shape and patting it down. Do the same for the other half of the third side, then turn and repeat the process for the fourth side.

6. When the web is completely tacked down, it will appear straight and even if it has been woven correctly. Do not expect blocking to cure a poorly woven edge. It may straighten it a little but it will not correct poor weaving.

7. When the edges have been tacked down, dampen the tapestry thoroughly with a sponge and warm water.

8. It will require several days for the tapestry to dry thoroughly. Do not hasten drying by placing the tapestry over a radiator or in the sun. Best results are obtained through slow drying. Stand the board on end. When thoroughly dry, withdraw the brads carefully.

Methods of Turning and Interlocking Weft Threads There are several methods of turning back or interlocking weft threads where pattern and background areas meet. Some of these methods are illustrated here and their applications to the various tapestry weaves are described later in the text.

TECHNIQUE Warp Lock

A. Slit—Straight

This is the most simple tapestry technique. Each weft thread turns around its own single warp thread where the color changes occur, leaving a slit in the web. The two areas of weaving separated by the slit may or may not be sewn together (Fig. 507).

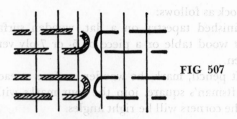

FIG 507

While a pattern area can be woven over two threads, four is a better number, especially for the beginner. A two-thread area, unless very carefully woven of fine thread, may twist and turn and, if the slits are sewn together, may be difficult to handle. Do not pull the weft threads too tight, or the straight lines at the edges of the units will pull in at a slant leaving gaps between the pattern areas. To sew the slits together, use either a buttonhole stitch, on the wrong side, or the French Gobelin method (page 501). If the buttonhole method is used, no stitches should show on the right side. After the sewing has been completed, the two sides of the seam should be pressed down flat. In the French Gobelin method, the stitches show on the right side.

B. Slit—Diagonal

This method is the same as technique *A* except that the right weft thread advances one warp thread further to the left with each shot, while the left weft thread covers one less warp thread in the same shed. The change is made as the weft proceeds from left to right (Fig. 508).

This method is used in Gobelin, the kilim where diagonals appear, and for the 40-deg. angle in the Navaho technique.

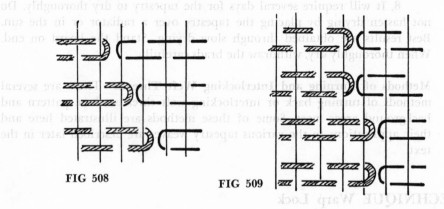

FIG 508   FIG 509

C. Slit—Diagonal in Pairs

Here the weft threads progress in pairs, leaving slightly longer slits than those produced by method *B*. This results in a more gradual angle. Method *C* (Fig. 509) is employed in the Gobelin and the Navaho.

D. Dovetail—Vertical Single Warp-Thread Turn

The weft threads are turned around the same warp thread making an interlocked turn. When the warp is beaten into position, there is a serrated line where the two colors alternate around the warp. Hard ridges can be felt when the finger is run along the edges of the pattern areas. Method *D* (Fig. 510) is used in the Navaho, sometimes combined with technique *F:* one technique being used on one side of the design, the other on the opposite side.

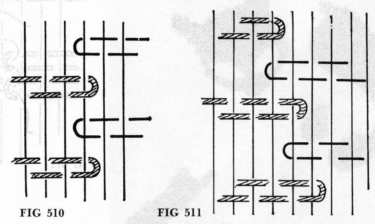

FIG 510   FIG 511

E. Dovetail on Diagonal

As with *B,* the weft threads advance on one side and recede on the other.

The weft threads lying in the same shed pass around the same warp thread to build up pointed designs (Fig. 511). To make a steep angle, as in the kilim, and for the 52.2 deg. of the Navaho designs, two shots of weft pass around the same warp thread before passing to the left or right to change the diagonal. It takes considerable practice to get the correct thread sequence.

This method is used in the Gobelin, the kilim, and the Navaho.

TECHNIQUE Weft Lock
F. Interlocking Weft

This interlocking weft method of turning the threads, when done on one shed only, does away with the ridge formed when the two weft threads are locked around the same warp thread (Fig. 510). Keep a straight line where the threads lock around each other. If these locks are not centered exactly between the warp threads, the edges of the pattern areas have a fuzzy appearance. Designs with angles can be woven with this technique by carrying the weft one warp thread further to the right or left.

This method is used for the åklae, the rölakan, and other techniques

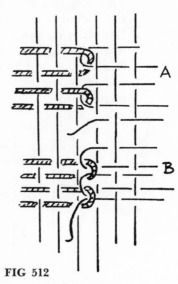

FIG 512

FIG. 513. Simple tapestry
showing various turning
techniques. Woven by Mary
E. Black, Nova Scotia.

to achieve special effects in modern tapestries. Low places in the weaving
can be brought to the fell level by weaving in short pieces of wool across
the area.

TYPE Tapestry · PATTERN Polish Kilim

The Polish kilim, to quote from an article by Halina Chybowska,[2] "is a
woven fabric that is neither carpet nor tapestry, but something between the
two.

"Kilim weaving, one of the oldest handicrafts known to man, was
popular among the Egyptians, the ancient Greeks, the Persians of old, and
the American Indians.

"In Europe, the kilim is virtually confined to Scandinavia, the
Ukraine, Rumania, part of the Balkans, and Southeastern Poland. Polish
kilims have long been considered among the most beautiful. . . .

"Polish kilim weaving is a native process the origin of which is lost in antiquity. It consists in interlacing woolen woof threads among warp threads so compactly that the warp does not show. The effect produced is that of an exquisitely soft but grainy surface. Woven into a rectangular space is a design consisting of rows of colored ornamental motifs arranged on a mono-chrome field and framed by a decorative border.

"Old Polish kilims were mostly the work of peasant craftsmen who, weaving in their cottages on simple wooden hand looms or in workshops of the nobility, produced without benefit of formal tuition, masterful pieces of color, texture, and composition."

Design Another writer has this to say about the Polish kilim, "It is their [the Polish peasants'] remarkable sensitivity to form, their insistence on decorative design at all costs of energy expended, which are the firm foundations of the quite remarkable art of Poland. If the peasants, in their bare and simple cottages, had not preserved for centuries certain mediaeval motifs and a highly developed manual dexterity, the modern weaving . . . would lack that very quality which . . . has won them such acclaim."

Practically all kilims have fringed ends and a border design with a scalloped or saw-toothed effect. Designs seldom are centered and there is no definite up or down. Favorite subjects for designs are birds, beasts, fish,

FIG. 514. A kilim of the peasant dance, with figures treated in a modernistic manner

FIG. 515. Kilim showing an Old Star motif

leaves, trees, and various geometric designs, all of which are highly stylized. Some of the older kilims woven in the homes of the nobility used heraldic motifs and were more similar in design and technique to the Gobelin or Flemish tapestries than to the original peasants' kilim characterized by the highly stylized, often repeated, design.

The Polish women, together with the Navaho women, have the distinction of being able to conceive a design in their minds and weave it without benefit of a cartoon. This is not true of all Polish weavers, of course, and many use a design which is slipped under or behind the warp and followed in the same manner as for the other types of tapestries.

Materials Originally, handspun, vegetable-dyed wool was used by the Polish weavers for their kilims; but, as in other countries, the advent of mechanically spun, factory-dyed wool which was cheap and labor-saving destroyed the true beauty of the kilim. However, the finer specimens of kilims have been and are being woven of hand-dyed homespun wool. Subtle coloring is achieved by uneven dyeing. Practically all the shades are derived from three dyes: cochineal, indigo, and onion skins. Dyeing wool is an art in itself and requires considerable time and skill, but the satisfaction obtained from weaving a kilim of home-dyed yarn more than offsets the extra work involved.

The weight desired for the finished kilim determines the size of wool. In general, kilims are fairly heavy so a heavy two-ply or fine three-ply wool can be used. Wool from a mill specializing in "homespun yarns" is preferable to yarn that has been highly processed. Homespun yarn has better body and dyes with a more interesting effect. Of course the ideal is an irregularly handspun yarn, dyed in the wool. The colors are beautiful and the texture unsurpassed. Heavy linen or hemp makes the most satisfactory warp.

Technique While it cannot be stated that all kilims are woven with a set technique wherein the weft threads are turned around their own warp thread (page 453), most of the samples studied have been woven in this way. Like other types of tapestries, the warp must be covered, so it is spaced at approximately 8 or 10 dents to the inch, according to the weft yarn being used. Where there are borders, and most kilim designs have borders, the weft threads are turned around a common warp thread (Fig. 510). This produces a firm edge. The slits in kilims are seldom, if ever, sewn together, for frequent changes in the design make this unnecessary. It is left to the individual weaver to decide whether to turn back and conceal the ends in the weft or to leave the ends loose on the back (Fig. 520). As the yarn is rather coarse, it is best to let the ends hang to prevent ridges along the pattern ridges. This is especially true if the design is a fine, complicated one with many color changes. Like the rölakan (page 471) and åklae (page 467), each row is woven across the entire width of the kilim, with the threads all going in the same direction and the turns made on the same shed.

Sample Illustrated (Fig. 519)

WARP	WEFT	REED (dents per inch)	SLEY
Hemp, fine, 3-ply	Wool, homespun, heavy, vegetable-dyed, 2-ply	8	Single

Number of Threads in Warp 148

The warp may be set on a high-warp loom if available, or threaded in a plain-weave threading (page 53) on a low-warp loom.

To Weave After the warp has been tied on and the threads are in order weave in five threads of warp to make a firm border against which to weave. In the sample, this heading has been left in at one end (Fig. 519). Next, weave in:

¼-in. white homespun wool,   2 rows blue homespun wool,
¼-in. yellow homespun wool,   ¾-in. yellow homespun wool.

This plain area can be woven in with a flat or boat shuttle, as can all the plain background areas which extend entirely across the width of the sample. The shed is changed with the treadles and is not finger-manipulated.

Work out the design on squared paper, allowing two threads to the square as for other tapestry weaves (page 450). Do not place the design under or behind the warp, but have it close at hand so the squares can be counted as the weaving proceeds.

The weft should be wound on bobbins or made into butterflies. Three yellow ones and two blue ones are required for the first two figures, and a rusty red for the center and end figures.

Like all tapestries, the kilim is woven with the wrong side toward the weaver.

Remember that each square on the graph paper represents two threads.

Open the shed and insert a yellow bobbin at *A* (Fig. 516) leaving an end long enough to turn around the edge warp thread and back into the shed (Fig. 44). Bring out the bobbin between the twelfth and thirteenth warp threads at *B*, turn the end around the warp, carry it for about ½ in. in the shed, bring it to the surface, and allow it to hang loose.

Next, insert a blue bobbin at *B*, carry it across 52 threads, and bring it out at *C*. This is the first row of the first pattern unit.

Insert the second bobbin of yellow weft at *C*, carry it across 20 threads, and bring it out at *D*.

Insert a second blue bobbin at *D*, carry it to the left, across 52 threads, and bring it to the surface at *E*. Enter the third yellow bobbin at *E*, pass it across 12 threads, and take it out at the left selvedge.

Tuck in all new ends at *B, C, D*, and *E*, as was done at *A*.

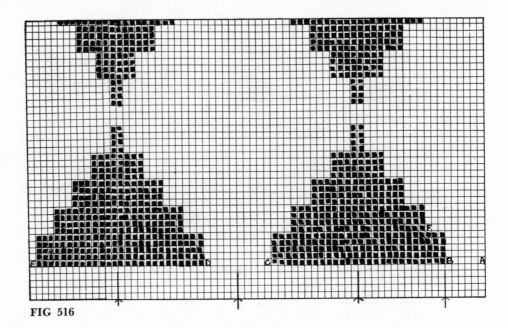

FIG 516

Comb back the weft loosely with the fingers and then beat with the reed, or with the fork or bobbins if there is no reed on the loom.

Change the shed and give the row a second beating.

Everything is now ready for the return of the bobbins from left to right. The procedure is exactly the same as for the first row.

The last bobbin now becomes the first, is passed through the shed, and is brought out between the threads at *E;* the first blue bobbin is passed through the shed and is brought out at *D;* the second yellow bobbin is brought out at *C;* the second blue bobbin at *B;* and the third yellow bobbin is brought out at the right selvedge. The beating is done and the shed changed. The third row now can be woven. Before proceeding, however, it is advisable to do a little checking.

Does a hole show at *B, C, D,* and *E?* If not, the bobbins have not been brought to the surface between the same threads as they were in the first row.

To have perfectly straight slits between the pattern units, the warp threads around which the weft turns (Fig. 507) should not be pulled either to the right or the left, but should be kept straight. The selvedge threads should not be drawn in, nor should loops appear along the selvedges. Remember that a straight selvedge is the mark of a good weaver. This is true particularly for weavers of wall tapestries.

The Polish kilim designs show a much freer interpretation than either the Swedish rölakan or the Norwegian åklae, so it is not necessary, unless the weaver so desires, to measure each pattern unit with a gauge. However, there should be some effort toward uniformity and, if this cannot be achieved without measuring, a gauge should be used (page 464).

The second unit of the design area, *F,* should be started. The bobbins travel from right to left, the first yellow bobbin covering 18 instead of 12 warp threads as in the first unit.

The blue bobbin thread, which had been cut after the last left-to-right row, starts new at *F.* All the bobbins must be started new where they enter the shed. This particular design is built up like steps on each side. When the second pattern is woven, it is in reverse of the first with the blue areas extending further out into the background as each pattern unit is woven.

It is suggested that the weaver learn to weave design units directly on the loom, without first working them out on paper. If simple designs are woven directly on the loom, the weaver will grow in knowledge and confidence and will be able, like the Polish and the Navaho women, the Zulus, and the Egyptian child weavers, to visualize and weave a kilim or rug without the aid of a prepared design.

To complete the sample, weave in five rows of the warp hemp.

The units of the sample are:

Crosses, probably the most simple designs to weave, are suitable for borders and corner designs. Eight warp threads are covered in the base, and each arm extends out eight threads to each side of the center (Fig. 517).

FIG 517

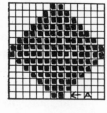 FIG 518

FIG 519

FIG 520

The small diamond-shaped design (Fig. 503), is woven according to the following directions.

First row: the weft thread passes over 4 warp threads.
Second row: the weft thread passes over 8 warp threads.
Third row: the weft thread passes over 12 warp threads.
Fourth row: the weft thread passes over 16 warp threads.
Fifth row: the weft thread passes over 20 warp threads.
Sixth row: the weft thread passes over 24 warp threads.
Seventh row: the weft thread passes over 28 warp threads.

At this point the diamond reverses back from the seventh to the first row.

The number of rows of weft in each "step" determines the angle of the diagonal (Fig. 518). If squared, a 45-deg. angle will result.

Problem   Set up a small warp and weave the above pattern units (Fig. 519).

TYPE Tapestry · PATTERN Norwegian Rölakan or Åklae

Lovely examples of rölakan, a traditional Scandinavian weave, are seen in wall hangings, rugs, table covers, upholstery, and cushion tops.

Although there are several types of rölakan, directions are given here for only one.[3] In all rölakans, the weft must completely cover the warp, though it should not cover it too easily or the material will tend to pack down, become spongy and too thick, and lose the identity of the design and the weave. When the weft has been laid in and beaten firmly, it should just cover the warp and no more. Rölakan is one of the most exacting of the tapestry weaves since each square must square up exactly according to measurement. Other types of tapestry allow much more freedom in the weaving than the rölakan or åklae; but, in the latter, the results in both design and fabric are superior.

Design   Rölakan designs are usually geometric arrangements of squares, crosses, stars, diamonds, and vertical and horizontal lines. Modern weavers employ geometric and highly stylized designs adapted from old or modern realistic designs.

All rölakan designs which use vertical and horizontal lines must be worked out on squared paper before the number of warp threads required can be computed (Fig. 521). In this text, each square of the design represents two warp threads. (With some methods, each square represents four threads.) For example, if there are 50 squares in the width of the design, 100 threads, plus four extra for the selvedges, would be required. The two or three outside threads on each side of the warp are doubled for all types of rölakan to prevent the edges from curling. For cushion tops, runners, or wall hangings in relatively lightweight material, it is sufficient to double two threads on each side; for rugs, three pairs may be necessary. However, when weaving the pattern, these pairs are considered as one thread.

The width of a design area should never be less than two squares wide and preferably not less than three or four squares wide. If the pattern areas are narrow it is difficult to lock the weft threads smoothly, and to get an even width.

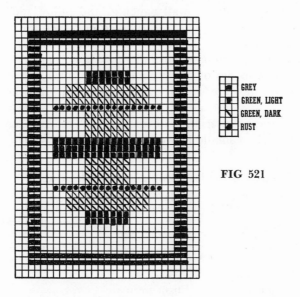

GREY
GREEN, LIGHT
GREEN, DARK
RUST

FIG 521

Technique Rölakan may be either reversible or nonreversible as desired; either weave is correct. The reversible is more difficult to weave, but the result is worth the extra work and care involved. Besides, most weavers make only one rölakan rug during a lifetime.

With the rölakan technique, the weft can be locked with a weft-lock going both ways (Fig. 512, B), resulting in a ridge on the back or working side of the material; or it can be locked only on the left-to-right shed (Fig. 512, A), producing a reversible fabric. The double weft-lock, called the Swedish rölakan, is easier to weave but not as practical. The single weft-lock, a Norwegian rölakan, is called åklae. The Norwegian technique is used in both countries. The Swedish rölakan is not used for rugs in either country because of the ridges caused by the interlocking weft threads.

Scandinavian weavers often refer to the shed in which the weft travels from right to left as the pattern shed, and the left-to-right shed as the locking shed, although other terms and methods can be used. The single weft-lock (Fig. 512, A) occurs as the weft travels from left to right on the locking shed. Pattern changes are made on the right-to-left pattern shed. The turning or locking must be done carefully so that it appears in a perfectly straight line between the two warp threads. If the weft-lock is pulled to either side, the finished design will have uneven sides.

Materials Hemp, linen, or jute are the best materials for the warp. The size depends upon the article being woven. A four-ply hemp is a satisfactory weight for a rug; a fine, two-ply linen for a wall hanging.

The ideal weft for rugs is the Swedish "nöthårsgarn" or cow-hair yarn which is now obtainable in this country in large quantities. However, commercial homespun yarns, ranging in size from heavy three-ply for heavy rugs to the fine single-ply for wall hangings and pillow tops are suitable and not too expensive. The ends or thrums from carpet mills are excellent. The difficulty with thrums, however, is that they must be purchased in fairly large quantities with no opportunity to choose colors.

Two or three shades of single homespun or thrums give more subtle color effects when they are twisted together than they do when laid in, in successive rows. Twisting is also the easier way to blend colors. Unless the weaver has a natural appreciation of color or has had considerable training in its use, a color chart should be worked out before the weaving begins.

Norwegian Rölakan or Åklae (Single-lock Technique)

WARP	WEFT	PATTERN	REED (*dents per inch*)	SLEY
Hemp-sizing twine, 4-ply	Homespun yarn, 2-ply, natural gray and cream	Carpet thrums, rust, dark green, and light green	8	Single

Threading Thread 4, 3, 2, 1 and repeat. When threading the outside pairs of threads, either thread the first two pairs double in the heddle or thread them 4, 4, 3, 3, 2, 1, then continue across the loom threading 4, 3, 2, 1, ending with 4, 4, 3, 3. Sley one thread per dent except for each side where the threads are sleyed two per dent twice on each selvedge.

Weaving Weave in ½ or ¾ in. of plain weave with the same thread used for the warp. If necessary, to keep the selvedges from pulling in, lay the weft in the shed in loose scallops so that it will cover the warp threads when beaten. This band of plain weave makes a firm foundation on which to weave, it helps regulate the width of the weaving, and holds it in place after the material is cut from the loom. The plain weave band is cut away before tying the fringe or hemming. As each pattern area of the rölakan weave must be exactly the same as the pattern, it is necessary to make and use a gauge. This is done by laying a piece of light cardboard or heavy paper on the warp in front of the reed. With a pen or pencil mark a line on the cardboard before every other dent (Fig. 522). The width of the two dents, or two warp threads, is the gauge for each square of the design, since each square in this sample represents two warp threads. The number of weft threads per inch or square cannot be the same as the number of warp threads, since the size of the weft varies considerably and the web is a weft-face weave, not a 50/50 plain weave. As the weaving proceeds, this cardboard gauge is used to measure the rows of weft. When the square has been completed, the weaver might assume that the next square can be started. However, other factors enter here. When the warp tension has been released, the square tends to flatten out. Also, the beating back of successive rows of weft will tend to pack down the block just woven. Therefore, it is wise to weave in an additional row or two before beginning the next square. An even number of rows is preferable, for it brings the bobbins into the correct position to start the next part of the design.

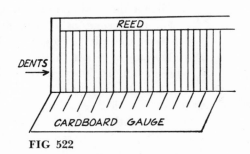

FIG 522

FIG 523

Weave the border in the width shown on the graph paper. This can be done with a shuttle or with a butterfly to avoid pulling in, since the weft goes across the entire piece from selvedge to selvedge. Measure with the gauge and allow at least two extra rows at the beginning since the successive rows will beat this further back than seems indicated.

When the border is finished start the pattern, remembering that the finished web is to be reversible and that all ends must be concealed.

At this point three butterflies (Fig. 143) or bobbins will be required: two gray and one white.

Try out the treadles to bring up the first and outside thread, or pair of threads, on the right-hand selvedge. As 50 threads and 4 border threads have been threaded for the sample, 25 will lie in the lower shed and 25 in the upper.

In the first or right-to-left row insert the first gray bobbin (or butterfly) into the shed from the right. Bring the bobbin to the upper surface between the 4th and 5th warp threads (not counting the selvedge threads), leaving an end sufficiently long to be turned back around the edge thread into the shed.

Insert the white bobbin in the shed between the 4th and 5th threads, where the gray bobbin was brought out, carry it along the shed to the left, to within four threads of the left selvedge, and bring it to the surface between the 46th and 47th warp threads. The end of this thread must be turned in and concealed in the shed. Now insert the second gray bobbin between the 46th and 47th threads, pass it through the shed, bring it out at the left selvedge, and conceal the end in the shed.

Comb the weft threads back with the fingers, leaving the threads rather loose or scallopy in the shed.

Check the ends carefully. All ends should be turned around the corner warp thread and tucked into the shed.

Change the shed and beat hard.

For the second or return, left-to-right row, insert the gray bobbin which is at the left selvedge and bring it out between the 4th and 5th threads from the left, actually between threads 46 and 47 where the bobbin had been entered in the first row. Bring the bobbin to the surface.

The rölakan sample is locked only on the left-to-right shed with a weft-lock (Fig. 512, A). The white thread and the gray thread are passed around each other midway between the two warp threads. Unless the locking, or turning, is centered exactly between the warp threads each time, the dividing lines between the design areas will be crooked. After the threads have been locked around each other, the gray bobbin is dropped and the white one is passed through the shed, from left to right, and is brought out between the 4th and 5th threads from the right, where it originally had been entered. Pass the white thread carefully around the gray, pick up the gray bobbin and pass it through the shed, bringing it out at the right selvedge. Comb the threads back with the fingers, change the shed, and beat hard three or four times.

One complete cycle has now been woven.

Starting again at the right, insert the bobbins in the same order as for the first row, bringing them out between the designated threads. Remember that there is no locking of threads on the right-to-left shed for this type of rölakan. Complete this cycle with a return row.

Continue this routine until the required width has been woven, as shown on the paper pattern between the border and the start of the center pattern. Measure carefully with the gauge.

At this point another white bobbin and a light green bobbin are introduced. All pattern changes take place on the right-to-left shed.

The gray bobbins on each selvedge, which weave the border, continue in the same routine as given above, being brought out between the 4th and 5th and 46th and 47th threads. The white bobbin is inserted between the 4th and 5th threads and brought out between the 18th and 19th threads; the light green bobbin is inserted between the 18th and 19th threads, passes through the shed, and is brought out between the 32nd and 33rd threads;

the second white bobbin is inserted between the 32nd and 33rd threads and is brought out at the 46th and 47th threads, where the left gray border begins.

Continue this routine until the green pattern area has been completed according to the gauge. Cut off the green thread, turning it back around the last warp thread which marks the pattern area and into the shed.

Follow the pattern from the graph paper, introducing all new colors when the bobbins are proceeding from right to left on the pattern shed.

When the sample has been completed, turn the end of the gray border thread around the selvedge thread and back into the shed (Fig. 44). Carefully turned in ends are the sign of a good weaver.

Weave in ¾ in. of hemp warp as at the beginning. Cut the tapestry from the loom, leaving the warp ends sufficiently long to tie into the desired type of fringe (page 586).

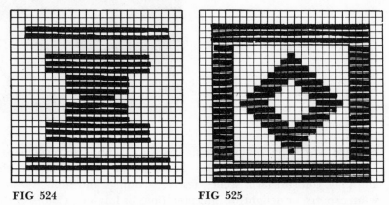

FIG 524   FIG 525

Problem Set up enough warp for two samples and weave one (Fig. 524) in two colors producing a completely reversible fabric.

Weave a second sample (Fig. 525) with four harmonious colors, tying off the ends and allowing them to hang loose on the back (page 505).

TYPE Tapestry · PATTERN Norwegian Åklae

Tapestry weaves are not for impatient weavers. They are time consuming, and patience and accuracy are required. The Norwegian åklae and the Swedish rölakan (page 462) demand more of the weaver than any other tapestry weave.

The beautiful Norwegian åklae wall hangings are well known to travelers who have visited the Scandinavian countries. They decorate both public buildings and homes, and are for sale in the many fine craft shops.

Design Old tapestries, woven originally for wall or bed coverings to keep out the intense cold of the long Norwegian winters, usually depicted

FIG. 526. From an ancient Norwegian tapestry

FIG. 527. Norwegian åklae weaving on a vertical loom

national sagas, mythological figures, or complicated geometric figures. Modern hangings, on the other hand, portray Norwegian youth at work and play, colorful farm scenes, festive weddings and holidays, summer and winter sports, or delightful interpretations of folklore. Colors in the modern pieces are lighter and gayer than those in the older tapestries, capturing the lighthearted, joyous spirit of modern Norway.

The designs are worked out in color on graph paper and are referred to constantly as the weaving proceeds. It is wise to mark each row as it is woven, either with a pin or by running a pencil line through the row. As with rölakan, each square on the paper represents two warp threads. The design, especially for the complicated geometric figures, must be worked out accurately. An error which will pass unnoticed on the paper will show up sharply in the weaving.

Materials Strong, tightly twisted cotton, hemp, jute, or linen threads are suitable for the warp.

If available weft should be of single-ply nöthårsgarn, a Scandinavian cowhair yarn with a lovely sheen. If nöthårsgarn is difficult to obtain, a satisfactory substitute is single-, two-, or three-ply homespun yarn, or some of the better commercial yarns. Colors should be soft and pleasing, not garish. The size of the threads depends entirely on the weight and purpose of the piece being woven. Those listed for the Swedish rölakan are suitable for the åklae as well. As with other types of tapestry weaving, the relationship between the warp, weft, and sleying must be such that the warp is completely covered.

The loveliest åklae hangings are, of course, those woven of vegetable-dyed, handspun wool. But here again, as in other countries, the time consumed in gathering the dyestuffs, dyeing, and spinning the wool makes the cost prohibitive. It is not surprising, therefore, that the completely hand-made pieces are woven only for special occasions and special people. Favorite colors of the Norwegian weavers are rust, green, brown, yellow, and medium blue, as well as white and enough black to balance the other colors.

The åklae and rölakan techniques are similar, therefore the directions will not be repeated. As with the rölakan there are several methods of weaving the åklae.

Those who are interested in rölakan and åklae are advised to consult the excellent packets on Scandinavian weaves prepared by Elmer W. Hickman. Clear, concise directions are given for the various weaves as well as sketches of the techniques, samples of the wools used, and a piece of the finished web.

Sample Illustrated (Fig. 529)   (Swedish rölakan, double-lock technique):

WARP	WEFT	REED (*dents per inch*)	SLEY
Linen, fine, 3-ply, tight-twist, natural color	Swedish weaving wool, best quality, fine, 2-ply, white, light buff, rose, green, blue	10	Single

The pillow cover (Fig. 529) is Swedish in design and is woven with Swedish yarns but in a rölakan technique. The edges of the design areas are straight and the colors harmonious and well balanced.

The turnings, or lockings, which are made on both the left-to-right and right-to-left sheds (Fig. 512, B), show up very plainly on the reverse side (Fig. 530). The ridge formed by the turnings can be felt easily with the fingers.

Lengths of the weft have been carried across from one completed pattern area to the start of the new one (Fig. 530). This procedure is correct, though very impractical if the wrong side of the material is subjected to any wear.

If a completely reversible hanging is desired, cut the weft ends about 1½ in. long and allow the ends to hang loosely from the weaving. The ends are not turned around the warp and into the shed, as before, but are concealed in the following way. After a few rows of weft have been woven beyond the place where the change occurs, thread the weft ends into a needle and pass it in beside the nearest warp thread. Bring the needle to the surface some rows below the weaving edge or fell and cut off the thread.

The end slips back into the weaving and is invisible. Do not draw the end down so tightly that the weaving is pulled out of line causing a hole; but do conceal the end well so that no loop shows at the darning point. All ends should be disposed of in this way for a completely reversible hanging.

If, on the other hand, a great many colors are used, as in the very beautiful Viking hanging woven by Elmer Hickman, no attempt should be made to conceal the ends as the result would be a very lumpy piece of work. To strengthen the hanging and prevent the ends from working through to the front, knot each end around the warp thread next to which it enters or leaves the shed at the beginning or end of the design area.

The knot is simple and can be made around either one or two warp threads. It should be tied after the warp thread has been entered in the shed and lies on top of the warp (Fig. 528).

FIG 528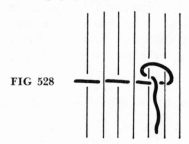

There is a method whereby, in changing colors from one pattern area to another, the old and new colors are carried along together, instead of cutting off the used color. Experienced weavers use this method since it is faster. This technique is difficult at first, but weavers who would like to try it can find explicit directions in current weaving literature.

The back of the pillow is a plain weft-face weave woven of cream-colored wool. The warp ends from both ends of the piece are knotted

FIG 529

FIG 530

together tightly to close the end of the case. If a visible fringe is desired, the ends are knotted on the right side; if not, the ends are knotted on the wrong side. The sides are sewn together. The size of the samples is approximately 15 by 15 in.

TYPE Tapestry ·
PATTERN Swedish Rölakan, Lightning;
Norwegian Lynildbordvevning

The lightning or *blixt* design of the Scandinavian weavers has a counterpart in the arrow design of the Indian weavers of southwestern United States. To the Indians, the design probably was suggested by the zigzag flashes of lightning against dark storm clouds and, to the Scandinavian weavers, the aurora borealis ascending and descending in colorful pageantry across the winter sky.

The directions given here and the illustrations (Figs. 537 and 538) are from a hanging woven by a Canadian weaver[4] while attending the Handarbetes Vänners Vävskola in Stockholm. This beautiful hanging is woven in soft green, yellow, creamy white, gray, and black wool.

The general information given for the Swedish rölakan applies also to the *blixt,* lightning, or zigzag rölakan. Almost any color combination can be used, even gray, black, and white with one bright color.

For the lightning rölakan, draw the design on plain paper to indicate both the color sequence and the zigzag sequence that is to be followed (Fig. 533). Do not place the design under the warp threads, but keep it nearby for reference.

Vary the design by lengthening or shortening the zigs or zags. The width of the stripe is always the same, except for the sides of the design where the diagonal stripe may run off.

The sample of the blixt technique described here (Fig. 533) has 144

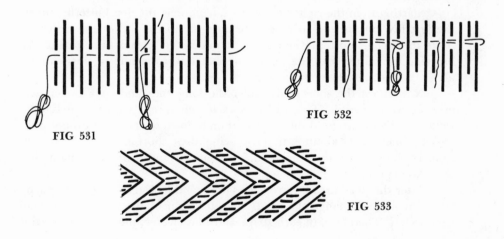

FIG 531

FIG 532

FIG 533

threads in the warp. However, since the two outside threads on each side are doubled and are woven as single threads, the piece is woven as though there were only 140 threads. There are 14 zigzags in the design with 10 warp threads in each stripe. Stripes can be woven in any desired length, but there must be an even number of warp threads in each stripe.

Materials Used in Sample (Fig. 538)

WARP	WEFT	REED *(dents per inch)*	SLEY
Linen, Swedish unbleached, 12/3	Wool, Swedish, 2-ply	10	Single

These materials are suitable in weight for a wall hanging or table cover.

Threading   Plain weave (page 53)

Weaving   Thread the loom on any threading that will produce a plain weave, and start the weaving with the pattern, with a border of plain stripe, or with stripes of plain weave in wool. Do not forget the band of plain weave which starts all tapestry weaves.

Rölakan is woven with the wrong side facing the weaver. It is much simpler this way.

As there are 14 zigzag stripes of 10 warp threads each, it is necessary to wind 14 bobbins or butterflies (Fig. 143). Then open one or the other of the sheds so that the first thread, actually the first pair of threads, on the right-hand side is up. Since each stripe is made up of 10 threads, there will be five *up* threads and five *down* threads in each stripe. The right-to-left shed is referred to as the *pattern* shed, and the left-to-right shed as the *locking* shed.

Starting from the right side of the warp, insert the first butterfly under the first five *up* threads, bringing the butterfly to the top of the material. Take the second butterfly and insert it under the second five *up* threads, bringing the butterfly to the top of the material. Continue in this manner across the width of the material (Fig. 531).

Now insert the short ends under the long ends and back under two or three warp threads. This will lock each weft thread with the preceding weft thread and also hold the short weft ends down so that they cannot pull out (Fig. 532). After about ¾ in. of weaving, these short ends may be cut off to make the weaving look neater and prevent the ends from catching under the weaving threads.

After the weft threads have been laid-in and locked all across the warp, beat sharply and change the shed. The direction of the diagonal is from right to left. Therefore, in each stripe and in each row, the weft thread will cover one more warp thread on the left side of the stripe and one less on the right side of the stripe. After the shed has been changed, the outside thread on the *left* side of the warp will be up.

Starting from the *left* side of the warp, insert the first butterfly under the first five *up* threads, bring the butterfly to the top of the material, and lay it across the second butterfly. Take the second butterfly from under the first (Fig. 534), insert it under the second five *up* threads, bring the butterfly to the top of the material, and lay it across the third butterfly. Continue in this manner across the warp, locking the weft threads as the weaving proceeds.

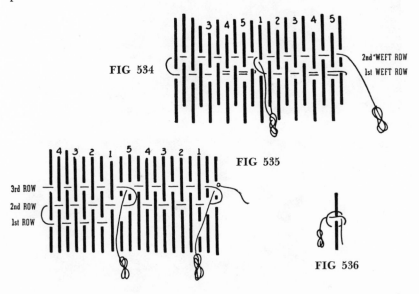

FIG 534

2nd ·WEFT ROW
1st WEFT ROW

FIG 535

3rd ROW
2nd ROW
1st ROW

FIG 536

Change the shed. To make the diagonal progress from right to left, another color stripe must be started. Tie the new butterfly around the first *up* right thread (Fig. 535), leaving the short end about 2 in. long. This short end can be darned up or down through the weft after weaving another inch or so. Bring the butterfly to the top of the material. Take the next butterfly across the top of the first butterfly and insert it under the next five *up* threads. Bring the butterfly to the top of the material. Take the third butterfly across the top of the second butterfly and under the next five threads, and so on, across the warp. Note that the last butterfly on the left-hand side will go under only four warp threads.

Continue in this manner. When the butterfly on the left side of the weaving comes to the last warp thread, tie it around that warp thread (Fig. 536). Leave a short end about 2 in. long to darn up or down into the web.

Continue the diagonal for the length desired, adding new colors on the right side where necessary and tying the thread off on the left side when a color ends.

To reverse the diagonal, start with the threads going from left to right, that is, through the shed where the outside left thread is up. Since the direction of the diagonal is now going from *left* to *right,* in each stripe and in each row, the weft thread will cover one more warp thread on the *right* side of the stripe and one less on the *left* side of each stripe.

To reverse the diagonal again, start the first reverse row from right to left, that is, in the same direction as the new diagonal.

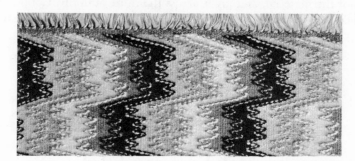

FIG 537

FIG 538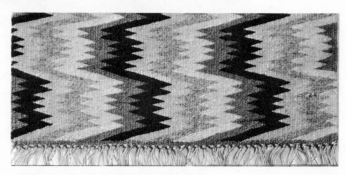

Finish the threads by locking them, as usual, in the last weft row. Then double back with each weft under two or three warp threads.

Weave in the border stripe or stripes to balance the beginning border, and then weave the tabby heading using the same material as the warp. Remember that this warp material is to be removed after the weaving is off the loom.

Problem Set up a warp and try a small sample to learn the technique.

TYPE Tapestry · PATTERN French Gobelin

In the Latin Quarter of Paris there is a tablet which reads "Jean and Philibert Gobelin, merchant dyers in scarlet, who have left their name to this quarter of Paris and to the manufacture of tapestries, had here their atelier, on the banks of the Bievre, at the end of the Fifteenth Century."

This tribute is the keynote to a long and fascinating history of the French Gobelin tapestry works and of a famous country during its most glorious and its saddest period.

These Gobelin brothers started what was to become one of the most famous European tapestry works. In 1667, during the reign of Louis XIV, the works was taken over by the State and Charles LeBrun was appointed director. The names of Gobelin and LeBrun are practically synonymous. His administrative ability, coupled with his innate feeling for the beauty to be expressed in properly designed and woven tapestry, made his a name to be looked up to, hated, or admired, depending upon whether the onlooker was weaving tapestries or buying them.

Fortunately much of the history of the European tapestry works has been preserved and much of this information is available to weavers through a text compiled and originally published in 1912 by Helen Churchill Candee.[5] While this text gives little information on the actual Gobelin weaving techniques, it provides background material concerning the history, the cartoons, dyeing, and use of colors, and contains many photographs of the world's famous tapestries.

The Design or Cartoon   LeBrun recognized the necessity of employing only the best talent to design the cartoons for the Gobelin tapestries. He found that a beautiful painting by a famous artist was still a painting when woven and not a tapestry. For a successful tapestry the cartoon must be designed by an artist who is familiar with the requirements of tapestry weaving, its possibilities and limitations. Beyond this, there must be complete understanding and recognition of their respective talents between the artist and weaver; the skill of one is useless without the skill of the other.

Any subject may be chosen for a tapestry, though the destination of the tapestry and the wishes of the customer also control the choice.

Tapestries with the traditional designs of fruits and flowers; human and animal figures; sport, hunting, and historical scenes do not fit too well into modern interiors.

These traditional designs have given way to the work of such moderns as Jean Lurçat,[6] who operates a small business, without State aid, at the old Aubusson tapestry works outside Paris.

There is little similarity in design and feeling between the Gobelin *mille fleurs* tapestries and the sometimes almost startling Lurçat tapestries, although Lurçat does uphold the old traditions of tapestry-weaving techniques much more than seems evident. Lurçat believes that the intelligent use of a few good colors is much more important than the unintelligent use of many. Was it not LeBrun who stated that in some of the most famous and beautifully colored Gobelins less than eighty colors were used?

The design for a first tapestry should be very simple and should embody the many problems which the student will meet. The tapestries shown in this text follow these precepts. The weaver should work out designs of a similar nature for his first tapestry. After the problems have been conquered, pictures of old and modern tapestries should be studied and designs formulated which embrace the principles shown.

An examination of old tapestries shows the use of bits of silk in various parts of the design to give strength and highlights not provided by the wool. Modern tapestry weavers interested in effect, rather than technique and the traditional use of wool, use whatever comes to hand to get the desired result.

The history, techniques, and general field of tapestry weaving are so extensive that it is possible, in a text of this size, to deal with only a short history and a few techniques.

The true Gobelin tapestry seems to have been woven originally on a high-warp loom, the haute-lisse, judging by the pictures of weavers painted during the early days of tapestry weaving. Later pictures show the low warp, the basse-lisse looms, in use as well.

Throughout the years, weavers have shown little interest in tapestry weaving. The reason for this may be that there has been no source from which to receive instruction and that written or verbal directions have shown considerable variation. Therefore it is particularly gratifying to be able to present weaving directions in this text for two of these techniques, the Swedish knot (page 480) and the nonshaded Gobelin (page 493).

FIG 539

These difficult techniques have recently been taught in America by Mrs. Albertine Durand Kelz, a pupil of the late Gaza Gilbert Foldes who studied at the Gobelin works (Fig. 539).

Materials and Colors   In the earliest tapestries a wool warp was used. After cotton was introduced to Europe, weavers adopted cotton since it was cheaper and easier to weave on. However, tapestries woven on wool are considered more beautiful than those woven on a cotton warp. Hard-twist 3- or 4-ply yarns, obtainable under the name of "tapestry wool," are used for wefts in Gobelins.

FIG. 540.   Front of loom with tapestry during weaving

FIG. 541.   Back of loom during weaving

Colors should be chosen to match the cartoon or vice versa. The Gothic designs, on which modern tapestries are based, used few colors and only wool. The better tapestries show a restrained use of color, the true Gothic showing less than one hundred shades, which is remarkable when a study of the subtle shading is made. Tapestry is shaded by "hatching" and by twisting fine threads of different shades together. The "hatching" process is involved and intricate and requires deep concentration to obtain the correct results. It should be studied under the personal direction of a competent instructor. For the benefit of weavers who do not have access to such professionals a directional chart is given here (Figs. 542 to 548).

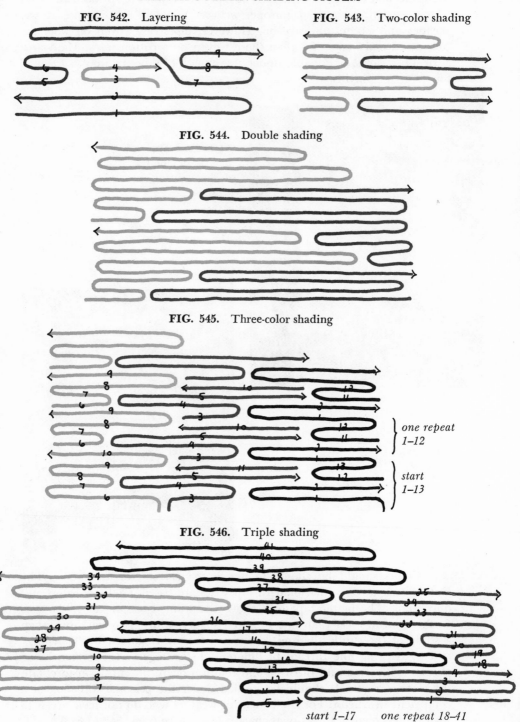

FIG. 542. Layering

FIG. 543. Two-color shading

FIG. 544. Double shading

FIG. 545. Three-color shading

} one repeat
1–12

} start
1–13

FIG. 546. Triple shading

start 1–17   one repeat 18–41

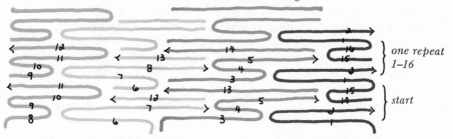

FIG. 547. Four-color shading

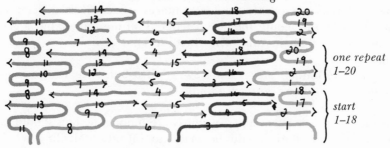

FIG. 548. Five-color shading

Shading and hatching charts prepared by Evelyn Longard, Nova Scotia

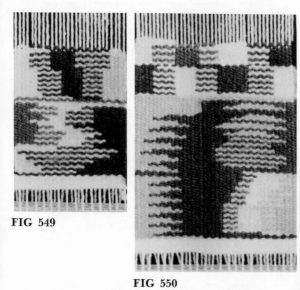

FIG 549

FIG 550

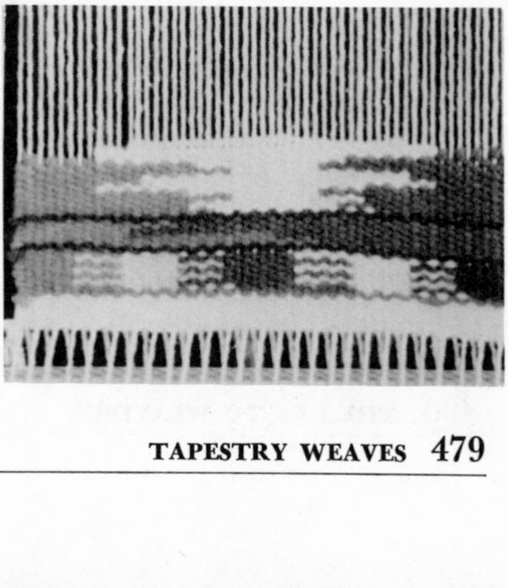

FIG 551

TYPE Tapestry · PATTERN French Gobelin—Swedish Knot

The reason for calling this type of tapestry weave the Swedish knot is obscure, since the technique is actually one of the first steps used in instructing students and apprentices in French Gobelin tapestry weaving.

This is a restful, fascinating type of weaving, little known to hand weavers. It is not used commercially because of the time element and because of the amount of wool required. For the home weaver or the semi-invalid, to whom time is not important, it is excellent.

The loom is small and light and can be carried easily from place to place.

Upholstery for home use, woven in this technique, has a long life if good, fast-colored wools are used. The technique also is suitable for handbags and purses. One of the disadvantages is that it is difficult for the average person to mount the heavy material on the frames, but a good bag manufacturer will do this. The Swedish knot also is suitable for wall hangings.

The technique may seem slow at first but once the processes are mastered the weaving proceeds rapidly.

Design   As this is essentially a primitive technique, designs should be kept simple and no effort should be made to introduce shading within the design areas. Colorful effects can be obtained through the introduction of areas of blended or contrasting colors. Stylized and abstract designs are best.

Materials for Samples Shown

WARP	WEFT	REED *(dents per inch)*
Cotton, 6-ply — Triton	Tapestry yarn, Bernat	13

Loom   The loom is a plain wooden frame, approximately 16 by 23 in. (outside measurements), similar to those used by artists on which to stretch their canvas. The pieces of the frame should be about 1½ in. wide and ¾ in. thick.

Once the frame is warped it should be guarded carefully and never left where an object might be placed on it. It should be protected from climatic changes, which will affect the tension, by slipping it into a plastic pillow case, a blanket bag with a zipper, or a plastic suit-length garment bag. Let the uninitiated laymen admire the weaving through the bag.

Dressing the Loom

1. *Assembling the Frame.* Assemble the canvas stretcher or frame. Using a wooden mallet, tap the corners into position so that the frame is

exactly square. *Do not use a frame in which the wood is warped.* Put a
½-in. screw in each corner, otherwise the tension of warp may move the
corners, or, if the frame is dropped, it may come apart.

2. *Marking 1-in. Marks on the Top and Bottom of the Frame.* On top
of the frame, make a pencil mark 3 in. in from the left side and every inch
up to within 3 in. from the right side. On each mark, rule a straight line
across the width of the top of the frame.

Turn the frame upside down. When marking the bottom edge be
sure to mark in from the *same* left side. Mark in the same manner as along
the top edge. Rule straight lines across the marks.

Turn the frame on its side, center it in the vise with a piece of felt
around it to prevent marring, and to hold it steady.

3. *Winding the Cotton in a Ball.* Wind the cotton warp into a tight
ball. Turn the ball constantly while winding it very tightly.

4. *Winding on the Warp.* Start at the upper left side (this will really
be the bottom of the frame) and tie the warp around the frame just below
the pencil mark. Tie two knots plus at least two extra slipknots with the
short end of the cotton, to prevent slipping.

Holding the warp *tight,* carry the ball to the back of the right frame,
to the front of the right frame, under the first warp thread, to the back of
the left frame, and then to the front of the left frame. This will make a
figure 8 in the warp. Continue this sequence, keeping an even tension on
the warp and pulling the thread constantly so that the warp will be as tight
as possible (Fig. 552).

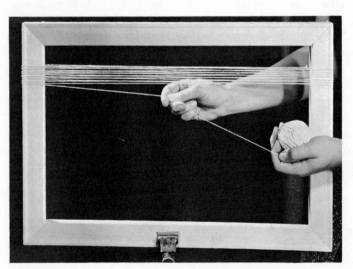

FIG 552

The Swedish knot, using 6-ply cotton for warp and Bernat's tapestry
yarn for weft, should be set at 13 threads per inch. In threading the loom,
the 13 threads will lie between the two inch marks at the top and bottom

ends of the loom frame, six between the inch with the seventh on the inch mark.

If the ball of warp is not long enough, tie on a new ball of warp and continue the warping. *Always* knot the new and old threads at the top or bottom of the frame.

Once the warp is started, it must be finished. The tension is lost if the warp slackens, and the entire warping must be done over again.

When the required number of threads have been wound on the frame cut the thread, allowing an extra 15 in. at the end of the warp. Tie the end around the frame twice. Tie two knots plus at least two extra slipknots on top of the first two knots so that it is impossible for the warp to slip.

Space the threads evenly at the top of the frame. A thread will rest on every other line. Be sure the threads are *straight*. Follow the same procedure along the bottom edge of the frame. Hold the frame between the knees while checking the threads.

Cotton Heading

1. Remove the frame from the vise. Wind the warp cotton on a netting shuttle. Hold the frame in weaving position. Tie a cotton end from the shuttle to the lower left side of the frame. Tie two knots plus two slipknots as before.

Make certain that the two left, outside threads are not together; that is, there should be one up and one down, or vice versa. This arrangement may be adjusted at the top left of the frame, where the knot is, by moving the outside thread up or down, as required.

Make any necessary adjustment for the outside right thread in the same way, with the knot at the bottom right side of the frame.

2. Insert the shuttle from the left through about 1 in. of threads bringing the figure 8 to the bottom of the frame. Drop the shuttle and, holding the weft thread in the left hand, beat down with the fork. Hold the fork loosely at the end of the handle and use a "throwing" motion when beating so that the weft will beat in firmly. Pick up another inch of threads, insert the shuttle, beat, and continue in this manner across the width of the warp.

Pull the weft tight and carry it around the right side of the frame twice. *Continue to hold* the cotton tight.

Pick up the opposite shed about an inch at a time and weave from right to left, beating as you do so.

Do not go around the right and left frame again, but continue weaving the tabby heading for about 5⁄16 in. The weft must completely cover the warp.

3. Tie the cotton thread around the right upright about 5 in. from the top of the frame. Weave this thread across the width of the loom, to put the shed into "neutral." Tie the end securely to the left upright and cut off the long end (Fig. 553).

FIG 553   FIG 554

Inking the Design Onto the Warp   The weaving is done with the wrong side facing the weaver, therefore care must be exercised when drawing on and inking in the design so that the pattern will be right side out when the weaving is finished. Particular attention should be paid to designs with letters, numerals, directional signs, or activities.

1. Draw the design on paper, then paint in the desired colors.

2. Trace the design onto tracing paper in black India ink with a fairly coarse pen to make wide lines.

3. When the ink has dried, carefully place and pin the tracing-paper design into position under the warp threads with the wrong side up. Before placing the design behind the warp, study it to determine the better way to weave it. Some designs weave better if placed as drawn, with the base of the design at the base of the weaving, while other designs should be placed with the side at the base of the weaving. Place a drawing pad under the warp to provide a firm, light-colored surface on which to work.

4. With a crow quill pen and dark blue India ink, mark a dot on each warp thread where it lies over the design line. Work from left to right to prevent possible smudging of the design (Fig. 554). Black India ink will smudge and spoil the design dots after a few rows of weaving. Red ink is reserved for correcting the design, if necessary, as the weaving proceeds.

5. After the design has been completely dotted onto the warp, remove the tracing paper and allow the ink to dry.

6. Now, ink the dot completely around the warp thread. This is done by twisting the thread several times toward the left with the left hand first

and then placing the point of the crow quill pen, which has been dipped in blue ink, exactly under the dot where it lies on the surface of the warp thread. As the thread untwists against the inked pen, a mark is made around the thread. The thread, not the pen, does the work. Do not try to maneuver the pen around the thread; it will leave a blot instead of a line. If the inked line is not thin and correctly placed, mistakes will be made in the weaving since the weaver will not know the exact spot where the pattern design stops. Remember to ink from left to right. After all the inking has been done, allow the ink to dry thoroughly before starting the weaving.

Winding the Bobbins Directions already have been given (page 128) for making butterflies for tapestry weaving, but these are not suitable for the Swedish knot technique. The bobbins should not be too large or there will be too much wear and tear on the wool. Bobbins are made by winding the wool around the fingers:

1. Take the end of the wool and wind it around the ends of the index and middle fingers of the left hand which have been placed closely together (Fig. 555).

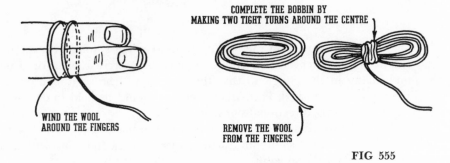

COMPLETE THE BOBBIN BY
MAKING TWO TIGHT TURNS AROUND THE CENTRE

WIND THE WOOL
AROUND THE FINGERS

REMOVE THE WOOL
FROM THE FINGERS

FIG 555

2. Make about 12 turns around the fingers, winding the yarn snugly yet not tight enough to stretch the wool. When the required number of turns have been made, slip the wool from the fingers and hold it at the center between the thumb and finger of the left hand. Make two very tight turns around the middle of the bobbin with the bight of yarn, ending with two or three looser turns. Cut the yarn from the skein leaving an end of about 8 or 10 in. with which to work.

3. When a bobbin is not in use, it is wise to make a half hitch around the middle with the bight to prevent its unwinding as it lies at the back of the work.

Weaving

1. Sit in a straight, comfortable chair and rest against the chair back to prevent fatigue. The top of the loom rests against the edge of a table and

the bottom in the weaver's lap. The under or wrong side of the loom faces the weaver.

2. Start weaving at the edge of the cotton warp heading, which was woven in when the loom was warped.

Take a bobbin in the color chosen for the border, and tie the end of the bobbin thread around the first warp thread close to the heading at the lower left-hand corner of the loom.

After having made this knot, put the "tail" in to the left, under the warp thread to which it is tied. Tie all new bobbins in the direction in which the weaving is going. The tails lie in the direction *from* which the weaving is coming.

Going from left to right, pass the bobbin under the warp thread so the tail end will be out at the left, take it over, under, and over the bight (Figs. 556 and 557).

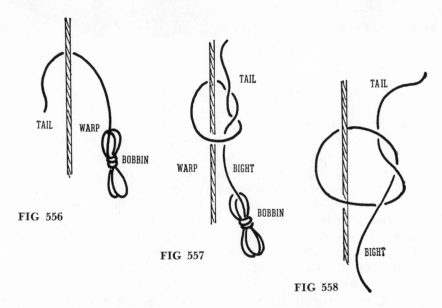

FIG 556

FIG 557

FIG 558

Going from right to left, pass the tail of the bobbin under the warp as before (Fig. 556), then pass the tail under, over, and under the bight (Fig. 558).

3. Pass the index and third fingers of the left hand, with the palm facing you, under the first and second warp threads at the left of the loom and about 5 or 6 in. up from the fell. Keep the thumb above the warp threads, the fourth and fifth fingers tucked back against the palm of the hand, out of the way.

4. With the index finger and the thumb, pull back to the left the first warp thread on the left, which already is covered by the knot. This separates the first warp thread from the second. Pick up the second warp thread and push it toward you with the third finger.

FIG 559   FIG 560

5. Carry the bobbin of weft thread along and slightly to the left of the warp thread, the bight of the bobbin thread and the warp lying parallel to each other (Fig. 559).

6. Lift the thumb off the warp thread and use it to hold the bobbin thread loosely against the first warp and the index finger; move the bobbin over the warp thread at right angles and to the right of the warp thread. This locks the weft thread in position for the knot to be tied.

Hold the bobbin in the center between the thumb and index finger and pass it under the warp thread from right to left, guiding it with the middle finger. When completely through the opening, take it again between the thumb and index finger of the right hand and slide it down to the fell of the weaving in a single swift motion ending in a knot. In bringing the bobbin down, the bight of weft is kept in direct alignment with the warp threads and is not allowed to angle to either the left or the right. The knot that is tied around the warp thread is actually a half hitch or, to those who are accustomed to embroidery stitches, a buttonhole stitch (Fig. 560).

7. The two warp threads around which knots have been tied are held in the crook of the middle finger of the left hand.

Bring a new warp thread forward into position, with the tip of the middle finger, so that it is ready to have the knot tied around it. The bight of the thread lies to the left of the third warp and is held, along with the first and second warps, with the index finger and thumb of the left hand, as before.

8. After knots have been tied around six or eight warp threads, drop them from the left hand and pick up new warp threads. Knotting continues across the entire warp, including the last thread at the right.

9. Examine both sides of the weaving frequently. The beginner sometimes discovers that a warp thread has been missed, leaving a white spot. Traditionally, errors of this type are referred to as "lice." Also, two warps may have been tied together. If mistakes are found, use a blunt-pointed tapestry needle to loosen the knots and unweave back to the error. Correct it and reweave.

10. To weave from right to left, the method of inserting the bobbin and tying the knot is reversed.

The fingers of the left hand are inserted as before, from the left to right, but in a higher position—about 8 to 10 in. from the fell—as the knot is made entirely below the left hand. Pick up the warp farthest to the right with the left hand; include the edge thread for a total of six or eight warp threads.

Hold the first thread on the right apart from the others with the middle finger of the left hand. Keep the weft bight parallel to and at the right of the outside warp thread by holding the bobbin with the thumb, index, and middle fingers of the right hand. The weft thread is looped over the back of this hand. Now pass the bobbin across the warp thread, under it, and out between the warp thread and the bight of the weft.

With a single motion draw it swiftly down the fell (Fig. 561). Drop the warp thread just knotted off the end of the finger.

FIG 561

11. Separate the next two warp threads. The left hand always holds the threads at about 8 or 10 in. from the fell to allow for the easy separation of the warp threads and for the easy insertion of the bobbin below the fingers holding the threads.

Make a knot around the second warp thread, pull it tight, and slip the warp thread from the finger in the same manner as for the first.

An examination of the right selvedge will show a knot or loop lying at right angles to the weaving and parallel to the warp. This is quite in order. A series of similar knots will continue along each selvedge for the entire length.

12. Continue across the warp from right to left, knotting around the last warp thread at the left as was done at the right selvedge, and pulling the threads snugly to prevent a ridge. Reverse the order of knotting, working from left to right. The rows of knotting are repeated in alternating succession from left to right and right to left until the border is the desired width.

End the weaving of the border at the left edge but do not cut the thread. This bobbin will be used to weave the left border.

13. Make a paper gauge the exact width of the border and turn it across the warp at right angles. Measure and count the number of warp threads that lie within the mark. Seven or eight is a good number for a border the size of the samples being woven.

14. Weave from left to right across the eight left warp threads with the bobbin. On the ninth warp thread, tie in the background bobbin and weave across to within eight warp threads of the right side.

15. Tie in a bobbin of the border color around the eighth thread from the right side, weave across these threads to the edge, turn, and weave back toward the left covering the eight threads a second time.

16. Pick up the background bobbin and pass it under, to the right, and above the border thread; start weaving toward the left. This is called interlocking. Pull these threads snugly together to prevent a ridge from developing at the point of interlocking. Reverse the method of interlocking weaving from left to right.

17. Continue across the background to the left border, interlock the threads again, and, with the border thread, weave to the left edge, turn, weave over the eight threads, and interlock the border and background threads. Continue back and forth across the entire warp up to the point where the first pattern dots begin.

Note that during the weaving the weft thread untwists when proceeding from left to right and twists in going from right to left. It is necessary to correct this twisting because the weft will show up on the right side as either thin, tight rows or as fuzzy areas.

As the weaving grows, the side edges roll under. To correct this, thread a tapestry needle with a piece of warp thread and run the needle through the border between the first and second warp threads. Tie the thread around the loom frame; it must not be tied too tightly. Make a similar tie on the opposite side of the weaving. If necessary, as the weaving grows, make these ties at intervals of 2½ or 3 in. along the border.

Stop within 1½ or 2 in. of the ends of the bobbins and let the end hang loose. Tie in the new bobbin according to directions (page 484). Do not tie in new bobbins at points where pattern areas are interlocked. Do not tie one new bobbin directly above another. Do not tie a new bobbin at the edge of the tapestry.

Weaving the Pattern   In the Swedish knot technique, each row of weaving does not always cross the entire warp from border to border thereby covering the colored design areas, as occurs in other tapestry weaving, for example, the kilim (page 458). Border, background, and design areas are built up as more or less separate units, depending greatly upon their relative positions because of the necessity of *interlocking wherever one color of the design meets another in a vertical position*. In other words, the parts of the design always are interlocked except for certain portions of diagonal lines, circles, and curves (Fig. 562). The wavy lines crossing the design lines (Fig. 563) show the points where interlocking takes place.

FIG 562

FIG 563

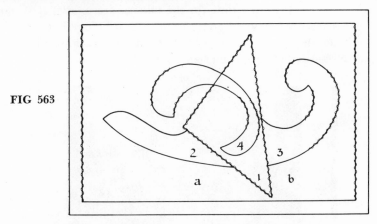

1. Following Fig. 563, weave from left to right up to the first pattern area 1 and tie in the new pattern thread. In the design shown, this thread goes around two warp threads. Make a second stitch around this thread; tie in a new bobbin for the background *b* and continue weaving to the right edge.

2. Weaving from right to left, follow the same sequence as in the preceding row, interlock at the right border and background *b*, at background *b* and pattern area 1, at pattern area 1 and background *a*, and at background *a* and the left border.

3. Continue in this manner, following the pattern dots up to pattern area 2. Note that, up to now, the weaving has proceeded back and forth across the loom. With the addition of pattern area 2 a new problem arises, that is "building up" and "filling in."

4. With the background *a* bobbin, build up the background area following the curve of pattern area 2, at the same time interlocking this thread with the left border thread. Note that when building the pattern 2 curve, weaving from right to left, weft skips develop and are unavoidable.

5. When filling in pattern area 2, the right side of the area will be interlocked with the diagonal line of pattern area 1. A new bobbin is tied in for 2 and woven to the built-up area of background *a*. When returning from left to right, the first knot of this second row is to be made in the same manner as the knots in the preceding row, thus joining the rows neatly. All other knots in this row are made in the usual manner when weaving from left to right. To complete the "filling in" of this area repeat these two rows.

6. When filling in pattern area 3 the above procedure is reversed:

The left side of the area is to be interlocked with the diagonal line of pattern area 1. A new bobbin is tied in for 3 and woven to the built-up area of background *b*. When returning from right to left, the first knot of this second row is to be made in the same manner as those of the preceding row. All other knots are to be made in the usual manner when weaving from right to left.

7. If at any time (in the pattern areas *only*) it is more convenient to start a new bobbin going from right to left rather than from left to right, do so; or, if it is more convenient to start a new bobbin going from left to right rather than from right to left, then do so.

FIG 564

The above information covers all the steps in tying in new threads, interlocking, building up, and filling in. If in doubt, it is better to interlock than run the risk of having a slit. No slits are permissible in the Swedish knot technique so the weaving and interlocking must proceed with thought and with careful and constant attention to the original cartoon as well as to the dots on the warp threads.

It is important that the student weaver start with designs which bring out the problems to be faced. Fig. 564 was designed by a student to point up these problems. Remember that all design dots must be covered completely before moving on to the adjacent design areas.

Curious as it may seem, the design will work out without trouble. Watch the design carefully where there are overhangs or widenings to be sure that the background or adjacent design areas which should be built up are woven before any attempt is made in filling in these areas. Proceed slowly, check the original design to be sure what the dots on the warp threads represent, and do not weave extensively in any one area in order to avoid the danger of failing to interlock with adjacent areas (Fig. 563).

Finishing

1. Upon completion of the pattern area, weave in a top border the same width as the bottom one.

2. Remove the piece of warp thread which was inserted when the loom was warped to hold the threads in a flat or "neutral" position (page 482).

3. Weave in the same number of rows of warp heading at the start. Beat tightly into place with fork (Figs. 565 and 566).

FIG 565

FIG 566

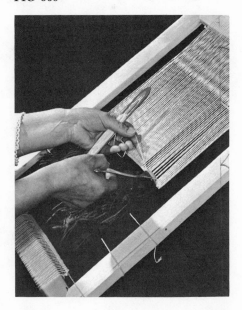

FIG 567

4. With a sharp-pointed shears cut the warp threads across the end of the loom where the weaving started (Fig. 567). Do not be alarmed when the piece rolls up like a mailing tube, it will straighten out later.

5. Tie together the last two warp threads at the left edge, the last two at the right edge, and the two threads at the center of the web to prevent the weft from slipping out.

6. Cut across the warp about 6 or 8 in. beyond the top of the weaving (Fig. 568) and tie groups of warp threads together as at the opposite end.

7. Gobelin tapestries are never finished with a fringe. Either of two methods may be employed to finish the ends: (1) Tie the warp ends in groups of two threads only completely across the web, or (2) machine stitch across the edge of the heading. In either case, turn the heading back far

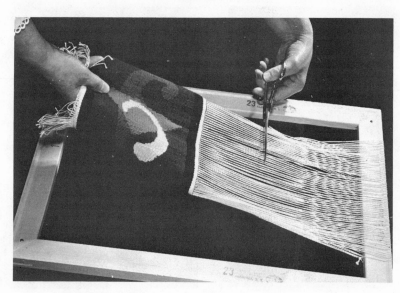

FIG 568

enough so it does not show from the front and sew it down against the underside of the tapestry. Cut the warp ends evenly and cover the ends and the warp heading with a piece of carpet binding, or conceal them inside the lining. Many tapestries are lined, some of the older ones with hand-woven linen.

8. It will be recalled that when new weft threads were required they were tied around the warp threads leaving approximately 2 in. of the "tail" hanging, as well as the end of the old bobbin thread. Tie these two threads together with a double knot to keep them from slipping through to the right side. The tapestry now is ready to be blocked (page 452).

Problem   Set up the loom and practice inking on the pattern and making knots. When you can do these skillfully, weave the sample.

TYPE Tapestry · PATTERN French Gobelin, Nonshaded

The experience which the weaver gains in learning the Swedish knot technique is valuable in learning the French Gobelin. While there is little similarity between the two techniques, the general process of building up the pattern areas, threading the loom and inking on the design, selecting colors and materials, accurately following the dots, and developing of self-discipline is all of value.

The French Gobelin requires a shed; it is woven with wooden bobbins; there is little or no interlocking of threads; and slits, which are not found in the Swedish knot technique, appear constantly in the French Gobelin.

After weaving a sample in each technique, the weaver may ask himself which technique he most enjoys weaving. The answer is not easy because each technique has fascinating appeal and only after considerable experience will the weaver be sure.

Materials for Samples Shown

WARP	WEFT	SLEY
Cotton, 6-ply — Triton	Tapestry yarn, Bernat	11 per inch

Loom   The loom is similar to the one used for the Swedish Knot (Fig. 553) and is threaded with the same materials in the same manner (pages 480 through 484).

For the French Gobelin sample there are 11 threads between each 2-in. mark at both the top and the bottom of the frame. The Swedish Knot had 13.

Provision must be made for a shed. Two wooden brackets are required with holes through each for the insertion of a ⅝-in. dowel (page 494).

Dressing the Loom

1. Assemble the frame in the same way as for the Swedish knot. Then, measure 3 in. down on the left upright from the top of the frame and place the bracket below the 3-in. mark, with the inside of the bracket flush with the inside of the frame. Make two holes through the bracket and into the frame. Insert screws, making certain that the screws do not go more than halfway through the frame. Put the right bracket on in the same way.

2. Pad the jaws of a vise with felt or rags, center the bottom of the frame in the vise, and tighten the vise.

Insert the dowel through the holes of the brackets.

Fasten a flat stick approximately 2 by ½ by 24 in. securely behind the warp threads so that the lower edge of the stick is parallel to the top of the dowel.

3. Wind the netting shuttle, using the same thread as is in the warp.

4. Tie the thread securely around the dowel outside the left bracket. Carry the thread across the dowel to the outside of the right bracket, around the dowel, back across to the outside of and around the left bracket; repeat these steps. Make two buttonhole stitches around the four threads outside the bracket.

There are four threads across the face of the dowel and fastened securely at both ends of it. These, for convenience, can be called "dowel threads."

Carry the shuttle over the bracket, over and back of the dowel, under and to the front of the dowel, making a buttonhole stitch at the dowel threads about 1 in. from the bracket. Pull the knot tight. The dowel threads do not yet lie tight against the dowel.

Make two buttonhole stitches around the dowel threads, pulling each tight and close against the preceding stitch.

Continue this sequence (once around the bar, twice around the four threads) until the dowel threads are tight against the dowel and the shuttle is lined up straight with the first *back* warp thread.

Put the point of the shuttle in to the *left* of the first back thread (Fig. 569) and let the shuttle rest on the dowel and the flat stick at the back of the loom. Separate the threads below the flat stick with the right hand. Bring the shuttle with the right hand to the *right* of the back thread and bring it forward through the warp threads and below the flat stick. Make a buttonhole stitch beside the last stitch. This makes one heddle. Make two stitches around the dowel threads. Make a heddle for the next *back* warp thread, following the directions for the first heddle, and make two stitches around the dowel threads. Continue in this way across the width of the warp. (NOTE: Occasionally it will be necessary to make an extra stitch on the dowel threads so that the heddle always is directly in line with the back warp thread.)

Every inch, make a buttonhole stitch around the dowel to hold the stitches tight against the dowel.

After the last heddle has been made, make two stitches around the

FIG 569

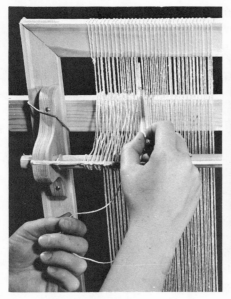

FIG 570

dowel threads, one around the dowel, two around the dowel threads, one around the dowel, and three around the dowel threads; then tie a firm knot so that the stitches cannot slip. Clip the end of the thread (Fig. 570).

5. *Test for and Correct Mistakes*. Obviously, there should be no mistakes. However, if there are any, they can be detected easily by inserting the hand in the open shed and drawing it down to the tabby heading. The mistakes will appear as twisted warp threads just above the heading.

If a mistake has been made near the beginning, it will probably make the rest of the warp twisted; in this case cut off the heddles and start again. If the mistake is near the end, rip back to it, tie on a new thread where the buttonhole stitches are, and restring the remaining heddles. If the mistake only involves one or two warp threads, without causing the rest of the warp to be incorrect, tie in a new heddle always tying it on the dowel bar beside the buttonhole stitches.

6. Tie a thread around the right upright just below the bracket and weave across the loom making a "neutral" shed as was done for the Swedish knot. This thread is removed after the design has been inked on the threads.

Inking the Design on the Warp   The design is inked onto the warp following the directions given for the Swedish knot technique (page 483). The designs used for the samples were especially planned to train the student to meet and overcome the various problems confronting the beginner.

Bobbins   Regulation Gobelin tapestry bobbins are used (Fig. 571). They should be well-balanced, smoothly finished wood. Keep the points smooth with a piece of fine sandpaper.

The bobbin is used to carry the weft thread, open up spaces between the warp threads, and beat the weft down into place. The conventional reed and beater are never used for Gobelin weaving as the fell of each design area lies at a different height on the warp.

The bobbin is wound around the yarn; to wind the yarn around the bobbin twists it too much. The end with which the weaving is done comes from underneath the neck. Wind only enough yarn on the bobbin to fill the area indicated with dotted lines on Fig. 571. If the bobbins are too full the wool scrapes against the warp threads and becomes fuzzy.

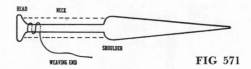

FIG 571

Do not stretch the wool when winding the bobbin. When the bobbins are not in use make a half hitch with the bight of the yarn around the neck of the bobbin; the bobbin can hang down in front of the loom without unwinding.

Weaving   As with the Swedish knot technique, the weaving starts with a heading of warp beaten tightly back against the lower inside edge of the loom frame (page 482).

Next comes the border. The width must first be decided upon, then the gauge made (page 488).

The Gobelin is a weft-face plain weave so it is necessary to have a shed. This is controlled by the string heddles which were tied in on the loom (page 494). An examination of the warp will show one row of threads in a front shed, a second row of threads in a back shed.

The front row of threads does not need a control as it lies high enough above the back row to be easily picked up before passing the bobbin in back of it.

1. Starting at the left-hand lower corner of the loom, insert the bobbin which carries the border weft into this shed, passing it under three or four warp threads and bringing it to the surface between the warp threads.

To handle the bobbin correctly turn the right palm up, lay the bobbin across the fingers, and hold it in place by closing the thumb and index finger onto the shoulder of the bobbin. Assuming that the shed is already open, with the warp threads resting on the left hand and the index finger lifting the warp to open a wider shed, pass the head of the bobbin through the opening from left to right followed by the body and then the point (Fig. 572).

2. Beat the weft back against the fell by inserting the bobbin between the warp threads up to the shoulder (for the wide areas) and at an angle almost parallel with the warp threads. Do not beat in the sense that other tapestries, the kilim (page 459) or the Navaho (page 514), for example, are

FIG 572   FIG 573

beaten but rather by withdrawing the bobbin with a quick forward motion
from the underside of the weft at the fell (Fig. 573).

The insertion and withdrawal of the bobbin are done in rapid succession and a few strokes will place the weft in the correct position. Once the
weft is in place, additional strokes are a waste of time. Be sure that the
bobbin is inserted deeply enough between the warp threads, particularly
in the wider areas of the design, so that they are spread far enough apart
to allow the weft threads to cover them completely. If warp threads show
in the finished areas it is because this rule has not been observed. In
narrow areas, such as the point of a design or in an eight- or ten-thread
border, do not go in as deeply or the area will spread out too wide. With
practice and care the weaver will soon learn the correct beating technique.

Fig. 573 shows how the bight of wool is held out of the way with the
right hand, while the left hand guides the thread through the shed.

When the beating is finished, pick up another group of three or four
threads with the left hand and pass the bobbin through from left to right.

In their haste to weave quickly, beginners sometimes run the shuttle
under more than three or four warp threads at a time in an attempt to
speed up their work. On the contrary, it slows the work down as more
beating is required. It is not easy to get the weft threads worked down
around the extra warp threads.

Beat again, remembering to thrust the bobbin well down between the
warp threads even up to the shoulder of the bobbin, especially when

FIG 574

FIG 575

FIG 576

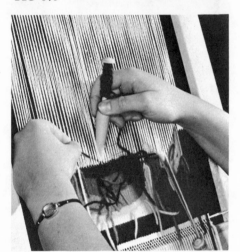

FIG 577

weaving wide areas. Continue across the width of the warp and take the bobbin out at the right side.

3. In weaving from right to left, the back row of threads must be lifted to make the opposite shed.

To do this, run the fingers of the right hand, which holds the bobbin, up the warp at the right of the loom and slip them in back of the first four or five heddles. Place the thumb against the heddle dowel, using it as a fulcrum to lift the heddles (Fig. 574).

Pass the fingers of the left hand under the four or five raised threads (Fig. 575), insert the bobbin into the shed from the right (Fig. 576), and bring it to the surface between the warp threads. After the bobbin has passed through the shed, whether from the left or the right side, pick it up with the right hand, in the position for beating. Remove the left fingers from under the raised warp threads and take the bight of the weft thread between the thumb and finger of the left hand. Gently draw it into a position which is at an angle of approximately 45 deg. to the fell (Fig. 577).

Beat, and repeat the operation completely across the warp to the left side. Continue back and forth across the warp until the border has been built up to the desired width. Measure after the weft has been well beaten back.

4. Wind a second bobbin with the border color and one with the background color. Remember to wind the bobbin around the wool and to have the thread come from underneath, not from the top of the bobbin (page 496).

5. The borders and the center of the web are woven independently from now on. If desired, the two side borders can be woven the entire length of the sample before the center with the design is started, or the design can be completed before the borders are started. It is advisable, however, for the beginner to weave 2 or 3 in. of the borders before starting the center. Figs. 578 and 579 show the upper and lower parts of the loom; Fig. 580, the front.

FIG 578

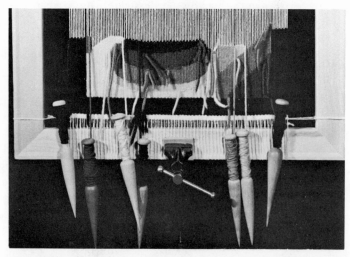

FIG 579

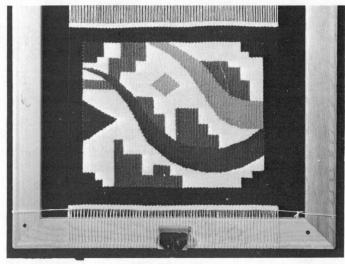

Weave the narrow borders carefully to keep the edges straight. If the selvedge threads can be moved up or down on the warp with the fingers, they are too loose; if the warp is not completely covered, the weft is too tight. If these mistakes have occurred, the weaving should be taken out and a second effort made. Do not expect perfection at first, however, as tapestry weaving requires practice and care.

6. Study the design (Fig. 580), a good one for the beginner, choose the colors, and determine which area to start first. Always keep the colored cartoon close at hand for reference.

In the Gobelin technique, whole pattern areas are woven in, regardless of the background or the other pattern areas in the design.

Judgment must be exercised in choosing the order in which the areas are to be built up to prevent overhangs when filling in the surrounding areas. The photograph and the diagram for the Swedish knot (Fig. 563) illustrate the order to follow in general.

All vertical lines in the design become slits which later are sewn together. It is permissible to interlock parts, whole borders, or parts of long vertical lines if desired.

The dots must be followed carefully, and covered completely before moving on to a new design area. Whereas warp and weft must always be at right angles to one another, curves are built up in steps. These may be one-, two-, three-, or four-thread steps depending entirely upon the placement of the dots. When filling in the background, or a second design area next to a part that is already built up, be sure to fill in each "riser" of the step with the same number of threads as appear in the original riser.

It is usually wise to use two weft shots where a sharp point occurs, such as the points of the diamond in the center of the design (Figs. 580 and 581). otherwise, the contour of the figure may be lost.

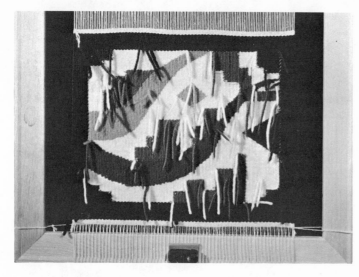

FIG 581

When the design and background have been completely filled in, end with a woven border to correspond in width with the border at the start, finishing with the ⁵⁄₁₆-in. warp heading.

Sewing the Slits One of the distinguishing marks of the true French Gobelin tapestry is the manner in which the slits are sewn together.

The stitching threads are parallel to the weft and are plainly visible on the right side. No effort is made to conceal them.

1. To sew the slits together use a medium-size tapestry needle with a semi-dull point. A sharp-pointed needle is likley to go through the warp and weft threads instead of between them.

2. Thread the needle with a length of gray or light tan, strong linen or cotton thread; 8/2 or 10/3 mercerized cotton is satisfactory. Tie a knot at the end as for sewing.

3. Hold the tapestry with the right side up; it need not be on the loom (Fig. 582). With the needle held under the work, sew up through the warp thread which lies at the top left of the slit being sewn.

FIG 582

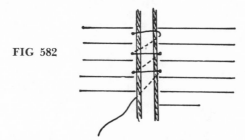

4. Pull the needle straight up through the warp until the knot tightens against the warp thread.

Carry the needle across to the other side of the slit and run it down between the first and second warp threads on the right of the slit, being careful to pass it between and not through the weft. Pull the thread until it is snug, with the two edges of the slit lying neatly together. Make certain that the thread lies in a straight line across the opening (Fig. 583).

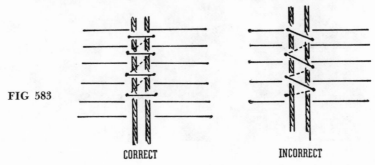

FIG 583

CORRECT   INCORRECT

Cross under the slit and bring the needle up about ¼ to ⅜ in. below the place where the first stitch was made. Bring the needle up between the warp and weft threads, but do not pass it through either of them. The stitching thread must always lie in perfect alignment with the weft threads.

Continue until the slit is sewn together. End on the right by sewing through the warp thread as was done at the start. Tie off the thread with a knot, adding an extra knot or two for security. All slits over ¼ or ⅜ in. long are sewn together in this manner. In the factory, long tapestries are stretched on special tables with rollers on both sides to facilitate sewing.

Finishing   The French Gobelin tapestries are finished in the same manner as the Swedish Knot (page 491). Block the tapestry (page 452).

Problem   Set up the loom and practice this technique.

TYPE Tapestry ·
PATTERN French, Swedish Adaptation, Shaded

In general, Swedish tapestry resembles the French, although there are variations in the technique, in the materials used, and in the manner of shading.

The sample shown (Fig. 585) was woven in Sweden at an accredited school[7] and can, therefore, be accepted as a correct interpretation of the Swedish-tapestry technique.

Design   The design used in this sample is a copy of a small part of an old Swedish tapestry.[8] As in the post-Gothic period of French tapestry (page

477), numerous colors and shadings were used. Two- and three-ply yarns split and twisted with other threads give subtle shading effects.

In the present world-wide renaissance of tapestry weaving, tapestry designers have reverted to the use of fewer colors and bolder designs. This is also true of the modern Swedish tapestries. The sample shown here would not be considered modern in design, although it certainly has the charm of its period.

Sample Illustrated (Fig. 585)

WARP	WEFT	REED
Linen, 3-ply	Swedish tapestry yarn, linen	15 per inch

The French tapestry (page 477) was woven on a cotton warp, while the Swedish is always woven on a linen warp. The French weavers feel that a cotton warp is superior since there is no danger of its cutting the weft threads. Swedish weavers feel that a linen warp is better than cotton, since it is more permanent for a piece of such lasting importance as the tapestry.

In the French tapestry, wool, silk, and, very occasionally, gold or silver threads are used in the weft. In the Swedish tapestry, both Swedish tapestry yarn and linen were used. The linen was used in certain areas of the design to bring out highlights such as the iris petals.

In contemporary Swedish tapestry, not only wool and linen are used, but various weights of these yarns are used in the same piece of tapestry. The variation in weight is not great but just enough to create interesting texture effects without destroying good workmanship in the weaving.

Loom   The loom used for the sample shown is essentially the same as the one described for the French Gobelin technique (page 480). It is a vertical or "haute-lisse" loom consisting of two sturdy upright supports between which one crossbar is attached about 2 ft. from the floor and another crossbar with pegs at the top of the loom (Fig. 503). For larger pieces of tapestry the lower bar is replaced with a cloth beam and the upper bar with a warp beam.

Dressing the Loom   The warp for the French tapestry practice frame was a continuous warp thread going around the top and bottom of the frame and crossing in the middle to make a figure 8.

In the Swedish tapestry the warp is made in the usual manner for weaving; that is, a continuous warp with a cross at one end.

The warp is transferred to the loom with the lower bar going through one end of the warp and two lease rods going through the cross in the middle of the warp. The other end of the warp is cut and tied in even groups with a half-hitch knot behind the pegs at the top crossbar. The lease sticks should be kept in a rigid position in the middle of the warp while dressing the loom.

A "reed" is made for the warp by tying a cotton thread around the right upright, carrying it over to the warp threads, and making an "Idiot's Delight" chain around each warp thread (Fig. 584). The reed is located below the weaving area and just above the lower crossbar. After the last stitch of the chain has been made, the cotton thread is carried out to the left upright and tied securely, making the chain taut.

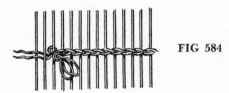

FIG 584

Care must be taken when making the chain to use a weight of cotton that will make the exact number of stitches or "dents" per inch as are necessary for the weight of warp and weft being used. A similar chain is made at the top of the warp just below the top crossbar.

Heddles are made from the dowel bar, in front of the loom, back around the warp threads, and around the lower lease rod going through the warp (page 494). This lease rod is removed after the heddles have been made. The upper lease rod is left in the warp but moved closer to the top of the loom (Fig. 503).

Preparing the Design The design is outlined in black India ink on tracing linen or tracing paper. If tracing paper is used it should be sewn onto another piece of more durable paper since the design takes a lot of hard wear as the weaving progresses. A colored cartoon should be kept for reference as the weaving progresses.

Bobbins The tapestry bobbin used (Fig. 504) is smaller than that used for French tapestry. The yarn is wound on the bobbin in the same manner as for the French technique and a half hitch is made around the neck of the bobbin to keep the wool from unwinding.

Weaving A tabby heading of the same material as the warp is made on top of the lower chain. The weft ends are turned back under four or five threads as is done in harness weaving when new threads are started. The weft is beaten down so that it will cover the warp.

The border of the design is woven in next. The weft is tied around the first warp thread as was done for the French-Swedish knot and the weaving proceeds back and forth across the warp until the border is complete. Whenever a new bobbin is started anywhere in the tapestry it is tied in as for the French-Swedish knot (Fig. 536).

The beating is done by using only the tip and up to about ½ in. of the bobbin. The bobbin is held at right angles to the warp and the weft thread picked or beaten into place. Care must be taken in beating. If the weft is beaten in too loosely, the finished tapestry will not lie flat; if beaten in too tightly, the warp threads will not be covered and the design will draw in.

When the border is the required width, start the design. Note that this sample (Fig. 585) was woven with the side of the design running across the warp. The building up and filling in are done in the same manners as for the French Gobelin.

Open the shed, lay in a length of wool which covers the pattern area, and beat it back with the bobbin. Change the shed and lay in the second row of weft. Here again, the weaver must be careful to insert and bring out the thread at the correct point on the pattern and to watch that the edge threads do not draw in, forming gaps between the pattern areas rather than holes or narrow slits. It is these vertical design lines which become the slits. To avoid the long slits which would occur between the right and left borders and the main design areas, the weft threads are interlocked. This shows plainly in the picture of the under, or reverse, side of the weaving (Fig. 586).

Continue weaving a design area until it has been built up to the required height, carefully following the colors of the cartoon and leaving all weft ends hanging loose on the back surface. The thread used for one colored area is *never* carried across the weaving to a second area of the same color; it is always cut off and started new.

Now start a second design area. Though it may seem confusing at first, each area of the design follows along logically, one after another, as the

FIG 585

FIG 586

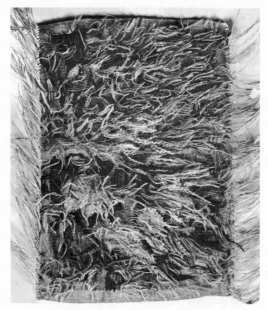

weaving proceeds. Do not let the border and/or background areas fall too far behind the design areas since the designs might extend quite far into the tapestry proper.

When the piece is finished, weave in a top border of the same width as the bottom border and finish with ¾ or 1 in. of warp to hold the weaving in place. Cut the tapestry from the loom.

If the piece is to be hemmed or backed, stitch the plain-weave ends on a machine to reinforce them. This machine stitching should be concealed inside the hem, under a strip of carpet binding, or inside the lining if the piece is to be lined.

On many Swedish tapestries the warp ends are knotted or tied into a fringe. Methods of tying fringes are shown later in the text (page 588).

Sew Slits With a fine but stout neutral-colored thread, catch the slits neatly together with a coarse buttonhole stitch. Leave the stitches loose enough so that the edges of the slits will just touch each other when the tapestry is laid on a flat surface.

Block the Tapestry (page 452)

Problem Plan and weave a small tapestry in the Swedish Gobelin technique using not more than six colors. Use either an original design or a detail of a larger design of an old Scandinavian Gobelin or Flemish tapestry.

TYPE Tapestry · PATTERN Navaho

The women of the Navaho Indian tribe are excellent weavers; their weaving is so tight and firm that the finished product is waterproof.

This is surprising since they work with crude implements, building up their looms from tree trunks and branches found around their hogans or in the woodlands and mountains. Their weaving techniques probably have changed less from the early primitive processes than those of any other ethnic group. Navaho girls start weaving almost as soon as they can walk, and have their own looms by the age of seven or eight.

The origin of the Navaho sheep is unknown. The breed is a mixed one, and varies somewhat, even on the same reservation. Its fleece is light and the wool staple long and wavy. The white wool responds more readily to the Navaho's primitive method of spinning than does the black sheep's wool which is of a shorter staple and inclined to be kinky. There is little oil in the fleece, which is an advantage in an area where water is scarce. While carding removes much of the dirt and the dyeing helps clean the wool, it is never thoroughly washed according to Old Country standards.

Spinning is carried on almost continuously, as a blanket requires considerable wool. The activity does not interfere with family or social groups as the simple, primitive stone spindle operates noiselessly. Although a great deal of imported wool is used today to weave articles for the tourist trade, the finest Navaho weaving still is done with handspun wool, hand-dyed by the weavers.

A Navaho woman does not use the conventional type of loom. Each time she weaves a piece, which may vary in size from a saddle blanket to a large bed blanket, rug, or hanging, she makes her loom.

First, she decides upon the size of the piece; then she uses part of the loom as a warping board. Because of the nature of the Navaho weave, a conventional warping board or loom would be of little use as the warp is continuous and there are no warp ends to be knotted or made into hems when the article is completed. A true Navaho piece always can be identified by the neat appearance of the selvedges with the added thread caught down at regular intervals, the ends without a knotted fringe or hems, and the woolen tassels at each corner.

Directions for the Navaho Weave   These directions have been simplified for the benefit of weavers who wish to learn this technique but are not in a position to weave a full-size Navaho rug or blanket on an outdoor loom. Those who wish to do so should study in detail the excellent description given by Gladys A. Reichard[9] who spent some time on a Navaho reservation learning this interesting technique.

Equipment Needed   1 sturdy wooden frame, approximately 18 in. wide by 24 in. long, with mitred or lapped corners; side and end pieces, 2 in. wide 8 pieces of ¾-in. sturdy tape, about 8 in. long, doubled and tacked four at each end to hold the rods

4 sturdy, nonbendable wood or iron rods, 20 in. long (Fig. 587, 1, 2, 3, 4)

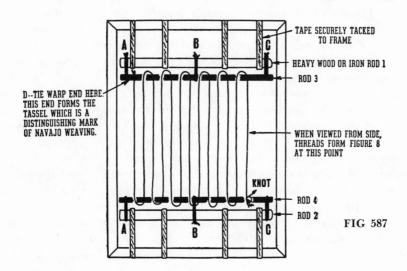

TAPE SECURELY TACKED TO FRAME

HEAVY WOOD OR IRON ROD 1

ROD 3

D--TIE WARP END HERE. THIS END FORMS THE TASSEL WHICH IS A DISTINGUISHING MARK OF NAVAJO WEAVING.

WHEN VIEWED FROM SIDE, THREADS FORM FIGURE 8 AT THIS POINT

KNOT

ROD 4

ROD 2

FIG 587

1 flat, polished piece of wood, the batten, 1½ in. wide by 20 in. long by ¹⁄₁₆ in. thick with tapered edge and end (Fig. 591, 7)

2 flat, polished pieces of wood, the shed sticks, ¾ in. wide by 20 in. long by ¹⁄₁₆ in. thick (Fig. 588, 5 and 6)

1 polished piece of wood, the heald, ¾ in. wide by 20 in. long by ¹⁄₁₆ in. thick

1 sturdy dinner fork

1 large tapestry or darning needle

1 umbrella rib or fine steel netting needle

Materials Heavy wrapping cord for lashing, fine polished cord for heald.

Since most weavers will make only one or two Navaho pieces, it seems wise to use the best materials available. Tightly spun, single-ply yarn for the warp and single-ply handspun wool for the weft in natural gray, white, and black sheep, or vegetable-dyed colors are suggested. Commercial yarns can be substituted, but they do not weave the hard, boardlike blanket or rug which is characteristic of the Navaho. Do not select harsh colors. In the best Navaho blankets and rugs the colors are muted.

Warping Decide on the size of the piece. Since it is necessary that all threads be exactly the same length and since none of the warp threads are cut, wind the warp directly on the loom bars.

Setting Up the Loom Lay the frame on a table and attach it with small clamps. Insert heavy wood or iron rods 1 and 2 in the tape loops at each end of the frame.

Take rod 3 and tie it at points *A, B,* and *C* to rod 1, measuring carefully so that the distance between the two rods is exactly the same at the middle and at each end. Now, tie rod 4 to rod 2 at the other end of the loom frame. The distance between these rods should be the length of the finished piece. Two sticks or dowels equal to the length of the finished piece can be used between the rods to assure an equal distance between the rods. Adjust the tying cords for the correct distance, since the cords cannot be changed once the warp is strung.

With a small ball of warp, start warping at *D.* Tie the warp to rod 3, carry it across the loom in a straight line over rod 4, then between rod 4 and rod 2, back over rod 3, then back again to 4. Continue in this way until the required number of threads has been wound (Fig. 587). Spread the warp evenly on the rods and at an even tension. Note that there is a crossing of threads at the center of the loom. If the loom is viewed from the side, the crossing resembles a figure 8. It is necessary to have each thread in its place, otherwise the weaving will be thrown off. Check the center of the 8. If any threads are not in the proper order, alternating one over, one under, remove the warp and start again. Remember to insert the warp spool over and down between the rods each time. When the warp is finished, tie the end to the rod around which it has been wound; rods 3 and 4 can be likened to the warp and cloth beam on an ordinary loom.

Securing the Shed Place shed stick 5 in the open shed above the figure 8 and shed stick 6 in the open shed below the figure 8. Bring the two sticks close together at the 8, and tie the ends together (Fig. 588).

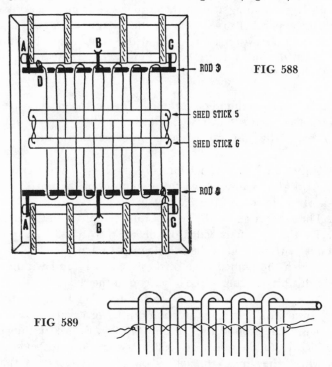

FIG 588

FIG 589

Reeding or Twining As there is no reed on this primitive type of loom, it is necessary to control the threads in some way so that the spacing between them will be equidistant. Fig. 589 illustrates twining.

Weavers who are familiar with basket weaving will recognize this as a pairing weave. Take a piece of warp wool four times the length of the finished piece. Double the strand and tie a knot about 1½ or 2 in. from the doubled end. Take the single ends, pass them around the outside warp thread on the left-hand side, and pull them toward the front until the knot is close to the warp thread. To begin the twining, take the thread lying at the left in front of the warp, pass it behind the second warp thread, bring it out to the front between the second and third warp threads, and drop it. Now take the strand at the left of the one just used, pass it behind the third warp thread, and bring it out to the front of the loom. Continue in this way, always using the left-hand thread, until the right edge of the loom has been reached.

As the twining proceeds, it is necessary to distribute the threads evenly along the bars. Measure the reed frequently, using a cardboard gauge (Fig. 161), so that the warp threads will run exactly eight to the inch. If the measurement is not accurate, either loosen or tighten the twining to correct the spacing. Once the spacing has been checked and found correct, tie the two ends of the wool strand together and cut off approximately 2 in. from the last knot, leaving the tassel.

Now begin twining at the other end of the loom. Check first to see that the threads lie parallel to the sides of the loom and that the warp measures the same width across rods 3 and 4 and the same length between these two rods at each side and in the middle. This is important if the piece is to be even.

Binding the Warp to the Loom Frame   The next step, after the twining has been completed, may seem drastic, but as it has been carried out successfully on wide warps by Navaho weavers for generations, there should be no trouble.

1. Untie rod 3 from rod 1 and slip the looped warp ends off the rod.

2. Work the twining down to the bottom of the warp loops and completely across the width of the warp.

3. Thread a large needle with a long length of doubled carpet warp.

4. Tie the right-hand edge of the warp to rod 3 (the rod which was slipped out) with the end of the double carpet warp.

5. Stretch the twined edge of the warp to its full width across rod 3 and tie with a bit of string to the other end of the rod.

6. Now sew the twined edge to the rod, beginning at the right and working toward the left (the direction can be reversed if more convenient), passing the needle around the bar and through the warp, thus binding the twining tightly to the rod (Fig. 590). Pass the needle between the warp threads where they form the loop. Sew completely across the warp and fasten the thread.

FIG 590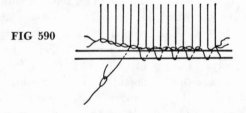

7. Tie rods 1 and 3 together with the heavy wrapping twine, keeping the rods equidistant from each other and the warp tense. The lacing will pass over the twining but this does not matter.

8. Repeat steps 1 to 7 at the other end of the loom, lacing very carefully to insure a good tension. Measure across the warp on rods 3 and 4. Also measure the length between rods 3 and 4 at each side. Check the measurements and if there is any variation of length or width make the necessary adjustments.

Making the Heald or Heddle   As the Navaho loom is not equipped with a harness to change the sheds, it is necessary to make one. Finely twisted, waxed wrapping cord is used for this purpose. At this stage, the two shed sticks, still tied together at the ends, lie in position in the middle of the loom on each side of the figure 8 (Fig. 588). To make the heald:

1. Insert the batten, 7, in the same shed and below the lower shed stick, 6 (Fig. 591).

2. Untie the cords that tie the shed sticks together.

3. Pull out the lower shed stick, 6, and push the other shed stick, 5, up close to the top of the loom where the twining lies, and tie it to the loom frame.

4. Turn the batten on edge to open a shed.

5. Take a ball of fine, highly polished cord, of which the heddle is to be made, and place the ball at the right side of the loom. Pass the end through the shed in back of the batten, working from right to left.

6. Tie the end of the cord around the end of shed stick 6 which was removed from the shed when the batten was put in and which is now at the left of the loom.

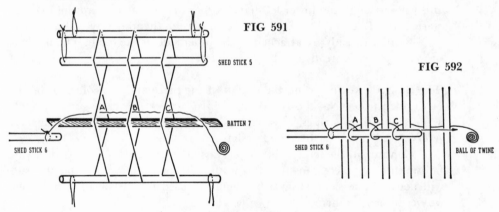

FIG 591

SHED STICK 5

BATTEN 7

SHED STICK 6

FIG 592

SHED STICK 6

BALL OF TWINE

7. Hold this shed stick in the left hand and, with the right forefinger, reach down between the warp threads at *A* (Fig. 592) and bring the cord up between the warp threads.

8. Twist the cord from left to right making a loop.

9. Slip the loop over the end of the shed stick 6 which is held in the left hand.

10. Proceed in this manner completely across the warp as at *B, C,* etc. (Fig. 592), taking care that the loops are made around each warp thread of the lower shed and that the loops are all the same length. The stick is gradually advanced from left to right as the loops are made. These loops make the heald, which is sometimes called the heddle. They answer the same purpose as heddles.

11. When all the loops have been made across the width of the warp, measure a length of the cord slightly longer than the length of the heddle

stick and cut it off. Pass the end through the hole in the shed stick and knot it. Pass the cut end through the hole in the other end of the shed stick, at the left side of the warp, and knot it. This prevents the loops from slipping off the heddle rod.

12. The batten can now be removed and the heald tested. All the threads should be even when the heald is lifted; if they are not, adjust the loops. Check to see that the loops pass around every warp thread of the lower or back shed. The upper row of threads is not shown in Fig. 592.

The loom is now threaded and in order; the shed stick is loosely tied at the upper part of the loom; the heald is in place in the middle of the loom with the heddles tied; and the batten is in readiness to open the shed when the weaving begins.

There is one more operation before the weaving can actually begin. This is the tying in of the wool warp threads at each side of the loom to provide the heavy whipped edge which is characteristic of Navaho weaving.

Cut and double a length of tightly twisted wool warp, over twice the length of the warp and not necessarily the same color as the background of the blanket. Tie a knot about 3 in. from the doubled end. Slip the ends of this wool through the lower left-hand corner of the warp where the twining started (rod 4), carry them up to rod 3, and fasten them loosely.

Similar threads are attached to the other side of the loom. The method of weaving these threads will be given later.

The Design At this point, the design of the piece and the coloring should be decided upon. Navaho rug designs have, across the years, gone through a transition from stripes, terraced designs, and diamonds to what Charles Avery Amsden[10] calls "bordered designs."

Contrary to general belief, the Navaho weaver does not weave symbolism into her pieces, for to do so would cheapen the symbol and this she will not do. The same basic tribal signs are used by all Navahos, but each weaver interprets them in her own way.

The accuracy of many weaving techniques is judged by their adherence to the 45-deg. angle. Navaho weaving, on the other hand, runs at 40-deg. and 52.5-deg. angles. Vertical stripes also are common. It is on these three principles that Navaho designs are based.

The Navaho weaver first visualizes her finished piece, then carries it through without a cartoon or drawing. For this reason, one weaver can never weave on another's project. As few of us can mentally picture the finished article, at least at first, the design and colors should be worked out on graph paper with the whole in proportion to the finished piece. The method used to prepare the cartoon for the rölakan (page 462) is satisfactory.

Before planning and weaving a Navaho piece, visit a museum, if possible, and examine pieces of Navaho weaving for design and color, technique and "feel." In contrast to other tapestries, the Navaho blanket or rug is very hard and boardlike; it is these characteristics which make it waterproof.

FIG. 593. A Navaho weaver. Note the primitive loom, spindles, and carding combs. (Photo from "Mission Fields at Home.")

In designing a Navaho piece, the weaver must consider correct balance, pleasing color arrangements, approved Navaho tradition, and the plotting of correct angles.

The colors of Navaho rugs may be bright or subdued, depending on whether they are being woven for the tourist market or for interior decorators. A large American dye firm produces special dyes blended to reproduce, as closely as possible, the original vegetable dyes obtained from the desert plants. Genuine natural dyes are difficult to obtain, for few sections of the Navaho reservation have the necessary variety or quantity of desert plants for mass production of dyes. Only the most expensive rugs and blankets are woven of vegetable-dyed yarns.

The Navaho weaver uses neither shuttle, bobbin, nor butterfly; she spins and uses her yarn in short pieces which she inserts with her fingers. When she weaves across the entire width of her web, she ties the end of her weft strand to a long stick which she passes through the shed. New threads are joined in the usual manner (Fig. 593). Since the wool is packed back very tightly into the shed, the joinings do not show.

Weaving The first four rows of weaving are done without the heald, since it is necessary to break up the pairs of warp threads. To do this use the batten to pick up a set of threads different from those picked up and controlled by the heddle.

1. Insert the batten from the right, passing on *top* of the first warp thread, under the second and third, over the fourth and fifth, under the sixth and seventh, and so on in pairs, across the entire warp.

2. When all the pairs of threads have been picked up, turn the batten on edge.

3. Starting at the right, insert a length of weft yarn into the shed, with the end extending about an inch outside the loom. After the thread is beaten down this end is turned back into the shed and beaten.

4. Using the fork, start at the side from which the thread was inserted (in this instance, the right side), and beat the yarn down tightly against the twining. Work toward the opposite side (in this instance the left side) of the loom. The yarn should be loose enough in the shed to allow it to be well beaten down between the warp threads, yet not so loose that it will protrude above the web in loops. A little practice will determine the correct tension. Remove the batten and give the weft a second beating with the fork.

5. Again insert the batten into the warp threads from the right, going *under* the first warp thread, over the second and third, under the fourth and fifth, over the sixth and seventh, and so on across the warp. Insert a weft thread from the left exactly opposite the first row and beat it into position with the fork. Remove the batten.

6. A total of four rows of weft are needed to separate the pairs completely. They are picked up in the same manner as the first two rows. Row 3 corresponds to row 1 and row 4 to row 2.

7. Remember the blanket or rug will end as well as begin with four rows of this weave. No harm is done if these four rows are woven in at the top of the loom at this time. If the loom is small and can be turned top for bottom, the process is exactly as described above. However, if the weaving is being done on a large stationary loom, it will be necessary to beat upward with the fork to get these threads in their proper place.

8. Now the weaving proper begins. Many weavers, seeing Navaho or other tapestry weaves being done for the first time, feel that the process must be very slow. All types of finger weaving are more slowly executed than those done with a shuttle and harnesses manipulated with treadles. Yet, it is surprising how quickly tapestry weaves progress once the various processes have been learned and the movements synchronized.

To Begin Weaving Check to see whether the loom frame is heavy enough to withstand the pull of weaving; if not, fasten it to the table so it will not tip forward. Grasp the heald in the left hand and pull it forward. Open the shed and pass the batten through it with the right hand, immediately turning it onto its thin edge with the same movement of the hand. Release the right hand. Insert the weft, beat down with the fork, remove the batten, and give the weft a second beating.

In all forms of tapestry weaving, two important things to remember are that all warp threads must be covered completely and that edges must not be drawn in. It takes a little practice to perfect these points so it is well to practice on a sample or two.

9. Pulling the heald forward makes one shed. The other shed is made by the shed stick which has been tied up to the upper beam of the loom. Loosen the shed stick, slip it down the warp to a point just behind the heald, and turn it on edge. This brings up the other set of warp threads. If the opening is too small the heald can be retied around a wider stick. Slip the batten into this shed, directly in front of the heald, and turn it on edge as was done for the previous row of weft. The two sheds should be perfectly clear, with the warp threads in alternating sequence. The ones that were up in the first row should be down in the second row, and so on. If they do not follow this sequence, check the heddle loops and correct them if necessary.

Assuming, for the first piece at least, that there will be a fairly wide border at each end, it is safe to proceed with several inches of plain weave. However, it is necessary to consider the heavy edge threads, if they are to be woven in correctly. The edge threads need not be woven into the first four

FIG. 594.   A Navaho woman weaving a rug

FIG. 595.   Navaho weaver using the batten

rows, which separate the pairs of warp threads, but should be bound in with the first row of weaving proper. To do this, twist the two strands at the edge, place a finger between to hold the strands in position, and slip the batten through. A twist has been formed close to the edge of the web. There is no rule stating how often this twist should be made, but it should be done at regular intervals and often enough so that the skip along the

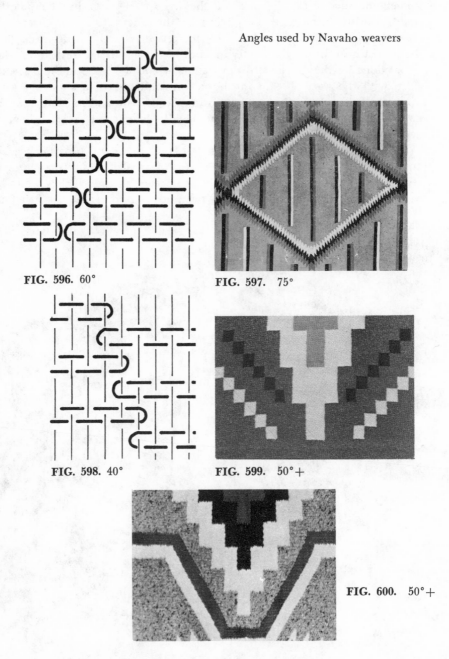

Angles used by Navaho weavers

FIG. 596. 60°

FIG. 597. 75°

FIG. 598. 40°

FIG. 599. 50°+

FIG. 600. 50°+

selvedge is not too long. Mrs. Reichard states that "the test of a blanket is its edge. If the edge strands are perfectly twisted at equal distances, and if the width of the blanket is the same throughout, it is perfect."

Beating   As has been stated, the beating is done with a fork. The Navaho forks, passed down through generations of the same family, are rather crudely made of desert wood. They become smooth and hard from use and the oil in the wool. A fork for a large piece of tapestry can be made from a thick piece of wood about 10 in. long, the tines cut into one end and a handle shaped on the other (Fig. 506). A heavy dinner fork with rounded tines is adequate for small pieces.

The Navaho weaver never puts her fork down. She holds it in her hand in an "at rest" position when inserting the batten, then moves it with only a slight finger motion to the "at use" position. Tapestry weavers should train themselves to do this from the beginning as the systematic use of tools and motion simplifies and hastens the weaving.

Technique   If a Navaho blanket is closely examined, small slits will be seen along the edges of the design. The slits are caused by turning the weft threads around the warp threads (Fig. 507). In Navaho weaving, we find the use of several techniques, this apparently both through custom and to achieve the correct angle. Techniques *A* (Fig. 507) and *D* (Fig. 510) are used where straight lines appear with technique *B* (Fig. 508) for the 40-deg. angle, and technique *F* (Fig. 510) for the 52.5-deg. angle.

As the weaving proceeds the warp becomes tighter and tighter and the weaving space smaller and smaller until it is necessary to remove the heald and use an umbrella rib or fine, steel netting needle to insert the weft. A steel knitting needle is used to press the weft down as the tines of the fork can no longer be inserted. It is an advantage to have the top border woven in before the main body of the sample is woven, yet, even when this is done it is difficult to fill in this last space neatly and tightly.

The average weaver is advised against attempting even a sample of the Navaho technique as it is difficult to obtain the correct wools and it takes a great deal of practice to achieve the hard, boardlike, waterproof web which is a distinguishing feature of the Navaho rug or blanket. The directions for the technique are given here as it is an interesting and true American weave.

TYPE Tapestry · PATTERN Chimayo

Contrary to the usual belief, the Chimayos are of Spanish descent and are not members of the southwestern American Indian tribes.

Originating in Spain, they have lived for many years in the Chimayo Valley of northern New Mexico, within sight of the Sangre de Cristo Mountains and within easy traveling distance of Los Alamos and Sante Fe.

Proximity to these centers, however, has not destroyed their love for their small farms nor their interest in weaving.

Unlike the Navaho weavers, who use a primitive loom, the Chimayo weavers use a 2-harness, treadle-type loom. The originals were brought with them when they immigrated to the American Southwest.

When Chimayo weaving was first discovered by tourists, the wools used were home grown, homespun, and dyed with vegetable dyes; but, like the Navahos, the demand for Chimayo weaving became so great that they resorted to commercial wools, usually of poor quality and crude color. The finest Chimayo weaving is found in museums (Fig. 601). There is, however, such a demand for their blankets, rugs, bags, coat materials, and runners, that much of the production now is carried on in factories. As could be expected, it does not require much weaving knowledge to distinguish the home-woven from the factory-woven. The wool in the factory weaves is a poor quality and the colors apt to be garish.

Many Chimayos, employed at steady work, add to their income by weaving at home during their leisure time. Most of them are good technicians and use a good quality commercial wool. Some of the older weavers will, upon occasion, accept orders for articles of homespun, vegetable-dyed yarn which they combine with the natural black, brown, and creamy white sheep's wool. These pieces are very expensive but, when compared with the average piece of Chimayo weaving, are gems of workmanship and color.

Sample Illustrated (Fig. 601)

WARP	WEFT	REED (dents per inch)	SLEY
Wool, tightly twisted, medium size, 2-ply	Wool, knitting, medium size, soft, 4-ply	10	Single: the two selvedge threads on each side are double sley

Number of Threads in Warp   50

Threading   Plain weave

Tie-Up   Plain weave

Technique   The Chimayos use the dovetail technique (Fig. 510), which gives a serrated line at the edge of the design areas. In one sample, a few places were found where the weft threads were turned around adjacent warp threads, rather than around common warp threads leaving slits. In this particular instance, the change in technique preserved the design contour better than the original technique would have done. The threads are locked at the edge of the various pattern areas on the locking left-to-right shed only.

Weaving Follow the general rules for tapestry weaving. Weave a band of tabby warp at the start and finish. Beat firmly, though not hard, so that all warp threads are covered. Carefully weave, or turn in, all ends so that the finished piece is completely reversible.

Design The colors in Fig. 601 are Oxford gray, black, white, scarlet, and crimson. Weave in as follows:
1. 1-in. Oxford gray
2. As follows:

ROWS	COLOR
2	white
2	black
4	white
4	scarlet
4	crimson
*4	black
2	white — center

From * reverse back to beginning.
3. 1-in. Oxford gray

FIG 601

The lower left-hand area of the design is white; the lower right, black. The center is scarlet bounded on the left by white, on the right by black up to the middle of the design where it reverses back to the beginning. The two halves of the design are exactly reversed.

To complete the sample, reverse the order of the colors, beginning with one inch of Oxford gray back to the start.

Finish Some Chimayo pieces are finished with a hem but most of them have a simple knotted fringe with from three to five warp threads in each knot.

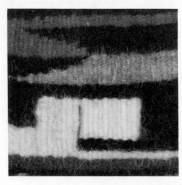

FIG 602

Problem   Set up a warp and weave a sample following the directions given above.

TYPE Tapestry · PATTERN Finnish

The strict rules and discipline which accompany the weaving of the rölakan, Gobelin, Soumak, and other finger-manipulated weaves can be disregarded when weaving modern tapestries.

Here the weaver can freely and imaginatively develop his theme. Teachers of modern tapestries contend that, if the weaver concentrates on the manual excellence of the tapestry, the design loses its natural motion and character and becomes stilted and lifeless. Technique, color, and material are all sublimated to the design; the mood of the finished tapestry is all that matters.

Design   Designs for modern tapestries can be of any subject, interpreted in whatever manner interests the weaver. They may be abstract, stylized, primitive, conventional, or photographic. But, regardless of the form, the weaver or designer—and it is preferable that the weaver be his own designer—should be completely familiar with the finer, more subtle characteristics of his subject and should clearly develop and accentuate these distinctions.

The number of colors used in modern tapestry weaving is unrestricted. The weaver may limit himself to a simple triad, or a few, subtly blended, vegetable-colored wools with an occasional sharp color contrast; or he may choose a blaze of rainbow hues. The color choice expresses the mood of the design.

Materials   Materials also express the mood and they can be as conventional or unorthodox as the weaver feels necessary. Linen or hemp are advised for the warp, because of their strength and stiffness, but, if 8/4 cotton is the only warp available, it is correct to use it.

Wools usually are used for the background of the tapestry, with strands of single-ply linen woven in at intervals to give added strength and firmness. To the wool and linen are added bits of cotton, perle cotton, rayon, nylon, other synthetics, and pieces of metallics for highlights. Three or more strands of the different shades are twisted together with no effort made to keep them uniform. Where shading is desired, it may be done by changing the order of the colors in the twisted strand. For instance, several rows can be woven with a strand composed of three dark colors, then two dark strands and one light, then two light and one dark, then all light.

Technique   Like the materials and designs, the weaver uses whatever technique best suits his purpose at the moment, changing from one to another if he finds a different one will emphasize a certain line or area. In general, either a warp-lock (Fig. 507) or a weft-lock (Fig. 512) technique is used, and the tapestry is woven with the wrong side facing the weaver. Headings and hems are woven or provision made for a fringe.

Sample Illustrated

WARP	WEFT	REED (dents per inch)	SLEY
Linen, 10/2	Homespun, vegetable-dyed, shades of tans, greens, and rusts, single-ply Linen, fine, natural, single-ply Linen, scarlet, separated and one or two strands used together	12	Single

In this modern tapestry the design is not built up in areas as was done in the Gobelin. Each row continues entirely across the warp and is beaten back in place with the beater. Bobbins can be used if desired, but as the colors and types of yarn are changed frequently it is just as easy to pick up the pieces, twist them together, and weave them in as is done by the Navaho women (page 513).

The design was placed sideways under the warp and the weft-lock tapestry technique was used (Fig. 512, A).

It is permissible, with this modern technique, to add threads with a needle to the surface of the finished tapestry after it is taken from the loom. To weave them in would present somewhat of a problem and slow the work considerably. Modern tapestries are designed to be woven up quickly.

Problem Weave a tapestry sample using the above method displaying ingenuity in design and choice of materials.

FIG 603

FIG. 604. Designed and woven by the late Martta Taipale, Finland

TYPE Tapestry · PATTERN Modern Egyptian

In 1941, a noted Egyptian architect, Ramses Wissa-Wassef, and his wife Sophie had the belief that if children were given the right work environment, proper materials, a minimum of instruction, and freedom to give full play to their imaginations and creativity, they could produce interesting work. To prove his theory, he built a workshop equipped with wooden frames for the small tapestries and high-warp looms for the larger pieces, and gathered together a group of children. These children were taught the fundamental weaving processes, supplied with wool, and told they could come to the workshop when and as they wished to weave, but must create their own designs. The three rules which were to be strictly followed were: no cartoons; no design influences from persons or books; and absolutely no criticism or interference from adults. The success of his venture far exceeded his wildest expectations and worldwide recognition has come to him, his wife, and the child weavers of Harrania.

The wool, obtained locally, is dyed in large vats located on the roof of one of the buildings. Only natural dyes are used: indigo for blue, weld for yellow, and madder and cochineal for red. All other colors are derived from various combinations of these three primary colors.

The designs which the children create in their minds are influenced by the life around them. Living as they do not far from Cairo, the Nile, and the great pyramids, it is not strange that these appear in one form or another in their tapestries. They never repeat a design and if questioned can describe exactly how the design they are working on will look when finished. They have confidence in their ability, and their work, done with consummate skill, radiates joy and happiness. They use many bright colors

FIG. 605. Detail of tapestry woven by Egyptian children

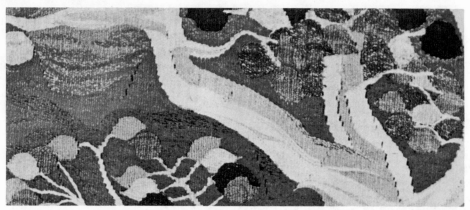

FIG. 606. Detail of tapestry woven by Egyptian children

and their innate color sense enables them to blend seemingly unrelated colors into a pleasing whole.

Each year new children come to the workshop where they are taught by an older brother or sister. When weavers reach adulthood, they move to other villages, thus forming a secondary group of producing weavers whose tapestries show sophistication, contrasting markedly with the naiveté of the children's work.

There is no inherent tradition of Egyptian crafts with which to compare these present-day tapestries unless one goes back to the Coptic school of weaving which flourished centuries ago and with which there is some similarity. However, a much greater resemblance appears between the children's work, the Zulu weavers, and tapestries woven in Norway during the sixteenth century.

TYPE Tapestry · PATTERN Bantu Zulu

The Bantu Zulus of the Republic of South Africa have inherited many traditional craft skills from their forebears. The articles they produce are much sought after by tourists and for sale overseas. In addition to their tapestries woven of vegetable-dyed native grasses, which are considered to be museum pieces, they weave two other quite different types of webs. For their lightweight tapestries designed for wall hangings, bedcovers, and other home uses, they use gaily colored figurative designs, and for the heavy floor mats nonfigurative geometric designs.

Their designs are original and are usually inspired by their surroundings. They tell a story, record a special event, a dance or religious service, or simply portray the village street on which the weaver lives (Fig. 607). Some of their designs find their origin in the tribal beadwork or pottery designs but these do not have any other meaning than being purely decorative. Like the Navaho and child weavers of Egypt, the Zulu weavers

FIG. 607. Bantu Zulu figurative design

FIG. 608. Bantu Zulu woodcut design for large tapestry

FIG. 609. Bantu Zulu floor covering, nonfigurative design

conceive and carry their designs in their minds, though for the larger designs they sometimes make a rough drawing on a scrap of paper to which they refer from time to time as the weaving progresses. Lino and woodcuts are also used (Fig. 609) but a design once used is discarded. As a result, their products retain a freshness and spontaniety, thus preventing their Center from developing into a factory.

Nonfigurative geometric designs composed of a combination of small design units are used for the heavy floor coverings (Fig. 609). These small designs are not components of the total design, as are the designs in the Navaho rugs, but each unit, in rich jewel-like colors, stands alone with a charm and interest of its own.

The tapestries are woven on the upright conventional type tapestry loom. Local wool, mostly karakul, is carded, spun, and dyed with commercial dyes at the weaving center. The colors are clear and bright. The yarn is spun very loosely with very little twist and is about the size of a slender pencil. The weaver does not twist the yarn during the weaving but because of its soft silky quality it packs back compactly into the shed. In 1962, under the auspices of the Church of Swedish Mission and the Committee for Bantu Arts and Crafts, a weaving workshop was established at Roke's Drift. Artist-craftsmen were sent from Sweden to help the people improve the mechanics and techniques of their crafts, to train them to administer the project in a businesslike manner, and to prepare the young people for remunerative vocations such as teaching at the Center and the nearby villages and weaving their own tapestries. The type of articles to be made, the designs, and the colors used were to be decided by the weavers themselves and there was to be no suggestion or criticisms from the artist-craftsmen, thus keeping the products free of outside influences and keeping alive and perpetuating the Zulu traditions.

The techniques used can be seen in the detailed cut (Fig. 610). A special native technique used for the heavy floor coverings is not evident in the cut.

FIG. 610. Bantu Zulu. Detail of figurative design tapestry showing techniques used.

TYPE Tapestry · PATTERN "Free" Techniques

This free and easy method of tapestry weaving will provide a welcome relief from the strict discipline required to master the various traditional techniques.

Weaving up very quickly, the webs are inexpensive, as both warp and weft can be cotton and wool yarns too short for most purposes. The webs can be used for zipper purses; shopping bags; pillow tops; coasters and so on.

The weaving can be done (1) on any loom with a plain weave threading and treadling (page 46); (2) on a French Gobelin frame which provides a shed (page 494), or (3) a plain sturdy wooden frame (page 480) where alternate threads are picked up with the fingers, point of the tapestry bobbin (page 451), or with a pickup stick. There is no interlocking around either warp or weft threads, and it is not necessary to ink the design on the warp or slip a colored cartoon under it.

For the heavier pieces, such as a shopping bag, use 8/4 or 12/4 cotton warp, sleyed from 10 to 12 threads per inch. Use finer yarns for warp, set somewhat closer, for the smaller pieces such as coasters. For weft, use pieces of tapestry, or other available yarns. If some seem a bit small, either twist two or even three strands together of the same color, or, to obtain a more interesting effect, twist strands of different shades together.

Start and finish the weaving with a ½- to ⅜-in. plain-weave heading of fine yarn which will do away with bulkiness. In the mind's eye conceive a design of hills and hollows, leaves, fat fish, or flowers, keeping the design simple and bold. Starting at the right-hand corner of the frame, open the shed and lay the weft thread in far enough to make the base of the first unit of the design. Beat thread back to hem line. Change shed, take weft back to right selvedge.

Beat, change shed, and continue this operation until figure is of desired height and shape. When last row is finished, let weft thread hang down under the web to be cut off later, leaving ends ½- to ⅜-in. long so they will not pull out. Start the second unit at the left of the first, using a different but blending color. Make the second unit a different size and shape and continue across the web with a variety of shapes and colors. Care must be taken that the correct shed opens when passing from unit to unit, otherwise two up or two down warp threads may come together. To correct this, weave in an additional row across the top of the unit just completed. This will bring up the correct set of threads. Use a tapestry bobbin (page 451) or small fork to beat the weft back to completely cover the warp. Take care when turning the weft around the warp threads not to pull it too tight thus distorting the edge of the unit design. The warp at all times should remain taut and parallel with the edges of the frame.

When the first row of hills, fat fish, or leaves has been woven, take a piece of wool of a contrasting color and slightly heavier thread, called for convenience a "binder" thread, and, starting at the right-hand side of the

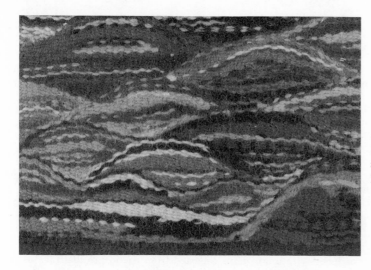

FIG. 611. Designed and woven by Mary E. Black, Nova Scotia

frame, weave it across the entire web. Leave it loose enough in the shed so it can be beaten down with the bobbin to the bottom of the hollows without destroying the contours of the units. After beating it into position, change the shed and weave the binder thread back to the right selvedge, turning the end into the web and cut off.

The next row of units will start at the bottom of the hollows and can be woven in any desired shape or size once it becomes higher than the surrounding units of the first row. Once this row is completed weave in another binder thread. Continue until the tapestry is the desired size.

This is a simple, relaxing, method of weaving a colorful web. The weaver will find, once the technique is understood, that threads, color, and design will flow into place with little effort. It is an excellent occupational therapy project and provides a good medium for color exploration. If the frame is not large, and it is advisable to use a small frame for the first project, it can be easily carried from place to place to work on.

TECHNIQUE Tapestry · PATTERN Mixed Techniques

Shown here (Fig. 612) is a tapestry which illustrates how a weaver's skill in combining a variety of tapestry and other weaving techniques together with a knowledge of natural dyeing, spinning, and a talent for painting enabled her to produce a beautiful piece of weaving. Because she was familiar with these many techniques, she was able to achieve the results she envisioned, even to the naturalness of the evergreen branches woven with the rya knot.

The tapestry depicts her three children relaxing on the grass between tall trees with bright sunshine streaming through. The tapestry measures roughly 4 by 5 ft. and she estimates that it required approximately 1300 hours to prepare the design and materials and weave the piece. She has donated the tapestry to a new local hospital to be hung in the guest alcove.

Dawn MacNutt has written the following about her tapestry:

"Once Upon a Time"

This pastoral tapestry was woven with handspun naturally dyed wool from Nova Scotian sheep. The one exception is the brown poodle wool in the little girl's shoes; it was spun from the pet which belongs to the weaver's daughter who modeled for the tapestry. The rest of the wool came from black, gray, and white sheep at several farms throughout the province.

After being spun on a hundred-and-twenty-year-old McIntosh wheel, the skeins were dipped in pots of color brewed from local plants. These included the blossoms from lilacs and lupins, buttercups and clover, hollyhocks and goldenrod, dahlias and marigolds, cockscomb and coreopsis, smartweed and beach pea, and some sweetfern and bracken from the back roads. The color range was broadened with onion skins collected from friends, rhubarb leaves, rose cuttings, sumac, privet berries, spruce needles, and branches. The rose shades came from umbilicaria, a lichen from our seacoast rocks, soft green from an innovation of a Navaho recipe from copper. And just as our ancestors did, precious blue came from indigo imported from overseas.

The design of the tapestry came from images of sunlight on trees in a wooded spot; it was inspired by the impressionist painters, the great Polish tapestries, but mostly by children and the nature of Nova Scotia itself.

FIG. 612. Designed and woven by Dawn Macnutt, Nova Scotia

chapter 14

Theory of Weaving

HOW TO READ AND UNDERSTAND THREADING DRAFTS

A threading or pattern draft is the set of marks or characters used to designate the order in which the threads are to be drawn into the heddles to form the weave. There is considerable variation in the manner in which threading drafts are recorded. Weavers in different countries, as well as in different parts of the same country and at different periods, have devised their own methods of draft writing. Some of these almost resemble shorthand in their brevity, while others are long and involved.

Any or all of them, differing from the usual method used on this continent, are likely to cause difficulty and much waste of time, particularly for the beginning weaver. Therefore, some of the more ordinary methods are explained in the text.

The three methods used most extensively for recording threading drafts in America and Canada are listed and explained first since the beginner will start with one of these.

Method 1 has the advantage of showing up the general characteristics of the pattern design. It is a visual type of recording (Fig. 613) but takes slightly longer to record than the other two methods.

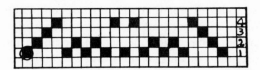

FIG 613

Many of the old drafts are found with the notations in the form of crosses. Method 2 employs this speedy method of writing down a draft and

529

is commonly used (Fig. 614). The beginning weaver should be careful not to confuse it with the tie-up draft (page 534).

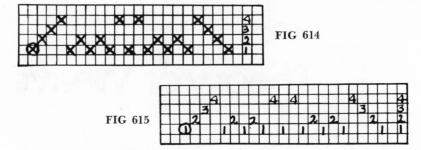

FIG 614

FIG 615

Method 3, in which numbers denote the position of the threads (Fig. 615), is a quick and simple way to record a draft and is easy to follow when threading. It reveals at a glance which harness combinations compose the various blocks. There is less chance of making a mistake when threading from numbers than from crosses or filled-in squares and the sequence of the numbers can be readily memorized. Generally, method 3 has been used throughout the text, though a few drafts have been written in other ways to familiarize the beginning weaver with the different methods. The weaver should learn to think of his weaving in terms of blocks and the combined movement of the harnesses and treadles which execute the desired pattern.

Note that, in all the above drafts, the last thread has been encircled. The circle indicates that this thread is not to be threaded until the last repeat of the pattern. If this heddle was threaded in each repeat of the draft, it would result in two threads on harness 1, instead of only one, since the pattern begins each time with a thread on harness 1. The last heddle is not shown on some drafts (Fig. 616). In this case, the weaver must remember to thread it at the end of the last repeat to balance the pattern.

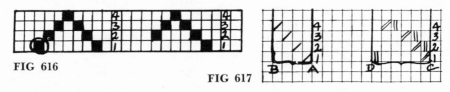

FIG 616

FIG 617

The Southern Mountain weavers use a method of draft writing similar to that in popular use today except that they do not completely fill in the squared space but draw a diagonal line across it, as shown in *A* to *B* (Fig. 617). *C* to *D* represents an abbreviated method of writing a pattern based on a twill. The two diagonals mean that the 1 and 2, 2 and 3, etc., are each repeated twice instead of only once as occurs in the *A–B* section.

It is difficult to figure out some of the old drafts found in remote areas. Once deciphered, it is wise to make a draw-down (page 535), since many contain mistakes.

Shortly before her death, Marguerite Davison studied a number of old drafts and pieces of weaving from which she recorded and published a book of overshot threadings.[1] She has used an abbreviated system of draft writing which has merit but has the disadvantage of being open to two interpretations. Unless the weaver is experienced, he should not attempt to thread from them. If incorrectly threaded, the last and first threads of adjoining blocks may not lie in the correct position to each other.

Mrs. Davison's method of recording drafts is shown in Fig. 618.

A simplified interpretation of this draft is given in Fig. 619.

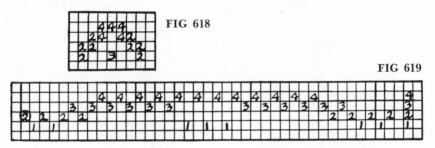

FIG 618

FIG 619

Note that there are 39 threads. Unless there is an uneven number of threads in the center turning block, it is impossible to obtain a completely balanced pattern. Many of the old drafts do not show this.

The methods used to write drafts in the Scandinavian countries are also quite varied. One thing to remember about these drafts, however, is that the harness next to the beater which we call 1 is their 4 or 8 as the case may be. Therefore, when using a Scandinavian draft, transpose it to our system. The simplest way of doing this is to jot down the draft and tie-up on graph paper as they are read off by an assistant.

Most Scandinavian books show the draft, tie-up, and treadling on the same chart. This system is good but it is not in general use on this continent. Other systems seem better suited to our purposes (page 533).

The drafts in Fig. 620 illustrate what would happen if twelve weavers, chosen at random, were asked to write down the threading draft and tie-up for the 1, 2, 3, 4 twill weave set on four harnesses. Twelve different methods!

There are probably additional ways in which the notation could be made but these drafts are sufficiently different to allow the beginning weaver to study and compare them so that the interpretation of drafts will not present a problem.

Note that the order of treadling is given for some of them; for instance, in the *Vävbok*. The strokes under the tie-up mean, reading from left to right and from top to bottom, that treadle 1 (harnesses 1 and 4) is treadled first; treadle 2 (harnesses 3 and 4) is next; treadle 3 (harnesses 2 and 3) follows; and treadle 4 (harnesses 1 and 2) is last. This routine is repeated as often as required to weave the desired length. This is a comparatively simple method of recording the treadling but one that is not generally used in this country.

FIG 620

1. VAVBOK—S. Palmgren

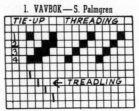

2. SWEDISH-PRAKISK VAVBOK—N. Engestrom

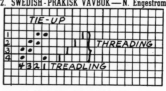

3. DEN STORA VAVBOKEN—M. Block

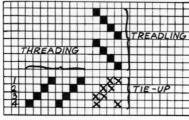

4. DANISH

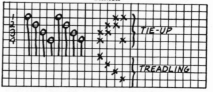

5. HOME WEAVING—O. Beriau

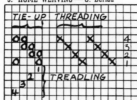

6. HANDWEAVERS' PATTERN BOOK—M. Davidson

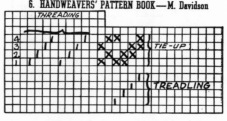

7. LOOM MUSIC

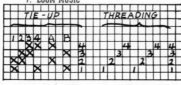

8. PENLAND SCHOOL OF HANDICRAFTS

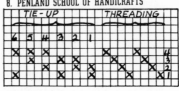

9. THE JOY OF HANDWEAVING—O. Gallinger

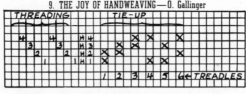

10. ADVENTURES IN WEAVING—G. Greer

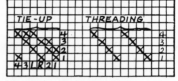

11. HAND-LOOM WEAVING—L. Hooper

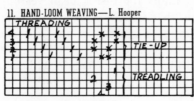

12. SHUTTLE CRAFT GUILD—H. Tidball

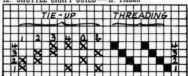

THE TIE-UP

In Chapter 2, a simple explanation of the tie-up is given together with directions for making the snitch knot and the method of keeping the harnesses and treadles level while tying.

Some rising-shed and jack-type looms do not require a tie-up because the harnesses are directly connected to the treadles with heavy metal rods and there are no lams. Harness 1 is connected to treadle 1, harness 2 is connected to treadle 2, and so on. This is called a direct tie-up and there are only four treadles. As a result, it is often necessary to use both feet simultaneously to depress the required treadles. When the pattern calls for three harnesses to be depressed at once, one foot depresses the two adjacent treadles, the other foot the third treadle.

Most sinking-shed counterbalanced looms have six treadles. On those which have only four the lams are tied directly one to each treadle. As a result it is often necessary, as with the jack and direct tie-up loom, to use both feet simultaneously to treadle the various blocks. In general, however, there are six treadles, and two or more pattern harnesses are tied to one treadle.

Oelsner and Dale[2] advise that it is much simpler, on a sinking-shed loom, to weave on three harnesses against one treadling by tying up the blank spaces instead of the crosses. This will weave the material wrong side up, but this is of little consequence as it can simply be turned over when taken from the loom.

As each weave has its own structure so also does it have its own standard tie-up. When treadled in the same sequence in which the pattern blocks are written, the tie-up produces a piece of cloth "woven as drawn-in," or, to use an expression of the weavers of the highlands in the southern United States, "tromp as writ." Special tie-ups and/or treadlings are used to obtain variations.

Directions for tie-ups are shown in a chart or diagram form and placed usually at the right or left side of the pattern draft. The system, or order, to be followed in tying up the treadles is one of the most controversial subjects among hand weavers.

Drafts are written to be threaded from right to left, as the weaver faces the loom, with block *A* written on harnesses 1 and 2. Therefore, it seems logical that harnesses 1 and 2 should be tied to the first treadle on the right, which is directly below these harnesses, and that treadling should begin with this treadle. Harnesses 2 and 3 are then tied to treadle 2; 3 and 4 to treadle 3; 4 and 1 to treadle 4; and plain-weave harnesses *a* and *b* to treadles 5 and 6 at the extreme left. This is the standard tie-up for twill, overshot, crackle, and other balanced weaves.

However, the human factor must be considered. The majority of people start walking by unconsciously extending the left foot. Also, we read from left to right which would indicate that the tie-up should conform. New weavers automatically start to treadle with the left foot unless otherwise instructed. With this human element being at variance with the logical system of the tie-up, it is difficult to know whether to follow logic or the human behavior pattern.

Furthermore, a study of many weaving books shows that there is considerable variation in the order in which the treadles are tied. Many weavers tie the first harness to the last treadle on the left and the tabby harnesses on the extreme right. Others tie the tabby treadles in the center, while some tie one tabby at the extreme right and the other at the extreme left. Those who weave for production often tie the harnesses so they can "walk" their treadles.

Throughout this text the tie-ups given below have been adapted as standard, but it is suggested that after the weaver has gained experience he should decide for himself which tie-up is most convenient. Often the placement of the treadles is governed somewhat by the weave.

Unless otherwise noted, tie-ups shown in most texts are for sinking-shed looms. X is the symbol used to designate the tie-up on the chart for a sinking-shed loom; O is the symbol used for a rising-shed loom.

Standard Tie-Up

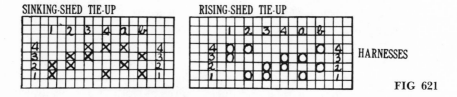

FIG 621

Note that the treadles for the rising-shed loom are tied in the opposite spaces from those for the sinking-shed. If there are no tie-up or treadling directions given for the rising-shed loom, use the blank spaces on the sinking-shed tie-up chart and treadle the two or more treadles or levers together. For instance, where 1 and 2 are shown on the chart for the sinking-shed loom, depress the opposite levers or treadles, 3 and 4 together, for the rising-shed loom. Sometimes the two are shown on the same chart (Fig. 622).

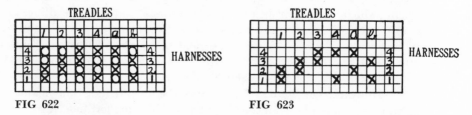

FIG 622

FIG 623

Standard tie-ups for the overshot, 2:2 twill, and crackle weaves are as shown in Fig. 623.

The tie-up given here for the 8-harness loom is for a rising-shed, as practically all multiple-harness looms (those with more than four harnesses) are rising-shed looms.

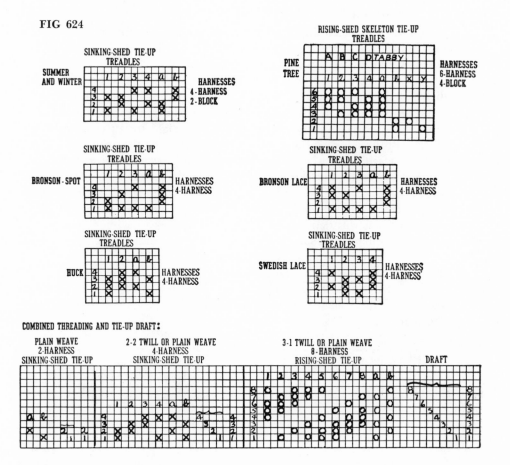

FIG 624

WEAVING ON PAPER OR THE DRAW-DOWN

Once the drafts and tie-ups are understood the next step is learning to weave on paper or, as the process is frequently called, making draw-downs. The principal advantages of understanding and making draw-downs are:

1. To prove the correctness of the pattern draft

2. To determine if the second repeat of the draft joins the first correctly

3. To check the arrangement of the blocks to determine whether or not they answer the purpose for which the weaving is intended

4. To present the pattern in a graphic manner

5. To check a pattern of unknown source written in a method with which the weaver is unfamiliar.

Draw-downs are not difficult if approached step by step, and the more often the beginning weaver makes them, the better will be his understanding of the structure of the various weaves, the meaning of pattern blocks, and the balancing of patterns.

It is advisable to think of the different weaves in terms of blocks, their limitations and possibilities for expansion. Once the mind is trained to do this, the weaver is free from the chore of following a set of numbers which at best seem unrelated to, and restrict, the development of the pattern.

There are two methods of making a draw-down. The first follows the diagonal of the weave from the top to the bottom of the graph paper, working from right to left. The other, which is described here, follows the draft horizontally across the graph paper from right to left in the direction of the weft thread when the shuttle is thrown through the open shed.

No matter which system is used, if it has been drawn correctly, the result is the same. The weaver will need graph paper, not finer than ten squares to the inch (eight to the inch has been used throughout this text), a medium-size lettering pen, and black India ink or a fine felt-tip pen. The size of the pen will depend upon whether the weaver wishes to fill in the squares completely or make lines across them to represent the weft threads.

For the first example, the 4-harness twill, which is familiar to all weavers but still simple, has been chosen to illustrate the procedure.

1. Write down three repeats of the threading at the top of a piece of graph paper (Fig. 625). For other longer drafts one-and-a-half repeats are sufficient.

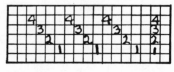

FIG 625

FIG 626

2. Thinking in terms of blocks and remembering that it requires at least two threads to form a block and that four blocks comprise the twill sequence on a 4-harness loom (page 165), encircle the threads which comprise these four blocks (Fig. 626):

Note that the last thread of each block becomes the first thread of the next block. This thread is referred to as a thread common to each block.

3. The next step is to weave these blocks on the graph paper in the same way that they are to be woven on the loom. The one difference is that on paper the weaving is done from the bottom of the draft down toward the weaver, while on the loom the weaving is done up or away from the weaver. In this particular instance, note that the twill as woven on paper emerges with a right-hand diagonal, while it weaves with a left-hand diagonal with the same treadling on the loom. To prove the accuracy of this, lightly sketch the draw-down strokes above rather than below the draft.

Starting at the right of the draw-down (Fig. 627), draw a line across the two spaces which lie directly under the first block to the right, which is the *A* block threaded on harnesses 1 and 2.

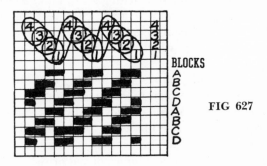

BLOCKS
A
B
C
D
A
B
C
D

FIG 627

As there are three repeats of the draft, the *A* block appears three times, so a line is drawn across each two spaces where it appears. This line corresponds to the weft thread which is thrown through the shed when treadle 1 is depressed, covering the two threads on harnesses 1 and 2 (block *A*) completely across the web regardless of its width.

Now the same procedure takes place for block *B* which is comprised of threads on harnesses 2 and 3; for block *C* which is comprised of threads on harnesses 3 and 4; followed by block *D* which is comprised of threads on harnesses 4 and 1.

At this point, recall the relationship between the harnesses and treadles. Harnesses 1 and 2 carrying block *A* are tied to treadle 1 which, when depressed, pulls down these harnesses (or block) so that the weft thread when passed through the shed covers them. Depressing treadles 2, 3, and 4 in sequence allows the weft to cover blocks *B*, *C*, and *D* in the actual weaving in the same manner in which the weaving is emerging on the paper.

With a more involved threading draft, proceed on the same premise as for the twill and encircle the various blocks (Fig. 628).

The first four blocks of this draft are two-thread blocks on the twill threading. These are followed by blocks with four and three threads each, which repeat at intervals across the entire draft.

Starting at the right with the *A*, 1 and 2 block, make a stroke under it across the two threads exactly as was done on the twill draw-down (Fig. 627). This block is followed by two spaces. Working toward the left, the next block is a four-thread block; make a stroke across the squares. Then there is a space, followed by another four-thread *A*, 1 and 2 block; and so on. Whenever an *A*, 1 and 2 block appears, a line is drawn under it covering the same number of squares as there are threads in the block. Where a single-thread of the block being analyzed appears alone, the square directly under it is filled in. This appears in the actual weaving as a dot, and is known as a half tone.

The same procedure is carried out for the next three rows of paper weaving, filling in the squares that lie beneath the *B,* 2 and 3 block; the *C,* 3 and 4 block; and the *D,* 1 and 4 block.

It is not until the fifth row is reached that a change occurs. Here we have worked from right to left, reaching an *A,* 1 and 2 block of four threads. In actual weaving this would be treadled three times with the pattern thread. Tabby threads treadled on 1 and 3 and 2 and 4 run between the pattern threads (page 231) when weaving on the loom but do not show on a draw-down.

It is one of the rules of overshot weaving that there is always one less pattern shot in the square than there are threads threaded in the block. A block with an even number of threads is always treadled with an uneven number of pattern shots. The blocks in which the pattern reverses back to the start should be threaded with an uneven number of threads, 3, 5, 7, 9, etc., and woven with an even number of pattern shots. They are just the opposite of the nonturning blocks.

To return to the draw-down, the sixth block, a *B,* 2 and 3 turning block of three threads, has now been reached. Two pattern shots only are thrown, one less than the number of warp threads in the block.

The next block is the "key" block for the line and it is the number of pattern shots that are entered for this block which controls the number of pattern shots in all *B* blocks across the entire warp, at this particular place in the weaving. Regardless of the block being inked in, always work from the "key" block to the left, then return to it and, working to the right,

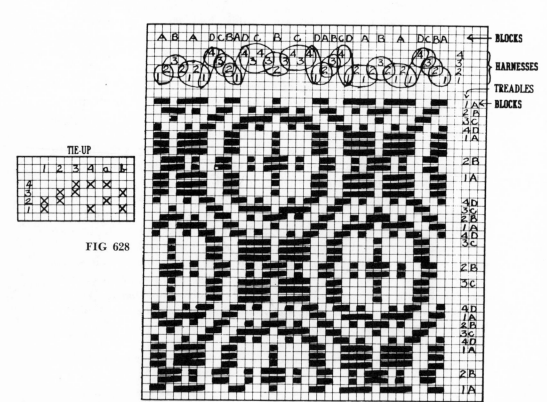

TIE-UP

FIG 628

FIG 629

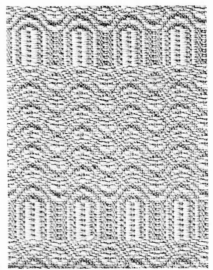

FIG 630

fill in all the squares lying under it that have the same harnesses as the key block.

Continue filling in the rows for the different squares until the block at the left-hand selvedge has been reached. Beginners, particularly, may have difficulty in following the squares across and down the draw-down. Cut a T square, or right angle, out of dark construction paper and use it as a guide, moving it from right to left and down the graph paper as the draw-down proceeds.

It is also a good plan to put a small check mark over the block letter at the top of the draw-down as soon as a block is "woven" so there will be no confusion as to which "key" block is being "woven."

While the weaver is practicing draw-downs it is advisable to use a soft pencil because once the squares are filled in with ink it is difficult to correct a mistake. Never try to erase a mistake on graph paper. Cut out a square or two or three or whatever number is needed and paste over the area where the mistake occurs. When dry, fill in the proper squares.

The draw-down can be checked by holding it at a little distance and following the diagonals with the eye. Mistakes will show up immediately. The draw-down shows the draft woven as-drawn-in, as does the photograph (Fig. 629).

Note here that there are several errors in the woven sample.

A further development of the draft is shown (Fig. 630). Once the weaver has worked out the draft into a "woven-as-drawn-in draw-down" he should experiment with original treadlings.

Problem Find the errors in the sample (Fig. 629) and weave a corrected sample from the draw-down.

FABRIC ANALYSIS

As the weaver progresses in knowledge and wisdom, he may wish to reproduce an heirloom bedspread or duplicate an attractive set of place mats.

The lack of details concerning threads, sley, threading, tie-up, and treadling need not prove a deterrent because, through the process of fabric analysis, they can all be brought to light. It will require a bit of time, care, and patience to make a fabric analysis but once the procedure is thoroughly understood it is not difficult.

Making the analysis can be greatly simplified if two people work together, one reading off the details from the materials and the other recording them on graph paper. Analysis can be done alone but at first it is best to have an assistant as it is confusing to keep track of both the counting and the recording.

FIG 631

A large piece of graph paper with eight or ten squares to the inch, straight pins, a soft-lead pencil, India ink and pen such as used for the draw-down, and a darning needle to separate and facilitate the counting of the threads are all needed.

Most important of all are good eyesight and patience. For fine materials a reading glass mounted on a frame is of great assistance. Do the first recording with a soft pencil. Mistakes will be made which can be easily erased; they are difficult to correct if they have been inked in.

It was mentioned, in the directions for a draw-down, that one of the reasons for so doing was to determine the accuracy of the woven piece.

It requires only a glance at the photograph of the piece of old quilt chosen for this analysis (Fig. 631) to immediately tell the weaver that there is something wrong with both threading and treadling. The table is not pleasing and there are obvious mistakes in the threading and weaving of the star section.

An analysis of the material will point out these errors, as well as instruct the weaver in the correct development of the threading draft, the tie-up, and the treadling.

To begin the analysis, choose a section of the fabric that shows the complete design with a bit of the beginning of the second repeat.

1. Pin the sample securely to a smooth working surface, such as a drawing board or piece of heavy cardboard.

2. Decide on the exact area to be analyzed and put pins through the material into the board at each of the four corners. To keep track of the analysis as it proceeds, stick a pin in the lower left corner of each block as soon as the thread counting is finished.

3. Prepare a large piece of graph paper and have it ready to jot down the notations as they are read off the fabric (Fig. 632).

4. At this point concentrate on "blocks." This should not be difficult as the squares of the table are so obviously pattern blocks. Review for a moment the making of a draw-down (page 535) in which a line was drawn across the squares of the graph paper to represent the number of threads. Each pattern block is then encircled on the draft.

Exactly the same thing happens here, except that no draft is available and the number of threads in each block is not known. To find out, count the number of warp threads in the sample over which the first pattern thread passes. In Fig. 631, ten warp threads have been passed over, so a stroke is made across ten squares of the graph paper at the upper right corner, beginning six squares down from the top and four squares in from the right-hand edge.

5. At this junction of squares write the figures 4, 3, 2, 1 from top to bottom to designate the harnesses in the customary manner.

From previous experience we know that each block is identified and that we logically start on the right with an *A* block, threaded on harnesses 1 and 2. Therefore, call the first block an *A* block and just above the first square of the ten across which the line was drawn, mark the figure 1, above the second square mark a 2 (on the harness-2 line), then a 1 again, and so on across the ten squares, ending with a 2 (Fig. 632). These represent the harnesses on which the first ten threads are entered for the *A* block.

6. Another study of the sample shows that this block has been treadled with seven pattern shots. This is the first mistake to appear in the draw-down but do not correct it now as the analysis of the fabric must be made exactly as it was woven. Thinking back to the tie-up (page 533), recall that block *A*, 1 and 2 is tied to treadle 1. Therefore treadle 1 was treadled seven

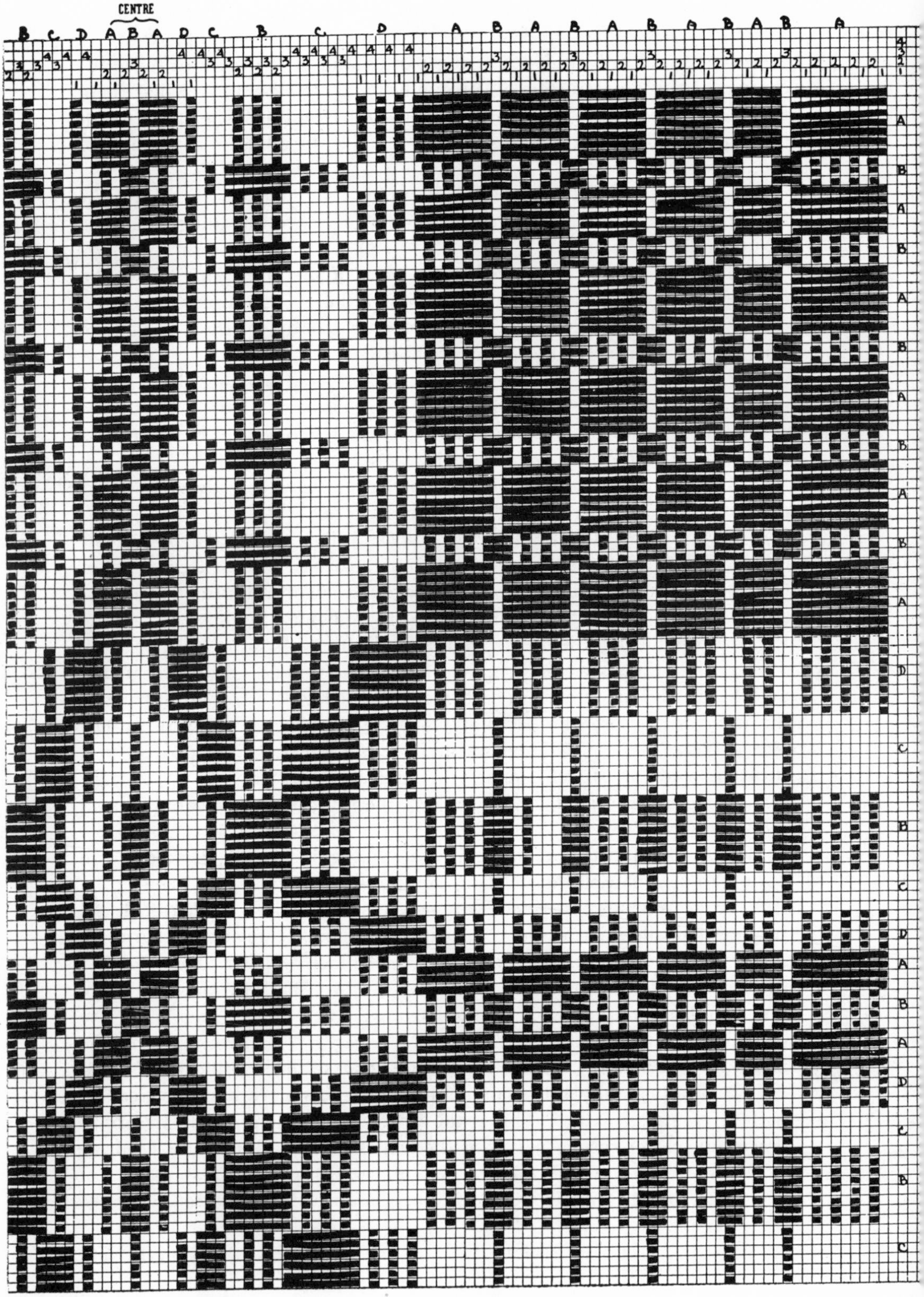

FIG 632

times for these seven pattern shots; draw a total of seven lines directly under one another across the ten squares.

Tabby shots are not shown in the draw-down for an overshot fabric.

7. This completes the drawing of the first block. Put a pin upright in the lower left corner of the block to indicate that the analysis of the block has been completed.

8. The first thread of the second block overlaps the last thread of the first block making it a thread common to both blocks, therefore it is known that the next block must follow the twill sequence and therefore becomes the *B*, 2 and 3 block. The pattern thread passes over only three warp threads, so the *B*, 2 and 3 block is written as a three-thread block, with the notation 2–3–2 jotted down in the proper squares on the threading draft. It has been treadled three times.

9. Encircle the first ten threads, or squares, on the draft and the 2–3–2 of the second block. Encircle each of the following blocks as they develop, as was done in the draw-down (Fig. 628).

10. It is obvious at this point that the rest of the table is a repetition of these two blocks, so they can be drawn in, one below another on the diagonal, until six have been recorded. However, recalling the admonition of a Swedish weaving teacher that "you do not take it for granted, you write down every thread," continue with the counting. In the sample we found that, due to errors in the threading, the second *A* block has only five threads; the third, fourth, and fifth *A* blocks, seven threads each; and the last one, eight threads.

It is due to these errors in threading and treadling on the part of the original weaver that the table looks odd. These errors must be corrected when the new draft is made. Notice also that, if a ruler is laid on the draw-down, extending from the first square at the top and right of the first *A* block to the last square at the left and bottom of the last *A* block, the intervening blocks do not lie along a perfect diagonal as they should.

11. The next block, which starts the second unit of the pattern, begins at the lower left-hand corner of the last *A* block. It covers eight warp threads, the first one being a thread in common with the last one of the *A* block. This thread was threaded on harness 1 so a new threading combination must be used, one which contains a thread on harness 1 plus one on some other harness. The combination 1 and 3 or 2 and 4 is never used for pattern harnesses for overshot, except when an entirely different system or a different technique is being used. This then leaves a 1 and 4 combination which is the threading for the *D* block.

12. Eight threads are covered by the pattern thread so this becomes an eight-thread *D*, 1 and 4 block. This *D* block, tied to treadle 4, was treadled eight times, so lines are drawn across the designated squares to represent this treadling. It is here and in the next two blocks that errors are apparent. The first *D* block should be treadled seven times, the *C* block seven times, and the next *B* block six times.

13. The *D*, 1 and 4 block ends on harness 4. The only combination

which has not been used so far is the 3 and 4 combination, so this block becomes the C, 3 and 4 block. It in turn contains eight threads and has been treadled eight times. The C block is tied to treadle 3.

14. The last block ended with a thread on harness 3 so the combination B, 3 and 2 is used again. This covers seven threads but was treadled eight times. This turning block should contain an uneven number of threads, which would be a total of six instead of the eight shown.

15. Continuing to the left and down, the next block of four threads is a C, 3 and 4 block, because the last thread of the previous block was on harness 3. This block was treadled four times instead of three.

16. The next block of four threads is a D, 1 and 4 block, treadled four times instead of three, and followed by an A, 1 and 2 block of four threads treadled four times, although three times would have been correct.

17. This brings the analysis to the center turning point of the star, set on B, 2 and 3, a block three warp threads wide, treadled four times; two shots would have been the correct number.

18. It is from this point that the pattern reverses back to the start.

19. Continuing on the diagonal, the A, 1 and 2 block of four threads treadled four times appears again, followed by the D, 1 and 4 block of four threads treadled four times, and the C, 3 and 4 block of four threads treadled four times.

20. A B, 2 and 3 block of seven threads treadled eight times brings the draw-down to the edge of the paper, but we have already gone four blocks beyond the B, 2 and 3 block, the point from which the pattern reverses back to the start.

21. The diagonal of the pattern being analyzed has now been sketched and numbered on the draw-down. The assistant called off the number of warp threads covering the pattern threads in each block. It is necessary now to fill in the rest of the draw-down. The method of doing this has been discussed on pages 537 and 538.

The weaver now possesses a picture or draw-down complete with a threading draft and treadling of the fabric to be reproduced. Determine the size and set of the threads as they are being counted.

The tie-up will not present a problem for, as is stated in the section on tie-ups:

BLOCK	HARNESSES	IS TIED TO TREADLE
A	1 and 2	1
B	2 and 3	2
C	3 and 4	3
D	1 and 4	4

The number of times each block is treadled is one less than the number of warp threads in each block. If the choice of materials, sleying, and beating are correct, the block should be square.

As pointed out at the beginning of the analysis, the sample chosen has obvious mistakes, but this might happen with any sample chosen for analysis. The final step, therefore, after the draw-down has been made is to study it, correct the structural errors, and rearrange the blocks if necessary to improve the design.

Problem Check the draw-down locating the mistakes, write a corrected draft observing rules for the overshot technique (page 226), thread the loom, and weave a sample.

THE SHORT DRAFT

Still another form of draft writing is the short draft which can be adapted to many different types of weaves. When thoroughly understood its use simplifies and hastens both threading and treadling.

The theory of the short draft is to use one filled-in square on the draft paper to represent that group of threads, usually written in a thread-by-thread manner, which forms one block of the weave structure.

Each mechanically produced weave has its own structure which is expressed through the order in which the heddles are threaded and the harnesses treadled.

The short draft is the common denominator whereby it is possible to weave a number of techniques to conform to the same design.

If the weaver has seen a particularly well-designed piece of weaving in, for example, the summer-and-winter technique but he feels it would suit his purpose better if woven in the Bronson lace or M's-and-O's technique, he can sketch down the summer-and-winter threading design in a short draft form and then arrange his chosen technique to follow the same layout.

Overshot and crackle techniques are the two weaves which do not lend themselves too well to short-draft conversion. It is quite possible to reduce these threadings to the short-draft system but, because of the overlapping of the blocks, the chances for misinterpretation and error in rethreading are many. The overshot (Fig. 642) and the crackle sample (Fig. 645) both were threaded and woven from the same short draft as the other weaves discussed in this section of the draft.

The weave which is most readily reduced to the short-draft form, and the one with which we are most familiar, is the summer-and-winter weave. A full description of its transition from a thread-by-thread draft to the shortened and more efficient short-draft form is discussed under summer-and-winter weaves (page 312). The Bronson weaves, the double weaves, damask, and demi-damask are all weaves that, especially in the multiple-harness types, are written in short-draft form.

An original short draft, in this case a more elaborate one perhaps than was necessary to illustrate the process, was designed and various samples and draw-downs, all woven as-drawn-in, were made. An examination of these draw-downs shows the same design in a variety of techniques.

The weaver is urged to design a simple short draft, weave samples, and make draw-downs in order to become completely familiar with the advantages of this method of draft writing.

Short-Draft Draw-Down   The thread-by-thread draw-down has been thoroughly discussed (page 535).

The short-draft draw-down is much more simple to execute and follow and its greatest advantage is that it shows an allover design in a much smaller space, a design not for any one particular weave but one which can be adapted to a number of different weaving techniques. The draw-down consists of squaring the blocks below the short draft in the order in which they lie (Fig. 633).

The squares forming the design remain constant in size and arrange-

FIG 633

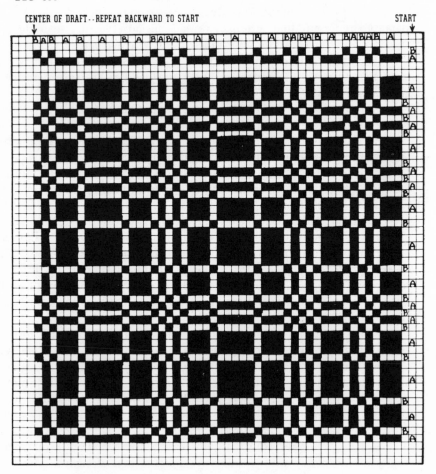

546   THE KEY TO WEAVING

ment, except where slight changes must be made to accommodate a weave structure or to control the size of the piece being woven.

The short-draft draw-down should not be confused with the profile draw-down in which a single horizontal stroke designates the width of the blocks (Figs. 188 and 646). In weaving, the blocks are squared with the required number of threads.

How a short draft was transposed to some of the more popular weaves is shown in the following pages.

Working from the 2-block short draft (Fig. 633) the first example is a 2-block, 4-harness summer-and-winter weave (Fig. 635).

Sample Illustrated (Fig. 635)

WARP	WEFT	PATTERN	REED (dents per inch)	SLEY
Cotton, 24/3	Cotton, 50/3	Wool, 2/16	15	Double

Threading The thread-by-thread structure of the blocks and tie-up is shown in Fig. 634.

The blocks are arranged in the order shown on the short draft (Fig. 633). The left side must end with the correct blocks to balance the right side.

Treadling Treadle blocks as-drawn-in (page 228). Details of the summer-and-winter weave have been given earlier in the text (page 311).

Two factors to be considered when converting the short draft into various weaves is the arrangement of the blocks into pleasing designs and the number of threads within each block. The M's-and-O's weave is a good example. The transposing of the summer-and-winter weave to the short

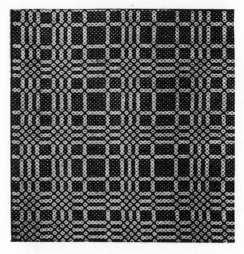

FIG 634

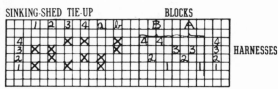

FIG 635

draft already has been discussed (page 313). This weave had four threads only in each block while the M's-and-O's has eight threads per block.

It follows, therefore, that in converting the M's-and-O's to the short draft, extra width will result unless fewer repeats of the draft are used. If all finished samples are to be the same width, the design must be changed accordingly.

The sample illustrated (Fig. 637) uses only a small part of the short draft (Fig. 633) although the width of the woven piece would have been the same as the other samples (Fig. 635), had the last *B* and the three *A* blocks been added to balance the design. Only one repeat and balance is used here, whereas the other samples use three repeats and balance.

Sample Illustrated (Fig. 637)

WARP	WEFT	REED (*dents per inch*)	SLEY
Cotton, 8/2	Dutch cotton, No. 8	18	Single

Threading   Thread the blocks in the following order:

To start—four threads for the right selvedge threaded 1, 2, 3, 4. The thread-by-thread draft for the blocks is given in Fig. 636.

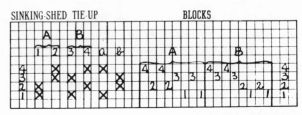

FIG 636

FIG 637

BLOCK	REPEAT	BLOCK	REPEAT
A	3×	B	1×
B	1×	A	3×
A	1×	B	1×
B	1×	A	1×
A	1×	B	1×
B	1×	A	1×
A	3×	B	1×
B	1×	A	3× to balance the design
A	5×		

To end—four threads for the left selvedge threaded 1, 2, 3, 4.

Treadling Treadle the blocks in the order in which they are drawn in. Alternate treadles 1 and 2 for eight shots for block *A;* and treadles 3 and 4 for eight shots for block *B*. The *a* and *b* treadles weave the headings. These instructions are for a sinking-shed loom. For a rising-shed loom tie the harnesses to blanks as shown in the tie-up and treadle in the same order as for a sinking-shed loom.

Details of the M's-and-O's technique have been given (page 378).

Problem Design a short draft suitable for a place mat. Use this draft as M's and O's, thread the loom, and weave a mat.

To give a greater design interest and to carry the study further into the field of 4-harness weaving, the 2-block short draft was extended to a 4-block arrangement.

A comparison of the 2-block (Fig. 633) and the 4-block (Fig. 639) draw-downs show that the essential characteristics of the original 2-block short-draft design can still be seen in the *C* and *D* blocks. The addition of the extra blocks results in more interesting designs.

Examples of summer-and-winter, M's-and-O's, overshot, and crackle weaves reduced to the same short-draft arrangement are shown, beginning with the 4-block, 6-harness summer-and-winter weave (Fig. 640).

Sample Illustrated (Fig. 640) Materials, reed, and sley as for 2-block summer-and-winter weave (page 314).

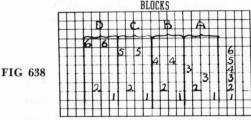

FIG 638

The thread-by-thread block structure for this weave is shown on Fig. 638.

Tie-Up As given for the 4-block 6-harness summer-and-winter weave (page 325).

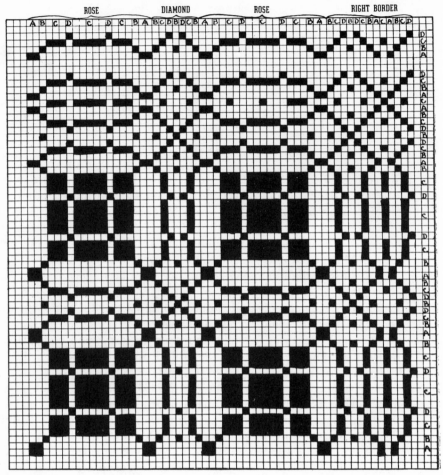

FIG 639

Treadling The blocks are treadled in the order in which they are drawn in. The method of treadling may be any one of the approved summer-and-winter methods preferred by the weaver (page 313).

Notice, when comparing the photograph (Fig. 640) with the draw-down (Fig. 639), that the complete pattern is not shown. This is because the photograph shows a center section of the weaving rather than an end with the border. Two blocks appear at the selvedges on the woven piece which are not shown on the draw-down. These were added to prevent the two edge blocks, *D* and *C*, from being lost in the selvedge. The extra blocks used were *D* and *B*.

The overshot, like the crackle, presents a problem when reduced to the short-draft form. The problem occurs when transposing the short into the thread-by-thread draft. Some of the weaves discussed in connection with this study have a definite number of threads in each block, but here, with the overshot, there is a choice of considering two threads, 1 and 2, or four threads, 1, 2, 1, 2, as one unit (Fig. 642).

FIG 640

If the short draft has many repeats of the same block, a two-thread unit is more satisfactory because it avoids long skips. If there are single blocks in the short draft, a four-thread unit is more satisfactory. In either case, it is necessary to add a thread to the two-thread unit, or subtract a thread from the four-thread block, so that a thread on harness 3 does not follow a thread on harness 1, or a thread on harness 4 follow a thread on harness 2 or vice versa.

The overlapping of blocks, which is an essential characteristic of overshot, causes difficulty in threading from the short draft because the last thread of one block is the first thread of the next block. It is sometimes more convenient to consider the threads in the reverse order, that is, block *A* may be threaded 1, 2, 1, 2 or 2, 1, 2, 1 depending on whether the next thread is on an odd- or an even-numbered harness.

The thread-by-thread draft and draw-down (Fig. 641) demonstrate how this particular design (Fig. 642) was worked out.

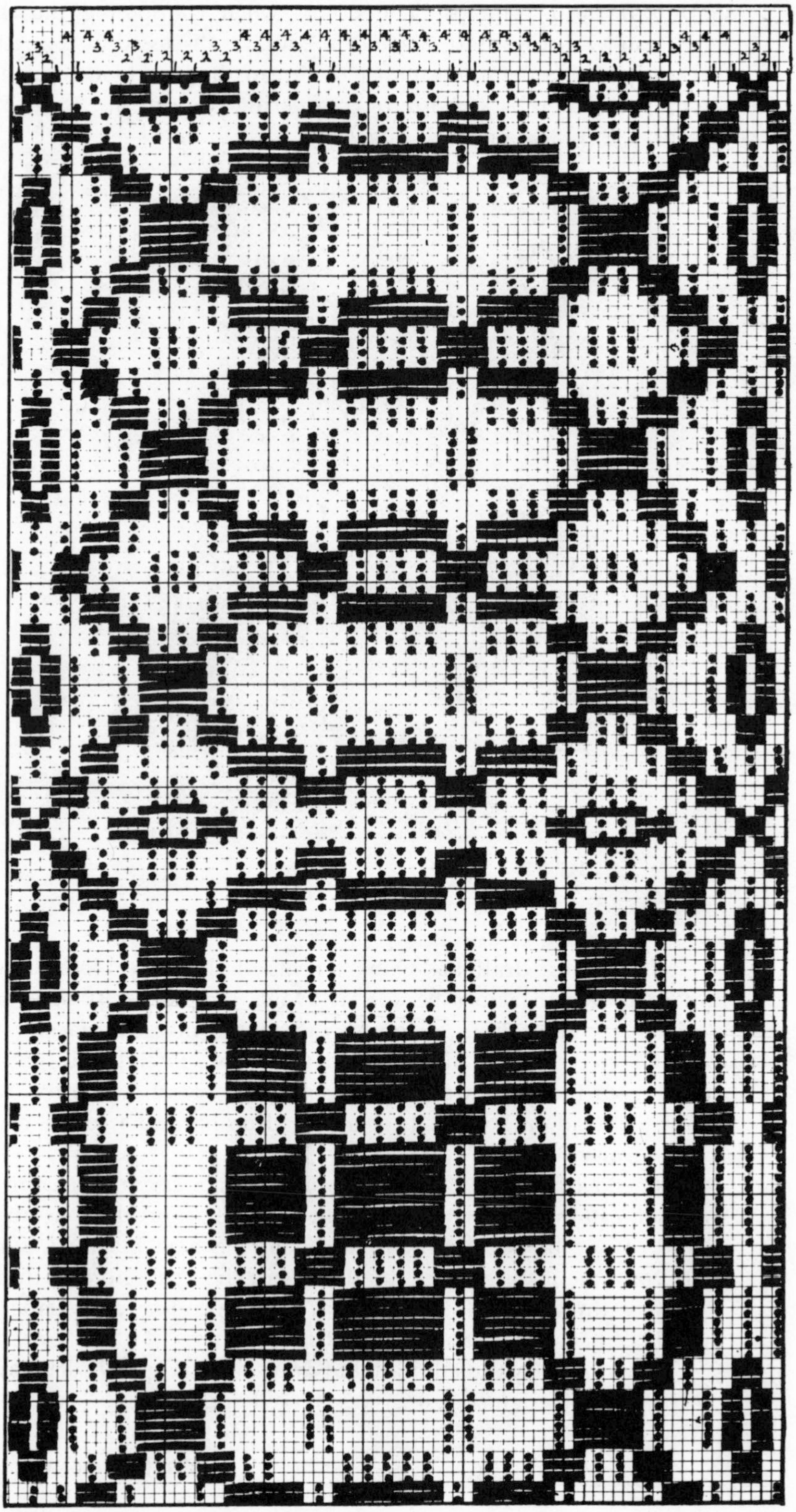

FIG 641

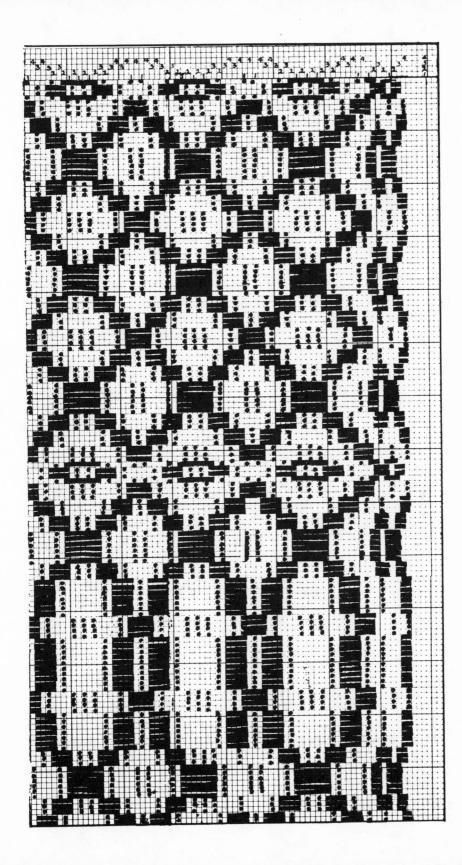

Sample Illustrated (Fig. 642)

WARP	WEFT	PATTERN	REED *(dents per inch)*	SLEY
Daisy crochet cotton, No. 40	Cotton, 24/2	Wool, 2/32, 3 strands together on bobbin	14	Double

The above materials and sleying will produce an overshot with a 45-deg. angle and blocks that square.

Threading The thread-by-thread draft is given at the top of the draw-down (Fig. 641).

Tie-Up Standard (Fig. 621)

Treadling Do not weave the first three threads; these are inserted only to prevent the first blocks of the pattern from becoming lost in the selvedge.

```
1 and 2 — 1  ⎫
2 and 3 — 2  ⎪
1 and 2 — 1  ⎪
1 and 4 — 3  ⎪
4 and 3 — 3  ⎪            1 and 4 —  3  ⎫
2 and 3 — 3  ⎪            3 and 4 —  3  ⎪
1 and 2 — 6  ⎪                          ⎪
2 and 3 — 3  ⎪            2 and 3 —  3  ⎫
3 and 4 — 3  ⎪            1 and 2 —  6  ⎬ Small Star
1 and 4 — 4  ⎪            2 and 3 —  3  ⎭
3 and 4 — 3  ⎪            3 and 4 —  7  ⎫
2 and 3 — 3  ⎪            1 and 4 —  4  ⎪
1 and 2 — 6  ⎬ Border    3 and 4 — 10  ⎬ Rose      Center, 6×
2 and 3 — 3  ⎪            1 and 4 —  4  ⎪
3 and 4 — 3  ⎪            3 and 4 —  7  ⎭
1 and 4 — 4  ⎪            2 and 3 —  3  ⎫
4 and 3 — 3  ⎪            1 and 2 —  6  ⎬ Small Star
2 and 3 — 3  ⎪            2 and 3 —  3  ⎭
1 and 2 — 6  ⎪            3 and 4 —  3
2 and 3 — 6  ⎪            1 and 4 —  3
3 and 4 — 3  ⎪            2 and 3 —  3
1 and 4 — 3  ⎪
1 and 2 — 1  ⎪
2 and 3 — 2  ⎪            End with border.
1 and 2 — 1  ⎭
```

Problem Originate a small short draft; thread and weave a sample in overshot.

It already has been mentioned that the crackle weave does not thread well from a short draft since there are too many chances for error because of the peculiar structure of the weave. However, Fig. 645 shows fairly good results.

A few minor changes were made, particularly in the border section. Also, to keep the sample to the size desired, the first and last *C* block in the rose was repeated only twice instead of three times, and the center *C* block three times instead of five.

In treadling, the rose section was woven as-drawn-in while the borders were woven according to the treadling given on the draft in order to obtain the desired effect.

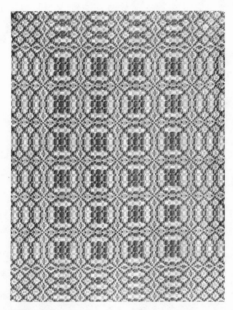

FIG 642

Sample Illustrated (Fig. 645)

WARP	WEFT	PATTERN	REED (*dents per inch*)	SLEY
Cotton, 30/3	Cotton, 30/3	Wool, 2/32, 2 strands together on bobbin	15	Double

Threading See thread-by-thread draft on draw-down (Fig. 643) from short draft (Fig. 633). The encircled numbers on the draft are the incidentals (page 309).

NOTE: The draw-down shows only the right border treadled once and one repeat of the rose-and-diamond design, while the photograph (Fig. 645)

FIG 643

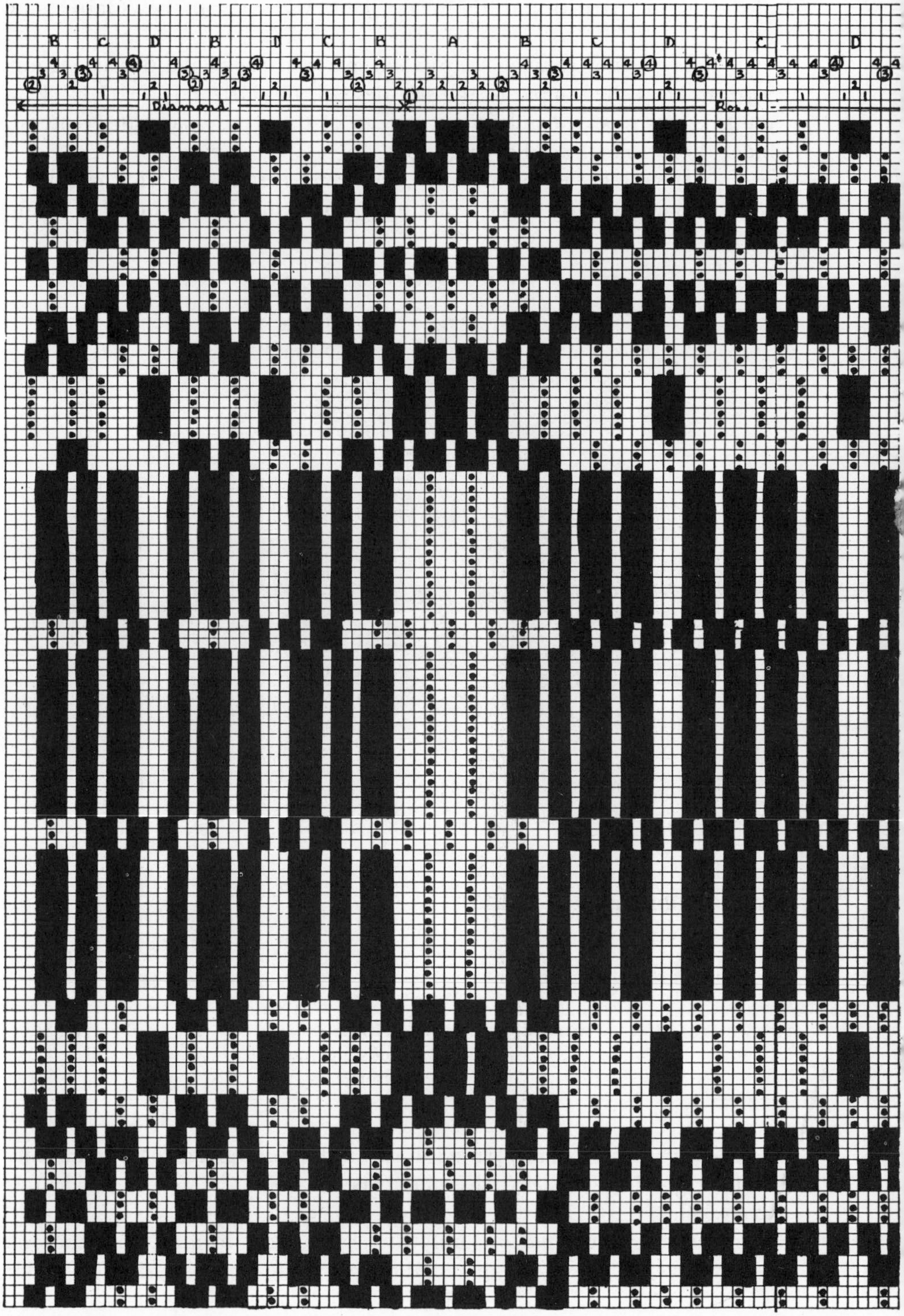

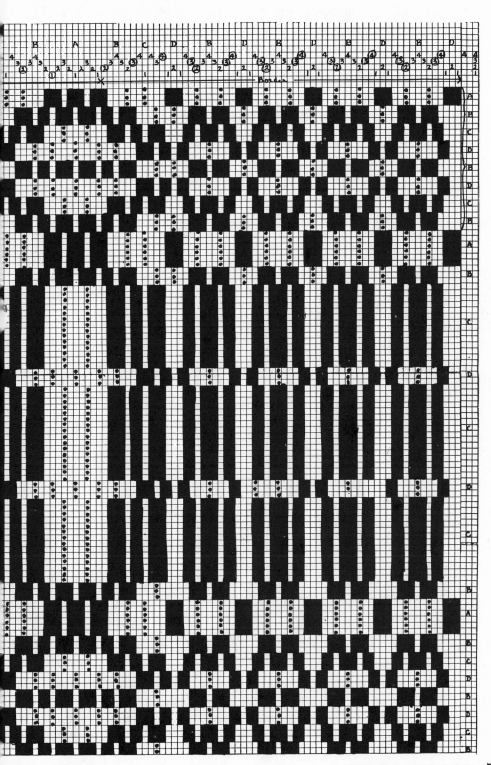

shows the sample threaded with both right and left borders repeated twice, with three complete roses.

SINKING-SHED TIE-UP

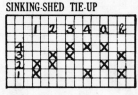

RISING-SHED TIE-UP

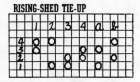

FIG 644

Treadling

BLOCK	TREADLE	REPEAT	
Border:			
A	1	3×	
B	2	3×	
C	3	3×	
D	4	3×	
B	2	3×	2×
D	4	3×	
C	3	3×	
B	2	3×	
Rose:			
A	1	6×	
B	2	3×	
C	3	14×	
D	4	3×	
C	3	16×	
D	4	3×	
C	3	14×	
B	2	3×	
A	1	6×	
Diamond:			
B	2	3×	
C	3	3×	
D	4	3×	
B	2	3×	
D	4	3×	
C	3	3×	
B	2	3×	

Repeat the rose and the diamond the required number of times and end with a rose to weave a piece in the desired length.

To Finish   Weave the border backward from the last block *B* to the start.

The basic structure of M's and O's has been described (page 318). Here we have an extension from the 4-harness to an 8-harness arrangement which is rather unusual. As derived from the 4-block short draft used in this study,

FIG 645

it somewhat resembles an overshot in that the threading on each side of the turning points must lie in reverse, that is, divergent from the turning point.

To accomplish this, it is necessary either to drop or add a half block. In either case, a balancing thread is needed so it seems easier to reduce the number to seven rather than increase the size of the blocks.

Block *B*, at the center of the diamond in the short draft, is the major turning point. In arranging the threading draft this block was used as a starting point and the draft worked out, proceeding first to the right, then to the left. Normally the *B* block is threaded 1, 3; 1, 3; 2, 4; 2, 4; a total of eight threads. But, as only seven are needed, the last 4 is omitted and the next two threads, which normally would be threaded 1, 3, are reversed to 3, 1.

Note that, in the draft (Fig. 646), the threads in the blocks to the right and left of the *B*-turning block now lie divergent to it.

In some places in the draft, a few threads are found to be common to two blocks. Although the draft was rearranged several times in an effort to avoid this, they still occur in one place or another. However, the design is balanced with similar threads on the opposite side of the weaving.

In the areas between the skips there appears a pleasing, textured effect which, with some color combinations, produces a result not normally found in other weaves.

It is not necessary to treadle the blocks "as-drawn-in" as shown in the sample (Fig. 647). There are many variations that can be woven. The "as-drawn-in" treadling was used so that the design of the finished piece would be similar to the other weaves set on the same short draft. Variations in treadling would, of course, be possible with all the other weaves discussed in the short-draft study.

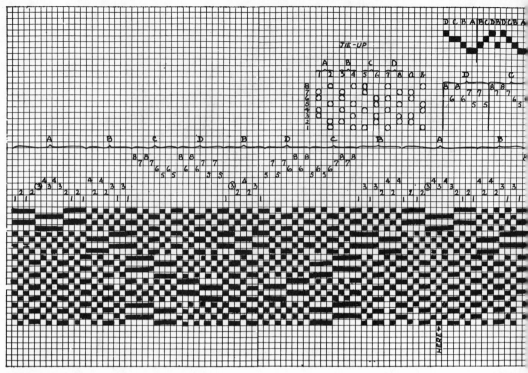

FIG 646

Sample Illustrated (Fig. 647)

WARP	WEFT	REED *(dents per inch)*	SLEY
Cotton, 8/2	Cotton, 8/2	12	Double

Threading Draft, Tie-Up, and Draw-Down The complete thread-by-thread draw-down is not given because, due to size, it is not possible to legibly reproduce it in the text. However, the weaver has progressed to the point where he should be able to complete the draw-down if it seems desirable to do so.

To complete the rose, this sample was threaded with four extra blocks before the main pattern block, *A*, was threaded *A, A, B, C, D, B,* the threading, as is customary, starting with *B* at the right and working toward the left. The draw-down was made and woven as if starting with block *A*. The extra blocks added at the left selvedge were threaded *B, D, C, B, A, A,* again reading from right to left with the threading ending on block *B*.

Tie-Up See the draw-down (Fig. 646).

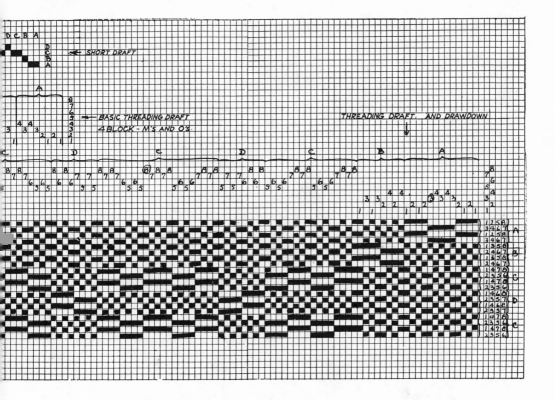

Treadling The blocks were treadled in the following order:

BLOCK	SHOTS	BLOCK	SHOTS
A	13	A	13
B	8	B	8
C	16	C	8
D	8	D	8
C	21	B	7
D	8	D	8
C	16	C	8
B	8	B	8

Repeat twice, starting at the top each time.
To balance, treadle once only:

BLOCK	SHOTS	BLOCK	SHOTS
A	13	D	8
B	8	C	16
C	16	B	8
D	8	A	13
C	21		

FIG 647

FIG 648

Interesting borders can be woven by choosing any section of the design and weaving it in a reverse-twill sequence (Fig. 648). These borders, in combination with the unusual background texture, make attractive towels and place mats.

Problem Thread the loom from a 4-harness short draft in M's and O's as given above and experiment with original treadlings.

The 6-block summer-and-winter weave requires eight harnesses, and the sample shown here (Fig. 651) has been threaded from a further extension of the original 2-block short draft (page 547).

This further extension produces a design which is a bit "spidery" but it serves as a guide toward the designing of multiple-harness patterns. A study like this emphasizes the advisability of making an actual sample before weaving large projects such as drapes, upholstery, and spreads. Unless the draw-down is done on very fine graph paper with the number of squares per inch equaling the number of threads, it is not possible to get an actual "to-size" result. The choice of color also influences the result. Where we see the dark figure on the light background in the draw-down

(Fig. 650) the balance of the design is much more pleasing than it is in the actual material (Fig. 651) where the light figure is against the dark background.

As an experiment in weaving the sample, the *F* block, between the units of the rose, was treadled in reverse of the usual order which is 1, 8; 2, 8; 2, 8; 1, 8; using instead 2, 8; 1, 8; 1, 8; 2, 8. This produces a different center from the 6-harness version and is pleasing on the dark side, but not on the light side as it disturbs the continuity of the background threads. Nor is it good technique, for once the routine of the treadling for summer-and-winter has been established there should be no variation in the piece.

The thread-by-thread structure of the individual blocks for the 6-block, 8-harness summer-and-winter sample (Fig. 649) is as follows:

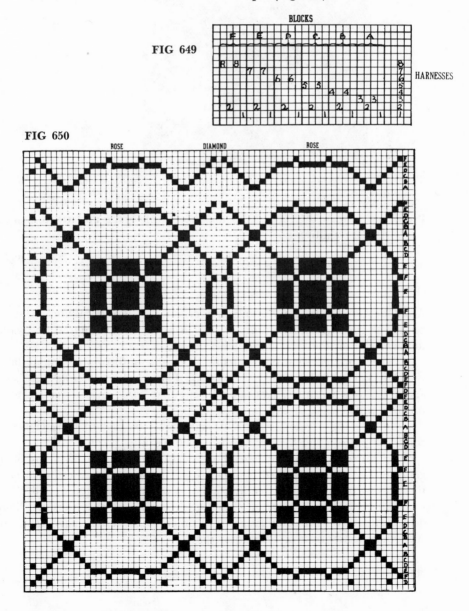

FIG 649

BLOCKS

HARNESSES

FIG 650

ROSE   DIAMOND   ROSE

Tie-Up As for the 6-block, 8-harness summer-and-winter weave (page 330).

Treadling Treadle the blocks in the order in which they are drawn-in (Fig. 650), using whichever method of weaving summer-and-winter is desired (page 313).

FIG 651

Problem Thread the loom from the short draft given and weave a piece with original treadling.

GAMPS

A well-designed, carefully woven gamp, or sampler, is a useful and treasured possession to hang on the studio wall. It is of particular interest and value to the teacher or the weaver who takes orders.

The word *gamp* takes its name from the multicolored umbrella of Charles Dickens's character Sairy Gamp. The word *sampler* is also used, and the words are interchangeable except that *gamp* may suggest a more intricate project.

In weaving a gamp, careful thought must be given to the choice of color and pattern and the arrangement of the drafts. It can be of any color, type of thread, design, and size. For general purposes, a 30-in. by 30-in. gamp is a good choice. Small gamps are not practical because the effect of the crossing of the various treadlings and colors in small squares is lost.

There are many types of gamps, each having its own purpose. Some deal exclusively with color (page 634), others with design (page 158), and still others concentrate on techniques (page 566).

A most interesting gamp, woven of heather yarns, is indispensable to the weaver of tweeds. Such a gamp set with fifteen 2-in. stripes of various shades of heather yarns and woven as-drawn-in will result in a gamp of 225 squares, each one different in color and design. This wool gamp has the two-fold value of showing the beautiful colors of one heather yarn crossing another set of different colors as well as one treadling crossing a different one. The effects achieved are quite striking.

Probably the most challenging gamp to weave is the one dealing with techniques (page 566). In this gamp, each band or stripe of warp is threaded with a different technique or draft. The desired width of the stripes is decided upon and the required number of threads for each wound accordingly. Each stripe may contain the same type of thread and/or color or a mixture of threads. These, however, should be kept reasonably similar, as some threads stretch more than others, thus resulting in a seersucker effect. Threading each side stripe in a plain twill threading and treadling with a similar weave at the heading and the bottom hem will ensure a uniform selvedge. The choice and arrangement of the drafts used in the stripes is an individual matter, but in changing from one draft to another avoid long skips and also avoid having two threads follow each other on the same harness. For instance, if one draft ends with a thread on harness four and the first thread of the next draft is also on harness four, start the new stripe with a thread on harness three or one.

Each square is treadled as-drawn-in. Some most interesting and unusual results are obtained where the treadling of one draft crosses that of a different draft. Often these crossings will be more attractive than those in which the treadling as-drawn-in is used.

It is advisable to separate the warp stripes and the squares, weftwise, with a single, slightly heavier, thread of a contrasting color, otherwise the squares will blend into one another, making it difficult to determine where one square begins and another ends.

Directions are not given for all the gamps shown throughout the text, as the greatest value the weaver can derive from weaving a gamp is the complete self-involvement required to work it out for oneself. Some of the more interesting gamps shown in the text are: 4-harness twill (page 170), 8-harness twill (page 207), overshot, honeysuckle (page 236), overshot, Whig Rose (page 250), summer-and-winter (page 331), Bronson (page 356), bound-weave (page 292), finger-manipulated weave (page 158), and the mixed technique (page 566).

FIG. 652. Section of a gamp designed and woven by Durene Lewis, Nova Scotia

chapter 15

General Information

JUDGING YOUR WEAVING

The best way to evaluate your weaving is to set up a study group within the local guild. Establish a set of points against which to measure the weaving. To be effective, all judging should be fair and unbiased.

Much can be learned from participation in local, state, and national exhibitions. Both winners and losers gain valuable experience. Those who live in a remote area might start a round-robin weaving letter, seek out a weaving pen pal, or join a national organization. It is advisable, too, to build up a library of good weaving books.

METHOD OF KEEPING THREADING DRAFTS AND SAMPLES

Every weaver interested in the articles he weaves will want to keep an accurate record of his pattern drafts, samples, and results. After experimenting for a period of years, the following method was found to be the most satisfactory.

The suggested outline for an index card (Fig. 653) records the essential facts. Thus information is readily available if pieces already woven are to be duplicated. There may be other details, such as the customer's name and address if articles are woven to be sold. The form is flexible and should be developed to aid the individual weaver.

Samples can be attached to the back of the card with paste, cellophane tape, or staples. To prevent raveling, stitch around the four sides of the sample, except where there are selvedge edges. Ravel all the threads back to the stitching, thus exposing the warp, weft, and pattern threads for study.

A coating of thin, clear nail polish along the cut edges will prevent raveling, and make it easy to study the threads.

While any size card can be used, the standard 8½ by 11 in. has proven to be the most satisfactory. Larger cards present a filing problem and smaller ones do not always hold all the desired information. The cards can be punched and inserted into loose-leaf notebooks but even the most conservative weaver soon finds his notes outgrowing the capacity of the covers. The holes break away from the rings and the whole thing becomes an untidy mess.

FIG 653

WEAVING RECORD

Weaving Library of _ _ _ _ _ _ _ _ _ _ _ _ _ _ _ _ _ Date started_ _ _ _ _ Finished _ _ _ _

Pattern Classification _ _ _ _ _ _ _ _ _ _ _ _ _ _Name _ _ _ _ _ _ _ _ Source _ _ _ _ _ _

WARP _ _ _ _ _ _ _ _ _ _ _ _ _ _ Size _ _ _ _ _ _ _ _ Color _ _ _ _ _ _ _ _ _ _ _ _ _

WEFT (1) _ _ _ _ _ _ _ _ _ _ _ _ Size _ _ _ _ _ _ _ _ Color _ _ _ _ _ _ _ _ _ _ _ _ _ _ _

(2) _ _ _ _ _ _ _ _ _ _ _ _ Size _ _ _ _ _ _ _ _ Color _ _ _ _ _ _ _ _ _ _ _ _ _

REED _ _ _ _ _ _ _ Sleying _ _ _ _ _ _ Width in reed _ _ _ _ _ _ No. of threads _ _ _ _ _

Length of warp _ _ _ _ _ _ _ _ _ Weight of warp _ _ _ _ _ _ Weight of weft _ _ _ _ _ _ _ _

THREADING DRAFT
One repeat _ _ _ _ threads   Border _ _ _ _ threads   Selvage _ _ _ _ threads

TIE- UP   TREADLING

ARTICLE ON LOOM   FINISHED ARTICLE AFTER WASHING
Width _ _ _ _ Length _ _ _ _   Width _ _ _ _ Length _ _ _ _

Weaving time _ _ _ _ _ _ hrs.   Finishing time _ _ _ _ _ _hrs.

No. yards woven or articles made _

COST per UNIT _ _ _ _ _ _   SALES PRICE per UNIT _ _ _ _ _ _

COMMENTS:

A better system is to purchase three-cut Manila filing folders and file them in a box. Note the contents of each folder on the tab and file them in order. It is then very simple to skip through the box of folders and find a particular pattern. Clippings and notes placed in the folders can be disposed of when they become obsolete. Materials to be discussed in study groups should also be kept in folders.

TO TIE STRING HEDDLES

Three types of heddles are in common use: string heddle, twisted wire, and flat steel (Figs. 7, 8, and 9).

Scandinavian and old Colonial looms are usually equipped with string heddles. For replacement purposes, these string heddles may be tied as follows:

Tie the heddles to a frame so as to get them a uniform length. To get the correct measurement, a heddle must be taken from the loom.

Measure the sample and add 2 in. to this length.

Wind a number of pieces of twine for the required number of heddles on the warping board. Cut the twine at one post. Heddles should be made of seine twine, although carpet warp is a fair substitute.

The length between pegs is determined by the sample heddle taken from the loom.

Pegs are ⅝-in. doweling sunk into and through a ¾-in. board of hardwood.

The frame must be sturdily made or the pegs will slant, causing heddles to be of varying lengths.

Pass a length of twine around peg *A* (Fig. 654), and even the ends.

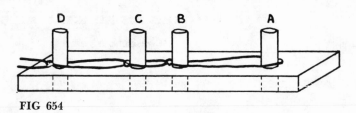

FIG 654

Carry the ends around peg *B,* and tie a square knot.

Continue and carry the ends around peg *C,* and tie a square knot. The space between these two square knots makes the eye of the heddle.

Continue and carry the ends around peg *D* and tie two square knots.

Tie eight or ten heddles before removing them from the frame.

To stiffen the heddles, string them onto a flat stick in such a manner that they do not touch, and dip them into a solution of thin glue mixed with hot wax or into thin shellac or varnish.

To Tie in a String Heddle to Replace a Heddle That Has Been Incorrectly Threaded   Cut a piece of 8/4 carpet warp or similar thread twice as long as the regular heddle plus about 4 in. Double this piece of warp and make a half hitch around the bottom heddle rod (Fig. 655).

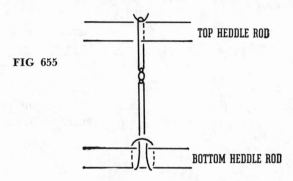

FIG 655

TOP HEDDLE ROD

BOTTOM HEDDLE ROD

Take the two ends in the right hand and slide the thumb and finger up the bight until they are even with the bottom of the heddle eye. Pass the threads that are between the right fingers around the bight at this point and make a knot. Be sure the knot is exactly on a level with the bottom of the heddle eye before tightening it.

In the same manner tie a knot level with the top of the heddle eye. Tie the ends around the top heddle bar with a square knot. Cut the surplus thread.

Be accurate in tying the knots or the warp thread threaded through this temporary heddle will not be in alignment in the shed with the rest of the warp.

To Hold Unused Heddles Out of the Way   Attach a large dress hook to one end of a stout rubber band with a slipknot, the eye to the other end of the band. Pass this around the harness frame and the extra heddles at the ends of each harness and hook. This is much easier than tying.

To Hold Overhead Beater Back   Attach a spiral screen door spring to each upright of the loom, attaching the other end with a hook to the swords of the beater. These springs hold the beater back leaving both hands free for weaving. Occupational therapists will find this idea useful to develop muscle tone by using springs of graded resistance.

REMOVE KNOTS WHILE WINDING WARP

If knots are found during the process of winding the warp, cut them away. The object of this is to remove any knots that would cause difficulty in passing back and forth through the beater when the weaving begins.

Cut the knot appearing at *A* (Fig. 656).

Remove the length of thread between *C* and *B*.

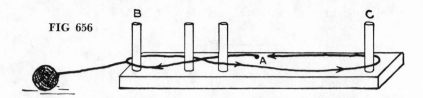

FIG 656

Retie the ends at post *C*. If a knot appears nearer the post where the warp is reversed for the return, cut the warp and retie it at this post instead of at post *C*.

TO CORRECT CROSSED HEDDLES

Sometimes, when threading a loom, two heddles will be found that do not separate and slide along the bar. This is an error which was made when threading the heddles onto the heddle bar. The tops of the heddles were threaded in proper sequence onto the bar, but the heddles were crossed before threading onto the bottom bar. The immediate remedy is to skip the two heddles and proceed to the next. The permanent remedy is to remove all preceding heddles, uncross the offenders, and thread heddles back in order onto the bar.

CROSSED THREADS IN THE SHED

After the loom has been threaded and the warp tied on, it is sometimes found, when the treadles are depressed, that one or more threads are crossed between the heddles and the reed thus preventing a clear passage of the shuttle (Fig. 657).

FIG 657

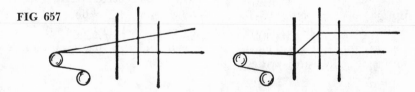

When such mistakes are made, the threads fail to follow in sequence.

To correct this, find the two threads that cross, and slip a warp hook under them.

Loosen the group of threads which contains the crossed threads from the cloth-beam rod, and gently draw the two threads involved toward the back of the loom, out of the reed, but not out of the heddles. Hold the group of threads tightly in the left hand, to prevent more than the two threads from being pulled out.

Retie the group of threads temporarily to the rod.

Pick up one of the withdrawn threads as it lies in front of the heddles, and rethread it back into the correct space in the reed. Draw the second thread back through the reed. To make certain that the threads are in the correct heddle, take the thread farthest to the right and thread it through the dent farthest to the right. Then the second thread will naturally belong in the one remaining empty dent.

Retie the group of warp ends, being sure to tie them at the same tension as the rest of the groups.

TO PREVENT THE LOOM FROM SLIPPING

A loom that continuously slips back against the weaver's knees is an annoying time-waster. It also interferes with regular and even beating.

To rectify this difficulty, place the loom with the light coming over the left shoulder (the right, if left-handed) in a north window if available.

Several methods can be used, but first, can the loom be permanently placed or must it be moved frequently? Is there a wall behind and fairly close to the weaver's back? Is it permissible to put permanent anchors into the floor, or must some other method be devised?

1. If the weaver's back is toward a wall, cut two pieces of board approximately 40 in. long and place one end of each board against each front post (or leg) of the loom with the opposite ends of the boards against the baseboard. In some instances, a ¾- or 1-in.-thick board would be best; for others, square-ended braces would be better depending on the size and shape of the loom post.

2. If feasible, two sturdy hooks and eyes can be used to fasten the loom to the floor. Screw the hooks into the back of the front posts of the loom and the eyes into the floor. Placing the hooks in the front posts does away with any danger of falling over them while working around the loom. In placing the loom for this method, leave room to pass around it easily for warping, threading, and cleaning, in addition to sufficient leeway to throw the shuttle without striking the wall.

3. A heavy wooden strip, slightly wider than the width across the front of the loom, nailed or screwed to the floor, provides a satisfactory brake.

4. Where it is not practical to use any of the above methods, place thick sponge rubber pads under each of the four posts. Cut these to extend about a quarter of an inch beyond each side of the posts. These are effective and can be renewed easily and inexpensively as they wear out.

TO CORRECT LOOPS WHICH APPEAR
INSIDE SELVEDGE EDGES

Loops which appear just inside the selvedge indicate that the weft thread has not been pulled quite tight enough (Fig. 658).

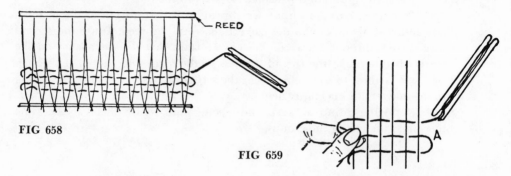

FIG 658

FIG 659

To remedy this, pull thread *A* to the left and hold it in place between the thumb and index finger of the left hand until the shuttle has been passed back to the right-hand side of the loom, the shed changed, and the thread beaten back in place (Fig. 659). If a loop appears on the right-hand side as well, repeat this process in reverse.

TO CORRECT ERRORS CAUSED BY
UNEVEN TYING AND FAULTY TENSION

The beginning weaver sometimes is puzzled by an unevenness in the weaving at the edge of the web next to the reed.

This may take any of the following forms:

1. The edge of the web runs at an angle to the reed or fell (Fig. 660).

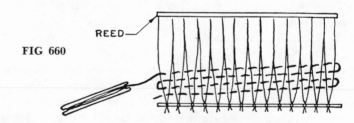

REED—

FIG 660

This is due to the fact that the beater has been grasped at one end instead of in the center, thus bringing more pressure to bear on the left side than on the right, or vice versa. This will occur only where there is a certain amount of play in the beater frame. Correct this error by grasping the beater either in the center with one hand, or at each end using both hands.

The slant edge also may have been caused by lack of care in beating the carpet rags back into correct alignment when the weaving was begun (page 46).

This can be corrected only by undoing the weaving back to the beginning and forcing the first row of rags into place; then weaving in the rest of the rows, carefully checking, as the weaving proceeds, to determine that the rags are close up against the reed all the way across the web. If the rags are out of line at any point, they should be pushed into position with the fingers. The first row of weft thread also must be in correct position at the beginning of the weaving.

Another cause of the foregoing difficulty may be that the warp has been tied with a tighter tension on one side of the loom than on the other. This can be corrected by retying the groups of warp threads involved.

2. Wavy lines at the edge of the weaving next to the reed (Fig. 661).

This is due to uneven tying of groups of warp ends. To remedy, retie the groups with an even tension.

3. Web higher at the center than at the edges (Fig. 662).

This is the result of the warp ends being tied tighter in the center than at the selvedges. To remedy, retie the warp with even tension.

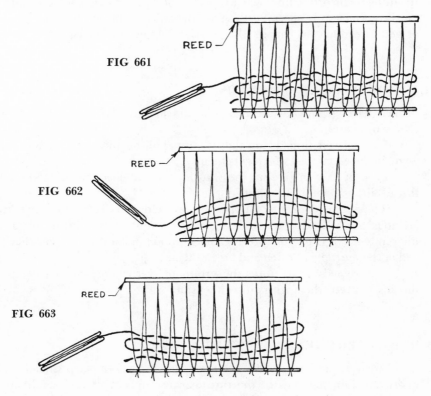

FIG 661

FIG 662

FIG 663

4. Web tighter at the edges than at the center (Fig. 663).

The warp has been tied tighter at the edges than in the center. To remedy, retie the warp with even tension.

UNEVEN SPACING OF WEFT THREADS IN WEB

This (Fig. 664) is caused by uneven beating. It can be corrected by more uniform beating.

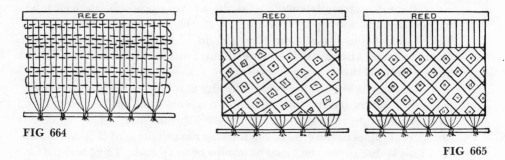

FIG 664

FIG 665

IMPERFECT DIAGONALS IN PATTERN WEAVING

This condition (Fig. 665) is caused either by incorrect sequence of pattern treadling or incorrect number of shots of each pattern change or sleying. It can be corrected by checking the pattern sequence or the number of shots of weft thread in each change. Diagonals should be at a 45-deg. angle.

CAUSES OF BROKEN THREADS

Broken selvedge threads are common and are usually due to one of the following causes:

Pulling weft threads too tightly, thus pulling the warp threads at an angle to the metal reed which cuts them.

Lack of care in passing the shuttle into the shed, catching the edge threads in the point of the shuttle.

Threads in the center of the web are seldom broken, but when they are it is probably due to carelessness in the use of the shuttle or to an uneven tension. If one or two threads are loose, it stands to reason that the end of the shuttle will catch and break them.

The remedy is to untie the group of warp ends which have loose threads and retie them with an even tension.

TO REPAIR BROKEN WARP THREADS

Every weaver, particularly the beginner, dreads broken warp threads. The knots that join the ends of the threads cause difficulties and are likely to pull apart as they pass back and forth through the reed.

The following simple method of repairing broken warp threads does away with these difficulties, and saves not only time but temper as well.

Assuming that the warp thread breaks midway between the heddles and the fell of the web (for example, on a large loom about 6 in. from the edge), the first step in making repairs is to draw one end of the broken thread out of the reed toward the front of the loom and the other end out toward the back of the loom.

Cut a new warp thread long enough to reach from the fell of the web back through the reed and heddles to the warp beam; to this, add 5 in. for knots, etc.

Tie the new warp thread onto the old at the edge of the web with a square knot. Pin the knot back onto the web. This prevents the warp from stretching thus allowing the knot to rub back and forth through the reed.

Thread the other end of the warp thread through the reed and heddle in the space left vacant by the broken warp thread.

Tie the end of the new warp thread, with a square knot, to the end of the broken thread at the back of the loom, but first examine it to discover and remove any frayed portions.

This new warp thread will be considerably longer than the rest of the warp. Carry this thread over the back beam and hang a weight on it (a C clamp will make a good weight). The weight should be heavy enough to give the same tension on this thread as on the other warp threads. Wind the remainder of the thread around the clamp to prevent its getting tangled.

Weave about 8 in., which is slightly more than the distance between the edge of the web and the place where the original warp thread broke. Unwind the surplus thread, and remove the clamp.

Stand in front of the loom, and gently draw the repaired thread through to the edge of the web, being careful to ease the knot through the heddle and the reed. If the web is loosely woven, draw the knot into the web and back a distance of an inch or so or until the thread is tight. If the web is tightly woven, it will be necessary to untie the knot and darn the end of the repaired thread into the web with a small blunt tapestry needle.

After being drawn to the same tension as the other warp threads, wind the end of the thread around a pin to prevent its slipping. Excess length can be cut off and the ends or knot cut after the web has been removed from the loom.

The broken thread has been repaired without any of the usual difficulties, and the weaving can now continue smoothly.

TO REPAIR WARP SLIPPING ON BEAM

This usually occurs when papers inserted to keep the layers of warp separated are not wound tightly enough during the warping of the beam. It can easily be remedied by tightening the warp on the beam through winding until all the slack has been taken up. Be sure that the dog on the cloth beam is secure before the winding begins.

TO ADD NEW WEFT THREADS

New weft threads can be added anywhere in the web, but in plain weaving it is advisable to do the splicing near the edge rather than in the center of the web as it shows less.

Continue with the weaving until the weft thread has been used up. Allow the end to lie in the shed. Pass the shuttle with the new thread through in the same direction allowing the old and new ends to lie beside each other for about 1 or 1½ in. (Fig. 666). Close the shed and beat the

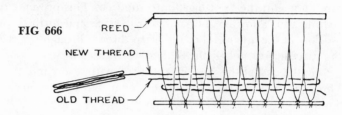

FIG 666   REED

NEW THREAD

OLD THREAD

thread back in the customary manner. Do not become disturbed if the ends stick out or if the splice seems loose in the shed. After an additional row or two of shots have been put through, pull the loose ends of the two threads in opposite directions until they are tight. They can be clipped later. The splice can hardly be seen; in an overshot pattern it does not show at all.

WINDING TWO THREADS TOGETHER ON THE SHUTTLE

To facilitate the winding of two threads together onto a shuttle, use the following method:

Place one spool inside a small box in the top of which a hole has been punched.

Draw the end of the thread through this hole.

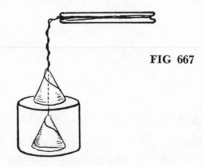

FIG 667

Pass this thread up through the center of a second spool that has been placed on the top of the box over the hole (Fig. 667).

Wind the two threads together onto the shuttle, being careful to hold the shuttle directly over the cones and drawing the thread in a direct line from them. If this is not done, the cones will upset.

The two threads twist around each other and will lie smoothly in the web.

TO PREVENT THREADS ON SHUTTLES FROM TANGLING WHEN PLACED IN A CUPBOARD

To prevent ends of threads from getting tangled when shuttles are placed in the cupboard, catch such ends under the threads that are wound on the shuttles. This is easily done and the threads are easy to untie:

Pass the first and second fingers of the left hand under the thread (from the left) as it lies on the shuttle.

Hold the thread at B (Fig. 668) under the thumb as it lies across the top and at right angles to the thread wound on the shuttle.

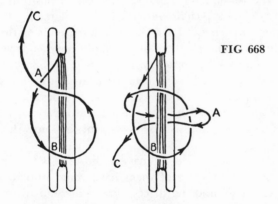

FIG 668

Take the thread at *A,* pass it under the thread on the shuttle with the fingers and pull it to the right. This will make loop *A,* and the end *C* will still be at the left.

Hold end *C,* and pull loop *A* to the right to tighten it.

To untie pull end *C.*

TYING NEW WARP ENDS ONTO OLD WARP ENDS

There are several reasons why the weaver may wish to tie a new warp onto the old warp ends. He may wish to weave additional webs with the same pattern or use the same pattern but in a different color, or he may wish to tie a plaid or stripe warp on a plain-color threading which was originally set up for either tabby or pattern weaving, or vice versa. Whatever the reason may be, the weaver who works alone can save considerable time by utilizing a threading that is in the loom.

Wind the warp according to any of the methods previously described (pages 17 and 23). Tie in the lease sticks and place them in position on the loom.

FOR NEW WARP TO BE TIED ONTO OLD WARP ENDS IN FRONT OF THE REED

This method saves time as the warp requires only one winding onto the warp beam.

1. Tie the beater close to the heddle frames.
2. Wind the completed web toward the cloth beam until there is about 8 or 10 in. of warp between the reed and the web.
3. Cut the web from the loom.
4. Loosely knot the warp ends in groups across the loom in front of the reed.
5. Place and tie new warp and leash sticks in position at the front of the loom, and tie the warp chain onto the breast beam.
6. Cut the warp chain. Take the new warp ends as they lie in order along the leash sticks and tie them onto the old warp ends with a square or weaver's knot. Test each knot after tying.
7. When all warp ends have been tied, untie the heavy cord holding the warp chain in place around the leash sticks and beam.
8. Slowly and gently wind the warp toward the warp beam, shaking the heddles, if necessary, to assist the passage of the knots through the dents and eyes.
9. When the knots have all passed through the reed and heddles, check to determine that none of them have come untied, leaving empty heddles or dents. If so, find the spaces, thread the ends through, and retie.
10. Complete by winding the warp onto the warp beam according to instructions (page 34).

FOR NEW WARP TO BE TIED ONTO OLD WARP ENDS ON THE BACK OF THE LOOM

1. Tie the beater close to the heddle frames.
2. Place new warp and leash sticks in position on the back of the loom.
3. Untie old warp ends from the warp-beam rod, and knot them loosely in groups close to the heddles.
4. Proceed as in steps 6 and 7 in the previous operation.
5. Slowly and gently wind the new warp toward the cloth beam, and gently shake the heddles, if necessary, to assist the passage of knots through the heddle eyes and dents.
6. Proceed as in step 9 in the previous operation.

7. After all warp ends have passed through, cut the web and remove it from the front of the loom.

8. Tie the new warp ends onto the cloth-beam rod.

9. Complete the winding of warp onto the cloth beam then reverse the operation winding this new warp back onto the proper warp beam. Insert papers or sticks (page 32).

TO THREAD A NEW PATTERN WITH WARP THAT IS ON THE BEAM

The weaver may wish to change the pattern threading while warp still remains on the beam. It may be that the pattern chosen does not work out satisfactorily, or that he has woven as many webs as he desires of this particular pattern. Or, he may be anxious to try out a new pattern on the end of an old warp, to determine its desirability before he commits himself to the winding and threading of new warp for it. No matter what the reason may be, it is a comparatively simple process to rethread a loom from the warp that is already wound on the beam.

1. Wind the completed web toward the breast beam on the front of the loom, until there are at least 10 in. of warp between the reed and the completed web.

2. Open up a shed (on a 2-harness loom this will be harness 1; on a 4-harness loom, harnesses 1 and 3; and on an 8-harness loom, harnesses 1, 3, 5, and 7).

3. Insert a lease stick in the shed behind the harnesses and in front of the warp beam.

4. Open up the opposite shed, and insert the other lease stick in front of the first stick. Insert the ends of the lease sticks into the wire or rope supports on the loom frame, and tie the ends securely, or

Cut a piece of cellophane tape, adhesive tape, or gummed paper as long as the width of the warp lying between the harnesses and warp beam. Stick this securely on top of the warp where it lies over the back beam.

Of the above two methods, the first method is preferred.

The object of the insertion of the lease sticks or use of the adhesive is to keep the warp ends in order as they come from the beam.

5. Cut the finished web from the cloth beam, and draw the warp ends through to the back of the loom.

6. Thread the heddles with the desired pattern sley and tie warp ends to cloth-beam rod (page 40).

SALVAGING SAMPLES

Small pieces of weaving that appear to have little value can be salvaged for table or lamp mats, pin cushions, etc. Cut an oval or round of cardboard, place it on the piece of weaving, mark around the cardboard with a pencil or chalk, and stitch around this line on a sewing machine (Fig. 669). Cover the row of machine stitching with a row of hand stitching as machine stitching should never appear on hand weaving. Cut the surplus material off ½ or ¾ in. beyond the stitching, and fringe out all around the piece. Trim the fringe.

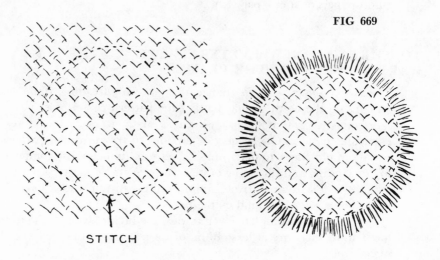

FIG 669

STITCH

TO KEEP WEAVING CLEAN

Purchase a piece of transparent pliofilm approximately 45 in. long by 49 to 54 in. wide. Directions given here are for a 45-in.-wide loom but can be easily adjusted to fit a loom of any size.

Baste a hem in each end of the pliofilm wide enough for the easy insertion of a "wind-in" stick (approx. 1¼ in. wide). The ends of the stick should extend 1½ in. beyond each side of the pliofilm.

Loosely tie pieces of stout cord or, preferably, wide tape around each end of the cloth beam, tying a knot about 1 in. away from the beam so that the cord or tape won't turn with the cloth when the beam is rolled.

Now tie the ends of these cords or tapes around each end of one of the "wind-in sticks" which has been inserted into the hem at one end of the pliofilm cover. Lift up the breast beam, slip a wide rubber band around each end of the beam, and replace the beam. If the beam is not removable, tie pieces of elastic around the beam instead. The elastic bands should clear the selvedges of the material by at least 1 or 2 in.

Slip the ends of the other "wind-in stick," which has been inserted into the second hem of the pliofilm, under these rubber bands. Make a few turns of the pliofilm around each stick until all slackness has been taken up and the protective cover lies close to the web. The edge of the "wind-in stick," which lies on the breast beam across the web, should run parallel with the inside edge of the beam.

It is not necessary to move the cover when rolling the finished web onto the cloth beam as the weaving proceeds since it will slide under easily.

At the close of the weaving period, unroll the pliofilm at the cloth beam far enough so that the "wind-in stick" can be laid up and over the finished cloth resting on the beam. Also unroll the pliofilm at the breast beam and carry the stick and material up close to the beater. If perishable material is being woven, a similar cover can be made for the back of the loom. When leaving the weaving for an indefinite period, open up the covers full length and bring them around the warp and cloth beams up to the beater in front and the harnesses in back. Attach clothespins at each selvedge to hold the cover close to the warp and the woven material.

The advantages of this pliofilm protective cover over one of cloth is that the finished material can be seen through it, it does not pick up lint, and it is smooth to the touch. Any dust that collects when the loom is not in use for a few days can be wiped off with a damp cloth.

TO DETERMINE CORRECT SLEYING FOR THREADS OF UNKNOWN SIZE

When in doubt as to the proper sleying to use to obtain a 50/50 plain weave with a thread of unknown size, wind it around a steel tape measure or ruler. Be sure each successive thread lies closely beside the last one without over-lapping. Count the number of threads that lie within an inch measurement on the tape and divide by two. The answer is the correct number of dents per inch at which the thread should be sleyed.

TO FIGURE AMOUNT OF MATERIAL TO WEAVE A GARMENT

Because of the variation in the weaving width of looms, garment styles, and the sizes of people, it is impractical to make up tables stating how many yards of material will be required for a given garment.

The most simple and accurate method is to purchase a paper pattern, open and spread it out on bed or floor, arranging it in various ways, then decide whether to weave a long narrow piece of material or a short wide one.

An average-size woman's suit or top coat requires approximately 6 yd. of 30 to 32-in. material. Tailors do not object to using 27- or 28-in. material as it is just one half the width of the 54-in. material to which they are accustomed.

Regardless of the method used to figure the amount of material needed, do allow plenty for loom waste, take-up, and shrinkage when the material is steam pressed. It is rather disconcerting to discover that the finished material is ¼ or ½ yd. too short!

Any extra length can be used for a vest, waistcoat, hat, bag, skirt, pants, or vest for a small child, or even to upholster a chair or cover a pillow.

FOLLOWING TREADLING DRAFT

If it is necessary to have a treadling draft to follow, write it in clear, dark figures on a narrow piece of paper. Slip paper under the edge of the web on top of the breast beam. As the block is woven, pull out the paper so that the edge of the web is directly under the next row or block to be woven.

TO MARK BLOCKS

A small hatpin with a large head can be dropped through the corner of the block just woven to keep track of the diagonal when weaving as-drawn-in without treadling directions. This is helpful with the crackle weave.

TO WEAVE TWO IDENTICAL PATTERN UNITS

Bedspreads, rugs, drapes, and sometimes large wall hangings are woven in two strips and joined together after removal from the loom. When this is done, it is necessary that the pattern units of the two pieces should match exactly.

This can be done in the following manner:

Cut a piece of cardboard, longer than the pattern unit and about 3 in. wide.

Place the cardboard at the edge of a completed unit, with the end on the first pattern thread of the unit being measured, and carefully mark the cardboard at the other end of the unit. Make marks with a heavy dark pencil between these two showing where the various changes occur.

Use this as a guide for measuring the remaining units.

The same method may be used by the beginner to measure the accuracy with which he is beating his pattern units.

TO WEAVE NARROW WEBS ON WIDE LOOMS

Cut and hem two canvas aprons about 12 in. wide and long enough to reach from the warp beam up over the back beam to within 6 in. of the harness frames.

Attach one of these aprons to the warp-beam rod and the other to the cloth-beam rod, placing them at the center of the beams. A 12-in. rod, similar to those used with the full-width apron, should be attached to each of the narrow aprons. Before using these narrow aprons, roll the wide aprons tightly around the warp and cloth beams respectively, and tie securely at each end of the beams. Continue threading in the usual manner, paying attention to careful warping and tension, etc.

TO UNWEAVE A WEB

From time to time it is inevitable that a web does not materialize as it was envisioned after the first ten or twelve inches have been woven, and the weaver realizes that it must be taken out. The following method of unweaving is suggested. It is especially good for wool or linen warps as it does away with frizzing and possible shuttle breakage; it is speedy and much less frustrating than unweaving with the shuttle.

With the fell of the material at least 12 in. from the beater, which as an added precaution has been tied securely to the loom frame, untie the warp bouts from the cloth-beam rod. Now sit as far as possible into the loom, with the woven piece resting on the knees. Start at the center of the woven piece and carefully pull out two or three of the warp threads, one at a time drawing them toward the reed. These first few threads may resist a bit but once they are out the rest will come out easily. Never start at the selvedge as the threads are much tighter there and may break. Continue withdrawing the warp threads from the center to the left for a few inches, then to the right, and so on until all the threads have been pulled out. If carefully done, the weft threads will all lie in perfect order on the knees and can be easily wound into balls ready to be reused.

KNOTS

A weaver who doesn't know his knots is like a ship without a rudder; neither gets very far. However, the weaver can get along nicely with three simple knots that are easily learned and remembered. It is difficult to describe knots, but the following sketches, if carefully analyzed, will give adequate instruction.

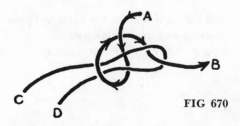

FIG 670

1. Weaver's Knot The weaver's knot (Fig. 670) is probably one of the oldest knots in existence, and it is always found where there are weavers, though seldom elsewhere. Unlike the square knot, it cannot be tied at a tension; nevertheless, it is very useful and once tied can be depended upon to stay tied, and it cannot slip.

2. Square Knot The square knot (Fig. 671) is a good general knot as useful around a loom as it is in everyday life. It can be tied at a tension and will not slip if correctly tied. If the two cords being tied together are of unequal size, it will be necessary to wrap the ends to the bight after tying.

FIG 671

An incorrectly tied square knot is known as a granny knot. This knot does not hold when subjected to strain. Some authorities advocate the granny knot rather than the square knot for tying string heddles (page 570), otherwise it has little or no value and should be avoided.

3. Snitch Knot The snitch knot (Fig. 672) is used universally to tie up lams and treadles. It as made as follows:

The loop *A* coming up from the treadles is doubled back across as shown at *A'*.

FIG 672

The two ends of the cord *B* from the lams are passed through loop *A'*. Loop *A'* is tightened and drawn downward.

The ends of loop *B* drawn through *A'* are tied with a square knot close to the bight.

FRINGE

Any twill and some of the finer overshot patterns are suitable for headings for fringe. Any of these can be easily worked out by the weaver once he has become familiar with the technique of fringe weaving and has gained a knowledge of the weaving of overshot patterns.

FIG 673

Uses   Fringe sometimes is used in place of gimp to finish off the edges of upholstered furniture. It is also used on the ends and sides of pillows, table covers, bags, etc.

Suitable Materials and Sleying   Any materials suitable in upholstery

The width of the fringe depends upon the number of dents skipped.

Use two shuttles which run in opposite directions but pass across the entire web and in the same shed (Fig. 674).

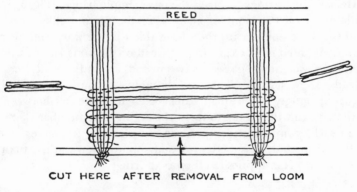

FIG 674

After every third shot, pass the shuttle around the inside edge of the six threads. This binds the inner edge of the fringe, making it firm and durable.

A good piece of weaving is judged by its finish, provided the warp is of good quality and closely spaced. A well-tied fringe adds greatly to the appearance of rugs, place mats, or runners. Fringes are not suitable on all articles.

Fringes can be simple, such as a hemstitched or a simple, knotted

FIG 675

FIG 676

fringe, or they can be quite complex like those used on some Scandinavian or Oriental rugs and wall hangings. Remember that the Gobelin tapestry pieces are *never* finished with a fringe.

To trim a fringe evenly, fold the article in half and place it on a table with the selvedge close to and parallel to the side of the table. The warp ends of the piece will then be at right angles to the end of the table and can be trimmed evenly.

1. Hemstitched Fringe   This is the most simple fringe, (Fig. 675) and can be made on or off the loom. If made after the piece is taken from the loom, hold the woven piece with the wrong side up, the warp ends away from the body. A pointed needle carrying a thread of the same color as the warp, but lighter in weight, is passed between and around the desired number of threads, from left to right, and brought to the surface. The thread is drawn up snugly and a small stitch taken into the fell between this group of threads and the next group to the right. The number of threads taken up in each group depends upon the coarseness of the material and the size of the warp, but it is better to take up too few rather than too many threads. This rule applies to all types of fringe.

2. Simple Knotted Fringe   Take the desired number of threads between the thumb and index finger of the left hand and twist them to the left. When the twist is tight and close to the fell take the end of the group in the right hand and carry it on top of the bight, close to the web, and pass it up through the circle thus formed (Fig. 676). Work the knot up close to the fell before tightening.

3. Double-Knotted Fringe   Tie the first part of the knot as for the simple knotted fringe. Take half the total number of threads from each of the two adjacent bouts, twist them together, and knot (Fig. 677).

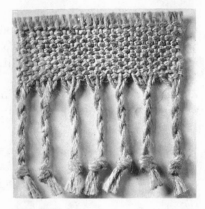

FIG 677

FIG 678

4. Twisted Fringe Pick up a group of threads and twist them to the right. Hold the end to prevent its untwisting. Pick up a second group of threads and twist tightly in the same direction as for the first group. Lay this group on top of the first group, still holding the ends, and twist the two around each other. This twist will go in the opposite direction from the first. Knot the ends together to prevent untwisting (Fig. 678).

5. Braided Fringe Take up three groups of two threads each and braid them. Keep the threads flat; do not crisscross them. Knot the ends of the braids to keep them from unraveling (Fig. 679). If desired, a four-strand braid can be made. In this case, four groups of two threads each are used.

6. Half-Hitch Knot Fringe This fringe can be tied quickly. It is not suitable for a slippery warp as it will not stay tied properly. It should be pressed when used on a wall hanging; walking, however, will soon press down the fringe on a rug (Fig. 680).

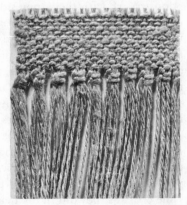

FIG 679

FIG 680

To tie this fringe, pick up a group of three warp threads. Take the thread lying at the left of the group and make two half hitches, or buttonhole stitches, around the other two threads. Tie the knot tightly, close to the fell. Take up a second group of threads and tie the next group.

7. Uncut Loop Fringe   This fringe is particularly good for ecclesiastical weaving or for synthetic warps which fray easily (Fig. 681).

FIG 681

Start the weaving with a heading about 1¼ in. wide. Cut a piece of stiff cardboard, twice the width of the desired fringe, and weave it in. Weave the body of the article. When the end is reached weave in a second piece of cardboard the same width as the first. End with a 1¼-in. heading. Follow with an inch or so of coarse weaving to hold the threads in place.

Remove the weaving from the loom and turn the hem back onto the body of the web, matching the two fells exactly. Baste the two fells together, then hemstitch as inconspicuously as possible. Repeat with the second end. Turn under and hem down the other side of the hem or line the article.

8. Swedish Fringe   There are several variations of the knotted Swedish border, some simple, some complex. The simple fringe given here is useful for flossa or rölakan rugs or hangings, and has within itself several variations. Work with the wrong side of the warp up, the warp ends toward the body. Take the first pair of threads at the left border, pass them to the right under the second pair of threads, over the third pair, and under the fourth pair. Bring the first pair to the surface; the ends will point toward the center of the rug. Now take the pair at the extreme left, pass them to the right under the next pair, over the next, under the next, and to the surface as was done for the first pair. Continue thus across the width of the rug. Keep the threads flat; do not crisscross them (Figs. 682 to 684).

When the right selvedge is reached, there will be four pairs of threads. Braid these pairs into a four-strand braid about 2 or 3 in. long. Tie a knot at the end. Start the braiding with the pair that lies at the top, that is, the pair nearest the fell. By doing this, the threads will continue to lie in the same order as they did in the heading.

One method of finishing the fringe is to cut these ends about ¾ in.

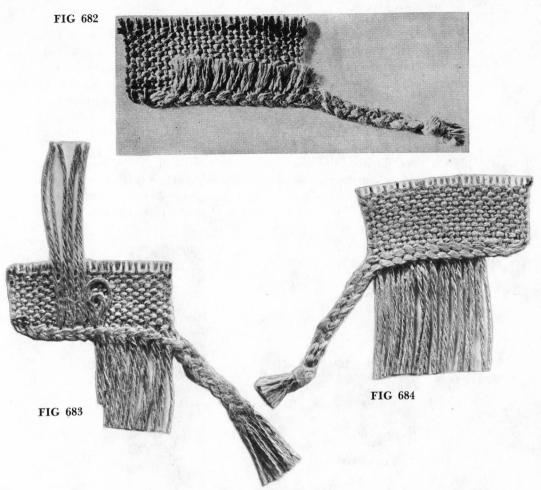

FIG 682

FIG 683

FIG 684

from the heading and tack them down to the back of the rug (Fig. 682). Cover the tacked ends with a piece of carpet binding or line the rug. If preferred, the warp ends can be threaded into a needle and drawn down through the heading to make a fringe (Figs. 683 and 684).

9. Flossa Fringe To obtain a heavier fringe than is possible by simply knotting the warp threads as shown previously, the insertion of one of two rows of flossa knots (page 142) can be tied in at any desired place in the web.

These threads can be of any type, color, or size. Gold thread is suggested for fringe on ecclesiastical articles as it adds richness, has good body, and is lasting.

Decide on the placement of the fringe and its depth. Cut a piece of cardboard around which to tie the knots. If the fringe is to be at the end of an article, first weave an inch or so of the web. This will later be turned back up under to form a hem. The knot itself forms a neat heading, but if a more decorative effect is desired weave in an extra row or two with the thread used for the fringe (Fig. 685). Where a really heavy fringe is desired, a second row of flossa knots can be tied in, weaving a few rows of the background web between (Fig. 686). If this is done, it will be necessary, in order to have both rows of fringe the same length, to cut a second piece of cardboard to tie the knots around, adding to its width the same amount as the width of the plain weave between the two rows of fringe. It is a matter of choice whether or not to cut the loops of the fringe.

Another easily made and effective fringe (Fig. 687), needs little explanation, as the method of making it can be clearly seen in the photograph. When removed from the loom, the hemstitched end of the lower part of the web, *A*, which forms the backing of the bookmark, is brought up at the back to meet the hemstitched end of the marker *B*, and carefully joined to it with small stitches. The steps required to complete the piece are the same as described previously.

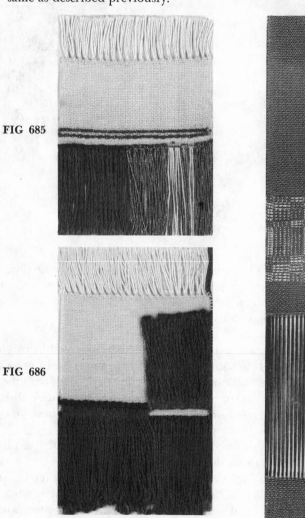

FIG 685

FIG 686

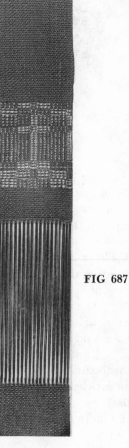

FIG 687

10. Auto Rug Fringe In keeping with tradition, wool auto rugs should be finished with a fringe at each end. These fringes are neither knotted nor whipped, but are twisted in the following manner.

Take two adjacent groups of from two to four threads each, depending upon the size of the wool warp used, twist the strands of each group separately, but in the same direction. When both the groups are tightly twisted, lay one group over the other and allow the two to twist around each other. They will twist in the opposite direction from which the two single groups are twisted. The initial twists must be very tight along the full length of the bouts. Some weavers feel the fringe will be tighter if the wool warp ends are wet before twisting.

FRINGE WOVEN ON FOUR SIDES

On certain types of place mats, napkins, and the like, it is sometimes considered desirable to have a fringe on all four sides. The technique of doing this is comparatively simple. The only requirement is a loom wide enough to allow for the extra threads needed to weave the fringe in addition to the width of the finished article itself.

Wind 38 threads for the sample illustrated (the weaver can determine the width of the material desired for himself).

Thread 30 threads single sley in the center of the loom.

Skip 10 dents on the left of the web which is centered in the reed, and thread in four threads at the left edge. Skip 10 dents on the right of the web and thread in four threads at the right edge. The width of the fringe can be controlled by the number of dents skipped between the main web and the extra warp threads threaded on both sides. These threads are tied in and wound around the warp roller along with the main warp threads.

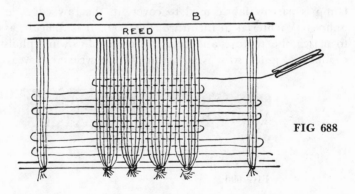

FIG 688

Method for Weaving In weaving, insert the shuttle at the lower right, and weave across and out at D. Change the shed, insert the shuttle at D, and weave across and out a A (Fig. 688).

Every fourth time, the shuttle does not pass completely across the web from *A* to *D* (or vice versa), but passes around the edge *C* or *B* of the inner or main web. The purpose of this is to fasten the edge threads of the web to prevent them from slipping. If this is not done, the edges must be hemstitched.

FIG 689

After the removal from the loom, the threads at *A* and *D* are removed, the loops are cut and fringed. The ends of the web are hemstitched before removal from the loom.

GIMP, TWO WEBS WOVEN SIMULTANEOUSLY

Gimp is narrow fabric used to cover up the raw edges left after tacking upholstery material to furniture (Fig. 690). It is difficult, as a general rule, to match the texture and coloring of hand-woven upholstery webs with commercial gimp, so it is advisable for the weaver to weave his own. The

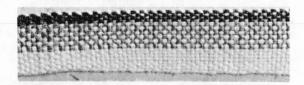

FIG 690

weaving of gimp is simple and proceeds rapidly. To shorten the process even more, however, two webs or lengths can be woven simultaneously. Gimp can be woven on a tabby, twill, or overshot threading. A very firm gimp can be woven on an 8-harness threading.

Uses For completing furniture, bags, purses, pillows, etc., and in a wider width for bag handles

Wind two lengths of warp of 10 threads each (width of gimp can be controlled by the number of threads threaded).

Sley one length of warp of 10 threads (or the number of threads required to make gimp in the desired width) 2 in. to the left of the center, and the other length 2 in. to the right of the center of the reed, for two webs. This will leave a space of 4 in. between the webs. It is not necessary to leave this much space between the webs, but it facilitates the manipulation of the shuttles. Two shuttles are required for the weaving, one for each web (Fig. 691).

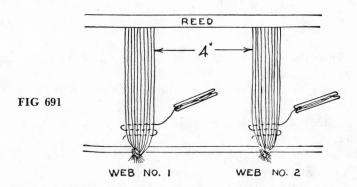

FIG 691

To Weave In weaving, pass the shuttle through the shed on the left-hand web; then the second shuttle through the shed on the right-hand web. Change the shed and beat. Repeat this procedure until the desired length has been woven. Both shuttles should enter the sheds from the same side, that is, both from the right or the left simultaneously.

SLITS OR HOLES

Occasionally it is desirable to weave slits or holes in a web for the insertion of a cord, for example, at the top of a drawstring bag.

The process involved is really a tapestry technique but the holes are not difficult to weave and the time used more than pays for itself in the neat manner in which the bag will draw up. If the bag is not too large, four holes equally spaced across the web should be sufficient. Weave the hem and heading of the bag.

Decide on the placement of the holes or slits and end the weaving of the last row with the shuttle on the right-hand side of the web. For four holes or slits, four butterflies (page 128) and the shuttle are required, as there are five areas which will be built up simultaneously. We will assume there are 50 threads in the sample for purposes of clarifying the instructions.

1. Open the shed and, starting from the right, enter the shuttle and bring it out to the left of the tenth thread (Fig. 692).

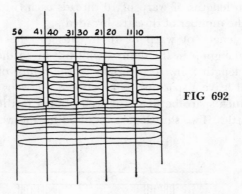

FIG 692

Enter the first butterfly at the right of thread 11 and bring it out at the left of thread 20.

Enter the second butterfly at the right of thread 21 and bring it out at the left of thread 30.

Enter the third butterfly at the right of thread 31 and bring it out at the left of thread 40.

Enter the fourth butterfly at the right of thread 41 and bring it out at the left selvedge.

2. Turn the ends of the butterfly threads back into the shed.

3. Close the shed and beat.

4. Open the alternate shed and:

Enter the fourth butterfly at the left selvedge and bring it out to the right of thread 41.

Enter the third butterfly at the left of thread 40 and bring it out to the right of thread 31.

Enter the second butterfly at the left of thread 30 and bring it out to the right of thread 21.

Enter the first butterfly at the left of thread 20 and bring it out to the right of thread 11.

Enter the shuttle at the left of thread 10 and bring it out at the right selvedge.

5. Close the shed and beat. This constitutes one complete cycle.

6. Repeat the cycle until the slit is the desired height, ending with the shuttle at the right selvedge.

7. Cut off the butterflies, leaving sufficient length to be tucked back into the shed.

8. Change the shed and beat.

9. Starting from the right, weave the body of the bag the required length.

10. Weave the slits for the other half of the bag top according to steps 1 to 6.

11. Weave the heading and hem of the bag.

If only a single slit is required in the material it may be woven according to the sketch shown (Fig. 693).

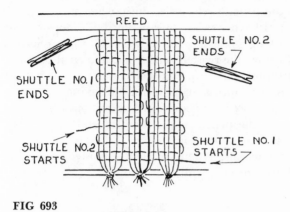

FIG 693

FIG 694

CORDS

Weavers find many uses for cords but at times are puzzled about finishing the ends, especially where a knot or tassel is neither desirable nor appropriate. In such cases a cord with two "butt ends" will solve the problem.

A "butt end" cord[1] can be twisted to any desired size but, in general, for a simple cord, the number of threads should be a multiple of four, and for a compound cord, a multiple of eight. The final length, size, and appearance of a cord will depend on how tight or loose the cord is twisted.

If two cords of identical length are needed, such as for bag handles, the exact number of turns used to twist the first cord must also be used for the second cord.

Calculate the number and length of threads required for the cord and wind them on a warping board. No cross is required. Tie the ends of the first and last threads together when the required number are wound. When the cord is finished, darn these ends into the bight of the cord where they cannot be seen.

The formula for calculating the number and length of threads needed for a simple cord is to wind only half the number of threads required in the finished cord, i.e., for a 24-thread cord wind only 12 threads. The threads should be 2½ times longer than the finished cord, i.e. for a 15-in. cord they should be 37½ in.

For a compound cord, wind only one-quarter the number of threads desired for the finished cord, i.e., for a 56-thread cord, wind only 14 threads. The length of the threads for a 12-in. compound cord should be 6¼ times longer than the length of the finished cord, 75 in.

To twist the cord, remove the threads from the warping board with a hand at each end of the loop. Hang one end of the loop over a hook, step back, keeping the threads taut, and insert a pencil through the other end of the loop. If two persons are working together, each puts a pencil through an end of the loop. Turn the pencil(s) clockwise until, when the tension is released experimentally, a satisfactory twist appears. Put both loops on one pencil or on the hook if working alone. The threads should, when released, twist around themselves. Remove the twisted cord from the pencil or hook, slip a piece of fine thread through the two end loops, and tie with a tight knot. This prevents the cord from untwisting until it is put to use.

For the compound cord, proceed as above until both loops are on one pencil or on the hook. Insert the pencil in the doubled end of the cord and twist with the cord at a slight tension but in the reverse direction (counterclockwise). Test at intervals. When sufficiently twisted, place the two ends together, slip a thread through both ends, and tie.

FIG. 695.   Simple eight-strand cord

Any number of kinds and colors of threads can be combined in a cord providing they are of the same size. Do not try to combine stretchy and nonstretchy threads.

chapter 16

Fibers

Threads are the weaver's medium. Upon an intelligent selection and use of them depends the success or failure of the woven web.

In all types of weaving there must be a correct relationship between thread, sleying, and beating. Obtaining this correct relationship is one of the most difficult problems confronting the new weaver. A thorough knowledge of threads and their characteristics comes only through study plus experimentation on the loom. Theory is necessary and good, but actual experimentation is better.

Spun fibers are known, commercially, as yarns—a term in our everyday vocabularies which we have been inclined to use only to designate threads of wool. However, regardless of the fiber from which the yarn is spun, handweavers usually refer to it as thread.

To obtain thread, the wool, cotton, or other fiber must be spun.

Many types of yarns, or threads are available to the weaver—smooth, rough, dull, shiny, large and small—but to meet commercial requirements a kind and size must be spun exactly to specification. It must have the same number of twists per inch. The twist may vary from only three to six per inch in some types of silk and up to forty to eighty twists in the fine silk used to weave crepe de chine. Yarns are twisted with either a clockwise twist called the Z twist, or a counterclockwise twist called the S twist.

Yarns are also plyed. This means that instead of remaining a single strand after spinning, two strands may be spun together. This is called a 2-ply yarn. Any number from 2 up to 12 strands and sometimes even more may be spun or plyed together. A 2-ply yarn usually consists of one S-twist strand and one Z-twist strand spun together. A 3-ply yarn may have one S and 2 Z strands or 1 Z strand and 2 S strands twisted together. Any com-

599

bination of S and Z strands may be twisted together, each producing a different thread or yarn with its own trade name. From the foregoing it is evident that yarn may be of a single, two, three, four, or more plys. Single ply yarns are usually soft and fuzzy and have little strength. They are mostly used for weft, though there are some single-ply linen and wool yarns which can be used successfully for warp by the experienced weaver. The plyed yarns are stronger and suitable for both warp and weft.

There are two main classifications of fibers, (1) natural and (2) man-made. The history of the source and use of natural fibers goes far back to antiquity; the history of man-made fibers falls largely within our own life span.

It is surprising how quickly and universally we have accepted the man-made fibers, and what a definite place they have come to fill. Practically every garment we wear, every bit of drapery material, car upholstery, and floor covering with which we come in contact contains at least a percentage of man-made yarns. These have come uninvited into our lives, but will doubtless remain. Some are durable, some have definite advantages over the natural fibers, particularly in laundering, but it is questionable if they will ever completely replace the natural fibers. Because of the easy accessibility and low cost of these fibers, the natural fibers, wool, cotton, linen, and silk, have now become the luxury fibers.

The handweaver should question the advisability of mixing man-made and natural fiber yarns. This is being done successfully by commercial mills so it seems logical for the handweaver to follow suit. In some cases the various fibers are mixed together during the spinning process to make the yarn; in others, the different yarns are mixed in the warps. There are, however, a few cardinal rules which should be observed before undertaking a web of mixed fibers: (1) The stretch of the two or three yarns chosen may be entirely different, in which case, to maintain an even tension, two warp beams will be required; (2) Due to the varying stretch of different yarns, a seersucker effect may appear when the web is removed from the loom or later during the finishing; (3) Dry cleaning is advised for some of the man-made fibers, so it is questionable whether or not they should be combined with yarns such as cottons or linens which thrive on soap and water; (4) Some of the man-made fibers require special equipment for finishing which is not available to the handweaver.

Because of the ever-changing nature of the man-made fibers, and the unsuitability of most of them for handweaving, these threads will not be discussed at length. This does not mean that the weaver should not experiment with them. It frequently happens that some threads, name unknown, may come to light in a bundle of odd-lot yarns that could be exactly what was needed for a certain project. Among the nylons and rayons are many yarns which are well suited to handweaving and which over a period of time have proven their worth. Yarns listed on sample cards from reliable dealers can be purchased and used with assurance that they will measure up to specifications.

Purchase of Yarns   Purchase only good yarns from reliable dealers. Do not be taken in by "come-on" advertisements for job lots of yarns at a low price. The weaver has little choice and the so-called bargain yarns may be dirty, of poor quality, and of dye lots which never can be matched. Frequently the dyes used are poor and will run when washed, while others will fade out after a few weeks' exposure to the light. If there is any doubt about the fastness of the colors, wash samples of the yarn in lukewarm water and good soap before using. There is one exception to the above. Should you be fortunate enough to live near a carpet factory whose products carry a recognized name for a good quality product, do not hesitate to take advantage of their thrum sales. These are a good buy, especially for the tapestry or rug weaver. They come in many attractive colors and although they can never be duplicated they are a joy for the creative weaver with a flair for color to work with.

If you sell your woven products, it is wise to keep a detailed record of your yarn purchases. Your weaving record card (page 569) lists all the information covering the use of your yarns, but you also need to have a record of the type of yarn, its size, and trade name; from whom purchased; date; cost per unit (skein, cone, spool); weight per unit; yardage per unit; color and dye lot number, if known.

As soon as a web is completed, remove all yarns from the shuttles, unless the next project calls for the same yarns, and store with the original cones or spools from which they were taken. These odd bits and pieces of yarns should be kept for such purposes as tapestry weaving, cords for bags, edgings, rug weaving, and so on. Check yarn supplies every few months and discard, or plan a special project for those which have not been used for a year or more. Gather up all short odds and ends of wool yarns, mix, card, and spin. Some amazing colors will emerge, especially good for tapestry weaving.

Care of Yarns   It pays to take care of weaving yarns. Store them in cupboards with doors. Where such are not available, store in uniform size paper cartons, covering them with fancy paper if they are to be stored on shelves in the studio, so they will not look objectionable. Label the boxes clearly so contents can be found easily. Light-colored threads should be wrapped in tissue paper or placed in cellophane bags. Some weavers store all their yarns in transparent bags, close with a twist-em, and hang on the wall or pegboard. This presents a colorful picture. Some weavers object to the use of tightly closed plastic bags, as they prevent the yarn from breathing. Avoid storing linens in a hot dry place, as heat removes the life from linen and makes it brittle. Wool and cotton, on the other hand, should not be stored in an excessively damp place.

While many of the weaving yarns available today have been mothproofed during manufacture, there are still some available which have not been. These, such as the tweed "yarns in oil," should be sprayed or sprinkled with moth repellent.

Comparison of Yarn Sizes The yardages given for various yarns, cotton, silk, jute, wool, etc., elsewhere in the text, will enable the weaver to match up any of his own threads to any unfamiliar ones listed in weaving instructions from a country outside his own. For example, a 2/32 worsted yarn with 8960 yards to a pound would compare favorably with a 2/30 lightweight weaving wool with 8400 yards per pound. The slight difference in size, if noticeable, could be easily resolved by using a reed with one more or one less dent per inch.

Should the weaver be confronted with matching up a thread from an unlabeled cone of thread with another of the same size or grist, a length of each of the two threads—about 10 in. or so of each—can be doubled, the two threads passing one through the other as in Fig. 696.

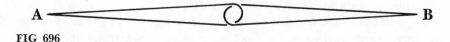

A   B

FIG 696

Hold thread A between the thumb and forefinger of the left hand, and thread B between the thumb and forefinger of the right hand. Give a sharp twist of A toward you and thread B away from you, and it can be seen at once whether or not the threads are of the same thickness.

It is handy, too, when there are two like threads—for example, 2/16 worsted—spun by different mills. They may both be labeled as 2/16 but one may have a looser or tighter twist than the other. The twist will affect sleying and ultimately the finished product. By twisting the two threads together, it can be determined whether it is necessary to substitute a finer or heavier thread than the one originally thought to be suitable or to change the sleying.

MAN-MADE FIBERS

New man-made yarns appear with such rapidity that it is impossible to keep up with them. Some of these are excellent, some are fair, and some will soon pass by the wayside. Few of them are available to handweavers, nor are suitable for handweaving, so we have little concern with them. Where the new yarns are available, venturesome weavers will try them and through the various weaving publications will make their findings available for the benefit of all weavers.

The color in most of the man-made yarns is incorporated into the solution of which the yarn is spun so colors should be and usually are clearer and more lasting than in yarns which are dyed in the skein. However, these yarns are not as a general rule guaranteed sunfast and will fade in strong sunlight. Some of the yarns will shrink a bit, which suggests the advisability of weaving a test sample which should be washed and ironed before starting a full-size web. Among the nylons and rayons are many yarns which are well suited to handweaving and over a period of years have proven their worth. Yarns listed on sample cards from reliable dealers can be purchased and used with assurance that they will measure up to the specifications of the information which accompanies them.

The production methods of the man-made fibers are so involved that it would be impractical to try to describe them here. Suffice it to say that the fluid from which the yarn is spun is, in general, ejected from spinnerets —a principle learned from the lowly silk worm.

MINERAL FIBERS

Aluminum It is always difficult to categorize anything and we run up against this difficulty with the mineral fibers. Some listings we have seen list glass and aluminum as natural fibers, while other equally reliable sources list them as man-made fibers. However, for our study of fibers, man-made or natural, a precise classification is not too important. For a number of years metallic yarns have been used in weaving and are found under various trade names. Some of these yarns are good, some fair, and some of very poor quality. Among the best are those with an aluminum base, reinforced with an extremely fine nylon thread. At Christmas the stores call our attention to the decorative value of festoons of narrow aluminum strips. Some of these are of natural aluminum, others in red, blue, or green. The strips are about ⅛-in. wide and inclined to be brittle. They do not lend themselves to winding on either bobbin or flat shuttle, so if they are used, cut off pieces of various lengths and lay them in the shed with the fingers to follow a chosen design, or lay them in at random. The strips do not turn around the selvedge threads successfully, so keep the design well inside the selvedges. These strips give a certain flair to Christmas tree skirts and Christmas card material, and are inexpensive. This material is suggested for theatrical curtains, screens, room dividers, or wall hangings. These should be designed to express whatever theme or mood the production calls for. A hanging in grays—shiny against dull yarns, or smooth against rough —could be very striking. And, in passing, it should be mentioned that your Christmas wrapping ribbons, some paper, some rayon, and some metallic, can be woven up into Christmas tree skirts, decorative wall hangings, and decorations for home use or gifts.

VEGETABLE FIBERS

Although there are many vegetable fibers which lend themselves to weaving, such as bark (coir, corn husks, etc.), roots and pine needles, rushes, and others, the ones with which we are most familiar are cotton, linen, and jute.

Cotton Cotton has been called the poor man's fiber. It is sturdy and long-wearing and suitable for many purposes. Because it is inexpensive and easy to handle, it is usually the first yarn handled by the novice weaver. During many critical periods in the world's history the financial stability of many countries has revolved around cotton. Some historians claim that the American Civil War was due to cotton, for example. In England during the eighteenth and nineteenth centuries, the cotton mills were considered by the socially conscious as a curse rather than a benefit to humanity.

Much has been done to develop plants which will produce cotton with a long, silky staple. Different types of cotton are grown for different purposes, some countries concentrating on one type and some on another, though this fluctuates from year to year. Some types of cotton are highly competitive and others are not. For many years Egypt has produced on the Nile Delta a very fine, long-staple cotton which has not been successfully duplicated elsewhere.

The cotton plant, which thrives in hot countries, grows from four to six feet tall, bearing both blossoms and seeds simultaneously. Modern machines now gather the bolls, a task that was for years delegated to humans, in particular in the U.S. to Negro slaves, a backbreaking job which had to be done during the heat of the day when the bolls were dry. After picking, the bolls are run through the cotton gin several times to ensure that all seeds, dirt, and lint are removed. This is usually done at the source before the cotton is compressed into bales for shipment. From the seeds is extracted cotton seed oil, vegetable oil, animal feeds, etc. Upon arriving at the mill, the bolls are put into a picking machine for further cleaning and to separate the tangled mass of fibers into some sort of order. The short and broken fibers, called "linters," are spun into string or yarns for cheap cloth, carded for cotton mattresses, made into gun cotton, or assigned to make a hundred and one other useful products. After the picking, the next process is carding or combing which converts the bolls into large, almost transparent, gauzelike sheets which are twisted into big, fat, soft ropes which pass through the spinners, emerging as firm yarn of many hundreds of sizes and kinds as required for commercial use. The finish required to prepare the yarns for each particular use ranges from ordinary washing to complicated mercerizing and Sanforizing. All these various finishes add to the cost of the yarns but give the user a wide variety of cottons with which to work.

Cotton is frequently mixed with other fibers, both natural and man-made, during either the spinning process or later in mixing various warp threads together when threading the loom. After some experience, the weaver will find himself eager to experiment with various types and sizes of yarns. To overcome any difference in the stretch of the warp when two types of cottons or a cotton and other type of yarn are used together, it is a good practice to use a loom equipped with two warp beams. Throughout the text there are listed many projects for which cotton yarns are suitable. The weaver will think of many others. A professional finish can be given cotton articles by pressing them under a damp cloth, then ironing them dry. Allowance must be made for shrinkage, as all cotton yarns are subject to some shrinkage. Cotton dyes quite well, though it is better to purchase commercially dyed yarns, as it is sometimes difficult to achieve an even color throughout.

Cotton, like all other yarns, has a "count" or unit of measurement. One strand of thread spun without noticeable twist is known as 1-ply, or singles, yarn. The heaviest weight in each singles thread is size 1. The number of yards required to make 1 pound of any size cotton is called the yarn count or count of thread. The count of thread for cotton and rayon is 840. This means that in 1 pound of cotton or rayon there are 840 yards. Size 2 indicates that there is twice the yardage and half the diameter of size 1; size 3 would have three times the yardage and one third the diameter; size 10 would have 10 times the yardage and one tenth the diameter; and so on. For example:

Size 1 cotton = 840 yards in one pound.
Size 2 cotton = 2 × 840 = 1680 yards in one pound.
Size 3 cotton = 3 × 840 = 2520 yards in 1 pound.
Size 10 cotton = 10 × 840 = 8400 yards in 1 pound.

When two strands of singles or 1-ply are twisted together, it is known as a 2-ply; three strands a 3-ply; and so on. 3-ply size 10 cotton is indicated as 10/3 cotton; 2-ply size 16 cotton is indicated as 16/2; etc.

The yardage for more than 1-ply thread is computed as follows:

10/3 cotton = *10* = 2800 yards per pound.
16/2 cotton = 840 × *16* = 6720 yards per pound.
20/2 cotton = 840 × *20* = 8400 yards per pound.
30/3 cotton = 840 × *30* = 8400 yards per pound.

The method of designating the size of cotton thread is sometimes written 2/16 instead of 16/2 or 2/20 instead of 20/2. This is due to either carelessness or local usage of terms and can easily lead to confusion. However, regardless of the sequence of numbers, the smaller number indicates the number of plys and the larger the size of the thread.

Coarse cotton yarns are suitable for the beginner. Sizes 8/2 and 8/4 do not snarl, break, or knot easily, and should they do so are not difficult to straighten out. They are inexpensive, easily woven, and show the structure of the weave to advantage. As experience is gained more glamorous threads can be used.

Jute This fiber is obtained from the stalk of the plant and is rippled, retted, scutched, and hackled in the same process as linen flax (page 606). Jute fiber is two to five times as long as flax fiber, but is not a strong fiber and disintegrates if exposed to moisture or water. Like hemp, it is difficult to bleach, but will bleach to a creamy white. It is used for carpet warp, for weaving burlap, and for rough textured effects in contemporary upholstery. It is rough on the hands and unpleasant to use.

Hemp   The outstanding quality of hemp is that it withstands water better than any other natural fiber. It is a long, coarse fiber which comes from just inside the outer bark of the plant. It is difficult to bleach. Though used mostly for rope, the most refined fibers are also used for woven textiles. The hemp plant, cannabis sativa, is the source of marijuana.

Coir   Coir is the fiber of the outer husk of the coconut. It is a rough, uneven fiber of variable strength. The coconut husks are steeped in water for as long as six months to a year, then beaten until the fibers separate. These fibers are twisted or spun into coir yarn or, as it is frequently called, cocoa-fiber. It is not affected by salt water, and aside from being used for certain types of ropes, brushes, and upholstery stuffing, coir yarn is used in the manufacture of cocoa matting door mats. These mats can be made on either a large, heavy, 2-harness loom or a sturdy upright frame-loom similar to a high-warp tapestry loom. If a floor loom is used, it will be necessary to purchase a special reed with widely spaced dents, about 4 or 5 to the inch. Various techniques are used but the most satisfactory are those with a pile. While coir yarn is somewhat rough, and strong hands and wrists are an advantage in weaving rugs, they are within the capabilities of the average home weaver.

Linen   Babylonia and many ancient civilizations prized and cultivated flax. The earliest record we have of cloth dates back to the Stone and Bronze ages, traces of it having been found in the Swiss lakes. Its history is long and interesting, much more so than we have room here to discuss. Linen is made from flax, many processes being involved. These are pulling, tying, rippling, shocking, retting, breaking and/or scutching, heckling, winding the fibers onto the distaff, spinning, and skeining. It is a long process which has shown little variation over the ages and in the production of one of the strongest, longest-wearing, and most beautiful of threads.

FIG. 697.   Mat woven with single-ply linen warp and meadow-grass weft.

Two types of linen thread emerge during the processing of the flax, the tow linen and the soft line linen. The tow linen is coarse and rough and contains bits of the outer covering of the stock. It is loosely spun and suitable only for weft. It lacks strength but is very absorbent and therefore quite suitable for towels as well as many other purposes. During pioneer days, it was from this tow linen that ticking and sheets were made for the hired help and itinerant travelers. These, in combination with blankets woven of the rough tag ends of wool, did not encourage lying abed! The term line linen applies to the soft single linen thread spun from the long flax fibers. The more care used in handling and spinning these fibers, the better the thread. When we read of using linen singles, it is this thread which is meant. There are two processes used in spinning linen; one is the dry, the other, the wet process. It is the latter method which produces the more beautiful and more expensive thread.

There is a third type of linen called ply linen. This is simply stranded linen, that is, two, three, or four or more strands of linen spun tightly together to form a single strong thread. Plyed linen is also known as round thread linen.

The count system for linen is called a lea. There are 300 yards in 1 lb. of #1 lea linen. Plyed linens, like cottons, are numbered with the size of the thread first, number of plys second. Thus, a #10/2 linen would be made up of two single linen threads of #10 linen spun tightly together. This size has 1500 yards per lb.

Linen may be purchased in a great variety of sizes and, as it is necessary to know how much to purchase for a specific purpose, the following table is given to help the weaver ascertain at a glance how many pounds or units of a pound of a given size will be required.

SIZE	YARDS PER POUND	SIZE	YARDS PER POUND	SIZE	YARDS PER POUND
1	300	15/2	2250	20/2	3000
10	3000	16	4800	30/2	4500
10/2	1500	18	5400	40/2	6000
12	3600	18/2	2700	40/3	4000
14	4200	20	6000	60/3	6000

The formula for figuring linen counts is:

$$\frac{\text{size of linen} \times 300}{\text{number of plys}} = \text{yards per pound}$$

that is, a 40/2 linen would be: $\frac{40 \times 300}{2} = 6000$ yards per pound. Linen is difficult to dye, therefore it is advisable to purchase only the best of colored linens and it is suggested that they be tested for colorfastness if two or more colors are to be used together. Poorly dyed linens will smut when run through the fingers. These are undesirable linens and should be avoided. A third type will show white along the inside of the strands when untwisted.

There are many shades among the natural linens, depending largely upon the country from which it is imported and the method of retting. Scandinavian weavers play up these nuances of color and some striking effects are obtained from the use of one natural shade for warp with a different shade for weft. Two or three delicately colored linen singles twisted together on the bobbin for weft will produce subtle colorings in the woven piece, most difficult to describe.

Linen does not possess the elastic properties of either cotton or wool so it is rather difficult for the experienced weaver to handle. However, experience cannot be gained without making a start. There is no reason why, with care taken in winding the warp to keep a good tension, and with careful handling, it cannot be successfully used. Avoid starting with a long, wide warp of fine linen. Start rather with coarse, plyed linen, winding enough only for one or two guest towels or place mats. The careless, impatient weaver will do best to avoid linens altogether, because they will fight back at the unsympathetic weaver! Experienced weavers have little difficulty with singles linen. Here, though, a careful choice must be made. The cheaper tow type, loosely spun linens are not suitable for warp. But on the sample cards will be found linen singles that are strong and evenly spun. These are quite suitable for warp. If they seem to fuzz up a bit or stick, a cold starch or linseed dressing (page 630) can be applied as the warp is rolled forward as the weaving proceeds. Some weavers weave with their warps wet and even keep their filled bobbins in a pan of water; others scorn this procedure and weave with both dry warp and weft. Each weaver will have to learn, through experience, which method is best for himself.

Linen is such a beautiful fiber in itself that it seems unnecessary to combine it with other fibers, especially synthetic or man-made ones. Linen provides a strong, long-wearing, nonstretching warp for rugs and tapestries. The harmony between rough linen and single-ply vegetable-dyed homespun wool is a happy one. All weaving techniques are not suited to linen weaving, but among those that are suitable are the balanced weaves—the M's & O's, the Atwater and Swedish laces, and spot weaves. Certain twill threadings are most effective, the plain 50/50 weave especially, when attractive color combinations are used. For multiple-harness and draw looms, there are the damask weaves. There are also the finger-manipulated weaves—Spanish lace, Brook's Bouquet, the leno weaves, etc.—which are most attractive when woven in a single color. Except in the hands of an experienced weaver, neither summer-and-winter nor overshot techniques lend themselves to linen weaving. However, some unusual and outstanding effects can be obtained when the designer-weaver takes over. It is perhaps the 2-harness loom weaver and the multiple-harness weavers who are the ones to explore and develop linen weaving to its fullest.

When first removed from the loom, linen pieces are apt to be disappointing. However, washing and ironing will soon remedy this and reassure the weaver that the result has been well worth the effort. Drastic washing methods are suggested. Begin by soaking the web overnight, well immersed in soapy water. In the morning, give it a vigorous rub in hot water with a good soap or detergent. Rinse thoroughly. Roll in a towel to remove excess water. Iron until dry with a hot iron, but watch out for scorching. When dry and smooth, and duly admired by friends, give it a second vigorous washing and rinsing, roll in a towel, and iron. It takes courage and fortitude to give it this second washing, but it will be noted immediately that there is considerable difference in softness and sheen. Never be afraid to launder your choice linens frequently; they improve with each washing.

Ramie Ramie is a natural fiber, a stingless member of the nettle family. It was cultivated and processed into cloth in China in Confucius's time (551–478 B.C.). Over the centuries the cultivation of ramie spread to East Asia and in the last hundred years to France, Italy, Central and South America, and to Florida in the United States. It has never been as well known or as popular as linen, largely because of the difficulty of separating the fiber from the gum which binds it firmly to the stalk. For centuries the Chinese people pounded the stalk with a heavy stick to separate it from the gum, but because of the time consumed in the processing it was found to be financially unfeasible. Shortly before World War II a successful degumming process was invented. This led to the planting of many large fields of ramie in various warm countries where, because of its rapid growth, three crops a year could be harvested. About this same time the man-made fibers began to appear and the popularity of the natural fiber yarns faded. This was unfortunate, as ramie has many excellent attributes, among them its great strength, which increases two-and-one-half times when wet, its high resistance to mildew and rot, and its high luster. Like linen, it improves with successive washings, using the same method as for linen. It has many uses commercially other than for clothing and household articles, and because of its close resemblance to linen can be woven in the same manner and for the same purposes.

The count of ramie is the same as for linen, and it is usually available in the same sizes as the linens and at the same price. Although advertised as colorfast, it is well to test the yarns before use as some of them do run and smut.

SILK

It seems ironic that one of the most beautiful and sturdy fibers we have should come from a worm! The silk worm, "bombyx mori," a small black worm which hatches from an egg, spends its short life of forty or so days munching on mulberry leaves. It is so sensitive to sounds, odors, and un-cleanliness that the young girls who work in the sericultural centers wear spotless white gowns and padded shoes. Four times during its short life span the worm, snakelike, sheds its skin. The food it consumes is gradually changed to cellulose which, when the time comes for it to spin its cocoon, is exuded from two tiny spinnerets, one on each side of its head. These filaments are thrown to points at quite some distance from its head, fasten-ing themselves to the nearest branch or stick. It takes about three days for the worm to complete its whole cocoon. During this time the plump little worm becomes a shriveled dark brown pupa. As soon as all movement ceases within the cocoon, it is ready for processing. The healthiest are selected for reproduction, while the others are sorted and the poor ones discarded. The chosen ones are placed in an oven, or under steam, sufficiently hot to kill the worm. Following this, the cocoons are "degummed" by placing them in warm water and stirring them around with a stick. This loosens the ends of the two filaments, which are then twisted together with the fingers to unite them into a single thread. This single twisted end is passed through a small metal or glass eye and fastened to a reeling machine. It requires both skill and care to wind these filaments from cocoon to reel, as the fibers are of varying length and strength. New threads must be added when broken ones occur and fastened together with the natural gum. This process is continued until a sizable skein is made. Each skein is then tied in the same manner in which we prepare skeins for washing or dyeing and is then washed in warm soft water with pure soap and rinsed. When dry, the skeins are put on large reels, or swifts, so they are tight, then wound off to the required measurement.

Like cotton, linen, wool and the man-made fibers, silk has a count of its own. It is measured in books.

30 skeins of raw silk make one book of 4.3 lbs.
30 books of raw silk make one bale.
100 kan (or 900 lbs.) of cocoons are required for one bale of raw silk.

The ends of the little silk books are sometimes covered with curious little caps formed from a single cocoon, and sometimes have even been manipulated into a single lacy cap large enough to cover a man's head!

The various uses for which the silk fiber is to be put control the processes through which it passes. These are many and varied and some-what complicated and will not be discussed here. The plyed silk yarn, which is the type the handweaver usually uses, requires no further spinning beyond that given the filament as it comes directly from the cocoon. This is a continuous very strong fiber, a lovely one with which to work, and handling it is no more difficult then handling other yarns. It does have a curious characteristic of standing off from the warping reel in a weird, frightening, but harmless manner which may well intimidate the novice weaver but it can be managed quite easily with patience. If the hands are inclined to be rough, use generous applications of hand lotion. The three pure silk fibers most easily available are the 12/2 or 12/3 running 9600 and 6400 yards to the pound; the tweeds 14/1 with 11200 yards to the pound; and a coarse shantung with 2400 yards to the pound. Considering the yardage of the silk yarns per pound, they are not expensive to buy. There are other silk yarns but they had best be left to the experienced weaver.

Suggested threadings for the silk yarns are 4-, 6-, and 8-harness plain and return twills, Bronson spot (page 345) and lace weaves (page 358) set at 40 ends per in. for a fabric where draping is desired; for a brocade-like fabric, use crackle (page 307), summer-and-winter (page 311), miniature overshots (page 226), set at 36 to 40 ends per inch. Long thread skips are to be avoided.

Silk and wool mixtures are beautiful. Combine a very fine wool warp with either the 12/3 or a flecked spun silk sleyed at 30 to 36 ends per inch for men's jackets or women's coatings. For a heavier weight material, use 2/16 or 2/18 wool with two strands of silk wound together on the bobbin. Combine silk with 30/3 Egyptian cotton, in any desired color, set 36 ends per inch; a 60/6 mercerized Egyptian set 36 ends per inch; or a comparable size linen. For neck and head scarves and for dress materials, set 12/3 silk at 30 ends per inch using same silk for weft. Silk is not difficult to dye using general directions given on the commercial package, or, better yet, weave the yardage and have it dyed commercially. In this manner you are assured of an evenly dyed piece of material.

Silk is durable—strand for strand, its tensile strength is equal to that of steel. Silk is easy to care for. Washing in warm water with a pure soap will freshen the garment. Most silks should be ironed on the wrong side while still damp, but tussah, pongee, and shantung should be ironed when bone dry. The heavier, more luxurious silk garments should be dry cleaned. Silk garments are excellent for traveling, as all wrinkles will disappear if the garment is hung on a hanger where the air can circulate around it. Silk is a natural insulator, cool in hot weather and warm in cold weather. It sheds dust and has no dust or fluff of its own. It's good for people allergic to other materials. Never buy cheap silk, as it is "weighed" or "filled," which means that it is filled with tin or other minerals to replace the natural weight lost during processing. Silk is long-wearing and gives the wearer a sense of being well dressed.

In 1972, Director Manjeet Jolly of India's Central Tasar Research Station announced that after considerable experimentation his scientists had successfully crossbred the Chinese-mulberry-leaf-eating silk worm, Antheraea permiji, with a silk worm common to India which subsists on the wild oak tree leaves. There is a vast untapped reserve of some two million of these wild oaks across the Himalayas waiting to feed this new hybrid worm. Its production is more reliable and of a quality superior to other known silk fiber. New techniques have been developed to raise the worms and process the silk, which means that this exotic fiber should now be more readily available, and hopefully at a lower cost, to weavers interested in weaving webs for household purposes and for high style garments.

ANIMAL FIBERS

In researching the animal fibers, the first thing which strikes the researcher is that the words fur, hair, and wool are used interchangeably with little regard to their proper application. The *Encyclopaedia Britannica* defines the words as follows:

> Epidermal hairs. Of these (a) wool, the protective covering of sheep, is the most important. The varying species of the animal produce wools of characteristic qualities, varying considerably in fineness, in length of staple, in composition, and in spinning quality. (b) An important group of raw material closely allied to the wools are the epidermal hairs of the Angora goat (mohair), the Llama and Alpaca. Owing to their form and the nature of the substance of which they are composed, they possess more luster than the wools. (c) Various animal hairs such as those of the cow, camel, and rabbit are also employed; the latter is largely worked into the class of fabrics known as pelts. (d) Horse hair is employed in its natural form as an individual filament or monofil. Hair and wool fibers are greatly influenced by climatic conditions. During hot dry weather they become dry and straight, while they soften and curl in dampness. The animal fleece or hair, acts as an insulator against both heat and cold, thus enabling the animal to live comfortably in a changing climate.

Among the animals the camel family has the distinction of contributing the finest, most luxurious class of fibers known to man. The hair of the desert camel, which is long-wearing, soft, and warm, should perhaps not be included in the luxury class, as most of us have been able to afford a camel hair coat at one time or another during our existence, like the famous Harris Tweed coat, "once possessed, never discarded."

Until recently it has been claimed that the camel's smaller relatives could boast of producing the most luxurious hair known, but now the hair of the musk ox, called quiviut (kee-vee-yute), has challenged this claim.

The musk ox, an animal which looks like a small buffalo and is thought to belong to the goat family, lives on Alaska's Bering Sea coast and in various parts of the Canadian Arctic.

Efforts to domesticate the animal have been successful, especially where they have been left near their native living and breeding grounds. The adult musk ox, weighing a half ton, is placid, yet wary of humans though conforming comfortably to domestication. The calves are intelligent, mischievous, and gentle enough for the local children to ride. Although the meat is a welcome addition to the diet of the Inuit (the designation preferred by the native people rather than Eskimo), the income received from the sale of the hair is more important. This hair, described as a "golden fleece," is harvested in the spring. With the coming of the sun, the qiviut, which is the underhair of the animal, loosens and falls off in large patches, catching on the bushes and rocks to be picked up by the women and children, while the hair from the domesticated animals is combed or groomed off by hand. Each animal produces about six pounds of hair a year during its life span of twenty years. This hair is so fine that a pound spins into ten miles of yarn and sells for $50 or more a pound. Both the American and Canadian governments have trained the Inuit women to card and spin the hair and knit it into attractive scarves and sweaters. One of these luxury scarves, 16 in. wide by 8½ ft. long and weighing less than four ounces, sold for $75. Super soft, ultra warm, light, and so sheer it can be drawn through a finger ring, it is truly the most beautiful of the luxury fibers. If and when it is procurable, the weaver will find that this fiber can be easily and successfully woven by using the same techniques as for the other fine fibers.

The alpaca, llama, and vicuna live in the rarefied air of the high Andes of South America. Nature has so constructed them that they are quite capable of meeting the problems of their environment. In general the characteristics of the three types are similar, though each has its own individual traits. The alpaca is noted for the length and fineness of its hair, which is of a lustrous silken texture, almost metallic in appearance. If shorn regularly, the hair, gray, black, yellowish, or grayish-white in color, averages a yearly growth of from twenty to thirty inches. These proud little animals are not easily domesticated unless captured while quite young and taken into the villages by the Indians, who are usually successful in training them. On the other hand, the llama has long been domesticated and used as a beast of burden. It is a clever and likable animal. If too heavily laden, it lies down and refuses to move! It grows to a height of about three feet. Its hair or fleece, inferior to that of the alpaca or vicuna, is in shades of yellow-black mix, rarely a clean-cut black or white. The vicuna, the third member of this group, is reported to be a much more beautiful animal than either the alpaca or llama. The vicuna, a hybrid combination of the llama and the alpaca, lives in the moist pastures lying between the high mountain peaks. Its short curly hair is very fine and silk-like, usually dark brown or black with white patches. Garments manufactured from the fleece of any of these animals definitely belong in the luxury class, with the vicuna the most expensive of the three. The yarn itself is expensive, but easy to weave. However, as the fibers are very fragile, they should not be used for warps. Very fine wool or worsted in a matching color is suggested for warp. And do weave carefully, enjoying the feel of it as you go!

Two other members of the goat family have made distinct contributions to the class of luxury fibers, the cashmere goat and the Angora goat.

The cashmere goat, a native of Kashmir, Tibet, the Himalayas, and outer Mongolia, is best known to us through the cashmere shawl of our grandmother's day, and, more recently, expensive cashmere sweaters, which are numbered among our most prized possessions. This cashmere goat wool is soft and light, has natural draping qualities, is gently warm, takes and retains the dye beautifully, and wears well if given proper care. It is its scarcity as well as its beauty which accounts for its luxury price. The fleece is combed or plucked by hand. Shepherds eagerly scour the rough countryside collecting the small bunches of hair which have stuck to rock or shrub in the rough areas where the goats feed. The animal, completely domesticated, is jealously guarded by the tribes whose living depends upon the sale of the fibers. The story of the dangerous route followed from the time the hair is plucked until it finally reaches its destination over dangerous mountain passes on small native horses, across the Gobi desert on camel, along the Great Silk Road, on small river craft to arrive finally at its destination at some large railway center on its way to its ultimate destination, is a thrilling saga. After reading it one wonders that we ever have it to enjoy. Like the camel family fibers, use a fine wool warp with cashmere. It too is fragile and soft.

The ibex goat, also native to Kashmir, produces a fiber called Shahtoosh, which has been named as the most precious fiber in the world. We hear little about it, as it produces only about two ounces of fiber a year.

Mohair is spun from the hair or wool fiber of the Angora goat. This animal originally inhabited that part of Asiatic Turkey of which Angora is the center. It was from this center, where the mohair wool trade flourished, that it received the name of Angora goat. Mohair fiber is somewhat like wool fiber, except that the scales along the fiber are not as fully developed. The lustrous fibers of almost clear, translucent white grow from 7 in. to 8 in. long. Like wool, there are many grades and varieties of mohair, but those available to the handweaver are soft, slightly wiry, and strong, and are easy to work with. They are suitable for coatings, scarves, and upholstery; are long-wearing and need little or no embellishment, as they are quite beautiful in themselves; and can be procured in natural creamy white, a variety of colors, and looped texture. These wools, when woven, drape nicely and should be sleyed to give a semifirm web for scarves and stoles, a firmer web for coatings, and the firmest web for upholstery. The wool is expensive, but it wears so well that if you can find an old sweater, wash it and ravel out and you have a good supply for scarves or whatever you wish to weave.

The fiber from the Angora rabbit is very soft and silky, but if spun without the addition of lamb's wool fiber, is apt to produce a rather heavy, lifeless web. The quantity of lamb's wool added may vary from 30 to 50 percent. The Angora rabbit wool business has been largely centered in France and Belgium and, more recently, in the U.S. The rabbits are likable little creatures, usually gentle, though upon provocation they will bite and scratch. The fiber can be cut, plucked, or combed. It does not hurt to pluck the animal as it is only the loose hairs that come out. The animal molts frequently and it is at the molting time that the fibers are gathered. Like the other luxury wool, it is expensive. Weave it across a fine wool warp, and when completed press under a damp cloth. When dry, brush lightly to raise the pile.

Cowhair A well-known and extensively used fiber in the Scandinavian countries, cowhair has only recently become easily available to Canadian and U.S. weavers. The staple is not as long as the sheep wool staple, but it is much stronger and better wearing if some sheep wool is included during the spinning process. It is less expensive than a comparable wool yarn. It is recommended for the weft in rölakan and rose-path rugs and for the binder thread in flossa and rya rugs. It is obtainable in 1-ply or singles yarn in sizes from heavy 1-ply tweed yarn to 3- or 4-ply rug yarn. It is available in an extensive range of natural and beautiful colors.

Horsehair This seldom found natural fiber was much better known in the nineteenth than it is in the present century. It was used extensively for upholstery, and not only gave long and satisfactory service but caused small boys and girls much discomfort with its pricking! It was also used for stiffening materials which are now made of the man-made fibers.

Dog Hair Owners of long-haired dogs have found pleasure in working with the combings from their pets. If the hair staple is of sufficient length, it can be spun without the addition of sheep fibers, but when the hairs are short it is best to add some sheep fiber to hold them together. Samoyed dog hair is very similar to, though somewhat coarser than, that of the Angora rabbit. In experiments using Samoyed hair for both warp and weft, it was found that the warp threads tended to pull apart under tension and beating, and the web seemed rather heavy and lifeless. To give the required strength, resiliency, and life to the fabric, use a fine worsted warp with the dog hair for the weft.

Sheep's Wool Sheep are covered with a thick fleece called wool. This fleece differs from hair in that it is finer, kinky, and, when viewed under a microscope, small scales or barbs, placed like shingles on a roof or scales on a fish, can be seen. These little barbs form air pockets which add to the insulating value of materials made from wool. Sheep's wool cloth is one of the few materials found on the market that admits the ultraviolet ray directly to the body.

There are some four hundred varieties of sheep—large and small, some with long hair, some with short, but each with its own mission to fulfill. Wool shorn from a live sheep is called fleece, and that taken from the slaughtered sheep is called dead wool. In their natural state, wool fleeces are flammable if stored away wet. Care should be taken, therefore, to see that they are perfectly dry before storing in a cool dry place. This heat-producing quality is of value in that it absorbs perspiration when worn next to the skin. If wool gets wet in icy water, it generates sufficient heat to raise the temperature from forty to forty-five degrees Fahrenheit. The Wool Bureau states without reservation that, "Wool has everything. . . . It is a truly versatile fiber, can be woven, knitted, felted . . . is tough and elastic, stands up to hard wear. . . . It is resilient, stretches as much as 30 percent and springs back to shape. Wrinkles shake out when garments are hung up, thus refreshing itself. Colors in wool are clear, vibrant, and lasting because the natural wool fiber, like human hair, has a central canal so the dye goes inside the fiber. Wool responds to every mood so it is very easy to understand why it is increasingly the favorite of outstanding designers."

Sheep's wool is processed into many different types of yarn, most of them suitable for and available to handweavers at reasonable prices, but care must be taken to purchase only from reputable dealers whose names have been obtained from experienced weavers or reliable firms whose advertisements appear in the various weaver's publications.

There are the very fine, silky combed worsted yarns, the fine carded yarns, the novelty yarns, and many others. There are many yarns suitable for weaving materials for clothing, blankets, wall hangings, rugs, pillow covers, and so on. In addition to the pure wool yarns, there are a great many blended yarns. These are composed of wool spun together with cotton, silk, linen, and other natural animal and vegetable fibers and blends of wool and man-made fibers.

Unlike cotton, which has an established count, wool has several systems. Among them the better-known ones are:

1. the American system, in which 1 cut, or single ply, has 1600 yds. per lb.

2. the Philadelphia system, in which 1 cut, or single ply, has 300 yds. per lb.

3. the Worsted system, in which 1 cut, or single ply, has 560 yds. per lb.

This information should be helpful when calculating the amount of yarn required for a given project.

Before wool yarn is ready for the weaver or knitter, it must pass through many processes which commercially require large and complicated machines and involved handling. Our pioneer ancestors worked out simple but efficient devices to process the fleeces from their sheep. These fortunately have been preserved and are available to today's weavers, many of whom are interested in repeating these various steps for themselves. No weaver can feel greater satisfaction, nor be more worthy of praise, than the one who holds up a carefully woven wool web and states, "I did it all myself, from the fleece to the finished web."

The initial process, after the sheep has been caught, subdued, and washed in the nearest stream or lake, is the shearing. This may be done with either hand clippers called "sheep shears" or, where power is available, with electric clippers.

An alert, well-trained person can shear from 175 to 200 sheep in a day with electric clippers without injuring the sheep.

The wool, when cut from the sheep, hangs together in a mat called a fleece.

Skirting occurs after the main fleece has been removed. This operation removes the torn, ragged, dirty parts, which are thrown together in a pile and sold as cheap wool. Following this, the fleeces are loosely tied together and graded and thrust into burlap sacks ready for shipping.

Sorting   Good sorters learn from experience, and work rapidly once they have learned the technique. They examine the wool to determine the fineness, elasticity, and strength and length of the fiber.

The finest quality of wool comes from the forehead of the sheep. It is from this very fine yarn that the gossamer Shetland shawls are made.

The side on which the sheep lies does not produce as fine a quality of wool as the other. Second-quality wool comes from the shoulders and sides. Other qualities in order, from the back, thighs, offals, belly, rear, and legs.

Scouring   A heavy, greasy substance, called lanolin, covers the wool of sheep. This must be removed before the wool can be properly washed. It responds best to a neutral soap or weak alkali, such as ammonia. A commercial cleanser called "Igepon," which can be used in water of any temperature or degree of hardness, is satisfactory for removing the lanolin. After the wool has aged for some time, this lanolin is much easier to remove, as it seems to deteriorate.

Washing   Wool should be thoroughly washed several times and given a good rinsing between soapings. Lukewarm water, running if possible, should be used, the same temperature sustained throughout. Soft water is preferable to hard, but, if hard water must be used, an alkali softener should be added. The wool should be tested between two sheets of blotting paper with a hot iron to determine if all grease has been removed.

The safest way to dry wool is to place it in flour or sugar sacks and hang in the shade where the wind can reach it. The bag should be shaken frequently so that the air will reach all parts of the wool. It will require several days to thoroughly dry the wool. Wool should never be hung out to dry in freezing temperatures nor should it be dried over or near extreme heat.

Oiling   If wool has been scoured with "Igepon" or other lanolin remover in warm water, much if not all of the natural oil has been removed. Before spinning, it will be necessary to replace some of this oil or the hairs will be too brittle and will break easily. In carding mills, a watering can is used to sprinkle oil over the wool which has previously been spread on the floor. "White wool oil" is used for this purpose. If wool is to be dyed after spinning, this oil must be removed. Therefore, it will be seen that it is easier and a time-saver to "dye-in-the-wool."

Picking   The best yarn obtainable is spun of hand-picked wool. The machine picker breaks up the burrs and twigs and scatters them all through the yarn. When picked by hand, this foreign matter is completely removed from the wool resulting in a clean soft yarn. An English authority on the processing of wool for weaving and knitting states that the machine picker destroys the life of the wool. Picking takes place after dyeing, if wool is to be dyed before spinning (Fig. 698).

FIG. 698. The whole family participates in the picking of raw wool

Carding The average wool fiber, suitable for carding, is about 5 in. in length. Longer fibers are combed, which is a process not used by the hand-craftsman.

The three methods used to card wool are:

a) *Hand Carding:* This, as implied, is done by hand. Two small boards, each with its own handle, and fitted with short wires, are needed for this process (Fig. 699).

b) *Hand Machine:* The hand-machine carder is a small reproduction of the machine-driven carder used in carding mills. Two rollers or drums, garnished with the same type of wire as the hand cards, turn against each other, pulling the fibers into place.

c) *Machine Carding.* Carding mills are usually equipped with three sets of carding drums, each one having a finer comb than the preceding one.

Some authorities claim that machine carding breaks the barbs and destroys the elasticity of the fiber. Hand carding, a slow process requiring five to seven carders to one weaver, is recommended for quality goods and where help is plentiful and time need not be considered.

The hand-carding machine cuts time and labor and is a satisfactory method, but where quantity is required for the production of the average utilitarian material, machine-carded wool is of value.

Hand-Carding Process

a) Place a small bunch of wool on the card that is held in the left hand resting on the lap with the wires up.

b) Hold the second card in the right hand with the wires down.

c) With this card, draw the wool lying on the first card away from yourself.

d) Repeat this process several times.

e) With the forefinger of the left hand, draw and twist the wool into a sliver. This is easily accomplished as the carding has pulled the fibers into parallel position. This sliver is also called a roll.

f) Lay the roll aside, place more wool on the card, and proceed as above. It will be noted that short fibers remain on the comb after each operation.

FIG. 699.   Carding wool

These gradually work up into the next roll, and the few remaining at the end of the process can be picked off with the fingers.

Hand-carded rolls are short, but machine-carded rolls run to about 20 in. or so.

Spinning Upon completion of the carding the wool is ready to be spun into yarn. This may be done on complicated machines; on the hand spinning wheels; or the drop spindle.

From the earliest recorded history we find carvings, paintings, and poems all depicting the women of the times with the ever-present spindle in their hands. This hand-spindle method of spinning is slow but effective. Wheel spinning methods were brought to America by the early settlers. Our word "spinster" was a designation placed upon the unmarried daughters of the household in early Colonial days who spun the wool and were ever mindful of the fact that it required the output of seven spinners to supply sufficient yarn to keep the itinerant weaver busy for one day!

As there are many good books dealing with spinning, and capable instructors available in most areas, the subject will be dealt with here only superficially.

There are two major operations to spinning:

a) Drawing out with the fingers.

b) Twisting by the spindle.

Spinning on the High Wheel

a) Attach the end of the rolls of carded wool (or sliver) to the spindle (Fig. 701).

b) Hold the opposite end in the left hand.

c) Start the wheel with the right hand.

FIG. 700. Spinning with the drop spindle

d) Step back several steps and draw out the wool at the same time. (Note how the spindle twists the wool.)

e) Step forward, and allow the twisted wool to wind onto the spindle. (The term used by spinners is "let the wool down.")

f) Repeat the process beginning at *c*.

FIG. 701. Spinning on the high wheel

FIG. 702. Spinning on the low wheel

Low Wheel The low wheel is composed of a simple wooden frame with three legs and a flywheel, treadle, and spindle (Fig. 702).

The treadle operates the flywheel or large wheel, which is connected by a belt to the flier spindle.

The flier spindle, to which the end of the sliver or roll is fastened, turns with a rapid twisting motion.

The length of fineness to which the roll is drawn out controls the size of the finished thread.

The secret of even spinning lies in the use of long rolls and the evenness with which the threads are drawn out.

When a two-ply thread is desired, two strands of the single-ply thread are twisted together. This is called doubling, and in this process the wheel is treadled in a direction opposite to that used for the spinning.

Bobbins for the shuttles can also be wound on the spinning wheel.

Homespun for warp should be spun tight, and that for weft more loosely.

Once the spindle is full, wind the spun yarn off onto a skein winder or click wheel. If it is desirable for each skein to have the same number of yards in it, it will be necessary to keep careful count of the number of turns made by the wheel. If using the click wheel, there is no problem as this old-fashioned wheel is so constructed as to "click" after a certain number of turns are made, thus informing the spinner that the length needed for the skein has been wound. In using the click wheel, care must be taken to have the clicking guage in the start position, that is at the point just after the "click" has occurred. Before removing the skein from the wheel, twist the end of the yarn around the skein a time or two to fasten it. Many spinners before tying the knot make three or four half hitches with this thread around the skein to hold the threads in position. To remove the skein from the winder, place one hand at the knot and the other at the opposite halfway point of the skein, slip the skein off the wheel, holding it taut, and twist it, the left hand twisting in a clockwise direction, the right hand twisting in the opposite direction. After a few twists, bring the two hands together and allow the skein to twist around itself into a compact unit. If, however, the skein is to be washed or dyed, it is necessary before removing it from the wheel to tie pieces of contrasting color wool very loosely around the bight in three or four places to hold the threads in position and prevent snarling. More ties are advised if the skein is to be dyed.

Nubbing We have all been annoyed at and puzzled by the little nubs which appear at times on even the most expensive wool sweaters after they have worn a while. The operator of a small rural carding-spinning mill, when questioned about this, replied that he "couldn't be sure but he felt that wool which nubbed came from older, sick, or poorly fed sheep, and there doesn't seem to be a thing you can do about it but patiently pluck them off."

WEAVING WITH WOOL

Each yarn has its own purpose. When purchasing a supply, be sure that the choice made is suitable for the project in mind. It is only through constant study and experimentation that the weaver can be sure.

Webs woven of either the fine worsted type of wool yarn or the homespun yarns are warm and durable and long-wearing. When soiled they can be handwashed in lukewarm water with a mild soap, dried, and pressed (page 626). Even after frequent washings they still retain their initial beauty. For some purposes the blended yarns will give better results than the pure wool yarns, as for instance if the articles woven of it are to be laundered in the washing machine. The weaver may ask, why then bother with the pure wool yarns? Pure wool yarns when properly woven will produce a prestige web, soft and luxurious to the touch and with superior draping characteristics. Once the weaver has mastered the intricacies of weaving with pure wool and experiences the superior "hand" of the beautiful material which has come from his loom, he will be loath to use other yarns.

For the first piece of wool weaving, it is advisable to start with a somewhat coarse yarn on a short narrow setting, the finished piece to be used for a shoulder bag, a child's skirt, or a scarf. Directions have been given (page 14) as to the method of calculating the length of warp, the number of threads required, and the allowance of loom waste. It is difficult to calculate the exact amount of shrinkage that will take place when a woolen web is washed, so it is necessary to make an extra allowance to cover. Some weavers figure an approximate shrinkage of from 2 to 4 in. in length per yard and 1 to 4 in. in width. Others claim all shrinkage takes place in the width and none in the length. In order to offset the many variables which may cause shrinkage, it is advisable to weave and thoroughly wash and press a generous sample, measuring it carefully both before and after pressing.

Explicit directions covering the purchase of yarns, sleying, and suitable threading for a specific project cannot be given here in detail, as each project requires its own combination. As mentioned above, the two most useful and important types of yarns that the weaver will come in contact with are the combed worsted and the carded homespun. The combed worsted yarns weave up into smooth, fine, but somewhat hard lustrous yardages, while the carded, shorter fibered yarns produce a fuzzy, more open type of cloth with air pockets permitting the wool to hold body heat. This guards the wearer against cold and storm. Cloth woven of worsted yarn is usually tailored into sophisticated garments for city wear, whereas cloth of the homespun tweedy type produces attractive clothing for country or sports wear. 28 to 30 in. is a good finished width for material for suits, coats, unless they are widely flared, and dresses. Instructions are given (page 583) as to how to calculate yardage and width required for garments.

Twills, of which there are many variations, the one-shuttle weaves, including the lace weaves and their derivatives, and any fine compact over-shot threading, woven with two shades of the same color, are all suggested threadings for yardages for garments. The twill weaves are recommended above the plain weaves for clothing as they are not as apt to stretch.

In general and in accordance with the size of the yarn being used, double sleying in a 9-, 10-, 11-, or 12-dent reed gives satisfactory results. Double sleying in a coarse reed prevents friction and wear on the yarn, and if there are any undetected knots or lumps in the warp they will slip back and forth through the coarser reed with little catching or breaking.

Experienced weavers are able to weave successfully on a single-ply homespun-type yarn without sizing it, but for the inexperienced weaver it is suggested that the warp chain be sized (page 630). Twisted plyed worsted or homespun yarns can be used without sizing and are almost as easy to work with as the cotton yarns.

Both the worsted and homespun yarns can be purchased in a wide selection of colors. Many weavers, however, prefer to purchase yarn in its natural state, a soft creamy white, and dye it with either a commercial or natural dye (page 627). All yarns should be tested before use to determine if they are colorfast. If not, and especially if they were advertised as being colorfast, they should be returned to the shop from which they were purchased for refund. Sometimes an overnight soaking in tepid water to which salt or vinegar has been added will stop the bleeding. However, it is not wise to take chances on yarn which is not colorfast. It is well to also make a close examination of the skein, ball, or cone before using. Does it show soil where it has rested on a shelf, or dust marks on the top of cone or along the length of the skeins? If so, after the warp has been wound, tie it in several places along its length as suggested for dyeing (page 627) and carefully wash it. Unless this is done, the woven web will have a streaked appearance which it is almost impossible to wash out. The same applies to the weft yarn. To wash, assuming the yarn is on a cone or tube, wind it in skeins, tie loosely in several places, and wash carefully in lukewarm water with a mild soap, and hang outside in a warm, airy, shady place to dry.

Once the project has been decided upon, the yarn purchased, all calculations checked, and the foregoing instructions completely understood, the warp can be wound (page 17). For best results, wind it snugly around the warping pegs, or reel, being careful not to stretch it. If pulled too tight, the natural elasticity of the yarn is lost and the finished cloth will be hard and lifeless. It is, however, advisable to wind the warp onto the warp beam (page 34) with a fairly good and even tension, otherwise it will be difficult to obtain a clear shed.

Once the loom has been dressed, the weaving (page 46) can proceed in the usual manner with special care being exercised with the throwing of the shuttle and with the beating. Beating should be well controlled with every effort made to establish a rhythm in order to obtain uniformity and evenness in the texture of the web. Lacking these, the web will have a streaked appearance. For fine wool fabrics for garments, press rather than beat the threads back into position. Heavier webs such as for floor rugs should be beaten very hard; upholstery should be firm and on the stiff side; webs for bags or pillow covers should be firm but not stiff. Some webs will be warp face (page 88), others weft face (page 61); some 50/50 and some with open spaces between the weft threads, or the warp threads. All are correct if suited to the project.

Even, regular selvedges are the mark of a good weaver. The competent weaver will be able to achieve good edges without giving them any thought. Good selvedges are a requirement on scarves and other articles where the edges show. However, it is not so important on webs which are to be tailored, as the selvedges are usually cut off or become part of the garment seam. Much breakage of warp threads can be avoided if the weft thread is left loose at the selvedge before the beater is brought forward and the shed changed. However, if the weaver does experience difficulty with breaking selvedge threads on a blanket or rug and cannot remedy the trouble with careful beating or with the aid of dressing (page 630), replace the four outside wool warp threads on each selvedge with a twisted commercial wool or cotton thread of the same grist and stretch as the wool warp.

If the threads in the shed stick together, especially if homespun, mohair, or other fuzzy yarn is being used, work the beater back and forth a few times after the shed has been changed and before the shuttle has been thrown. Exercise care in throwing the shuttle into the shed, to prevent the end from catching a single thread thus breaking it.

It is best to roll the woven web back at frequent intervals before the point is reached when the fell of the web is so close to the beater that it is difficult to insert the shuttle. Some weavers feel the warp tension should be released at the end of the weaving period, others say this is not necessary. The important point here is that the weaver be able to establish the same tempo and rhythm of beating upon returning to the loom after a rest period as he was using before.

When the web is finished and removed from the loom, examine it by holding it up to the light in front of a window. Check for broken threads, which should be darned in. At the same time, check the beating. If streaks show and some parts of the web are stiff and other parts soft and sleazy, it is a sign that the weaver needs to exert more care in beating. Smooth rhythmic beating comes with practice as well as with care. If, however, the warp and weft threads cross each other at regular intervals and the web, if intended for garments, is soft, pliable, with good draping qualities, the weaver has every right to be pleased with his accomplishment.

FINISHING THE WEB

The utmost care must be taken in finishing handwoven homespun or fine wool webs, as a poor finish can easily destroy the beauty of a well-woven piece of material.

The following directions for washing and pressing pure wool webs are those used by a well known Nova Scotian weaver[1] whose specialty was "one-of-a-kind" tweed suit and coat yardages.

A bathtub is an excellent vessel in which to wash tweed lengths, blankets, or other woolen webs. Run enough quite warm, not hot, water into the tub to cover the web, adding sufficient liquid soap (page 631) to make a good suds. Put the length of tweed in the suds, keeping it as flat and smooth as possible. Work the web by tramping it with the hands in the same manner as pioneer women would have done with their feet when washing their blankets in a nearby stream or lake. Procure a smoothly planed board with rounded edges about six or seven inches wide and the length of the top of the tub. After tramping long enough to allow the suds to completely permeate the web, wind it around the board by turning the board over and over. When the web is all wound around the board, fasten the end securely to the body of the web with three large safety pins. Stand the board on one end for about ten minutes to let the soapy water drain off. Then reverse the board. When it stops draining, run fresh warm water into the tub, unwind the web from the board, and again tramp it with the hands. (No rule against getting into the tub and tramping with the feet if desired!) Drain off the rinse water from the tub without disturbing the tweed, run in more rinse water, tramp, and drain. This second rinse water should be free of soap. Again wind the tweed carefully and tightly onto the board, spreading it so all patterns and lines are straight and selvedges even. Pin the end as before with the safety pins. Stand the board on one end in the tub. After a few hours, turn the board end for end and leave overnight.

In the morning, carefully unwind the web into a washtub or clothes-basket and hang to dry. Take the board on which the web was wound, and with two stout pieces of cord tie it to the clothesline with the flat side up. Hang the web over this board rather than to the line, to avoid a sharp crease which is difficult to press out. Choose a dull day with a gentle breeze to avoid any sunburn. When the web appears to be dry, lay the *width* on the ironing board with the end of the web at the further side of the board. Spread a sheet or clean wrapping paper on the floor for the web to fall on. Place a thin damp cloth over the web with a sheet of brown wrapping paper over the cloth. Press lengthwise, that is, with the warp, with a hot iron. Once the web is pressed, remove the paper and damp cloth. To dry the web completely, give it a second pressing, this time using only the brown paper between iron and web. When finished, roll the web on a mailing tube or roll of paper. This is preferable to folding, as it avoids any creases.

Wrap the roll in a clean cloth or wrapping paper. Do not tie with cord, pin with safety pins.

A few rules to remember: do not use *hot* water; do not let the web stand in water to soak; do not wash in a washing machine; do not run through a dryer or wringer; do not wring by hand; do not press the web without first covering it with wet cloth and paper, do not use newspapers for any of the finishing operations as the ink can easily rub off.

Careful finishing (page 626) will not only enhance the beauty of the material but will remove any soil which may have been in the yarn or was acquired during the weaving.

DYEING

Dyeing, like spinning, is a craft in its own right with many ramifications and problems, each requiring its own specific skills. There are many publications available from bookstores and libraries which deal adequately with the various dyeing processes, so they will not be discussed here in detail.

There are many methods of dyeing. The better-known ones are as follows.

Dyed-in-the-Wool   As its name implies, the wool is dyed as it is taken from the sheep (the fleece), following a good washing to remove the oil and dirt, but before the carding and spinning. The most attractive and higher priced yarns are dyed-in-the-wool.

Skein Dyeing   This takes place after the wool or other fiber is spun. One commercial method is to hang the skeins from a large wheel which, when set in motion, dips each skein in succession into a trough of hot dye. This method results in an evenly dyed skein.

Dope Dyeing   This refers to the inclusion of the dye in the "dope" from which the yarn is spun and is the method used for dyeing the man-made fibers. The dye is well mixed into the "dope," following which the whole mixture is exuded through spinnerets, then dried. Thus the color is actually a part of the fiber itself, as color and fiber are well bonded together, so much so in fact that it is practically impossible to remove the color if it is desired to re-dye the goods. Dope-dyed yarns hold their color well, though there is some fading from sunlight.

Piece Dyeing   This is the immersion of a finished web of cloth into a large pot of steaming dye, followed by a thorough rinsing and pressing.

Vegetable Dyeing   Yarn or fleece, after a soaking for the designated length of time in a mordant which fixes the color, is immersed in a hot dye bath in which the leaves, roots, or bark of a plant or tree have been steeped.

Many craftsmen have achieved excellent results with home dyeing because they have a natural instinct for it and a deep interest and have developed their skills to a high degree. This is not a craft to be lightly undertaken. Considerable equipment, much of which can be homemade or assembled, is required. There are certain dangerous elements associated with dyeing: burns from scalding hot dye baths; careless use of mordants, some of which are poisonous; and danger to children and animals, who should be kept well away from the dyeing area. It requires a great deal of experience, care, and patience to obtain an evenly dyed piece of material, garment, or skein of yarn. It is also difficult to achieve colors which are bright and clear and will not run or smut.

Because of the many variables which exist in dyeing with natural dyes, the results are seldom as hoped for. Results may be disappointing or, on the other hand, may yield an unexpectedly beautiful color.

Many neophyte dyers cannot understand why, when given a recipe said to produce a certain color from some common, local plant, the result will be far from the original. Some variables causing this may be: different type of soil; seasonal rainfall, or lack of it; difference in mean temperature from the previous year; date on which the plant is harvested; insect interference; and so on. No one can fully explain why a color will vary when identical methods are used, any more than it can be explained why wine of one year varies from that of another year.

As it is difficult, almost impossible, to reproduce an exact shade in natural dyes, the amount of yarn needed for a project should all be dyed at one time. If wool is too light in color, redye it in the same dye bath to darken it.

It is pleasant to work outdoors, but the dye bath should be kept in the shade, or the dyeing will be uneven. Wet wool is darker than dry. The final shade cannot be determined until the wool has dried. The color of woven material, however, can be determined while still wet by holding it to the light and looking through it.

Handspun wool accepts dye exceptionally well, and added interest is obtained by dyeing-in-the-wool (page 627), then carding and spinning various colors together to obtain heather effects, a type of yarn very popular in Scotland. When dyed with natural dyes, the colors are softer and more lasting and seem more suitable for this type of fiber than commercial dyes. A faded natural dye takes on a softness and beauty of its own, while a faded commercial dye renders a garment useless.

The material photographed here was woven[2] of various types of handspun wool from sheep native to Cape Breton, together with imported mohair wools to give contrast. All were dyed with natural dyes: ferns; goldenrod leaves and flowers; beets; bayberry; cochineal; barks; lichens; and old man's beard. Alum, salt, and vinegar were the mordants used.

A variety of colors and shades were obtained by dyeing several skeins

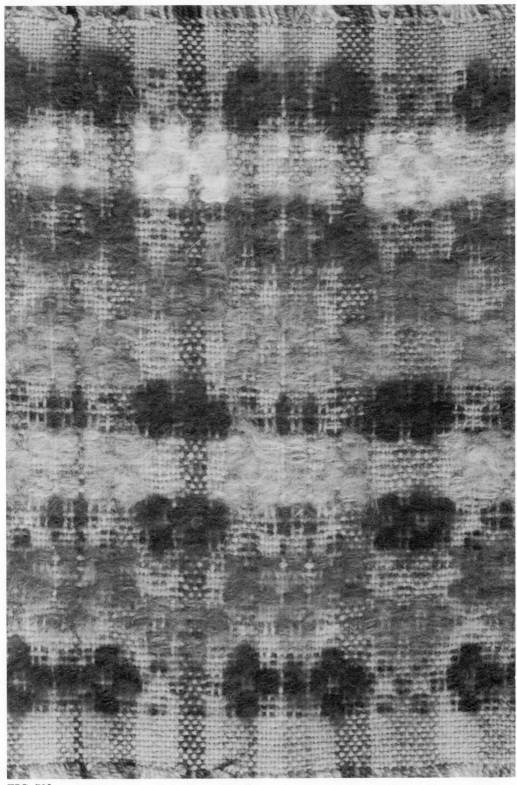

FIG 703

in one pot of dye, removing them, and dyeing a single skein of a different type of wool in the remaining dye bath. Some skeins were overdyed in a dye bath of a color different from the first dyeing. Unfortunately, a photograph cannot do justice to the subtle coloring of this woven piece.

TO PREPARE WARP CHAIN FOR DYEING

Wind the warp in the customary manner.

Tie the lease *loosely* with a shoelace.

Chain the warp very loosely.

Tie the last loop of the chain into the first loop made when passing the threads around the first peg.

Immerse the chain in warm water and let it soak for several hours, or overnight, if possible.

Wash the warp with soap flakes and rinse it thoroughly.

Immerse the chain in the dye bath while it is still wet.

Stir constantly, working the dye bath between the strands with a stick. This permits the dye to permeate all parts of the chain.

When dyeing has been completed, rinse the warp thoroughly according to directions given with the dye, and hang it in the air to dry.

It is very necessary that chaining and tying be done loosely or the warp will be spotted.

SIZING

Weaving with a single-ply natural linen or homespun yarn warp presents a problem, especially for the beginner. These yarns tangle and break easily. The linen is springy and difficult to tie and keep tied, while the hairy nature of homespun yarn causes it to stick together. In both cases it is difficult to get a good shed.

A sizing made of flaxseed (below) answers well for the warp of good quality, but a glue size is preferable for most homespun warps, and even the poorest warps can be successfully woven with a minimum of breakage if a glue size is used.

Soak half a pound of sheet glue in sufficient cold water to cover. It will be necessary to add water, as the glue absorbs some and it must be kept well covered while soaking. Let stand overnight. When ready to use, pour two quarts of boiling water over the glue and cold water in which it is soaking. Stir until well dissolved. This amount should stiffen five or six pounds of wool. It may be necessary to experiment a bit to get the right consistency, as some wools will absorb more than others.

The flaxseed sizing is made by soaking and boiling flaxseed until it reaches the consistency of coffee cream. As this solution spoils quickly, prepare only the estimated quantity required to dip and thoroughly permeate the warp chain.

When the solution is ready, immerse the warp chain in it and, with the hands, work the sizing well into and through the chain, being sure to reach all the inside parts. When the chain is thoroughly saturated, run the warp through a wringer, or, if one is not available, squeeze the solution out of the skein by drawing the hand tightly down the warp rather than wringing it.

Dry outdoors, if possible, but never in frost, bright sun, or wind. Hang a weight at the end of the warp to prevent tangling.

A word of caution—be sure that the warp chain has a goodly number of cross ties along its entire length, tied in loosely before the chain is taken from the warper, otherwise it will become tangled and unmanageable.

Some weavers prefer to sponge the solution directly onto the warp as it is wound onto the beam rather than immersing it. Others use plastic spray starch or hair spray with good results, spraying it on as the warp is rolled forward. Regardless of the method used, it is better that it dries before weaving begins. None of these sizings leave a residue. Experienced linen or wool weavers seldom bother to size their warps. Through experience they learn to handle them without breakage.

HOMEMADE SOAP

Homemade soap far surpasses commercial soap or detergent for washing handspun and other fine wool webs and garments.

To make the soap, render, or try out, 3½ lbs. of beef suet in a kettle large enough to hold 1½ gallons of water. Use extreme care during the rendering process, as the hot fat may splash and cause nasty burns. Once the suet is completely rendered, remove and discard what is left of the original lump of fat. Combine with the suet in the kettle 2 tbsp. Borax, ½ lb. resin, one can of Gilletts Lye, and one gallon of soft water. Stir all together with a wooden spoon. If rainwater is procurable, it is best; avoid chemically softened water. Boil mixture slowly and carefully for two hours. Remove from stove and let cool to a temperature where there is no danger from burns should the liquid splash or be spilled. Put greased wax paper in the bottom of any straight-sided pan and carefully pour in the cooled liquid. Cover pan with an old blanket, rug, or what have you, and leave for two days to harden. When firmly set, cut into pieces of desired size with a sharp knife and stack to dry in an airy place.

To use the soap, shave off the required amount—experience will soon show how much is required—put in a small kettle with water to cover, and bring gradually to a boil. Let cool, then add to water in container in which web is to be washed.

In pioneer days, to be assured of good results it was considered advisable to make the soap just before a full moon, and to make as much as there was suet for, because the longer the soap was kept the better it became.

Burning Tests for Fibers

FIBER	DESCRIPTION OF FLAME	DESCRIPTION OF SMOKE	SMELL	METHOD OF BURNING
Acetate	Burns with pale yellow flame, mauve or blue at bottom.	Blue wispy bits of smoke after flame is out.	Acetic.	Ignites easily and is not self-extinguishing, seems to melt rather than burn, leaving charred beads.
Acrylic (Acrilon)	Yellow flame.	Black smoke.	Similar to burnt hair.	Does not ignite easily, burns out leaving tarlike residue.
Cotton	Orange yellow. Mantle and bottom edges orange. Mauve tints at base not apparent with very well bleached samples.	Wisps of bluish smoke after flame extinguished.	Burnt paper.	Ignites readily. Not self-extinguishing. Burns steadily. Leaves delicate black or grayish ash skeleton. Little or no ash from very well bleached samples.
Flax	Orange yellow. Edges orange. Orange and yellow sparkling.	Bluish smoke on removal from flame.	Burnt grass.	Ignites readily. Self-extinguishing. Burns with crackle and smolders on removal from flame. Delicate grayish ash skeleton.
Glass	Does not burn.	Orange.	None.	Softens, forming round bead, glows red then orange, leaves hard white bead.
Hemp & Sisal	Orange yellow. Mantle and bottom edges orange.	Wisps of bluish smoke after flame extinguished.	Burnt paper.	Ignites readily. Not self-extinguishing. Burns steadily leaving delicate white ash skeleton.
Jute	Orange yellow. Mantle and bottom edges orange with mauve tints.	Wisps of bluish smoke after flame extinguished.	Burnt paper.	Ignites very readily. Not self-extinguishing. Burns steadily. Delicate blackish skeleton smoldering to blue color.

Fiber	Flame	Smoke	Odor	Burning Behavior
Kapok	Orange yellow. Mantle and bottom edges orange with mauve tints.	Wisps of bluish smoke after flame extinguished.	Burnt paper.	Ignites readily. Not self-extinguishing. Burns steadily leaving delicate black or grayish skeleton.
Polyamide (Nylon)	Orange edges, blue body with orange tip. Hisses while burning.	Gray-blue puffs.	Like fresh celery.	Does not ignite easily, shrinks from flame, and is self-extinguishing, no ash, melts leaving bead.
Polyestis (Dacron)	Burns with yellow body and orange tip.	Black.	Aromatic.	Difficult to light and self-extinguishing, melts forming bead.
Polyvinyl (Saran)	Burns with bright yellow orange tip. Bottom and edges green, spurting yellow and green sparkling.	Puffs of blue smoke on removal from flame.	Hyacinth.	Moderately difficult to ignite, self-extinguishing.
Ramie	Orange yellow. Mantle and bottom edges orange.	Wisps of bluish smoke after flame extinguished.	Burnt paper.	Ignites very readily. Not self-extinguishing. Burns steadily and fairly quickly. Delicate black ash skeleton.
Rayon	Occasional sparks with orange and yellow edges and orange center.	Bluish smoke after flame is out.	Resembles burnt paper.	Ignites and burns readily, and is not self-extinguishing, black or gray ash.
Silk	Orange yellow. Orange mantle. Sparkling.	Bluish gray on removal from flame.	Burnt hair.	Ignites readily. Self-extinguishing. Burns steadily with very slight sizzle.
Wool	Yellow. Orange mantle. Bottom edges bluish or purplish.	Bluish gray, rising in clouds on removal from flame.	Burnt hair.	Ignites readily. Self-extinguishing. Swells. Coarsest varieties burn with slight crackle. Leaves irregular crisp black inflated mass.

chapter 17

Color in Weaving

Much of the success or failure of the woven piece, aside from its design and mechanical accuracy, lies in the use or misuse of color. To handle color efficiently, the weaver must have either an innate "color sense" or spend considerable time in learning about color and actually experimenting with it.[1]

What is color? Technically, color is the response of vision to wavelengths of light. The wavelengths of light which the human eye can see make up the spectrum, the familiar rainbow colors which start at red and go through orange, yellow, green, blue, and violet. When a ray of light passes through a prism, it is broken up into the orderly color sequences of the rainbow. Each color has its own wavelength, beginning with red which has the longest and strongest, and ending with violet which has the shortest.

Because of the length and complexity of the subject, it is not possible to delve into all its ramifications in this text, but the information which is given should serve to start the weaver off on the right track. It would be an advantage to be able to include actual woven samples to illustrate the results of the experiments described in the text, but to do so is impossible in a bound book. The alternative is for the weaver to turn to other sources. An art teacher or the local librarian can recommend the name of a clearly written, comprehensive book on color such as those used in the secondary school or in art, design, and craft schools. If the book does not contain a *good* color wheel with the primary, secondary, and tertiary colors shown in their correct positions, one should be purchased. There are several color systems, the best-known of which are those based on light (in which the primary colors are red, green, and blue-violet), on vision (primaries are red, green, blue, and yellow), and on pigments (in which the primaries are red, yellow, and blue). It is the last system, based on pigments, which concerns us here and on which instructions in this text are based. So, when buying a color wheel, be sure that its primary colors are red, yellow, and blue. The color wheel should be studied carefully while following the written directions in order to thoroughly understand the close relationship between the two.

Colors are classified into groups. The *primary colors*—red, yellow, blue—are not derived from the mixing together of any other colors. They are the pure colors and placed on the color wheel with the lightest (yellow) at the top and the darker colors (red and blue) spaced to make an equilateral triangle.

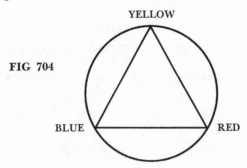

FIG 704

Next on the color wheel are three additional colors which lie between the first three and are obtained by mixing together any two of the primary colors which lie next to each other in the color wheel. These are called the *secondary* or binary colors. Their color names are orange, green, and violet. Orange is obtained by mixing together red and yellow. Green is obtained by mixing yellow and blue together. Violet is obtained by mixing blue and red together. Theoretically, *equal* parts of each primary color are mixed to achieve the right secondary color. In practice, however, this is not the case

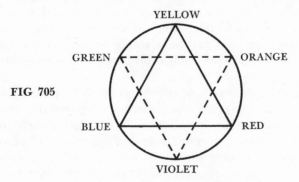

FIG 705

because yellow is a lighter color than red or blue so that more yellow is needed than the other two primaries to obtain orange and green. Similarly, red is a bit lighter than blue and hence more red than blue is needed to obtain violet.

A further blending of two colors—one primary and one secondary—

produces still a third group known as the *tertiary* colors. These again lie on the color wheel between the other sets of color. Their names are:

> red orange—a mixture of red and orange
> yellow orange—a mixture of yellow and orange
> yellow green—a mixture of yellow and green
> blue green—a mixture of blue and green
> blue violet—a mixture of blue and violet
> red violet—a mixture of red and violet

Twelve colors now appear on the color wheel.

YELLOW

YELLOW GREEN YELLOW ORANGE

GREEN ORANGE

BLUE GREEN RED ORANGE

FIG 706 BLUE RED

BLUE VIOLET RED VIOLET

VIOLET

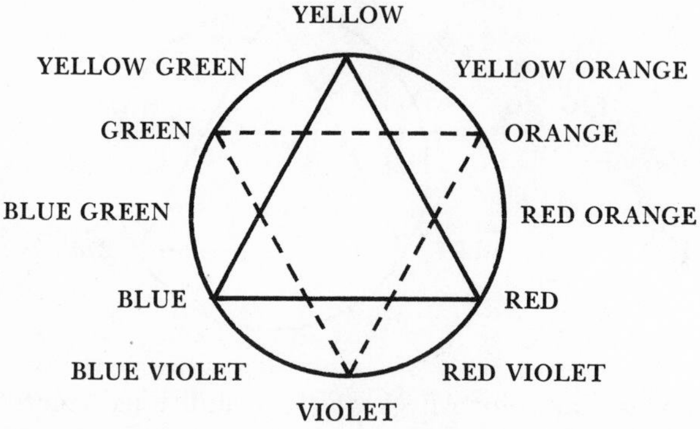

In addition to the primary, secondary, and tertiary colors, a further set of colors can be obtained by mixing the pairs of secondaries: green and violet to make "slate," violet and orange to make "russet," and orange and green to make "olive." These colors are considerably softer than those on the color wheel and are ideal for tweed and dress yardages. The mixing of various combinations of the primary, secondary, and tertiary colors can continue almost indefinitely. Some of the results will be beautiful and pleasing, others just so-so, and some will be impossible. But no matter what the result the complete personal involvement of the weaver in the exercise will be most satisfying.

So far only the theory of colors has been dealt with and in order to better understand the practical aspects it is suggested that the weaver plan and weave three gamps (page 564). The threads chosen for the gamps should be of uniform size and type and of the purest colors available. The colors printed on a color wheel will not exactly match the colors of the threads on a thread sample card simply because the light rays are reflected from two very different backgrounds. However, make the choice from the clearest and brightest colors on the sample card. Because twelve colors will be required, purchase only a small quantity of each.

For the three gamps, wind a warp of 290 threads at least 2½ yds. long.

Color order for warp:	Color order for weft:
*25 threads yellow	24 threads yellow green
24 threads orange yellow	24 threads green
24 threads orange	24 threads blue green
24 threads red orange	24 threads blue
24 threads red	24 threads violet blue
24 threads red violet	24 threads violet
24 threads violet	24 threads red violet
24 threads violet blue	24 threads red
24 threads blue	24 threads red orange
24 threads blue green	24 threads orange
24 threads green	24 threads orange yellow
*25 threads yellow green	24 threads yellow

Threading Draft   4-harness twill

Reed   16 dent, single sley

Gamp One   Start the weaving in the usual manner. Insert a 4-in. piece of cardboard followed by three or four threads the same size as the warp. Color does not matter as these threads are removed later. Hemstitch across the fell to prevent raveling when the gamp is handled. It is an advantage to have fringe at the bottom of the gamp so that the color and texture of the warp can be seen clearly for study purposes. End gamp with plain weave heading wide enough to insert a rod or flat wooden stick from which to hang the gamp.

It is necessary to enter the weft colors in the opposite order as used for the warp so that the yellow square, when the weaver faces the loom, will appear in the upper-left-hand corner. This square will be followed by the yellow orange, the orange, and so on. Reading from left to right, this color arrangement will be the same as the colors on the color wheel.

Weave the squares using a plain weave, 1 and 3, 2 and 4 treadling. After the first 24 threads have been woven and beaten into position, slacken the warp tension and measure the square. Theoretically, it should be a square with 24 warp and 24 weft threads, and if sleying, beating and yarn are all correct. If there is any deviation and the square is not square, look for the error and correct it.

Gamp Two   This is woven in the same manner and color sequence as gamp one except that the standard twill treadling 12; 23; 34; 41 is used instead

---

* Extra threads added at selvedges to offset draw-in.

of the plain weave treadling. This treadling should also produce a 50/50 fabric.

Gamp Three At the end of gamp two, weave in five or six threads in any color, then repeat the treadling and color sequence as for gamp one. End this gamp with a few threads as at the beginning. This gamp is to be cut up, so no hem nor fringe is required.

Cut the three gamps from the loom and retie the remaining warp for further experimentation. Cut the three gamps apart, hem the first two, press and mount each on a large sheet of white cardboard or sheet, hang on wall, stand back, and admire!

On a third sheet of cardboard, with a compass draw a large circle. There are 144 squares in each gamp, 12 of which are the primary, secondary, and tertiary colors. These are the ones (cut from gamp three), which are to be mounted on the large circle. To find these squares on the gamp, start at the yellow square in the upper left-hand corner of the gamp and follow diagonally across and down the gamp to the yellow green square which is the bottom square, right-hand side of the gamp. These squares are the ones where warp and weft of the same color cross each other. The dotted line on the chart (Fig. 707) shows this. At this point, before the squares are cut apart, mark those to be fastened to the color wheel with a piece of thread, pin, or tape so it will not be necessary to search through the pile of 144 squares to find them. The remainder of the squares provide a valuable set of color samples for future reference and study.

To determine what colors of warp and weft are crossed to produce a certain square, choose one at random, as, for example, the square marked "X" on the chart. Trace the warp in a straight line to the top of the chart where the heading "blue violet" appears. Then, to determine the weft, start again at the square and trace to the left in a straight line to the edge of the gamp where "orange" appears. This is shown by the dotted line on the chart. It would be well to mount the squares as they are cut, listing the colors of both warp and weft used in each one. This may seem to be somewhat of a chore but will provide a permanent record. Pleasing combinations can be used again and unpleasant ones discarded.

After the color wheel has been completed, hang the three cardboards side by side and study each in relation to its adjoining and surrounding squares, noting the effect of the gamps as a whole. Note the difference between the one woven in plain weave and the one in twill. Note the color combinations that are most appealing. Actually, most of them will be and will suggest check combinations for household linens, head and neck scarves, wool shirts and skirts, and so on. Stand back five, ten, even twenty-five feet and study the effects at a distance. The colors blend more as the distance increases, and this quality should be remembered if weaving something to be viewed from a distance. If drapery is to be seen only at close range, small pattern and color areas may be used, but these will blend into an allover general color at a distance. This may or may not be desir-

	Yellow	Yellow orange	Orange	Red orange	Red	Red violet	Violet	Blue violet	Blue	Blue green	Green	Yellow green
Yellow												
Yellow orange												
Orange								X				
Red orange												
Red												
Red violet												
Violet												
Blue violet												
Blue												
Blue green												
Green												
Yellow green												

FIG 707

able. If the checks seem to vibrate or jump at close range on the loom, avoid that particular combination, as they will probably also jump when the material is off the loom. It will be noted also that those squares which have one color in the warp and a second color in the weft have more life and sparkle than those which have the same color in both warp and weft. Scandinavian weavers have for years mixed two colors or two tones of one color instead of using one flat color. Because of this their bright colors as well as their darker colors tend to become brighter and more sparkling, and, conversely, the light, soft, and dull colors tend to be softer and more pleasing. The various combinations which the weaver can try are almost without limit. No color is unpleasant or distasteful in itself. It is the colors with which it is associated that determine its character.

Thus far only the pure colors and methods of mixing them to produce other colors have been discussed. This knowledge is important in itself as it is of help in combining threads to achieve a specific color and is important also as a basis for understanding and working out color schemes. But there are other qualities of color which must be considered. These are: hue, value, and intensity.

Hue is the name of a color, such as red, yellow, green, etc., with no qualifications as to darkness, lightness, dullness, brightness, and so on.

Value is the measure of lightness or darkness of a hue. Look at the color wheel and you will see the color of lightest value (yellow) is at the top of the wheel and the darkest color (violet) at the bottom of the wheel. If horizontal lines were drawn across the circle, a pretty accurate light-to-dark scale of colors (plus white and black) would be as follows:

White	Red
Yellow	**Blue**
Yellow orange	Red violet
Yellow green	Blue violet
Orange	Violet
Green	Black
Red orange	
Blue green	

Value also refers to the lightness or darkness of any single color. Any color to which white is added is called a *tint* of that color. If black is added you have a *shade* of the pure color. For example, sky blue is a tint of blue, while navy blue is a shade of blue; and pink and maroon are a tint and shade of red. If black and white are added to a pure color, a tone is produced. (Note that if you should try to *dye* tints of colors, there is no such thing as a white dye. You must use more dilute dyes for tints than for pure hues and you must dye on white fibers.)

In addition to the foregoing, there is *intensity,* also called saturation or chroma, which refers to the brilliance or dullness (or sharpness or softness) of a color. An intense or full-saturation color is one which contains very little or no gray. These are the pure colors as found in the color wheel or a very close tint or shade of a pure color. For example, emerald green, a sharp color, is a full-saturation green. A color of dull saturation, a dull color, is dull because it contains some gray or "degrading factor." It can be either a tint such as tan, old rose, powder blue, jade green, etc., or a shade such as brown, raspberry, hunter green, and so on.

When combining threads to produce an intense color (for instance a bright orange), the weaver should choose the two primary colors which have a tendency toward orange. That is, the red should have a yellowish cast and the yellow should have a reddish cast to produce the most brilliant orange. Conversely, if a dulled orange is desired, choose a yellow and a red with a little blue (the third primary) in them, that is, a yellow with a greenish cast, and a red with a bluish cast.

Colors can be dulled by the addition of a proportion of black or gray, but generally they will not only dull the color but also deaden it. The best way to dull a color is to add a small proportion of its *complementary* color, that is, the color which lies directly opposite on the color wheel. When mixing threads, avoid using an equal proportion of two complementary colors, as they tend either to neutralize each other or to produce a cheap bargain-basement effect.

Until some experience in working with color has been gained, it is as well to combine hues of more or less the same intensity and value.

COLOR SCHEMES

There are two general types of color schemes: arrangements of similarity which include the analogous and monochromatic color schemes, and arrangements of difference which include the complementary, split complementary, and triadic color schemes.

Color harmony profiles (Figs. 708 and 709) placed over the color wheel will help determine at a glance which color choice is most pleasing or most suitable for the piece being woven.

Arrangements of Similarity

Analogous The word itself, according to Webster, means "linked by resemblance."

Referring to the color wheel and the color harmony profiles, an analogous color scheme is one made up of three adjoining colors on the color wheel, yellow green, green, and blue green, for example. All colors in an analogous color scheme have one color in common, in this case green. An analogous color scheme is very useful and can have dozens of applications in weaving. For example, in tweeds and dress materials woven in plain weave, the warp and weft order could be made up of one thread yellow, one thread yellow green, one thread green, to produce an allover bright yellow green material. Various combinations of these three colors could be extended to check weaves, also to plaids and in softened shades for woolen skirts and in softened tints for woolen head squares, scarves, or gossamer shawls. It is also a useful color scheme for borders in place mats, aprons, draperies as, for example, one stripe red, one stripe red orange, and one stripe orange in muted hues. Think also of autumn colors, the colors of distant hills, and the sea colors.

Monochromatic This color scheme is made up of various tints, shades, and intensities—usually three—of a single color. A monochromatic color scheme can be soothing or exciting depending on the intensities, shades, and tints used. For example, a quiet, almost genteel combination can be made of three tints of blue, all cool colors, while a more exciting combination can be made using warm colors such as orange, burnt orange, and dark orange, depending on how far apart in value the hues are. A monochromatic arrangement of neutral colors can be either retiring or aggressive. While the monochromatic color scheme is probably the easiest one to understand, it is also the easiest to become boring and tiresome. For even though there can be wide contrast in shade, tint, and intensity, there is no contrast in hue. On the plus side, however, color arrangements of similarity may also be a lot easier to live with than color arrangements of difference.

Arrangements of Difference

Complementary The complement of one color is the color which lies directly opposite it on the color wheel. That is, the complement of red is green, of orange is blue, of yellow green is red violet, and so on. Thus a complementary color scheme is made up of any two complementary colors. Complementaries are also sometimes explained as being the color or combination of colors lacking in the original color. For example, yellow contains neither blue nor red, thus its complement would be violet, which represents both blue and red. When mixed in equal proportions, i.e. warp in one color, weft in its complement, woven in 50/50 plain weave (page 59), complementary colors tend to neutralize each other. However, when used side by side complementary colors result in very brilliant effects, as for example with Christmas red and green; both the red and the green seem to be intensified when used together. In the yellow and violet (purple) associated with Easter, both these colors seem to become more brilliant when used together. Thus, when using a complementary color scheme, it is best to use one color plus just enough of its complement to set it off, or use a tint or shade of the complement or a tint and/or shade of both colors. Both colors will still appear clear and bright though they won't appear to vibrate. The greatest vibration of colors occurs when the complements of closest value and greatest intensity are used, that is, full-saturation red orange and blue green.

Split Complementary A split-complementary color scheme is made up of three colors: one basic color plus one from each side of its complement, such as green, red orange, and red violet, or blue violet, yellow, and orange. Both the split-complementary and triadic color schemes are more tricky to work out successfully than any of the other color schemes, and for this reason one may find them the most challenging. Perhaps the most important factor to remember in planning these schemes is to keep the intensity and value of all colors the same for any one project. It is possible, of course, to make color schemes using different saturations and values, but it is probably wise to understand and use the single saturation/value color arrangements successfully before going on to schemes using several color intensities and values. It takes real skill and practice to do this.

Suggested split-complementary color schemes might be: a warp of a light shade of orange with weft pattern stripes of blue green and rusty red;

or a warp of a medium tint of orange and pattern borders in blue green and a tint of blue violet; or a knee rug or throw of lightweight mohair in a big bold check of pale yellow and pale green with a narrow overcheck in a slightly muted tint or shade of red violet.

Triadic or *triad* color schemes are made up of three colors forming an equilateral triangle on the color wheel: red, blue, and yellow; green, violet, orange; yellow green, blue violet, and red orange; etc. As with the complementary colors, when three triadic colors are mixed together in equal proportions they will produce a neutral color. As a result, (1) smaller quantities of at least one of the triad should be used, and/or (2) a tint of at least one of the dark colors should be used.

Suggested color schemes might be a medium blue tint for warp with overshot borders using rosy red and smaller borders of yellow; women's fall suiting of orange warp, violet weft, and green overcheck or green warp, violet weft, and orange overcheck; a soft woolen shawl in pastel stripes of lavender (blue violet), salmon pink (red orange), and very pale yellow green woven in any one of the warp colors or a slightly deeper tint of one of them.

Although it is always unwise to make dogmatic statements where aesthetics are concerned, it may be a helpful rule of thumb to remember that in all three of the color schemes of difference—complementary, split-complementary, and triad—the saturation and value of each color should probably be the same for any one article, and the proportion of each color should be varied. Equal proportions often appear to be either neutral or too garish.

If the weaver has difficulty in choosing which intensities, values, and proportions of each color to use, there is no better teacher than nature. In nature one will very rarely if ever find disharmony in color combinations. Look at a single flower or bowl of flowers or a combination of plants in the garden and observe the values, intensities and color schemes and proportions of each color which combine to make each attractive. Look at the plumage of birds, the color in distant fields and hills, the pattern, texture, and color in slate roofs, in the copper greens of towers and spires, in an old red brick wall, in deep water, in shallow water, in a field of waving grain. Look, too, at paintings that you like and ask yourself critically which colors were used? What proportions of colors were used? Which color went beside which color? How was it applied? In dots or blotches (texture and pattern)? With a spray gun (plain weave with warp of one color and weft of another color)? With long smooth strokes (solid color such as satin weave or weft or warp face weaves)? Another help in choosing colors is the old and still good rule of "a light, a dark, and a bright color" for each color combination. Color schemes of difference are usually more interesting than color schemes of similarity (analogous and monochromatic). Color schemes of difference are also a little more difficult to work out successfully, but with some practice and experience in weaving with color in order to understand value, saturation, and proportion thoroughly, the weaver is well on his way to good color schemes.

OTHER FACTORS WHICH AFFECT COLOR

We have seen how various colors can be mixed to produce other colors, how individual colors can vary in lightness, darkness, brilliance, and dullness, and finally how a variety of color schemes may produce pleasing color combinations in handweaving. However, this is treating color in a somewhat isolated way, since color in weaving never exists by itself but is always affected by some other factor than the pure color itself. Other factors which may and do affect color are the following.

Texture The surface texture of a fabric may be rough, smooth, shiny, or dull. (Dull in the sense of being non-shiny and not in the sense of being dull or bright in color.) Rough textures produce shadows, making the color appear darker than a smooth surface. Shiny surfaces reflect light and make colors appear lighter than the dull surfaces. A combination rough and dull surface will appear darker than a rough and shiny surface will, and a smooth dull surface will appear darker (though not as dark as rough and dull) than a smooth shiny surface. The smoother and shinier the material, the more light it will reflect, and thus the lighter it will appear. If, for example, metallic threads are woven on rayon or mercerized cotton warp, the color will appear lighter, especially under artificial light, than if rayon is woven on rayon.

Draping In addition to surface texture, the draping qualities of the fabric must be considered. A limp fabric will drape in soft, deep folds, producing darker shadows, thus producing a darker value in the color, than will a stiff, crisp fabric.

Thinness or Heaviness The weight of a fabric also affects the apparent color of the surface. Heavy yarns when interwoven will produce small surface shadows which will make a fabric appear darker than if a finer material is used. When used for large projects like drapery, the folds in the heavy material will also, of course, produce much darker shadows than those of the thinner material.

Whether a fabric is transparent, translucent, or opaque also has a bearing on the color. Colored objects, colored lights, and shadows behind translucent and transparent fabrics will change the apparent color or hue of the fabric, while none of these will affect an opaque fabric.

Lighting The lighting under which a woven article is seen has a very definite affect on the color of the woven piece. The "value" of a color is the measure of lightness or darkness of a hue, and hues to which black has been added are called shades. Thus if a fabric is in shadow, it will appear to be of darker value than if seen in full light. It also follows that a fabric seen under an intensely bright light, as is often the case in exhibitions or store display, will appear to be lighter than a fabric seen in daylight. The choice of colored threads to be used in weaving, especially in the experimental weaving of color combinations, should be done in daylight, preferably in north light.

Distance A color seen at close range will appear more brilliant than the same color viewed from a distance. This is observed in color schemes where two or more colors are used in a single piece of weaving. At close range the separate colors are clearly visible; at a distance they blend together in one allover color. This is especially noticeable in the Scottish tartans worn by a kilted band. Most tartans are on the bright side, but when seen from a distance they take on the predominant color or dim into a neutral hue. Most handweaving is, of course, not meant to be viewed from a distance, but the distance factor should be kept in mind when weaving fabrics for a large room, hall, or church.

Area or Size The larger the area of color, the stronger the color will appear to be. If two areas of the same color, one large and one small, appear side by side, the larger one will seem darker than the smaller. If one wishes both colors to appear the same, the larger one should be made lighter or the smaller one darker. With strong and weak colors, the strong color area should not be as large as the weak area. Though the strong color may be just right as an accent, it may prove too much of a muchness when covering a large area. This is important, for example, when weaving drapery to cover a large picture window. The color (and pattern and texture) must not be so dramatic that other parts of the room are not noticed. This same principle also applies to the weave and pattern used. A weave with small warp and weft floats, such as plain weave, will not show the color of warp and weft as much as will a weave with long warp or weft floats, such as overshot, even though both are woven using equal quantities of the same two colors. This is especially evident in patterns which have no halftones such as Monk's Belt.

Warm and Cool Colors All the gradations of color on the color wheel between yellow through orange to red and red violet are warm or aggressive or advancing colors, and all the gradations of color on the color wheel between yellow green through green and blue to violet are cool or retiring or receding colors. The exceptions to the rule are yellow and violet, which are right on the border and which may tend toward being either warm or cool. When equal quantities of warm (or advancing) and cool (or receding) colors are seen side by side, the warm colors will appear to be slightly larger or nearer than the cool colors. This is, of course, an optical illusion but can be of importance, especially when weaving large articles.

Effect of Surrounding and Adjoining Colors Color never exists by itself but is always influenced by surrounding and adjoining colors. Both of these will affect the apparent hue, value, and intensity of a color.

As noted earlier, complementary hues when placed together in the same proportion and value tend to jump or vibrate. Two nearby hues on the color wheel seem to be affected by absorbing some of the complement of each other. For example, when yellow and orange are placed next to each other the yellow seems to pick up some of the complement of orange —blue—which makes the yellow greenish; and the orange seems to pick up some of the complement of yellow—violet—which will add a russet cast to the orange. Gray has a tendency to pick up some of the complement of the color with which it is seen. This is especially apparent with strong colors. A gray beside red will make the gray appear greenish. To offset this, the gray should have a little red added to it, i.e., a pinkish gray. If gray is to harmonize with blue, it should have some blue added to it; gray with yellow should have yellow added to it; and so on.

Value   The tendency of gray to pick up the complement of a tint rather than of an intense color is not nearly so conspicuous, since they are closer together on the value scale. If a light color, e.g., yellow, and a dark color, e.g., blue violet, are used together, it will make the light color seem lighter and the dark color darker. When colors are not so far apart on the value scale, say yellow and orange, there is not so conspicuous an illusion of change in color value.

Intensity   The apparent intensity of colors is also influenced by adjoining colors. If a bright color—emerald green—and a dull color—jade green— are used together, the bright color will seem brighter and the dull color duller. In a 50/50 mixture—warp in one color, weft in another color, woven in plain weave or twill—the resulting color is usually neither one nor the other but a rather muddy-looking hybrid.

The influence of surrounding colors on a color are much the same as those of adjoining colors, except that the effect is heightened simply because there is more color.

The foregoing is at best only a cursory study of color as applied to weaving, but it should serve as an introduction to this intricate subject. No matter how good the weaver's color ideas and how thorough the technical knowledge of color and weaving, one can never be sure exactly what will happen to colored threads until they are woven. The thread as seen on the cone does not look the same when it is woven. Every new type of thread, every change of threading and sleying will produce a different effect. The only way to determine that it is what is required is to weave a generous sample, study it carefully in the place where it is to be used, and, once satisfied that it is what is needed, then, and only then, go ahead.

COLOR HARMONY PROFILES

These profiles, used in conjunction with the color wheel, will assist in determining harmonic color arrangements.

To make them, trace the outlines as shown here onto tracing paper, then transfer onto heavy white or light natural color paper. Cut carefully around the outline. To use, insert the point of a glass-headed pushpin through the dot in the center of the profile, then through the corresponding dot in the center of the color wheel. The profile can then be turned from group to group of colors until a pleasing arrangement emerges. If colors to be chosen are to go with a specific background, it would be advisable to cut a special profile of that color so that the true relationship of the colors can be seen.

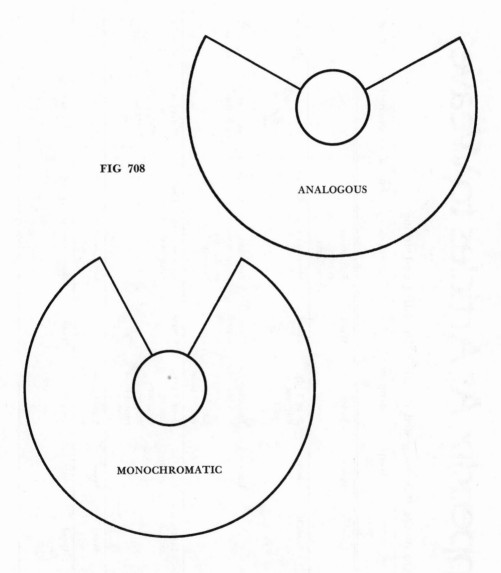

FIG 708

ANALOGOUS

MONOCHROMATIC

Appendix A: Articles to Weave

Articles to Weave, With Suggested Materials, Threading, and Sleying

Article	Description	Warp	Description	Weft	Description	Pattern	Description	Reed	Sley	Suggested Threading
Afghans	Wool	Wool	3-ply, medium weight	Wool	Soft, loosely twisted, medium			12 to in.	Single	Twills, surface weaves
Aprons	Peasant	Linen	2- or 3-ply, fine, round twist	Linen	Same as warp	Cotton	Mercerized, Nos. 3 or 5, or 6-strand perle	15 to in.	Double	50/50 plain weave, tartan, overshot bands, summer-and-winter
		Cotton	Egyptian, 2- or 3-ply, fine or medium weight, round twist	Linen or cotton	Egyptian, same as warp or slightly heavier	Cotton	Nos. 3 or 5, or 6-strand perle	12 or 15 to in.	Double	
Baby bibs	Linen or cotton	Linen or cotton	2- or 3-ply, fine or medium-weight, round twist	Cotton	Same as warp Same as warp	Cotton	Mercerized, fine or medium, or 3-strand perle	15 to in.	Double	Twills, fine overshot summer-and-winter, tapestry, dukagång, finger weaves
Baby blankets	Wool	Wool	Shetland or Germantown	Wool	Same as warp			12 or 15 to in.	Single	Twills, honeycomb, tabby
Baby bonnets	Wool	Wool	Very fine	Wool	Same as warp	Wool	Same as warp	18 to in.	Single	Twills, fine overshots, summer-and-winter

Article										Weaves
Baby-carriage covers	Wool	Wool	Germantown	Wool	Same as warp	Wool	Same as warp	12 to in.	Single	Twills, 50/50 plain weave, overshots with short skips, honeycomb, waffle, summer-and-winter, tapestry
Baby coats	Wool	Wool	Shetland or slightly heavier	Wool	Same as warp	Wool	Same as warp	12 to in.	Single	Twills, 50/50 plain weave, overshots (fine)
Bags	Knitting	Wool	Germantown	Wool	Same as warp			12 to in.	Single	Twills, 50/50 plain weave, tapestry
	Knitting	Cotton	Carpet warp	Cotton	Carpet warp			12 or 15 to in.	Single or double	Twills, log cabin, waffle, tartans
	Knitting	Cotton	Egyptian, medium and heavy	Cotton	Egyptian, fine, medium, or heavy	Wool	Germantown or lighter	12 to in.	Double	Fine overshots, tapestry, summer-and-winter, 50/50 plain weave, tartans
	Evening	Cotton	Fine	Rayon	Fine	Rayon Metallic	Many kinds	15 to in.	Double	
Belts	Wool	Wool	Fingering or Germantown	Wool	Same as warp	Wool	Same as warp	12 to in.	Double	Twills, tabby, warp face
	Wool	Wool	Fine	Wool	Same as warp	Wool	Fingering	15 to in.	Double	Fine overshots, summer-and-winter, twills, tapestry
	Metallic	Cotton	Fine	Wool	Fine	Metallic	Varied	15 to in.	Double	
	Cotton	Cotton	Carpet warp	Cotton	Carpet warp			12 or 15 to in.	Double	
	Cotton	Cotton	Egyptian, coarse	Cotton	Egyptian, coarse	Wool perle	Fine, medium, 6-strand	15 to in.	Double	50/50 plain weave, tartans, checks, stripes

Articles to Weave, With Suggested Materials, Threading, and Sleying (Cont'd)

Article	Description	Warp	Description	Weft	Description	Pattern	Description	Reed	Sley	Suggested Threading
(Belts cont'd)	Linen	Linen	3-ply, coarse or medium	Linen	Same as warp			15 to in.	Double	
Blouses	Peasant	Linen	Round thread, very fine	Linen	Fine, softer twist than warp	Perle	Medium, 6-strand	20 to in.	Double or triple	50/50 plain weave, with bands in summer-and-winter, fine overshot, twills
	Peasant	Cotton	Egyptian, very fine	Cotton	Fine, softer twist than warp	Perle	Medium, 6-strand	18 to in.	Double	
Bonnets	Peasant	Wool	3-ply, fine, tight twist	Wool	2-ply, fine, soft	Wool	Loosely twisted; homespun	15 to in.	Single or double	50/50 plain weave, twills, tartans, fine overshots, summer-and-winter
Book covers	Linen	Linen	Very fine, round thread	Linen	Same as warp	Perle	Fine, 3- or 6-strand	18 to in.	Double	50/50 plain weave, twills, tartans, very fine overshots, summer-and-winter, tapestry weaves in keeping with subject matter, if possible
	Cotton	Cotton	Egyptian, round thread	Cotton	Same as warp	Perle	Fine, 6-strand	18 to in.	Double	
Book-marks	As above for book covers			Should be very fine web, well woven						
Caps and berets	As for peasant bonnets									
Cards	Christmas	Cotton	Egyptian, fine	Cotton	Same as warp	Perle Metallic	Very fine, 3-strand Varied	15 to in.	Double	Stick or dukagång, tapestry

Chair seats	Linen	Linen	Fine, round thread	Linen	Same as warp	Perle	Fine, 3- or 6-strand	18 to in.	Double or triple	Twills, very fine overshots, summer-and-winter, double weaves
	Cotton	Cotton	Egyptian, 3-ply, fine	Cotton	Same as warp	Perle	Fine, 3- or 6-strand	18 to in.	Double	
	Wool	Cotton	Egyptian, 3-ply, medium	Cotton	Same as warp	Wool	Very fine, soft twist	18 to in.	Double	
Chair sets	3-piece	Linen	Round thread, medium or coarse	Linen	Same as warp	Wool, perle	Fine, soft, 6-strand	15 or 18 to in.	Double	Twills, very fine overshots, summer-and-winter, plain weave with stripes or colored borders, tapestry weaves
		Cotton	Egyptian, medium or coarse	Cotton	(as above)					
Church linens	Linen	Linen	Very fine, pure white	Linen	Same as warp			20 or 22 to in.	Double or triple	Plain insignias in finger weave. Must be perfectly woven. Maltese cross
Runners Kneelers	Cotton	Cotton	Fine	Cotton	Fine	Wool	Fine	15 to in.	Double	
	Wool	Cotton	Fine	Cotton	Fine	Wool	Rich reds			
Cloth	Dress	Wool	2-ply, very fine	Wool	Single-ply, fine, soft, homespun	Metallic	Varied in stripes	10 to in. / 14 to in.	Double / Double	50/50 plain weave, stripe, tartan, twills. Weave firm but not hard
	Suit	Homespun wool	3-ply, fine	Wool	Single-ply, fine, soft, homespun			9 or 10 to in.	Double	Overshot weaves, unless specially arranged, not suitable for dress, suit, or coat material
	Coat	Homespun or other wool	2- or 3-ply twist, medium weight	Wool	Single-ply, medium weight, fairly coarse, homespun			12 to in.	Single or double	

Articles to Weave, With Suggested Materials, Threading, and Sleying (Cont'd)

Article	Description	Warp	Description	Weft	Description	Pattern	Description	Reed	Sley	Suggested Threading
(Cloth cont'd)	Dress	Linen	Fine, 2- or 3-ply	Linen	Same as warp	Perle	No. 3 or 5, 6-strand	18 to in.	Double	50/50 plain weave, twill, tartan. Fine overshots used in borders only
	Coat or suit	Linen	3-ply, coarse	Linen	Same as warp	Perle	·	10–15 to in.	Double	
Covers	Bureau	Linen	3-ply, fine, medium, or coarse	Linen	Same as warp	Perle	No. 3 or 5, 6-strand	12 or 15 to in.	Single or double	50/50 plain weave, twills, stripes, tartans, overshots, summer-and-winter, double. Patterns in borders or all over. Crackle, Bronson lace
	Table	Cotton	3-ply, fine, medium, or coarse	Cotton	Same as warp	Wool	Fine wool; rayon	18 to in.		
	Footstool	See Upholstery								
Coverlets	Bed	Cotton	Egyptian, 2- or 3-ply twist	Cotton	Same as warp	Wool	Fine, soft or fine homespun wool	15 to in.	Double	Overshots in large designs, summer-and-winter, double weave. Crackle
Curtains or drapes	Window	Cotton	Egyptian, 10/2, carpet warp	Cotton, wool, rags, or heavy linen	Great variety of all types, preferably heavy and rough textured	Wool, rayon, linen	Coarse, rough / Coarse	12 or 15 to in. / 15 to in. (drapes)	Single / Double	Patterns suggesting texture, rather than definite design; allover or overshot borders. Much opportunity for originality in choice of materials
Curtain tiebacks	To match curtains									

Diapers	Baby	Linen	2- or 3-ply, very fine	Linen	Very fine, soft, single- or 2-ply twist		20 to in.	Double	Bird's-eye
Dish-cloths	Kitchen	Cotton	Soft knitting, medium	Cotton	Same as warp		12 to in.	Single	50/50 plain weave, simple twill, loose
Dressing gowns	See dress materials								
Hot-plate mats	Table	Cotton	Knitting, coarse	Cotton	Cotton warp or knitting cotton	Carpet warp or knitting cotton, rags	12 to in.	Single	Waffle weave, honeycomb
Holders	Hot pot	Cotton	Knitting, coarse waste string or carpet warp	Cotton			12 to in.	Single	50/50 plain weave, twill, stripes. Good use for odds and ends of thread
House-coats	See dress materials								
Jackets	See dress materials								
Kilts	Wool	Heavy	2/16 for men	Same as warp			18 to in.	Double	Must be on twill, all blocks squared and at a 45-deg. angle
Kilts	Wool	Light	2/16 for boys				16 to in.	Double	
Lunch cloths	Table	Linen	2-ply, very fine, 3-ply very coarse	Linen, perle	Same as warp	Coarser than warp, No. 3 or 5, 6-strand	15 or 20 to in.	Single or double	50/50 plain weave, twill, stripes, tartans, fine overshots, summer-and-winter in allover or borders. Lace weaves, crackle, and Bronson. Opportunity for originality in choice of materials, designs, and colorings
		Cotton	As for linen	Cotton, perle	Same as warp	Coarser than warp, No. 3 or 5, 6-strand	15 or 20 to in.	Single or double	

Articles to Weave, With Suggested Materials, Threading, and Sleying (Cont'd)

Article	Description	Warp	Description	Weft	Description	Pattern	Description	Reed	Sley	Suggested Threading
Mats and sets		Linen or cotton as above		Cotton	Same as warp		Variety materials such as cellophane, rags, heavy floss, etc.	15 to in.	Single or double	
Neckties	Men's	Wool	Very fine, firm twist	Wool	Same as warp			18 or 20 to in.	Single	Twill, 50/50 plain weave, stripes, tartans
Pillow-cases	Bed	Linen	2-ply, very fine twist	Linen	Very fine, soft twist			20 to in.	Double	Tubular weave
Pillow covers	Porch, etc.	Cotton	Egyptian, 2-ply, fine to coarse carpet warp	Cotton	Same as warp	Perle	Coarse	12 to in.	Double	Allover overshots, summer-and-winter with or without borders.
		Wool	2- or 3-ply, medium, tight twist	Wool	Same as warp	Wool	Coarse, soft twist; homespun	12 or 15 to in.	Single	Fairly large patterns
Purses	Many kinds	Linen, cotton, wool	Fine	Linen, cotton, Wool	Same as warp	Perle, wool	No. 3 or 5, fine or medium soft, 6-strand	12 or 18 to in.	Single and/or double	Plain weave in warp face; twills, fine overshots summer-and-winter, double. Much opportunity for originality. Should be firm weave
Rugs	Car	Wool	Heavy, double-twist homespun	Wool	Coarse, soft homespun			8 or 10 to in.		50/50 plain weave, twill, tartans

Floor	Cotton	Carpet warp	Cotton or rags	Carpet warp, cotton or wool rags, silk socks, or underwear	Rags	Cotton, wool, or silk	15 to in.	Single	50/50 plain weave, twill, overshots with short skips, log cabin, laid-in, Swedish flossa, Polish kilim, Navaho, Swedish, mattor, rya
Bath	Cotton	Carpet warp	Wool	Carpet warp	Wool	Heavy rug yarn, medium	12 to in.	Single	
	Linen	Jute	Wool	Homespun	Wool	Vegetable dye	8 to in.	Single	
	Cotton	Carpet warp	Cotton	Candlewick, chenille	Cotton	Candlewick	12 to in.	Single	
Scarves — Neck	Wool	Very fine, soft, but well twisted	Wool	Fine, soft			15 to in.	Single	Twills, log cabin, or basket weave. No overshots. Weave loosely
Table	See covers								
Shawls and stoles — Shoulder	Wool	Very fine, soft	Wool	Same as warp	Rayon Metallic	Varied Varied	12 to 18 to in.	Single	50/50 plain weave or twills, basket weave, lace weave. Weave very loosely but firmly. Should be very soft
Skirts	See dress materials								
Smocks	See blouses								
Towels — Hand	Linen	2- or 3-ply, fine, medium	Linen	Same as warp	Perle	No. 3 or 5, 6-strand	18 or 20 to in.	Double	Twills of all kinds, huck, lace Bronson, summer-and-winter. No overshots except borders
	Cotton	2- or 3-ply, fine, medium	Linen or cotton	Same as warp	Perle	No. 3 or 5, 6-strand	15 or 18 to in.	Double	Should be woven firm but not harsh

Articles to Weave, With Suggested Materials, Threading, and Sleying (Cont'd)

Article	Description	Warp	Description	Weft	Description	Pattern	Description	Reed	Sley	Suggested Threading
(Towels cont'd)	Dish	Linen	2- or 3-ply, unbleached	Linen	Slightly coarser and softer than warp			12 or 15 to in.	Double	50/50 plain weave, checks, stripes, twills
Up-holstery	Furniture	Cotton	Egyptian, 2- or 3-ply, fine	Cotton	Same as warp	Wool	Fine and soft to pack	15 or 18 to in.	Double	Fine allover patterns, twills, summer-and-winter, Bronson, crackle, or texture. Should be woven firm and tight
						Perle	No. 3 or 5, 6-strand			
						Metallic	Varied			
						Bouclé	Varied			
Wall-hangings		Cotton	Egyptian, coarse	Wool Cotton	Tapestry Egyptian, medium	Wool	Tapestry, fine	12 to in. 15 to in.	Single	Tapestry patterns, summer-and-winter, double, or overshot
							Soft			
		Linen	Jute	Wool	Homespun	Wool	Vegetable dyed	8 to in.	Single	

Appendix B:

Ready Reference Tables[1]

TABLE 1 *Yardage Table*

COTTON AND RAYON		WOOL (WORSTED)		LINEN, HEMP, JUTE, RAMIE	
SIZE	YARDS PER LB.	SIZE	YARDS PER LB.	SIZE	YARDS PER LB.
1	840	1	560	1	300
4/4	840	10	5600	10	3000
4/12	280	10/2	2800	10/2	1500
8/2	3360	10/4	1400	12	3600
8/4	1680	12/2	3360	14	4200
8/8	840	12/3	2240	15/2	2250
10	8400	15/2	4200	16	4800
10/2	4200	16/2	4480	18	5400
10/3	2800	18/2	5040	18/2	2700
12/4	2520	32/2	8960	20	6000
16/2	6720			20/2	3000
16/4	3360			30/2	4500
16/6	2240			40/2	6000
20/2	8400			40/3	4000
20/3	5600			60/3	6000
20/6	2800				
24/3	6720				
30/3	8400				
50/3	14000				

TABLE 2 *Formula for Calculating Warp Requirements*

To determine the number of threads needed to weave a piece a given width:

multiply the width of the material by the number of threads per inch in the reed to be used, i.e.:

width of material	10″
multiplied by threads per inch	15
	150 threads required

To the above must be added extra threads to allow for draw-in or to balance pattern design.

To determine the number of yards of thread required:

multiply the number of threads required	150
by the length of the finished article	36″
	5400″

To this must be added extra length to allow for take-up in weaving, loom waste, fringe or hems, and samples. Divide the total number by 36.

The yardage per pound of various materials has been given in table 2.

TABLE 3 *Number of Threads Required to Weave Material a Given Width*

REED DENTS PER INCH	GIVEN WIDTH								
	10″	12″	18″	20″	24″	30″	36″	40″	45″
8	80	96	144	160	192	240	288	320	360
9	90	108	162	180	216	270	324	360	405
10	100	120	180	200	240	300	360	400	450
12	120	144	216	240	288	360	432	480	540
14	140	168	252	280	336	420	504	560	630
15	150	180	270	300	360	450	540	600	675
16	160	192	288	320	384	480	576	640	720
18	180	216	324	360	432	540	648	720	810
20	200	240	360	400	480	600	720	800	900

If threads are to be double sley, i.e. two threads per dent, double the numbers given above. If triple sley, multiply the number by three and so on.

TABLE 4 *Reed Size Table*

The following table gives a quick reference for the number of threads per inch that can be sleyed in commonly used reeds.

REED NO.	THREADS PER DENT						
	1–0	1	1–2	2	2–3	3	4
6	3	6	9	12	15	18	24
7	3½	7	10½	14	17½	21	28
8	4	8	12	16	20	24	32
9	4½	9	13½	18	22½	27	36
10	5	10	15	20	25	30	40
11	5½	11	16½	22	27½	33	44
12	6	12	18	24	30	36	48
14	7	14	21	28	35	42	56
15	7½	15	22½	30	37½	45	60
16	8	16	24	32	40	48	64
18	9	18	27	36	45	54	72
20	10	20	30	40	50	60	80

Threads per dent are as follows:

1–0 means: 1 thread in first dent, skip second dent, repeat.
1   means: 1 thread per dent throughout.
1–2 means: 1 thread in first dent, 2 in second dent, repeat.
2   means: 2 threads per dent throughout.
2–3 means: 2 threads in first dent, 3 in second dent, repeat.
3   means: 3 threads per dent throughout.
4   means: 4 threads per dent throughout.

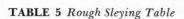

TABLE 5 *Rough Sleying Table*

The following table is for the use of weavers who make a chain warp (i.e. not sectional warp method) and rough sley the warp through the reed, either by the Beriau or Swedish methods, preparatory to rolling the warp on the back beam.

REED NO.	THREADS PER DENT						
	2–0–0–0	2–0 4–0–0–0 6–0–0–0–0–0 8–0–0–0–0–0–0–0	2–2–2–0	2 4–0 6–0–0 8–0–0–0	2–2–2–4	2–4 6–0	4 8–0
6	3	6	9	12	15	18	24
7	3½	7	10½	14	17½	21	28
8	4	8	12	16	20	24	32
9	4½	9	13½	18	22½	27	36
10	5	10	15	20	25	30	40

THREADS PER DENT

REED NO.	2–0–0–0 2–0 4–0–0–0 6–0–0–0–0–0 8–0–0–0–0–0–0–0	2–2–2–0	2 4–0 6–0–0 8–0–0–0	2–2–2–4	2–4 6–0	4 8–0
11	5½	11	16½	22	27½	33	44
12	6	12	18	24	30	36	48
14	7	14	21	28	35	42	56
15	7½	15	22½	30	37½	45	60
16	8	16	24	32	40	48	64
18	9	18	27	36	45	54	72
20	10	20	30	40	50	60	80

Threads per dent are as follows:

2 means: 2 threads per dent throughout.

2–0 means: 2 threads in first dent, skip second dent, repeat.

2–0–0–0 means: 2 threads in first dent, skip three dents, repeat

2–4 means: 2 threads in first dent, 4 threads in second dent, repeat.

2–2–2–0 means: 2 threads in first dent, 2 threads in second dent, 2 threads in third dent, skip fourth dent, repeat.

2–2–2–4 means: 2 threads in first dent, 2 threads in second dent, 2 threads in third dent, 4 threads in fourth dent, repeat.

4 means: 4 threads per dent throughout.

4–0 means: 4 threads in first dent, skip second dent, repeat.

4–0–0–0 means: 4 threads in first dent, skip three dents, repeat.

6–0 means: 6 threads in first dent, skip second dent, repeat.

6–0–0 means: 6 threads in first dent, skip two dents, repeat.

6–0–0–0–0–0 means: 6 threads in first dent, skip 5 dents, repeat.

8–0 means: 8 threads in first dent, skip one dent, repeat.

8–0–0–0 means: 8 threads in first dent, skip three dents, repeat.

8–0–0–0–0–0–0–0 means: 8 threads in first dent, skip seven dents, repeat.

TABLE 6 *Conversion Table: Reed Numbers from Swedish to English*

Notice that in this table, the dents in the metric system are given for 10 cm rather than 1 cm. This is because sleying in the Swedish weaving books is almost always given for a 10 cm width. (The exception to this being for extremely fine materials such as damask.) For example, in the Swedish texts you see: "Sked: 90 ror pa 10 cm." This means: "Reed: 90 dents in 10 cm." Or sometimes you will see: "Sked: 90/10." This means: "Reed: 90/10" which is a quick way of writing 90 dents in 10 cm.

To convert Swedish dents per 10 cm to English dents per inch use either of two methods:

1. Divide the dents in 10 cm by 10 and multiply by 2.54 (1 inch equals 2.54 cm); or,

2. multiply the dents in 10 cm by 10 and divide by 39.4 (1 meter equals 39.4 inches).

Although either of these methods gives the correct conversion from centimeters to inches, many of the sleys are very awkward when written in the English system. These awkward sleys would have to be sleyed in the closest reed size available to North American weavers.

The following table covers reeds most commonly found in Swedish books. Any other reed sizes may be converted by either of the methods described above.

In each case the "dents per inch" have been figured to the nearest ½ inch.

DENTS PER 10 CM.	=	DENTS PER INCH.	DENTS PER 10 CM.	=	DENTS PER INCH.
18		4.5	60		15
20		5	65		16.5
22		5.5	66		16.75
24		6	70		18
25		6.3	75		19
30		7.5	80		20
34		8.5	85		21.5
35		9	90		22.5
36		9	95		24
40		10	100		25.5
44		11	105		26.5
45		11.5	110		28
50		12.5	120		30.5
55		14	130		33
56		14			

The warp settings can be single sleyed, double sleyed, and so on in the above table, as per the directions given in the Swedish text.

Refer to Reed Size Table for the closest warp setting to that desired in the above Conversion Table.

TABLE 7 *Sleying Table*

SIZE	THREAD	PLAIN WEAVE LOOSE	PLAIN WEAVE FIRM	TWILL
8/2	Cotton	20	24	28
8/4	"	14	16	18
10/2	"	24	27	30
10/3	"	20	22½	24
16/2	"	28	30	32
20/2	"	30	32–34	36
20/3	"	22	24	28
20/6	"	20	22½	24

SIZE	THREAD	PLAIN WEAVE LOOSE	PLAIN WEAVE FIRM	TWILL
24/2	"	30	36	40
24/3	"	28	30	32
30/3	"	30	32	36
1½/1	Linen	6		
7/1	"	20	22½	25
10/1	"	24	27	30
12/1	"	25	28	32
12/2	"	20	22	24
14/2	"	20	22½	25
18/2	"	22½	24	27
20/2	"	24	26	30
30/2	"	28	30	32
40/2	"	32	36	40–45
50/3	"	35	37½	45
Lily's Art 110	Worsted	18	20	24
				(28 for kilts)
16/2	"	24	28	32
				(36 for kilts)
Bernat Fabri	"	20	24	27–30
Bernat Afghan	"	28	30	36
32/2	"	30	32	32–36
English knicker 9/1	Wool	14	16	18
Briggs & Little 8/1	"	16	18	20
Harris 9 cut	"	16	18	20
Cheviot 11 cut	"	18	20	24
12 cut	"	18	20	24
Cheviot 16 cut	"	24	27	30
Botany 20/2	"	24	27	30
Botany 12/2	"	22½	24	27

TABLE 8 *Cloth Measure*

2½ inches	=	1 nail
4 nails	=	1 quarter
3 quarters	=	1 Flemish ell
4 quarters	=	1 yard
5 quarters	=	1 English ell
6 quarters	=	1 French ell
37 inches	=	1 Scotch ell

TABLE 9 *Metric Table*

Measures of length

10 *millimeters* (mm)	=	1 *centimeter*	(cm)
10 centimeters	=	1 decimeter	(dm)
10 decimeters	=	1 *meter*	(m)
10 meters	=	1 decameter	(dkm)
10 dekameters	=	1 hectometer	(hm)
10 hectometers	=	1 *kilometer*	(km)

Measures of capacity

10 *milliliters* (ml)	=	1 *centiliter*	(cl)
10 centiliters	=	1 deciliter	(dl)
10 deciliters	=	1 *liter*	(l)
10 liters	=	1 decaliter	(dkl)
10 decaliters	=	1 hectoliter	(hl)
10 hectoliters	=	1 kiloliter	(kl)

Measures of weight

10 *milligrams* (mg)	=	1 *centigram*	(cg)
10 centigrams	=	1 decigram	(dg)
10 decigrams	=	1 *gram*	(g or gm)
10 grams	=	1 decagram	(dkg)
10 decagrams	=	1 hectogram	(hg)
10 hectograms	=	1 kilogram or kilo	(kg)
10 kilograms	=	1 myriagram	(myg)
10 myriagrams	=	1 quintal	(q)
10 quintals or 1000 kg	=	1 *metric ton*	(mt)

Measures of volume

1000 *cu. millimeter* (mm^3)	=	1 *cu. centimeter*	(cm^3 or cc)
1000 cc's	=	1 *cu. decimeter*	(dm^3)
1000 dm^3's	=	1 cu. meter	(m^3)

TABLE 10 *Metric System with Approximate U.S. Equivalents*

UNIT	NUMBER		U.S. EQUIVALENT	
Length				
kilometer	1,000	meters	0.62	miles
hectometer	100	meters	109.36	yards
decameter	10	meters	32.81	feet
meter	1	meter	39.37	inches
decimeter	0.1	meters	3.94	inches
centimeter	0.01	meters	0.39	inches
millimeter	0.001	meters	0.04	inches

TABLE 10 *Metric System with Approximate U.S. Equivalents*

UNIT	NUMBER	U.S. EQUIVALENT
Area		
square kilometer	1,000,000 sq. meters	0.3861 sq. miles
are	100 sq. meters	119.60 square yards
centare	1 sq. meter	10.76 square feet
square centimeter	0.0001 sq. meters	0.155 square inches
Volume		
decastere	10 cubic meters	13.10 cubic yards
stere	1 cubic meter	1.31 cubic yards
decistere	0.10 cubic meters	3.53 cubic feet
cubic centimeter	0.000001 cubic meters	0.610 cubic inches

Capacity		cubic	dry	liquid
kiloliter	1,000 liters	1.31 cu. yds.		
hectoliter	100 liters	3.53 cu. ft.	2.84 bu.	
decaliter	10 liters	0.35 cu. ft.	1.14 pecks	2.64 gal.
liter	1 liter	61.02 cu. in.	0.908 qts.	1.057 qts.
deciliter	0.10 liters	6.1 cu. in.	0.18 pts.	0.21 pts.
centiliter	0.01 liters	0.6 cu. in.		0.338 fl. oz.
milliliter	0.001 liters	0.06 cu. in.		0.27 fl. dr.

Mass Weight		
metric ton	1,000,000 grams	1.1 tons
quintal	100,000 grams	220.46 pounds
kilogram	1,000 grams	2.2046 pounds
hectogram	100 grams	3.527 ounces
decagram	10 grams	0.353 ounces
gram	1 gram	0.035 ounces
decigram	0.10 grams	1.543 grains
centigram	0.01 grams	0.154 grains
milligram	0.001 grams	0.015 grains

U.S. Measures & Weights with Their Metric Equivalents

U.S. UNIT	METRIC EQUIVALENT	U.S. UNIT	METRIC EQUIVALENT
Length		**Volume**	
mile	1.609 kilometers	cubic yard	0.765 cubic meters
rod	5.029 meters	cubic foot	0.028 cubic meters
yard	0.914 meters	cubic inch	16.387 cubic centimeters
foot	30.480 centimeters		
inch	2.540 centimeters	**Weight**	
		ton, short	0.907 metric tons
Area		ton, long	1.016 metric tons
		hundredweight,	
square mile	2.590 square kilometers	short	45.359 kilograms
acre	0.405 hectares, 4047 square	hundredweight,	
	meters	long	50.802 kilograms
square rod	25.293 square meters	pound	0.453 kilograms
square yard	0.836 square meters	ounce	28.349 grams
square foot	0.093 square meters	dram	1.771 grams
square inch	6.451 square centimeters	grain	0.0648 grams

U.S. UNIT	METRIC EQUIVALENT	U.S. UNIT	METRIC EQUIVALENT
Capacity, Liquid		**Capacity, Dry**	
gallon	3.785 liters	bushel	35.238 liters
quart	0.946 liters	peck	8.809 liters
pint	0.473 liters	quart	1.101 liters
		pint	0.550 liters

TABLE 11 *Temperature*

Ander Celsius, the nineteenth-century astronomer who devised the metric temperature scale, originally called it Centigrade. In honor of its inventor, °C is now designated as degrees Celsius. The following will give a feeling for the ambience of various Celsius temperatures.

100°C water boils
40°C an uncomfortably hot day
30°C a good day for a swim
20°C room temperature
10°C an early spring or fall day
0°C water freezes

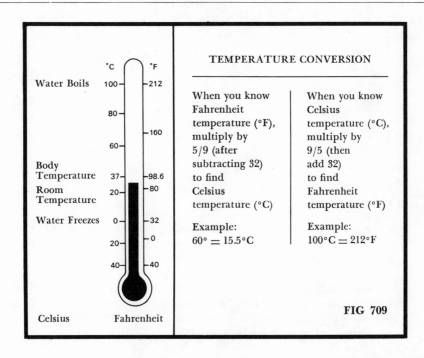

TEMPERATURE CONVERSION

When you know Fahrenheit temperature (°F), multiply by 5/9 (after subtracting 32) to find Celsius temperature (°C)

Example:
60° = 15.5°C

When you know Celsius temperature (°C), multiply by 9/5 (then add 32) to find Fahrenheit temperature (°F)

Example:
100°C = 212°F

FIG 709

TABLE 12 *Decimal Equivalents*

1/64...................	.015625	33/64.................	.515625
1/32...................	.03125	17/32.................	.53125
3/64................	.046875	35/64................	.546875
1/16.................	.0625	9/16.................	.5625
5/64................	.078125	37/64................	.578125
3/32................	.09375	19/32.................	.59375
7/64...............	.109375	39/64................	.609375
1/8.................	.125	5/8.................	.625
9/64................	.140625	41/64................	.640625
5/32................	.15625	21/32.................	.65625
11/64................	.171875	43/64...............	.671875
3/16.................	.1875	11/16.................	.6875
13/64................	.203125	45/64................	.703125
7/32................	.21875	23/32.................	.71875
15/64................	.234375	47/64................	.734375
1/4.................	.25	3/4.................	.75
17/64................	.265625	49/64................	.765625
9/32................	.28125	25/32.................	.78125
19/64................	.296875	51/64................	.796875
5/16.................	.3125	13/16.................	.8125
21/64................	.328125	53/64................	.828125
11/32................	.34375	27/32.................	.84375
23/64................	.359375	55/64................	.859375
3/8.................	.375	7/8.................	.875
25/64................	.390625	57/64................	.890625
13/32................	.40625	29/32.................	.90625
27/64................	.421875	59/64................	.921875
7/16.................	.4375	15/16.................	.9375
29/64................	.453125	61/64...............	.953125
15/32................	.46875	31/32.................	.96875
31/64................	.484375	63/64................	.984375
1/2.................	.5	1	1.

TABLE 13 *Multiplication & Division Table*

A number in the top line (19) multiplied by a number in the last column on the left (18) produces the number where the top line and the side line meet (342), and so on throughout the table.

A number in the table (342) divided by the number at the top of that column (19) results in the number (18) at the extreme left; also, a number in the table (342) divided by the number (18) at the extreme left gives the number (19) at the top of the column, and so on throughout the table.

1	25	24	23	22	21	20	19	18	17	16	15	14	13	12	11	10	9	8	7	6	5	4	3	2
2	50	48	46	44	42	40	38	36	34	32	30	28	26	24	22	20	18	16	14	12	10	8	6	4
3	75	72	69	66	63	60	57	54	51	48	45	42	39	36	33	30	27	24	21	18	15	12	9	6
4	100	96	92	88	84	80	76	72	68	64	60	56	52	48	44	40	36	32	28	24	20	16	12	8
5	125	120	115	110	105	100	95	90	85	80	75	70	65	60	55	50	45	40	35	30	25	20	15	10
6	150	144	138	132	126	120	114	108	102	96	90	84	78	72	66	60	54	48	42	36	30	24	18	12
7	175	168	161	154	147	140	133	126	119	112	105	98	91	84	77	70	63	56	49	42	35	28	21	14
8	200	192	184	176	168	160	152	144	136	128	120	112	104	96	88	80	72	64	56	48	40	32	24	16
9	225	216	207	198	189	180	171	162	153	144	135	126	117	108	99	90	81	72	63	54	45	36	27	18
10	250	240	230	220	210	200	190	180	170	160	150	140	130	120	110	100	90	80	70	60	50	40	30	20
11	275	264	253	242	231	220	209	198	187	176	165	154	143	132	121	110	99	88	77	66	55	44	33	22
12	300	288	276	264	252	240	228	216	204	192	180	168	156	144	132	120	108	96	84	72	60	48	36	24
13	325	312	299	286	273	260	247	234	221	208	195	182	169	156	143	130	117	104	91	78	65	52	39	26
14	350	336	322	308	294	280	266	252	238	224	210	196	182	168	154	140	126	112	98	84	70	56	42	28
15	375	360	345	330	315	300	285	270	255	240	225	210	195	180	165	150	135	120	105	90	75	60	45	30
16	400	384	368	352	336	320	304	288	272	256	240	224	208	192	176	160	144	128	112	96	80	64	48	32
17	425	408	391	374	357	340	323	306	289	272	255	238	221	204	187	170	153	136	119	102	85	68	51	34
18	450	432	414	396	378	360	342	324	306	288	270	252	234	216	198	180	162	144	126	108	90	72	54	36
19	475	456	437	418	399	380	361	342	323	304	285	266	247	228	209	190	171	152	133	114	95	76	57	38
20	500	480	460	440	420	400	380	360	340	320	300	280	260	240	220	200	180	160	140	120	100	80	60	40
21	525	504	483	462	441	420	399	378	357	336	315	294	273	252	231	210	189	168	147	126	105	84	63	42
22	550	528	506	484	462	440	418	396	374	352	330	308	286	264	242	220	198	176	154	132	110	88	66	44
23	575	552	529	506	483	460	437	414	391	368	345	322	299	276	253	230	207	184	161	138	115	92	69	46
24	600	576	552	528	504	480	456	432	408	384	360	336	312	288	264	240	216	192	168	144	120	96	72	48
25	625	600	575	550	525	500	475	450	425	400	375	350	325	300	275	250	225	200	175	150	125	100	75	50
1	25	24	23	22	21	20	19	18	17	16	15	14	13	12	11	10	9	8	7	6	5	4	3	2

Notes

CHAPTER 1 The Loom

1. Harriet Tidball, *If You Plan to Buy a Loom* and *To Build or Buy a Loom*; Edward F. Worst, *How to Build a Loom* (Pacific, Calif.: Select Books).

CHAPTER 3 Plain Weaves—Loom Controlled

1. Consult local weaving group, library, bookmobile, or government craft department for names and addresses of current weaving publications.
2. Märta Brodén and Gertrud Ingers, *Trasmattor* (Västerås, Sweden: ICA-Förlaget, 1955); Malin Selander, *Vävmonster* (Göteborg, Sweden: Wezäta Förlag, 1954).
3. T. Tanaka, *A Study of Okinawan Textile Fabrics* (Tokyo, 1953).
4. E. Henderson and M. Sandin, *Loom Music* (Edmonton, Alberta, Canada: University of Alberta), Vol. 2, No. 11.

CHAPTER 4 Plain Weaves—Finger Manipulated

1. Victoria and Albert Museum, *Guide to Chinese Woven Fabrics*.

CHAPTER 5 Twill

1. Marguerite Porter Davison, *A Handweaver's Pattern Book* (Swarthmore, Pa.: M. P. Davison, 1950).
2. Mary M. Atwater, *The Shuttle-Craft Book of American Hand Weaving* (New York: Macmillan Publishing Co., Inc., 1951); Marguerite P. Davison, *A Handweaver's Pattern Book* (Swarthmore, Pa.: M. P. Davison, 1950).
3. G. Ingers and J. Becker, *Damast* (Motala, Sweden: Broderna Borgströms Boktryckeri, 1955).
4. Designed and woven by Elizabeth Wittenberg, California.

CHAPTER 6 Overshot

1. Mary M. Atwater, *The Shuttle-Craft Book of American Handweaving*, rev. ed. (New York: Macmillan Publishing Co., Inc., 1951).
2. Mary M. Atwater, *The Shuttle-Craft Book of American Handweaving*, rev ed.

(New York: Macmillan Publishing Co., Inc., 1951); Marguerite P. Davison, *A Handweaver's Pattern Book* (Swarthmore, Pa.: M. P. Davison, 1950).

3. Marguerite Davison, *A Handweaver's Pattern Book* (Swarthmore, Pa.: M. P. Davison, 1950).
4. Designed and woven by Bessie R. Murray, Halifax, Nova Scotia.
5. Harriet Tidball, *Weaver's Word Finder* (Big Sur, Calif.: Craft and Hobby Books).
6. Marguerite P. Davison, *A Handweaver's Pattern Book* (Swarthmore, Pa.: M. P. Davison, 1950).
7. Winogene Redding, Massachusetts.
8. Gertrude Greer, *Adventures in Weaving* (Peoria, Ill.: Chas. A. Bennett Co., Inc., 1951).

CHAPTER 7   Variations and Extensions on Twill Threadings
1. Dorothy Oliver, Nova Scotia.
2. Designed and woven by the late Helen M. MacDonald, Nova Scotia.
3. Minnie Simpson, York, England.
4. Marian Powell, Mexico.
5. Minnie Simpson, York, England.

CHAPTER 8   Crackle Weave
1. Sigrid Palmgren, *Vävbok* (Norrköping, Sweden: U. & S. Palmgren, 1939); Mary M. Atwater, *The Shuttle-Craft Book of American Hand Weaving* (New York: Macmillan Publishing Co., Inc., 1951).

CHAPTER 9   Summer-and-Winter Weaves
1. Mary M. Atwater, *The Shuttle-Craft Book of American Hand Weaving* (New York: Macmillan Publishing Co., Inc., 1951).
2. *Ibid.*

CHAPTER 10   Bronson
1. J. and R. Bronson, *The Domestic Manufacturer's Assistant and Family Director on the Art of Weaving and Dyeing*, rev. ed. (Boston: Charles T. Branford Co., 1949).

CHAPTER 11   Miscellaneous Weaves
1. Marguerite P. Davison, *A Handweaver's Pattern Book* (Swarthmore, Pa.: M. P. Davison, 1950).
2. Evelyn Neher, *Four-Harness Huck* (New Canaan, Conn.: Evelyn Neher, 1953).
3. Davison, *op. cit.*
4. Arrangement by Mary Sandin, Alberta, Canada.
5. Ester Perheentupa, *Kutokaa Kuviollisia Kankaita* (Helsinki, Finland: W. S. Osakeyhtiö, 1950).
6. Davison, *op. cit.*
7. Sigrid Palmgren, *Vävbok* (Norrköping, Sweden: S. Palmgren, 1939).
8. Arranged by the late Mrs. Bradford Eldridge, Nova Scotia.

CHAPTER 12   Tartan Weaves
1. D. C. Stewart, *The Setts of the Scottish Tartans* (London: Oliver and Boyd, 1950).

2. Frank Adam and Sir Thomas Innes of Learney, *The Clans, Septs and Regiments of the Scottish Highlands* (Edinburgh: W. & A. K. Johnston, 1952); Robert Bain and Margaret MacDougall, *Clans and Tartans of Scotland* (London and Glasgow: Collins Publishing Co., 1938); Mary E. Black, *The Sett and Weaving of Tartans* (Shelby, N. C.: Lily Mills).

3. Stewart, *op. cit.*

4. *Ibid.*

5. Logan, *Description of Clan Tartans* (Glasgow: Collins, 1949).

6. Logan, *op. cit.*

7. By Dorothy Hill, Nova Scotia.

8. G. H. Oelsner and S. S. Dale, *A Handbook on Weaves* (New York: Dover Publications, Ltd., 1951).

CHAPTER 13 Tapestry Weaves

1. Helen Churchill Candee, *The Tapestry Book* (New York: Tudor Publishing Co., 1935).

2. Reprinted by permission of Legation of Poland, Ottawa, Canada.

3. Text on Scandinavian åklae and rölakan checked by Fröken Ann-Beat Carlson, Handarbetets Vänners Vävskola, Stockholm, Sweden.

4. Joyce Chown, Nova Scotia.

5. Helen Churchill Candee, *The Tapestry Book* (New York: Tudor Publishing Company, 1935).

6. Jean Lurçat, *Designing Tapestry* (London: Rockliff, 1950).

7. Handarbetets Vänners Vävskola, Stockholm, Sweden, 1952.

8. Designed and woven by Joyce Chown, Nova Scotia.

9. Gladys, A. Reichard, *Navajo Shepherd and Weaver* (New York: J. J. Augustin, Publisher, 1936).

10. Charles Avery Amsden, *Navajo Weaving* (Albuquerque, N. Mex.: University of New Mexico Press, 1934).

CHAPTER 14 Theory of Weaving

1. Marguerite Davison, *A Handweaver's Source Book* (Swarthmore, Pa.: M. Davison, 1953).

2. G. H. Oelsner and S. S. Dale, *A Handbook of Weaves* (New York City: Dover Publications, Ltd., 1951).

CHAPTER 15 General Information

1. Minnie Simpson, York, England.

CHAPTER 16 Fibers

1. The late May Stronach, Nova Scotia.

2. Designed and woven by Florence Mackley, Cape Breton, Nova Scotia.

CHAPTER 17 Color in Weaving

1. Much of the material here is from "Color Guide for Handweavers" by Joyce Chown and Mary E. Black (Out of Print, 1958).

2. Woven by Daurene Lewis, Nova Scotia.

APPENDIX B Ready Reference Tables

1. Originally published in leaflet form titled "Ready Reference Tables for Handweavers" by Mary E. Black and Joyce Chown (Canada, 1958).

Glossary

apron Piece of canvas attached to the warp and cloth beams to which the warp ends are tied.

batten See **beater.** English, "lay" or "laith."

beam, breast Beam at front of loom, between beater and cloth beam, over which web passes to the cloth beam.

beam, cloth The front roller on which the cloth is wound as it is being woven. The roller holds the web at the correct tension.

beam, knee Beam at front of loom between breast and cloth beams to keep web away from the weaver's knees.

beam, warp Beam at back of loom around which warp is wound.

beam, whip Beam at back of loom directly above warp beam; corresponds in position to breast beam at front of loom; also called "slab" or back beam.

beater Frame holding reed. Used to "beat" weft thread back into place in the web.

bight (1) Group of warp ends, usually ready for tying. (2) The middle part of a rope, the ends being fast elsewhere.

binder See **tabby.**

bobbin A reel, quill, or spool to carry weft thread.

bobbin carrier A shuttle.

breaking Pounding of flax to break it up.

capes Side uprights of a loom.

card boy Youth who arranges the cards on a Jacquard loom.

carding Preparation of wool for spinning.

cards (1) Instruments for combing cotton, wool, flax, hair, etc., into rolls preparatory to spinning. (2) Perforated cards on a Jacquard loom used to produce figures.

cartoon Full-size drawing used in connection with tapestry.

castle, top Beam across top of loom on which are hung the jacks, coups, or harnesses.

chain Warp as taken from the warping board or reel chained to shorten and prevent tangling.

cord, Maitland   Cord on which string heddles are run.

counter march   A short lower lever in a loom.

cross, porrey   Crossing of threads at start of warp during winding to form a lease.

cross, portee   Alternate crossings of threads at end of warp during winding to form a lease.

cut   Small skein or part of a skein.

dent   Single space in a reed.

dent, strong   Dent with more than the required number of threads.

dent, weak   Dent with less than the required number of threads.

dog or pawl   Catch fastened to side of loom to act as a brake for ratchet wheel.

doup   Upper and lower parts of a string heddle as distinguished from the eye. Also applies to special heedle used for gauze weaving.

draft   Drawing on ruled paper indicating the placement of the threads in the harnesses used in threading loom.

dressing   Preparing loom for weaving.

ends, warp   Ends of warp, after cutting, in the chain.

entering   Threading warp ends through heddles and reed.

fell   The edge of the weaving where the warp threads cross after the shed is changed after the insertion of the last thread.

Finnish pukko knife   Small hunting knife.

float   See **overshot.**

flossa   A knotted-rug technique thought to have originated in Sweden.

gating   Adjusting a loom.

graph paper   Paper marked off in squares of various sizes by printed lines. Also spoken of as squared paper. Paper with rectangular, instead of squared spaces is used for some types of weaving.

grist   Size or thickness of threads.

ground work   Principal or body part of web on which the pattern is superimposed or interwoven.

hackles   Heavy combs across which flax is drawn to separate it into lengths.

half flossa   A knotted rug in which only the pattern areas are knotted.

half hitch   A simple knot or noose so made as to be easily unfastened.

harness   Frames on which heddles are hung.

heedle eye   Loop or opening in center of heddle.

heddle gauge   Frame on which string heddles are tied.

heddles   Wire, twine, or flat pieces of steel with holes or eyes in center through which warp ends are threaded.

hook, warp   Flat metal hook used to pull warp ends through the reed.

knot   Term used by professional weavers, meaning 80 warp threads 1 yd. long. When applied to reed, means 80 spaces.

knot, snitch   Knot used to tie lams to treadles.

knot, weaver's   Knot commonly used by weavers for many purposes around the loom.

lams   Horizontal levers tied between harnesses and treadles.

lash   A shot running back and forth in the same shed. Usually an error.

lay or laith   English or Scotch term for beater.

lease   Crossing of warp threads during winding between warping posts to keep them in order during threading.

lease sticks   Two thin sticks used in the cross or shed to keep the threads in order; also called shed sticks.

leisures Selvedges on very fine weaving.

loom Upright frame or machine of wood or other media on which a weaver works thread into a web.

loom, Jacquard Loom perfected by Mon. Jacquard to simplify a type of weaving done with cards.

loom waste That length of warp thread which lies between the back and breast beam, plus the amount of warp used for knots, plus allowance for take-up. This varies considerably between looms, weavers, type of thread, and technique. In winding warps it is better to err through allowing too much rather than not enough.

mail Eye of a string heddle through which the warp passes.

marches English, Scotch, and Scandinavian term for lams.

mesh Fineness or coarseness of web as measured by number of threads to the inch.

niddy noddy Old Colonial term for hand reel for winding skeins.

overshot Term used to describe thread passing over two or more warp threads to form a pattern. Also called a float.

pick Single shot of weft thread through shed across top of stretched warp threads. Usually applied to power looms.

quill Paper tube on which weft is wound for insertion in boat shuttle.

race, shuttle Bottom crosspiece of beater on which shuttle runs back and forth on an automatic loom.

rack, spool Frame with rods to hold spools when winding warp directly onto warp beam.

raddle Bar with row of upright pegs to separate warp into designated sections and prevent it from tangling during the process of winding onto the warp beam.

reed Comblike piece set in the beater to separate warp threads and used to beat threads together to form web.

reel, drum-warping Large barrel-like revolving wheel around which long lengths of warp are wound.

retting Immersion of flax in water to separate straw from fiber.

rya A knotted rug similar to the flossa rug but with longer pile.

section or bout Fractional part of entire length of web.

selvedge or selvage Edge of web.

set Refers to the number of warp threads threaded per inch through the dents in the reed.

sett The count of threads, in terms of color, in Scottish tartans as approved by the Court of the Lord Lyon.

shed Opening formed in warp, by raising or depressing harnesses, through which the shuttle is passed.

shed, rising A shed in which part of the warp rises as on a hand or rising-shed loom, the rest of the warp remaining stationary.

shed, sinking Opposite of above.

shed sticks See **lease sticks.**

shot Passage of shuttle through shed with one weft or pattern thread.

shuttle Instrument for carrying weft thread.

shuttle, fly Boat shuttle thrown from one end of shuttle race to the other by contact with rawhide picks on automatic looms.

shuttle race The shelf on a beater along which a fly shuttle runs.

skein Loosely wound "knot" or number of "knots" as measured on the swift, of linen, silk, or yarn.

slab beam   Supporting beam at back of loom over which warp travels.

slack   Loosely drawn thread.

spinning   Twisting of fiber to make thread.

splicing   Joining of weft threads by overlapping the ends.

sley (noun)   Number of warp ends per inch drawn through spaces or dents in reed.

sley (verb)   To draw threads through dents in the reed with warp hook.

sley, double   Two threads in each dent of the reed.

sley, single   One thread in each dent of the reed.

sticks, lease   Narrow, flat, smooth sticks inserted into the warp (as it lies on the warping board) on each side of the cross threads; later inserted behind harnesses to keep threads in position during threading.

stock, slab   Beam at back over which warp passes between the warp beam and harnesses.

swift   Adjustable wheel mounted on frame to hold yarn for unwinding.

swords   Sidepieces of beater; also, the sticks used on primitive looms for beating.

tabby   Often used to describe plain weave. In this text, applies to thread inserted between pattern threads.

taut   Tightly drawn threads.

teasel brush   A wire brush used to nap woolen webs, used in place of teasel pods.

teasing   Fluffing or napping a woolen web for which the seed pods of the teasel were originally used.

temple or stretcher   Adjustable wooden bar with nails in ends placed across web during weaving to prevent selvedges drawing in.

texture   Character or feel of finished web.

tie-up   Tying of lams to treadles.

treadles   Pedals used to raise or lower harnesses on looms. Operated by hand on hand loom to raise harness. Also called levers on hand loom.

twill   A web in which the weft threads form a diagonal pattern. Referred to in foreign weaving books as "Serge."

warp   System of threads running lengthwise in loom across which weft threads are passed to form web or cloth.

warping board or bar   Heavy wooden frame with pegs spaced at intervals around which warp is wound.

warp measure   Metal gauge used to measure length of warp as it is being wound directly onto warp beam.

weave, plain   The basic or fundamental weave which forms the background of many other weaves. Frequently referred to as the tabby weave.

web   Piece of woven cloth.

weft or woof   Threads woven across warp threads to form cloth.

wheel, ratchet   Wheel with teeth, fastened to ends of warp and cloth beams to hold warp at proper tension.

wheel, spooling   Machine for winding warp on spools or bobbins.

yarn   Thread of any kind, produced by spinning. Frequently refers only to woolen thread.

Weaving Terms in Foreign Languages

English	Gaelic	Norwegian	Swedish	Danish	French	German
beater	crannslinn	slagbom	vävsked	slagbord	ros	
black	dhu	sort	svart	sort	noir	schwarz
bleached	ghlan	bleket	vitblekt	bleget	blanchi	gebleicht
blue	gorm	blå	blått	blaa	bleu	blau
border	bordair	bord	bard	bort	bordure	Bord
brown	donn	brun	brun	brun	brun	braun
cloth	clo	tøi	tyg	tøj	tissu	Web
colors	dathan	farver	farjer	farver	couleurs	Farben
cotton	cotan	bomull	bomull	bomuld	coton	Baumwolle
curtain	curtair	gardin	gardin	gardin	rideau	Gardine
dark	dorcha	mörk	mörk	mork	fonce	dunkel
dents	slinn	tind	rostandtänder	rit	peus	
draft threading	snadadh-na-slinn	hooling	soloning	sølning	tracé	Einzüge
drill	joll	dreiel	dräll	drejl	serge	
green	uaine	grön	grön	grøn	vert	grün
gray	glas	graa	grå	graa	gris	grau
harness	iomalinnin	skaft	skaft	skaft	lame	Schafte
heddle eye	iomal suil	hovel oie	solv	søl óje	lisse	Litz
light	ban	lyst	ljus	lys	pâle	leicht
linen	lion	lin	lingarn	linned or laerred	lin	Leinen
loom	bearta	vevstol	vävstol	vaev	métier	Webstuhl
mat	maat	gulveteppe	matta	maatte	tapis	Teppich
orange	dath	orange	orangeförjad	orange	orangé	

English	Gaelic	Norwegian	Swedish	Danish	French	German
pattern	pathern	mønster	mönster	mønster	patronmodel	Muster
red	dearg	rodt	röd-rött	rødt	rouge	rot
rep		rips	rips	reps		Rips
rose	ros	rosenröd	ljus röd	rosa	rose	rosa
rug	bratteallaich	loper, tepper, gulv		lóber taeppe	tapis	Teppich
satin	seorsa	atlask	atlas	atlask	satin	Atlas
shuttle	spal	skytler	skyttel	skytte	navette	Schiffchen, Schütze
silk	sioda	silke	siden	silke	soie	Seide
sleying			skedtathet	indskyde	passage en ros	
swift	grad	garnvinde		garnvinde	devidoir or tournette	Garnwinder
tabby	seorsa, siodh	bunnan	bundväv	bundvaev	liaison	
tan	gartaih	lysebrun	ljus brun	lysebrun	bronzé	hellbraun
thread	snath	trad	trad	traad	fils	Faden
tie-up	ceanchhlsuas	opknyting	uppknytning	opbinding	attachage	Kette Einteilung
treadles	casachanan	troer	trampor	skamler	marches	Pedale
twill	twill	dreiel	kypert	drejl	serge	Koper
unbleached	neo-ghlan	ublelet	oblekt	ubleget	naturel	ungebleicht
violet	sail chuaich	fiolet	violet	violet	violet	violett
warp	dluth	renning	varp	trend	chaine	Kette
weave	fihidh	lerret	väv	vaeve	tisser	Flecht
weaving	fihidhearachd	vevning	vävning	vaevning	tissage	weben
weft	snathcuire	islett	väft	indslag islaet	duitetrame	Schlussfaden
wheel, spinning	cuidheal snidmh	spinnehjul		spindehjul	rouet	Spinnrad
white	geal	hoit	vit	hvid	blanc	weiss
wool	cloidh	ull	ull-ylle	uld	laine	Wolle
yarn	snathcloimh	garn	garn	garn	fils	Garn
yellow	buidhe	gult	gult	gul	jaune	gelb

Bibliography

This bibliography lists only those books which deal principally with technique or with the history of weaving, such books as have been accepted by weavers as the books on which our working knowledge of handweaving has been based. Even this list, condensed as it is, contains some books which are difficult to obtain. Local guilds and guild members usually have their own libraries which they make available to the beginning weaver, and local, national, state, or university libraries can be helpful in supplying names of firms and individuals which issue catalogues of currently available as well as hard-to-find books. The larger libraries will sometimes procure out-of-print books, though it may take some months to find the requested publication and a fee is usually charged for the service.

Never overlook the opportunity of searching through the book tables at auctions, garage sales, old book shops, and attic sales. Many valuable books have come to light in such places.

Although some of the publications listed are not printed in English, the advanced weaver can glean much useful information from the drafts and illustrations. Those which are printed in color are an inspiration to the weaver seeking attractive color arrangements.

Allen, Helen L. *American and European Hand Weaving*. Rev. ed. 1939.

Amsden, C. A. *Navaho Weaving*. Albuquerque, New Mexico: University of New Mexico, 1934.

Atwater, Mary Meigs. *Byways in Hand Weaving*. New York: Macmillan Co., 1954.

———. *Finneweave and Mexican Double Weave*. Privately printed.

———. *Guatemala Visited*. Privately printed.

———. *Handweaving*. New York: Macmillan Co.

———. *Shuttle Craft Book of American Handweaving*. New York: Macmillan Co., 1951.

Beriau, Oscar. *Home Weaving*. Quebec, Canada: Arts & Crafts of Gardenvale, Inc., 1939.

――――. *Tissage Domestique.* Quebec, Canada: Ministere De L'Agriculture, 1933.

Black, Mary E. *Key to Weaving.* New York: Macmillan Co., 1945.

――――. *Sett and Weaving of Tartans.* Shelby, N.C.: Lily Mills Co., 1958.

――――. *Weaving for Beginners.* Ottawa, Canada: Dept. National Health and Welfare, 1954.

Black, Mary E., and Murray, Bessie R. *You Can Weave.* Toronto, Canada: McClelland & Stewart Ltd., 1974.

Block, Mary. *Den Stora Vävboken.* Sweden, Bokförlaget Natur och Kultur, 1939.

Bronson, J. R. *Domestic Manufacturers Assistant and Family Directory in the Arts of Weaving and Dyeing.* Boston, Mass.: Charles T. Brandford, 1949.

Brown, H. J. *Handweaving for Pleasure & Profit.* New York: Harper & Bros., 1952.

Collin, Maria. *Flamskväv Och Finnväv.* Stockholm, Sweden: Ahlen & Åkerlunds, Förlag, 1927.

Cyrus, Ulla. *Manual of Swedish Hand Weaving.* Boston, Mass.: Chas. T. Brandford Co., 1956.

Davison, Marguerite Porter. *A Handweaver's Pattern Book.* Swarthmore, Pa.: Privately printed, 1950.

――――. *A Handweaver's Source Book.* Swarthmore, Pa.: Privately printed, 1953.

Engestrom, Nina. *Praktise Vävbok.* Stockholm, Sweden: C. E. Fritzes, Bokförlags, 1913.

France, L. *Weaver's Complete Guide, or The Web Analyzed.* Burrillville, R.I., 1814.

Frey, Berta. *Design & Drafting for Handweavers.* New York: Macmillan Co., 1958.

――――. *Seven Projects in Rosecraft.* Privately printed, 1948.

Gallinger, Osma C. *Joy of Handweaving.* Scranton, Pa.: International Textbook Co., 1950.

Halvorsen, Caroline. *Handbook I Veving.* Oslo, Norway: J. W. Capplens, Förlag, 1934.

Hooper, Luther. *Handloom Weaving.* London, England: Pitman, 1920.

――――. *The New Draw Loom.* London, England: Pitman, 1932.

――――. *Weaving for Beginners.* London, England: Pitman, 1934.

House, Florence. *Notes on Weaving Techniques.* New York: Columbia University, 1954.

Ingers, Gertrud, and Becker, John. *Damast.* Vasteras, Sweden: I.C.A. Förlaget, 1955.

Klein, Bernat. *Eye for Color.* Edinburgh, Scotland: Pillans & Wilson Ltd.

Lurçat, J. *Designing Tapestry.* London, England: Rockliff, 1950.

Mackley, Florence. *Cape Breton Coverlet Patterns.* Sydney, Nova Scotia: Commercial Printers, 1952.

――――. *Handweaving in Cape Breton.* Sydney, Nova Scotia: Commercial Printers, 1967.

Montell, Aina. *Vävboken.* Stockholm, Sweden: Albert Bonniers, Förlag, 1925.

Neher, Evelyn. *Four-Harness Huck.* New Canaan, Conn.: Privately printed, 1953.

Oelsner, G. H., and Dale, S. S. *A Handbook of Weaves.* New York: Dover Publishing Ltd., 1951.

Palmgrens, Sigrid. *Väv Bok.* Norrköping, Sweden: Utgiven av Sigrid Palgrens, 1939.

Pendleton, Mary. *Navajo and Hopi Weaving Techniques.* New York: Collier, Macmillan, 1974.

Perheentupa, Ester. *Kutokaa Kuviollisia Kankaita.* Helsinki, Finland: Porvoo, 1950.

Pritchard, M. E. *A Short Dictionary of Weaving.* London, England: Philosophical Library, 1956.

Reichard, G. A. *Navajo Sheperd and Weaver.* New York: J. J. Augustin, 1936.

Rodier, Paul. *The Romance of French Weaving*. New York: Tudor Publishing, 1936.

Selander, Malin. *Swedish Handweaving*. Goteberg, Sweden: Wezäta Förlag, 1954.

Stewart, Donald C. *The Setts of the Scottish Tartans*. Edinburgh, Scotland: Oliver & Boyd, 1950.

Tate, Louise. *Kentucky Coverlets*. Louisville, Ky.: Privately printed.

Tidball, Harriet. *Foundations for Handweavers*. Privately printed, 1955.

———. *Handweaver's Instruction Manual*. Privately printed.

———. *Interior Decoration, The Handloom Way*. Privately printed.

———. *The Weaver's Book*. New York: Macmillan Publishing Co., 1961.

———. *Weaver's Word Finder*. Privately printed.

Tilquist, Hilda, and Wålstedt, Lars. *Yllevävar*. Västeras, Sweden: I.C.A. Förlagets.

Van Cleve, Kate. *Published Notes on Handloom Weaving*. Privately printed.

Victoria and Albert Museum. *Guide to Chinese Woven Fabrics*. London, England.

Worst, Edward F. *Foot-Power Loom Weaving*. New York: Macmillan Publishing Co., 1924.

———. *How to Weave Linens*. New York: Macmillan Publishing Co., 1926.

Wulff, Hans E. *The Traditional Crafts of Persia*. Cambridge, Mass.: M.I.T. Press.

Zielinski, S. A. *Encyclopaedia of Hand-Weaving*. Toronto, Canada: Ryerson Press, 1959.

Index

sample, in MacPherson Clan tartan sett, 434–35
yardage table for, 657
yarn, formula for counting yardage, 16
Counterbalanced foot loom, 45
Counterbalanced loom, 4, 6
Coverlets, weaving, 652
Covers, weaving, 652
Cowhair, 614–15
Crackle weave (Jämtlandsväv), 307–10. *See also* Weaving
Crank, 8
Cross beams, 6
Curtains or drapes, weaving, 652
Curtain tiebacks, weaving, 653

Danish medallion pattern, in pattern threads inserted into web weaves, 117–20
Davison, Marguerite Porter, 160, 337
Decimal equivalents table, 666
Description of Clan Tartans (Logan), 413–14
Design threads inserted into web weaves, 120–22. *See also* Pattern threads; Pattern threads on surface; Pattern threads on surface, knotted
Diagonals in pattern weaving, imperfect, correcting, 576
Diamond and cross, in overshot weave, 235–39
honeysuckle or pine bloom pattern, 235–37
orange pattern, 237–39
Diapers, weaving, 653
Dishcloths, weaving, 653
Distance, color and, 645
District checks of tartan weave, 444–46
Glenfeshie pattern, 444–45
Glen Urquhart (small) pattern, 445–46
Dog hair, 615
Dogs or pawls of loom, 6, 7
Dope dyeing, 627
Dornik and broken pattern, in 4-, 6-, 8-harness twill, 209–10
Double-knotted fringe, 588
Double plain weave, tubular, in 4-harness twill, 184–86
Double point, extended pattern, in 8-harness twill, 202–203
Double warp-and-weft face, in 8-harness, 8-block twill, 213–15
Double weave
Finnväv and Mexican pattern, in 4-harness twill, 219–23

in MacPherson, Cluny sett, in tartan weave, 437–40
interlocking pattern, in 4-harness twill, 180–82
2-block pattern, in 8-harness twill, 210–13
Double-width web pattern, in 4-harness twill, 182–84
Drafts, frames for holding, 12
Draft writing. *See* Draw-downs; Short draft; Threading drafts
Drapes or curtains, weaving, 652
Draping, color and, 644
Draw-downs, 535-39
Dressing gowns, weaving, 653
Dressing loom. *See* Loom, dressing
Dukagång and half-Dukagång pattern, in pattern threads on surface weave, 130–35
Dyed-in-the-wool, 627
Dyeing, 627–30
preparing warp chain for, 630

Egyptian, modern, pattern, in tapestry weaves, 522–23
8-harness, 8-block twill, 213–15
8-harness, 4-block, M's and O's pattern, in miscellaneous weaves, 385–90
8-harness, point, spot setting pattern, in Bronson weave, 345–47
8-harness grouped warp and weft threads, basket weave pattern, in miscellaneous weaves, 366–67
8-harness loom, 5
8-harness summer-winter weave, 329–33
6-block, spider web pattern, 329–30
6-block, treadling variation on spider web pattern, 331–33
8-harness twill, 194–208, 210–213, 216–18
double point, extended pattern, 202–203
double weave 2-block pattern, 210–13
extended point, sampler pattern, 208–209
extended point, Swedish Rosenkransen M's and W's pattern, 205–207
false damask pattern, 218
interlocking double weave pattern, 216–17
plain pattern, 194–97
point, herringbone pattern, in 8-harness twill, 200–201
Swedish Kypert—reverse twill pattern, 198–99
triple point, extended pattern, 204–205
8-harness waffle weave pattern, in miscellaneous weaves, 394–95
Evaluation of weaving, 568